Handbook of Self-Determination Research

Handbook of Self-Determination Research

Edited by
Edward L. Deci
Richard M. Ryan

 THE UNIVERSITY OF ROCHESTER PRESS

First published 2002
by the University of Rochester Press.
Softcover edition published 2004.

The University of Rochester Press
668 Mount Hope Avenue, Rochester, NY 14620, USA
www.urpress.com
and Boydell & Brewer, Ltd.
P.O. Box 9, Woodbridge, Suffolk IP12 3DF, UK

ISBN 1-58046-108-5 (Hard cover)
ISBN 1-58046-156-5 (Soft cover)

Library of Congress Cataloging-in-Publication Data

Handbook of self-determination research / Edward L. Deci and Richard M. Ryan, editors.-- Soft cover ed.
    p. cm.
Includes bibliographical references and indexes.
ISBN 1-58046-156-5 (pbk. : alk. paper)
1. Autonomy (Psychology) I. Deci, Edward L. II. Ryan, Richard M.

BF575.A88H36 2004
155.2'5--dc22
                                                          2003027192

British Library Cataloging-in-Publication Data
A catalogue record for this item is available from the British Library

Designed and typeset by Christine Menendez
Printed in the United States of America
This publication is printed on acid-free paper.

For all those individuals who have been interested in and engaged with work on Self-Determination Theory.

Contents

PREFACE

In April, 1999, the first conference devoted exclusively to a discussion of research on self-determination theory (SDT) was held at the University of Rochester. Approximately 75 researchers—faculty, post-docs, and graduate students—from 20 universities in the United States, Canada, Germany, and Israel assembled for two long days of discussions and debates, examining findings and mapping directions for future research.

People came with a shared vocabulary, a shared set of concepts, a shared system of thought, and a shared familiarity with an extensive research literature. This allowed everyone to begin immediately discussing important and penetrating issues. Each person had been engaged in his or her unique research program—on values, psychosocial medical interventions, self-regulatory styles, coping processes, the self, organizational dynamics, and so forth—and each of the research programs was briefly reviewed and discussed in relation to the others. Some issues were discussed by several researchers; others were addressed by only one or two. In each case, the issues were the basis for rich and stimulating dialogue, and some led to the specification of empirical questions that are already under examination in various labs.

So exciting were the presentations and discussions that the group decided it was time to prepare a volume that would draw together the results of several research programs as they relate to and have been organized by SDT. This volume is the result of that decision.

It begins with a brief overview of the theory. Then, 17 specific chapters, covering a broad range of topics, are organized into three sections. The first set deals with specific theoretical issues related to SDT. In each of those chapters, the researchers review work that has taken the theory into new directions, expanding or organizing specific aspects of it. The second set deals with the application of SDT to various applied domains, including parenting, education, environmentally friendly behaving, health care, management of for-profit and not-for-profit organizations, and exercise programs. Although SDT has been developed using a basic-science approach, we have always believed that it is important for theories to be formulated in a way that makes them useful for informing interpersonal dynamics and the design of social settings. The set of chapters concerned with applying SDT in various domains makes clear how broadly relevant the theory is for real, human concerns. The third set of chapters relates SDT to some other theoretical perspectives and other areas of research. The first presents a discussion of the relation between self-determination and perceived control and shows the importance of self-determination (in addition to perceived control) for effective coping. Then, the importance of differentiating the concept of self-esteem is discussed along with the relevance of SDT for doing so. Third, the concept of competence as a need and process is examined within the context of achievement research, followed by a discussion of human agency as it relates to perceived control, resource control, and self-determination. The final chapter in this section relates SDT to research on interest that began in the European tradition.

It is our hope that this volume will not only convey a sense of the breadth of the research on SDT that has already been performed, but even more importantly that it will stimulate readers to ask new questions and develop new paradigms for investigating additional issues that tie into the basic themes of this field of inquiry.

There are many people who were of great help both in organizing the conference and in preparing this volume. The Department of Clinical and Social Sciences in Psychology at the University of Rochester provided substantial resources for the conference; we thank Miron Zuckerman, chair of the department, and other members of the faculty. Phyllis Joe worked hard on organizational matters. Graduate students and post-doctoral fellows in the Human Motivation Program did many tasks to ensure that everything went well during the conference. Presenters and audience members participated enthusiastically in the discussions, making the event stimulating and rewarding. Timothy Madigan, our editor at the University of Rochester Press, and Elizabeth Whitehead, who has done expert editorial work on the SDT project for the past 25 years, worked hard in preparing this volume. We are grateful for all these contributions.

Edward L. Deci
Richard M. Ryan
September, 2001

PART I

❖ ❖ ❖

INTRODUCTION

1: Overview of Self-Determination Theory: An Organismic Dialectical Perspective

Richard M. Ryan
Edward L. Deci
University of Rochester

In the classical, Aristotelian, view of human development, people are assumed to possess an active tendency toward psychological growth and integration. Endowed with an innate striving to exercise and elaborate their interests, individuals tend naturally to seek challenges, to discover new perspectives, and to actively internalize and transform cultural practices. By stretching their capacities and expressing their talents and propensities, people actualize their human potentials. Within this perspective, active growth is complemented by a tendency toward synthesis, organization, or relative unity of both knowledge and personality. Moreover, the integration of that which is experienced provides the basis for a coherent sense of self—a sense of wholeness, vitality, and integrity. To the degree that individuals have attained a sense of self, they can act in accord with, or be "true" to, that self.

This general view of an active, integrating organism with the potential to act from a coherent sense of self can be found in psychodynamic and humanistic theories of personality and in cognitive theories of development. For example, psychoanalytic theorists posit inherent activity and a synthetic function of the ego (Freud, 1927; Nunberg, 1931; Meissner, 1981; White, 1963), and humanistic psychologists postulate an actualizing tendency (Angyal, 1963; Maslow, 1955; Rogers, 1963). Similarly, many cognitive developmental theories emphasize an organizational or integrative tendency as an endogenous feature of the organism, proposing that development is characterized by an overarching organization function through which new self-extensions are brought into coherence with other cognitive structures (Piaget, 1971; Werner, 1948).

Preparation of this chapter was supported in part by a research grant from the National Institute of Mental Health (MH-53385).

To varying degrees, some recent theories have continued to embrace such assumptions (e.g., Ford, 1992; Loevinger & Blasi, 1991; Kuhl & Fuhrmann, 1998), recognizing the intrinsic propensities of people to engage in active, curiosity-based exploration and to integrate new experiences to the self.

Despite its longevity and seeming popularity, the assumption of innate tendencies toward growth and integration is not without its critics. Among the more staunch opponents of constructs concerning growth and integration have been operant behaviorists who assume there is no inherent direction to development and suggest that behavioral regulation and personality are a function of reinforcement histories and current contingencies (e.g., Skinner, 1953). For them, any appearance of an inner organization to personality is attributable not to a presumed integrative tendency but rather to the fact that the relevant contingencies people encountered in their environments were organized and systematic.

Similarly, contemporary social-cognitive approaches portray personality not in terms of a self-unifying system, but rather as a collection of selves or self-schemas that are activated by cues. Personality is viewed as a repository for schemata related to various goals and identities, each of which can be elicited by features of the social contexts (Bandura, 1989; Higgins, 1987; Markus & Nurius, 1986; Mischel & Shoda, 1995). Unlike their operant predecessors, such social-cognitive theories do not deny the idea of a synthetic tendency in development, but instead peripheralize it, focusing on the unified properties within isolated goal schemata or regulatory structures rather than among such schemata or structures.

Finally, and perhaps most importantly, the concept of endogenous tendencies toward psychological growth and unity in development seems to fly in the face of everyday behavioral observations. Ambient evidence could readily support the view that people are no more characterized by tendencies toward growth and integrity than by propensities to be controlled, fragmented, and stagnated in development. Everywhere, we see signs of divided functioning, of inner conflict and a lack of concern with responsibility and community. These widespread symptoms are echoed in psychological theories (e.g., Broughton, 1987; Greenwald, 1982). In fact, Gergen (1993) viewed the metaphor of a core or true self that grows and struggles for unity as a post-romantic view that should be replaced by the acceptance of a postmodern perspective in which the self is more aptly described as fragmented, saturated, and diversely populated by identities that are imputed by the social world.

It seems indeed that the field of psychology is quite widely divided on the issues of inherent tendencies toward psychological growth, a unified self, and autonomous, responsible behavior. Whereas some theorists see our nature as including a self-organizing, growth promoting tendency, others see us as wholly lacking such an endowment, and thus as mere conditioned or reactive reflections of our surroundings. Importantly, each position seems to have some prima facie evidence in its favor.

This set of issues concerning the degree to which there are inherent tendencies toward growth and integration is important not only theoretically, but also practically. Insofar as practitioners believe people have a natural tendency toward gaining integrity and enhancing their human potentials, they will orient to supporting and facilitating that endogenous tendency across a variety of settings, including homes, schools, work organizations, and therapy clinics. In contrast, insofar as practitioners assume no such inner tendency toward growth, self-construction, and inner coherence, then educational, therapeutic, and other practical intervention strategies will focus on exogenous means of training, shaping, controlling, and directing behavior towards ends deemed to be of value.

The Organismic Dialectic: An Integrating Perspective

The primary agenda of self-determination theory (SDT; Deci & Ryan, 1985b; Ryan & Deci, 2000b) has been to provide an account of the seemingly discrepant viewpoints characterized, on the one hand, by the humanistic, psychoanalytic, and developmental theories that employ an organismic metatheory and, on the other hand, by the behavioral, cognitive, and post-modern theories that do not. In other words, recognizing that there is compelling evidence in favor of human tendencies toward active engagement and development and that there is, as well, manifold indication of fragmentation and conditioned responses, SDT provides a framework that integrates the phenomena illuminated by these discrepant viewpoints.

SDT begins by embracing the assumption that all individuals have natural, innate, and constructive tendencies to develop an ever more elaborated and unified sense of self. That is, we assume people have a primary propensity to forge interconnections among aspects of their own psyches as well as with other individuals and groups in their social worlds. Drawing on terms used by Angyal (1963), we characterize this tendency toward integration as involving both autonomy (tending toward inner organization and holistic self-regulation) and homonomy (tending toward integration of oneself with others). Healthy development involves the complementary functioning of these two aspects of the integrative tendency.

However, although SDT accepts this general integrative tendency as a fundamental aspect of human life, the theory also suggests that this tendency cannot be taken for granted. On the contrary, SDT posits that there are clear and specifiable social-contextual factors that support this innate tendency, and that there are other specifiable factors that thwart or hinder this fundamental process of human nature. Accordingly, SDT predicts a broad array of developmental outcomes, ranging from a relatively active and integrated self to a highly fragmented and sometimes passive, reactive, or alienated self, as a function of social-environmental conditions.

Another way of stating this is that the foundations of SDT reside in a dialectical view which concerns the interaction between an active, integrating human nature and social contexts that either nurture or impede the organism's active nature. Social environments can, according to this perspective, either facilitate and enable the growth and integration propensities with which the human psyche is endowed, or they can disrupt, forestall, and fragment these processes resulting in behaviors and inner experiences that represent the darker side of humanity. As such, psychological growth and integration in personality should neither be taken as a given, as something that will happen automatically, nor should it be assumed not to exist. Instead, it must be viewed as a dynamic potential that requires proximal and distal conditions of nurturance. In this, we fully agree with Allport (1961) who suggested that unity in personality is a matter of degree and should not be exaggerated. We add, however, that whatever the attained unity of the psyche, the importance of the issue of integration within personality cannot be over emphasized when one is attempting to understand the processes of healthy psychological and social development. As well, the issue is important for examining applied questions related to effective parenting, education, work, health care, exercise regimens, environmentalism, religiosity, psychotherapy, and other significant human endeavors.

Basic Needs and Social Contexts

Approaches to describing environments that support versus thwart effective or healthy functioning have been numerous in the social, personality, and developmental literatures. In SDT, the descriptions are organized with respect to the concept of basic or fundamental psychological needs. The theory posits three such needs, each of which has shown itself to be essential for integrating a variety of empirically illuminated phenomena. These needs—the needs for competence, relatedness, and autonomy—provide the basis for categorizing aspects of the environment as supportive versus antagonistic to integrated and vital human functioning. Social environments that allow satisfaction of the three basic needs are predicted to support such healthy functioning, whereas factors associated with need thwarting or conflict are predicted to be antagonistic. Thus, the concept of basic needs provides a critical linking pin within the organismic dialectic and is the basis for making predictions about the conditions that promote optimal versus nonoptimal outcomes in terms of both personality development and the quality of behavior and experience within a specific situation.

The nature of needs. Among the fundamental properties that separate the animate from the inanimate is the dependence of the animate on nutriments. Living beings must engage in continual exchanges with their environment to draw from it those necessities that allow them to preserve, maintain, and enhance their functioning. Stated differently, living things have *needs* that must be fulfilled if they are to persist and thrive (Jacob, 1973).

The concept of needs is relatively noncontroversial in the field of biology, a field that focuses primarily on the survival and reproduction of the physical structure of the organism. One can verify empirically that there are certain specifiable requirements, such as hydration, for organisms to survive and thrive. Withholding such an element will lead reliably to deterioration of growth and integrity, whereas making it available will lead to maintenance or enhancement. As such, the concept of needs is important because it supplies a criterion for specifying what is essential to life. At the same time, the concept says something about organismic nature because it is reasonable to argue that organisms are "built for" the satisfaction of needs—that is, that they have evolved functional structures and sensitivities that can lead to sustenance and integrity (see, e.g., Deci & Ryan, 2000).

The concept of needs has received far less attention and acceptance regarding essential psychological nutriments than essential physiological ones. SDT maintains, however, that there are necessary conditions for the growth and well-being of people's personalities and cognitive structures, just as there are for their physical development and functioning. These nutriments are referred to within SDT as *basic psychological needs*. By this SDT definition, basic needs are universal—that is, they represent innate requirements rather than acquired motives. As such, they are expected to be evident in all cultures and in all developmental periods. Although they may have different expressions or different vehicles through which they are satisfied, their core character is unchanging. Clearly, this is a very restrictive definition, which is why the list of psychological needs within SDT is thus far so short, including only competence, relatedness, and autonomy. In humans, the concept of psychological needs further suggests that, whether or not people are explicitly conscious of needs as goal objects, the healthy human psyche ongoingly strives for these nutriments and, when possible, gravitates toward situations that provide them.

Competence refers to feeling effective in one's ongoing interactions with the social environment and experiencing opportunities to exercise and express one's capacities (Deci, 1975; Harter, 1983; White, 1959). The need for competence leads people to seek challenges that are optimal for their capacities and to persistently attempt to maintain and enhance those skills and capacities through activity. Competence is not, then, an attained skill or capability, but rather is a felt sense of confidence and effectance in action.

Relatedness refers to feeling connected to others, to caring for and being cared for by those others, to having a sense of belongingness both with other individuals and with one's community (Baumeister & Leary, 1995; Bowlby, 1979; Harlow, 1958; Ryan, 1995). Relatedness reflects the homonomous aspect of the integrative tendency of life, the tendency to connect with and be integral to and accepted by others. The need to feel oneself as being in relation to others is thus not concerned with the attainment of a certain outcome (e.g., sex) or a formal status (e.g., becoming a spouse, or a group member), but instead concerns the psychological sense of being with others in secure communion or unity.

Finally, *autonomy* refers to being the perceived origin or source of one's own behavior (deCharms, 1968; Deci & Ryan, 1985b; Ryan & Connell, 1989). Autonomy concerns acting from interest and integrated values. When autonomous, individuals experience their behavior as an expression of the self, such that, even when actions are influenced by outside sources, the actors concur with those influences, feeling both initiative and value with regard to them. Autonomy is often confused with, or melded together with, the quite different concept of independence (which means not relying on external sources or influences), but the SDT view considers there to be no necessary antagonism between autonomy and dependence. Indeed, one can quite autonomously enact values and behaviors that others have requested or forwarded, provided that one congruently endorses them. On the other hand, one can of course rely on others for directions or opinions in such a way that autonomy is not experienced, as is the case with mere compliance or conformity. In short, independence versus dependence is a dimension that is seen within SDT as being largely orthogonal to the issue of autonomy versus heteronomy (Ryan & Lynch, 1989; Ryan, 1993).

Needs and motives. Our concept of basic psychological needs is quite different from the broader idea of personal motives, desires, or strivings. Although people may formulate motives or strivings to satisfy basic needs, it is also clear that there are many motives that do not fit the criterion of being essential for well-being and may, indeed, be inimical to it. In other words, some motives may distract people from activities that could provide basic need fulfillment and thus detract from their well-being. Even when people are highly efficacious at satisfying motives, the motives may still be detrimental to well-being if they interfere with people's autonomy or relatedness. This is an extremely important point, because it makes clear that attaining one's goals efficaciously is not enough to ensure psychological well-being. As such, many motives and goals that organize behavior must be viewed dynamically either as being peripheral to psychological need satisfaction or as being need substitutes that developed as compensations when basic needs were thwarted (Deci, 1980; Ryan, Sheldon, Kasser, & Deci, 1996).

Summary

To summarize, SDT embraces both an organismic and a dialectical framework for the study of personality growth and development. As an organismic view, SDT conceives of humans as active, growth-oriented organisms, that innately seek and engage challenges in their environments, attempting to actualize their potentialities, capacities, and sensibilities. However, this organismic tendency toward actualization represents only one pole of a dialectical interface, the other being social environments which can either facilitate the individuals' synthetic tendencies, or alternatively wither, block, or overwhelm them.

The concept of psychological needs provides the basis for describing characteristics of the environment that support versus undermine the organism's attempts to master or engage each new situation. To the extent that an aspect of the social context allows need fulfillment, it yields engagement, mastery, and synthesis; whereas, to the extent that it thwarts need fulfillment, it diminishes the individual's motivation, growth, integrity, and well-being.

Within SDT, the specification of needs and the study of need-related behavioral dynamics has been pursued as an empirical endeavor. The specification of needs, along with a stringent functional definition of what qualifies as a psychological need, has led to quite exacting, if sometimes counter-intuitive predictions about human behavior and the effects of social contexts. That is, by evoking needs and applying appropriate criteria, SDT research has been able to pinpoint and examine factors in social environments that facilitate self-motivation and well-being, and those that thwart initiative and positive experience across diverse settings, domains, and cultures.

The Basic Components of Self-Determination Theory

SDT has evolved over the past three decades in the form of mini-theories, each of which relates to specific phenomena. The mini-theories are linked in that they all share organismic and dialectical assumptions and all involve the concept of basic psychological needs. When coordinated, they cover all types of human behavior in all domains. Thus, together, the mini-theories constitute SDT. Specification of separate mini-theories was, historically, a consequence of building a broad theory in an inductive fashion. That is, our approach has been to research phenomena, construct mini-theories to account for them, and then derive hypotheses about related phenomena. Throughout this process, basic assumptions and approaches remained constant, so the mini-theories were logically coherent and readily integratable each with the others. As such, each represents a piece of the overall SDT framework.

In our writings, various aspects or propositions of the mini-theories have at times been presented with the terminology of the relevant mini-theories, but often they have simply been presented under the rubric of SDT. At this time, SDT comprises four mini-theories. *Cognitive evaluation theory*, the first, was formulated to describe the effects of social contexts on people's intrinsic motivation (Deci, 1975; Deci & Ryan, 1980). It describes contextual elements as autonomy supportive (informational), controlling, and amotivating, and it links these types of contextual elements to the different motivations. *Organismic integration theory* (Deci & Ryan, 1985b; Ryan & Connell, 1989) concerns internalization and integration of values and regulations, and was formulated to explain the development and dynamics of extrinsic motivation; the degree to which individuals' experience autonomy while engaging in extrinsically motivated behaviors; and the processes through which people take on the values and mores of their groups and cultures. *Causality orientations theory* (Deci & Ryan, 1985a) was formulated to describe individual differences in people's tendencies to orient toward the social environment in ways that support their own autonomy, control their behavior, or are amotivating. This mini-theory allows for prediction of experience and behavior from enduring orientations of the person. Finally, *basic needs theory* (Ryan & Deci, 2000b) was formulated to explain the relation of motivation and goals to health and well-being, in part by describing associations of value configurations and regulatory styles to psychological health, across time, gender, situations, and culture. We address each mini-theory in turn.

Cognitive Evaluation Theory

Intrinsically motivated behaviors are those whose motivation is based in the inherent satisfactions of the behaviors *per se*, rather than in contingencies or reinforcements that are operationally separable form those activities. Intrinsic motivation represents a prototype of self-determined activity, in that, when intrinsically motivated, people engage in activities freely, being sustained by the experience of interest and enjoyment. Thus, as it is classically defined (see Ryan & Deci, 2000a), intrinsic motivation is noninstrumentally focused, instead originating autotelically from satisfactions inherent in action, whereas extrinsic motivation is focused toward and dependent on contingent outcomes that are separable from the action *per se*. DeCharms (1968) used Heider's (1958) concept of perceived locus of causality to describe the two types of motivation: with extrinsic motivation, deCharms suggested, people perceive the locus of initiation and regulation of their behavior to be external to themselves, whereas with intrinsic motivation, they perceive the locus to be within themselves. SDT has followed deCharms' perspective only in part. We agree with him that intrinsically motivated actions invariantly entail an internal perceived locus of causality, and that intrinsic motivation tends to be undermined when factors conduce toward an external perceived locus of causality. However, our view of extrinsic motivation is more differentiated, as we shall describe in our coverage of Organismic Integration Theory.

The intrinsic-extrinsic distinction provided the basis for the first experiments in the field. Specifically, research began with the question of how extrinsic rewards would affect people's intrinsic motivation for an interesting activity. In other words, if someone engaged in an activity freely without being rewarded and found it highly interesting and enjoyable, the person would clearly be intrinsically motivated. If he or she were then offered an extrinsic reward for doing the activity, what would happen to the person's intrinsic motivation?

The initial studies (Deci, 1971, 1972a, 1972b; Kruglanski, Friedman, & Zeevi, 1971; Lepper, Greene, & Nisbett, 1973) all found that tangible rewards—

whether concrete, such as money (Deci), or symbolic, such as good player awards (Lepper et al.)—decreased intrinsic motivation so long as they were expected and their receipt required engaging in the activity. However, the initial Deci studies also showed that positive feedback—or what is sometimes referred to as verbal rewards or praise—enhanced rather than undermined intrinsic motivation.

The undermining of intrinsic motivation by extrinsic rewards has been a controversial issue from the time the initial studies were published, in part because the finding appeared to fly in the face of operant theory which had a strong presence in empirical psychology at that time. In spite of the controversy and some fatally flawed attempts to deny the undermining phenomenon (e.g. Eisenberger & Cameron, 1996), a meta-analysis of 128 experiments confirmed that expected tangible rewards which require engaging in the target activity do indeed undermine intrinsic motivation for that activity, whereas verbal rewards tend to enhance intrinsic motivation (Deci, Koestner, & Ryan, 1999).

Perceived Causality and Perceived Competence

Cognitive evaluation theory (CET: Deci, 1975; Deci & Ryan, 1980), which expanded upon deCharms' analysis of perceived locus of causality, was initially formulated to account for reward effects on intrinsic motivation, as well as various other results that extended these phenomena. The theory suggests that the needs for competence and autonomy are integrally involved in intrinsic motivation and that contextual events, such as the offer of a reward, the provision of positive feedback, or the imposition of a deadline, are likely to affect intrinsic motivation to the extent that they are experienced as supporting versus thwarting satisfaction of these needs.

More specifically, Deci and Ryan (1980) suggested that there are two primary cognitive processes through which contextual factors affect intrinsic motivation. Change in *perceived locus of causality* relates to the need for autonomy: when an event prompts a change in perceptions toward a more external locus, intrinsic motivation will be undermined; whereas, when an event prompts a change toward a more internal perceived locus, intrinsic motivation will be enhanced. Tangible rewards, which were typically found to decrease intrinsic motivation, were theorized to have their effect by prompting a shift toward a more external perceived locus of causality for the rewarded activity. The second process, change in *perceived competence*, relates to the need for competence: when an event increases perceived competence, intrinsic motivation will tend to be enhanced; whereas, when an event diminishes perceived competence, intrinsic motivation will be undermined. According to CET, however, positive feedback is predicted to enhance intrinsic motivation only when people feel a sense of autonomy with respect to the activity for which they perceived themselves to be competent, a proposition upheld in various studies (e.g., Fisher, 1978; Ryan, 1982).

As initially presented, CET further specified that contextual events or climates contain both a *controlling* aspect and an *informational* aspect and that it is the relative salience of these two aspects of social contexts that determines the effects of the context on perceptions of causality and competence, and thus on intrinsic motivation. The controlling aspects of social environments are those that represent pressure toward specified outcomes, and thus conduce to a shift toward a more external perceived locus of causality. Features of the social environment that have controlling salience undermine intrinsic motivation. The informational aspect of social contexts pertains to effectance-relevant inputs. Specifically, informational events and communications provide feedback that supports people's experience of competent engagement. In discussions of CET, the concept of *functional significance* is used to convey the idea that individuals will actively construe social-contextual inputs in terms of their informational and controlling meanings, and that it is the relative salience of informational versus controlling components that will, in large part, determine subsequent intrinsic motivation. For example, an event such as the offer of a tangible reward (which studies have found to be controlling) is, on average, said to have a controlling functional significance; whereas, the functional significance of positive feedback is, on average, said to be informational. Accordingly rewards are predicted to undermine intrinsic motivation in many circumstances, whereas positive performance feedback is expected to enhance it.

The bulk of the experimental studies on intrinsic motivation has focused on the undermining of intrinsic motivation when the controlling aspect of an event is salient. Thus, in addition to the studies of expected rewards, others have shown that threats of punishment (Deci & Cascio, 1972), deadlines (Amabile, DeJong, & Lepper, 1976), imposed goals (Mossholder, 1980), surveillance (Lepper & Greene, 1975; Plant & Ryan, 1985), competition (Deci, Betley, Kahle, Abrams, & Porac, 1981), and evaluation (Smith, 1975; Ryan, 1982) all decreased intrinsic motivation, presumably because they were experienced as controls. Relatively little attention has been given to events that enhance intrinsic motivation through a shift toward a more internal perceived locus of causality. However, Zuckerman, Porac, Lathin, Smith, and Deci (1978) and Swann and Pittman (1977) reported that providing choice about what to do or how to do it enhanced intrinsic motivation, and Koestner, Ryan, Bernieri, and Holt (1984) showed that empathy and noncontrollingness can help maintain intrinsic motivation.

Furthermore, most feedback studies have focused on positive feedback, with only a few assessing the effects of negative feedback on intrinsic motivation. However, Deci and Cascio (1972) found negative feedback to undermine intrinsic motivation, and Vallerand and Reid (1984) found the undermining by negative feedback to be mediated by a decrease in perceived competence.

Social Contexts and Internal Events

CET was elaborated in the early 1980s in two important ways. First, it was suggested that although events such as rewards, deadlines, or positive feedback tend to have a particular functional significance, the interpersonal climate within which they are administered can significantly influence it. Thus, for example, Ryan (1982) showed that, whereas positive feedback is typically experienced as informational, if it is administered within a pressuring climate, emphasizing for example that people "should do well," the positive feedback tends to be experienced as controlling. Similarly, Ryan, Mims, and Koestner (1983) showed that although tangible rewards tend to be experienced as controlling, if they are administered in a non-evaluative context that supports autonomy, they tend not to be undermining. Furthermore, subsequent studies showed that limit setting will have a significantly different effect depending on whether the interpersonal context is informational or controlling (Koestner, Ryan, Bernieri, & Holt, 1984) and that competition can also be experienced as either informational or controlling, depending on the interpersonal climate (Reeve & Deci, 1996).

The second important extension of CET concerned internal initiating events. Specifically, Ryan (1982) suggested that people can initiate and regulate their actions in different ways that are relatively independent of the social context. For example, people can become ego-involved in an activity and its outcome. That is, their feelings of self-worth can become hinged to their performance such that they do the activity to prove to themselves that they are good at the activity and thus worthy individuals. Ryan contrasted this with task-involvement in which people are more involved with the task itself rather than with its implications for their own feelings of worth. He suggested that when the initiation and regulation of behavior is ego-involved the functional significance will be controlling relative to when the initiation and regulation is task-involved, and results confirmed this reasoning (Plant & Ryan, 1985; Ryan, 1982). A recent meta-analysis of experimental studies confirmed the CET proposition concerning the effects of ego versus task involvement on subsequent intrinsic motivation (Rawsthorne & Elliot, 1999). More generally, CET holds that self-controlling forms of regulation will be associated with diminished intrinsic motivation, whereas more autonomous forms of self-regulation will maintain or enhance intrinsic motivation.

Relatedness

As noted, we theorized that intrinsic motivation is integrally connected to the needs for competence and autonomy, and research has indicated that aspects of the social context which influence perceptions of competence and autonomy do indeed affect intrinsic motivation. There remains, however, the question of how the need for relatedness is involved in intrinsic motivation. We have emphasized that all three needs are essential for growth and development, so one would expect relatedness to play a role in intrinsic motivation. Indeed, evidence from studies with infants indicates that exploratory behavior (i.e., intrinsically motivated curiosity) tends to be in evidence to the degree that the children are securely attached to a primary caregiver. For example, Frodi, Bridges, and Grolnick (1985) found that security of attachment, which implied relational satisfaction, was associated with exploratory behaviors. In other words, when the infants experienced a general sense of satisfaction of the relatedness need, they were more likely to display intrinsically motivated exploration.

A serendipitous finding from a laboratory experiment by Anderson, Manoogian, and Reznick (1976) indicated that when children worked on an interesting activity in the presence of a previously unknown adult experimenter who ignored them, the children displayed a very low level of intrinsic motivation, suggesting therefore that thwarting of the need for relatedness can have a deleterious effect on intrinsic motivation. Still, evidence which closely links competence and autonomy to intrinsic motivation is considerably more plentiful than that linking relatedness to intrinsic motivation, and there do appear to be many solitary types of activities for which people maintain high intrinsic motivation in spite of not relating to others while doing them. Accordingly, we (Deci & Ryan, 2000) have suggested that relatedness typically plays a more distal role in the promotion of intrinsic motivation than do competence and autonomy, although there are some interpersonal activities for which satisfaction of the need for relatedness is crucial for maintaining intrinsic motivation.

Organismic Integration Theory

As noted, CET focuses on the effects of social-contextual variables on intrinsically motivated behaviors. It thus applies primarily to activities that people find interesting, optimally challenging, or aesthetically pleasing. Activities that are not so experienced will not be intrinsically motivated and are thus unlikely to be performed unless there is an extrinsic reason for doing them. Still, socializing agents frequently find it necessary to promote these uninteresting behaviors, so they face the issue not only of how to prompt the behaviors but, even more importantly, how to promote self-regulation of the behaviors so they will persist over the long term.

Because early discussions of intrinsic motivation contrasted it with extrinsic motivation, and because extrinsic motivation has frequently been shown to relate negatively to intrinsic motivation, many commentators (beginning with deCharms, 1968) have characterized extrinsic motivation as being nonautonomous—as being antithetical to self-determination. Indeed, research does make clear that extrinsic motivation in the form of working to attain tangible rewards is generally nonautonomous, for it tends to undermine intrinsic motivation (Deci et al., 1999). Nonetheless, we have assumed from the time we began this research that it is possible to be autonomously extrinsically motivated, and research within organismic integration theory has examined that issue extensively.

Internalization

Organismic integration theory (OIT) is based on the assumption that people are naturally inclined to integrate their ongoing experiences, assuming they have the necessary nutriments to do so. Accordingly, we postulated that if external prompts are used by significant others or salient reference groups to encourage people to do an uninteresting activity—an activity for which they are not intrinsically motivated—the individuals will tend to internalize the activity's initially external regulation. That is, people will tend to take in the regulation and integrate it with their sense of self. To the extent that this occurs, the individuals would be autonomous when enacting this extrinsically motivated behavior. Accordingly, in line with our active-organism metatheory, we view the phenomenon of internalization as a natural process in which people work to actively transform external regulation into self-regulation (Schafer, 1968), becoming more integrated as they do so.

An important element of OIT is that, unlike most other theories of internalization (e.g., Bandura, 1996), it views internalization not in terms of a dichotomy but rather in terms of a continuum. The more fully a regulation (or the value underlying it) is internalized, the more it becomes part of the integrated self and the more it is the basis for self-determined behavior. From this perspective, then, it is possible for individuals to internalize regulations without having them become part of the self. Regulations that have been taken in by an individual but not integrated with the self would not be the basis for autonomous self-regulation but would instead function more as controllers of behavior. Thus, extrinsically motivated behaviors for which the regulations have been internalized to differing degrees would differ in their relative autonomy. Those for which the regulations have been well integrated would be the basis for autonomous extrinsically motivated behavior, whereas those for which the regulations have been less fully internalized would be the basis for more controlled forms of extrinsic motivation.

Accordingly, OIT proposes a taxonomy of types of regulation for extrinsic motivation which differ in the degree to which they represent autonomy. Figure 1-1 presents the OIT taxonomy, arranged from left to right in terms of the extent to which the motivation for a behavior emanates from the self (i.e., is autonomous).

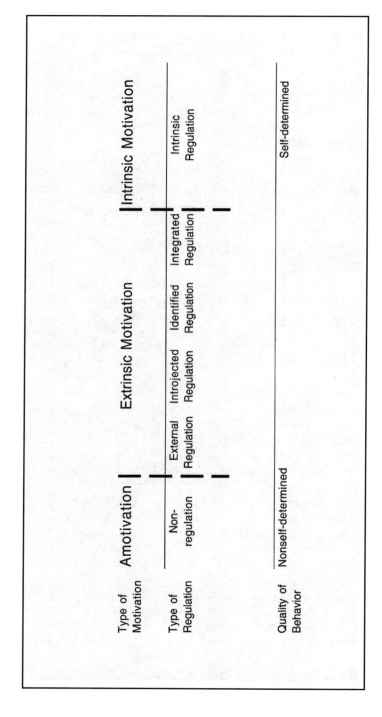

Figure 1.1. The Self-Determination Continuum, with Types of Motivation and Types of Regulation.

At the left end is *amotivation*, the state of lacking the intention to act. When people are amotivated, either they do not act at all or they act passively—that is, they go through the motions with no sense of intending to do what they are doing. Amotivation results from feeling either that they are unable to achieve desired outcomes because of a lack of contingency (Rotter, 1966; Seligman, 1975) or a lack of perceived competence (Bandura, 1977; Deci, 1975) or that they do not value the activity or the outcomes it would yield (Ryan, 1995).

The other five points on the continuum refer to classifications of motivated behavior. Each of these describes a theoretically, experientially, and functionally distinct type of regulation. At the right end of the continuum is *intrinsic motivation*, which we have already discussed as the state of doing an activity out of interest and inherent satisfaction. It is the prototype of autonomous or self-determined behavior. Extrinsically motivated behaviors, which are characterized by four types of regulation, fall along the self-determination continuum between amotivation and intrinsic motivation.

External regulation is the least autonomous form of extrinsic motivation and includes the classic instance of being motivated to obtain rewards or avoid punishments. More generally, external regulation is in evidence when one's reason for doing a behavior is to satisfy an external demand or a socially constructed contingency. External regulation has an external perceived locus of causality, is the type of regulation that is central to operant theory (e.g., Skinner, 1953), and is the form of extrinsic motivation that was contrasted with intrinsic motivation in the early discussions of the topic (e.g., deCharms, 1968).

Introjected regulation involves an external regulation having been internalized but not, in a much deeper sense, truly accepted as one's own. It is a type of extrinsic motivation that, having been partially internalized, is within the person but is not considered part of the integrated self. Introjection is a form of internalized regulation that is theorized to be quite controlling. Introjection-based behaviors are performed to avoid guilt and shame or to attain ego enhancements and feelings of worth. In other words, this type of regulation is based in contingent self-esteem (Deci & Ryan, 1995). Studies by Ryan (1982) and others have shown that, when ego-involved in an outcome, which is a form of introjected regulation, people tend to lose intrinsic motivation for the target activity, thus indicating that this type of regulation is, in fact, quite controlling.

Regulation through identification is a more self-determined form of extrinsic motivation, for it involves a conscious valuing of a behavioral goal or regulation, an acceptance of the behavior as personally important. Identification represents an important aspect of the process of transforming external regulation into true self-regulation. When a person identifies with an action or the value it expresses, they, at least at a conscious level, are personally endorsing it, and thus identifications are accompanied by a high degree of perceived autonomy. That is, identifications tend to have a relatively internal perceived locus of causality. However, SDT suggests that some identifications can be relatively compartmentalized or separated from one's other beliefs and values, in which case they may not reflect the person's overarching values in a given situation. Nonetheless, relative to external and introjected regulations, behavior that stems from identifications tends to be relatively autonomous or self-determined.

Integrated regulation provides the basis for the most autonomous form of extrinsically motivated behavior. It results when identifications have been evaluated and brought into congruence with the personally endorsed values, goals, and needs that are already part of the self. Research has shown extrinsically motivated behaviors that are integrated to be associated with more positive experiences than the less fully internalized forms of extrinsic motivation. Integrated extrinsic motivation also shares many qualities with intrinsic motivation. Nonetheless, although behaviors governed by integrated regulations are performed volitionally, they are still considered extrinsic because they are done to attain personally important outcomes rather than for their inherent interest and enjoyment. In other words, they are still instrumental to a separable outcome whose value is well integrated with the self.

It is important to recognize that the relative autonomy continuum is intended descriptively, to organize types of regulation with respect to the concept of self-determination. We do not suggest that it is a developmental continuum *per se,* nor that people must progress through each stage of internalization with respect to each regulation. Rather, it is possible for people to take in a regulation at any point along this continuum, assuming they have relevant prior experience and the immediate interpersonal climate is sufficiently supportive (Deci & Ryan, 1991; Ryan, 1995). We assume that the range of behaviors that can be assimilated to the self does increase over time as a function of greater cognitive and ego development (e.g., Loevinger & Blasi, 1991; Piaget, 1971), and there is evidence that children's general regulatory style tends to become more internalized with age (e.g., Chandler & Connell, 1987).

Ryan and Connell (1989) developed an approach to assessing regulatory styles, and thus the relative autonomy of one's regulation for a behavior or class of behaviors, treating regulatory styles as behavior-specific individual differences. They then used the approach to show that these different types of regulation lie along a continuum of relative autonomy. Specifically, they found that the different regulatory styles were intercorrelated according to a quasi-simplex pattern, correlating most strongly with those other styles that were theoretically closest to them in terms of the underlying relative autonomy continuum.

The Ryan and Connell approach has been extremely useful for examining OIT in various applied domains, such as education (Miserandino, 1996; Ryan & Connell, 1989), child rearing (Grolnick & Ryan, 1989), health care (Williams, Grow, Freedman, Ryan, & Deci, 1996; Williams, Rodin, Ryan, Grolnick, & Deci, 1998), intimate relationships (Blais, Sabourin, Boucher, & Vallerand, 1990), religious behavior (Ryan, Rigby, & King, 1993), physical exercise (Chatzisarantis, Biddle, & Meek, 1997), political behavior (Koestner, Losier, Vallerand, &

Carducci, 1996), and environmentally friendly activity (Green-Demers, Pelletier, & Menard, 1997). Consistently, the research has shown varied advantages to being autonomously motivated, relative to controlled, including more volitional persistence, better relationships in one's social groups, more effective perform-ance, and greater health and well-being.

Promoting Integrated Regulation

Because extrinsically motivated behaviors are not inherently interesting, people are unlikely to do them if the behaviors are not instrumental for a desired outcome. Thus, initially, such behaviors are typically prompted by significant oth-ers, whether with a simple request, the offer of a reward, or the fact that the oth-ers demonstrate their valuing of the activity by performing it regularly. That is, the dynamic involved in prompting such behaviors involves a significant other or group endorsing an action and in some way conveying their endorsement to the target individual. The individual, in turn, out of feeling related to the other per-son or the group, or out of the desire for such relatedness, will likely engage in the behavior with the expectation of gaining implicit or explicit approval for doing so. This suggests that the need for relatedness to others is centrally impor-tant for internalization. OIT proposes that supports for feelings of relatedness are, indeed, crucial for promoting internalization. In fact, a study by Ryan, Stiller and Lynch (1994) showed that children who felt securely connected to, and cared for by, their parents and teachers were the ones who more fully internalized the regulation for positive school-related behaviors. It seems that, whereas relatedness is less central than the other two needs for maintaining intrinsic motivation, it is very much central for promoting internalization.

Still, relatedness alone is not enough to ensure a full internalization of extrin-sic motivation. As well, people will need to feel competent with respect to behav-iors valued by a significant other if they are to engage in and accept responsibil-ity for those behaviors. Thus, OIT suggests that support for competence will con-tribute to the facilitation of internalization and the subsequent self-regulation of extrinsically motivated activities. If people do not feel competent to perform a target behavior, they are unlikely to internalize regulation of the behavior; in fact, they will likely find an excuse not to do the behavior at all, even in the presence of the significant other.

Finally, from the perspective of OIT, perceptions of autonomy play an extremely important role in the processes of internalization and integration. As already noted, internalization can take the form of introjection, resulting in con-trolled regulation, or it can involve a much fuller internalization and integration. According to the theory, support for autonomy is the critical factor for determin-ing whether the internalization that is promoted by supports for relatedness and competence will be only partial (as in introjection) or will be much fuller (as in integration). Thus, although some internalization may occur without autonomy support, the type of internalization that will result in persistence, flexibility, and vitality—those being the factors that characterize self-determination—will be in evidence to the degree that supports for autonomy are present. Stated differently, to integrate the regulation of a behavior, people must grasp its meaning for themselves personally, and they must synthesize that meaning with other aspects of their psychic makeup. This type of engagement with the activity and with the process of internalization is most likely to occur when people experience a sense of choice, volition, and freedom from external demands. Accordingly, autonomy support is the basis for people's actively transforming a value and regulation into their own.

To summarize, external regulation is likely to occur when people feel competent enough to perform the requisite action, assuming there are salient consequences such as implicit approval from significant others. Further, with supports for relatedness as well as competence, introjection is a likely outcome. Only when the social climate also provides support for autonomy is there likely to be integration of the relevant regulation, thus providing the foundation for subsequent selfdetermined behavior.

Various studies have provided evidence for this reasoning. For example, Grolnick and Ryan (1989) found greater internalization and integration of school-related values among children whose parents were more supportive of autonomy and relatedness, and Williams and Deci (1996), using a longitudinal design, demonstrated greater internalization of biopsychosocial values among medical students whose instructors were more supportive of autonomy.

Deci, Eghrari, Patrick, and Leone (1994) performed a laboratory experiment with an uninteresting activity in which they manipulated the presence versus absence of three supportive factors—a meaningful rationale, acknowledgement of the person's perspective, and provision of choice rather than pressure. The researchers found internalization, as measured by subsequent behavioral persistence, to be a function of the number of facilitating factors. However, they also found that with relatively little support, whatever internalization occurred was in the form of introjection, whereas with relatively more support, the internalization was likely to involve integration.

Causality Orientations Theory

Self-determination theory, with its various mini-theories, has devoted considerable attention to the influence of social contexts both on motivation, behavior, and experience in a particular situation and on the development of personality over time. Whereas CET is concerned primarily with the effects of specific social context on motivation, behavior, and experience, OIT is concerned more with the differentiation of extrinsic motivation in accord with internalization and on the influence of social contexts on the internalization of extrinsic motivation. More specifically, OIT posits that different regulatory styles for extrinsically motivated behaviors are developmental outcomes, and researchers have used those styles as individual differences to predict performance and well-being.

Throughout the development of SDT, we have assumed that a person's motivation, behavior, and experience in a particular situation is a function both of the immediate social context and of the person's inner resources that have developed over time as a function of prior interactions with social contexts. Causality orientations theory was developed as a descriptive account of these inner resources—that is, of relatively stable individual differences in one's motivational orientations toward the social world. Based on it, we developed an individual difference measure, the General Causality Orientations Scale (GCOS) that has been used for predictive purposes in numerous studies (Deci & Ryan, 1985a).

The causality orientations approach is intended to index aspects of personality that are broadly integral to the regulation of behavior and experience. It specifies three orientations that differ in the degree to which they represent self-determination—namely, the autonomous, controlled, and impersonal causality orientations—and people are assumed to have each of these orientations, to some degree. The *autonomy orientation* involves regulating behavior on the basis of interests and self-endorsed values; it serves to index a person's general tendencies toward intrinsic motivation and well integrated extrinsic motivation. The *controlled orientation* involves orienting toward controls and directives concerning how one should behave; it relates to external and introjected regulation. The *impersonal orientation* involves focusing on indicators of ineffectance and not behaving intentionally; it relates to amotivation and lack of intentional action.

Individuals get a score on each of the three orientations reflecting the strength of each general tendency for themselves. In the initial research by Deci and Ryan (1985a) the autonomy orientation was found to relate positively to self-actualization, self-esteem, ego development, and other indicators of well-being. As expected, the controlled orientation was not positively associated with well-being but instead was related to public self-consciousness and the Type-A coronary prone behavior pattern, indicating that the focus tends to be outward and pressured. The impersonal orientation was related to self-derogation, low self-esteem, and depression.

Koestner, Bernieri, and Zuckerman (1992) explored the relation of the autonomy and controlled orientations to integration in personality, hypothesizing that autonomy, relative, to control, would be associated with greater integration. They began by creating two groups, one of individuals who tended to be more autonomous and one of individuals who tended to be more controlled, based on a comparison of their standardized scores for the two orientations. The researchers then examined the consistency among behaviors, traits, and attitudes within the two groups. Results indicated that autonomy-oriented individuals displayed a strong positive relation among behaviors and self-reports of traits or attitudes, whereas control-oriented individuals displayed weak or even negative relations among these various personality aspects. Thus, the studies drew an empirical link between the concepts of autonomy and integration by showing greater congruence among personality, awareness, and behavior for autonomy-oriented than for control-oriented individuals.

Numerous investigators have related general causality orientations to specific regulatory styles, to behavioral outcomes, to aspects of personality, and to well-being indicators, and much of that research is described in various chapters of this volume.

Basic Needs Theory

The concept of basic psychological needs has played an important, though often implicit, role in SDT and each of its mini-theories from the time the work began. The relatively recent formalization of this mini-theory was done to clarify the meaning of the concept and to detail its dynamic relation to mental health and well-being.

To qualify as a need, a motivating force must have a direct relation to well-being. Needs, when satisfied, promote well-being, but when thwarted, lead to negative consequences. Further, because needs are hypothesized to be universal, this relation between satisfaction and well-being must apply across ages, genders, and cultures. Of course, the means through which needs are satisfied (versus thwarted) vary as a function of age, gender, and culture. Thus, in an extreme case, it is possible for the same behavior to be need satisfying for one group and need thwarting for another. Still, the underlying process in which need satisfaction promotes health is theorized to be the same across all these groups.

Well-being

Recent research on well-being has been plentiful, although the concept of well-being has been treated in two different ways by different researchers (see Ryan & Deci, 2001). One approach focuses on hedonic or subjective well-being and essentially equates it with happiness (e.g., Kahneman, Diener, & Schwarz, 1999), whereas the other approach focuses on eudaimonic well-being and equates it with being fully functioning (e.g., Ryff & Singer, 1998). Although there is substantial intersection of the two concepts, we endorse the eudaimonic conception, and much of our recent research has served to establish a clear empirical link between satisfaction of autonomy, competence, and relatedness needs, on the one hand, and eudaimonic well-being, on the other. In so doing, we have not used a specific measure of eudaimonic well-being, but have instead used several measures of positive affect and mental health to index the general organismic concept that involves people detecting the degree of their own vitality, psychological flexibility, and deep inner sense of wellness (Ryan & Frederick, 1997; Ryan, Deci, & Grolnick, 1995).

Research on Basic Needs Theory

Research on basic needs theory has thus far fallen into three categories. First, diary procedures have been used to examine whether daily variations in need satisfaction predict daily fluctuations in well-being. In other words, this research has considered the within-person relations between experienced need satisfaction and well-being over time, as well as the more standard between-person relations. Second, studies have explored the relation between the pursuit and attainment of specific goal contents, on the one hand, and well-being, on the other. Whereas most theories do not differentiate goal contents, suggesting simply a positive relation between the attainment of valued goals and well-being, basic needs theory suggests that there will be a positive relation between goal attainment and well-being only for those goals that satisfy basic psychological needs. In fact, pursuit of some valent goals may be negatively related to well-being if the goals distract people from satisfaction of the basic needs. Third, we have begun to examine need satisfaction across cultures, hypothesizing that need satisfaction will relate to well-being regardless of culture.

Need Satisfaction and Well-being

In two studies (Sheldon, Ryan, & Reis, 1996; Reis, Sheldon, Gable, Roscoe, & Ryan, 2000), multilevel modeling was used to relate variations in need satisfaction to well-being. At both the between-person (i.e., individual-difference) level and the within-person (i.e., daily-fluctuation) level, measures of basic-need satisfaction related to positive affect, vitality, and the inverse of negative affect and symptomatology. These studies confirmed both that general satisfaction of each basic need contributed to general well-being and that daily satisfaction of each basic need explained daily fluctuations in well-being over time.

In other, between-person, studies, V. Kasser and Ryan (1999) found that satisfaction of the needs for autonomy and relatedness in the daily lives of residents of a nursing home were positively related to their well-being and perceived health. Two studies (Baard, Deci, & Ryan, 2000; Ilardi, Leone, Kasser, & Ryan,

1993) have further found that employees' reports of satisfaction of their basic needs in the workplace related to self-esteem, general health, vitality, and the inverse of anxiety and somatization. Thus, within the specific settings of nursing homes and workplaces, the evidence supports the hypothesis that satisfaction of the needs for autonomy, competence, and relatedness will predict psychological health.

Aspirations and Basic Needs

The relation of goal contents to well-being has been examined in a series of studies by Kasser and Ryan (1993, 1996) and others, concerning people's aspirations or life goals. Research on these issues is also discussed in the chapter by Kasser in this volume. Kasser and Ryan suggested that there are two types of aspirations, namely, *intrinsic aspirations*, which provide relatively direct satisfaction of the basic needs, and *extrinsic aspirations*, which are more related to obtaining external signs of worth and are less likely to provide direct need satisfaction. Examples of intrinsic aspirations are affiliation, personal growth, and community contribution, and examples of extrinsic aspirations (at least within the American culture) are wealth, fame, and image. Kasser and Ryan argued that, because of the hypothesized links of intrinsic aspirations to basic need satisfaction, pursuit and attainment of those aspirations, relative to extrinsic aspirations, should be more strongly associated with well-being. Whereas people might feel happy about attaining their extrinsic aspirations, the theory suggests that pursuit and attainment of extrinsic aspiration will not contribute to eudaimonic well-being.

Kasser and Ryan (1996) had individuals rate how important, in terms of their own lives, they considered each of a set of life goals. Using items related to three intrinsic aspirations (affiliation, personal growth, and community) and three extrinsic aspirations (wealth, fame, and image), they calculated how strong each aspiration was relative to all others. The critical issue in this program of research, then, is not so much the actual strength of an aspiration, but rather, where it stands relative to the others: is it, for example, unusually strong and thus out of balance with the others?

Kasser and Ryan (1993, 1996) found that the relative strength of intrinsic aspirations was significantly positively related to well-being indicators, such as self-actualization and vitality, and were significantly negatively related to anxiety, depression, and physical symptoms. In contrast, the index for the extrinsic aspirations showed the opposite pattern of relations. One of the studies in the series used clinical indicators, finding that a strong relative extrinsic aspiration for wealth related positively to conduct disorders and negatively to global social functioning and social productivity. These studies converged on the finding that placing high importance on extrinsic outcomes, relative to intrinsic ones, was related to poorer well-being. Furthermore, the research showed that the effects on well-being of the relative strengths of aspirations was not accounted for by people's feelings of efficacy with respect to attaining the goals.

The aspirations studies reviewed thus far examined the relative *importance* to individuals of different aspirations or life goals, whereas other studies have shown that the *attainment* of intrinsic versus extrinsic aspirations also relates differentially to well-being. For example, Kasser and Ryan (2001) found that perceived current attainment of intrinsic aspirations was positively associated with well-being, but rated current attainment of extrinsic aspirations was not. Sheldon and Kasser (1998) found that well-being was enhanced by the actual attainment of intrinsic goals, whereas attainment of extrinsic goals provided little benefit. Together, these results suggest that pursuit and attainment of valued goals does not ensure well-being. The content of the goal itself makes a difference, and we theorize that this is because some goals (which we label intrinsic) provide more need satisfaction, whereas others (which we label extrinsic) provide less need satisfaction. In fact, the pursuit and attainment of extrinsic aspirations may actually detract from need satisfaction by keeping people focused on goals that are not directly need related.

Need substitutes. According to basic needs theory, extrinsic aspirations, which can be highly motivating, are likely to develop as substitutes for basic needs (Deci, 1980) under developmental conditions in which need satisfaction is relatively unavailable. As such, they can provide collateral satisfaction, but they do not provide the direct satisfaction of basic needs that are necessary for promotion of well-being.

Kasser, Ryan, Zax, and Sameroff (1995) studied teenagers and their mothers to test this reasoning by examining the developmental antecedents of placing high relative importance on extrinsic aspirations. They found, using both teens' perceptions of their mothers and also the mothers' self-reports of their parenting styles, that when the mothers were democratic, noncontrolling, and warm (thus being supportive of basic need satisfaction), the teens placed significantly less relative importance on extrinsic aspirations. The results suggest that parenting styles that thwart children's need satisfaction lead the children to develop extrinsic aspirations, such as wealth, that are visible indicators of "worth" and may represent substitutes for basic need satisfaction. These, in turn, are expected to perpetuate the lack of need satisfaction and exacerbate the negative, ill-being consequences.

Williams, Cox, Hedberg, and Deci (2000) studied high school students to test the hypotheses (a) that need-thwarting parental styles would lead to stronger relative extrinsic aspirations and (b) that this pattern of aspirations would promote risky behaviors that could further interfere with basic need satisfaction and health. Results of the study yielded a significant relation between the students' perceiving their parents as controlling and the students' having strong relative extrinsic aspirations. Further, students with less autonomy-supportive parents and stronger extrinsic aspirations reported more health-compromising behaviors, including the use of tobacco, alcohol, and marijuana. It does appear, therefore, that social contexts that thwart need satisfaction can lead to goals that are compensatory and may involve serious risks to physical and psychological well-being.

Need Satisfaction Across Cultures

According to the basic needs perspective, a need is by definition universal and thus the relation between need satisfaction and well-being must apply in all cultures. There can, however, be considerable variability in the values and goals held within different cultures such that the means through which people satisfy basic needs will differ among cultures. In other words, the relations between specific behaviors and satisfaction of underlying needs may be different in different cultures because the behaviors come to have different meanings in accord with culturally endorsed values and practices. Recent research on motivation has begun to explore the relations between need satisfaction and well-being across cultures.

In some studies, investigators have examined issues in Asian or European cultures that had previously been studied in North America. By finding results that are similar to those from American samples, these studies provide initial evidence in support of the cross-cultural validity of propositions from basic needs theory. For example, Hayamizu (1997) used the self-regulation questionnaire to assess the motivation of junior high school students in Japan and found that the autonomous forms of motivation were associated with positive coping whereas the controlled forms were associated with maladaptive coping, thus replicating findings from the United States by Ryan and Connell (1989). Similar results were also found in Japanese children by Yamauchi and Tanaka (1998).

Chirkov and Ryan (2001) found that Russian and American students who experienced their parents and teachers as more autonomy supportive displayed greater well-being than those who experienced them as less autonomy supportive. Although there were mean level differences in the amount of perceived autonomy support, with Russians perceiving less, both the constructs and the relations between autonomy support and well-being were comparable across cultures. The importance of this and other Russian replications of SDT studies in the United States is that traditionally Russia has been an authoritarian, or vertical culture, which has led some theorists (e.g., Miller, 1997) to argue that autonomy should not matter there. However, showing parallel functions of autonomy support versus control suggests that such cultural or historical backdrops do not negate this basic dynamic of human nature.

A recent study of workers in Bulgarian state-owned companies operating in accord with central-planning principles investigated the relations among social contexts, need satisfaction on the job, and well-being (Deci, Ryan, Gagne, Leone, Usunov, & Kornazheva, 2001). Results of this study indicated construct comparability between Bulgarian and American samples and supported the model in which contextual supports predict basic need satisfaction, which in turn predicts work engagement and well-being. In other words, employees in both Bulgaria and the United States who reported greater satisfaction of the competence, autonomy, and relatedness needs while on the job were more motivated and evidenced greater psychological health.

Other research has examined the relation of aspirations to well-being in different cultures. For example, Ryan, Chirkov, Little, Sheldon, Timoshina, and Deci (1999) found in Russian college students that those individuals whose life goals were focused more on relationships, growth, and community than on wealth, image, and fame evidenced greater well-being. Of course, aspiring for specific outcomes such as accumulating wealth can have different meaning for basic need satisfaction in different cultures, so we would not necessarily expect an invariant relation between aspirations and well-being across cultures (although we would expect invariance in the relation between need satisfaction and well-being). Thus, it is interesting that the results for these Russian college students largely replicated those for Americans, even though the two cultures are so different.

Summary

Self-determination theory focuses on the dialectic between the active, growth-oriented human organism and social contexts that either support or undermine people's attempts to master and integrate their experiences into a coherent sense of self. The concept of basic psychological needs for competence, autonomy, and relatedness serves to define those contextual factors that tend to support versus undermine motivation, performance, and well-being. SDT was formulated in terms of four mini-theories that share the organismic-dialectical metatheory and the concept of basic needs. Each of the metatheories was developed to explain a set of motivationally based phenomena that emerged from laboratory and field research and focused on different issues. Cognitive evaluation theory addresses the effects of social contexts on intrinsic motivation; organismic integration theory addresses the concept of internalization especially with respect to the development of extrinsic motivation. Causality orientations theory describes individual differences in people's tendencies toward self-determined behavior and toward orienting to the environment in ways that support their self-determination. And basic needs theory elaborates the concept of basic needs and its relation to life goals and daily behaviors, specifying the essential role of needs to psychological health and well-being.

About this Book

In this volume, researchers summarize their own contributions to the field of motivation and self-determination. Some chapters represent specific extensions of SDT by formulating theoretical models that systematize relations among SDT variables, elaborate a piece of the theory, or apply the concepts to new phenomena. Other chapters use the concepts and measures of SDT to shed important light on various applied problems or areas, helping to provide solutions for profound problems facing society. A final set of chapters adds significantly to the explication of SDT by relating its concepts to the concepts of other theoretical perspectives or fields of research. Each of these chapters describes exciting, programmatic, research that is helping to provide a comprehensive and meaningful system of psychological thought.

References

Allport, G. (1961). *Pattern and growth in personality*. New York: Holt, Rinehart & Winston.

Amabile, T. M., DeJong, W., & Lepper, M. (1976). Effects of externally imposed deadlines on subsequent intrinsic motivation. *Journal of Personality and Social Psychology, 34*, 92-98.

Anderson, R., Manoogian, S. T., & Reznick, J. S. (1976). The undermining and enhancing of intrinsic motivation in preschool children. *Journal of Personality and Social Psychology, 34*, 915-922.

Angyal, A. (1965). *Neurosis and treatment: A holistic theory*. New York: Wiley.

Baard, P. P., Deci, E. L., & Ryan, R. M. (2000). The relation of intrinsic need satisfaction to performance and well-being in two work settings. Unpublished manuscript, Fordham.

Bandura, A. (1977). Self-efficacy: Toward a unifying theory of behavioral change. *Psychological Review, 84*, 191-215.

Bandura, A. (1989). Human agency in social cognitive theory. *American Psychologist, 44*, 1175-1184.

Bandura, A. (1996). *Self-efficacy: The exercise of control*. New York: Freeman.

Baumeister, R., & Leary, M. R. (1995). The need to belong: Desire for interpersonal attachments as a fundamental human motivation. *Psychological Bulletin, 117*, 497-529.

Blais, M. R., Sabourin S., Boucher, C., & Vallerand, R. (1990). Toward a motivational model of couple happiness. *Journal of Personality and Social Psychology, 59*, 1021-1031.

Bowlby, J. (1979). *The making and breaking of affectional bonds*. London: Tavistock.

Broughton, J. M. (1987). *Critical theories of psychological development*. New York: Plenum.

Chandler, C. L., & Connell, J. P. (1987). Children's intrinsic, extrinsic and internalized motivation: A developmental study of children's reasons for liked and disliked behaviours. *British Journal of Developmental Psychology, 5*, 357-365.

Chatzisarantis, N. L. D., & Biddle, S. J. H., & Meek, G.A. (1997). A self-determination theory approach to the study of intentions and the intention-behaviour relationship in children's physical activity. *British Journal of Health Psychology, 2*, 343-360.

Chirkov, V. I., & Ryan, R.M. (2001). Parent and teacher automony support in Russian and U.S. adolescents. *Journal of Cross-Cultural Psychology, 32*, 618-635.

deCharms, R. (1968). *Personal causation: The internal affective determinants of behavior.* New York: Academic Press.

Deci, E. L. (1971). Effects of externally mediated rewards on intrinsic motivation. *Journal of Personality and Social Psychology, 18*, 105- 115.

Deci, E. L. (1972a). Effects of contingent and non-contingent rewards and controls on intrinsic motivation. *Organizational Behavior and Human Performance, 8*, 217-229.

Deci, E. L. (1972b). Intrinsic motivation, extrinsic reinforcement, and inequity. *Journal of Personality and Social Psychology, 22*, 113- 120.

Deci, E. L. (1975). *Intrinsic motivation.* New York: Plenum.

Deci, E. L. (1980). *The psychology of self-determination.* Lexington, MA: D.C. Heath.

Deci, E. L., Betley, G., Kahle, J., Abrams, L., & Porac, J. (1981). When trying to win: Competition and intrinsic motivation. *Personality and Social Psychology Bulletin, 7*, 79-83.

Deci, E. L, & Cascio, W. F. (1972, April). *Changes in intrinsic motivation as a function of negative feedback and threats.* Presented at the Eastern Psychological Association, Boston.

Deci, E. L., Eghrari, H., Patrick, B. C., & Leone, D. R. (1994). Facilitating internalization: The self-determination theory perspective. *Journal of Personality, 62*, 119-142.

Deci, E. L., Koestner, R., & Ryan, R. M. (1999). A meta-analytic review of experiments examining the effects of extrinsic rewards on intrinsic motivation. *Psychological Bulletin, 125*, 627-668.

Deci, E. L., & Ryan, R. M. (1980). The empirical exploration of intrinsic motivational processes. In L. Berkowitz (Ed.), *Advances in experimental social psychology* (Vol. 13, pp. 39-80). New York: Academic Press.

Deci, E. L., & Ryan, R. M. (1985a). The general causality orientations scale: Self-determination in personality. *Journal of Research in Personality, 19*, 109-134.

Deci, E. L., & Ryan, R. M. (1985b). *Intrinsic motivation and self-determination in human behavior.* New York: Plenum.

Deci, E. L., & Ryan, R. M. (1991). A motivational approach to self: Integration in personality. In R. Dienstbier (Ed.), *Nebraska symposium on motivation: Vol. 38. Perspectives on motivation* (pp. 237-288). Lincoln, NE: University of Nebraska Press.

Deci, E. L., & Ryan, R. M. (1995). Human autonomy: The basis for true self-esteem. In M. Kernis (Ed.), *Efficacy, agency, and self-esteem* (pp. 31-49). New York: Plenum.

Deci, E. L., & Ryan, R. M. (2000). The "what" and "why" of goal pursuits: Human needs and the self-determination of behavior. *Psychological Inquiry, 11*, 227-268.

Deci, E. L., Ryan, R. M., Gagné, M., Leone, D. R., Usunov, J., & Kornazheva, B. P. (2001). Need satisfaction, motivation, and well-being in the work organizations of a former Eastern Bloc country. *Personality and Social Psychology Bulletin, 27*, 930-942.

Eisenberger, R., & Cameron, J. (1996). Detrimental effects of reward: Reality or myth? *American Psychologist, 51*, 1153-1166.

Fisher, C. D. (1978). The effects of personal control, competence, and extrinsic reward systems on intrinsic motivation. *Organizational Behavior and Human Performance, 21*, 273-288.

Frodi, A., Bridges, L., & Grolnick, W.S. (1985). Correlates of mastery-related behavior: A short term longitudinal study of infants in their second year. *Child Development, 56*, 1291-1298.

Ford, M. E. (1992). *Motivating humans: Goals, emotions, and personal agency beliefs.* Newbury Park, CA: Sage.

Freud, S. (1927). *The ego and the id.* London: Institute for Psychoanalysis and Hogarth Press.

Gergen, K. J. (1993). *The saturated self.* New York: Basic Books.

Green-Demers, I., Pelletier, L. G., & Menard, S. (1997). The impact of behavioral difficulty on the saliency of the association between self-determined motivation and environmental behaviors. *Canadian Journal of Behavioural Science, 29,* 157-166.

Greenwald, A. G. (1982). Ego task analysis: An integration of research on ego-involvement and self-awareness. In A. H. Hastorf & A. M. Isen (Eds.), *Cognitive social psychology,* (pp. 109-147). New York: Elsevier.

Grolnick, W. S., & Ryan, R. M. (1989). Parent styles associated with children's self-regulation and competence in school. *Journal of Educational Psychology, 81,* 143-154.

Harlow, H. F. (1958). The nature of love. *American Psychologist, 13,* 673-685.

Harter, S. (1983). Developmental perspectives on the self-system. In E. M. Hetherington (Ed.), *Handbook of child psychology. Vol. 4. Socialization, personality and social development* (4th ed., pp. 275-386). New York: Wiley.

Hayamizu, T. (1997). Between intrinsic and extrinsic motivation: Examination of reasons for academic study based on the theory of internalization. *Japanese Psychological Research, 39,* 98-108.

Heider, F. (1958). *The psychology of interpersonal relations.* New York: Wiley.

Higgins, E. T. (1987). Self-discrepancy theory: A theory relating self and affect. *Psychological Review, 94,* 319-340.

Ilardi, B. C., Leone, D., Kasser, T., & Ryan, R. M. (1993). Employee and supervisor ratings of motivation: Main effects and discrepancies associated with job satisfaction and adjustment in a factory setting. *Journal of Applied Social Psychology, 23,* 1789-1805.

Jacob, F. (1973). *The logic of life: A history of heredity.* New York: Pantheon.

Kahneman, D., Diener, E., & Schwarz, N. (Eds), (1999). *Well-being: The foundations of hedonic psychology.* New York: Russell Sage Foundation.

Kasser, T., & Ryan, R. M. (1993). A dark side of the American dream: Correlates of financial success as a central life aspiration. *Journal of Personality and Social Psychology, 65,* 410422.

Kasser, T., & Ryan, R. M. (1996). Further examining the American dream: Differential correlates of intrinsic and extrinsic goals. *Personality and Social Psychology Bulletin 22,* 80-87.

Kasser, T., & Ryan, R. M. (2001). Be careful what you wish for: Optimal functioning and the relative attainment of intrinsic and extrinsic goals. In P. Schmuck & K. M. Sheldon (Eds.), *Life goals and well-being* (pp. 116-131). Göttingen: Hogrefe and Huber.

Kasser, T., Ryan, R. M., Zax, M., & Sameroff, A. J. (1995). The relations of maternal and social environments to late adolescents' materialistic and prosocial values. *Developmental Psychology, 31,* 907-914.

Kasser, V., & Ryan, R. M. (1999). The relation of psychological needs for autonomy and relatedness to vitality, well-being, and mortality in a nursing home. *Journal of Applied Social Psychology, 29,* 935-954.

Koestner, R., Bernieri, F., & Zuckerman, M. (1992). Self-determination and consistency between attitudes, traits, and behaviors. *Personality and Social Psychology Bulletin, 18,* 52-59.

Koestner, R., Losier, G. F., Vallerand, R. J., & Carducci. D. (1996). Identified and introjected forms of political internalization: Extending self-determination theory. *Journal of Personality and Social Psychology, 70*, 1025-1036.

Koestner, R., Ryan, R. M., Bernieri, F., & Holt, K. (1984). Setting limits on children's behavior: The differential effects of controlling versus informational styles on intrinsic motivation and creativity. *Journal of Personality, 52*, 233-248.

Kruglanski, A. W., Friedman, I., & Zeevi, G. (1971). The effects of extrinsic incentive on some qualitative aspects of task performance. *Journal of Personality, 39*, 606-617.

Kuhl, J., & Fuhrmann, A. (1998). Decomposing self-regulation and self-control: The theoretical and empirical basis of the Volitional Components Checklist. In J. Heckhausen & C. Dweck (Eds.), *Motivation and self-regulation across the life-span (pp. 15-49)*. New York: Cambridge University Press.

Lepper, M. R. & Greene, D. (1975). Turning play into work: Effects of adult surveillance and extrinsic rewards on children's intrinsic motivation. *Journal of Personality and Social Psychology, 31*, 479- 486.

Lepper, M. R., Greene, D., & Nisbett, R. E. (1973). Undermining children's intrinsic interest with extrinsic rewards: A test of the "overjustification" hypothesis. *Journal of Personality and Social Psychology, 28*, 129-137.

Loevinger, J., & Blasi, A. (1991). Development of the self as subject. In J. Strauss & G. R. Goethals (Eds.), *The self: Interdisciplinary approaches* (pp. 150-167). New York: Springer-Verlag.

Markus, H. R., & Nurius, P. S. (1986). Self-understanding and self-regulation in middle childhood. In W. A. Collins (Ed.), *Development during middle childhood*. Washington, DC: National Academy Press.

Maslow, A. H. (1955). Deficiency motivation and growth motivation. In M. R. Jones (Ed.), *Nebraska symposium on motivation*, (Vol. 3, pp. 1-30). Lincoln: University of Nebraska Press.

Meissner, W. W. (1981). *Internalization in psychoanalysis*. New York: International Universities Press.

Miller, J. G. (1997). Cultural conceptions of duty: Implications for motivation and morality. In D. Munro, J. F. Schumaker, & A. C. Carr (Eds.), *Motivation and culture*, (pp. 178-192). New York: Routledge.

Mischel, W., & Shoda, Y. (1995). A cognitive-affective system theory of personality: Reconceptualizing situations, dispositions, dynamics, and invariance in personality structure. *Psychological Review, 102*, 246-268.

Miserandino, M. (1996). Children who do well in school: Individual differences in perceived competence and autonomy in above average children. *Journal of Educational Psychology, 88*, 203-214.

Mossholder, K. W. (1980). Effects of externally mediated goal setting on intrinsic motivation: A laboratory experiment. *Journal of Applied Psychology, 65*, 202-210.

Nunberg, H. (1931). The synthetic function of the ego. *International Journal of Psycho-Analysis, 12*, 123-140.

Piaget, J. (1971). *Biology and knowledge*. Chicago: University of Chicago Press.

Plant, R., & Ryan, R. M. (1985). Intrinsic motivation and the effects of self-consciousness, self-awareness, and ego-involvement: An investigation of internally controlling styles. *Journal of Personality, 53*, 435-449.

Rawsthorne, L. J., & Elliot, A. J. (1999). Achievement goals and intrinsic motivation: A meta-analytic review. *Personality and Social Psychology Review, 3*, 326-344.

Reeve, J., & Deci, E. L. (1996). Elements within the competitive situation that affect intrinsic motivation. *Personality and Social Psychology Bulletin, 22*, 24-33.

Reis, H. T., Sheldon, K. M., Gable, S. L., Roscoe, J., & Ryan, R. M. (2000). Daily well-being: The role of autonomy, competence, and relatedness. *Personality and Social Psychology Bulletin, 26*, 419-435.

Rogers, C. (1963). The actualizing tendency in relation to "motives" and to con-sciousness. In M. R. Jones (Ed.), *Nebraska symposium on motivation* (Vol. 11, pp. 1-24). Lincoln, NE: University of Nebraska Press.

Rotter, J. (1966). Generalized expectancies for internal versus external control of reinforcement. *Psychological Monographs, 80* (1, Whole No. 609). Pp. 1-28.

Ryan, R. M. (1982). Control and information in the intrapersonal sphere: An exten-sion of cognitive evaluation theory. *Journal of Personality and Social Psychology, 43*, 450-461.

Ryan, R. M. (1993). Agency and organization: Intrinsic motivation, autonomy and the self in psychological development. In J. Jacobs (Ed.), *Nebraska symposium on motivation: Developmental perspectives on motivation* (Vol. 40, pp. 1-56). Lincoln, NE: University of Nebraska Press.

Ryan, R. M. (1995). Psychological needs and the facilitation of integrative processes. *Journal of Personality, 63*, 397-427.

Ryan, R. M., Chirkov, V. I., Little, T. D., Sheldon, K. M., Timoshina, E., & Deci, E. L. (1999). The American dream in Russia: Extrinsic aspirations and well-being in two cultures. *Personality and Social Psychology Bulletin, 25*, 1509-1524.

Ryan, R. M., & Connell, J. P. (1989). Perceived locus of causality and internalization: Examining reasons for acting in two domains. *Journal of Personality and Social Psychology, 57*, 749-761.

Ryan, R. M., & Deci, E. L. (2000a). Intrinsic and extrinsic motivations: Classic def-initions and new directions. *Contemporary Educational Psychology, 25*, 54-67.

Ryan, R. M., & Deci, E. L. (2000b). Self-determination theory and the facilitation of intrinsic motivation, social development, and well-being. *American Psychologist, 55*, 68-78.

Ryan, R. M., & Deci, E. L. (2001). To be happy or to be self-fulfilled: A review of research on hedonic and eudaimonic well-being. In S. Fiske (Ed.), *Annual Review of Psychology* (Vol. 52; pp. 141-166). Palo Alto, CA: Annual Reviews, Inc.

Ryan, R. M., Deci, E. L., & Grolnick, W. S. (1995). Autonomy, relatedness, and the self: Their relation to development and psychopathology. In D. Cicchetti & D. J. Cohen (Eds.), *Developmental psychopathology Vol. 1.* (pp. 618-655). New York: Wiley.

Ryan, R. M., & Frederick, C. M. (1997). On energy, personality, and health: Subjective vitality as a dynamic reflection of well-being. *Journal of Personality, 65*, 529-565.

Ryan, R. M., & Lynch, J. H. (1989). Emotional autonomy versus detachment: Revisiting the vicissitudes of adolescence and young adulthood. *Child Development, 60*, 340-356.

Ryan, R. M., Mims, V., & Koestner, R. (1983). Relation of reward contingency and interpersonal context to intrinsic motivation: A review and test using cognitive evaluation theory. *Journal of Personality and Social Psychology, 45*, 736-750.

Ryan, R. M., Rigby, S., & King, K. (1993). Two types of religious internalization and their relations to religious orientations and mental health. *Journal of Personality and Social Psychology, 65*, 586-596.

Ryan, R. M., Sheldon, K. M., Kasser, T., & Deci, E. L. (1996). All goals are not created equal: An organismic perspective on the nature of goals and their regulation. In P. M. Gollwitzer & J. A. Bargh (Eds.), *The psychology of action: Linking cognition and motivation to behavior* (pp. 7-26). New York: Guilford.

Ryan, R. M., Stiller, J., & Lynch, J. H. (1994). Representations of relationships to teachers, parents, and friends as predictors of academic motivation and self-esteem. *Journal of Early Adolescence, 14*, 226-249.

Ryff, C. D., & Singer, B. (1998). The contours of positive human health. *Psychological. Inquiry , 9*, 1-28.

Schafer, R. (1968). *Aspects of internalization*. New York: International Universities Press.

Seligman, M. E. P. (1975). *Helplessness*. San Francisco: Freeman.

Sheldon, K. M., & Kasser, T. (1998). Pursuing personal goals: Skills enable progress but not all progress is beneficial. *Personality and Social Psychology Bulletin, 24*, 1319-1331.

Sheldon, K. M., Ryan, R. M., & Reis, H. T. (1996). What makes for a good day? Competence and autonomy in the day and in the person. *Personality and Social Psychology Bulletin, 22*, 1270-1279.

Skinner, B. F. (1953). *Science and human behavior*. New York: Macmillan.

Smith, W. E. (1975). *The effect of anticipated vs. unanticipated social reward on subsequent intrinsic motivation*. Unpublished dissertation, Cornell University.

Swann, W. B., & Pittman, T. S. (1977). Initiating play activity of children: The moderating influence of verbal cues on intrinsic motivation. *Child Development, 48*, 1128-1132.

Vallerand, R. J., & Reid, G. (1984). On the causal effects of perceived competence on intrinsic motivation: A test of cognitive evaluation theory. *Journal of Sport Psychology, 6*, 94-102.

Werner, H. (1948). *Comparative psychology of mental development*. New York: International Universities Press.

White, R. W. (1959). Motivation reconsidered: The concept of competence. *Psychological Review, 66*, 297-333.

White, R. W. (1963). *Ego and reality in psychoanalytic theory*. New York: International Universities Press.

Williams, G. C., Cox, E. M., Hedberg, V., & Deci, E. L. (2000). Extrinsic life goals and health risk behaviors in adolescents. *Journal of Applied Social Psychology, 30*, 1756-1771.

Williams, G. C., & Deci, E. L. (1996). Internalization of biopsychosocial values by medical students: A test of self-determination theory. *Journal of Personality and Social Psychology, 70*, 767-779.

Williams, G. C., Grow, V. M., Freedman, Z. R., Ryan, R. M., & Deci, E. L. (1996). Motivational predictors of weight loss and weight-loss maintenance. *Journal of Personality and Social Psychology, 70*, 115-126.

Williams, G. C., Rodin, G. C., Ryan, R. M., Grolnick, W. S., & Deci, E. L. (1998). Autonomous regulation and long-term medication adherence in adult osutpatients. *Health Psychology, 17*, 269-276.

Yamauchi, H., & Tanaka, K. (1998). Relations of autonomy, self-referenced beliefs and self-regulated learning among Japanese children. *Psychological Reports, 82*, 803-816.

Zuckerman, M., Porac, J., Lathin, D., Smith, R., & Deci, E. L. (1978). On the importance of self-determination for intrinsically motivated behavior. *Personality and Social Psychology Bulletin, 4*, 443-446.

PART II

❖ ❖ ❖

THEORETICAL ISSUES AND CONSIDERATIONS

2: Intrinsic and Extrinsic Motivation: A Hierarchical Model

Robert J. Vallerand
Catherine F. Ratelle
Université du Québec à Montréal

For almost three decades, two distinct types of motivation have been of interest to researchers in psychology: intrinsic motivation and extrinsic motivation (Deci & Ryan, 2000; Vallerand, 1997). The concept of intrinsic motivation (IM) refers to behaviors performed out of interest and enjoyment. In contrast, extrinsic motivation (EM) pertains to behaviors carried out to attain contingent outcomes (Deci, 1971). The purpose of this chapter is to present the Hierarchical Model of Intrinsic and Extrinsic Motivation (Vallerand, 1997). The model facilitates the integration of findings from various theoretical perspectives in the intrinsic-extrinsic motivation literature, and it provides novel and testable hypotheses to orient future research on IM and EM. This model addresses the multiplicity of ways to represent motivation in individuals, as well as the structure, determinants, and consequences of these different representations. Selected empirical studies that support the Hierarchical Model are presented to illustrate how motivational phenomena can be understood within the framework of this model. As we will see, the model embraces several of the elements of Self-Determination Theory (Deci & Ryan, 1985b, 1991).

Before introducing the model in its full length, we provide an example that illustrates the kind of issues that the model deals with. Take the case of a sixteen-year-old named Amanda. In general, she is the kind of person who engages in activities because she likes them. She therefore interacts with friends, plays sports, and goes to school because of the pleasure inherent in these activities. As a result, these activities are a great source of enjoyment and satisfaction for her. This is, however, not the case when it comes to playing the piano. Amanda plays the piano because she feels obliged to, certainly not because she likes it. In fact, she really plays the piano for her parents (especially her father, a former piano virtuoso). In addition, she feels pressured by her piano instructor who never appears to be satisfied by her performance. Ever since she started piano lessons, Amanda has had Ms. Verkawski, a very controlling woman, as an instructor. The teacher never provides her pupils with opportunities to experience choice, and she gives poor competence feedback. She always pushes Amanda to play musical pieces that are out of her realm of skills. Playing the piano is thus associated with feelings of being controlled and lacking autonomy and competence. As a consequence, her performances were never very good and the satisfaction derived from playing music has been virtually absent.

However, things have started to change recently. For the last two months, Ms. Verkawski has been afflicted with pneumonia and Amanda has been taking her piano lessons with a new instructor, Mr. McConnell. Amanda's new teacher is more autonomy-supportive, giving her more freedom to express herself and letting her explore new avenues. In contrast to Ms. Verkawski, Mr. McConnell often lets Amanda choose among a wide array of musical pieces, including more contemporary genres. For years, this is what Amanda had been wanting. More and more, Amanda goes to her piano lessons out of choice and sometimes experiences pleasure. Consequently, her performance has improved dramatically and she has started to enjoy herself more at her lessons.

A few weeks ago on a Sunday, Mr. McConnell asked Amanda if she would like to perform in a student recital and asked her to choose a musical piece to present. She opted for Harry Connick Jr.'s "It Had to Be You", one of her favorite jazz numbers. Amanda experienced feelings of autonomy because her teacher provided her with the opportunity to choose whether to participate and to choose a piece to play. During the weeks prior to the recital, Amanda devoted considerable time and energy to practicing and perfecting her number. She was nevertheless very stressed at the idea of performing in public. On recital day, before it was her turn, Mr. McConnell told Amanda that she did not have to play if she did not want to. It relieved her from a lot of stress. She chose to play anyway and it went well. During her musical number, she felt deeply concentrated on the rhythms and subtleties of the arrangements in this piece. Even though she did not put enough emphasis on the decrescendo at the end, Amanda was happy and satisfied with her performance. After the recital, Amanda felt inclined to practice more and she became more fully engaged in piano playing. In fact, at home after the recital, Amanda went straight to the piano to play some more.

The Hierarchical Model of Intrinsic and Extrinsic Motivation Outlined

Several motivational features can be derived from the above example. The first feature concerns the complexity of the motivation construct. Referring to motivation as a general, unitary concept is insufficient to explain such complexity.

Instead, we need to focus on a collection of motivations differing in types and levels of generality. In the example above, Amanda manifests IM toward school, interpersonal relationships, and sports. At the same time, she displays EM toward playing the piano. Each of these different motivations constitutes an aspect of Amanda and must be addressed if we want to fully understand who she really is. Furthermore, it would appear that different motivations exist at three levels of generality, namely the global, contextual, and situational levels. For example, we mentioned that, in general, Amanda engages in activities out of enjoyment. Consequently, Amanda can be said to have, at the global level, an intrinsically motivated personality, which predisposes her to be intrinsically motivated in her many life contexts. Indeed, we saw that at the contextual level Amanda seems typically to be motivated in an intrinsic way in several contexts such as in education, sports, and interpersonal relationships. Distinguishing between motivations toward different life contexts is important. Indeed, focusing uniquely on her contextual motivation toward piano playing might mistakenly lead one to conclude that Amanda is an extrinsically motivated person when, in fact, this is the only domain in which she is not intrinsically motivated. Finally, at the situational level, during the recital, Amanda was intrinsically motivated to perform her musical piece.

A second feature of motivation is that other individuals can have a substantial impact on our many motivations. Such was the case for Amanda and her piano instructor, Ms. Verkawski. Despite the fact that Amanda is intrinsically motivated in general, the impact of her piano instructor was powerful enough to make her become extrinsically motivated in this life domain. At each level of generality, corresponding social factors function as significant motivational determinants. Thus, at the situational level, Mr. McConnell's support in providing Amanda choice about whether to be in the recital and about what to play had the beneficial effect of facilitating her intrinsic motivation toward practicing, leading her to finally enjoy playing the piano. He was very influential in shaping Amanda's situational motivation in playing the piano at the student recital too. Mr. McConnell's support allowed her to feel autonomous in her decision to play, which made her intrinsically motivated to play on that day.

A third feature of motivation is that it yields important consequences occurring at three levels of generality. At the global level, motivation is considered an individual difference that applies across situations and yield's general consequences. At the contextual level, these consequences differ according to the context which influences motivation at the corresponding level. In the example, we saw that Amanda experienced positive consequences such as satisfaction and enjoyment when she engaged in school activities, sports, and interpersonal relationships. It was however not the case with piano playing, where her motivation was extrinsic. She experienced dissatisfaction and her performance was poor. However, the change in piano instructor (which constitutes a change in contextual factors) shifted her motivation from an extrinsic orientation to a more intrinsic one. As a consequence, she started enjoying playing the piano more and her performance reached higher levels. At the situational level, the day of the recital, Amanda's IM led her to be deeply concentrated on playing, to feel good about herself, and to want to practice some more at home. Thus, motivation is associated with important consequences.

A fourth motivational feature concerns the recursive bottom-up influence of situational motivation on contextual motivation. Repeatedly engaging in intrinsically motivating activities (at the situational level), together with experiencing their beneficial consequences will play a role in facilitating contextual intrinsic motivation. It may not come as a surprise that Amanda is now more intrinsically motivated in general toward playing the piano. Indeed, experiencing situational intrinsic motivation in a repeated manner, such as having numerous enjoyable piano rehearsals and recitals, has had recursive positive effects on her contextual motivation toward playing the piano, although her contextual-level intrinsic motivation may not be as strong as her situational-level intrinsic motivation because she has been with her new teacher for only a short time.

The example presented above illustrates some of the elements of the Hierarchical Model of Intrinsic and Extrinsic Motivation (Vallerand, 1997). This coherent framework for integrating social psychological and personality perspectives on motivation is outlined in Figure 2-1 and is described more thoroughly by means of 5 postulates.

The Importance of Distinguishing Intrinsic Motivation, Extrinsic Motivation, and Amotivation

In order to provide a complete analysis of motivational processes, three important constructs must be considered: IM, EM, and amotivation (AM). The importance of clearly distinguishing all three concepts is supported by (1) their ability to explain a considerable range of human behaviors; (2) their capacity to represent essential aspects of human experience; and (3) the variety of important consequences they engender. This brings us to the first postulate.

Postulate 1: A Complete Analysis of Motivation Must Include Intrinsic and Extrinsic Motivation, and Amotivation

Here, the focus is on the conceptual distinction between IM, EM, and AM. First, we describe and differentiate each construct as well as discuss their multidimensional nature. Second, the issue of levels of generality is addressed. Finally, we discuss measurement issues.

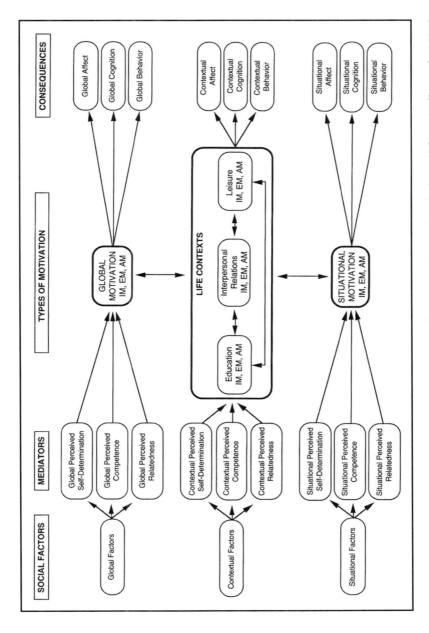

Figure 2.1 The Hierarchical Model of Intrinsic and Extrinsic Motivation (adapted from Vallerand, 1995).

A Multidimensional Perspective on IM, EM, and AM

Intrinsic Motivation. IM implies engaging in an activity for the pleasure and satisfaction inherent in the activity (e.g., Deci, 1975; Deci & Ryan, 1985b). Students doing their homework because they enjoy it and find that learning new things is interesting and satisfying are said to be intrinsically motivated. Although the majority of researchers advocate a global, unitary IM construct, Vallerand and his colleagues (Vallerand, 1993; Vallerand, Blais, Brière, & Pelletier, 1989; Vallerand, Pelletier, Blais, Brière, Senécal, & Vallières, 1992) have suggested a tripartite taxonomy of IM. First, *IM to know* implies engaging in activities because of the pleasure and satisfaction derived from learning, exploring, and understanding new things. Second, *IM to accomplish* things refers to engaging in activities because of the pleasure and satisfaction derived from trying to surpass oneself, creating, or accomplishing something. Third, *IM to experience stimulation* operates when one is engaged in an activity because of the stimulating sensations associated with it.

Extrinsic Motivation. In contrast to IM, EM refers to a broad array of behaviors having in common the fact that activities are engaged in not for reasons inherent in them but for instrumental reasons. Extrinsically motivated behaviors are undertaken to attain an end state that is separate from the actual behavior. In early discussions of the topic, it was thought that behaviors performed with a lack of choice were the only type of extrinsically motivated behaviors, so that all EM behaviors were evoked by contingencies. However, research and thinking by Deci, Ryan, and their colleagues (Deci & Ryan, 1985b, 1991) have put forth a more complex typology of EM where some types of extrinsically motivated acts involve self-determination and choice. They identified four types of extrinsic motivations that vary in their degree of self-determination and can be ordered along a self-determination continuum ranging from non self-determined to self-determined forms of extrinsic motivation.

The first type of EM is *external regulation*. When someone is externally regulated, acts are performed to attain a positive end state (e.g., to get money) or to avoid a negative end state (e.g., to avoid a parent's reprimands) which are separate from the activity itself. External regulation lies at the nonself-determined end of the continuum because it is the least self-determined type of extrinsic motivation. This type of regulation is typically how EM is being portrayed in the literature.

The second type of EM, *introjected regulation*, represents the first stage of the internalization process, where individuals take prompts from their environment and bring them inside themselves. With this type of motivation, individuals start to internalize the reasons for their behaviors. However, motivation is still not self-determined because this type of regulation deals with past external contingencies that have now been internalized inside the person. The person acts out of obligation, in order to avoid feeling shame and internal pressure. For example, a woman may vote at municipal elections because she feels she has to, because it is her duty as a citizen. This elector can be said to be introjected toward municipal politics.

The third type of EM is *identified regulation*. When the reasons to engage in an activity are internalized such that the activity is judged valuable by the person, he or she will perform the activity with a sense of choice and the behavior is said to be regulated through identification with the activity. The person acting out of identified reasons is said to be relatively self-determined. For instance, a boy in high school who decides to get up an hour earlier to review his chemistry notes because he feels it is personally important to do so is regulated by identification.

Although identification implies choice, choices to engage in some activities are not necessarily coherent with other self-structures. When such coherence is reached, however, the choice underlying behavior is in harmony with other structures within the self. This type of extrinsic motivation refers to *integrated regulation*. For example, a ballet dancer might choose not to go to a party with friends in order to be in shape for dance class early on the next morning. Integrated regulation is the most self-determined type of EM.

It is important to note that, although these types of external motivation can be ordered along a self-determination continuum, one need not go through them successively for each behavior. For example, when a young man who has not had much experience painting houses is offered a job painting the house of a family friend he may readily become identified in his regulation of the activity (because he personally values doing the job well for his father's long-time friend).

Amotivation. Deci and Ryan (1985b) proposed that a third motivational construct, AM, should be considered when trying to understand human behavior. Amotivation is at work when individuals display a relative absence of motivation. In such instances, individuals do not perceive a contingency between their behaviors and outcomes, so they do not act with the intention to attain an outcome. AM is a construct similar in many ways to learned helplessness (Abramson, Seligman, & Teasdale, 1978), mostly because amotivated individuals feel incompetent and act like they have little or no control. Their behaviors are perceived to be caused by forces outside themselves. They begin to feel helpless and may start to question the usefulness of engaging in the activity in the first place. A highly probable consequence of AM is to quit the activity toward which the individual is amotivated. Examples of amotivated individuals are students who, because they cannot see what staying in school will bring to their future, decide to drop out of high school.

Over the years, numerous studies have provided empirical support for the first postulate of the model. As such, results from confirmatory factor analyses on the different motivation scales that have been validated using the present perspective have consistently provided support for the existence of IM, EM, and AM (see Vallerand, 1997). In addition, as we will see later, confirmation of predictions about the determinants and consequences of specific motivational types provides support for the construct validity of these motivational types.

Of importance for the model is the SDT proposition that the different motivational orientations represent different levels of self-determination, which can be ordered along a self-determination continuum. Thus, IM is the most self-determined motivational type, followed by integrated regulation, identified regulation, introjected regulation, and external regulation. AM involves a complete lack of self-determination. As we will see in Postulate 5, this continuum allows us to predict the impact of the different types of motivation on important consequences.

Motivation at Three Levels of Generality

Over the past 20 years or so, research and theories on the self have represented self-regulation processes at different levels of a hierarchy. Carver and Scheier (1981), for example, suggested a hierarchy of self-regulatory processes while Shavelson and Marsh (1986) proposed a hierarchy of self-concepts which includes the global level, the academic and non-academic level, and the specific activity level. In concordance with such theorizing and with past research conducted in the motivation area, the second postulate proposes that IM, EM, and AM are represented within the individual at three hierarchical levels of generality: the global, the contextual, and the situational levels.

Postulate 2: Intrinsic Motivation, Extrinsic Motivation, and Amotivation Exist at Three Levels of Generality: The Global, Contextual, and Situational Levels.

The global level. At this level of the hierarchy, the individual is seen as having developed a global (or general) motivational orientation to interact with the environment in an intrinsic, extrinsic, and/or amotivated fashion. Research on the General Causality Orientation Scale (GCOS; Deci & Ryan, 1985a) conducted by the members of the Rochester group (e.g., Hodgins & Deci, 1999; Hodgins, Liebeskind, & Schwartz, 1996; Knee & Zuckerman, 1996, 1998), and that of Guay, Blais, Vallerand, and Pelletier (1999) with the Global Motivation Scale (GMS), illustrate research carried out at this level of generality. Motivation at the global level is expected to be the most stable.

The contextual level. Several studies performed in the last 20 years have examined motivation at the contextual level of generality. Here, we use the word "context" to refer to "a distinct sphere of human activity" (Emmons, 1995). Although many different life contexts exist, research with young adults has revealed that the three most important contexts are education, leisure, and interpersonal relationships (Blais, Vallerand, Gagnon, Brière, & Pelletier, 1990). Individuals develop motivational orientations toward each life context that are moderately stable, although they can be influenced to an extent by social factors that are specific to each context. At the contextual level, motivation is influenced by contextual determinants and leads to contextual consequences (the issue of motivational determinants and consequences is discussed further in the next two sections). Studies on motivation in intimate relationships by Blais, Sabourin, Boucher, and Vallerand (1990), and in education by Vallerand and his colleagues (e.g., Vallerand, Fortier, & Guay, 1997) are examples of research studying motivation at the contextual level.

The situational level. When studying motivation at the situational (or state) level of generality, we are interested in understanding why individuals engage in a specific activity at a particular time. Motivation at this level is assumed to be unstable because of its responsiveness to the environment. A study by Guay, Vallerand, and Blanchard (2000, Study 2), conducted in the educational setting, is one example of research studying motivation at the situational level. In this study, a self-report measure of situational motivation was given to students 35 minutes after their class had begun in order to measure their motivation toward the educational task they were engaged in at that specific point in time.

In sum, the present model posits that it is useful to study motivation at three different levels of generality: the global (or personality) level, the contextual (or life domains) level, and the situational (or state) level. Distinguishing among levels of the hierarchy becomes important, particularly when specifying determinants and consequences. For example, it is important to accurately identify a student as being externally regulated toward education in order to use the appropriate teaching strategy that will lead him or her to become more self-determined toward school. Looking only at this student's global intrinsic motivation would have led one to neglect some very useful information.

Measuring Intrinsic Motivation, Extrinsic Motivation, and Amotivation

Measuring motivation at each level of the hierarchy, requires use of the appropriate scales. For instance, if a researcher is interested in studying students' usual motivation toward school, it would be appropriate to use a contextual measure rather than either a global measure which is too broad in focus or a situational measure which is too narrow.

In order to empirically test postulates from the Hierarchical Model, it was necessary to assess the different motivations at each level of generality. Therefore, we developed and validated scales that assess the different motivations discussed above at global, contextual, and situational levels. At the global level, we developed the Global Motivation Scale (GMS; Guay, Blais, et al., 1999). It assesses the 3 different types of IM, and the identified, introjected, and external types of EM, as well as AM toward life in general. Results with the GMS indicate that the scale is both reliable and valid. Furthermore, its factorial structure indicates that an independent assessment of the different motivational types is provided. Internal consistency and temporal stability were also found to be adequate. Furthermore, the different subscales of the GMS were found to be unrelated to scores on the Social Desirability Scale (Crowne & Marlowe, 1960).

Scales assessing motivation at the contextual level have also been developed. Because we were interested primarily in college students and research revealed that education, leisure, and interpersonal relationships were the three main life contexts for this age group (Blais, Vallerand, et al., 1990), scales were developed to measure motivation in these contexts. For instance, the Academic Motivation Scale (Vallerand et al., 1989, 1992, 1993) assesses contextual motivation toward education, the Interpersonal Motivation Inventory (Blais, Vallerand, Pelletier, & Brière, 1994) assesses contextual motivation in interpersonal relationships, and the Leisure Motivation Scale (Pelletier, Vallerand, Blais, Brière, Green-Demers, 1996) measures contextual motivation toward leisure activities. Contextual measures of motivation have been developed for other life domains, as well. Examples are the Sport Motivation Scale (Brière, Vallerand, Blais, & Pelletier, 1995; Pelletier et al., 1995; see also Frederick, this volume), the Blais Work Motivation Inventory (Blais, Brière, Lachance, Riddle, & Vallerand, 1993), the Gambling Motivation Scale (Chantal & Vallerand, 1996), the Volunteering Motivation Scale (Chantal & Vallerand, 2000), the Motivation Toward the Environment Scale (Pelletier, Green-Demers, & Béland, 1997; Pelletier, Tuson, Green-Demers, Noels, & Beaton, 1998), the Political Motivation Scale (Koestner, Losier, Vallerand, & Carducci, 1996), and the Elderly Motivation Scale (Vallerand & O'Connor, 1991; Vallerand, O'Connor, & Hamel, 1995). Indices of reliability and validity have been found to be acceptable for all of these scales (see Vallerand, 1997).

At the situational level, two main techniques have been used to measure motivation. The first approach measures situational motivation by way of the free-choice measure (Deci, 1971), which measures the amount of time an individual has spent on an activity during a free-choice period. The assumption underlying this measure is that individuals intrinsically motivated toward an activity will return to the activity when they are free to do so. However, this measurement approach can be problematic in distinguishing between types of motivation (see Vallerand, 1997; Vallerand & Fortier, 1998). Indeed, research has shown that, under some circumstances, the free-choice measure, besides being associated with IM, can also reflect introjection (Ryan, Koestner, & Deci, 1991) as well as identified regulation (Deci, Eghrari, Patrick, & Leone, 1994). Another way to measure situational motivation is with a self-report measure. By using such a technique, it becomes possible to consider the multidimensional aspect of motivation. We thus developed the Situational Motivation Scale (SIMS; Guay et al., 2000) which measures IM (without distinguishing types of IM), identified and external types of EM, as well as AM. The choice to measure only 4 motivational types was dictated by the need to keep the scale as brief as possible in order to capture situational motivation in many lab or field situations. Indices of reliability and validity have been found to be very satisfactory (see Guay et al., 2000).

Sometimes, researchers will integrate the different types of motivation (at one specific level) into a single motivation index, called the Self-Determination Index .[1] The advantage of using such an index is the significant reduction of variables needed to represent the different types of motivation at a given level. To do so, a different weight is allocated to each subscale, with the autonomous subscales having positive weights and the nonself-determined having negative weights (e.g., Grolnick & Ryan, 1987; Vallerand & Bissonnette, 1992; also see Vallerand, 1997 on this topic). Thus in one approach, a weight of +2 is awarded to the intrinsic motivation subscale because this construct represents the highest level of self-determination. A weight of +1 is assigned to the identified regulation subscale; a weight of -1 is allocated to the external regulation subscale; and a weight of -2 is awarded to the amotivation subscale, because it represents the lowest level of self-determination. Multiplying the score for each subscale by its corresponding weight and adding all the products yields an index for the individual's self-determined motivation. This procedure can be used at each level of the hierarchy.

The Determinants of IM, EM, and AM

The present section introduces determinants, or antecedents of IM, EM, and AM. We highlight studies that have measured motivational determinants and their impact on motivation at the three levels of generality. The goal is not to review all studies on the determinants but rather to demonstrate the heuristic nature of the Hierarchical Model as an integrative framework.

Postulate 3: Motivation at a Given Level Results from Two Sources: (1) Social Factors and (2) Top Down Effects from Motivation at the Proximal Level

The third postulate of the model tackles the role of motivational determinants on the different motivational orientations. It is subdivided into three corollaries.

---

1. The "Self-Determination Index" is also called the "Relative Autonomy Index" by the Rochester group.

Corollary 3.1: _Motivation at a Given Level Can Result from Social Factors Which Can Be_ _Global, Contextual, or Situational Depending on the Level in the Hierarchy._ The term "social factors" is used to refer to both human and nonhuman factors encountered in one's social environment, such as comments from another person (human) or instructions on a sign (nonhuman). These factors can also be distinguished according to their level of generality. _Situational social factors_ concern transient variables encountered in a specific activity, at a specific time, that may not remain constant. Receiving an ovation after a clarinet solo represents an example of a situational factor. _Contextual factors_ refer to recurrent variables that are systematically encountered in a specific life context but not in others. For example, a controlling third-grade teacher is a social factor in a student's academic context but she is not in this student's leisure context. _Global factors_ pertain to social factors whose impact extends across several life domains. Parents represent such a factor during our upbringing. Because they are initially involved in most of our activities, parents can have a profound effect on our global motivation (see Grolnick & Apostoleris, this volume). Nursing homes for senior residents also represent a global factor. Having all activities take place within a single social environment can strongly affect global motivation. It is crucial to take social factors into account at each level of generality because they have been found to have a deep impact on motivation (see Deci & Ryan, 1985b; Vallerand, 1997).

We believe that clearly discerning the level of generality of social factors is of great importance when it comes to making predictions regarding the types of factors that should influence motivation at each level of the hierarchy. Empirical support for the first corollary has been provided by results from a study that examined the effects of success/failure, a situational variable, on situational, contextual, and global motivations (Vallerand, 1996). These findings revealed that failing at a task significantly undermined situational IM but increased AM, relative to succeeding at the task. However, contextual and global motivations were not significantly affected by this situational social factor.

Corollary 3.2: _The Impact of Social Factors on Motivation is Mediated by Perceptions of_ _Competence, Autonomy, and Relatedness._ According to Cognitive Evaluation Theory, a subtheory of Self-Determination Theory (CET; Deci, 1975; Deci & Ryan, 1985b, 1991), the impact of situational factors on motivation is mediated by perceptions of autonomy, competence, and relatedness. These perceptions relate to basic psychological human needs. The _need for competence_ pertains to the human desire to efficiently interact with one's environment so as to feel competent in producing desired outcomes and preventing undesired outcomes (Connell & Wellborn, 1991; Deci, 1975; Deci & Ryan, 1985b; Harter, 1978; White, 1959). The _need for autonomy_ refers to the human desire to be the origin of one's behaviors (deCharms, 1968; Deci, 1975, 1980; Deci & Ryan, 1985b). Finally, the _need_ _for relatedness_ implies a desire to feel connected to significant individuals (for recent reviews on belongingness and/or relatedness, see Baumeister & Leary, 1995; Richer & Vallerand, 1998; Ryan, 1993).

CET proposes that, to the extent that social factors foster perceptions of competence, autonomy, and relatedness in individuals, self-determined types of motivation (IM as well as integrated and identified regulation) will be enhanced whereas nonself-determined types of motivation (introjected and external regulations, and AM) will be diminished (see Deci, Vallerand, Pelletier, & Ryan, 1991). Thus, an activity that promotes perceptions of autonomy, competence, and relatedness, is performed volitionally because it nurtures these three basic psychological needs. The Hierarchical Model further posits that such mediating effects take place at each of the three levels in the hierarchy.

Much research has brought empirical support for CET at the situational level (see Vallerand, 1997). The study of Vallerand and Reid (1984) exemplifies such support. In this study, participants engaged in a motor task during a pretest and a posttest. In the posttest, they received either positive, negative, or no performance feedback. Individuals' perceptions of competence and IM were measured after both the pretest and the posttest. Results of path analyses revealed that positive feedback led participants to feel more competent, which in turn, led them to be more intrinsically motivated. Studies by Vallerand and Reid (1988) and by Whitehead and Corbin (1991) have provided replications of the mediating role of perceived competence. These findings are even stronger when individuals strive to achieve competence (Sansone, 1986) and when the environment supports individuals' autonomy (Ryan, 1982).

The mediating role of perceived autonomy at the situational level was empirically tested in a study by Reeve and Deci (1996). They examined the impact of competition on situational motivation, as mediated by perceptions of competence and autonomy. They found support for the mediating role of these variables. With regard to perceptions of relatedness, results of a study by Blanchard and Vallerand (1996a, Study 2) revealed that the extent to which the individual feels connected to other teammates mediates the impact of individual and team performance on self-determined forms of motivation (as evidenced by the self-determination index) in basketball players.

At the contextual level, several studies have examined whether the impact of social factors on motivation was mediated by perceived autonomy, competence, and relatedness. In Blanchard and Vallerand (1996b), basketball players completed questionnaires assessing contextual measures of perceived competence, autonomy, and relatedness, and self-determined motivation toward basketball, as well as their perceptions of their coach's autonomy-supportive style. Results provided support for the proposed causal sequence where social factors determined perceptions of competence, autonomy, and relatedness, which in turn influenced self-determined motivation. Other studies in the academic setting have provided support for this mediation link (Guay & Vallerand, 1997; Vallerand, Fortier, &

Guay, 1997). Finally, support for the mediating role of perceptions of competence at the global level of the hierarchy has also been reported (Ratelle, Vallerand, Chantal, & Provencher, 2002).

Overall, these results indicate that perceptions of competence, autonomy, and relatedness mediate the impact of social factors on motivation, at situational, contextual, and global levels. Future research is needed to further establish the validity of these results, especially at the global level of the model.

Corollary 3.3: In Addition to the Influence of Social Factors and Their Psychological Mediators, Motivation at a Given Level also Results from Top Down Effects from Motivation at the Proximal Level Higher in the Hierarchy. One important novel contribution of the model is that it acknowledges the possibility of top-down effects with motivation at one level of the hierarchy affecting motivation at the next lower level. Thus, global motivation should have a stronger impact on contextual motivation than on situational motivation and contextual motivation should influence situational motivation. To illustrate such effects, we can take the example of someone who is globally motivated in an intrinsic way. We can expect this individual to be intrinsically motivated in several life contexts as well, because the top-down effect of motivation is assumed to go from the global to the contextual level. Similarly, we can expect the person who is intrinsically motivated at the contextual level in education to also be intrinsically motivated at the situational level on educational tasks.

Conceptual links can be drawn between Corollary 3.3 and research on self-regulatory processes, which has shown that global properties of the self can shape more specific self attributes (Brown, 1993; Brown & Dutton, 1995; Sansone & Harackiewicz, 1996). Few studies have tested Corollary 3.3. One of them (Williams, Grow, Freedman, Ryan, & Deci, 1996), measured obese patients' global motivation and their contextual motivation toward the medical treatment. Path analyses revealed that being motivated in a self-determined fashion at the global level predicted a self-determined contextual motivation toward the treatment at a later time. Similar findings were reported by Blanchard, Vallerand, and Provencher (1998) in the context of sport. Altogether, these results provide empirical support for the top-down effect of motivation at higher levels on motivation at the next lower level. Although these findings are encouraging, experimental studies are nevertheless necessary to firmly establish the validity of this postulate.

It thus appears that Postulate 3 and its corollaries have been empirically supported by several studies. In addition, the heuristic nature of the distinction between social factors at global, contextual, and situational levels of generality was underscored. Furthermore, evidence was found for the role of perceptions of competence, autonomy, and relatedness as psychological mediators of social factors' impact on motivation at the three levels of generality. Finally, the top-down effect of motivation at higher levels on motivation at the proximal lower level has been supported.

Postulate 4: There is a Recursive Bottom Up Relationship Between Motivation at One Level and Motivation at the Next Higher Level in the Hierarchy

According to this postulate, we need to consider these recursive effects—the situational level on the contextual and global levels and the contextual level on the global level—in order to explain the motivational changes likely to take place over time. The specific goal of this postulate is to specify how the dynamics between motivation at the various levels of generality can account for these motivational changes.

As an illustration of this recursive effect, let's take the example of a man who is about to teach his first high school English class of the semester. He is generally intrinsically motivated toward teaching, but he has been warned that this particular class is really something else and that he should be ready for it. As he is walking down the corridor, he can hear students talking loudly and desks being moved around. Upon entering in the classroom, he is hit by a flying eraser. The class starts to laugh. Students then go back to what they were doing, that is, talking and shouting. The teacher begins to speak, asking everyone to sit and stop talking. He cannot get any response as student are totally uninterested in him. He is disappointed because he was looking forward to meeting his new students. It finally took ten minutes to get them to listen to what he had to say. The class was, in all, disastrous. The next morning, as he was going over in his head what had happened the day before in class, he felt anxious. He was afraid that the next class with this group would be just as bad. Unfortunately, his fears were concretized the next day. At the end of the period, his situational motivation was at its lowest. He did not feel like teaching them: he was completely amotivated. Later that night, as he was preparing for the third class with this group of students, he started to wonder if he would be able to put up with them for the whole year. Within a few weeks he had begun, for the first time in his career, to question whether teaching was really for him. Perhaps working in a private company would suit him better. Maybe it was time to grasp new opportunities and take up new challenges. And that's what he did: he updated his résumé, applied for jobs in the private sector, and wrote his resignation letter.

How did the teacher come to such a decision? First, at the situational level, the totally disinterested attitude of his students as well as their lack of respect represent crucial social factors that had a negative impact on the teacher's situational motivation. He felt incompetent and experienced repeated instances of decreased IM and increased AM at the situational level. In turn, his situational nonself-determined motivation had a recursive negative impact (Postulate 4) on his contextual motivation toward teaching. Because his contextual motivation toward teaching has now become nonself-determined, the teacher decided to quit his job (an important behavioral consequence of motivation, which will be examined in Postulate 5).

Empirical support has been provided for this fourth postulate. In a first study with basketball players, Blanchard, Vallerand, and Provencher (1998, Study 1) assessed contextual motivation toward basketball before a tournament, as well as situational motivation and contextual sport motivation after each of the two games of the tournament. Finally, contextual motivation was assessed 10 days after the tournament. Results revealed that situational motivation had a recursive bottom-up effect on contextual motivation toward basketball after each of the two games, as well as 10 days after the tournament. These results have been replicated over a complete season (Blanchard, Vallerand, & Provencher, 1998, Study 2). Similar findings at the contextual and global levels have also been found by Blanchard and Vallerand (1998), who tested the postulate with individuals engaged in an exercise program. They measured global motivation at times 1 and 3 and contextual motivation toward exercising at time 2. Results showed that global motivation influenced contextual motivation toward exercising (Postulate 3), which in turn had a recursive bottom-up effect on the global motivational orientation (Postulate 4). Thus, Postulate 4 has been supported by empirical evidence involving all three levels of the hierarchy.

The Consequences of IM, EM, and AM

Thus far, attention has been devoted to determinants of the types of motivation, as well as to the psychological processes responsible for their effects. We now turn to motivational consequences.

Postulate 5: Motivation Leads to Important Consequences

The postulate that motivation produces consequences is supported by at least two types of evidence. First, it appears intuitively appropriate to view variables such as attention, satisfaction, and behavioral persistence as being affected by motivation. Thus, a ballet dancer motivated in an intrinsic fashion would be expected to concentrate more during practice than one who is amotivated for dance and could not care less about it. Second, research has shown that motivation leads to a host of consequences such as creativity (Amabile, 1985; Hennessey, 1989), learning (see Lepper, 1994), and smoking abstinence (Curry,

Wagner, & Grothaus, 1991; Harackiewicz, Sansone, Blair, Epstein, & Manderlink, 1987). For instance, writers for whom EM was induced produced poems of lower quality than intrinsically motivated or control-group participants (Amabile, 1985). Other studies provided support for the causal effect of motivation on consequences (Curry et al., 1991; Lepper & Cordova, 1992). Thus, motivation does lead to important consequences and researchers in the IM/EM literature have isolated cognitive (e.g., concentration, attention, and memory), affective (e.g., interest, satisfaction, and positive emotions), and behavioral (e.g., choice of behavior, persistence at a task, intensity, task complexity, behavioral intentions, and performance) consequences (see Vallerand, 1997 for a review).

Corollary 5.1:   *Consequences Are Decreasingly Positive From Intrinsic Motivation to Amotivation.* This first corollary relates motivational consequences to types of motivation. Deci and Ryan's (1985b) self-determination continuum is particularly useful when predicting motivational consequences. Because we know the location of the different types of motivation on the self-determination continuum and that self-determination is associated with enhanced psychological functioning (Deci, 1980; Ryan, Deci, & Grolnick, 1995), we can predict the impact of the different types of motivation on consequences. More specifically, IM is expected to lead to the most positive consequences, followed by integration and identification. External regulation should be associated with negative consequences, and AM with the most negative ones. Introjection is hypothesized to lead to consequences that lie between those generated by external regulation and identification.

Much support exists for Corollary 5.1 For instance, in the context of couple relationships, a study by Blais, Sabourin, et al. (1990) revealed that the most self-determined types of motivation (IM, integration, and identification) led to the most positive consequences (i.e., positive interpersonal behaviors, couple happiness) whereas nonself-determined types of motivation (introjection, external regulation, and AM) yielded the most negative consequences. Several other studies have provided empirical support for this corollary (see Ryan, 1995; Vallerand, 1993, 1997) in life domains such as work (Blais et al., 1993), leisure (Pelletier, Vallerand, Green-Demers, Brière, & Blais, 1995), education (Vallerand & Bissonnette, 1992), environmental protection (Pelletier et al., 1998), and aging (Vallerand et al., 1995).

Corollary 5.2:   *Motivational Consequences Exist at Three Levels of the Hierarchy, and the Level of Generality of the Consequences Depends on the Level of the Motivation That Has Produced Them.* This second corollary pertains to the levels of generality of motivational consequences. The level of generality of a particular consequence is a function of the level of generality of the motivation that produced that particular consequence. Thus, consequences of situational motivation will be situational. They will include feelings of satisfaction, level of attention, and behavioral persistence with respect to a particular task at a specific point in time. Likewise, contextual consequences, resulting from contextual motivation, will be specific to the context at hand, and will be of moderate generality. Lastly, consequences at the global level of generality, resulting from global motivation, will be the most general.

Support for this second corollary has been provided by Chantal, Guay, and Vallerand (1995). In this study, students' global motivation, as well as contextual motivations toward education and interpersonal relationships were measured. Five weeks later, educational and relational consequences were measured. Results showed that contextual educational consequences were better predicted by contextual educational motivation than by contextual motivation toward interpersonal relationships. Similarly, relational consequences were better predicted by contextual motivation toward interpersonal relationships. Finally, global motivation did not affect the different types of consequences.

Further support was provided for Corollary 5.2 in a study by Vallerand and Blanchard (1998) in which exercise participants completed motivation and consequences scales at the three different levels of generality, at three points in time. At Time 1, they completed the Global Motivation Scale (Guay et al., 1999) as well as a scale assessing contextual motivation toward exercise (adapted from the Sport Motivation Scale; Brière et al., 1995). At Time 2, four weeks later, participants completed the Situational Motivation Scale (Guay et al., 1999) and scales assessing situational consequences such as concentration and positive emotions. Finally, at Time 3 (four weeks later), they completed scales assessing global consequences (i.e., global negative affect), and contextual consequences pertaining to exercise. Regression analyses showed that global motivation was the best predictor of global consequences, contextual motivation toward exercise was the best predictor of contextual consequences related to exercise, and situational motivation was the most important predictor of situational consequences.

In sum, Postulate 5 and its corollaries have been supported by numerous research findings. It thus appears safe to conclude that motivation leads to important cognitive, affective, or behavioral consequences. Consistent with the level of generality of the motivation that produced them, it is also possible to distinguish among consequences occurring at the global, contextual, and situational levels of the hierarchy. Furthermore, motivational consequences were found to be increasingly positive as we go from AM to IM.[2] Future research is nevertheless needed to validate these results, using other types of consequences.

---

2. Although the majority of research findings indicated that IM leads to the most positive consequences, Koestner, Losier, Vallerand, and Carducci (1996) reported that in the political domain, identification leads to more positive behavioral consequences than IM. The same was true for research in the domain of environmental protection (Pelletier, Tuson, Green-Demers, Noels, & Beaton, 1998). These results are explained by Vallerand (1997) as resulting at least in part from the nature of the task. When some aspects of a task are perceived as uninteresting, identified regulation may be required for individuals to experience positive outcomes. Future research is needed to test this hypothesis.

Integrative Studies

In this section, additional studies are reviewed which have examined more than one postulate and corollary of the model and have included all three levels of generality (for a more complete analysis of integrative studies, refer to Vallerand, 1997).

A first integrative study was conducted by Vallerand, Guay, Blanchard, & Cadorette (2002, Study 1) in the education domain. In this study, several postulates and corollaries of the model were tested simultaneously. College students involved in an educational task in class completed scales assessing situational level mediators (perceptions of autonomy, competence, and relatedness), motivations, and consequences (concentration, positive affect, and behavioral intentions of engagement in the activity). Furthermore, contextual-level motivations and mediators (perceived competence, autonomy, and relatedness) toward leisure, education, and interpersonal relationships were also measured. Finally, global-level motivations and mediators were measured. Thus, motivation as well as psychological mediators were measured at each level of the hierarchy and for each of the three life contexts. In addition, situational consequences were assessed.

Results from a structural equation modeling analysis (with EQS) provided strong support for the Hierarchical Model. First, it was possible to distinguish motivation at the global, contextual, and situational levels, thereby providing support for the hierarchical structure of the model (Postulate 2). Second, at each level, perceptions of autonomy, competence, and relatedness were found to predict motivation (Corollary 3.2). There was also support for the fact that perceptions of autonomy, competence, and relatedness for each of the different contexts affected only motivation that was relevant to that context. The top-down hypothesis (Corollary 3.3) where global motivation influenced each of the three contextual motivations also was supported. Of interest is that only motivation in education was found to significantly influence situational motivation toward an educational task (as proposed by the specificity hypothesis). Analysis also confirmed the hypothesized consequence aspects of the model. First, it was possible to distinguish the three types of consequences, namely affect, cognition, and behavior, at the situational level (Postulate 5). Second, Corollary 5.1 was supported in that situational self-determined motivation was found to positively influence affect, cognition, and behavioral intentions. Finally, there was support for Corollary 5.2 in that only situational motivation affected situational consequences. Neither global nor any of the contextual motivations influenced situational consequences.

Although the study by Vallerand et al. (2002, Study 1) provided support for several of the postulates and corollaries of the Hierarchical Model, all measures were assessed at the same time, so support for the direction of causality among variables was far from perfect. In a second study, Vallerand et al. (2002, Study 2) used a prospective design to test some of the postulates and corollaries of the model. One hundred and seventy-eight college students completed scales assessing motivation at the global and contextual levels (toward education, leisure, and interpersonal relationships). Five months later, they were contacted again and asked to complete scales assessing situational motivation and consequences (positive affect and behavioral intentions) toward a leisure activity they had just been engaged in. Thus, the measures assessed in this second study were similar to those used in the first study, except that perceptions of competence, autonomy, and relatedness were not assessed and situational measures dealt with a leisure activity instead of an educational activity. The results from a path analysis (with EQS) were almost identical to those obtained in the first study. Further, alternative models were tested and yielded poorer fit indices than the hypothesized model.

In sum, findings from the above two studies provide strong support for the Hierarchical Model. In fact, combined, the two studies empirically support most of the model's postulates and corollaries including: Postulate 1 (on the importance of including IM, EM, and AM for a complete analysis of motivation), Postulate 2 (on the three levels of generality of motivation), Corollary 3.2 (on the mediating role of perceived competence, autonomy, and relatedness), Corollary 3.3 (on the top down effect of motivation), and Postulate 5 (on motivational consequences) However, additional research is needed in order to more fully understand some of the intricacies of the model. We now turn to this issue.

Future Research on the Hierarchical Model

As evidenced by the studies reviewed above, there is empirical support for the postulates and corollaries of the Hierarchical Model of Intrinsic and Extrinsic Motivation. Thus, we believe that the theoretical framework provided by the model is a reliable and robust one in that it allows the integration of research findings on IM and EM. Furthermore, it can lead to novel and testable research hypotheses in the area of IM/EM. Here are a few research directions based on the model.

A first research avenue would be to investigate the interaction between social factors and personality variables. It is possible that, at a given level such as the contextual level, motivation results from the interplay of social factors at that level (e.g., contextual social factors) and personal forces at the higher level (i.e., global motivation). For example, Williams and Deci (1996) have shown how medical students' global motivational orientations and the interpersonal style of their professor (being autonomy supportive vs. controlling) have additive effects on students' contextual motivation toward their interviewing course. However, little is known about the interaction of these two variables on motivation. Similarly, testing whether social factors at the situational level influence situational motivation differently as a function of contextual motivation could also lead to new and interesting research. For instance, are people with self-determined contextual motivation relatively immune to the impact of situational factors on situational motivation?

A second research direction involves motivational conflict. So far, the model has looked at how contextual and situational motivation can influence each other through top-down and bottom-up effects. However, little attention has been devoted to the interplay of different contextual motivations and their influence on situational motivation. For example, a girl involved with a tedious algebra assignment who is brought to think about participating in a soccer game is likely to experience motivational conflict. Her situational motivation will then be a function of her contextual motivations both toward school and toward sports. The relative strength of each contextual motivation will dictate which of these two contexts will have the most prevalent effect on situational motivation. To the extent that the student's contextual motivation toward school (and algebra) is less self-determined than that toward sports (and soccer in particular), she will experience a drop in IM toward her assignment. In a recent study (Ratelle, Rousseau, Vallerand, & Provencher, 2002), we examined the consequences of a motivational conflict between education and leisure activities. Participants involved in an educational task were led to think about an attractive leisure activity through a priming procedure, after which they were to return to the educational activity. Results have shown that participants who were led to think about an interesting leisure activity experienced significant drops in IM toward the educational task. These results indicate that experiencing a conflict between two motivations (e.g., motivation toward education and motivation toward leisure) can lead to negative consequences, especially if the person has to remain engaged in the less interesting activity.

A third promising area of research is that of motivational compensation. Compensation effects can result from a dynamic interplay between contextual motivations. From the model's perspective, losses in self-determined motivation in one context can lead a person to compensate in another context by becoming more intrinsically motivated there. Such a phenomenon allows individuals to restore (or keep) their global motivation at a certain (self-determined) level. A preliminary study by Blanchard, Vallerand, and Provencher (1998) seems to support such compensatory effects within the self. Basketball players completed scales assessing their contextual motivation and their perceptions of competence toward education and sports on two separate occasions. They were also asked to rate their school performance at Time 2. Individuals who experienced failure in the academic context at Time 2, and who perceived themselves as competent in sports (basketball) at Time 1, reported a small increase in contextual motivation toward sports. No other group experienced an increase in contextual sport motivation. Losses of competence and self-determined motivation in one domain (school) may have motivated individuals to restore their sense of self and, consequently, to experience an increase in self-determined motivation toward the other context (sport). However, such an effect seems to take place in life domains in which people feel competent. More research on this issue is needed.

A final research avenue concerns the testing of the "Social Factor → Psychological Mediators → Motivation → Consequences" sequence within the confines of the same study. Several studies in the motivation literature have looked at subparts of this sequence but only one, to our knowledge, has tested the whole sequence. In this study by Grouzet, Vallerand, and Thill (1999), social factors were manipulated such that participants were put either in a success or in a failure condition to perform the NINA task (drawings in which the word NINA is embedded several times). Perceptions of competence and autonomy (psychological mediators), self-determined situational motivation, and concentration and intentions of future persistence (motivational consequences) were measured. Structural Equation Modeling provided support for the sequence. More specifically, the success/failure variable influenced perceptions of competence and autonomy, which affected situational self-determined motivation. In turn, motivation predicted concentration and future behavioral intentions. Replication at other levels of the hierarchy are needed to further establish the validity of the sequence.

Conclusion

The purpose of the present chapter was to present the Hierarchical Model of Intrinsic and Extrinsic Motivation (Vallerand, 1997) along with related evidence. In the introduction, we identified two functions of the model. First, the model provides a conceptual framework for organizing and understanding the core mechanisms underlying intrinsic and extrinsic motivational processes. Overall, the research evidence reviewed in the present chapter provided support for the postulates and corollaries of the Hierarchical Model. A second function of the model lies in its heuristic nature. From the framework provided by the model, we can derive new and testable hypotheses. One of the ways through which testing such new hypotheses becomes possible is through conceptual and methodological progressions. From a methodological standpoint, the tools needed to study the model's postulates and corollaries are now available. Scales have been developed in order to measure motivation at each level of the hierarchy. From a conceptual standpoint, the framework provided by the Hierarchical Model provides the means to study motivation from a multidimensional and hierarchical perspective. It is hoped that the model and the research that it will generate will lead us to a better understanding of the psychological processes underlying motivated behavior.

References

Abramson, L. Y., Seligman, M. E. P., & Teasdale, J. D. (1978). Learned helplessness in humans: Critique and reformulation. *Journal of Abnormal Psychology, 87,* 49-74.

Amabile, T. M. (1985). Motivation and creativity: Effects of motivational orientation on creative writers. *Journal of Personality and Social Psychology, 48,* 393-399.

Baumeister, R. F., & Leary, M. R. (1995). The need to belong: Desire for interpersonal attachments as a fundamental human motivation. *Psychological Bulletin, 117,* 497-529.

Blais, M. R., Brière, N. M., Lachance, L., Riddle, A. S., & Vallerand, R. J. (1993). L'Inventaire des motivations au travail de Blais (The Blais Work Motivation Inventory). *Revue Québécoise de Psychologie, 14,* 185-215.

Blais, M. R., Sabourin, S., Boucher, C., & Vallerand, R. J. (1990). Toward a motivational model of couple happiness. *Journal of Personality and Social Psychology, 59,* 1021-1031.

Blais, M. R., Vallerand, R. J., Gagnon, A., Brière, N. M., & Pelletier, L. G. (1990). Significance, structure, and gender differences in life domains of college students. *Sex Roles, 22,* 199-212

Blais, M. R., Vallerand, R. J., Pelletier, L. G., & Brière, N. M. (1994). *Construction et validation de l'Inventaire des Motivations Interpersonnelles* (Construction and validation of the Inventory of Interpersonal Motivations). Unpublished manuscript, Université du Québec à Montréal.

Blanchard, C., & Vallerand, R. J. (1996a). *The mediating effects of perceptions of competence, autonomy, and relatedness on the social factors-self-determined situational motivation relationship.* Unpublished manuscript, Université du Québec à Montréal.

Blanchard, C., & Vallerand, R. J. (1996b). *Perceptions of competence, autonomy, and relatedness as psychological mediators of the social factors-contextual motivation relationship.* Unpublished manuscript, Université du Québec à Montréal.

Blanchard, C., & Vallerand, R. J. (1998). *On the recursive relations between global motivation and contextual exercise motivation.* Raw data, Université du Québec à Montréal.

Blanchard, C., Vallerand, R. J., & Provencher, P. (1998). *Une analyse des effets bidirectionnels entre la motivation contextuelle et la motivation situationnelle en milieu naturel* (An analysis of the bi-directional effects between contextual and situational motivation in a natural setting). Unpublished manuscript, Université du Québec à Montréal.

Brière, N. M. , Vallerand, R. J., Blais, M. R., & Pelletier, L. G. (1995). Développement et validation d'une mesure de motivation intrinsèque, extrinsèque et d'amotivation en contexte sportif: l'Échelle de motivation dans les sports (EMS) (On the development and validation of the French form of the Sport Motivation Scale). *International Journal of Sport Psychology, 26,* 465-489.

Brown, J. D. (1993). Self-esteem and self-evaluation: Feeling is believing. In J. Suls (Ed.), *Psychological perspectives on the self* (vol. 4, pp. 27-58). Hillsdale, NJ: Erlbaum.

Brown, J. D., & Dutton, K. A. (1995). Global self-esteem and specific self-views as determinants of people's reactions to success and failure. *Journal of Personality and Social Psychology, 73,* 139-148.

Carver, C. S., & Scheier, M. F. (1981). *Attention and self-regulation.* New-York: Springer-Verlag.

Chantal, Y., Guay, F., & Vallerand, R. J. (1995). *Contextes de vie et situations: Une analyse portant sur la spécificité de leurs liens motivationnels.* [Life contexts and situations: An analysis of the specificity of their motivational relations]. Paper presented at meeting of the Société québécoise de la recherche en psychologie [Québec Society for Research in Psychology], Ottawa, Ontario, October 27-29, 1995

Chantal, Y., & Vallerand, R. J. (1996). Skill versus luck: A motivational analysis of gambling involvement. *Journal of Gambling Studies, 4*, 407-418.

Chantal, Y., & Vallerand, R. J. (2000). Construction et validation de l'échelle de motivation envers l'action bénévole (ÉMAB). [Construction and validation of the volunteering motivation scale.] *Society and Leisure, 23*, 477-508.

Connell, J. P., & Wellborn, J. G. (1991). Competence, autonomy, and relatedness: A motivational analysis of self-esteem processes. In M. R. Gunnar & L. A. Sroufe (Eds.), *The Minnesota symposium on child psychology: vol. 22. Self-processes in development* (pp. 43-77). Hillsdale, NJ: Erlbaum.

Crowne, D. P., & Marlowe, D. (1960). A new scale of social desirability independent of psychopathology. *Journal of Consulting Psychology, 24*, 349-354.

Curry, S. J., Wagner, E. H., & Grothaus, L. C. (1991). Evaluation of intrinsic and extrinsic motivation interventions with a self-help smoking cessation program. *Journal of Consulting and Clinical Psychology, 59*, 318-324.

deCharms, R. (1968). *Personal causation: The internal affective determinants of behavior.* New York: Academic Press.

Deci, E. L. (1971). Effects of externally mediated rewards on intrinsic motivation. *Journal of Personality and Social Psychology, 18*, 105-115.

Deci, E. L. (1975). *Intrinsic motivation.* New York: Plenum.

Deci, E. L. (1980). *The psychology of self-determination.* Lexington, MA: D. C. Heath.

Deci, E. L., Eghrari, E., Patrick, B. C., & Leone, D. R. (1994). Facilitating internalization: The self-determination perspective. *Journal of Personality, 62*, 119-142.

Deci, E. L., & Ryan, R. M. (1985a). The General Causality Orientations Scale: Self-determination in personality. *Journal of Research in Personality, 19*, 109-134.

Deci, E. L., & Ryan, R. M. (1985b). *Intrinsic motivation and self-determination in human behavior.* New York: Plenum.

Deci, E. L., & Ryan, R. M. (1991). A motivational approach to self: Integration in personality. In R. Dienstbier (Ed.), *Nebraska symposium on motivation: Vol. 38. Perspectives on motivation* (pp. 237-288). Lincoln, NE: University of Nebraska Press.

Deci, E. L., & Ryan, R. M. (2000). The "what" and "why" of goal pursuits: Human needs and the self-determination of behavior. *Psychological Inquiry, 11*, 227-268.

Deci, E. L., Vallerand, R. J., Pelletier, L. G., & Ryan, R. M. (1991). Motivation and education: The self-determination theory perspective. *Educational Psychologist, 26*, 325-346.

Emmons, R. A. (1995). Levels and domains in personality: An introduction. *Journal of Personality, 63*, 341-364.

Grolnick, W. S., & Ryan, R. M. (1987). Autonomy in children's learning: An experimental and individual difference investigation. *Journal of Personality and Social Psychology, 52*, 890-898.

Grouzet, F. M. E., Vallerand, R. J., & Thill, E. E. (1999). *From social factors to situational consequences: The role of motivation.* Paper presented at the XIth Annual Convention of the American Psychological Society (APS), Denver (CO), June 3-6 1999.

Guay, F., Blais, M. R., Vallerand, R. J., & Pelletier, L. G. (1999). *The Global Motivation Scale.* Unpublished manuscript, Université du Québec à Montréal.

Guay, F., & Vallerand, R. J. (1997). Social context, student's motivation and academic achievement: Toward a process model. *Social Psychology of Education, 1*, 211-233.

Guay, F., Vallerand, R. J., & Blanchard, C. (2000). On the assessment of situational intrinsic and extrinsic motivation: The Situational Motivation Scale (SIMS). *Motivation and Emotion, 24,* 175-213.

Harackiewicz, J. M., Sansone, C., Blair, L. W., Epstein, J. A., & Manderlink, G. (1987). Attributional processes in behavior change and maintenance: Smoking cessation and continued abstinence. *Journal of Consulting and Clinical Psychology, 55,* 372-378.

Harter, S. (1978). Effectance motivation reconsidered: Toward a developmental model. *Human Development, 1,* 34-64.

Hennessey, B. A. (1989). The effect of extrinsic constraints on children creativity while using a computer. *Creativity Research Journal, 2,* 151-168.

Hodgins, H. S., & Deci, E. L. (1999). *Generosity toward others: The influence of causality orientations on attributions.* Unpublished manuscript, Skidmore College.

Hodgins, H. S., Liebieskind, E., & Schwartz, W. (1996). Getting out of hot water: Facework in social predicaments. *Journal of Personality and Social Psychology, 71,* 300-314.

Knee, C. R., & Zuckerman, M. (1996). Causality orientations and the disappearance of the self-serving bias. *Journal of Research in Personality, 30,* 76-87.

Knee, C. R., & Zuckerman, M. (1998). A nondefensive personality: Autonomy and control as moderators of defensive coping and self-handicapping. *Journal of Research in Personality, 32,* 115-130.

Koestner, R., Losier, G. F., Vallerand, R. J., & Carducci, D. (1996). Identified and introjected forms of political internalization: Extending self-determination theory. *Journal of Personality and Social Psychology, 70,* 1025-1036.

Lepper, M. R. (1994). The "hot" versus "cold" cognition: An Abelsonian voyage. In R. C. Shank, & E. Langer (Eds), *Beliefs, reasoning, and decision making: Psycho-logic in honor of Bob Abelson* (pp. 237-275). Hillsdale, NJ: Erlbaum.

Lepper, M. R., & Cordova, D. I. (1992). A desire to be taught: Instructional consequences of intrinsic motivation. *Motivation and Emotion, 16,* 187-208.

Pelletier, L. G., Fortier, M. S., Vallerand, R. J., Tuson, K. M., Brière, N. M., & Blais, M. R. (1995). Toward a new measure of intrinsic motivation, extrinsic motivation, and amotivation in sports: The Sport Motivation Scale (SMS). *Journal of Sport & Exercise Psychology, 17,* 35-53.

Pelletier, L. G., Green-Demers, I., & Béland, A. (1997). Pourquoi adoptez-vous des comportements écologiques? Validation en langue française de l'échelle de motivation vis-à-vis les comportements écologiques. [Why do people adopt certain environmental behaviors?: A French validation of the Motivation Towards the Environment Scale]. *Canadian Journal of Behavioral Science, 29,* 145-156.

Pelletier, L. G., Tuson, K. M., Green-Demers, I., Noels, K., & Beaton, A. M. (1998). Why are you doing things for the environment?: The Motivation Towards the Environment Scale (MTES). *Journal of Applied Social Psychology, 28,* 437-468.

Pelletier, L. G., Vallerand, R. J., Blais, M. R., Brière, N. M., & Green-Demers, I. (1996). Vers une conceptualisation motivationnelle multidimensionnelle du loisir: Construction et validation de l'Échelle de motivation vis-à-vis des loisirs (EML) (Construction and validation of the Leisure Motivation Scale). *Loisir et Société, 19,* 559-585.

Pelletier, L. G., Vallerand, R. J., Green-Demers, I., Brière, N. M., & Blais, M. R. (1995). Loisirs et santé mentale: Les relations entre la motivation pour la pratique des loisirs et le bien-être psychologique (Leisure and mental health: Relationships between leisure involvement and psychological well-being). *Canadian Journal of Behavioural Science, 27,* 214-225.

Ratelle, C. F., Rousseau, F. L., Vallerand, R. J. & Provencher, P. (2002). *The affective, cognitive, and behavioral consequences of a motivational conflict: Implications for the Hierarchical Model of intrinsic and extrinsic motivation.* Unpublished manuscript, Université du Québec à Montréal.

Ratelle, C. F., Vallerand, R. J., Chantal, Y., & Provencher, P. (2002). *Toward a motivational model of positive illusions and mental health.* Unpublished manuscript, Université du Québec à Montréal.

Reeve, J., & Deci, E. L. (1996). Elements of the competitive situation that affect intrinsic motivation. *Personality and Social Psychology Bulletin, 22,* 24-33.

Richer, S., & Vallerand, R. J. (1998). Construction et validation de l'Échelle du sentiment d'appartenance sociale [Construction and validation of the Relatedness Feeling Scale]. *Revue Européenne de Psychologie Appliquée, 48,* 129-137.

Ryan, R. M. (1982). Control and information in the intrapersonal sphere: An extension of cognitive evaluation theory. *Journal of Personality and Social Psychology, 43,* 450-461.

Ryan, R. M. (1993). Agency and organization: Intrinsic motivation, autonomy and the self in psychological development. In R. Dientsbier (Ed.), *The Nebraska symposium on motivation* (vol. 40, pp. 1-56). Lincoln, NE: University of Nebraska Press.

Ryan, R. M. (1995). The integration of behavioral regulation within life domains. *Journal of Personality, 63,* 397-429.

Ryan, R. M., Deci, E. L., & Grolnick, W. S. (1995). Autonomy, relatedness, and the self: Their relation to development and psychopathology. In D. Cicchetti, & D. J. Cohen (Eds.), *Developmental Psychopathology - Vol. 1: Theory and methods* (pp. 618-655). New York: Wiley.

Ryan, R. M., Koestner, R., & Deci, E. L. (1991). Ego-involved persistence: When free-choice behavior is not intrinsically motivated. *Motivation and Emotion, 15,* 185-205.

Sansone, C. (1986). A question of competence: The effects of competence and task feedback on intrinsic interest. *Journal of Personality and Social Psychology, 51,* 918-931.

Sansone, C., & Harackiewicz, J. M. (1996). "I don't feel like it": The function of interest in self-regulation. In L. Martin & A. Tesser (Eds.), *Striving and feeling: Interactions between goals and affect.* Hillsdale, NJ: Erlbaum.

Shavelson, R. J., & Marsh, H. W. (1986). On the structure of self-concept. In R. Schwarzer (Ed.), *Anxiety and cognitions* (pp. 305-330). Hillsdale, NJ: Erlbaum.

Vallerand, R. J. (1993). La motivation intrinsèque et extrinsèque en contexte naturel: Implications pour les contextes de l'éducation, du travail, des relations interpersonnelles et des loisirs (Intrinsic and extrinsic motivation in natural contexts: Implications for the education, work, interpersonal relationships, and leisure contexts). In R. J. Vallerand, & E. E. Thill (Eds.), *Introduction à la psychologie de la motivation* (Introduction to the psychology of motivation) (pp. 533-582). Laval, Qué.: Etudes Vivantes.

Vallerand, R. J. (1995, June). *Toward a hierarchical model of intrinsic and extrinsic motivation.* A theory/review paper presented at the Canadian Psychological Association annual conference, Charlottetown, PEI, Canada.

Vallerand, R. J. (1996). *On the effects of success/failure on motivation at three levels of generality.* Unpublished raw data, Université du Québec à Montréal.

Vallerand, R. J. (1997). Toward a Hierarchical model of intrinsic and extrinsic motivation. In M. P. Zanna (Ed.), *Advances in experimental social psychology: vol. 29* (pp. 271-360). San Diego: Academic Press.

Vallerand, R. J., & Bissonnette, R. (1992). Intrinsic, extrinsic, and amotivational styles as predictors of behavior: A prospective study. *Journal of Personality, 60,* 599-620.

Vallerand, R. J., Blais, M. R., Brière, N. M., & Pelletier, L. G. (1989). Construction et validation de l'Echelle de motivation en éducation (EME) (On the construction and validation of the French form of the Academic Motivation Scale). *Canadian Journal of Behavioural Science, 21*, 323-349.

Vallerand, R. J., & Blanchard, C. (1998). *A test of the motivation-consequences relationship at three levels of generality.* Unpublished raw data, Université du Québec à Montréal.

Vallerand, R. J., Fortier, M. S. (1998). Measures of intrinsic and extrinsic motivation in sport and physical activity: A review and critique. In J. Duda (Ed.), *Advancements in sport and exercise psychology measurement* (pp. 83-100). Morgantown, WV: Fitness Information Technology.

Vallerand, R. J., Fortier, M., & Guay, F. (1997). Self-determination and persistence in a real-life setting: Toward a motivational model of high school dropout. *Journal of Personality and Social Psychology, 72*, 1161-1176.

Vallerand, R. J., Guay, F., Blanchard, C., & Cadorette, I. (2002). Self-regulatory processes in human behavior: A confimatory test of some elements of the hierarchical model of intrinsic and extrinsic motivation. Unpublished manuscript, Université du Québec à Montréal.

Vallerand, R. J., & O'Connor, B. P. (1991). Construction et validation de l'Échelle de motivation pour les personnes âgées (EMPA). [Construction and validation of the Elderly Motivation Scale]. *International Journal of Psychology, 26*, 219-240.

Vallerand, R. J., O'Connor, B. P., & Hamel, M. (1995). Motivation in later life: Theory and assessment. *International Journal of Aging and Human Development, 41*, 221-238.

Vallerand, R. J., Pelletier, L. G., Blais, M. R., Brière, N. M., Senécal, C., & Vallières, E. F. (1992). The Academic Motivation Scale: A measure of intrinsic, extrinsic, and amotivation in education. *Educational and Psychological Measurement, 52*, 1003-1019.

Vallerand, R. J., Pelletier, L. G., Blais, M. R., Brière, N. M., Senécal, C., & Vallières, E. F. (1993). On the assessment of intrinsic, extrinsic, and amotivation in education: Evidence on the concurrent and construct validity of the Academic Motivation Scale. *Educational and Psychological Measurement, 53*, 159-172.

Vallerand, R. J., & Reid, G. (1984). On the causal effects of perceived competence on intrinsic motivation: A test of cognitive evaluation theory. *Journal of Sport Psychology, 6*, 94-102.

Vallerand, R. J., & Reid, G. (1988). On the relative effects of positive and negative verbal feedback on males and females' intrinsic motivation. *Canadian Journal of Behavioural Sciences, 20*, 239-250.

White, R. W. (1959). Motivation reconsidered: The concept of competence. *Psychological Review, 66*, 297-333.

Whitehead, J. R., & Corbin, C. B. (1991). Youth fitness testing: The effect of percentile-based evaluative feedback on intrinsic motivation. *Research Quarterly for Exercise and Sport, 62*, 225-231.

Williams, G. C., & Deci, E. L. (1996). Internalization of biopsychological values by medical students: A test of self-determination theory. *Journal of Personality and Social Psychology, 70*, 767-779.

Williams, G. C., Grow, V. M., Freedman, Z. R., Ryan, R. M., & Deci, E. L. (1996). Motivational predictors of weight loss and weight-loss maintenance. *Journal of Personality and Social Psychology, 70*, 115-126.

3: The Self-Concordance Model of Healthy Goal Striving: When Personal Goals Correctly Represent the Person

Kennon M. Sheldon
University of Missouri-Columbia

How do people decide what to strive for in their lives, and how can this process go awry? In this chapter I discuss the self-concordance model of goal-striving (Sheldon & Elliot, 1999), which addresses these questions by building from and extending self-determination theory (SDT). Specifically, the model attempts to account for longitudinal increases in levels of well-being and personality development, issues that have received relatively little research attention from self-determination researchers. The model focuses on the idiographic personal goals that individuals set and pursue, devoting special attention to the perceived locus of causality (PLOC) that they have for those goals. As will be shown below, people sometimes fail to select goals that are appropriate to their true or actual needs, values, and interests, which can have profound costs for their adjustment and growth. Before considering these theoretical issues, however, it is first necessary to consider the nature of idiographic goal-assessment procedures.

Idiographic Goals as Units of Motivational Analysis

Idiographic goal methodologies begin by asking participants to list the salient personal goals (Brunstein, 1993), life-tasks (Cantor & Blanton, 1996), personal strivings (Emmons, 1989), personal projects (Little, 1993), or current concerns (Klinger, 1977) that they engage in or will be engaging in. These idiographic methodologies offer a number of important advantages for motivational researchers. First, they are *personologically valid*, given that individuals themselves provide the units of analysis and are thus typically invested in them. This links the approach to one of the most respected traditions of personality psychology

(Allport, 1937; Murray, 1938), in which researchers attempt to understand persons in their own terms (King & Napa, 1998). Second, these goal methodologies are *flexible*, in that once participants provide the basic "stems," a variety of issues can be explored. By aggregating a participant's appraisals across the multiple goals in his or her system, a researcher can gain reliable trait-level information about many constructs of interest (Sheldon & Elliot, 2000). Third, goal methodologies lend themselves well to *longitudinal* research, given that the goals specified naturally occupy participants' attention over time. Thus, these methodologies open up a potentially powerful window into the temporal dynamics of basic personality functioning, and they also offer a focus for conceptualizing and measuring the entire process of proactive adaptation in which individuals engage (Aspinwall & Taylor, 1997; Snyder & Cantor, 1998). Fourth, as will be argued below, personal goal methodologies have the potential to shed new light on important *conceptual* issues not yet addressed by self-determination researchers. An encapsulated review of SDT's development helps illustrate this claim.

Self-Determination Theory
and the Proactive Individual

SDT began in the realm of social psychology, examining the impact of potentially controlling situational forces upon intrinsic motivation, adjustment, and performance (Deci, 1975; Deci & Ryan, 1980). The theory began to move deeper into the person when Ryan (1982) showed that people can also be controlled by internal forces, that could be aroused by ego-involving situational manipulations. The PLOC internalization continuum (Ryan & Connell, 1989) and the organismic integration concept (Deci & Ryan, 1985b, 1991) took the theory to the very core of person-hood, as researchers explored the motivational dynamics of religious behavior (Ryan, Rigby & King, 1993), the internalization of family values (Grolnick, Deci, & Ryan, 1997), the nature of psychological vitality (Ryan & Frederick, 1997), and many other issues. These theoretical developments helped shed important new light on a host of basic personality and self-regulatory processes.

However one process not extensively addressed by self-determination researchers is that by which individuals proactively select new life-directions for themselves from among the potentially bewildering variety of possible choices (Schwartz, 2000). That is, how do people generate personal initiatives, initiatives that will hopefully serve to advance them in their own developmental process and give broad meaning and purpose to their lives (Ryff & Singer, 1998)? Given the wide freedom that people have in selecting such initiatives (Schwartz, 2000), is it possible for them to choose the "wrong" goals for themselves? If individuals do in fact generate self-inappropriate goals even in the absence of any contextual controls or constraints (as is the case during open-ended goal-assessment), then there would appear to be important personality factors involved in proper goal-selection, factors that have received little attention in prior SDT research.

Of course idiographic goal-assessment procedures may indeed have some controlling aspects, in that some people may feel forced to come up with goals "for the experimenter" when they would not have generated goals, otherwise. However two facts are worth noting in this regard. First, participants in our longitudinal goal-studies typically rate themselves as being quite committed and involved in the goals they generate. That is, at least initially, they tend to view their participation in the study as an interesting and even exciting opportunity—a chance to devote focused effort on getting what they want—although, unfortunately, this initial rush of enthusiasm does not necessarily last. Second, because of the ambiguity of the situation and the paucity of information given participants regarding *what* goals to list, the procedure bears important similarities to projective testing (Emmons & McAdams, 1991). That is, participants must of necessity project their underlying desires and inclinations onto the sheet of paper. Along with other goal researchers I assume that such information is important and revealing, regardless of participants' conscious attitude towards the task.

The PLOC Methodology Applied to Personal Goals

An important concept within SDT concerns individuals' perceived locus of causality for their behavior (Ryan & Connell, 1989). According to this view, behaviors vary on a continuum of internalization, ranging from noninternalized (or controlled) to fully internalized (or autonomous). PLOC concerns the degree to which the regulation of a behavior is external or noninternalized versus internal or fully internalized. The PLOC methodology has now been applied to study the quality or degree of internalized motivation within a wide variety of specific domains or contexts. These include school (Vallerand, Fortier, & Guay, 1997), work (Baard, Deci, & Ryan, 2000), sports (Pelletier, Fortier, Vallerand, & Tuson, 1995), environmentalism (Seguin, Pelletier, & Hunsley, 1998), dyadic relationships (Blais, Sabourin, Boucher, & Vallerand, 1990), medical regimens (Williams, Rodin, Ryan, Grolnick, & Deci, 1998), and political behavior (Koestner, Losier, Vallerand, & Carducci, 1996). Typically in such research a scale is developed so that people can rate why they behave within the particular domain being studied. Scale items tend to focus people's attention upon the forces and contingencies residing within that domain, as well as the reasons they behave in the context of those forces. The basic issue concerns whether people can feel self-determined in the face of these situational influences. A measure of felt self-determination within that domain is derived, often by subtracting the strength of controlled reasons from that of autonomous reasons.

However, as noted above, my program of research takes leave of particular domains and instead asks people to list (6 to 10) broad personal goals. These idiographic stems then become the focus of PLOC appraisals; that is, participants proceed to rate the extent to which they pursue each goal for autonomous vs. controlled reasons. Because the goals concern participants' entire lives (i.e., they represent a variety of life-domains and/or address trans-domain issues), such appraisals, when aggregated across the goal-system, take on the status of *trait* measurements similar to the Autonomy orientation and Control Orientation subscales of the General Causality Orientations Scale (Deci & Ryan, 1985a). Again, however, I argue that trait motivation measures based on idiographic goals may have especially desirable properties, given that they concretely represent participants' proactive growth attempts, and naturally occupy participants' attention over time.

Conceptualizing Self-Concordance

The goal-PLOC variable discussed in this chapter was originally called goal self-determination (Sheldon & Kasser, 1995, 1998). However, in later work we were led to revise this term (Sheldon & Elliot, 1999; Sheldon & Houser-Marko, 2001), in order to avoid ambiguity and to better capture the desired meaning. One ambiguity was that during goal assessment individuals project a set of goals, with almost no guidance, onto the assessment form (Emmons 1989). Thus, in one sense, *all* personal goals are self-determined, at least nominally so, in that they are created *ex nihilo* by the person himself or herself. Because of this, and also because we wished to focus on the issue of whether chosen goals are congruent or concordant with the person's deeper or true condition, we have now adopted the term "self-concordance." The basic question becomes, can the individual correctly perceive his or her own needs and developmental trends, thereby generating self-concordant goals that will remain salient over time and, if attained will satisfy the person's needs? As will be illustrated below, this under-studied self-perceptual ability has important implications for positive functioning, psychological adjustment, and personality growth.

Figure 3-1 provides a graphic illustration of the concept of self-concordance, which includes four salient aspects of the PLOC continuum. Self-concordant goals are defined as those that are inspired by a person's lifelong evolving interests (Gruber & Wallace, 1999) and deeply-felt core values (Little, 1993; Lydon & Zanna, 1990). In other words, they are goals underlain by intrinsic and/or identified motivation. Such goals are assumed to represent the "best" of people, proactively shaping themselves and their environments to permit further growth and expansion. As can also be seen in Figure 3-1, however, not all goals are integrated with the self. Specifically, some goals are felt to be compelled by external or introjected forces, and are not felt to reflect core values or deeper interests. In our research, we typically compute an aggregate self-concordance variable for each participant, by summing the intrinsic and identified ratings the person makes for each of his or her (6 to 10) goals, and subtracting the external and introjected ratings.

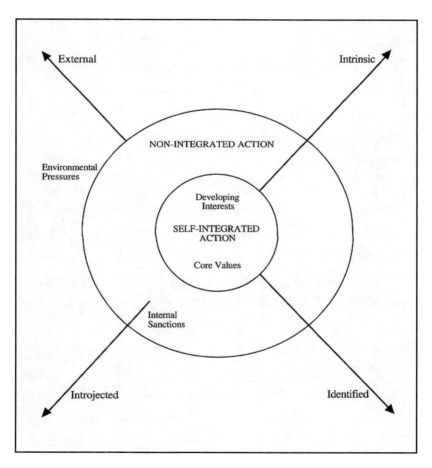

Figure 3.1. A Spatial Relationship of Self-Concordance

Self-Concordance and Well-being

Logically, non-concordant goal pursuit should present substantial problems for individuals. This is because the process of pursuing personal goals can consume a considerable amount of one's limited self-regulatory (Baumeister, Bratslavsky, Muraven, & Tice, 1998) and functional (Wilensky, 1983) resources. If a person's goals do not accurately represent the interests and values of his or her deeper self, then that person may be unable to meet his or her deeper organismic needs through the goal pursuits. Thus, the person may exhaust important psychological and physical resources, in vain. If this view is correct, then clearly, whether or not a person pursues concordant goals has important implications for that person's well-being and personal thriving.

Self-Concordance and Concurrent Well-being

Sheldon and Kasser (1995) found support for this idea in a cross-sectional study of participants' personal strivings (i.e., the enduring teleological trends that characterize their personalities; Emmons, 1989). Specifically, self-concordant individuals were higher on a wide variety of well-being and healthy personality characteristics, such as openness, empathy, self-actualization, positive mood, vitality, and role-system integration. Sheldon and Kasser suggested that self-concordant people appear healthier because they are better satisfying their organismic needs via their goal pursuits.

A limitation of this study was that it was purely cross-sectional, that is, it focused on individuals' personal strivings and their well-being at a single moment in time. Because of this, Sheldon and Kasser were unable to establish the direction of any causal relationship between self-concordance and well-being. In fact the relation may go the other way: perhaps those higher in dispositional well-being (apparently a highly heritable trait; Lykken & Tellegen, 1996) naturally report that they better enjoy and more strongly identify with their strivings. Thus, an important next step was to examine the potential causal influence of self-concordance upon well-being in a longitudinal context, using more concrete and focused personal initiatives.

Self-Concordance and Longitudinal Well-being

Sheldon and Kasser (1998) conducted a short-term prospective study of well-being, using the time-delimited personal project (Little, 1993) construct as a vehicle. Guided by Brunstein's (1993) findings, they hypothesized that longitudinal attainment promotes positive *change* in well-being. More importantly, they also hypothesized that "not all progress is beneficial"—that is, that only individuals attaining self-concordant goals would experience enhanced well-being. This was based on the assumption that concordant goals, when obtained, would be more satisfying of individuals' organismic needs than less concordant goals. Again, concordant goals were assumed to better represent the individuals' true values, interests, and developmental trends, so attaining them should provide more emotional benefits for the person.

Figure 3-2 illustrates the support that Sheldon and Kasser (1998) found for their hypotheses. As can be seen, a significant interaction emerged such that individuals increased in their well-being from the beginning to the end of the study only if their goals were, as a set, largely self-concordant. Notably, Sheldon and Kasser also showed that self-concordance was *not* a mere proxy for self-reported goal commitment—apparently self-concordance provides motivational resources that go beyond participants' conscious estimations of their personal commitment to the goals. Interestingly, the data in Figure 3-2 also suggest that concordant individuals are at risk for reduced well-being, if they fail to attain their goals. Sheldon and Kasser argued that this illustrates the deeper investment that individuals have in concordant goals. For example, a person seeking to transform a romantic relationship or grow in a new direction may feel substantial (legitimate) disappointment if he or she fails in those aims. To paraphrase an old saying, "no risk of pain, no potential for gain."

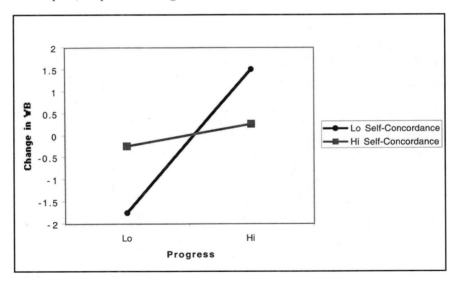

Figure 3.2 Change in Well-Being for Four Hypothetical Participants Who Made Low or High Amounts of Progress in Goals Low or HIgh in Self-Concordance.

Conceptualizing and Measuring Need Satisfaction

As noted above, Sheldon and Kasser (1998) assumed that concordant goal-attainment influences well-being because people better satisfy their needs as they pursue self-concordant goals. However, in their research they did not attempt to measure or model need-satisfaction. In fact, there is substantial confusion in the field regarding how to conceptualize and measure psychological needs. Are needs acquired motive dispositions or "pushes," to be measured by thematic methods as are the needs for intimacy, power, and achievement (Smith, 1994)? Or are they instead universal requirements or "inputs," to be measured with reference to phenomenological experience (Deci & Ryan, 1991) and tested as predictors of thriving? I briefly diverge from goal-related research and the self-concordance issue in order to address this question. Its relevance for the final self-concordance model will become apparent afterwards.

I and many of my colleagues have conditionally accepted self-determination theory's assumption that humans have three basic types of needs or motives, for autonomy, competence, and relatedness (Deci & Ryan, 1991). That is, humans are happiest and healthiest when environments, and their own inner processes, permit them to feel effective, choiceful, and connected in their ongoing experience. Where did these three needs come from? One can easily argue that they are evolved—that, on the behavioral output side, they were selected for because of the unique adaptive benefits associated with the behaviors that provide each type of experience and that, on the experiential input side, they were selected for because the rewarding aspect of these three feelings reinforces much adaptive learning. Unfortunately, space does not permit further development of these ideas here.

Sheldon, Ryan, and Reis (1996) and Reis, Sheldon, Roscoe, Gable, and Ryan (2000) found new support for the proposition that humans "need" these three types of experiences by showing that the activity-based feelings of autonomy, competence, and relatedness occurring during a given day each predicted well-being on that day. Specifically, these investigators pioneered a daily diary method by which the need-fulfilling quality of an individual's time-consuming activities on a given day could be assessed. They found that each of these qualities of daily activities (i.e., experiential autonomy, competence, and relatedness) had its own independent effect on positive mood, negative mood, vitality, and symptomology during that day, and they also found that the effect persisted when trait levels of need-satisfaction were controlled (Sheldon et al., 1996). Sheldon and Elliot extended these findings to the longitudinal realm (1999, Study 2 and Study 3), using a daily diary method to show that need-satisfying experiences accumulating over a period of time predict changes in global well-being at the end of that time. In short, the above findings are consistent with SDT's proposal that need-satisfaction is essential, so we have recently integrated need-satisfaction constructs into our goal research. Before discussing this integration, however, I first return to the topic of self-concordant goal pursuit and its relations with sustained effort.

Self-Concordance and Goal Attainment

Sheldon and Elliot (1998) studied the process by which personal goals are or are not attained over time. Specifically, they conducted a month-long study of personal projects, focusing their analyses on single rather than aggregated goals. To measure goal attainment by the most objective means possible, they used the goal attainment scaling procedure (Kiresuk, Smith, & Cardillo, 1994), in which participants pre-specify and scale the concrete outcomes by which later success (or lack of it) is finally determined. In their study Sheldon and Elliot divided the self-concordance variable into autonomous (intrinsic and identified) and controlled (external and introjected) facets, examining each separately as predictors of initial intended effort, actual later effort, and final attainment.

As expected, Sheldon and Elliot (1998) found that the degree of autonomous or concordant motivation associated with a goal predicted initial effort intentions regarding that goal. Interestingly, strong *controlled* motivation was also associated with strong effort intentions. Nevertheless, assessments revealed that controlled motivation did not predict *actual* effort, two and four weeks later, although autonomous motivation did. Sheldon and Elliot argued that this pattern of findings occurred because "not all personal goals are personal," that is, goals that do not contact people's enduring values and deeper interests may fail to contact enduring sources of energy, instead falling by the wayside in the manner of many New Year's resolutions. Because such non-self-representative goals do not have the person's full emotional backing and volitional support, such goals are not likely to be well-energized, protected, and attained.

Putting the Self-Concordance Model Together

Sheldon and Elliot (1999) assembled all of these findings (re: goal-attainment, need-satisfaction processes, and well-being changes) into a single path model. Figure 3-3 presents their integrated LISREL model, with the parameter estimates that were generated in a successful semester-long test of the model. In this research, all earlier results were simultaneously replicated: that is, the degree of self-concordance of participants' goals predicted concurrent well-being (Sheldon & Kasser, 1995) and also predicted sustained effort in those goals, which in turn predicted goal-attainment (Sheldon & Elliot, 1998); goal attainment in turn led to increased well-being, and self-concordance again moderated the effects of attainment upon increased well-being (Sheldon & Kasser, 1998). In addition, need-satisfaction constructs (i.e., accumulated activity-based experiences of autonomy, competence, and relatedness) were shown to be integratable into the model: goal-attainment, especially concordant attainment, predicted cumulative need-satisfaction, which in turn predicted changes in rated global well-being at the end of the semester. Sheldon and Elliot argued that their model and method provides a useful framework for testing many personality-developmental issues and outcomes.

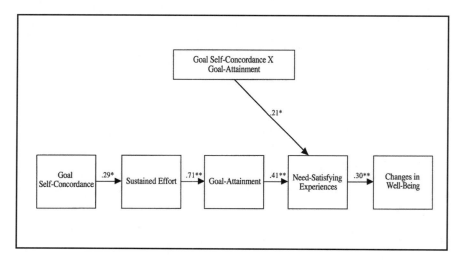

Figure 3.3. The Self-Concordance Model: LISREL Parameter Estimates

To summarize, the self-concordance of a person's personal goals has thus far been shown to be associated with three positive outcomes. First, self-concordance is correlated with positive concurrent well-being, indicating that positive mood states may enhance individuals' ability to select goals that well-represent their deeper values and interests, or vice versa. Second, self-concordance enables individuals to put sustained effort into their goals over time, enhancing the likelihood that those goals will be attained. Third, self-concordance makes goals more satisfying as they are attained, leading to enhanced well-being via the cumulation of need-satisfying experiences that occur during the period of striving. Notably, Sheldon and Elliot (1999) showed that these positive effects of self-concordance were not reducible to the effects of strong life-skills, efficacy-expectations, implementation intentions, or approach orientation; that is, self-concordance provides not only *important* but also *unique* motivational resources.

Bottom-up versus Top-down Routes to Enhanced Well-being

The results presented so far are consistent with bottom-up models of well-being (Diener, 1984), which say that happiness results from the accumulation of many small positive events. In other words, from this perspective, well-being is no more than the sum effect of the many daily events that make up an individual's life. Diener, Sandvik, and Pavot (1990) advanced a memory-based explanation of this process, assuming that when people make global well-being judgments they do it by recalling salient positive and negative experiences that occurred in the recent past, then basing their judgments on the proportion of each type which come to mind. Sheldon and Elliot (1999) suggested that accumulated daily experiences of autonomy, competence, and relatedness are exactly the kinds of salient emotional events that should contribute to this memory-based appraisal process, and their data, based on eight samplings of daily activity occurring during the study, supported that claim.

However, I now suggest another explanation for the bottom-up effects of need-satisfaction on well-being, namely, that people who have many such experiences literally experience greater "organismic thriving and health" as a result, that is, they may experience higher immune and neurocognitive as well as enhanced psychological functioning (Ryan, Kuhl, & Deci 1997; Ryff & Singer, 1998). Thus, a recently satisfied person's reports of greater well-being may be based on accurate perceptions of his or her current psychophysical state, in addition to being influenced by the retrospective memorial and self-perceptive processes outlined by the Diener et al. (1990) Model. Ryan's (1995) plant metaphor is apt in this context: those who regularly experience autonomy, competence, and relatedness may thrive to a greater extent than those who do not, in the same way that a plant thrives given regular sunlight and watering, compared to plants that do not get such nutriments.

In contrast, top-down models of well-being say that happiness is more a function of global attitudes or life-circumstances, rather than being the mere sum of small positive (or negative) events that occur to one (Diener, 1984). From this perspective, new levels of happiness may result when radical changes occur within one's life-situation, evaluative attitudes, or self-concept. Notably, Sheldon and Elliot (1999) found a *direct* path from goal-attainment to increased well-being, a path that by-passed cumulative need-satisfaction. They suggested that this indicates that attaining goals can have top-down influences in addition to bottom-up influences on global well-being. For example, personal goal-attainment may help people alter their basic attitudes or evaluative baselines which can bring about relatively sudden changes in global well-being. The idea that more self-concordant individuals are more poised for top-down transformations in their levels or stages of happiness, self-development, and personality integration will be discussed in greater detail below.

The above results suggest that the ability to select concordant goals is an important skill, one that is not necessarily to be taken for granted. What kinds of more specific abilities enable individuals to select the best goals for themselves? This interesting question is now considered.

Skills Required for Self-Concordant Goal-Selection

I suggest that generating concordant or health-producing goals requires at least three component skills or abilities. First, one must be able to distinguish lasting and broadly-representative impulses from more transient or superficial impulses; that is, one must be able to recognize what one's enduring values and interests are, in contrast to more momentary whims. By so doing, one is able to resist squandering motivational energy upon dead-ends or blind alleys and to avoid the volitional confusions that may result (Kuhl, 2000). Second, one must also be able to distinguish accurately between "me" and "not-me," that is, between goals that represent one's *own* interests and values, and goals that instead represent *others'* interests and values. By so doing, one is able to resist others' or the culture's attempts to implant goals in one, goals that may not be in one's own best interest (Kuhl & Kazen, 1994). Of course, while many good ideas for action can be identified by observing or listening to others (i.e., actions consistent with one's own needs and growth trends), it is also the case that many conformist and even harmful impulses are taken in from the environment. Thus, it is important to learn to tell the difference.

A third important skill that enhances self-concordance is that of selecting goals whose *contents* are consistent with basic needs and motives within the human personality (Ryan, 1995). To understand this, it is necessary to distinguish between the "what" or explicit object of goals, and the "why" or motives behind goals (Ryan, Sheldon, Kasser, & Deci, 1996). The self-concordance model focuses primarily on the "why" of goals, specifically, the sense of ownership that the person does or does not feel concerning goals. However, the content of goals is also important; for example, extrinsic goals, which concern money, appearance, or popularity, tend to be less salubrious than intrinsic goals, which concern intimacy, community, and personal growth (Kasser & Ryan, 1993, 1996; Sheldon & Kasser, 1998) .

Notably, the what and why dimensions are conceptually distinct. Thus, a person might conceivably pursue goals with strongly extrinsic content, yet feel quite self-concordant in doing so. For example, a thief might feel strong intrinsic motivation for stealing (if he enjoys the challenge) and strong identification with that process (if he believes that the rich have acquired their wealth by illegitimate means). Conversely, a person might pursue goals with intrinsic content, for non-concordant reasons. For example, a philanthropist might pursue the goal of supporting social causes out of a sense of guilt (if he believes his wealth is illegitimate) or coercion (if he believes his friends will not like him if he does not give to charity). Despite their conceptual separability, the data show that goals with intrinsic content are usually pursued for self-concordant reasons (Sheldon & Kasser, 1995, 1998). Thus, the ability to focus in healthy content areas can also be viewed as a skill that conduces to self-concordant goal-selection.

Enhancing Self-Concordance

Below I describe a program of research in which an intervention was tested to help individuals become more self-concordant in their personal goals (Sheldon, Kasser, Smith, & Share, 2002). Specifically, a randomly-assigned experimental group of participants attended two sessions run by graduate counseling students, in which they were taught strategies for regulating their goal-related experience during the upcoming semester (control participants also generated personal goals but then took part in other studies rather than attending the training sessions). The primary aim of the program was to enhance participants' goal-attainment, which was hypothesized to offer a *pro*active route to personal growth or personality development (notably, most extant theories of personal growth focus on individuals' *re*actions to trauma or stress). Of the four self-regulatory strategies taught, two correspond to the positive motivational forces specified by the self-concordance model (i.e., identified and intrinsic motivation). Specifically, participants were encouraged to try to "own the goal" and "make it fun" at times when goal pursuit felt onerous or when they were tempted to abandon the goal.

As expected, goal-attainment predicted positive longitudinal increases in psychosocial well-being, vitality, and self-actualization and also predicted positive increases in self-concordance (to test this PLOC was assessed a second time near the end of the semester). Thus, it appears that being successful in one's goals is one way to enhance one's sense of self-concordance regarding those goals. Surprisingly, the goal-training program had no main effects on attainment (compared with the control group). However, *some* participants benefited—namely, those who were already quite self-concordant at the beginning of the study! This was manifested in a significant interaction between self-concordance and intervention-participation in predicting goal-progress, such that the concordant individuals receiving the intervention manifested the most goal-progress in the study (which in turn led to more growth). These results suggest that the "strong get stronger"—that is, those who are already self-concordant are best poised (Holt, 1998) to profit from learning opportunities (such as our intervention), thus better attaining their goals and becoming even *more* self-concordant in the process.

Sheldon et al. (2002) conceptualized the "strong get stronger" effect in terms of dynamic systems models of personal functioning (Vallacher & Nowak, 1994; Read & Miller, 1998). Specifically, they postulated that self-concordant individuals are in a state of dynamic equilibrium in which they readily move to new phases or levels of organization, in part via their own process of goal-pursuit. In contrast, non-concordant individuals are in a more static form of equilibrium, resisting change and clinging to the status quo. Thus, they may be less able to actualize their own potential. In other words, self-concordant individuals are growing already, are receiving ample "psychological nutrition," and are thus poised to take advantage of an opportunity to grow even further. Non-concordant individuals may be "stalled," afraid of losing what little nutrition they do receive, and thus may be unprepared to take advantage of new growth opportunities.

Notably, participating in the intervention did not enhance participants' sense of self-concordance directly; that is, there was no main effect of program-participation on program-participants' later self-concordance ratings, compared to control group participants. Although this was contrary to our expectations it can be viewed as a desirable outcome, one that in a way, supports the validity of the self-concordance model. That is, it is perhaps comforting that people cannot be simply "talked into" greater self-concordance. Indeed, if the self-concordance model is correct in assuming that a person's goals can really fail to represent his or her values and interests, then such facile re-framings should have limited effectiveness. Instead, these results suggest that people must *work* for greater self-concordance or self-integration, achieving it in part via their goal-attainments. Again, those who were already more concordant showed the greatest ability to use the self-regulatory tools that we supplied in the goal-training program. This can be viewed as yet a fourth positive benefit of self-concordance.

Does the strong-get-stronger finding mean that self-concordant individuals spiral up indefinitely, on a happy trail to ultimate virtue and self-actualization? No, of course not. Although more concordant individuals are better poised to make further gains, there are many factors that can dis-entrain them from the upward path. That is, perpetual growth is a single (probably rare) outcome among many possible outcomes, and I would expect that few manage to fit themselves into the perpetual growth track. Furthermore, *non*concordant goal-selection doubtless has an important role in growth—as the saying goes, we learn from our mistakes. More specifically, the process of pursuing unsatisfying goals can supply information that can help a person identify better goals the next time. Notably, the self-concordance model does not yet have a means of incorporating such dialectical processes. However we are currently conducting studies to track multiple cycles of goal pursuit, hoping to open a window into the dynamic waxing and waning of personal goal-functioning.

Self-Concordance: Measurement Issues and Current Research

One important future issue for the self-concordance model concerns measurement. Again, the aim is to capture the extent to which a person's chosen goals correctly represent his or her underlying or "true" interests, values, and commitments. In effect, we are relying on PLOC ratings to tell us when a person's chosen goals, in aggregate, do not match the person's developmental core, that is, his or her enduring values and evolving interests (Gruber & Wallace, 1999). Obviously, however, these kinds of ratings are susceptible to a number of influences that might bias the assessment of the fit between self and goals.

For example, it is likely that some self-concordant individuals are not so concordant after all. Rather, they may suffer from "illusory mental health" (Shedler, Mayman, & Manis, 1993), in which their self-reported well-being is much more positive than their clinical and physiological profiles actually suggest. Similar illusions might come into play when people make PLOC ratings regarding important personal initiatives. To the extent that "false positive" strivers are intermixed with true positives, self-report measures of self-concordance may have reduced explanatory power. Relatedly, some individuals may have "closed identifications" in which their claimed values are not open for reflective consideration but, instead, are rigorously defended. In such foreclosed cases (Marcia, 1994), goals that are rated as highly identified might actually be highly introjected, again limiting the validity of the self-report measure. Finally, another problem concerns the referent. Whose interests and values are being modeled via participants' PLOC ratings—the self-concepts' or those of the underlying organism? To the extent that the individual's self-concept is out of touch with the organism, these ratings may actually reverse their meaning.

The fact that research thus far has supported the predictions of the self-concordance model indicates that these potential measurement problems are not serious. Nevertheless, the considerations outlined above suggest that non-self-report measures of self-concordance would be very desirable. Are there any indirect but reliable means of revealing a person's "disattunement" from his or her underlying organismic condition? Several research projects, pertinent to these questions, are discussed below.

One way to test the concordance of a goal with the organism of the person who listed it might be to use galvanic skin response (GSR) or lie-detector methodologies. Although such devices are too unreliable for legal purposes, they may often provide useful research data (Iacono & Lykken, 1997). Kasser and Sheldon (2002) collected data using a design in which participants are interviewed regarding their goals as their GSR, heart rate, and breathing rate are monitored. Participants are questioned about goals that were rated as high in identification and low in introjection, relative to other goals within the subject's goal-system.

Thus, there is an opportunity to observe participants' arousal level as they are challenged about goals that they may be "falsely positive" about.

Because goals with intrinsic content are assumed to be more directly expressive of people's organismic nature, one can hypothesize that individual's low ratings on introjection for these intrinsic goals would more likely be veridical. In other words, there should be less arousal when people are challenged about the low introjection ratings on their intrinsic goals than on their extrinsic goals. Kasser and Sheldons' (2002) preliminary data are consistent with their hypothesis that extrinsic goals (concerning money, beauty, and popularity) are more likely to be false positives than are intrinsic goals (concerning self-knowledge, intimacy, and community). That is, extrinsic goals are more likely to be "introjects disguised as identifications." Conversely, participants are more likely to be correct when they rate intrinsic goals as being motivated by identified but not introjected motivation. Thus, these preliminary results support the suggestion, made above, that the ability to select goals with intrinsic content is indeed a "skill" that conduces to self-concordant goal selection.

A second planned program of research will employ Kuhl and colleagues' "self-infiltration" methodology (Kuhl & Kazen, 1994; Kazen, Baumann, & Kuhl, 1999), as a way of assessing the meaning of self-concordance ratings. In this methodology a sophisticated computer program is used in a subtle attempt to implant false memories into participants. These memories are of a particular type concerning whether an intended action was originally self-generated or other-generated. Kuhl and Kazen's (1994) program first presents a list of "office activities," whose attractiveness the participant rates, and a subset of which he or she selects for later execution. Participants are then given information regarding a so-called experts' opinions of each action. They are then presented with the original list of activities and asked to recall which ones they originally selected. The program automatically counterbalances and controls a host of within-subject variables, enabling the researcher to clearly identify which actions the participants mistakenly believe were originally their own ideas.

Results thus far indicate that some people indeed make such memory errors, particularly under alienating conditions that inhibit "self-compatibility checking." Kuhl and Kazen called this "self-infiltration," in which a person incorporates the recommendations of an authority figure while believing that they were the his or her own idea, rather than the authority's idea. Kuhl and Kazen suggested that in many such instances, the partially-internalized action is actually incompatible with the person's true emotional preferences. Kazen, Baumann, and Kuhl (2002) found evidence to support this idea, showing that falsely-remembered action-elements are often ones that the participant originally rated as unappealing. Kuhl et al. interpret these effects in terms of their Personality Systems Interaction theory, which provides a fascinating neuropsychological complement to self-determination theory and the self-concordance model. Unfortunately there is not room here to sketch out the many interesting convergences between these theoretical perspectives.

Kuhl and colleagues' findings appear to have many implications for the question of how and why people might adopt goals that are incompatible with their true interests and values (Brunstein, Schultheiss, & Graessman, 1998). Specifically, they suggest that people may mistakenly come to believe that others' goal-recommendations were originally their own idea, thereby uncritically adopting goals that do not correctly represent their own values and interests. In other words, such persons may lack the second "skill" discussed above, that of discriminating "me" from "not-me" in making volitional choices.

To test this idea, a modified version of Kuhl and Kazen's (1994) computer program is being constructed, to address participants' personal goals instead of trivial office activities. The revised program will first ask participants to generate a list of personal goals that they would like to pursue in the near future and will then present a list of "expert recommended" goals. Finally, both self-generated and expert-recommended goals will be intermixed and presented to participants, who will be asked to pick out the goals that they originally identified themselves. The primary measurements of interest derived from this procedure will be (a) the number of alien goals, overall, that become infiltrated into a participant's goal-system (a between-subjects variable), and (b) the within-subject distinction between self-generated and self-infiltrated goals.

Several interesting questions will be addressed by this research, including (a) what types of individuals are most susceptible to goal self-infiltration? (b) what conditions tend to induce self-infiltration? and (c) how are self-infiltrated goals appraised on PLOC, compared to the person's other goals? The latter question has particular relevance for examining the degree of self-deception involved in participants' ratings of self-concordance. In effect, this experimental methodology will identify a clear subset of goals that are known to be "alien" within the person's system. If self-concordance ratings are reasonably accurate representations of the person's organismic condition, then infiltrated goals should be higher in external and introjected motivation and lower in intrinsic and identified motivation, compared to the person's "native" goals. However if infiltrated goals are instead rated as more self-concordant, then some prior findings of self-determination theory researchers (including myself!) would be called into question.

Yet another planned program of research will employ latency measures and priming manipulations to examine the unconscious dynamics of goal-pursuit (Chartrand & Bargh, 1996; Bargh & Barndollar, 1996). One interesting question is, how long does it take participants to correctly identify one of their own goals, flashed on a screen, as belonging to them? The theorizing outlined in this chapter suggests that goals that are less representative or less closely tied to the organism's "true" condition should be slower to be claimed, compared to more central goals. A related technique is to compare two groups of participants: those primed with the word "myself," and those primed with some other word (Fenigstein & Levine, 1984). The self-concordance model would predict that participants will be slower to claim their external or introjected goals, or goals with extrinsic content (Kasser & Ryan, 1996) after being exposed to the "myself" prime.

As can be seen, there are a number of potentially interesting developments underway in the measurement of self-concordance. Ultimately, it would be desirable to be able to objectively assess a person's degree of attunement or alignment with his or her own underlying developmental needs and processes, using indirect indicators and personal goal methodologies, in order to pinpoint areas of difficulty within a person's motivational system. One can even imagine 22nd century individuals "going in to get their selves aligned," just as we now take our automobiles in for alignment! We in my lab are excited about beginning to get answers to some of these fascinating questions.

Conclusion

As should be clear by now, research on the self-concordance model has just begun, and far more questions exist than do answers. Hopefully, however, it is also clear that this way of viewing matters has substantial promise for understanding how humans can become "disattuned" from themselves, such that their conscious goals are out of step with the deeper needs, preferences, and values of their own organism. Of course, discovering what is truly inside oneself may not necessarily correct one's problems, if what is inside is corrupt or false. However more often than not, I would argue, a person who succeeds in contacting deep and enduring sources of meaning and interest within himself or herself will also be a person who appreciates and expresses the profounder "being" values about which so many theorists have written. Folk wisdom says we should try to "be ourselves," and the self-concordance model concurs. Although the task of aligning one's goals and phenomenal self with one's underlying organism is not easy, it may hold the key to positive living.

References

Allport, F. (1937). Teleonomic description in the study of personality. *Character and personality, 5*, 202-214.

Aspinwall, L. G., & Taylor, S. E. (1997). A stitch in time: Self-regulation and proactive coping. *Psychological Bulletin, 121*, 417-436.

Baard, P., Deci, E. L., & Ryan, R. M. (2000). The relation of intrinsic need satisfaction to performance and well-being in two work settings. Unpublished manuscript, Fordham University

Bargh, J. A., & Barndollar, K. (1996). Automaticity in action: The unconscious as repository of chronic goals and motives. In P. Gollwitzer & J. Bargh (Eds.), *The psychology of action: Linking cognition and motivation to behavior* (pp. 457-481). New York, NY,: Guilford.

Baumeister, R. F., Bratslavsky, E., Muraven, M., & Tice, D. M. (1998). Ego depletion: Is the active self a limited resource? *Journal of Personality and Social Psychology, 74,* 1252-1265.

Blais, M. R., Sabourin, S., Boucher, C., & Vallerand, R. J. (1990). Toward a motivational model of couple happiness. *Journal of Personality and Social Psychology, 59,* 1021-1031.

Brunstein, J. (1993). Personal goals and subjective well-being: A longitudinal study. *Journal of Personality and Social Psychology, 65,* 1061-1070.

Brunstein, J. C., Schultheiss, O. C., & Graessman, R. (1998). Personal goals and emotional well-being: The moderating role of motive dispositions. *Journal of Personality and Social Psychology, 75,* 494-508.

Cantor, N., & Blanton, H. (1996). Effortful pursuit of personal goals in daily life. In P. Gollwitzer & J. Bargh (Eds.), *The psychology of action: Linking cognition and motivation to behavior.* New York: Guilford.

Chartrand, T. L., & Bargh, J. A. (1996). Automatic activation of impression formation and memorization goals: Non conscious goal priming reproduces effects of explicit task instructions. *Journal of Personality and Social Psychology, 71,* 464-478.

Deci, E. L. (1975). *Intrinsic motivation.* New York: Plenum Press.

Deci, E. L., & Ryan, R. M. (1980). The empirical exploration of intrinsic motivational processes. In L. Berkowitz (Ed.), *Advances in experimental social psychology* (Vol. 13). New York: Academic Press.

Deci, E. L., & Ryan, R. M. (1985a). The general causality orientations scale: Self-determination in personality. *Journal of Research in Personality, 19,* 109-134.

Deci, E. L., & Ryan, R. M. (1985b). *Intrinsic motivation and self-determination in human behavior.* New York: Plenum.

Deci, E. L., & Ryan, R. M. (1991). A motivational approach to self: Integration in personality. In R. Dienstbier (Ed.), *Nebraska symposium on motivation: Vol. 38. Perspectives on motivation* (pp. 237-288). Lincoln, NE: University of Nebraska Press.

Diener, E. (1984). Subjective well-being. *Psychological Bulletin, 95,* 542-575.

Diener, E., Sandvik, E., & Pavot, W. (1990). Happiness is the frequency, not the intensity, of positive versus negative affect. In F. Strack, M. Argyle, & N. Schwarz (Eds.), *Subjective well-being: An interdisciplinary perspective.* New York: Pergamon Press.

Emmons, R. A. (1989). The personal strivings approach to personality. In L. A. Pervin (Ed.) *Goal concepts in personality and social psychology.* Hillsdale, NJ: Erlbaum.

Emmons, R. A., & McAdams, D. (1991). Personal strivings and motive dispositions: Exploring the links. *Personality and Social Psychology Bulletin, 17,* 648-654.

Fenigstein, A., & Levine, M. P. (1984). Self-attention, concept activation, and the causal self. *Journal of Experimental Social Psychology, 20,* 231-245.

Grolnick, W. S., Deci, E. L., & Ryan, R. M. (1997). Internalization within the family: The self-determination theory perspective. In J. E. Grusec, & L. Kuczynski (Eds.), *Parenting and children's internalization of values: A handbook of contemporary theory* (pp. 135-161). New York, NY: John Wiley & Sons.

Gruber, H. E., & Wallace, D. B. (1999). The case study method and evolving systems approach for understanding unique creative people at work. In R. Sternberg (Ed.), *Handbook of creativity* (pp. 93-115). New York, NY: Cambridge University Press.

Holt, R. R. (1998). Loevinger's conception of ego development and general systems theory. In P.,M. Westenberg, A. Blasi, & L.,D.Cohn (Eds.), *Personality development: Theoretical, empirical, and clinical investigations of Loevinger's conception of ego development.* Mahwah, NJ: Erlbaum.

Iacono, W. G., & Lykken, D. T. (1997). The validity of the lie detector: Two surveys of scientific opinion. *Journal of Applied Psychology, 82,* 426-433.

Kasser, T., & Ryan, R. M. (1993). A dark side of the American dream: Correlates of financial success as a central life aspiration. *Journal of Personality and Social Psychology, 65,* 410-422.

Kasser, T., & Ryan, R. M. (1996). Further examining the American dream: Well-being correlates of intrinsic and extrinsic goals. *Personality and Social Psychology Bulletin, 22,* 281-288.

Kasser, T., & Sheldon, K. (2002). Autonomic reactivity regarding extrinsic vs. intrinsic goals. Unpublished data.

Kazen, M., Baumann, N., & Kuhl, J. (2002). Determinants of self-infiltration and autonoetic interference: The roles of personality and affect in goal pursuit and attitude change. Unpublished manuscript, University of Osnabrück.

King, L. A., & Napa, C. (1998). What makes a life good? *Journal of Personality and Social Psychology, 75,* 156-165.

Kiresuk, T., Smith, A., & Cardillo, A. (1994). Goal attainment scaling: Applications, theory, and measurement. Hillsdale, NJ: Erlbaum.

Klinger, E. (1977). *Meaning and void: Inner experience and the incentives in people's lives.* Minneapolis, MN: University of Minnesota Press.

Koestner, R., Losier, G. F., Vallerand, R. J., & Carducci, D. (1996). Identified and introjected forms of political internalization: Extending self-determination theory. *Journal of Personality and Social Psychology, 70,* 1025-1036.

Kuhl, J. (2000). A functional-design approach to motivation and self-regulation: The dynamics of personality systems interactions. In M. Boekaerts, P. R. Pintrich, & M. Zeidner (Eds.), *Handbook of Self-Regulation* (pp. 111-169). San Diego, CA: Academic Press.

Kuhl, J., & Kazen, M. (1994). Self-discrimination and memory: State orientation and false self-ascription of assigned activities. *Journal of Personality and Social Psychology, 66,* 1103-1115.

Little, B. R. (1993). Personal projects and the distributed self: Aspects of a conative psychology. In J. Suls (Ed.), *The self in social perspective: Psychological perspectives on the self* (Vol. 4, pp 157-185).

Lydon, J., & Zanna, M. (1990). Commitment in the face of adversity: A value-affirmation approach. *Journal of Personality and Social Psychology, 58,* 1040-1047.

Lykken, D., & Tellegen, A. (1996). Happiness is a stochastic phenomenon. *Psychological Science, 7,* 186-189.

Marcia, J. E. (1994). Ego identity and object relations. In J. M. Masling, & R. F. Bornstein (Eds.), *Empirical studies of psychoanalytic theories* (pp. 59-103). Washington, DC: American Psychological Association.

Murray, H. A. (1938). *Explorations in personality.* New York: Oxford University Press.

Pelletier, L. G., Fortier, M. S., Vallerand, R. J., & Tuson, K. M. (1995). Toward a new measure of intrinsic motivation, extrinsic motivation, and amotivation in sports: The Sport Motivation Scale (SMS). *Journal of Sport and Exercise Psychology, 17,* 35-53.

Read, S. J., & Miller, L. C. (1998). *Connectionist models of social reasoning and social behavior.* Mahwah, NJ: Erlbaum.

Reis, H. T., Sheldon, K. M., Gable, S. L., Roscoe, J., & Ryan, R. M. (2000). Daily well being: The role of autonomy, competence, and relatedness. *Personality and Social*

Psychology Bulletin, 26, 419-435.

Ryan, R. M. (1982). Control and information in the intrapersonal sphere: An extension of cognitive evaluation theory. *Journal of Personality and Social Psychology, 34*, 430-461.

Ryan, R. M. (1995). Psychological needs and the facilitation of integrative processes. *Journal of Personality, 63*, 397-427.

Ryan, R. M., & Connell, J. P. (1989). Perceived locus of causality and internalization: Examining reasons for acting in two domains. *Journal of Personality and Social Psychology, 57*, 749-761.

Ryan, R. M., & Frederick, C. (1997). On energy, personality, and health: Subjective vitality as a dynamic reflection of well-being. *Journal of Personality, 65*, 529-565.

Ryan, R. M., Kuhl, J., & Deci, E. L. (1997). Nature and autonomy: An organizational view of social and neurobiological aspects of self-regulation in behavior and development. *Development and Psychopathology, 9*, 701-728.

Ryan, R. M., Rigby, S., & King, K. (1993). Two types of religious internalization and their relations to religious orientations and mental health. *Journal of Personality and Social Psychology, 65*, 586-596.

Ryan, R. M., Sheldon, K. M., Kasser, T., & Deci, E. L. (1996). All goals were not created equal: An organismic perspective on the nature of goals and their regulation. In P. M. Gollwitzer & J. A. Bargh (Eds.), *The Psychology of action: Linking motivation and cognition to behavior*. New York: Guilford.

Ryff, C. D., & Singer, B. (1998). The role of purpose in life and personal growth in positive human health. In P. T. P. Wong, & P. S. Fry (Eds.). *The human quest for meaning: A handbook of psychological research and clinical applications* (pp. 213-235). Mahwah, NJ: Erlbaum.

Schwartz, B. (2000). Self-determination: The tyranny of freedom. *American Psychologist, 55*, 79-88.

Seguin, C., Pelletier, L. G., & Hunsley, J. (1998). Toward a model of environmental activism. *Environment & Behavior*, 30, 628-652.

Shedler, J., Mayman, M., & Manis, M. (1993). The illusion of mental health. *American Psychologist, 48*, 1117-1131.

Sheldon, K. M., & Elliot, A. J. (1998). Not all personal goals are personal: Comparing autonomous and controlled reasons as predictors of effort and attainment. *Personality and Social Psychology Bulletin, 24*, 546-557.

Sheldon, K. M., & Elliot, A. J. (1999). Goal striving, need-satisfaction, and longitudinal well-being: The Self-Concordance Model. *Journal of Personality and Social Psychology, 76*, 482-497.

Sheldon, K. M., & Elliot, A. J. (2000). Personal goals in social roles: Divergences and convergences across roles and levels of analysis. *Journal of Personality, 68*, 51-84.

Sheldon, K. M., & Houser-Marko, L. (2001). Self-concordance, goal attainment, and the pursuit of happiness: Can their be an upward spiral? *Journal of Personality and Social Psychology, 80*, 152-165.

Sheldon, K. M., & Kasser, T. (1995). Coherence and congruence: Two aspects of personality integration. *Journal of Personality and Social Psychology, 68*, 531-543.

Sheldon, K. M., & Kasser, T. (1998). Pursuing personal goals: Skills enable progress but not all progress is beneficial. *Personality and Social Psychology Bulletin.*

Sheldon, K. M., Kasser, T., Smith, K., & Share, T. (2002). Personal goals and psychological growth: Testing an intervention to enhance goal-attainment and personality integration. *Journal of Personality, 70*, 5-31.

Sheldon, K. M., Ryan, R. M., & Reis, H. T. (1996). What makes for a good day?

Competence and autonomy in the day and in the person. *Personality and Social Psychology Bulletin, 22,* 1270-1279.

Smith, C. (1994). *Motivation and personality: Handbook of thematic content analysis.* Cambridge, UK: Cambridge University Press.

Snyder, M., & Cantor, N. (1998). Understanding personality and social behavior: A functionalist strategy. In D. T. Gilbert, & S. T. Fiske (Eds.). *The handbook of social psychology,* (Vol. 2, 4th ed., pp. 635-679). Boston, MA: McGraw-Hill.

Vallacher, R. R., & Nowak, A. (1994). *Dynamical systems in social psychology.* New York: Academic Press.

Vallerand, R. J., Fortier, M. S., & Guay, F. (1997). Self-determination and persistence in a real-life setting: Toward a motivational model of high school dropout. *Journal of Personality and Social Psychology, 72,* 1161-1176.

Wilensky, R. (1983). *Planning and understanding: A computational approach to human reasoning.* Reading, MA: Addison-Wesley.

Williams, G. C., Rodin, G. C., Ryan, R. M., Grolnick, W. S., & Deci, E. L. (1998). Autonomous regulation and long-term medication adherence in adult outpatients. *Health Psychology, 17,* 269-276.

4: The Integrating Self and Conscious Experience

Holley S. Hodgins
Skidmore College

C. Raymond Knee
University of Houston

One of the central assumptions of Self Determination Theory (SDT) is that the core self includes intrinsic integrative tendencies that motivate individuals to assimilate ongoing experience into increasingly elaborated and integrated self-structures (Deci & Ryan, 1985b; Ryan, Deci, & Grolnick, 1995). In other words, there is a basic human tendency to proceed toward higher-order organization. The organismic integration process through which this tendency is actualized involves aspects of the self becoming more complex and interrelated with one another and with aspects of the social world.

The idea of increasingly organized self-structures is congruent with another SDT postulate, namely that there are innate psychological needs for competence, self-determination, and relatedness, and SDT proposes that the integrative tendency will function most effectively in social contexts that allow satisfaction of these needs. Hence, the process of organismic integration underlies healthy psychological development, is optimized when people are able to satisfy their basic needs, and results in a sense of self that is integrated, authentic, and congruent with intrinsic aspects of the core self (Deci & Ryan, 1991; Ryan, 1991, 1993, 1995; Ryan et al., 1995).

As individuals develop in the direction of greater autonomy, their sense of self-worth is based on organismic functioning, that is, on simply "being" what they are by nature as they act choicefully in integrated ways and fulfill potentialities (Maslow, 1968). This means, that when autonomous, people experience themselves as valuable for being who they are rather than only for doing particular activities or appearing certain ways to others or to themselves. Thus, secure self-worth based on "being" accompanies the development of self-structures that are authentic (i.e., congruent with the core self) and autonomous.

The Integrating Self and Openness

We propose that the conceptualization of an authentic, integrated self with self-worth rooted in "being" has important implications for the way individuals encounter ongoing conscious experience, broadly speaking. Being conscious involves a constant stream of experience including perceptual, cognitive, emotional, and social information. This stream of experience, and consequently, our intrapersonal and interpersonal worlds, constantly change as novel challenges and experiences arise. The external and internal changes sometimes are discrepant with self-structures and require assimilation into the working sense of self and the social world. Thus, it is possible to be "integrated" only in relation to past experiences before novel experiences come along that require further integration.

We suggest that the motivation underlying self-structures is relevant to how individuals encounter ongoing conscious experiences, especially novel ones. Specifically, to the extent that individuals are oriented toward organismic growth and integration, they will meet the continually changing stream of conscious experience with openness. By "openness" we mean a readiness to perceive ongoing experience accurately, without distorting or attempting to avoid the experience, and a willingness to assimilate novel experiences into self-structures. Another way of stating this is that when individuals function autonomously, they are open to experience what is occurring in the current moment. This openness is similar to what has been called "mindfulness" in both Buddhist writings (e.g., Gunaratana, 1992; Kabat-Zinn, 1994; Maitreya, 1995) and empirical psychology (for review see Langer, 1989). It also relates to the personality dimension of openness (e.g., see McCrae, 1994) and to Roger's (1961) suggestion that a fully functioning person is able to encounter experience honestly. However, our discussion differs from past conceptualizations in that it situates openness in the context of an empirically testable organismic theory of human motivation that explains development and functioning.

According to our perspective, openness to experience is possible because of the inner confidence produced by organismic functioning based simply on individuals' being who they are as they move toward fulfillment of their intrinsic needs and potentials. To the extent that an individual is connected to his or her core self, self-worth is rooted simply in "being" and the individual is less likely to be threatened by novel inputs or experiences. Rather, experiences of all types can be considered and encountered as opportunities. Through integration of what "is" in the moment, individuals grow toward greater unity in understanding and functioning. This stance toward reality was described by Rogers (1961) as the working assumption that "all the facts are friendly"(p. 25). When the self is open to reality, that is, to simply seeing what "is" in the present moment, individuals have a high tolerance for encountering experience without being threatened or defending against it. Individuals who are functioning autonomously, therefore, are responsive to reality rather than directed by ego-invested, preconceived notions. In empirical psychology this approach to information has been termed "bottom-up" or data-driven functioning (Sorrentino, Holmes, Hanna, & Sharp, 1995) or as having accuracy goals (e.g., Kunda, 1990) as opposed to categorical or conclusion-driven functioning (Sorrentino et al.) or having directional goals (Kunda).

Consequences of Openness to Experience

The openness, or willingness to experience what is occurring in the current moment, which accompanies autonomous functioning should have consequences across a broad range of events and behaviors, both intrapersonal and interpersonal. For example, to the extent that individuals function autonomously and are open to experience, they should show less evidence of trying to escape awareness of the present moment with mood-altering substances, with distracting activities such as television viewing, video games, or movies, or with compulsive behaviors regarding food, sex, and work.

Furthermore, to the extent that individuals function autonomously they should show less cognitive defensiveness including less self-serving and in-group bias in explaining their own and others' behavior, less distortion in recall and recognition, decreased primacy effects, and less use of stereotypic information in forming judgments.

Autonomous functioning also should be associated with lower emotional defensiveness including denial, criticism of others, justification of one's own behavior, and avoidance of emotions. Of course, low defensiveness toward emotional experience means that the so-called negative emotions will be *experienced* for what they are; thus, regulating emotions by experiencing them fully may be painful in the short term. In other words, autonomous self-regulation does not necessarily protect individuals from experiencing sadness, anger, or fear, for example; after all, emotions can only be integrated through the process of experiencing them. However, the integrating self's openness to experience what "is" in the present moment without defending against it should facilitate integration over time.

Although autonomy is associated with openness to experiencing emotions, autonomously functioning individuals also should have higher thresholds for experiencing threat and thus may experience some emotions less readily. That is, to the extent that a given emotion (e.g., anger or fear) arises as a response of an ego-invested aspect of self to a perceived threat (e.g., failure), autonomously functioning individuals may respond less readily or with less intensity compared to individuals who are functioning in a more control-oriented manner. Stated differently, the lower ego-involvement that is associated with autonomous functioning should result in lower emotional reactivity and this relation should be mediated by lower readiness to perceive threat.

Another implication of the openness associated with autonomous functioning is that it should be associated with less defensive projection onto others. There is evidence that people are most critical of those traits in others that are most undesired in themselves (Newman, Duff, & Baumeister, 1997), especially when they try to avoid their own unwanted traits. To the extent that individuals are honest about themselves and take responsibility for their own qualities and behaviors (i.e., function autonomously), they should show a lesser degree of defensive projection of their undesired traits onto others.

In addition to emotional regulation, there are important effects of openness on social and interpersonal experience, with autonomy being associated with greater honesty in interpersonal interactions of all types. To the extent that behavior emanates from integrated self-structures, individuals feel choiceful and endorsing of their behavior. Hence, they are more likely to take responsibility for their emotions and behaviors and not hide or distort information to deceive others. Additionally, the secure self-worth in "being" that accompanies autonomy decreases the fear of others' judgment that might otherwise result in attempts to manipulate impressions.

We also expect that autonomous functioning will be associated with choosing interpersonal interactions and partners that are congruent with integrated self-structures and with the need for relatedness. This should manifest in preferences for friendships, sexual and romantic relationships, and work relationships that promote organismic growth. Specifically, autonomously functioning individuals will seek relationships that are based on shared values and that fulfill intrinsic needs rather than relationships that primarily support ego-invested or extrinsic goals such as, image, reactive independence, and wealth (see Kasser & Ryan, 1996). For example, in sexual or love relationships, this might show up as a preference for an intimate connection with a growth-oriented partner rather than a partner with particular physical attributes, wealth, or social standing.

We have said that autonomous functioning is associated with a reality-based approach to experience, that is, being open to what "is" without avoiding or distorting. Another implication of this for intimate love relationships would be that autonomously oriented individuals would have less need of the positive, idealized illusions that have been proposed to be necessary for well-being and adjustment in romantic relationships (see, e.g., Murray, Holmes, & Griffin, 1996). Indeed, to the extent that positive illusions distort reality, they may be a defense used to avoid ambiguity and preserve rigid notions that are consistent with a more ego-involved, less-integrated self. Preserving illusions, however, forfeits the opportunity to intimately know and love another person in all of his or her glorious imperfection.

In summary, we think it useful to speak of the authentic self underlying autonomy motivation as an "integrating" self in order to predict how a broad range of ongoing experience will be encountered and responded to. We have proposed that autonomous functioning allows for openness to ongoing experience, or a willingness to experience what is occurring in the current moment without distorting or defending against it.

Ego-Invested Self-Structures

Some human behavior, however, does not emerge from integrated needs and organismic functioning. When environmental conditions do not facilitate integration, people behave according to external pressures and introjected demands. When individuals lack a sense of self-determination they may fail to choose goals that are relevant to their intrinsic needs and that promote organismic growth (Sheldon & Elliot, 1999; Sheldon & Kasser, 1995). Controlling environments therefore contribute to the development of very different kinds of self-structures (Deci & Ryan, 1991; Ryan, 1991, 1993, 1995; Ryan et al., 1995).

The lack of fulfillment of intrinsic needs and consequent disconnection from organismic being precludes a sense of self-worth based in being (see Sheldon, this volume). Instead, as a substitute for self-worth, individuals develop an ego-invested or false self (Ryan et al., 1995) that is based on doing particular activities in particular ways, being perceived by others in particular ways, or, perhaps most importantly, perceiving themselves in certain ways. The very existence of ego-invested self-structures can be considered a defense against the underlying insecurity of disconnection from one's intrinsic core self. Nonetheless, under control-oriented functioning it is necessary to protect and defend the ego-invested self in order to preserve the sense of self-worth it provides (albeit an artificial and very vulnerable one).

Conditional Approach to Reality

This characterization of an ego-invested self has very different implications for how conscious experience will be met and managed. A person operating in a controlled manner from a false self needs to muster all of his or her resources in the service of propping up and defending the false self from challenges because this constructed self provides some level of self-worth. Hence, under controlled functioning individuals want to experience what is occurring in the current moment only if it validates ego-invested self-structures. Novel inputs in the stream of conscious experience (e.g., cognitive, emotional, social, etc.) which are discrepant from ego-invested self-structures will be defended against as enemies of (simulated) self-worth. Controlled functioning therefore includes regulating conscious experience by avoiding or denying events and information that do not concur with the constructed reality of the ego-invested self.

Conversely, to the extent that experience *coincides* with ego-invested self-structures, individuals operating in a controlled manner will embrace the moment with eager and fervent enthusiasm. This seeking, clutching, and grasping of ego-affirming moments could be called an addiction in the sense that the ego-invested self requires these experiences for the seeming reassurance they give about self-worth. Stated differently, under controlled functioning, the current moment is not experienced neutrally for what it is but for its relevance to the false self. These tendencies either to reject or cling to experience could be described as relating conditionally to reality. That is, under controlled functioning people accept reality to the extent that it matches ego-invested aspects of themselves, but to the extent that reality diverges from their false selves, they deny and avoid it.

Consequences of Conditional Reality

Behaviorally, then, self-worth acquired through ego-invested self-structures results in rigid functioning. Sometimes this will manifest in general defensiveness under threat, in a range of behaviors that may include perceptual, cognitive, emotional, and interpersonal aspects. For example, controlled functioning would be associated with cognitive defenses including the use of self-serving attributional biases, selective information processing and memory, greater use of heuristics and stereotypes, construing events egocentrically, and inflating the importance of self in activities.

Similarly, controlled functioning produces emotional defensiveness so that under perceived threat individuals respond reactively in self-protection. Because most emotional defensiveness occurs in relation to others, practically speaking, emotional and interpersonal defensiveness are inseparable. Examples of defensive behaviors include self-justification, projection of one's own emotions onto others, intellectualizing experiences, failing to understand others' perspectives, outward-directed anger and blame, deception intended to avoid consequences, and lack of apology for wrongdoing.

As mentioned above, the corollary of rigid defense against ego-discrepant experiences is a resolute of ego-affirming experiences, which provide sustenance for the primary basis of self-worth. Behaviorally, this addiction to experiences that concur with ego-involved self-aspects might manifest in susceptibility to flattery, poor ability to perceive and interpret situations accurately, and seeking feedback that confirms egoistic self-aspects. In the relationship domain, to the extent people are ego-affirmation dependent, they might form relationships to validate ego-invested self-aspects even though these do not fulfill intrinsic, organismic needs. Similarly, people might choose a career for the financial wealth, prestige, or social power it offers, even if the work is inconsistent with their interests and with the intrinsic needs for competence, self-determination, and relatedness.

It seems paradoxical that people would neglect basic, intrinsic needs in order to serve ego-involved self-aspects. However, as a consequence of early experiences of thwarted need satisfaction, rigid and defensive self-structures develop that continually seek their own affirmation and consequently do not allow contact with and thus true satisfaction of the basic needs. Although people develop rigid self-structures initially in an attempt to compensate for the lack of basic need satisfaction, subsequently they must maintain these compensatory structures in order to preserve the self and sense of worth. It is as if people become psychologically addicted to ego-affirmation at the expense of their overall well-being, much as people can become physically addicted to substances that interfere with their general health.

In addition to compulsive seeking of ego-affirmation, relating to reality conditionally might manifest phenomenologically in a basic lack of trust or confidence in one's own intuitive judgment. That is, because the fundamental deception of a false self precludes contact with one's own experience, faith in one's intuitive functioning would be impaired, including the abilities to trust one's own perceptions about people and situations and to act upon one's desires.

The Lack of a Coherent Self

The construction of an ego-invested self can be considered a (perhaps valiant) adaptation in an environment that does not support self-determination. That is, it is a solution to the predicament of disconnection from one's own organismic being that at least allows for a sense of effecting outcomes and maintaining some level of self-worth, albeit artificial, vulnerable, and requiring vigilant protection.

In contrast, in environments that lack not only autonomy support but also block effectance and relatedness, people become impersonally oriented and amotivated (Deci & Ryan, 1985a). This is the least integrated mode of functioning, with individuals lacking not only self-determination but also a sense of intentionality (Deci & Ryan, 1991). Impersonal functioning is the consequence of being disconnected from one's organismic being and also being unable to construct an effective (albeit defensive) ego-invested self. Hence, impersonal functioning reflects the lack of an underlying cohesive self, either authentic or false.

In terms of meeting ongoing experience, then, impersonal functioning would be associated with being overwhelmed by and unable to regulate experiences effectively. It is possible that impersonal, like control-oriented functioning, might involve the use of defenses, but they likely would be ineffective and used inconsistently. Hence, under impersonal functioning individuals might show helplessness or defensiveness or vacillation between the two, with lots of negative affect.

Although impersonal functioning can arise from the trait-like, chronic lack of a cohesive self, any human can function impersonally when an experience is too discrepant to be integrated (e.g., after tremendous loss). To the extent that impersonal functioning is a transitory state, negative affect can be reduced in either of two ways. Through willingness to experience what is, individuals can integrate emotion over time into more elaborated self-structures and reestablish autonomous functioning. Alternatively, through defensive responses, some might reestablish and elaborate ego-invested self-aspects and thus maneuver out of helplessness and back into controlled functioning. Individuals who do not have either of these resolution strategies available may remain in a state of helplessness, immersed in and overwhelmed by negative affect.

In summary, characterization of the self according to Self-Determination Theory allows predictions about how individuals encounter conscious experience. The idea that an integrating self underlies self-determination suggests that to the extent we function autonomously, we will meet novel experiences openly and allow their integration into our sense of selves. Thus, the authentic self, with self-worth based in "being," which underlies autonomous functioning is responsive to reality. To the extent that we are control-oriented and our self-worth is dependent on ego-invested self-aspects, we are compelled to encounter ongoing experience according to its relevance for the false self: We defend and self-protect against ego-discrepant experiences and cling to ego-affirming ones. And when experiences provide challenges too great to be integrated and impossible to be defended against, we function impersonally and are overwhelmed by the experience, at least initially.

These three styles of functioning and experiencing parallel what Deci and Ryan (1985a, 1985b) have characterized with the concept of general causality orientations. Autonomy orientation refers to the tendency to initiate behavior with a sense of choice, based on an awareness of one's needs, feelings, and integrated goals. In contrast, control orientation describes the tendency to seek out external controls and to experience events as pressures that determine behavior and feelings. Impersonal orientation describes the general tendency to experience desired outcomes as unattainable and to display little sense of intentionality. In the past, autonomy has correlated positively with self-evaluation, self-awareness, self-actualization and ego development (Deci & Ryan, 1985a), as well as consistency among attitudes, traits, and behaviors (Koestner, Bernieri, & Zuckerman, 1992). In contrast, control has related to lack of self-awareness (Deci & Ryan, 1985b), regulation of social behavior by external cues (Zuckerman, Gioioso, & Tellini, 1988), and inconsistency among attitudes, traits, and behaviors (Koestner et al.). Finally, the impersonal orientation has related to self-derogation, social anxiety, external locus of control (Deci & Ryan, 1985b), and restrictive anorexia (Strauss & Ryan, 1987).

Although our model ambitiously discusses the regulation of conscious experience, broadly defined, it makes specific predictions about behavioral manifestations of the postulated openness to and defensiveness against experience. Below we review various studies that have examined general causality orientations and have supported our model of conscious experience. Finally, we discuss ways in which the model can be tested further.

Empirical Support

Several studies provide evidence for the prediction that autonomous functioning is associated with less defensiveness and controlled functioning with more. For example, Knee and Zuckerman (1996) examined autonomy and control orientations as moderators of the self-serving bias, a defensive attributional tendency in which people take more responsibility for success than for failure. It was hypothesized that self-determined individuals (those high in autonomy and low in control orientation) would display less self-serving tendency. Participants were randomly assigned to succeed or fail on a task, and their attributions were measured. Consistent with predictions, self-serving biases were evident for everyone except self-determined individuals, who made fewer self-enhancing attributions for success and fewer defensive attributions for failure. Thus, attributions of self-determined individuals did not vary according to the favorability of the performance feedback they received. Rather, these individuals attributed their performance similarly regardless of feedback, giving evidence that self-determination is associated with low cognitive defensiveness.

Consistent with the direction of the finding for cognitive defensiveness, there is evidence that lack of self-determination is associated with using a greater number of defensive coping strategies. In a one-semester longitudinal study, Knee and Zuckerman (1998) examined undergraduates' use of avoidant coping, including mental and behavioral disengagement and denial. They reasoned that the latter part of the semester is the most stressful for students, and they found, as predicted, that self-determination (high autonomy and low control orientation) was associated with less use of avoidant coping over the semester.

Additionally, Knee and Zuckerman (1998) examined the use of self-handicapping, which is the tendency to erect impediments to one's own success in order to provide an excuse for failure. Hence, self-handicapping can be considered a defensive preparation to maintain self-esteem in case of later failure. Consistent with our model, the results showed that self-determined individuals used less self-handicapping. Taken together, the results show that self-determination is associated with lower use of defensive coping strategies. This is consistent with the proposal that an integrating self underlies autonomous functioning and has less need to defend against ongoing experience.

In a somewhat different context, Knee, Neighbors, and Vietor (2001) examined driving anger and aggressive driving behaviors as a function of autonomy and control orientations, expecting that controlled functioning would be associated with reactive emotions and behavior. Reactivity in emotion and behavior can be considered symptoms of a nonintegrated, ego-invested, and defensive self. Results showed that (1) control orientation was associated with more driving anger as a result of other drivers' actions; (2) control orientation was associated with more aggressive driving behaviors and more traffic citations; (3) the relation between control orientation and aggressive driving was mediated by driving anger; and (4) self-esteem and social anxiety did not account for the results of motivational orientations. Thus, a less integrating, more controlled self was linked to experiencing more reactive emotion, which in turn was linked to reactive behavior.

The openness to, versus defensiveness against, experience seen in the above studies can also be found in studies that examine a different domain of functioning, that of interpersonal behavior. This work has shown that self-determined functioning is associated with openness, honesty, and taking responsibility for one's interpersonal behavior. For example, Hodgins, Koestner, and Duncan (1996) examined experiences in naturally-occurring social interaction in two samples as a function of autonomy and control orientations. The results showed that autonomy predicted experiencing greater pleasantness, higher self-honesty and other-honesty, and greater felt-esteem in college students' interactions with their parents during a 3-week period. In contrast, college students high on control orientation responded defensively in interactions initiated by their parents: The students were less honest and disclosing, felt lower esteem, and rated the interactions as less pleasant when parents initiated interactions compared to when students initiated.

The effects of general motivational orientation were not limited to parent interactions, however; a second undergraduate sample recorded all interactions during one week. The results showed that autonomy predicted (1) higher ratings of pleasantness and felt-esteem; (2) disclosure that was higher but selectively more appropriate with others who were close, honest, and also disclosing; (3) greater self-honesty regardless of relationship closeness; and (4) perception of higher other-honesty overall, but also selective trust in the honesty of others who were more closely related. In contrast, control orientation was associated with (1) rating one's own influence in interactions higher than the other's influence; and (2) giving lower ratings of felt-esteem and pleasantness during interactions that were high in honesty and disclosure.

Taken together, the results of Hodgins, Koestner, & Duncan, (1996) support our model: Autonomy is associated with greater enjoyment, honesty, and openness in social experience across a broad range of relationships. In contrast, an orientation toward control predicts greater attention to the initiation and influence aspects of interaction and a defensive dislike of honesty and disclosure.

Another important aspect of interpersonal relations is the process of conflict negotiation and accounting for behavior that is necessary when people have harmed another. Several studies have now examined the effect of motivational orientation on accounting behavior (Hodgins & Liebeskind, in press; Hodgins, Liebeskind, & Schwartz, 1996; Hixon, Hodgins, & Otto, 2002). The authors predicted that those higher on autonomy would take responsibility for their behavior rather than defend or justify themselves after harming someone. In contrast, those higher in control orientation were expected to show defensive self-protection, as evidenced in a lack of apology for their own wrongdoing. Thus, the studies examined an interpersonal aspect of the openness versus defensiveness that is predicted by our model of motivation and the regulation of ongoing experience.

Results confirmed the predictions: Self-determination was related to a greater number of and more complex apologies both in adults (Hodgins & Liebeskind, in press, Study 1; Hodgins, Liebeskind, & Schwartz, 1996) and in 5th and 6th grade children (Hixon et al., 2002), whereas control and impersonal orientations predicted greater defensiveness (i.e., less apology) in accounting (Hodgins & Liebeskind, in press; Hodgins, Liebeskind, & Schwartz, 1996). The pattern of deception, which is a defensive strategy that seeks to avoid consequences, lends further support for our model: Autonomy was associated with using fewer lies in accounts for wrongdoing, whereas control orientation predicted greater use of deception, especially with acquaintances (Hodgins & Liebeskind, in press; Hodgins, Liebeskind, & Schwartz, 1996).

The studies on naturally occurring social interaction and accounting for wrongdoing converge on the same understanding: Autonomy is associated with interpersonal openness and honesty whereas control orientation predicts interpersonal defensiveness. Together with the studies on attributions, coping strategies, and driving behavior, they provide evidence for some of the predictions of our model of motivation and ongoing conscious experience. Of course, several aspects of the model remain to be tested.

Future Directions

Throughout this chapter we have alluded to numerous behavioral manifestations predicted on the basis of openness versus defensiveness to experience. The predictions are empirically testable and future research is necessary to establish the full validity of our model. In addition, there are a few aspects that require empirical support not explicitly mentioned above. For example, one important aspect of the model is the idea that self-worth is based in the state of "being" when one is autonomously functioning, is based in "doing" or "appearing" when one is controlled, and is lacking under impersonal functioning. This assumption requires testing, but self-report measures of self-esteem may not be useful in this regard given the postulated relation between motivation and defensiveness. Rather, it will be important to create or adapt implicit measures of self-worth (e.g., Farnham, Greenwald, & Banaji, 1999) in order to circumvent defensiveness in self-report about self-esteem.

Another aspect of the model yet to be tested is the prediction that controlled functioning will be associated with clinging to ego-affirming experiences. So far our research has focused on defensiveness and the avoidance of threatening experience, but it will be important also to examine the grasping of ego-affirmation, which is part of relating to reality conditionally. The prediction that judgments and behaviors are overly influenced by flattery or others' positive opinions under controlled functioning can be examined in a number of different domains (e.g., social, relationship, learning tasks, etc.).

Finally, thus far our research has used the revised General Causality Orientations Scale (GCOS; Deci & Ryan, 1985a; Ryan, 1989) to measure motivational orientations and has taken an individual differences approach to examining predictions. Empirical support would be strengthened by showing that manipulated situational differences in autonomy, controlled, and impersonal functioning produce similar effects in openness versus defensiveness or clinging to experience.

One curious aspect of maturing is the realization that we will never attain the psychologically static place implicitly contained in childhood expectations of adulthood. That is, we never arrive at some stationary state through securing a particular job or promotion, having certain types of relationships, or acquiring material possessions. Rather, life is an ongoing process in which experiences inside us and around us constantly change. We have suggested that the way in which one meets these ever-changing experiences is a function of whether the self-aspects one is operating from in that moment are integrated, ego-invested, or lacking cohesion. Testing the validity of this assertion will, appropriately enough, be a process that unfolds in the future.

References

Deci, E. L., & Ryan, R. M. (1985a). The general causality orientations scale: Self-determination in personality. *Journal of Research in Personality*, *19*, 109-134.

Deci, E. L., & Ryan, R. M. (1985b). *Intrinsic Motivation and Self-Determination in Human Behavior*. New York: Plenum Press.

Deci, E. L., & Ryan, R. M. (1991). A motivational approach to self: Integration in personality. In R. Dienstbier (Ed.) *Nebraska Symposium on Motivation, Vol. 38. Perspectives on motivation* (pp. 237-288). Lincoln: University of Nebraska Press.

Farnham, S. D., Greenwald, A. G., & Banaji, M. R. (1999). Implicit self-esteem. In D. Abrams & M. A. Hogg (Eds.), *Social identity and social cognition* (pp. 230-248). Malden: Blackwell Publishers, Inc.

Gunaratana, H. (1992). *Mindfulness in plain English*. Boston: Wisdom Publications.

Hixon, E. J., Hodgins, H. S., & Otto, A. L. (2002). Children's facework in social predicaments. Unpublished manuscript, Skidmore College.

Hodgins, H. S., Koestner, R., & Duncan, N. (1996). On the compatibility of autonomy and relatedness. *Personality and Social Psychology Bulletin, 22*, 227-237.

Hodgins, H. S., & Liebeskind, E. (In press). Apology versus defense: Antecedents and consequences. *Journal of Experimental Social Psychology*.

Hodgins, H. S., Liebeskind, E., & Schwartz, W. (1996). Getting out of hot water: Facework in social predicaments. *Journal of Personality and Social Psychology, 71*, 300-314.

Kabat-Zinn, J. (1994). *Wherever you go there you are*. New York: Hyperion.

Kasser, T., & Ryan, R.M. (1996). Further examining the American dream: Differential correlates of intrinsic and extrinsic goals. *Personality and Social Psychology Bulletin, 22*, 280-287.

Knee, C. R., Neighbors, C., & Vietor, N. (2001). Self-determination theory as a framework for understanding road rage. *Journal of Applied Social Psychology, 31*, 889-904.

Knee, C. R., & Zuckerman, M. (1996). Causality orientations and the disappearance of the self-serving bias. *Journal of Research in Personality, 30*, 76-87.

Knee, C. R., & Zuckerman, M. (1998). A nondefensive personality: Autonomy and control as moderators of defensive coping and self-handicapping. *Journal of Research in Personality 32*, 115-130.

Koestner, R., Bernieri, F., & Zuckerman, M. (1992). Self-regulation and consistency between attitudes, traits and behaviors. *Personality and Social Psychology Bulletin, 18*,52-59.

Kunda, Z. (1990). The case for motivated reasoning. *Psychological Bulletin, 108*, 480-498.

Langer, E. J. (1989). Minding matters: The consequences of mindlessness-mindfulness. In L. Berkowitz (Ed.), *Advances in Experimental Social Psychology: Vol. 22*, (pp. 137-173). San Diego: Academic Press, Inc.

Maitreya, B. A. (Trans). (1995). *The Dhammapada: The path of truth*. Berkeley, CA: Parallax Press.

Maslow, A. H. (1968). *Toward a psychology of being*. Princeton: Van Nostrand.

McCrae, R. R. (1994). Openness to experience as a basic dimension of personality. *Imagination, Cognition and Personality, 13*, 39-55.

Murray, S. L., Holmes, J.G., & Griffin, D. W. (1996). The self-fulfilling nature of positive illusions in romantic relationships: Love is not blind but prescient, *Journal of Personality and Social Psychology, 71*, 1155-1180.

Newman, L. S., Duff, K. J., & Baumeister, R. F. (1997). A new look at defensive projection: Thought suppression, accessibility and biased person perception. *Journal of Personality and Social Psychology, 72*, 980-1001.

Rogers, C. R. (1961). *On becoming a person*. Boston: Houghton Mifflin Co.

Ryan, R. M. (1989). The revised 17-item General Causality Orientations Scale. Unpublished manuscript, University of Rochester.

Ryan, R. M. (1991). The nature of the self in autonomy and relatedness. In J. Strauss & G. R. Goethals (Eds.), *The self: Interdisciplinary approaches* (pp. 208-238). New York: Springer-Verlag.

Ryan, R. M. (1993). Agency and organization: Intrinsic motivation, autonomy and the self in psychological development. In J. E. Jacobs (Ed.), *Nebraska Symposium on Motivation: Vol. 40, Developmental perspectives on motivation* (pp. 1-56). Lincoln: University of Nebraska Press.

Ryan, R. M. (1995). Psychological needs and the facilitation of integrative processes. *Journal of Personality, 63*, 397-427.

Ryan, R. M., Deci. E. L., & Grolnick, W. S. (1995). Autonomy, relatedness, and the self: Their relation to development and psychopathology. In D. Cicchetti & D. J. Cohen (Eds.), *Developmental psychopathology, Volume 1: Theory and methods* (pp 618-655). New York: John Wiley & Sons, Inc.

Sheldon, K. M., & Elliot, A. J. (1999). Goal striving, need satisfaction, and longitudinal well-being: The self-concordance model. *Journal of Personality and Social Psychology, 76*, 482-497.

Sheldon, K. M., & Kasser, T. (1995). Coherence and congruence: Two aspects of personality integration. *Journal of Personality and Social Psychology, 68*, 531-543.

Sorrentino, R. M., Holmes, J. G., Hanna, S. E., & Sharp, A. (1995). Uncertainty orientation and trust in close relationships: Individual differences in cognitive styles. *Journal of Personality and Social Psychology, 68*, 314-327.

Strauss, J., & Ryan, R. M. (1987). Autonomy disturbances in subtypes of anorexia nervosa. *Journal of Abnormal Psychology, 96*, 254-258.

Zuckerman, M., Gioioso, C., & Tellini, S. (1988). Control orientation, self-monitoring, and preference for image versus quality approach to advertising. *Journal of Research in Personality, 22*, 89-100.

5: Distinguishing Three Ways of Being Internally Motivated: A Closer Look at Introjection, Identification, and Intrinsic Motivation

Richard Koestner
McGill University

Gaëtan F. Losier
Université de Moncton

Self-determination theory (SDT; Deci & Ryan, 2000) posits two innate growth tendencies to explain people's vitality, development, and psychological adaptation, namely intrinsic motivation and internalization. Intrinsic motivation refers to the innate energy that people demonstrate when they pursue a goal or an activity because it is interesting or fun. Intrinsic motivation is manifest as curiosity, pursuit of challenge, and competence development. Internalization refers to the natural tendency to strive to integrate (or take into one's self) socially-valued regulations that are initially perceived as being external. Successful internalization fosters responsible, conscientious behavior that allows people to function effectively within their social groups. According to SDT, vitality, development, and adaptation are facilitated to the extent that both intrinsic motivation and internalization function optimally, and for this to occur the social environment must provide essential psychological nutrients in the form of experiences that will satisfy the basic human needs of autonomy, competence, and relatedness (Deci & Ryan, 2000). Thus, understanding how to maintain or enhance intrinsic motivation and to facilitate successful internalization requires a consideration of the extent to which the social environment supports satisfaction of the fundamental needs.

This work was funded by grants to Richard Koestner from the Social Science and Humanities Research Council of Canada and from the Fonds pour la Formation de chercheurs et l'Aide à la Recherche of Québec. Gaëtan F. Losier was funded by the Université de Moncton. The Commission permanente de coopération Québec/Nouveau-Brunswick also provided funding for this research with traveling grants from each province to the two authors, respectively.

The distinction between intrinsic motivation and internalization revolves around the way an individual becomes drawn to engage a given activity. To the extent that an activity is inherently rewarding, such as recreational activities are for many people, it is likely that processes related to intrinsic motivation will energize and direct a person's involvement with the activity. However, to the extent that an activity lacks intrinsic appeal but is highly valued by one's social group, as may be the case with many school-related tasks, it is likely that internalization will have to provide the basis for effective self-regulation. In this case, it is the perception of the activity as valuable or meaningful that drives one to engage and persist at it. Of course, there are individual differences in what people find interesting and there are cultural differences in what groups find valuable, so it is difficult to determine à priori whether engagement with a particular activity will be regulated by intrinsic motivation or internalization.

Self-determination theory asserts that people are inherently motivated to internalize the regulation of uninteresting though important activities. Thus, it is thought that socializing agents do not have to compel individuals to internalize important values and guidelines. Rather, individuals have a spontaneous tendency to internalize such activities because of their desire to relate effectively to their social groups (Deci & Ryan, 2000). The success of this internalization process can vary, however. Identification describes the process wherein people accept the value of an activity as their own so that they can more easily assimilate it with their core sense of self (it becomes integrated with their values, beliefs, and personal goals). Introjection refers to a less successful internalization in which a value or regulatory process is taken in but not accepted as one's own. Identification results in a sense of personal endorsement of one's actions whereas introjection yields a controlled form of behavior regulation that is laced with feelings of pressure or compulsion (Deci & Ryan, 1985, 1991). The internalization process thus results in regulatory styles that reflect varying degrees of self-determination depending on the degree to which resolution of the process has been successful.

The purpose of this chapter is to review recent findings on the distinct affective, cognitive, and behavioral consequences associated with intrinsic motivation, identification (i.e., more successful internalization), and introjection (i.e., the less successful internalization). More specifically, we review findings in the domains of politics and education by highlighting similarities and distinctions among the three regulatory styles. It is expected that this review will shed light on the complementary role of intrinsic motivation and internalization in promoting vitality, development, and psychological adaptation.

Conceptual Features of Introjection, Identification, and Intrinsic Motivation

To illustrate some of the issues that will be discussed, we begin with an example. Dominique and Michelle have been good friends since kindergarten. Now in high school, they still very much enjoy doing recreational activities together such as skiing. It is while doing these activities that they feel most alert and vibrant, with both of them experiencing competence and having fun. Since kindergarten however, they have grown to experience school very differently. Dominique experiences a sense of obligation toward her school activities. She does not find them interesting and often feels anxious about her performance. Michelle does not find school thrilling either, but she is comfortable there and relatively confident about her performance. Although both have much in common when it comes to skiing, they show distinct approaches toward school. Dominique feels compelled to go to school and behaves as if she must perform well in this domain in order to feel like a good person. Michelle, however, chooses to go to school because she feels it is important for the career she wants to pursue, and she is relatively satisfied about her involvement. How can these two long time friends share so much in their experience of leisure activities and yet share so little about school? What led them to grow together in recreation and to grow apart in school?

The bulk of contemporary motivation research has examined the extent to which people are motivated versus amotivated. The results of this research indicate that there are powerful effects of contingency, control, and competence variables on whether people will be motivated (Bandura, 1997). However, Ryan (1995) has argued that important distinctions still need to be made among different forms of motivation. Such distinctions revolve around one acts, and reflect the relative integration of intentional actions. Distinctions among introjected, identified, and intrinsic forms of regulation focus not on the amount of motivation that individuals possess but, rather, on variations in the orientation of their motivation (Ryan, 1995). All three forms of regulation are expected to promote involvement and persistence in a given domain. Nonetheless, different experiential and performance consequences are expected to be uniquely associated with different forms of self-regulation. Stated differently, although it is clearly important to determine whether or not an individual is highly motivated, it is also of great consequence to consider whether the form of this motivation is in introjected, identified, or intrinsic regulation.

For instance, the two friends described above are highly motivated toward both recreational and school activities, however, their orientation leads them to experience the two domains very differently. Dominique is introjected toward school; she feels pressured to attend and to perform successfully in order to feel good about herself. For her, school is neither a choice nor fun; she gets nervous about school and feels it is something she must do. Michelle does not find school fun either, but she chooses to attend because she believes a good education is important for her career goals. Her orientation toward school reflects identification and leads her to feel confident and relatively satisfied about her involvement in school. However, both friends are intrinsically motivated when it comes to skiing, and this leads them both to experience a sense of competence and enjoyment while doing it.

Table 1 presents a summary of the similar and distinct conceptual features of introjection, identification, and intrinsic motivation. We first note that all three regulatory styles can promote high involvement and task-engagement. For example, Ryan and Connell (1989) found that parents' ratings of children's motivation toward school were significantly positively associated with the extent to which children expressed introjected, identified, and intrinsic reasons for doing school work. However, there was also evidence that intrinsic motivation and identification were associated with greater school enjoyment whereas introjection was associated with greater school anxiety. Subsequent studies confirmed that intrinsic and identified reasons were significantly associated with positive emotions while at school whereas introjection was associated with negative emotions and certain learning difficulties (Connell & Illardi, 1987; Grolnick & Ryan, 1987; Patrick, Skinner, & Connell, 1993).

These results suggest that high involvement can lead to different outcomes depending on people's subjective experience with the activity. Using deCharms' (1968) terminology, we can state that although all three types of regulatory styles govern intentional actions, both identification and intrinsic motivation reflect an internal locus of causality wherein individuals feel like an origin of their actions, whereas introjection reflects a more external locus of causality wherein the person feels like a pawn. Similarly, SDT explains this in terms of different regulatory styles that vary in their degrees of self-determination, with introjection representing a less self-determined form of instrumental behavior regulation than identification (Deci & Ryan, 2000). Intrinsic motivation is considered the most self-determined form of behavioral regulation because it involves spontaneous actions that are not based on internalized (or instrumental) processes.

Table 1 further distinguishes the motivating forces, regulatory guides, and goal orientations associated with the three regulatory styles. For introjection, commitment toward an activity or domain is based on feelings of guilt and compulsion. When introjected, the person feels pressured to do the activity in order to feel good about himself or herself, but would rather not have to do it. This results in a conflicted or ambivalent goal orientation characterized by both approach and avoidance motives. For identification, commitment toward an activity or domain is based on its perceived meaning in relation to one's goals, values, and identity. When identified, the person chooses to do the activity because it is personally important and useful. This choice likely reflects a consideration of the long-term outcomes one hopes to achieve for the activity, or in the domain. Identification is thought to result in an unconflicted goal orientation

Conceptual features	Regulatory styles		
	Introjection	Identification	Intrinsic
Involvement level	High	High	High
Emotional experience	Negative	Positive	Positive
Locus of causality	External	Internal	Internal
	(Controlled)	(Autonomous)	(Autonomous)
Motivating force	Compulsion	Personal importance	Attraction (interest)
Regulatory guide	Conditional self-regard	Values & identity	Emergent emotions
	(Learned)	(Learned)	(Innate)
Goal orientations	Approach/avoidance	Approach	Approach
	(Conflicted)	(Long-term\outcome)	(Short-term\process)
Needs implicated	Autonomy vs relatedness	Autonomy & relatedness	Autonomy & competence
	(Conflicted)	(Congruent)	(Congruent)

Table 5.1. Conceptual Characteristics of the Three Regulatory Styles.

characterized primarily by approach motives. For intrinsic motivation, the attractiveness of the activity is sufficient to elicit task engagement and the resulting positive emotions serve to sustain continued involvement. The goals of the intrinsically motivated individual tend to be relatively non-conscious, in-the-moment, and process-focused. When intrinsically motivated, one is completely absorbed in the task at hand, without necessarily reflecting on its meaning or significance.

Finally, Table 5-1 indicates the fundamental needs that are most salient to the emergence and sustenance of each type of regulatory style. Among the three fundamental needs, SDT posits that satisfaction of the need for autonomy is the most central nutrient to the person's growth (Deci & Ryan, 2000). Therefore, it is considered salient in all three types of regulatory styles dealt with here. However, because both introjected and identified regulations represent extrinsic (or instrumental) types of motivation based on an internalization (or learning) process, inputs or instructions from significant others (e.g., parents, teachers, coaches, supervisors) are often implicated. Thus, in relation to the internalized regulations, relatedness and autonomy are the two most salient needs. There is a central difference, however, in how these needs are aligned when one is introjected versus identified. With introjection, the satisfaction of the needs for autonomy and relatedness have typically been pitted against one another, such as in the case of conditional love (Deci & Ryan, 2000). This oppositional relationship between fundamental needs gives rise to ego involvement, contingent self-esteem, and vulnerability to guilt (Ryan, 1982). With identification, satisfaction of the needs for autonomy and relatedness is achieved harmoniously, as is typically the case under supportive environmental conditions (Hodgins, Koestner, & Duncan, 1996). The need for relatedness is not as essential for intrinsic motivation. Intrinsic motivation involves being spontaneously drawn toward activities that provide optimal challenge, opportunities for unencumbered action, and the possibility of testing one's skills with a reasonable chance of success. Therefore, it is the need for competence that more centrally combines with autonomy to influence intrinsic motivation (Koestner & McClelland, 1990).

Distinguishing Outcomes Related to the Three Types of Regulation

Our empirical work has focused on distinguishing the affective, cognitive, and behavioral consequences of introjection, identification, and intrinsic motivation in two domains, namely, politics and education. Self-regulation is assessed by asking participants to rate their reasons for participating in domain-relevant activities (e.g., "Why do you follow political events?"). Introjected reasons reflect pressure and compulsion ("I follow politics because it is something I should do"); identified reasons reflect consideration of important personal values and goals ("I go to school because this will help me make a better choice regarding my career orientation"); and intrinsic reasons reflect a natural inclination to pursue domain-relevant activities ("I choose to follow politics for the pleasure of doing it"). Our statistical analyses control for the overlap among the three regulatory styles because significant positive correlations are typically found between identification and intrinsic motivation, and, occasionally, between identification and introjection.

Political Domain

We conducted five separate short-term prospective studies to examine motivational outcomes in the political domain. A few weeks prior to an election or referendum, participants' reasons for following politics were assessed along with measures of information seeking, knowledge of events, and emotional experiences. Immediately after the election or referendum, participants were followed up to determine whether they had voted and how they felt about the outcome. Our goal was to determine whether the three regulatory styles led individuals to: (a) adopt different strategies in forming their opinions, (b) form different knowledge and attitude structures regarding political events, (c) experience different patterns of emotions regarding the anticipated and actual outcomes of the elections or referendum, and (d) vary in their tendency to actually cast their vote. Our guiding hypothesis was that both identification and intrinsic motivation would be associated with more active, differentiated, committed, and effective political participation than would introjection.

We assumed that college students were an appropriate sample for exploring self-regulation toward politics. The internalization process is thought to be influenced by developmental considerations, with different developmental stages calling for a focus on internalizing certain types of regulations and values. For example, late childhood primarily requires the internalization of relatively concrete regulations regarding conscientious and agreeable behavior, whereas late adolescence and early adulthood call for internalization of more abstract concerns such as the development of a coherent and personally meaningful set of religious and political beliefs (Marcia, 1980). The question "Why do you consider it important to follow political events?" becomes an important issue during the late teenage years.

Table 5-2 summarizes the correlates of introjection, identification, and intrinsic motivation in the political domain. Introjection was found to be associated with a distinctly different pattern of preparing to participate in a political campaign than were identification and intrinsic motivation. That is, introjection was associated with passively relying on authority figures such as parents when making voting decisions, whereas identification and intrinsic motivation were associated with actively pursuing information by reading newspapers, watching debates, and requesting information from political parties. Interestingly, the vigorous pursuit of information appears to be used for somewhat different purposes by highly identified versus intrinsically motivated voters. Intrinsic motivation was associated with forming an accurate base of knowledge about the political parties and current issues, whereas identification was associated with developing highly differentiated opinions about which party to support on various issues. That is, a highly intrinsically motivated voter was more likely to be able to correctly answer "which party or parties supports increased education funding?" whereas a highly identified voter was more likely to be able to specify which party he or she supported on the issue of education funding. This implies that intrinsic motivation and identification lead individuals to place somewhat different emphases on cultivating factual information versus personal opinions about political issues.

Political	Self-Regulatory Style		
Outcomes	Introjected	Identified	Intrinsic
Passive Reliance on Others	+	-	0
Information Seeking	0	+	+
Differentiation of Attitudes	0	+	0
Accuracy of Knowledge	0	0	+
Vulnerability to Persuasion	+	-	+
Emotional Experiences	-	+	+
Coping with Critical Vote	0	+	-
Voting	0	+	0

Note: "+" indicates that a significant positive relation was obtained; "-" indicates a significant negative relation was obtained; "0" indicates that a non-significant relation was obtained.

Table 5.2. Summary of the Correlates for the Three Self-Regulatory Styles in the Political Domain.

A complex set of findings emerged across three studies regarding the relation of self- regulatory styles to vulnerability and resistance to persuasion. Generally, introjection was found to be associated with increased vulnerability to persuasion whereas identification appeared to inoculate young adults against certain forms of persuasive appeal. Thus, in one study, highly introjected individuals who watched a televised debate just prior to a federal election tended to report significantly more positive views of these politicians shortly after the debate but before the election (Koestner, Losier, Vallerand, & Carducci, 1996: Study 2). In another study, highly introjected individuals who favored government policies about recycling were found to be particularly vulnerable to persuasion by an attractive, credible spokesperson (Koestner, Houlfort, Paquet, & Knight, 2002). Identification, however, was associated with highly stable political attitudes over time (Losier, Perreault, Koestner, & Vallerand, 2001). Intrinsic motivation was not related to vulnerability to direct persuasive appeals but, surprisingly, one study found that it was positively associated with greater influence by an incidental priming manipulation (Ratelle, Debeis, Koestner,& Losier, 1999). Specifically, the stated support of intrinsically motivated voters for the reelection of Montreal's mayor was significantly influenced by whether the participants had just written about their experiences during Montreal's 1998 ice storm (negative prime) or their experiences during the 1998 summer festivals in Montreal (positive prime). That is, intrinsically motivated voters were significantly more likely to support the mayor's reelection if they had reminisced about summer festivals rather than the winter ice storm. It seems that their interest in issues led them to behave in accord with whatever issue they were focused on.

Voters' emotional experiences before and after an election or referendum were importantly influenced by their self-regulation patterns. Voters high in introjection experienced a conflicted pattern of both pleasant and unpleasant emotions when the side they favored was victorious in the 1993 Canadian Referendum on constitutional reform (Koestner et al., 1996: study 1). Feeling pressured in their involvement thus had its affective costs even when their side won. Voters high in introjection who were on the losing side of this referendum experienced only greater negative emotions. In contrast, identification and intrinsic motivation were associated with positive emotional experiences for voters who were on the winning side of the referendum, but there was no association of identification or intrinsic motivation with affective experience for voters who were on the losing side. A subsequent study confirmed that identification was associated with experiencing positive emotions even in the context of a highly significant political event such as the 1995 Quebec Referendum which concerned the possible separation of the province from the rest of Canada (Losier & Koestner, 1999). Thus, even though the vote represented only a narrow victory for most participants in our sample, identification was associated with reporting pleasant emotions about the outcome. By contrast, we were surprised to find that intrinsically motivated voters in this study reported unpleasant emotions following this referendum outcome when their side won, despite the fact that they had anticipated having highly positive emotions under these circumstances. This finding led us to wonder whether intrinsic motivation toward politics may not have been sufficient to prompt voters to participate effectively in a consequential event such as voting on the future of their country, so we began a series of studies to investigate the issue.

Intrinsic motivation and internalization. The possibility that intrinsic motivation alone may not prepare people to participate fully and effectively in the political process was further suggested by the results for voting behavior. In two studies with over 500 participants we found that identification, but not intrinsic motivation, was significantly positively related to voting behavior (Koestner et al., 1996; Losier & Koestner, 1999). Introjection was also unrelated to voting behavior. Thus, whether participants viewed following politics as personally important was a better predictor of voting than whether they found politics interesting. It is puzzling that people who naturally enjoy following politics would spontaneously gather information and become emotionally involved in political issues, but not be more likely to follow through to cast their ballot in elections and referenda. We have speculated that people who are identified with respect to politics have accepted the importance of the political process and of their role in it, so they act accordingly, for example, by voting. However, those who are highly intrinsically motivated to follow politics take an interest in issues, are eager to find out information about the different sides, and may become emotionally involved in rooting for their side, but they are not more likely to engage in behaviors such as voting than are others low in intrinsic motivation if they have not internalized the importance of such behaviors. This speculation would suggest that in terms of the democratic ideal of fostering an electorate made up of involved participants who voice their opinions in elections, it may be important to promote identified reasons for following politics, even if a young person has a strong natural interest in the process. That is, it is important for citizens to see not only that politics can be interesting but that what happens is personally important to them.

Educational Domain

We conducted two separate long-term longitudinal studies with students who were making a transition either at the end of high school or the end of college (Koestner, Losier, Fichman, & Mallet, 2002). Participants' reasons for being in school were assessed along with measures of school satisfaction and general psychological distress. Participants were later followed up to determine if they continued in school, if their reports of satisfaction had changed, and if they showed any variation in their level of psychological distress. Our guiding hypothesis was that identification and intrinsic motivation would be associated with making school transitions more effectively than introjection.

Transitions for high school students. Graduation from high school or college is viewed by developmental researchers as a particularly significant transition because of powerful sociocultural expectations involving economic independence and establishing emotional attachments beyond one's family (Gore, Aseltine, Colten, & Lin, 1997). Not surprisingly, several studies have shown that these school transitions can result in increased psychological distress (Larose & Boivin, 1998). Such findings have led researchers to argue that high school and college graduation may represent a critical time period for ensuring successful adaptation to future adult roles (Seidman & French, 1997).

Table 3 summarizes our results in the educational domain. The reported results were obtained after controlling for overlap among the three regulatory styles and for general personality factors, such as optimism and dependency, that have been shown to influence adaptation. The general pattern of findings supported the prediction that identification and intrinsic motivation would be associated with superior outcomes relative to introjection. However, as in the political domain, there was evidence that it was particularly identification rather than intrinsic motivation that promoted positive engagement with academic activities, continued persistence in school, and successful adaptation to school transitions (Koestner, Losier, et al., 2002).

Outcome	Introjected	Identified	Intrinsic
High School Students			
Academic Satisfaction in College	0	+	0
Continuation to College (at 6 mth follow-up)	0	+	+
Continuation in College (at 18 mth follow-up)	0	+	0
Psych Distress in College at 6 mths	+	-	0
Psych Distress in College at 18 mths	+	-	0
College Students			
GPA	0	0	0
Psych Distress in School Over Time	+	-	0
Psych Distress After Graduation	+	-	0

Note: "+" indicates that a significant positive relation was obtained; "-" indicates a significant negative relation was obtained; "0" indicates that a non-significant relation was obtained.

Table 5.3. Correlates for the Three Self-Regulatory Styles.

It can be seen in Table 5-3 that only identification was significantly positively associated with reported satisfaction after students made the transition to college. Regarding continuing in school, identified and intrinsic regulation were both predictive of enrollment in college at the six-month follow-up, but only identification predicted continued enrollment in college at the 18 month follow-up. Introjection was unrelated to school persistence at both follow-ups.

An interesting pattern of results emerged on reports of psychological distress after students made the transition to college. Introjection was significantly related to later reports of heightened distress at both the six and 18 month follow-ups whereas identification was significantly associated with reporting lower levels of distress. Intrinsic motivation was unrelated to later reports of distress. These results only partially confirmed our hypothesis. Successful internalization of the value of being in school, as evidenced in endorsing identified rather than introjected reasons for school involvement, appeared to facilitate making a smooth transition to college. However, intrinsic motivation, which typically promotes positive school experiences, did not provide any benefit for high school students as they wrestled with the challenge of adapting to college (Koestner, Losier, et al., 2002).

Transitions for college students. Our second study followed college students either as they went from their junior year to their senior year or from their senior year to post graduation. Table 5-3 shows that the way students had internalized the value of school participation had long-ranging effects on their later adjustment regardless of whether they continued college or graduated. Highly introjected college students, who viewed school participation as something they do, reported higher levels of distress over time regardless of whether they were in their final year or had graduated. That introjection was significantly negatively related to adjustment even among college students who had graduated suggests that the emotional toll of adopting a controlling style of self-regulation in an important life domain may continue to be felt even after one departs the domain. Identification, which is reflected in viewing school participation as personally meaningful, was significantly associated with superior adjustment over time regardless of whether students remained in school or graduated. As in the first study, intrinsic motivation was unrelated to later reports of distress (Koestner, Losier, et al., 2002).

Together, the two studies yielded the surprising conclusion that whether or not young people successfully internalize the value of school participation is more important to their psychological growth and development than whether they remain intrinsically motivated about school. That is, whether students are able to view school activities as personally meaningful rather than something they feel coerced to do is a more important predictor of later adaptation than whether they find school activities naturally interesting and enjoyable. That identification rather than intrinsic motivation emerged as the best predictor of successful long-term adaptation in the academic domain echoed the earlier findings from the political domain which had suggested that identification (rather than intrinsic motivation) was especially associated with responsible and effective political participation (as reflected in forming differentiated opinions, casting one's vote on election day, and feeling positive emotions when one's side wins).

Conclusions and Implications for SDT

The results of our studies provided evidence that introjection placed individuals at risk for negative emotional, cognitive, and behavioral outcomes in both the political and academic domains. Although previous studies had demonstrated the negative consequences of introjection (Ryan, 1982; Ryan & Connell, 1989; Ryan, Rigby, & King., 1993), our political studies were the first to explicitly link this regulatory style with conflicted emotions and vulnerability to persuasion. The harshly evaluative and pressured character of an introjected self-regulatory style appears to compromise people's information processing and disrupt their emotional experiences in this domain. Furthermore, our academic studies were the first to demonstrate that introjection placed young people at risk when negotiating important developmental transitions such as entering into or graduating from college. Specifically, students who were pursuing their education because of internal pressures related to guilt avoidance and self-esteem maintenance showed a pattern of heightened psychological distress as they made normative school transitions. The impact of introjected academic regulation was not restricted to school-related emotions but instead radiated to undermine global adjustment. Such radiation effects from a specific domain to more global functioning have been outlined in a recent multi-level analysis of motivational phenomena (Vallerand, 1997). The way one has internalized the value of school activities exerts a wide-ranging impact on individuals' growth and development because of the centrality of the academic domain in Western cultures. The possession of an introjected regulatory style in a more peripheral domain, such as politics, may not exert such a wide-ranging effect on psychological adjustment.

There was also evidence that in both the political and academic domains, intrinsic and identified regulation conduce toward positive outcomes such as active information processing, the experience of positive emotions, and successful adaptation to school transitions. There was a consistent thread of evidence, however, suggesting that identified regulation was more important than intrinsic motivation in promoting responsible behavior and healthy adaptation. Thus, only identification was significantly positively related to forming differentiated political opinions and actually voting in elections, and, in the academic domain, only identification was consistently associated with higher levels of psychological adjustment as students made school transitions. This is not to say that intrinsic motivation was negatively associated with adaptive outcomes in any of these cases, instead, it was simply that intrinsic motivation did not exert a consistently significant impact on these outcomes. The stronger results for identification were a surprise. We had expected that intrinsic motivation would prove to be more advantageous than identification in promoting successful adaptation.

The Importance of Identification

The fact that identification was the best predictor of adaptive outcomes in our studies suggests reexamining some common assumptions regarding the relation of intrinsic motivation to internalization processes. Intrinsic motivation refers to behaviors that are performed for their inherent satisfaction and are thus not the product of internalization (Ryan, 1995). If someone is spontaneously drawn to perform an activity it is thought to be unnecessary for the individual to learn to acquire the regulation of that activity through the processes of acceptance and personal valuing that define identification. Although this may be true at the level of a specific activity, a potential difficulty arises when one considers that domains such as politics or academics encompass a wide range of activities that vary in terms of their intrinsic appeal. There are some aspects of these domains, such as registering to vote or rereading a chapter in preparation for an exam, that are likely to be perceived as quite uninteresting, yet that are essential to effective involvement in the domain. With such activities, it is likely that the extent to which individuals have consciously integrated the value of domain-relevant activities into their personal goals and values will be more important than their intrinsic interest in the domain. Our results suggest that someone who is highly identified toward a given domain is likely to persist at even the uninteresting activities within the domain whereas there is a risk that someone whose regulation is exclusively based on intrinsic motivation will invest themselves only in those domain-relevant activities that are interesting to them. This line of thinking suggests that it is important for socializing agents to promote successful internalization even if a young person is highly intrinsically motivated.

Autonomy Support and Structure

But how does one promote successful internalization? Grolnick and Ryan (1989) found that parental levels of autonomy-support were highly predictive of children reporting greater identification for achievement tasks, and also of better teacher-rated adjustment and performance in class. Williams and Deci (1996) showed that supervisors' level of autonomy support led to the development of identified regulation among medical students. Experimental studies similarly highlighted the critical role played by autonomy support in promoting identified regulation (Deci, Eghari, Patrick, & Leone, 1994). However, autonomy support has similarly been shown to be the critical factor in promoting intrinsic motivation (Reeve & Deci, 1996), thus begging the question of what social factors are *uniquely* associated with promoting successful internalization rather than intrinsic motivation.

We suspect that the distinction between autonomy support and structure is critical here. Autonomy support refers to the degree to which socializing agents encourage independent problem solving, choice, and participation in decisions (Grolnick & Ryan, 1989). Structure refers to the extent to which socializing agents provide consistent guidelines, expectations, and rules for behavior, without respect to the style in which they are promoted. Examples of providing structure include offering children a rationale for why certain uninteresting activities are important to perform and modeling engagement in such activities (Koestner, Ryan, Bernieri, & Holt, 1984). We would hypothesize that high levels of both autonomy support and structure are required to promote successful internalization. High levels of autonomy support without the provision of structure may result in a high level of intrinsic motivation toward certain activities within a domain but will not promote an understanding of why it is personally important and meaningful to perform even the uninteresting activities that are central to the domain. On the other hand, high levels of structure without an autonomy-supportive interpersonal context is likely to result in introjected self-regulation (Deci et al., 1994).

Intrinsic Motivation and Identification

Promoting high levels of *both* intrinsic motivation and integrated identifications seems like the appropriate goal for socializing agents to work toward. Indeed, we conceptualize intrinsic motivation and internalization as working in a complementary fashion to promote vitality, growth, and adaptation. Intrinsic motivation promotes a focus on short-term, process goals and yields energizing emotions such as interest and excitement, whereas identification keeps one oriented toward the long-term significance of one's current pursuits and fosters positive emotions such as pride in one's accomplishments in the domain. Possessing high levels of both intrinsic motivation and identification would seem to allow one to flexibly adapt to the wide diversity of situations that all domains typically offer. Three recent longitudinal studies by Sheldon and Elliot (1999) showed the adaptive value of combining these two forms of self-congruent regulation styles when pursuing personal goals.

Support for the adaptive value of possessing both intrinsic and more instrumental motives or goals is also provided by motivation researchers who do not use Self-Determination Theory as their starting point. For example, in a longitudinal study of talented teenagers, Wong and Csikszentmihalyi (1991) distinguished two forms of academic motivation, intrinsic motivation and work orientation. They argued that intrinsic motivation is based in the rewards of ongoing experience, whereas work orientation reflects an investment in long-term goals such as fulfilling one's career expectations or psychological needs. Their results showed that work orientation, which we would liken to identified regulation, was significantly associated with the amount of time students spent studying but was unrelated to their experience while studying. By contrast, intrinsic motivation was related to enjoyable studying experiences but not the amount of time spent studying.

A similar pattern of results was obtained in research on achievement goals. Thus, two recent studies demonstrated that college students' grades were predicted by performance goals, which involve demonstrating competence relative to others, whereas their positive emotions about school involvement were predicted by learning goals, which concern a desire to develop competence (Elliot & Church, 1997; Harackiewicz, Barron, Carter, Lehto, & Elliot, 1997).

To be able to achieve good grades and simultaneously enjoy the process seems to require combining self-regulation strategies that focus both on immediate experience (i.e., intrinsic motivation) and long-term goals (i.e., identification).

Although our research indicates that it is important to develop an identified regulatory style toward academics and politics, it is natural to wonder whether the same would be true in other domains, particularly those that consist largely of tasks that naturally elicit intrinsic motivation. For example, does identification have a role to play in relation to the way people pursue their leisure activities? We would argue that even domains consisting of highly interesting activities will still require internalization. Consider the example of a young girl who is passionate about playing tennis. Although her initial experiences may be driven by the natural pleasure of hitting the tennis ball, the girl will at some point want to extend her skills in order to pursue greater challenges. There is considerable evidence that long-term skill improvement will, however, require more than playful engagement in the domain. Thus, Ericcson and Charness (1994) have argued that the development of expertise in sports or performing arts is directly related to the amount of deliberate practice one performs in a domain, with deliberate practice being defined as specific training activities recommended by a knowledgeable instructor. These activities share little with the concept of intrinsic motivation; instead, they tend to be goal-oriented, repetitive, and highly effortful (e.g., hitting 100 consecutive backhand strokes to a coach). Interestingly, Bloom (1985) found that parents play a critical role in youngsters' learning to dedicate themselves to deliberate practice. Parents need to help children understand the relation between their practice and later improved performance, as well as to assist children in learning how to schedule practice activities into their daily lives. We would argue that the extent to which individuals are able to dedicate themselves to deliberate practice will hinge upon the degree to which the individuals are identified rather than intrinsically motivated toward the domain.

Having discussed the potential value of becoming identified in a domain that was primarily intrinsically motivating, it is important to consider whether the reverse also holds. Should one try to cultivate intrinsic motivation for activities that are socially valued but generally uninteresting? Is it even possible to become intrinsically motivated about an activity that one originally became involved with only because of its perceived social importance? The answer to both questions appears to be Yes. Thus, Lepper and Gilovich (1982) demonstrated that structuring children's chores so they involve an engaging fantasy resulted in superior internalization over time. Cordova and Lepper (1996) showed that adding an engaging fantasy context to a math activity led to greater interest and better learning. Other studies found that college students were able to generate their own strategies, such as varying their approach to the task in order to enhance the interest value of boring activities (Green-Demers, Pelletier, Stewart, & Gushue, 1998; Sansone, Weir, Harpster, & Morgan, 1992). Csikszentmihalyi (1997) has argued that even the most mundane of activities, such as working on an assembly line, can be made into a enjoyable flow experience if actors focus their attention on setting challenging goals and monitoring performance in relation to these goals. These results suggest that it is useful to supplement identified regulation with intrinsic motivation.

Future Research

There are three directions we would recommend for future research based on SDT. First, it seems important to reexamine commonly held beliefs about intrinsic motivation and adaptation. Our results suggest that intrinsic motivation is only partially responsible for psychological adjustment and that identified regulation can make a major contribution in certain domains. Future research should examine the complementary or synergistic roles of intrinsic motivation and internalization for growth and adaptation. Perhaps intrinsic motivation is most important for the energization and regulation of short-term goals related to interesting activities, whereas identification has more to do with delayed gratification and the attainment of long-term goals. The adaptive advantage of a dual-process motivational system consisting of both intrinsic motivation and internalization could be to provide flexibility in one's regulation of goal pursuits.

Second, future research should focus on the distinct regulatory styles, rather than relying on a composite score such as the Relative Autonomy Index (RAI). The RAI takes into account a person's endorsement of the different types of reasons by weighing the autonomous reasons positively and the controlled reasons negatively and then combining them into an overall score. Although the RAI can provide useful information about the "big picture", important distinctions concerning the relative contribution of each type of motivation may be overlooked. We particularly encourage researchers to examine the relative influence of intrinsic motivation versus successful internalization (identification rather than introjection) on adaptation in various domains.

Third, research should examine the distinct regulatory styles at different levels of personality to take into account not only domain specific factors, but also situational and dispositional influences (Vallerand, 1997). Exploring the relative influence of intrinsic motivation and internalization at a more global level of personality functioning is particularly interesting to us because of our previous work with the General Causality Orientations Scale. The GCOS was developed to measure individual differences in people's general orientation toward autonomous functioning (Deci & Ryan, 1985). The autonomy scale of the GCOS has been associated with a high degree of integration in personality, a persistent approach toward one's goals, flexible decision-making, and positive social relations with both peers and superiors (Koestner, Bernieri, & Zuckerman, 1992; Koestner, Gingras, et al., 1999; Koestner & Losier, 1996; Koestner & Zuckerman, 1994). Although these studies confirm an association between autonomy and adaptive functioning, they are uninformative regarding the relative role of intrinsic motivation versus identification because the GCOS autonomy scale includes item content related to both regulation styles. Separating the autonomy scale into distinct intrinsic and identified subscales might shed light on which aspects of adaptive functioning are more or less influenced by these two forms of self-regulation.

Conclusion

The present chapter has focused on distinguishing introjection, identification, and intrinsic motivation. Introjected regulation involves pursuing an activity because of feelings of pressure or compulsion. Identified regulation involves integrating important activities with one's personal values and goals. Intrinsic motivation involves pursuing an activity because it is interesting and fun. In a series of studies, it was shown that it is possible to isolate some relatively distinctive affective, cognitive, and behavioral features of these three forms of self-regulation. Introjection was uniquely associated with adverse outcomes such as conflicted emotional experiences, vulnerability to persuasion, and poor adaptation to school transitions, whereas identification was associated with adaptive outcomes such as resistance to persuasion about some personally important issues and flexible adaptation to school transitions. Intrinsic motivation, like identification, was associated with generally positive emotional experiences, but failed to predict voting behavior in the domain of politics or successful long-term adaptation in the domain of education. This last pair of findings suggests that it may be important to promote identified reasons for engaging in various activities even if a person displays high levels of intrinsic motivation. Our discussion highlighted the need for research to more closely explore the interplay between intrinsic motivation and internalization, the two innate growth tendencies that together explain much of the variance in people's vitality, development, and psychological adaptation.

References

Bandura, A. (1997). *Self-efficacy: The exercise of control*. NY: W.H. Freeman.

Bloom, B. S. (1985). *Developing talent in young people*. New York: Ballantine.

Connell, J. P., & Illardi, B. C. (1987). Self-system concomitants of discrepancies between children's and teachers' evaluations of academic competence. *Child Development*, *58*, 1297-1307.

Cordova, D. I., & Lepper, M. R. (1996). Intrinsic motivation and the process of learning: Beneficial effects of contextualization, personalization, and choice. *Journal of Educational Psychology*, *88*, 715-730.

Csikszentmihalyi, M. (1997). *Finding flow: The psychology of engagement with everyday life*. New York: Basic Books.

de Charms, R. (1968). *Personal causation: the internal affective determinants of behavior*. NY: Academic press.

Deci, E. L., Eghari, H., Patrick, P. C., & Leone, D. R. (1994). Facilitating internalization: The self-determination theory perspective. *Journal of Personality*, *62*, 119-142.

Deci, E. L., & Ryan, R. M. (1985). *Intrinsic motivation and self-determination in human behavior*. NY: Plenum.

Deci, E. L., & Ryan, R. M. (1991). A motivational approach to self: Integration in personality. In R. A. Dienstbier (Ed.), *Nebraska Symposium on Motivation* (pp. 237-288). Lincoln, NE: University of Nebraska Press.

Deci, E. L., & Ryan, R. M. (2000). The "what" and "why" of goal pursuits: Human needs and the self-determination of behavior. *Psychological Inquiry*, *11*, 227-268.

Elliot, A., & Church, M. (1997). A hierarchical model of approach and avoidance achievement motivation. *Journal of Personality and Social Psychology*, *72*, 218-232.

Ericcson, K. A., & Charness, N. (1994). Expert performance: Its structure and acquisition. *American Psychologist*, *49*, 725-747.

Gore, S., Aseltine, R., Colten, M., & Lin, B. (1997). Life after high school: Development, stress, and well-being. In I. H. Gotlib & B. Wheaton (Eds.), *Stress and adversity over the life course: Trajectories and turning points* (pp. 197-214). New York: Cambridge University Press.

Green-Demers, I., Pelletier, L. G., Stewart, D. G., & Gushue, N. R. (1998). Coping with the less interesting aspects of training: Towards a model of interest and motivation enhancement in individual sports. *Basic and Applied Social Psychology*, *20*, 251-261.

Grolnick, W. S., & Ryan, R. M. (1987). Autonomy in children's learning: An experimental and individual difference investigation. *Journal of Personality and Social Psychology*, *52*, 890- 898.

Grolnick, W. S., & Ryan, R. M. (1989). Parent styles associated with children's self-regulation and competence in school. *Journal of Educational Psychology, 81*, 143-154.

Harackiewicz, J., Barron, K., Carter, S., Lehto, A., & Elliot, A. (1997). Determinants and consequences of achievement goals in the college classroom. *Journal of Personality and Social Psychology, 73*, 1284-1295.

Hodgins, H., Koestner, R., & Duncan, N. (1996). On the compatibility of autonomy and relatedness. *Personality and Social Psychology Bulletin, 22*, 227-237.

Koestner, R., Bernieri, F., & Zuckerman, M. (1992). Self-regulation and consistency between attitudes, traits and behaviors. *Personality and Social Psychology Bulletin, 18*, 52-59.

Koestner, R., Gingras, I., Abutaa, R, Losier, G. F., DiDio, L., & Gagné, M. (1999). To follow expert advice when making a decision: An examination of reactive vs reflective autonomy. *Journal of Personality, 67*, 849-870.

Koestner, R., Houlfort, N., Paquet, S., & Knight, C. (2002). On the risks of recycling because of guilt: An examination of the consequences of introjection. *Journal of Applied Social Psychology,* in press.

Koestner, R., & Losier, G. F. (1996). Distinguishing reactive vs reflective autonomy. *Journal of Personality, 64*, 465-494.

Koestner, R., Losier, G. F., Fichman, L., & Mallet, M. (2002). Internalization and adaptation: Finding personal meaning in school activities. Unpublished manuscript, McGill University.

Koestner, R., Losier, G. F., Vallerand, R. J., & Carducci, D. (1996). Identified and introjected forms of political internalization: Extending self-determination theory. *Journal of Personality and Social Psychology, 70*, 1025-1036.

Koestner, R., & McClelland, D. C. (1990). Perspectives on competence motivation. In L. A. Pervin (Ed.), *Handbook of personality theory and research*, 527-548, NY: Guilford.

Koestner, R., Ryan, R., Bernieri, F., & Holt, K. (1984). The effects of controlling vs informational limit-setting styles on children's intrinsic motivation and creativity. *Journal of Personality, 52*, 233-247.

Koestner, R., & Zuckerman, M. (1994). Causality orientations, failure, and achievement. *Journal of Personality, 62*, 321-346.

Larose, S., & Boivin, M. (1998). Attachment to parents, social support expectations, and socioemotional adjustment during the high school-college transition. *Journal of Research on Adolescence, 8*, 1-27.

Lepper, M. R., & Gilovich, T. (1982). Accentuating the positive: Eliciting generalized compliance from children through activity-oriented requests. *Journal of Personality and Social Psychology, 42*, 248-259.

Losier, G. F., & Koestner, R. (1999). Intrinsic versus identified regulation in distinct political campaigns: The consequences of following politics for pleasure versus personal meaningfulness. *Personality and Social Psychology Bulletin, 25*, 287-298.

Losier, G. F., Perreault, S., Koestner, R., & Vallerand, R. J. (2001). Examining individual differences in the internalization of political values: Validation of the self-determination scale of political motivation. *Journal of Research in Personality, 35*, 41-61.

Marcia, J. E. (1980). Identity in adolescence. In J. Abelson (Ed.), *Handbook of adolescent psychology* (pp. 159-187). NY: Wiley.

Patrick, B. C., Skinner, E. A., & Connell, J. P. (1993). What motivates children's behavior and emotion? Joint effects of perceived control and autonomy in the academic domain. *Journal of Personality and Social Psychology, 65*, 781-791.

Ratelle, C., Debeis, P., Koestner, R., & Losier, G. F. (1999). Priming and persuasion during a mayoral election. Unpublished manuscript, McGill University.

Reeve, J., & Deci, E. L. (1996). Elements of the competitive situation that affect intrinsic motivation. *Personality and Social Psychology Bulletin, 22*, 24-33.

Ryan, R. M. (1982). Control and information in the intrapersonal sphere: An extension of cognitive evaluation theory. *Journal of Personality and Social Psychology, 43*, 450-461.

Ryan, R. M. (1995). Psychological needs and the facilitation of integrative processes. *Journal of Personality, 63*, 397-429.

Ryan, R. M., & Connell, J. P. (1989). Perceived locus of causality and internalization: Examining reasons for acting in two domains. *Journal of Personality and Social Psychology, 57*, 749-761.

Ryan, R. M., Rigby, S., & King, K. (1993). Two types of religious internalization and their relations to religious orientations and mental health. *Journal of Personality and Social Psychology, 65*, 586-596.

Sansone, C., Weir, C., Harpster, L., & Morgan, C. (1992). Once a boring task always a boring task?: Interest as a self-regulatory mechanism. *Journal of Personality and Social Psychology, 63*, 379-390.

Seidman, E., & French, S. E. (1997). Normative school transitions among urban adolescents: When, where, and how to intervene. In H. J. Walberg & O. Reyes (Eds.), *Children and youth: Interdisciplinary perspectives* (pp. 166-189). Thousand Oaks: CA: Sage Publications.

Sheldon, K. M., & Elliot, A .J. (1999). Goal striving, need satisfaction, and longitudinal well-being: The self-concordance model. *Journal of Personality and Social Psychology, 76*, 482-497.

Vallerand, R. J. (1997). Toward a hierarchical model of intrinsic and extrinsic motivation. In M. P. Zanna (Ed.), *Advances in Experimental Social Psychology* (pp. 271-360). New York: Academic Press.

Williams, G. C., & Deci, E. L. (1996). Internalization of biopsychosocial values by medical students: A test of self-determination theory. *Journal of Personality and Social Psychology, 70*, 767-779.

Wong, M. M., & Csikszentmihalyi, M. (1991). Motivation and academic achievement: The effects of personality traits and the quality of experience. *Journal of Personality, 59*, 539-574.

6: Sketches for a Self-Determination Theory of Values

Tim Kasser
Knox College

This chapter sketches out what a self-determination theory of values might entail. I begin by introducing the concept of values and discussing how researchers and theorists have understood the construct. Then six propositions derived from self-determination theory (SDT) are presented which could form the primary brush strokes needed for a self-determination theory of values. Review of the literature demonstrates that these six propositions are indeed consistent with much extant theorizing and research on values.

Values

Values were defined by Rokeach (1973) as beliefs "that a specific mode of conduct or end-state of existence is personally or socially preferable to an opposite or converse mode of conduct or end-state of existence."(p. 5) These guiding principles of life organize people's attitudes, emotions, and behaviors, and typically endure across time and situations. That is, someone with a particular value is expected to consistently express behavior relevant to that value in a variety of situations over time. According to Feather (1992, 1995), values lead to specific behaviors and experiences by influencing the valences that individuals assign to the desirability of specific objects and situations. For example, if a woman holds being attractive as an important value (i.e., an important end-state of existence she would like to personally attain), the valences she attaches to shopping for clothes, looking at magazines such as *Cosmopolitan*, and dating handsome men will likely be quite high. As a consequence of these valences, she will be more likely to engage in behaviors relevant to this value than will another person who views this pursuit as less worthy. Values may also influence behavior through the goals they organize (Emmons, 1989). For example, a person who strongly values personal growth is highly likely to proactively engage in a number of specific goals relevant to that overarching aim, such as going into therapy, meditating daily, and reading self-help books. These goals will influence behavior by activating specific action systems that lead the individual to actually engage in goal-relevant (and thus value-relevant) behavior (Carver & Scheier, 1982).

While individual values provide some information about people's experience and behavior, most values theorists emphasize that it is best to assess the entire organization of values a person holds, that is, the person's value system. To understand an individual's choice of career, for example, we would want to know about the entire system of the person's values, as all the values together and their relative importance to each other influence this decision. Thus the person who believes that the ideal societal end state of world peace is more important than the personal end-state of being wealthy will be more likely to choose a lower-paying job working as an activist than will someone whose value system is oriented in the opposite direction. And a third person who views these two values as equally important will be more influenced by other aspects of the job (e.g., opportunities for freedom, fame, etc.) and how they fit with his or her value system.

Using these concepts as starting points, values researchers have conducted more fine-grained analyses of how values influence attitudes and behavior, how they cohere in systems, and how their internalization is influenced by different environmental factors (see Seligman, Olson, & Zanna, 1996 for an overview). Unfortunately, values remain a rather neglected topic in mainstream psychology, as far more energy has been devoted to other issues of the self-concept, other types of beliefs, and other types of motivational dynamics. I believe there are three reasons for this. First, research on values is often said to be too subjective for a scientific enterprise that strives for objectivity. The idea that values are too subjective to be studied is obviously untenable, as the scientific method has been applied to values just as it has to many other aspects of personality. A second reason values have not attracted greater attention in psychology may be that most theories of values are mini-theories with nomological networks that do not extend far beyond value constructs (e.g., Rokeach, 1973; Schwartz, 1992, 1994, 1996). As such, these theories do not provide a very comprehensive explanation of human experience and behavior. Third, the grander theories of human behavior which do incorporate the concept of values (e.g., Maslow, 1954; Rogers, 1964) have been derived from theoretical orientations whose proponents often do not submit their formulations to empirical tests.

My intention in this chapter is to suggest that SDT is consistent with a great deal of what past students of values have proposed theoretically and found empirically, and that the attainment of greater integration between SDT and values research could be mutually beneficial. Research on values would be enhanced by being grounded in an empirically supported motivational theory that has implications for many aspects of human experience and behavior. SDT would in turn benefit by obtaining further support for its tenets and by incorporating a cognitive/affective construct that would help explain enduring personality functioning and social behavior.

Toward a Self-Determination Theory of Values

To this end, I present six propositions about values. My belief is that they are all consistent both with the existing literature on values and with previous theorizing and research conducted from the self-determination perspective. In order to support these propositions, I review the research my colleagues and I have conducted, in addition to that of a variety of other investigators whose writings have not been explicitly informed by SDT.

Proposition I: Valuing Originally and Ideally Emerges from the Self

At the core of SDT, both literally and figuratively, is the self. The self has been defined as the integrative center of the organism, the set of psychological processes that is attempting to make experience whole, to feel authentically behind its behaviors, and to grow (Ryan, 1995). In the attempt to integrate and grow, the self engages in behaviors that it finds intrinsically motivating—that is, behaviors that are fun, enjoyable, and valuable as ends in and of themselves.

One way to understand the attempts of the self to grow by engaging in activities it finds intrinsically motivating is to say that the self seeks out activities that it values. Rogers (1964) theorized that individuals are born with an organismic valuing process which helps guide infants' behavior. For example, hunger, pain, bitter tastes, and loud sounds are negatively valued, while security and food are usually positively valued. I say usually, because Rogers believed that the valuing process is a flexible one that depends on the organism's current state. Thus, once hunger is satisfied, food becomes negatively valued, as any parent well knows. Similarly, infants typically value security, but once they feel secure, they oftentimes turn to exploring their environment (see also Maslow, 1956), thus valuing intrinsically motivated activity. Naturally, we cannot speak of infants as having true concepts or beliefs at this stage of cognitive development, and thus no values as typically defined, but certainly they have feelings about what is and what is not desirable. According to Rogers, this valuing process acts in the service of helping the infant to continue to grow and satisfy its needs (as will be discussed in Proposition Two).

Hermans (1987) has also defined the process of valuing as a function of the self, emphasizing that by self he means the experiencing "I" rather than the looking glass "Me," a point that relates to Ryan's (1995) characterization of the self of SDT as the "I" and not the "Me." According to Hermans, the I is sometimes evaluating an external object, such as a car, and is other times evaluating the Me. That is, the I is at times evaluating its own ideas and behavior, judging for example whether the chapter one is writing is of high quality. This valuing is necessary for, and indeed central to, Hermans' concept of the person.

Thus, Hermans (1987) and Ryan (1995) agree that valuing emerges developmentally from the true self as a means of helping the young organism know what it likes and does not like, what will help it grow and what will not. Valuing can thus be understood as an evaluative function of the self which aids in its growth, in part by selecting which activities will be beneficial and which will not. From the perspective of SDT, the behaviors most likely to benefit the self are those that are intrinsically motivated—that is, those that are interesting, fun, and valued for their own sake.

SDT has been careful to recognize that not all activities that emerge from the self are intrinsically motivated, however. That is, although not all behaviors are intrinsically motivating, there are times when people still feel authentic and agentic about engaging in them. Feelings of agency for such behaviors, according to Ryan and Connell (1989), can occur when people feel identified with their behaviors. In the case of identification, a person is said to wholeheartedly endorse a course of action, or to engage in it because he or she values it, or because his or her whole self is behind it. Thus, just as infants' valuing originally emerges from the self, an adult's values may still emanate from the self if the person feels identified with the course of action. It is important to emphasize, however, that not all the values a person holds will necessarily feel agentic and owned. For example, two people may both hold the value of being religious, but one may do so out of a sense of felt pressure because he or she lives in a society where nonconformity leads to imprisonment, whereas the other authentically believes that spirituality is an essential part of his or her true being. Only in this latter case can the self be said to be the source of the valuing. As we will see in later propositions, the extent to which the valuing process continues to represent the self's growth processes throughout development is an important issue.

Proposition Two: Values Derive, in part, from Needs

Fundamental to SDT is the idea that all people possess psychological needs that help guide the organismic integration process and are "nutriments or conditions that are essential to an entity's growth" (Ryan, 1995, p. 410). Specifically, for the self to grow and integrate experience in an optimal manner, psychological needs for autonomy, relatedness, and competence must be satisfied. People need to feel that they freely choose their behaviors, that they have close connections with others, and that they are effective in the activities they undertake. Thus, a self-determination theory of values must relate people's value systems to psychological needs.

Indeed, values scholars commonly state that values stem in part from people's needs. For example, White's (1951) list of values is adapted from Murray's (1938) conceptions of needs, and Maslow (1959) often went so far as to use the terms values and needs almost interchangeably, believing that people's values are strongly determined by their place on his well-known need hierarchy. Schwartz (1992, p. 4) stated that "values represent, in the form of conscious goals, three universal requirements of human existence to which all individuals and societies must be responsive: needs of individuals as biological organisms, requisites of coordinated social interaction, and survival and welfare needs of the group." Perhaps most cogently, Rokeach (1973, p. 20) wrote: "Values are the cognitive representations and transformations of needs."

Valuing and values can therefore be seen as ways that the self goes about trying to grow and satisfy its needs. Values give expression to needs, helping the self select experiences that are desirable and supportive of need satisfaction, and avoid experiences that are neither desirable nor conducive to growth and need satisfaction. Most likely, values work in this regard by influencing the valences people attach to more specific activities and objects, as suggested by Feather (1995). For example, most people would place low valences on the activity of "spending time in prison" because such an activity does not typically work to satisfy the self's need for autonomy. In contrast, higher valences would likely be placed on the activity of "spending time with friends," as this activity is more likely to satisfy the need for relatedness. In essence, I am suggesting that both valuing and values are cognitive/affective tools by which the self can fulfill its aims of growth and need satisfaction and that these tools work by orienting the person towards some behaviors and away from others.

Proposition Three: Values Reflect Both Intrinsic and Extrinsic Motivations

Self-determination theory recognizes that people's behavior is not always intrinsically motivated. Ideally, people act out of the self's inherent tendencies to grow and integrate experience, to feel intrinsically motivated for their behavior, and to satisfy needs for autonomy, relatedness, and competence. However, it is (perhaps too) frequently the case that people's behavior arises not from the authentic strivings of the self but instead from feelings of coercion, control, and pressure. In such cases, individuals are said to be extrinsically motivated. Extrinsic motivation involves engagement in behaviors in order to obtain rewards or praise, or to avoid criticism or punishment (Deci & Ryan, 1985). Such behaviors are seen by SDT as alienated from the self and its needs and as being problematic in many regards well-reviewed in other chapters of this volume. Thus, a self-determination theory of values must recognize that some values are conducive to growthful, intrinsically motivated actions and others tend to prompt extrinsically motivated behaviors focused on rewards and people's praise. In other words, values sometimes emerge from and reflect the self, and sometimes they emerge from and reflect coercive processes.

Values theorists have noted a similar distinction. For example, Rogers (1964, p. 162) believed that individuals often give up their own internal locus of evaluation in order to obtain the love and affection of others, and thus hold *introjected values* which are based more on what others value than on what would facilitate actualization of the true self. We can see here quite well the distinction between values based in the self's own needs and those based in extrinsically motivated action. Similarly, Rokeach (1973) proposed three motivational functions of values: to self-actualize, to adjust to societal demands and group pressures, and to defend the ego. Obviously the first function is closest to what SDT would see as valuing based in autonomous motivation, while the latter two relate to valuing based in controlled motivations. This is because extrinsic motivation results from the pressures of either outside forces (i.e., society or the group) or from introjected beliefs that are not an integrated part of the self (i.e., ego-defensive motivations).

Thus, values sometimes express growth motivation and the self's needs and other times serve other functions that are extrinsically motivated and oftentimes at odds with the growth of the self. My colleagues and I have represented this distinction by identifying values that are *intrinsic* and *extrinsic*. Kasser and Ryan (1996, p. 280) defined intrinsic values as "expressive of desires congruent with actualizing and growth tendencies natural to humans. As such, intrinsic goals are likely to satisfy basic and inherent psychological needs." Examples of intrinsic values include those for self-acceptance, affiliation, and community feeling. Self-acceptance values are those that concern growth, autonomy, and self-regard; affiliation values involve having good relationships with friends and family; and community feeling values focus on improving the world through activism or generativity. In contrast to these values that stem largely from the self's tendency to grow and directly satisfy its needs, extrinsic values "do not provide satisfaction in and of themselves; instead, their allure usually lies in the presumed admiration that attends them or in the power and sense of worth that can be derived from attaining them" (Kasser & Ryan, 1996, p. 280). Three examples of extrinsic values are: financial success, the concern to accumulate wealth and possessions; image, the desire to look attractive in terms of one's body and clothing; and social recognition, the aim of being famous and well-known. As can be seen, all of these values express a concern with the attainment of external rewards and praise.

In order to test the notion that values can be classified into intrinsic and extrinsic types, Kasser and Ryan (1996) asked participants to rate the importance of different aspirations reflecting these values. Importance ratings were then submitted to a higher-order factor analysis. Two factors resulted, which were easily interpretable as representing intrinsic and extrinsic values. That is, the intrinsic values of self-acceptance, affiliation, and community feeling were highly associated with one another and empirically distinguishable from the extrinsic values of financial success, appearance, and social recognition, which also cohered with one another. This result has been demonstrated with U.S. college students and adults (Kasser & Ryan, 1996) and with students from Germany (Schmuck, Kasser, & Ryan, 2000) and Russia (Ryan, Chirkov, Little, Sheldon, Timoshina, & Deci, 1999).

The finding that intrinsic and extrinsic values form separate factors is only one piece of evidence supporting the validity of this distinction, however. Recall that, theoretically, intrinsic values are more likely than extrinsic values to satisfy the self's needs. Research indeed supports this claim, especially for autonomy and relatedness needs.

With regard to autonomy, intrinsic and extrinsic values have been associated with two important measures derived from SDT that assess feelings of autonomy. The first of these is the General Causality Orientations Scale (GCOS; Deci & Ryan, 1985a), which measures people's orientations toward autonomy (i.e., being motivated by challenges and opportunities for freedom) versus control (i.e., being motivated by rewards, praise, and external incentives). Kasser and Ryan (1993) showed that people who highly valued the intrinsic pursuits of self-acceptance, affiliation, and community feeling scored relatively low on measures of control orientation, whereas the reverse was true for people who highly valued the extrinsic aspiration of financial success. Similarly, Sheldon and Kasser (1995) demonstrated in two studies that people with personal goals aimed at intrinsic "possible futures" were more autonomy oriented, while people with personal goals aimed at extrinsic values were more control oriented. The second measure of autonomy used to support the validity of the intrinsic/extrinsic distinction derives from Ryan and Connell's (1989) measure of whether the perceived locus of causality (PLOC) for behavior is internal or external. Sheldon and Kasser (1995, 1998) have consistently found that people with intrinsically oriented goals also report more self-determined reasons for pursuing their goals (i.e., a more internal PLOC), while people with extrinsically oriented goals report more controlled reasons for pursuing their goals (i.e., a more external PLOC). In sum, research with both the GCOS and the PLOC shows that intrinsic values are more autonomous and self-determined than are extrinsic values.

Research has also demonstrated that people oriented toward intrinsic and extrinsic values have different experiences of relatedness as well. Here I will review only three relevant findings. First, Kasser and Ryan (2001) assessed the quality of people's relationships with friends and lovers by measuring length of relationships and characteristics such as trust, acceptance, and jealousy. Results showed positive correlations between the quality of both types of relationships and the importance participants placed on intrinsic goals, and negative correlations between these outcomes and the importance placed on extrinsic goals. Second, Sheldon and Kasser (1995) reported that people whose goals were very extrinsically oriented were less empathic, whereas intrinsically oriented individuals were not only more empathic, but also more likely to help friends with their problems. Finally, assessing only the extrinsic value of financial success, Richins and Dawson (1992) showed that materialists placed less emphasis on having intimate, close relationships with others.

Together, the studies just reviewed show, as predicted, that people oriented toward intrinsic values are likely to differ from those oriented toward extrinsic values in terms of their experience of needs for autonomy and relatedness. Regarding the need for competence, however, the picture remains unclear. On one hand, people generally report being less confident that they will attain their extrinsic aspirations than their intrinsic aspirations (Kasser & Ryan, 1996; Schmuck et al., 2000) suggesting that feelings of competence may decline when one pursues extrinsic goals. On the other hand, there is no theoretical reason that intrinsic and extrinsic values could not be equally effective in helping people to satisfy the need for competence. For example, individuals are likely to feel just as efficacious if they close a big business deal or lose 15 pounds to be more fashionable as if they make new friends or help someone at a soup kitchen. The allure of extrinsic values may in fact be that they help people who are questioning their own self-worth to feel competent in culturally sanctioned pursuits such as wealth and attractiveness.

Despite the fact that the bulk of research distinguishing between intrinsic and extrinsic values has been explicitly derived from SDT, a reinterpretation of results reported by Schwartz (1992, 1994) can provide additional support for the proposal that values reflect intrinsic and extrinsic motivations. Schwartz asked participants to rate the importance of a number of guiding principles in their lives, and then submitted these ratings to a "smallest space analysis" (Guttman, 1968) which organizes the values into a circumplex structure reflecting how values cohere together or oppose each other. Consistent with his theory, Schwartz has found 10 domains of values in this analysis: stimulation (novelty and challenge); self-direction (exploring and feeling choiceful); universalism (a desire to improve the welfare of all people and the world); benevolence (a desire to improve the welfare of those close to the person); tradition (commitment to the customs and ideas of a culture); conformity (restraining impulses and actions based on social norms); security (feeling safe and that one's life is stable); power (the desire for prestige and domination over others); achievement (personal success through demonstrated competence); and hedonism (pleasure and sensual gratification).

Interestingly, Schwartz (1994) believes that values of stimulation and self-direction reflect needs of the organism to seek out novelty and be in charge of one's life, which SDT would label as autonomy and which Kasser and Ryan (1996) assessed via "self-acceptance" values. Similarly, Schwartz considers the values of universalism and benevolence to satisfy needs of the organism to be connected with others, parallel with Kasser and Ryan's (1996) affiliation and community feeling values fulfilling relatedness needs. Extrinsic values are also represented in Schwartz's research. Specifically, Schwartz's definition of power values bears a strong resemblance to extrinsic aspirations, as do achievement and conformity/tradition values, which highly involve others' reactions to the person's own status and behavior.

Schwartz's (1996) circumplex model of value configurations, which has been validated in 41 countries, can also be interpreted in a way consistent with Kasser and Ryan's (1996) distinction between intrinsic and extrinsic values. In the circumplex, when values are close to each other, they are viewed by individuals as compatible, while when values are on opposite sides of the circumplex, they are in conflict with each other. Among other findings, the circumplex reveals that stimulation, self-direction, universalism, and benevolence all cluster together and are thus seen by individuals as mutually compatible. As mentioned above, these values can be seen as representing autonomy and relatedness needs, which conceptually replicates Kasser and Ryan's (1996) factor analyses showing that affiliation, community feeling, and self-acceptance load on one factor. What's more, the values most similar to extrinsic values, namely power, achievement, and conformity/tradition, also cluster together and are on the opposite side of the circumplex from the intrinsic values. Further, it is interesting that Kasser and Ryan (1996) suggested that feelings of insecurity are associated with extrinsic goals, and Schwartz (1996) showed that security and power values are right next to each other in the circumplex. In sum, although Schwartz's value model was not designed to test ideas deriving from SDT, many of his results can be interpreted in a manner consistent with the theory.

To summarize this section, people's values can be conceived of as intrinsic, thereby serving growth motivations and needs for autonomy and relatedness, or as extrinsic and focused on praise, rewards, and security. Substantial research with a diverse array of instruments supports this claim.

Proposition Four: On Average, People are More Oriented Toward Intrinsic Values than toward Extrinsic Values

Self-determination theory assumes that the basic trajectory of individuals is towards growth and integration. As noted above, growth and integration involve behavior organized by intrinsic motivation and the needs for autonomy, competence, and relatedness. Thus, when asking people about their values, we should find that they rate as most important values expressive of intrinsic motivation and the self's needs and are less interested in values concerning extrinsic motives. There are important qualifications to this proposition, as will be noted in Proposition Five, but generally speaking people should value intrinsic contents more than extrinsic contents.

Thus far, support for this proposition has been strong. For example, using the Aspiration Index, Ryan et al. (1999) compared the values of Russian and U.S.

college students, and Schmuck et al. (2000) compared the values of German and U.S. college students. In all four samples, intrinsic aspirations were more highly valued than were extrinsic aspirations. Further, in all four samples, affiliation and self-acceptance aspirations were rated as the two most important values, and the extrinsic goals of social recognition and appearance were the two least valued pursuits.

While not explicitly designed to test this proposition, two studies using Schwartz's value survey have reported results consistent with the idea that people view intrinsic values as more important than extrinsic values. Feather (1995) reported the ordering of Schwartz's values by their importance in a sample of Australian students, and Schwartz, Sagiv, and Boehnke (2000) reported similar information in seven samples composed of Israeli and German adults and students and Russians who were recent immigrants to Israel. Recall that self-direction and benevolence values are those which, in Schwartz's typology, most closely parallel Kasser and Ryan's (1996) intrinsic values of self-acceptance and affiliation, respectively. In five of the eight samples using the Schwartz measure, self-direction and benevolence were the two most important values, and in the other three samples, these two were both listed among the top three values. Recall also that power and tradition/conformity values bear strong resemblances to extrinsic values. As would be expected, these three contents were generally least valued, falling in the bottom three values in five of the eight samples, with at least two of these values in the bottom three in the other three samples.

These findings are quite compatible with SDT, which maintains that people in all cultures have the same psychological needs and tendencies towards growth and integration. Thus, people will orient most toward values that support growth and integrative processes and fulfill universal human needs but will tend not to focus on values that are counter to the development of the self and the fulfillment of basic needs. Further work is needed, but our preliminary analyses of cross-cultural data suggest that, as in individualistic cultures, people in collectivistic cultures are also more likely to place greater importance on intrinsic than extrinsic values.

Proposition Five: When Environmental Conditions Thwart Need Satisfaction, People Will Increasingly Orient toward Extrinsic Values

The origins of SDT lie in the discovery that controlling environmental conditions undermine intrinsically motivated activity. Deci (1971) found that rewarding people for engaging in enjoyable, fun activities decreased their likelihood of future engagement in these activities. Naming this phenomenon the "undermining effect," he explained that rewards change the perceived locus of causality for the behavior from internal to external, and thus undermine feelings of autonomy. Substantial research has expanded upon this phenomenon, showing that a variety of controlling conditions can undermine intrinsic motivation in different domains of life, including school, work, health care settings, and sports (see other chapters in this volume).

Similar dynamics are likely at work when individuals view extrinsic pursuits as highly valuable. For example, Rogers (1964) and Maslow (1956) both believed that when parents do not provide supportive environments, their children forego their own values expressive of growth motivation and instead focus on security and others' values. Research also supports the idea that a variety of environmental conditions that do not support psychological need satisfaction result in an increased focus on extrinsically oriented values. Much of this work has examined how environmental factors influence the extrinsic values of materialism and financial success.

At the level of the family, Kasser, Ryan, Zax, and Sameroff (1995) assessed the values of a heterogeneous group of 18 year olds, comparing teens who highly valued materialistic goals with those more oriented toward the intrinsic values of self-acceptance, affiliation, and community involvement. The teens' mothers were assessed for *nurturance* by interviews with the mothers and surveys the mothers completed. As expected, teens who were especially focused on the extrinsic value of financial success had less nurturant mothers. Similar results have been reported by Williams, Cox, Hedberg, and Deci (2000), who found that high school students highly oriented toward extrinsic values, in comparison to intrinsic values, perceived their parents as relatively low in autonomy support. Other research not informed by SDT similarly shows that materialistic children are more likely to have experienced family situations less supportive of the self's needs and desires for growth and integration. For example, Rindfleisch, Burroughs, and Denton (1997) found that materialistic children were likely to come from homes broken by divorce, and Cohen and Cohen (1996) reported that materialistic children had more punishing and possessive parents. Our understanding of these results is that nonnurturant families do not provide environments conducive to personal growth, self-expression, and feeling free and close to others. As a consequence of these experiences of control, children are less likely to pursue activities relevant to the self's growth motivations, and instead focus on materialistic and extrinsic pursuits, in line with capitalistic societies' suggestion that such pursuits provide a sense of worth and security.

Extra-familial factors have also been associated with a stronger focus on the extrinsic value of materialism. For example, both Kasser et al. (1995) and Cohen and Cohen (1996) found that materialistic children were more likely to come from disadvantaged socio-economic backgrounds. Interestingly, in longitudinal and cross-cultural studies of national materialism, the political scientists Abramson and Inglehart (1995) similarly showed that people living in relatively poor nations or economically difficult times were highly likely to value materialistic pursuits for their governments. Along with these political scientists, we suggest that living in disadvantaged socio-economic situations may ultimately result in less satisfaction of the self's needs for growth and integration, as poverty and dangerous neighborhoods can lead people to feel less secure, less trusting of others, and less able to express themselves. Further, individuals may look to wealth as a means to feel good about themselves, escape their insecure situation, and provide themselves with the food, shelter, and clothing that are necessary to survive in this world.

Two other national characteristics have recently been identified that thwart need satisfaction and are in turn associated with materialistic values. First, Khanna and Kasser (1999) reanalyzed Abramson and Inglehart's (1995) data and showed that nations that have experienced significant national upheaval since World War II were more likely to be materialistic, even after controlling for national wealth. Being occupied or invaded by a foreign power and undergoing internal revolutions are obviously unlikely to provide many opportunities for citizens to express their strivings for growth and autonomy. Second, Kasser and Sharma (1999) found that females were especially likely to desire wealthy, high-status mates when they lived in nations that did not support reproductive freedom or provide equal opportunity for female education. Thus, it appears that when women do not have the opportunity to control their own destiny (i.e., do not have satisfaction of the autonomy need) they will become more extrinsic and materialistic in their values and thus in the valences they place on various potential mates.

In sum, studies investigating characteristics of people's families, socio-economic situations, and nations support the proposition that people are more likely to orient toward extrinsic values when environmental conditions do not support their needs, as would be suggested by almost three decades of laboratory and field research from the self-determination perspective. Why is this the case? It seems most likely that when individuals see that the inherent desires for growth, expression, autonomy, and relatedness are unlikely to be satisfied in the present situation, they turn towards extrinsic values as a compensatory strategy to attain at least some satisfaction and some feelings of worth and security. Extrinsic values may seem to hold the promise of providing security, love, and feelings of self-worth, but as we will see momentarily, extrinsic values do not keep this promise.

Proposition Six: People Oriented Toward Intrinsic Values Experience Greater Well-being than People Oriented Toward Extrinsic Values

As described throughout this paper, self-determination theory maintains that optimal growth and well-being occur when the self is intrinsically motivated, expressing its integrative tendencies and satisfying its psychological needs for autonomy, competence, and relatedness. Research on the reasons people engage in a variety of activities supports the idea that people who feel more autonomous about their behaviors also report greater well-being, as does recent work demonstrating that positive experiences of autonomy, competence, and relatedness all help an individual have a "good day" (see Sheldon, this volume).

Above, I reviewed evidence that intrinsic values are associated with greater satisfaction of needs for autonomy and relatedness, while the reverse is true for extrinsic values. This suggests that people who pursue intrinsic values should have relatively high well-being, as their values are likely to lead them to engage in experiences associated with greater need satisfaction and more opportunities for intrinsic motivation and integration, the very experiences the self needs in order to thrive. In contrast, people who have relatively high values for extrinsic pursuits should have relatively low well-being, for such a value configuration signals an alienation from the growth processes of the true self and prompts more frequent engagement in activities counter to, or at least unrelated to, need satisfaction. Indeed, research from a number of investigators strongly supports this proposition, as briefly reviewed below.

In the first demonstration of this phenomenon, Kasser and Ryan (1993) found in two samples of college students that intrinsically oriented individuals reported more self-actualization, more subjective vitality, less anxiety, and less depression than individuals who placed a high value on financial success. Following up on these results with a heterogeneous sample of 18-year-olds, Kasser and Ryan (1993) showed in a third study that intrinsically oriented late adolescents were more socially productive, had fewer conduct disorders, and were rated by interviewers as showing higher overall global functioning.

While this research examined only the extrinsic value of financial success, later work has examined a fuller array of values. For example, in two studies, Sheldon and Kasser (1995) showed that the more people's personal strivings (Emmons, 1989) helped bring them towards intrinsically oriented possible futures, the higher their self-actualization, positive affect, openness to experience, and life satisfaction. In contrast, an extrinsic orientation was associated with less self-actualization and openness to experience and with more frequent engagement in distracting activities such as smoking and drinking. Kasser and Ryan (1996) expanded on these results by showing in a sample of adults that relatively high importance ratings for intrinsic values were associated with greater self-actualization and vitality and with less depression and physical symptoms, while the reverse was true for extrinsic values. In a second study, with college students, Kasser and Ryan (1996) replicated these results and showed that intrinsically oriented people were less narcissistic and less likely to report physical symptoms in diary reports than were extrinsically oriented people. Finally, Kasser and Ryan (2001) have shown that intrinsically oriented values were associated with greater self-esteem and well-being and with less drug and alcohol use, while the reverse was true for extrinsically oriented values. In sum, a wide variety of indicators of quality of life have been consistently associated with people's values, such that intrinsic values were associated with greater well-being and less distress, while the reverse was true of extrinsic values.

Notably, all of the results reported above have come from samples composed of U.S. citizens. More recently, however, this basic pattern of results has been replicated for German (Schmuck et al., 2000) and Russian (Ryan et al., 1999) college students. Parallel results have also been found in preliminary analyses of South Korean students (Kim, Kasser, & Lee, 2002) and Singaporeans studying marketing (Kasser & Ahuvia, 2002). Cross-cultural replications of findings originally demonstrated in the U.S. thus support the idea that the dynamics posited by SDT may be universal, as opposed to culturally specific.

As with the other propositions, researchers using different theories and different operational definitions of values and well-being have found results similar to those reported above, although they have focused primarily on the extrinsic value of financial success. For example, in their study of the *Diagnostic and Statistical Manual* diagnoses of adolescents with different value systems, Cohen and Cohen (1996) concluded that "the priority put on being rich was related positively to almost every Axis I and Axis II diagnosis assessed in this study, for the most part significantly so" (p. 139). Similarly, investigators in the area of consumer research have consistently documented negative relations between well-being and materialistic values (see Sirgy, 1999 for a review).

The "what" and the "why" of values. One interesting area of research relevant to this sixth proposition, but still in its infancy, concerns whether the relations of value and goal contents to well-being might depend on the *reasons* one pursues the values. That is, the basic thrust of the work reviewed thus far suggests that when people are highly focused on intrinsic values, their well-being will be relatively high, whereas when people are highly focused on extrinsic values, their well-being will be relatively low. Self-determination research also suggests, however, that pursuing goals for autonomous, well-internalized reasons (i.e., because it feels like a true choice) is more beneficial for well-being than pursuing goals for controlled, poorly-internalized reasons (i.e., because of external or introjected pressures and compulsions; see Sheldon, this volume). Thus, the benefit of pursuing intrinsic values may be mitigated when such values are nonself-determined, while the negative effects of a strong focus on extrinsic values may be lessened if such values are autonomously regulated.

Carver and Baird (1998) recently examined this possibility by examining how college students' self-actualization was related to: (a) the value they placed on financial success and community feeling aspirations; and (b) the reasons they pursued each of these aspirations. Replicating previous work, Carver and Baird showed that the relative centrality of financial success aspirations was negatively correlated with self-actualization, while the reverse was true for community feeling aspirations. Further, individuals who reported pursuing either aspiration for autonomous, well-internalized reasons scored high in self-actualization, while individuals who reported pursuing either aspiration for controlled, poorly internalized reasons scored low in self-actualization. Notably, however, regression analyses showed relatively little decrease in the strength of the negative relation between financial success values and self-actualization, even after controlling for the reasons the values were pursued. Thus, it appears that both the "what" and the "why" of values and goals play important roles in understanding people's well-being (Ryan, Sheldon, Kasser, & Deci, 1996).

Conclusions

In this chapter I have tried to sketch out what a self-determination theory of values might look like, in the hopes that further work can better integrate this theory with the extant literature on values. I hope to have shown that some basic tenets of SDT are echoed in what other value theoreticians have suggested and that much empirical research on values is consistent with the self-determination perspective.

To summarize, I suggested that valuing is ideally a function of the self, which is that integrative center that is attempting to actualize itself, be intrinsically motivated, and satisfy its needs for autonomy, competence, and relatedness. When the self is the source of valuing, people are likely to hold intrinsic values strongly in their system of values and thus engage in behaviors that support growth and satisfy needs. As a consequence, intrinsically oriented people are likely to experience greater well-being. However, people are sometimes exposed to controlling, nonsupportive environments and as a result hold extrinsic values, concerned with rewards and praise, as more central to their sense of what is important in life. Because extrinsic values typically orient people away from the self's growth and needs, such a focus is associated with lower well-being.

Much of the research reviewed in the context of the six propositions provides additional support for some fundamental aspects of SDT. For example, cross-cultural replication of the organization of values in terms of the intrinsic/extrinsic distinction and of their differential relationships with well-being is important evidence that the psychological needs that SDT claims to be universal may indeed be so. Additionally, the fact that both Schwartz (1996) and Kasser and Ryan (1996) empirically documented that values representing autonomy and relatedness needs were highly associated in people's value systems supports Ryan's (1993) claim that these two needs are not necessarily in conflict, as some theorists had suggested. Further, the fact that controlling characteristics of familial, socio-economic, and national environments predict a focus on extrinsic values in a manner parallel to research on the undermining of intrinsic motivation supports the generalizability of this phenomenon. Finally, the possibility that valuing can be a means by which the self selects experiences supportive of growth and avoids experiences that work against growth expands SDT's understanding of how to facilitate well-being and health.

To conclude, I by no means believe that the six propositions made here provide a comprehensive theory of values. Nor do I believe that they successfully explain all of the findings and suggestions in the value literature. However, I do hope that these propositions sketch out a picture that integrates existing work and allows for a fuller portrait of values to emerge in the future.

References

Abramson, P. R., & Inglehart, R. (1995). *Value change in global perspective.* Ann Arbor, MI: The University of Michigan Press.

Carver, C. S., & Baird, E. (1998). The American dream revisited: Is it what you want or why you want it that matters? *Psychological Science, 9,* 289-292.

Carver, C. S., & Scheier, M. (1982). Control theory: A useful conceptual framework for personality, social, clinical and health psychology. *Psychological Bulletin, 92,* 111-135.

Cohen, P., & Cohen, J. (1996). *Life values and adolescent mental health.* Mahwah, NJ: Lawrence Erlbaum.

Deci, E. L. (1971). Effects of externally mediated rewards on intrinsic motivation. *Journal of Personality and Social Psychology, 18,* 105-115.

Deci, E. L., & Ryan, R. M. (1985a). The general causality orientations scale: Self-determination in personality. *Journal of Research in Personality, 19,* 109-134.

Deci, E. L., & Ryan, R. M. (1985b). *Intrinsic motivation and self-determination in human behavior.* New York: Plenum.

Emmons, R. A. (1989). The personal strivings approach to personality. In L. A. Pervin (Ed.) *Goal concepts in personality and social psychology* (pp. 87-126). Hillsdale, NJ: Erlbaum.

Feather, N. T. (1992). Values, valences, expectations, and actions. *Journal of Social Issues, 48,* 109-124.

Feather, N. T. (1995). Values, valences, and choice: The influence of values on the perceived attractiveness and choice of alternatives. *Journal of Personality and Social Psychology, 68,* 1135-1151.

Guttman, L. (1968). A general nonmetric technique for finding the smallest coordinate space for a configuration of points. *Psychometrica, 33,* 469-506.

Hermans, H. J. M. (1987). Self as an organized system of valuations: Toward a dialogue with the person. *Journal of Counseling Psychology, 34,* 10-19.

Kasser, T., & Ahuvia, A. (2002). Materialistic values and well-being in business students. *European Journal of Social Psychology, 32,* 137-146.

Kasser, T., & Ryan, R. M. (1993). A dark side of the American dream: Correlates of financial success as a central life aspiration. *Journal of Personality and Social Psychology, 65,* 410-422.

Kasser, T., & Ryan, R. M. (1996). Further examining the American dream: Differential correlates of intrinsic and extrinsic goals. *Personality and Social Psychology Bulletin, 22,* 280-287.

Kasser, T., & Ryan, R. M. (2001). Be careful what you wish for: Optimal functioning and the relative attainment of intrinsic and extrinsic goals. In P. Schmuck & K. M. Sheldon (Eds.), *Life goals and well-being.* Göttingen: Hogrefe and Huber.

Kasser, T., Ryan, R. M., Zax, M., & Sameroff, A. J. (1995). The relations of maternal and social environments to late adolescents' materialistic and prosocial aspirations. *Developmental Psychology, 31*, 907-914.

Kasser, T., & Sharma, Y. S. (1999). Reproductive freedom, educational equality, and females' preference for mates high in resource acquisition characteristics. *Psychological Science, 10*, 374-377.

Khanna, S., & Kasser, T. (1999). *National upheaval and materialism.* Manuscript in preparation, Knox College, Galesburg, IL.

Kim, Y., Kasser, T., & Lee, H. (2002). *Self-concepts, aspirations, and well-being in South Korea and the United States.* Unpublished manuscript, University of Rochester.

Maslow, A. H. (1954). *Motivation and personality.* New York: Harper & Row.

Maslow, A. H. (1956). Defense and growth. *Merrill-Palmer Quarterly, 3*, 36-47.

Maslow, A. H., (Ed.) (1959). *New knowledge in human values.* New York: Harper.

Murray, H. A. (1938). *Explorations in personality.* New York: Oxford University Press.

Richins, M. L., & Dawson, S. (1992). A consumer values orientation for materialism and its measurement: Scale development and validation. *Journal of Consumer Research, 19*, 303-316.

Rindfleisch, A., Burroughs, J. E., & Denton, F. (1997). Family structure, materialism, and compulsive consumption. *Journal of Consumer Research, 23*, 312-325.

Rogers, C. R. (1964). Toward a modern approach to values: The valuing process in the mature person. *Journal of Abnormal and Social Psychology, 68*, 160-167.

Rokeach, M. (1973). *The nature of human values.* New York: Free Press.

Ryan, R. M. (1993). Agency and organization: Intrinsic motivation, autonomy, and the self in psychological development. In J. Jacobs (Ed.), *Nebraska symposium on motivation: Developmental perspectives on motivation* (Vol. 40, pp. 1-56). Lincoln: University of Nebraska Press.

Ryan, R. M. (1995). Psychological needs and the facilitation of integrative processes. *Journal of Personality, 63*, 397-427.

Ryan, R. M., Chirkov, V. I., Little, T. D., Sheldon, K. M., Timoshina, E., and Deci, E. L. (1999). The American dream in Russia: Extrinsic aspirations and well-being in two cultures. *Personality and Social Psychology Bulletin, 25*, 1509-1524.

Ryan, R. M., & Connell, J. P. (1989). Perceived locus of causality and internalization: Examining reasons for acting in two domains. *Journal of Personality and Social Psychology, 57*, 749-761.

Ryan, R. M., Sheldon, K. M., Kasser, T., & Deci, E. L. (1996). All goals are not created equal: An organismic perspective on the nature of goals and their regulation. In P. M. Gollwitzer & J. A. Bargh (Eds.), *The psychology of action: Linking cognition and motivation to behavior* (pp. 7-26). New York: Guilford.

Schmuck, P., Kasser, T., & Ryan, R. M. (2000). Intrinsic and extrinsic goals: Their structure and relationship to well-being in German and U.S. college students. *Social Indicators Research, 50*, 225-241.

Schwartz, S. H. (1992). Universals in the content and structure of values: Theory and empirical tests in 20 countries. In M. Zanna (Ed.), *Advances in experimental social psychology (Vol. 25)* (pp. 1-65). New York: Academic Press.

Schwartz, S. H. (1994). Are there universal aspects in the content and structure of values? *Journal of Social Issues, 50*, 19-45.

Schwartz, S. H. (1996). Value priorities and behavior: Applying a theory of integrated value systems. In C. Seligman, J. M. Olson, & M. P. Zanna (Eds.), *The psychology of values: The Ontario symposium, Vol. 8* (pp. 1-24). Hillsdale, NJ: Erlbaum.

Schwartz, S. H., Sagiv, L., & Boehnke, K. (2000). Worries and values. *Journal of Personality, 68*, 309-346.

Seligman, C., Olson, J. M., & Zanna, M. P. (Eds.) (1996). *The psychology of values: The Ontario symposium, Vol. 8.* Hillsdale, NJ: Erlbaum.

Sheldon, K. M., & Kasser, T. (1995). Coherence and congruence: Two aspects of personality integration. *Journal of Personality and Social Psychology, 68*, 531-543.

Sheldon, K. M., & Kasser, T. (1998). Pursuing personal goals: Skills enable progress, but not all progress is beneficial. *Personality and Social Psychology Bulletin, 24*, 1319-1331.

Sirgy, M. J. (1998). Materialism and quality of life. *Social Indicators Research, 43*, 227-260.

White, R. K. (1951). *Value analysis, the nature and use of the method.* Glen Gardner, NJ: Libertarian Press.

Williams, G. C., Cox, E. M., Hedberg, V. A., & Deci, E. L. (2000). Extrinsic life goals and health risk behaviors in adolescents. *Journal of Applied Social Psychology, 30*, 1756-1771.

7: Social Contagion of Motivational Orientations

T. Cameron Wild
Michael E. Enzle
University of Alberta

The pursuit of activities 'for their own sake' is a compelling human phenomenon that has been a focus of scholarly attention by a variety of philosophers and psychologists (Berlyne, 1966; Dewey, 1934; White, 1959). The appeal of such intrinsically motivated behavior lies partly in our beliefs that it facilitates creativity and aesthetic sensitivity, empathy and depth in interpersonal relations, and personal well-being. Empirical studies reviewed in this volume and elsewhere (Hodgins, Koestner, & Duncan, 1996; Sheldon & Elliot, 1999; Wild, Kuiken, & Schopflocher, 1995) suggest that these beliefs are correct and that intrinsic motivation is indeed associated with these outcomes. Thus, there has been longstanding interest in studying the conditions that foster or impede intrinsically motivated behavior.

One significant line of inquiry has focused on the interface between social events and motivational processes. Over a quarter century of research shows the detrimental effects of social controls on intrinsically motivated behavior. These detrimental effects on interest and involvement in activities have been demonstrated for a variety of social controls, including contingent rewards (Deci, 1971; Lepper, Greene, & Nisbett, 1973), deadlines (Amabile, DeJong, & Lepper, 1976), surveillance (Lepper & Greene, 1975), and imposed performance evaluation (Amabile, 1979; Harackiewicz, Manderlink, & Sansone, 1984). In contrast, intrinsic motivation is preserved or enhanced when social events minimize control, promote choice, and acknowledge feelings (Koestner, Ryan, Bernieri, & Holt, 1984; Zuckerman, Porac, Lathin, Smith, & Deci, 1978). Self-determination theory (SDT) (Deci & Ryan, 1985, 1987) provides an influential account of these findings. From this perspective, controlling social events undermine personal

Preparation of the chapter was supported in part by a grant from the Social Sciences and Humanities Research Council of Canada (#410-92-0464) to the second author.

autonomy, producing an internal-to-external shift in the perceived locus of causality for one's behavior (deCharms, 1968; Heider, 1958), with a corresponding decrease in intrinsic motivation.

It is tempting to conclude from the preceding evidence that the objective presence or absence of controlling social events is the key factor influencing changes in intrinsic motivation. Indeed, this conclusion is implicit in recent critiques of research on the influence of task rewards on intrinsic motivation (e.g., Eisenberger & Cameron, 1996), which assume that motivational processes are determined only by objective characteristics of rewards, such that we can determine when "reinforcement might have a detrimental effect, no effect, or an incremental effect" on intrinsic motivation (p. 1164). A closer reading of the literature suggests, however, that one's experience of social events must be taken into account when discussing changes in intrinsic motivation prompted by rewards or other events (Deci, Koestner, & Ryan, 1999). In particular, the locus of undermining effects appears to lie not in the *objective facts* of social control or choice, but rather in one's *subjective interpretation* of the context of activity engagement. Thus, when people believe that performance-contingent rewards affirm their competence, rather than control their behavior, no attenuation of intrinsic motivation occurs (Harackiewicz, 1979; Ryan, Mims, & Koestner, 1983). Similarly, intrinsic motivation is not undermined when adults set limits on children's behavior by using informational feedback, as opposed to controlling feedback (Koestner, Ryan, Bernieri, & Holt, 1984). Other research shows that the mere presence of surveillance does not undermine intrinsic motivation if people believe that they are being watched out of curiosity, rather than with an intent to control their behavior (Enzle & Anderson, 1993). Finally, provision of choice does not enhance intrinsic motivation for individuals with an interdependent sense of self, but does among individuals who have an independent sense of self (Iyengar & Lepper, 1999).

Self-determination theory accounts for the malleability of effects of social events on motivational processes by invoking the concept of *functional significance*. Thus, events related to the initiation and regulation of behavior can facilitate informational, controlling, or amotivating construals, and the "relative salience of these three aspects to a person determines the functional significance of the event" with regard to intrinsic motivation (Deci & Ryan, 1985, p. 64). The program of research described in this chapter takes its starting point from this phenomenological aspect of self-determination theory and the importance of construal processes as mediators of the relationship between social events and motivational orientations. Of particular interest to us is the ability of interpersonal cues about others' motives to shape the functional significance of social events in subtle ways that lead people to either become imaginatively involved in activities or to devalue them. We also suspect that the functional significance of social events does not solely depend on the *direct* application of social controls on individuals. Instead, we propose a more insidious route to undermining effects wherein people self-generate changes in intrinsic motivation on the basis of perceiving others' motives for engaging in activities. The implications of this approach include the idea that motivational orientations toward activities can spontaneously spread from person to person solely on the basis of interpersonal cues. In the following sections, we (a) review some of the literature on the importance of construal processes as determinants of motivational orientations toward activities, (b) review research demonstrating the impact of perceiving others' motives on the perceiver's own motivational orientation to activities, (c) review evidence supporting our account of the mechanism underlying these behavioral results: a self-generated expectancy formation process during social interaction, (d) highlight theoretical implications of this model in relation to attribution theory, behavioral confirmation, and modeling, and (e) outline new directions for work in this area.

Contextual Framing of Activities and Intrinsic Motivation

The importance of construal processes in mediating the relation between social events and motivational orientations toward activities has been demonstrated in many studies. One important approach to this issue has emphasized the impact of task labels and activity goals on intrinsic motivation (Sansone & Harackiewicz, 1995; Harackiewicz & Sansone, 1991). For example, if people are induced to ascribe boredom and obligation to a task, they are less intrinsically motivated than if they ascribe enjoyment, challenge, and interest to the same activity (Porac & Meindl, 1982). Tang and Baumeister (1984) similarly found that merely labeling an activity as work increased intrinsic motivation for those who held positive attitudes toward work, compared to individuals who did not hold such attitudes. Sansone, Sachau, and Weir (1989, Study 2) labeled a computer game as an index of skill or as a fantasy-related pastime and observed that task instructions designed to enhance performance decreased intrinsic motivation under the fantasy label but increased intrinsic motivation under the skill label. More recently, Harackiewicz and Elliot (1993) manipulated the extent to which people viewed a task as demonstrating ability (performance goals) or as an opportunity to develop one's skills (mastery goals) and found that performance goals enhanced intrinsic motivation among individuals scoring high in achievement motivation, while mastery goals enhanced intrinsic motivation for individuals low in achievement orientation (for additional work along these lines and expansion to approach and avoidance performance goals, see Elliot & Harackiewicz, 1994, 1996).

The preceding research is consistent with the notion that contextual framing of activities can be a potent source of influence on intrinsic motivation. However, these findings may have limited ecological validity because in all cases contextual interpretations of the activity were directly provided for people. That is, the experimenters provided task labels or activity goals to respondents, who were then evaluated with regard to interest in the task. These experimental operations raise the important question of how task labels become salient to individuals in the first instance, during unconstrained social interactions. In at least a partial answer, we propose a social contagion model that differentially cues interpretations of activities and activates cognitive-perceptual 'sets' that can undermine intrinsic motivation.

Social Contagion of Motivational Orientations Via Person Perception

An assumption underlying much of the experimental literature on intrinsic motivation is that undermining effects depend on the *direct* application of social controls to people. Thus, in a typical study, people are or are not constrained—by task rewards, task labels, performance feedback, activity goals, activity choice, and so on—and then are assessed to determine the motivational impact of these events. In contrast, our conceptual approach assumes that direct constraints such as these can be sufficient, but are not necessary, to undermine interest and creativity during activity engagement. For example, all that may be required to undermine intrinsic motivation are perceptions that *others* in one's shared social environment are extrinsically motivated. We devised a simple method to assess this prediction. People were brought into the laboratory ostensibly to participate in a teaching-learning session. The teacher, actually an experimental confederate, was portrayed as either an intrinsically motivated volunteer, or (in another condition) as extrinsically motivated to engage in the teaching session. Then, all individuals received a standardized lesson that instructed them to a standard criterion level of performance. A central aim of the research was to rule out alternative explanations of contagion effects based on exposure to different teaching styles. Therefore, confederate teachers were blind to conditions so they could not portray different motivational orientations in different conditions. Only participants' beliefs about their teacher's motivational orientation (rather than actual teacher behaviors) were manipulated. We then assessed the social perceiver's intrinsic motivation in relation to the activity that had just been learned. Of particular interest was the extent to which perceptions of the teacher's motivation affected students' interest in the activity.

In the first study in this series (Wild, Enzle, & Hawkins, 1992), musical novices were taught an introductory piano lesson. In a perceived intrinsically motivated teacher condition, participants were led to believe that the teacher had volunteered to develop and deliver piano lessons in the laboratory. In a perceived extrinsically motivated teacher condition, participants believed that the teacher had agreed to the same activities in return for $25. Teachers themselves were blind to conditions and were trained in a neutral teaching style that was neither autonomy supportive nor controlling. All participants received this standardized lesson in which they were familiarized with the keyboard and were taught a short song. After all participants met a skill acquisition criterion of playing the song correctly twice, the teacher was led to another room, ostensibly for an interview about the teaching process. Perceiver-students were then left alone in the laboratory for 10 minutes, and a concealed audiotape machine recorded participants' free-play behavior on the piano. Then, participants were administered a short questionnaire to assess their enjoyment and interest in learning, their perceptions of the teacher, and their mood following the lesson.

Results showed that perceiver-subjects in both conditions required the same number of trials and time to learn the song to the criterion level. However, participants who perceived their teacher as intrinsically motivated enjoyed the lesson more, reported more positive affect following the lesson, and reported that they were more interested in learning new piano skills, compared to participants who perceived their teacher as extrinsically motivated. Analyzing the free-play activity revealed that perceiver-subjects in both conditions exhibited the same duration of piano playing. However, participants who learned from a teacher they believed to be intrinsically motivated engaged in greater creativity and exploratory behavior. In contrast, participants who learned from a teacher they believed to be extrinsically motivated exhibited "functional fixedness" (McGraw, 1978) in their activity engagement. They merely played the criterion song repeatedly. Recall that these effects on perceivers' intrinsic motivation did *not* occur as a function of real differences in teaching content or teaching style, nor were they related to any direct constraints, task labels, or activity goals provided to participants. Instead, participants appear to have *self-generated* motivational orientations toward learning on the basis of their perceptions of the teacher's motivation for engaging in the activity. In short, the motivational orientation of the teacher appeared to have "infected" the student, despite the fact that no labels or goals were provided to participants and that all learners received the same standardized lesson and learned to the same criterion level.

Another study in this series (Wild, Enzle, Nix, & Deci, 1997, Study 2) attempted to replicate these results using a different task. This study also extended the focus to determine whether the social contagion of motivational orientations toward learning could spontaneously spread from person to person during social interaction. To accomplish this goal, we used a serial teaching-learning procedure in which a confederate teacher taught a skill to a first learner, who was then asked to instruct a second learner. This study used a rope-restoration magic trick as the focal task, and as in the first study, the cover story emphasized that the researchers were interested in the teacher's performance. The perceived motivation manipulation was exactly the same as used in Wild et al. (1992). All perceivers were taught using a neutral teaching style, and received the same standardized lesson. After meeting a learning criterion of performing the magic trick correctly twice, learners were asked whether they would be willing to teach another person the rope restoration illusion. All participants agreed, and the first learner then had 10 minutes to teach a second participant the skill. Following the transmission teaching session, both sets of learners were given a questionnaire to assess enjoyment, interest in learning, and mood.

Results from this study replicated effects of perceived motivation on self-reported measures of intrinsic motivation found in Wild et al. (1992). Specifically, first-generation learners who were taught the magic trick by an apparently intrinsically motivated teacher reported greater levels of enjoyment and interest in learning than those taught by a supposedly extrinsically motivated teacher, despite receiving identical lessons and learning to the same criterion level. In addition, we found that lower levels of task enjoyment, interest in learning, and positive mood were also exhibited by the second generation learners in the educational chain. As in the first study in this series, effects on first-generation perceivers' intrinsic motivation were *not* exhibited as a function of differential teaching content or teaching style, nor were they related to any direct constraints, task labels, or activity goals provided to participants. As before, participants appear to have *self-generated* motivational orientations toward learning on the basis of their perceptions of the teacher's motivation for engaging in the activity. But in addition, the motivational orientation toward the activity adopted by the first learner also influenced the second learner in the chain, lending support to our proposal that the social contagion of motivational orientations toward learning can spontaneously spread from person to person during social interactions, without providing task labels or activity goals to participants.

Taken together, these studies provide support for the proposal that direct application of social controls—task rewards, task labels, performance feedback, activity goals, activity choice, and so on—can be sufficient, but are not necessary to undermine intrinsic motivation. Evidently, learners in these two studies closely calibrated their own level of interest in the activity to the motivational orientation perceived in their teachers. The mere perception of another person's motivation for engaging in an activity affected the perceiver's own intrinsic motivation.

Expectancy Formation Processes Underlying the Social Contagion Effect

The preceding studies clearly show that there are significant consequences to perceiving others' motives for engaging in activities and that these consequences can spread from person to person in unconstrained social interaction.

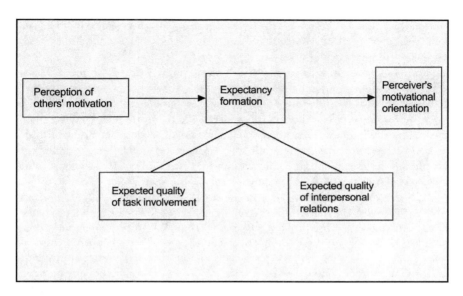

Figure 7.1. Social Contagion Model

The next step in the development of our model was to examine mechanisms that underlie this social contagion effect. We propose that, in many common dyadic interactions (e.g., between a teacher and student, a parent and child, a health care provider and patient, a manager and subordinate), perceptions of the other's motivation affects the formation of expectancies that shape the functional significance (Deci & Ryan, 1985, 1987) of events in that social context. As shown in Figure 7-1, perceiving others' motives for engaging in an activity cues differential expectancies for (a) quality of involvement (i.e., interest, pleasure) that the perceiver is likely to experience herself or himself during task engagement, and (b) quality of interpersonal relations (i.e., control or autonomy support) that is likely to ensue during social interaction. This account assumes that memories of past episodes of social control or autonomy support are blended with current perceptions of others' motives to form temporary expectations about how enjoyable and interesting an activity is likely to be, how controlling or autonomy supportive the other person is likely to be, and so forth. In turn, these expectancies form a cognitive "set" that is used to interpret subsequent activity involvement and interpersonal relations, thus affecting the perceiver's own intrinsic motivation.

We devised a story comprehension task to assess the proposed expectancy-cueing mechanism, wherein participants read a short story depicting an individual who adopted either an extrinsic or an intrinsic motivational orientation toward an activity. Immediately after reading the story, participants were asked to generate interpretations of this interpersonal target's motives and/or to rate expectations about the target's quality of involvement and quality of interpersonal relations (i.e., expected interest and expected support of autonomy) that were likely to occur in the described situation.

The first study in this series (Wild, Enzle, Nix, & Deci, 1997) used a two-group experimental design paralleling the behavioral studies reviewed earlier (extrinsic versus intrinsic motivation of an interpersonal target; Wild et al., 1992). Each version depicted an interpersonal target, Pat, who was a student spending the summer by working and giving walking tours of Nantucket Island. In one condition, three story excerpts were written to facilitate perceptions of extrinsic motivation for engaging in the tour activity: (1) "After his regular job, Pat spends his afternoons as a paid tour guide for the Historical Society on Nantucket Island," (2) "Pat earns $25 for each two-hour tour he conducts," and (3) "The last stop on the tour is the Ship's Inn, where Pat often stays afterward to reflect on the money he'll have acquired by the end of the summer." In the other condition, the same three excerpts were altered to facilitate perceptions of intrinsic motivation: (1) "After his regular job, Pat spends his afternoons as a volunteer tour guide for the Historical Society on Nantucket Island," (2) "Pat volunteers two hours of his time for each tour he conducts," and (3) "The last stop on the tour is the Ship's Inn, where Pat often stays afterward to reflect on the experiences he'll have acquired by the end of the summer." Aside from these alterations, both versions of the story were identical in content. Immediately after reading the story, participants were asked an open-ended question to assess perceived motivation of the interpersonal target: "Why did Pat give tours on Nantucket Island?" Then, participants completed a series of scale items to assess expectancies elicited following the reading of each vignette (e.g., expected enjoyment during activity engagement).

Free responses generated to the question "Why did Pat give the tours on Nantucket Island?" were rated by five judges who were blind to the hypotheses of the study and to experimental conditions. Each judge independently rated the free responses for intrinsic motivation, defined as activity engagement done solely for the interest or enjoyment of doing the task itself (e.g., "he enjoyed giving tours;" "because it was fun"), and for extrinsic motivation, defined as engaging in the activity for some type of external reward or contingency apart from the task itself (e.g., "for the money" or "for the cash he received" or "to get something on his resume"). Each rating was completed on a nine-point scale, where higher scores indicated increasing levels of intrinsic or extrinsic motivation represented by the response. Intraclass correlations across the five raters were $r = .87$ for both the intrinsic and the extrinsic motivation scores, indicating adequate interrater reliability. Composite perceived intrinsic and extrinsic scores were formed by averaging the intrinsic ratings and the extrinsic ratings across the five raters. Because the composite intrinsic and extrinsic motivation scores were very highly correlated ($r = -.98$), perceived extrinsic motivation scores were reverse scored and then averaged with the intrinsic scores to form a single perceived motivation score derived from the free responses, where higher scores indicate greater perceived intrinsic motivation in subjects' free responses.

As anticipated, greater perceptions of intrinsic motivation were judged in response to the free report item after reading about a volunteer than after reading about a paid employee. Results also revealed the predicted main effect of story type on expected enjoyment and value affixed to the activity, such that readers believed that giving tours would be an enjoyable and valuable activity to a greater extent when they read about a volunteer as opposed to a paid employee. Hierarchical multiple regression analyses were used to determine whether perceived motivation of the interpersonal target mediated expectancy formation. Perceived motivation predicted enjoyment-value when controlling for the effects of the independent variables, and most importantly, controlling for perceived motivation completely removed the effect of story type on expectations of enjoyment and value of the activity. Thus, perceptions of the interpersonal target's motivation (elicited via free-report) do mediate the relationship between exposure to an interpersonal target's motivation and beliefs about enjoyment and value of the activity.

Our second study in this series (Wild et al., 1997), attempted to replicate these findings using a different story context, and extended the research by taking into account a large literature demonstrating that people actively revise impressions of others during social perception (Fiske & Neuberg, 1990; Miller & Turnbull, 1986). Specifically, we wanted to determine whether the process of expectancy formation is malleable, depending on additional perceptions of the interpersonal target's motivation. The story materials described a protagonist who phoned a community college to inquire about receiving American Sign Language (ASL) lessons and an initial meeting with the ASL instructor, who represented the interpersonal target for the protagonist. Six versions of the story were designed, corresponding to a 2 (paid versus volunteer ASL instructor) X 3 (confirming, disconfirming, or no subsequent information about the instructor's motivation) factorial design. After reading one of the six versions of the story, participants were asked to respond to a free-report item, "Why did the instructor give ASL lessons?" and rated expectations about task involvement and quality of interpersonal relations on a battery of scales. Exactly the same coding procedure was used as in the first study to develop reliable measures of perceived motivation of the target, using the free response measures.

Results showed that participants who read about an extrinsically motivated instructor expected that task enjoyment and interest would be lower and that they would experience less positive affect and poorer quality of interpersonal relations, compared to participants who read about an intrinsically motivated instructor. Notably, these effects were completely reversed when additional information presented in the story disconfirmed the initial motivational orientation of the interpersonal target. As in the first study in this series, described above, mediational analyses demonstrated that controlling for perceived motivation of the interpersonal target completely removed or substantially reduced effects of the story materials on expectancy judgements.

A third study in this series provided further support for our expectancy formation model using a context and task with considerably more psychological interest and complexity: seeking treatment for alcohol problems (Wild, Cunningham, & Hobdon, 1998; Wild, Roberts, & Cooper, in press). In this context, clients often enter treatment due to formal and informal pressures to change their alcohol use (Weisner, 1990; Wild, Newton-Taylor, & Alletto, 1998). Similarly, counselors themselves can be constrained by external events (e.g., reward and schedule structures) to engage in treatment activities. In this study, we examined whether participants (i.e., the social perceivers) would believe that alcohol treatment is especially effective when both clients and counselors are perceived as adopting an intrinsic motivational orientation toward the activity. All participants read a short story depicting a drunk-driving offender (Chris) seeking help for alcohol problems. A 3 X 2 experimental design was used to portray one of three types of client motivation (Chris was interested in seeking help, Chris was ordered by a judge to seek help, Chris sought help to make a good impression on the court) and one of two types of counselor motivation (the counselor was paid or was a volunteer). Two scales were derived from a factor analysis to assess (a) expected interest in treatment, and (b) expected level of behavior change following treatment.

Results showed that maximal treatment efficacy was expected when readers perceived both clients and counselors as intrinsically motivated. In contrast, minimal treatment efficacy was expected when the client was believed to enter treatment only to manage impressions and when the counselor was perceived as extrinsically motivated. An interesting parallel to the second study in this series was that counselors who were perceived as intrinsically motivated were expected to reverse the detrimental effects of compulsory treatment and impression management on interest and efficacy of alcohol treatment.

The preceding results provide good support for the link between perceptions of others' motives and expectancy formation depicted in Figure 7-1. Across a wide variety of scenarios, people generate expectations of low levels of intrinsic motivation whenever they perceive that interpersonal targets have adopted an extrinsic motivational orientation toward activities. However, it also appears that the expectancy formation process is malleable, depending on additional perceptions of the interpersonal target's motives. Thus, two studies showed that expectancy formation effects can be reversed when information that disconfirms a target's motives is perceived.

Relation To Other Theoretical Accounts

The first series of studies described earlier demonstrates that direct constraints (e.g., rewards, task goals, task labels, etc.) are not necessary to undermine intrinsic motivation. Instead, undermining effects can occur when people merely perceive that an interpersonal target has adopted an extrinsic motivational orientation to an activity. The second series of studies illustrates mechanisms underlying this social contagion effect. When people perceive others' motives, they self-generate expectations about quality of task involvement and quality of interpersonal relations that put into place cognitive-perceptual sets that they use to interpret subsequent activity engagement. Thus, the functional significance (Deci & Ryan, 1985, 1987) of social events is in part determined by perceptions of others' motives as autonomy supportive or controlling. Taken as a whole, the research suggests an elaboration of self-determination theory wherein interpersonal contextual cues affect motivational processes in activity contexts in which no task labels or activity goals are provided for people. As such, the model has important implications for understanding motivational dynamics in a variety of settings in which dyadic interpersonal relations are at issue: teaching and learning, management, counseling, and parenting. In particular, the social contagion effect may play an important, though typically unacknowledged, role in determining outcomes in each of these domains. We turn now to a consideration of the relations between this approach and other possible accounts, derived from alternative theories.

Modeling and Imitative Learning

Perhaps the most obvious alternative account of some of the findings reported in this chapter comes from the perspective of behavioral imitation and modeling (Bandura, 1977; Bandura, Ross, & Ross, 1963; Hatfield, Cacioppo, & Rapson, 1994). From this viewpoint, perceptions of an interpersonal target's motivation and behavior cause people to imitate and model that individual's behavior. Cellar and Wade (1988) conducted a study that is relevant in this context. These researchers had participants perform a task after watching a videotape portraying an interpersonal target exhibiting either an intrinsic or extrinsic motivational orientation toward the activity. When perceivers saw the target exhibiting enjoyment and persistence, the perceiver-subjects also exhibited intrinsic motivation. Cellar and Wade (1988) proposed that perceptions of the target's activities led perceivers to imitate the model by constructing "work" or "play" scripts that guided their own behavior during activity engagement.

Imitation is a plausible contextual influence on motivational processes, but this account requires that interpersonal targets actually behave in a manner that demonstrates their intrinsic or extrinsic motivational orientation as they engage in the activity. Imitation cannot be a possible mechanism for the piano and magic learning results described earlier, however, because the teacher was blind to conditions and participants received identical instructional content and style across conditions. These aspects of the research reviewed earlier preclude an imitative modeling account of the social infection of motivational orientations. Indeed, a key difference between these accounts is that in the present model, people *self-generate* expectations in response to initial cues about an interpersonal target's motivation.

Behavioral Confirmation

Another relevant theoretical perspective on the social contagion model of intrinsic motivation is provided by research on interpersonal expectancies and behavioral confirmation (for reviews, see Fiske & Neuberg, 1990; Harris & Rosenthal, 1985; Hilton & Darley, 1991; Rosenthal & Rubin, 1978; Snyder, 1984, 1992; Snyder & Haugen, 1995). In a recent application of behavioral confirmation to intrinsic motivation, Pelletier and Vallerand (1996) used a teaching-learning task in which supervisors (teachers) were given no information about the student's motivation or were told that the student was either extrinsically motivated or intrinsically motivated. Their results showed that students who were believed by their teacher to be intrinsically motivated perceived their teacher as being more autonomy supportive and evidenced more intrinsic motivation, compared to students who were believed by their teachers to be extrinsically motivated. Pelletier and Vallerand (1996) argued that beliefs about the student's motivation initiated a behavioral confirmation process wherein teachers actually behaved in either a more controlling or a more autonomy supportive manner, thus influencing the student's own motivation toward the activity. This is an intriguing study suggesting that teacher expectations can influence their behavior, unwittingly confirming biased information about students' intrinsic motivation. However, it is limited by the same concerns raised earlier about ecological validity: the researchers provided information directly to social perceivers. In contrast, the present model provides an account of how perceiver's self-generate expectations and beliefs about interest and quality of interpersonal relations.

Imitative learning and behavioral confirmation theories are clearly relevant to the phenomenon under study because it is quite plausible that in unconstrained social interactions, people can model an interpersonal target's behavior and can use interpersonal cues to initiate a behavioral confirmation process. However, the research reviewed earlier demonstrates that there is another, typically unacknowledged, source of contextual interpersonal influence on intrinsic motivation. Merely perceiving another person's motivational orientation toward an activity elicits a cognitive set that provides a self-generated source of influence on intrinsic motivation.

Future Directions

The social contagion model described in this chapter provides a compelling and ecologically valid account of how interpersonal cues shape construal processes and how these mediate the relationship between social events and motivational processes. Nevertheless, there are many outstanding issues that need to be addressed in future work. On the antecedent side of the model, we need to arrive at a better understanding of the diverse factors that can affect whether or not people pay attention to others' motives. At a mundane level, cognitive load and attentional capacity demands might prevent individuals from perceiving interpersonal cues about others' motivation. In addition, there are plausible situational factors and personal characteristics that could make cues about others' motives more or less salient to the social perceiver. For example, the type of interpersonal relationship that exists between individuals will probably affect the extent to which perceivers pay attention to motivational orientation of others. Interactions among friends with an extensive history may well be less likely to elicit these effects than interactions among individuals who are not well acquainted or who are in differential positions of power (e.g., a manager and subordinate). Individual differences in social comparison orientation and/or perspective taking may moderate the effects described earlier. On the consequences side of the model, further research is required to understand the interplay of expectancies and behavior. One outstanding issue involves sorting out whether motivational effects of social perception occur just for a focal task or whether they generalize across different activities. Another issue involves the extent to which self-perceptions during activity engagement can shift cognitive sets previously elicited by perceiving others' motives. For example, it may be that certain kinds of activities or self-generated strategies can counter the detrimental effects of perceiving others' motives during activity engagement. By considering all of these issues, a better understanding of the boundary conditions of the theory will be achieved.

Conclusion

Teaching and learning occur in a wide variety of contexts both inside and outside the classroom, and the social contagion model outlined in this chapter has broad implications for educational interactions. Some educational contexts are defined mainly in terms of contractual obligations, as occurs in piano lessons taken from a paid teacher and coursework in the school system. Other educational contexts are defined without any reference to contractual obligations, as when friends share knowledge and skill with each other. This distinction may usefully be considered as a difference between *formal* and *informal* education. The social contagion model indicates that contextual knowledge about the presence or absence of extrinsic motivation on the part of teachers cues students' expectations about quality of task engagement (e.g., interest, curiosity) and about quality of interpersonal relations. The preceding research suggests that these expectancy-driven changes in cognitive "set" will produce learners who will approach their educational experience in a less intrinsically motivated manner than would be the case in informal educational contexts. However, the expectancy-cueing aspect of the model also suggests that these expectancies can be modified, depending on independent sources of confirming and disconfirming cues. Thus, informal educators can override initial expectations about high levels of task involvement and quality of interpersonal relations by engaging in a teaching style that is controlling, or by direct statements that contradict initial expectations of interest. Indeed, other educational research clearly shows the detrimental impact of controlling teaching styles on quality of learning (Flink, Boggiano, & Barrett, 1990). Conversely, formal educators could override initial student expectations of an uninteresting learning experience by demonstrating their own keen excitement about the topic and by encouraging self-determination in the learning process.

The implications of the social contagion model of motivation also extend beyond teaching and learning to the general issue of socialization and internalization of values, norms, knowledge, and skills. Socialization involves internalizing a set of core knowledge and skills from the cultural surround. In this context, "an important problem for adaptation and development is the promotion of a shift from regulation by external factors to self-regulation by internal factors" (Deci & Ryan, 1985, p. 129). The social contagion model has broad implications for understanding how people integrate the knowledge, skills, and values of their cultural context. In particular, we propose that the model is relevant for understanding the dynamic interplay that exists between cultural "stakeholders" (e.g., educators, parents, managers, health care providers) and individuals in the process of acculturation. Specifically, the social contagion model implies that the transmission of cultural knowledge and skills never takes place in a neutral context. Instead, it appears that people are easily able to self-generate expectations that will allow them to "tune out" or "tune into" the process of learning new cultural skills and knowledge depending on whether they believe they are participating in social interactions where educators, managers, health care professionals, and parents are extrinsically motivated. Thus, we believe that a better understanding of the process of internalizing cultural values, knowledge, and skills could be achieved by studying how people perceive the motives of cultural stakeholders.

References

Amabile, T. M. (1979). Effects of external evaluations on artistic creativity. *Journal of Personality and Social Psychology, 37*, 221-233.

Amabile, T. M., DeJong, W., & Lepper, M. R. (1976). Effects of externally imposed deadlines on intrinsic motivation. *Journal of Personality and Social Psychology, 34*, 92-98.

Bandura, A. (1977). *Social learning theory*. Englewood Cliffs, NJ: Prentice-Hall.

Bandura, A., Ross, D., & Ross, S. A. (1963). Vicarious reinforcement and imitative learning. *Journal of Abnormal and Social Psychology, 66*, 3-11.

Berlyne, D. E. (1966). Exploration and curiosity. *Science, 153*, 25-33.

Cellar, D. F., & Wade, K. (1988). Effect of behavioral modeling on intrinsic motivation and script-related recognition. *Journal of Applied Psychology, 73*, 181-192.

deCharms, R. (1968). *Personal causation: The internal affective determinants of behavior*. New York: Academic Press.

Deci, E. L. (1971). Effects of externally mediated rewards on intrinsic motivation. *Journal of Personality and Social Psychology, 18*, 105-115.

Deci, E. L., Koestner, R., & Ryan, R. M. (1999). A meta-analytic review of experiments examining the effects of extrinsic rewards on intrinsic motivation. *Psychological Bulletin, 125*, 627-668.

Deci, E. L., & Ryan, R. M. (1985). *Intrinsic motivation and self-determination in human behavior*. New York: Plenum.

Deci, E. L., & Ryan, R. M. (1987). The support of autonomy and the control of behavior. *Journal of Personality and Social Psychology, 53*, 1024-1037.

Dewey, J. (1934). *Art as experience*. New York: Capricorn Books.

Eisenberger, R., & Cameron, J. (1996). Detrimental effects of reward: Myth or reality? *American Psychologist, 51*, 1153-1166.

Elliot, A. J. & Harackiewicz, J. M. (1994). Goal setting, achievement orientation, and intrinsic motivation: A mediational analysis. *Journal of Personality and Social Psychology, 66*, 968-980.

Elliot, A. J. & Harackiewicz, J. M. (1996). Approach and avoidance achievement goals and intrinsic motivation: A mediational analysis. *Journal of Personality and Social Psychology, 70*, 461-475.

Enzle, M. E., & Anderson, S. C. (1993). Surveillant intentions and intrinsic motivation. *Journal of Personality and Social Psychology, 64*, 257-266.

Fiske, S. T., & Neuberg, S. L. (1990). A continuum of impression formation, from category-based to individuating processes: Influences of information and motivation on attention and interpretation. In M. Zanna (ed.), *Advances in experimental social psychology*, (Vol. 23). New York: Academic Press.

Flink, C. F., Boggiano, A. K., & Barrett, M. (1990). Controlling teaching strategies: Undermining children's self-determination and performance. *Journal of Personality and Social Psychology, 59*, 916-924.

Harackiewicz, J. (1979). The effects of reward contingency and performance feedback on intrinsic motivation. *Journal of Personality and Social Psychology, 37*, 1352-1363.

Harackiewicz, J. M. & Elliot, A. J. (1993). Achievement goals and intrinsic motivation. *Journal of Personality and Social Psychology, 65*, 904-915.

Harackiewicz, J., Manderlink, G., & Sansone, C. (1984). Rewarding pinball wizardry: The effects of evaluation on intrinsic interest. *Journal of Personality and Social Psychology, 47*, 287-300.

Harackiewicz, J. M. & Sansone, C. (1991). Goals and intrinsic motivation: You *can* get there from here. In M. L. Maehr & P. R. Pintrich (eds.), *Advances in motivation and education* (Vol. 7). Greenwich, CT: JAI Press.

Harris, M. J., & Rosenthal, R. (1985). Mediators of interpersonal expectancy effects: 31 meta-analyses. *Psychological Bulletin, 97*, 363-386.

Hatfield, E., Cacioppo, J. T., & Rapson, R. L. (1994). *Emotional contagion.* Paris: Cambridge University Press.

Heider, F. (1958). *The psychology of interpersonal relations.* New York: Wiley.

Hilton, J., & Darley, J. (1991). The effects of interaction goals on person perception. In M. P. Zanna (ed.), *Advances in experimental social psychology* (Vol. 23). New York: Academic Press.

Hodgins, H. S., Koestner, R., & Duncan, N. (1996). On the compatibility of autonomy and relatedness. *Personality and Social Psychology Bulletin, 22*, 227-237.

Iyengar, S. S., & Lepper, M. R. (1999). Rethinking the value of choice: A cultural perspective on intrinsic motivation. *Journal of Personality and Social Psychology, 76*, 349-366.

Koestner, R., Ryan, R. M., Bernieri, F., & Holt, K. (1984). Setting limits on children's behavior: The differential effects of controlling versus informational styles on intrinsic motivation and creativity. *Journal of Personality, 52*, 233-248.

Lepper, M. R., & Greene, D. (1975). Turning play into work: Effects of adult surveillance and extrinsic rewards on intrinsic motivation. *Journal of Personality and Social Psychology, 31*, 479-486.

Lepper, M. R., Greene, D., & Nisbett, R. E. (1973). Undermining children's intrinsic interest with extrinsic rewards: A test of the "overjustification" hypothesis. *Journal of Personality and Social Psychology, 28*, 129-137.

McGraw, K. O. (1978). The detrimental effects of reward on performance: A literature review and prediction model. In M. Lepper & D. Greene (eds.), *The hidden costs of reward: New perspectives on the psychology of human motivation.* Hillsdale, N.J: Erlbaum.

Miller, D. T., & Turnbull, W. (1986). Expectancies and interpersonal processes. *Annual Review of Psychology, 37*, 233-256.

Pelletier, L. G., & Vallerand, R. J. (1996). Supervisors' beliefs and subordinates' intrinsic motivation: A behavioral confirmation analysis. *Journal of Personality and Social Psychology, 71*, 331-340.

Porac, J. F., & Meindl, J. (1982). Undermining overjustification: Inducing intrinsic and extrinsic task representations. *Organizational Behavior and Human Performance, 29*, 208-226.

Rosenthal, R., & Rubin, D. B. (1978). Interpersonal expectancy effects: The first 345 studies. *Behavioral and Brain Sciences, 3*, 377-388.

Ryan, R. M., Mims, V., & Koestner, R. (1983). Relation of reward contingency and interpersonal context to intrinsic motivation: A review and test using cognitive evaluation theory. *Journal of Personality and Social Psychology, 45*, 736-750.

Sansone, C., & Harackiewicz, J. M. (1995). "I don't feel like it": The function of interest in self-regulation. In L. L. Martin & A. Tesser (eds.), *Striving and feeling: Interactions among goals, affect, and self-regulation.* Hillsdale, N.J: Erlbaum.

Sansone, C., Sachau, D. A., & Weir, C. (1989). Effects of instruction on intrinsic interest: The importance of context. *Journal of Personality and Social Psychology, 57*, 819-829.

Sheldon, K. M., & Elliot, A. J. (1999). Goal striving, need satisfaction, and longitudinal well-being: The self-concordance model. *Journal of Personality and Social Psychology, 76*, 482-497.

Snyder, M. (1984). When belief creates reality. In L. Berkowitz (ed.), *Advances in experimental social psychology* (Vol. 18). New York: Academic Press.

Snyder, M. (1992). Motivational foundations of behavioral confirmation. In M. P. Zanna (ed.), *Advances in experimental social psychology* (Vol. 25). New York: Academic Press.

Snyder, M., & Haugen, J. A. (1995). Why does behavioral confirmation occur? A functional perspective on the role of the target. *Personality and Social Psychology Bulletin, 21,* 963-974.

Tang, T. L., & Baumeister, R. F. (1984). Effects of personal values, perceived surveillance, and task labels on task preference: The ideology of turning play into work. *Journal of Applied Psychology, 69,* 99-105.

Weisner, C. (1990). Coercion in alcohol treatment. In Institute of Medicine (ed.), *Broadening the base of treatment for alcohol problems.* Washington, DC: National Academy Press.

White, R. W. (1959). Motivation reconsidered: The concept of competence. *Psychological Review, 66,* 297-333.

Wild, T. C., Cunningham, J., & Hobdon, K. (1998). When do people believe that alcohol treatment is effective? The importance of perceived client and therapist motivation. *Psychology of Addictive Behaviors, 12,* 93-100.

Wild, T. C., Enzle, M. E., & Hawkins, W. (1992). Effects of perceived extrinsic versus intrinsic teacher motivation on student reactions to skill acquisition. *Personality and Social Psychology Bulletin, 18,* 245-251.

Wild, T. C., Enzle, M. E., Nix, G., & Deci, E. L. (1997). Perceiving others as intrinsically or extrinsically motivated: Effects on expectancy formation and task engagement. *Personality and Social Psychology Bulletin, 23,* 837-848.

Wild, T. C., Kuiken, D., & Schopflocher, D. (1995). The role of absorption in experiential involvement. *Journal of Personality and Social Psychology, 69,* 569-579.

Wild, T. C., Newton-Taylor, B., & Alletto, R. (1998). Perceived coercion among clients entering substance abuse treatment: Structural and psychological determinants. *Addictive Behaviors, 23,* 81-95.

Wild, T. C., Roberts, A. B., & Cooper, E. L. (in press). Compulsory substance abuse treatment: An overview of recent findings and issues. *European Addiction Reasearch.*

Zuckerman, M., Porac, J., Lathin, D., Smith, R., & Deci, E. L. (1978). On the importance of self-determination for intrinsically motivated behavior. *Personality and Social Psychology Bulletin, 4,* 443-446.

PART III

❖   ❖   ❖

SELF-DETERMINATION
IN LIFE DOMAINS

8: What Makes Parents Controlling?

Wendy S. Grolnick
Nicholas H. Apostoleris
Clark University

Self-determination theory describes the motivationally facilitative environment as one that supports individuals' inherent needs for autonomy by providing choice and minimizing the use of controls (Deci & Ryan, 1985b). A wide variety of studies have supported the importance of autonomy supportive environments in various interpersonal interactions including those with teachers (e.g., Deci, Nezlek, & Sheinman, 1981), physicians (e.g., Williams, Rodin, Ryan, Grolnick, & Deci, 1998), and supervisors (Deci, Connell, & Ryan, 1989). Not surprisingly, because parents are children's primary socializers, the autonomy supportive versus controlling environment that parents provide their children has been the target of much research.

When parents are autonomy supportive, they value children's autonomy, encourage children to solve their own problems, take children's perspectives, and minimize the use of pressures and controls. When parents are controlling, on the other hand, they value obedience and conformity, solve children's problems for them, take the lead in interactions, and parent from their own, rather than the children's, perspectives (Grolnick & Ryan, 1989). Accumulating evidence confirms the positive effects of autonomy support and the negative effects of parental control on children. More specifically, controlling parents are likely to create an external perceived locus of causality in their children and to undermine their children's confidence in their abilities. Consistent with this thinking, we have found that parents who were rated by interviewers as more controlling had children who were less self-regulated in school, higher in acting out, lower in teacher-rated competence, and lower in achievement and grades (Grolnick & Ryan, 1989). Similarly, children who perceived their mothers and fathers as autonomy supportive exhibited more autonomous self-regulation, less unknown control, higher perceived competence, and higher school achievement (Grolnick, Ryan, & Deci, 1991).

Autonomy supportive parenting, then, has many positive ramifications. Yet many well-meaning parents behave in a controlling manner toward their children. The question we are going to address in this paper is, what makes parents autonomy supportive or controlling? In addressing this question, we review research on factors in parents' environments, in the children themselves, and in the psychology of parents that make for autonomy support or control. Following this, we present new theoretical ideas about some ways in which parents may be predisposed to become ego-involved in their children's performance and how that might play out in controlling parenting.

The clinical literature has provided us with at least two models for understanding parental control. Object relations theorists such as Margaret Mahler (1968) and Alice Miller (1981) have suggested that parents who have difficulty separating their own needs from those of their children have a hard time taking children's perspectives and acting in ways that are in the children's best interests. Miller's (1981) book, *The Drama of the Gifted Child*, portrays the narcissistic mother who uses her child to fulfill her own egoistic needs. Such a mother cannot see the child for who he or she is because the child is not a person in his or her own right but rather is a self-object for the mother. Similarly, the family therapy literature describes the enmeshed family. Such families do not recognize the boundaries between family members, and the thoughts and behaviors of parents are confused with those of children. In such families, parents intrude into children's lives and feelings and are unable to see children for who they are (Minuchin, 1974).

These pathological models for understanding controlling parents are certainly reasonable for a subset of parents. However, we need another model to understand how relatively healthy parents, even those who value autonomy in their children and believe autonomy supportive parenting works, can sometimes behave in a controlling manner, pressuring their children, standing over them while they do their homework, making sure they wear the right clothes. So what can it be that creates control in parents who aim to support their children's autonomy?

One possibility is that the same kinds of contextual factors that create controlling environments for children and undermine their motivation can impact on the parent. Thus, in the same way that pressure and evaluation undermine children's intrinsic motivation, they can also undermine parents' abilities to provide autonomy supportive parenting. But what kind of pressure? We present three types: pressure from without, pressure from below, and pressure from within.

Pressure from Without

Ecological theorists such as Bronfenbrenner (1986) stress that parents do not raise their children in a vacuum but are vulnerable to the stresses around them.

How does stress and pressure on the parents relate to control? We argue that stress and other pressures, including economic pressures, usurp the time and psychological availability necessary for autonomy supportive parenting. First, such pressures focus parents on their own immediate predicaments making it more difficult for them to take their children's perspectives. Second, allowing children to solve their own problems is likely to require more time and patience than solving the problems for them, and these parental resources may be undermined by stress.

This idea is consistent with several studies in the developmental literature. Although most of the studies that have looked at stress or economic pressure looked at positive parenting more generally (e.g., nurturance, responsivity) and not at autonomy support per se, some studies have examined dimensions relevant to autonomy support, such as punitiveness and harsh parenting which would be on the controlling end of the dimension. McLoyd and Wilson (1991) studied 92 mothers and children all being assisted by Aid to Families with Dependent Children (AFDC). They examined the level of economic hardship the families suffered, asking them questions such as, "How difficult is it for you to meet monthly payments on your family's bills?" They also considered parenting on the dimension of nurturance to punitiveness and the level of mother's psychological distress. Using a path model, they found that economic hardship was predictive of psychological distress, which was then associated with punitive parenting. A subsequent study with mothers of adolescents (McLoyd , Jayaratne, Ceballo, & Borquez, 1994) supported a similar model in which mothers' unemployment was associated with their own increased depressive symptoms, which then predicted increased punishment of adolescents. Two other studies supported similar models for severe socioeconomic disadvantage (Dodge, Pettit, & Bates, 1994), and economic hardship (Conger, Ge, Elder, Lorenz, & Simons, 1994). Elder's study of the Great Depression found that financial loss resulted in more irritability and tension and an increased tendency to treat children punitively.

Thus, these studies illustrate that when parents suffer economic distress, they may experience depressed, anxious, and irritable moods which then lead to harsher and more punitive parenting. These studies support the idea that autonomy supportive parenting is undermined by stressful life situations.

Whereas economic disadvantage is one type of external pressure that can lead parents to be controlling, other stresses, such as negative life events, to which parents are subjected is another type. Recently, we looked at such stress in a study of predictors of parenting styles in parents of adolescents (Grolnick, Weiss, McKenzie, & Wrightman, 1996). Fifty-three mothers and 38 fathers, along with their adolescents (ages 13-18) participated. Parents were interviewed separately in their homes by two interviewers. The structured interview asked a set of open-ended questions for each of five areas relevant to adolescents' lives: school, friends, dating, curfew, and chores. For each area the parent was asked how he or she motivates the child in that area, whether he or she has any rules or expectations in the area, and how he or she responds to positive or negative behaviors or outcomes (e.g., good or poor report card). For each area the parent was also asked to describe the most recent conflict or disagreement he or she had with the adolescent and how it was handled.

From audiotapes of the interviews, raters rated each parent on three 5-point scales. The "values autonomy" scale concerns the extent to which the parent expresses a value for autonomy and sees its promotion as a goal versus places preeminent value on obedience and conformity. The "autonomy supportive techniques" scale assesses the degree to which parents use more autonomy supportive methods, such as reasoning and limit setting, versus relying on controlling, power assertive motivational and disciplinary techniques such as rewards and threats. The third scale, "nondirectiveness," concerns the extent to which the parent includes the child in decision making versus imposes his or her own agenda on the child and allows for few choices. These scales were averaged to form a summary autonomy support versus control score. Parents' provision of structure, defined as the provision of rules, guidelines, and expectations in the home, as well as their involvement, defined as the dedication of resources to children, were also rated from the interviews.

Parents also completed questionnaires on stressful life events—the number of negative events that occurred in the last three months (e.g., death in the family, illness, repossession of their home)—and the social support they received. They also described their adolescents, but we will talk about the findings for these descriptions in the next section.

We were interested in finding out whether parents who experienced more stressful events were more controlling than those who experienced fewer events, even beyond the influence of economic disadvantage. Thus, in our analyses, we controlled for the effects of the socioeconomic status (SES) of the families. Results suggested that the more negative life events mothers reported, the less autonomy supportive they were rated (controlling for SES). Negative events were also associated with less provision of structure. There were no significant relations between stressful events and controlling behavior for fathers. The results suggest that mothers, who are likely to be the children's primary caretakers, spending the most time with them, may be especially vulnerable to the undermining effects of stressful life events. Interestingly, fathers who experienced more social support were rated as more involved with their adolescents. This suggests that a supportive environment for fathers helped them be able to spend time with their adolescents. Given that fathers may have more latitude in their parenting roles than mothers (Almeida & Galambos, 1991), their involvement may be more dependent on a supportive environment than is that of mothers.

In this study, then, stress was negatively associated with mothers' provision of autonomy supportive parenting to their children. Studies that have examined processes through which stress might affect parental control have identified parental mood and well-being as key mediators. The findings support our contention that autonomy support requires psychological availability and time, resources undermined by stressful conditions. Rather than interpreting the use of controlling techniques as resulting from ignorance about parenting (e.g., Piuck, 1975), it is important to recognize contextual constraints. Poor families are often aware of the fact that they are using problematic parenting strategies, yet are unable to change their use of such strategies (Longfellow, Zelkowitz, & Saunders, 1982) given the situations in which they find themselves.

Pressure from Below

Since Richard Bell's pioneering work in the late 1960's (e.g., 1968), we have come to accept that not only do parents affect children but children also affect parents. This is certainly likely to be the case with control. Children who are cooperative, who do their work or their chores, and who don't talk back may be the recipients of more autonomy support, while those who are uncooperative, test parents' patience, and don't take responsibility for their work may elicit more control. It is likely to be easier to involve children in decisions and take their viewpoints if they are agreeable and tend to cooperate readily.

In studying how characteristics of children impact on parenting, it would be optimal to find characteristics that are innate and not influenced by the children's environment. Unfortunately, it is impossible to find such characteristics because, even before birth, the environment is impacting on the child. However, researchers have delineated characteristics, such as temperament, that are *relatively* stable and are likely to be heritable (though most researchers acknowledge that temperamental characteristics are somewhat changeable). Thomas, Chess, and Birch (1968) described one set of temperamental features—high intensity, negative mood, high withdrawal, and low malleability—which cluster together to form the "difficult child." This cluster of characteristics may be a prime candidate for affecting levels of parental control.

Correlational studies support the relation between child difficulty and parental control. Rutter and Quinton (1984), in their 4-year longitudinal study of children of mentally ill parents, showed that children with adverse temperamental features (composite of low regularity, low malleability, negative mood, and low fastidiousness) were more likely than other children to be targets of parental hostility, criticism, and irritability.

Further evidence comes from the infancy literature. Bates (1980) found that at 6 and 13 months there were few relations between infant difficulty and mother behavior. By 24 months, however, there was more conflict between mothers and children who were described as difficult. Mothers of more difficult 24 month olds had relatively higher scores on power assertion, including frequent use of control efforts, frequent repetitions, prohibitions, and more frequent taking away of objects. Buss (1981) showed that power struggles were more frequent between children and their mothers and fathers when the children had higher scores on activity. Lee and Bates (1985) found that toddlers with difficult temperaments were more resistant to maternal attempts to exert authority than were toddlers with easy temperaments, and this negative behavior of those with difficult temperaments was likely to be met with coercive responses by mothers. Finally, on the opposite end of the spectrum, children's fearfulness (as reported by mothers and observed in unfamiliar situations in the laboratory) was positively associated with the use of gentle discipline that deemphasized power assertion as observed in the lab and at home (Kochanska, 1995).

In our own adolescent project, we took the perspective that the way parents experience and label a child's behavior is likely to be most proximally related to their parenting. We thus asked mothers and fathers about the "difficulty" of their adolescents (e.g., my child is even-tempered and not moody), and about their views of adolescence—specifically whether they believe adolescence is a difficult stage (e.g., adolescence is a difficult time of life for children and their parents). Results indicated that mothers who believed their adolescents were difficult were more controlling than mothers who rated their adolescents as easier. The finding did not hold true for fathers. For fathers, there was a significant negative relation between difficulty and involvement, suggesting that when fathers felt their own children were difficult they were likely to withdraw from interacting with them rather than controlling them. Fathers (but not mothers) who saw adolescence as a difficult time were more controlling with their adolescents, indicating that fathers are more influenced by their stereotypes of adolescents than by their own children's actual features. This may be a function of fathers' lesser experiences with adolescents in that they spend markedly less time with them relative to mothers (Montemayor, 1982).

In this same study we examined whether there would be transactions between the environment in which parents parented and the characteristics of the adolescents. More specifically, we wondered whether in nonstressful environments, parents would tailor their parenting to qualities of their adolescents, whereas in less conducive environments the parents would be less likely to do so. To examine this question, correlations between difficulty and parenting were computed within high and low stress groups. First, median splits on negative life events, social support, and marital satisfaction were conducted. Next, correlations between child difficulty and parenting within the high and low groups were computed (analyses were conducted for mothers only since the number of fathers did not allow for these analyses). Results indicated links between perceived difficulty and parenting in the "conducive" contexts but not the "nonconducive" contexts. More specifically, in low stress environments, there was a significant negative relationship between difficulty and autonomy support ($r = -.47$), whereas in high stress environments, this relation was nonsignificant. A similar pattern held for high and low social support and high and low marital satisfaction. Thus, within supportive environments parenting appears to be more regulated by characteristics of the adolescent than in nonsupportive environments.

Of course, all of these studies are correlational in nature. While parents who have difficult children may respond with more control, it is also plausible that parents who are more controlling increase reactance, whereby adolescents attempt to restore their freedom by engaging in negative behaviors. Thus, more controlling parents may actually create more difficulty in their children. When we see children and parents in our studies, we catch them in cycles of parent-to-child and child-to-parent influence. Sequential analyses of parent-child interaction show that oppositionality leads to irritable behavior, which evokes control, which sustains noncompliance (Patterson, 1982).

While it is significant that parents' experiences of their adolescents are predictive of control, one way to get around the *theoretical* problem of bidirectional influences is to experimentally manipulate the "difficultness" of the children. Jelsma (1982) did just this in a study in which she gave mothers the task of teaching anagrams to children (ages 9 to 11 years). Each mother taught one child. The children were confederates—half were trained to be difficult, uncooperative, and disinterested and the other half to be easy, cooperative, and interested. Tapes of the interactions showed that mothers were more controlling with the more difficult children.

Anderson, Lytton, and Romney (1986) had mothers of normal children and mothers of conduct disordered children interact in the laboratory with their own or others' children. Results showed more controlling responses to the conduct disordered children whether or not they were the mothers' own or others' children. In addition, mothers showed fewer positive behaviors to their own children whether or not they were conduct disordered. This study provides further indication that control is at least in part driven by child behavior.

Pressure from Within

While external pressure and characteristics of the children themselves may lead parents to become more or less controlling, we now focus on another type of pressure, that from within. Internal pressure from within parents to have their children perform in specified ways may also determine parenting patterns. One of the concepts that has been linked to internal pressure is that of ego involvement (Sherif & Cantril, 1947). When people are ego-involved, their performance has ramifications for their own self-esteem. In other words, they hinge their self-esteem on some outcome. People will feel proud and good about themselves if they perform well, but ashamed, perhaps embarrassed, and bad about themselves if they perform poorly. Thus, the outcome of the activity poses a threat to self-esteem and people are highly motivated to protect their self-esteem by creating a positive outcome. By contrast, when people are involved in the activity, they engage in it out of interest rather than a desire to display positive performance.

The Effects of Ego-Involvement

Ryan (1982) linked the concept of ego-involvement with internal control in which rewards, pressures, and other controlling contingencies come from within the person but function much like externally furnished contingencies to create an external locus of causality for behavior. Consistent with this idea, a number of studies have shown that the state of ego-involvement, with its accompanying internal stress and pressure, is undermining of intrinsic motivation (e.g., Plant & Ryan, 1985; Ryan, 1982).

For example, Ryan (1982) had college students solve hidden-figure puzzles in either an ego-involved (performance said to be linked to IQ) or task-involved (no performance-IQ link) condition. He showed that ego-involvement in the task resulted not only in greater feelings of pressure and tension than task-involvement, but also in lower intrinsic motivation to pursue the task in a subsequent free-choice session. In this study, participants became ego-involved when their own performance had ramifications outside of the task itself—that is, when their own performance had the potential to make them feel that they would be seen as either "smart" or "dumb." However, there are a variety of instances in which people's feelings hinge not on their own performance, but on the performance of another. For example, how a student performs on a test might affect how the teacher assesses his or her teaching, and how a child dresses might affect how the parent feels he or she will be judged as a parent. In these examples, teachers and parents become ego-involved in children's performance, behavior, or outcomes, and this ego-involvement is likely to influence the way the teachers and parents interact with children.

Deci, Speigel, Ryan, Koestner, and Kauffman (1982) examined a related phenomenon in an analog study of teachers. College students were told that they would be "teaching" other students to solve puzzles. Teachers were then given one of two orientations to their task; one emphasized performance standards and the other did not mention specific performance requirements. Those in the role of teacher then taught another college student to solve the puzzles. Presumably, teachers who were told they were responsible for students' performing up to standards would feel they were not good teachers if their students did not perform well. Thus, they would likely be invested (i.e., ego-involved) in the students' performance for their own views of themselves. Conversely, participants in the role of teacher who had been led to believe that there were no specific performance requirements would not feel their worth was linked to their students' performance.

Teaching sessions were audiotaped and later coded. Teachers in the performance-standards condition were judged to be more demanding and controlling, talked more, let students work alone less, used three times as many directives and "should" type statements, and two and a half times more criticisms than those in the control condition. Students assembled more puzzles with the help of the teacher but actually solved fewer puzzles on their own. Thus, when teachers are pressured and led to believe students' performance has meaning for their own worth, they are likely to be more controlling.

We would like to point out some other interesting results from this study, namely, ratings by teachers following the teaching sessions showed that teachers in the performance standards condition liked their students more than those in the control condition, presumably because they "performed" for the teachers. Further, there were no differences between teachers in the two conditions on reported enjoyment, effectiveness, rated interest in the puzzles, or willingness to take part in similar studies. Thus, the state of having performance standards did not appear to be especially aversive to these teachers even though they became more controlling with the students. We will come back to this point later.

A study conducted by Winch and Grolnick (1993) used another kind of analog, that of a counseling situation. A set of participants were given unsolvable anagrams to work on prior to talking with a simulated counselor. College-student "counselors" were then given the task of interacting individually with participants to find out what their experiences had been with the anagrams. Half the counselors were ego-involved and told that the session was a "test of how good they were at interacting with another person" and that such a skill would have implications for other important life skills. The task-involved counselors were told that we were interested in how people disclosed information about their experiences.

Interactions between counselors and counselees were audiotaped and later coded. The ego-involved counselors were judged to be more controlling than the task-involved counselors. However, while the ego-involved counselors rated themselves as more pressured and anxious immediately after receiving the ego-involving manipulation, they did not rate themselves as more pressured or anxious or as enjoying themselves less during the interaction.

Parents' Ego-Involvement

So what about parents interacting with their children? Will parents who are ego-involved in their children's performance show more control? And how will this affect the children? We examined just this issue in a recent study (Grolnick,

Gurland, DeCourcey, & Jacob, in press), one of a set of studies on parent involvement. Before describing the study, the manipulation used to create ego-involvement in the parents requires explanation.

In the educational literature, Dweck and her colleagues (Diener & Dweck, 1978; Dweck, 1975) have distinguished between children who have a mastery approach toward pursuing their schoolwork and those who take a helpless approach to tasks. A mastery approach involves the seeking out of challenging tasks and the maintenance of effective striving under failure. The helpless pattern is characterized by avoidance of challenge and deterioration in the face of obstacles. Dweck and Elliott (1983) have linked these patterns to the different goals children have when pursuing tasks. When children hold performance goals, they are concerned with gaining favorable judgements of their competence, so their goal in learning activities is to be sure they look competent (i.e., to prove their ability). By contrast, when children hold learning goals, they are concerned with increasing their competence, so their goal is to acquire new skills or extend their mastery.

Ames and Archer (1988) extended this work on students' goals to the goal orientation of the classroom environment. These researchers assessed children's perceptions of the classroom goal structure (whether it was experienced as performance or mastery oriented). The researchers found that when students perceived their class as emphasizing a mastery goal, they were more likely to report using effective learning strategies, prefer tasks that offer challenge, like their class more, and believe that effort and success are positively related. Further, when a performance orientation was salient to students, they tended to focus on ability and to cite their inability as a cause for failure.

For our study, we used these ideas to develop inductions that would give parents either an ego-involved or a nonego-involved orientation toward working with their child. We reasoned that an evaluative environment in which the parents felt responsible for the child's performance would make parents invested in the outcome of the task, that is, become ego-involved in the performance of their children. Thus, we created high and low performance-pressure conditions to facilitate ego-involved and nonego-involved orientations, respectively.

Sixty mothers and their third grade children participated in the study, conducted at our Child and Family Development Laboratory. Upon arriving at the laboratory, mothers rated their attitudes toward supporting versus controlling children. Children rated their mothers' autonomy support and completed questionnaires about their own motivational qualities. Each mother-child dyad then completed two homework-like tasks, similar to those that a third-grader might bring home from school: a map task, which required them to give directions to different locations on a large map, and a poem task, requiring them to label rhyming patterns of poems and then write a quatrain (four-line poem with a particular pattern). The order of the two tasks was counterbalanced. Each mother was assigned to either a high performance-pressure condition or a low performance-pressure condition. In the high-pressure condition, the mother was told, "Your role is to ensure that ___ learns to give directions (write a poem). We will be testing ____ after to make sure that he/she performs well enough." In the low-pressure condition, the mother was told, "Your role is to help _____ learn how to give directions (write a poem). We will be asking _____ some questions after but there is no particular level at which he/she needs to perform." After the induction, mothers completed an affect rating scale. Following this, the mother and child completed the task. Next, mothers and children separately completed questionnaires about their experience of the tasks including their competence, feelings of enjoyment, pressure and tension and effort expended. Finally, the mother left the room and the child was given a new task of the same type to solve on his or her own (e.g., give directions, write a quatrain). This task was included to determine whether children's internalization of what they had learned differed as a function of the condition under which the dyad worked.

A videotape was made of each mother and child dyad working on the tasks, and the verbal and nonverbal behaviors of the mothers were coded during each five-second interval in terms of the number of controlling and the number of autonomy supportive behaviors displayed by the mothers during that period. Verbal behaviors were coded as controlling if they involved directives, taking over (e.g., reading the items instead of allowing the child to do so), and telling the answers, whereas they were coded as autonomy supportive if they involved giving information and providing feedback. Controlling nonverbal behaviors included leading, taking over, and showing the child the answer, whereas autonomy supportive nonverbal behaviors included being available to provide assistance, pointing out information, and providing nonverbal feedback (e.g., nodding one's head). In addition to this coding, for each five-second interval, the mothers were given ratings for the degree to which they were controlling versus autonomy supportive in their verbal and nonverbal behaviors. Finally, dyadic and child performance on the map and poem tasks were coded, and the creativity of the poem the child wrote alone was rated using Amabile's (1983) system of consensual validation.

We expected that mothers in the high-pressure condition would use more controlling verbal and nonverbal behaviors and be rated as more controlling than those in the low-pressure condition. We also expected that mothers who came into the session with more controlling styles would be more controlling in our session. As well, we tested for possible interactions between the experimental conditions and individual differences in controlling styles.

In order to test for these effects, a series of Analyses of Covariance (ANCOVAs) were performed with condition (high- vs. low-pressure), autonomy supportive styles (high vs. low) and the interaction between condition and styles. Because mothers' behavior was correlated with children's grades in school, (suggesting that more competent children are provided more autonomy support), we entered children's grades as a covariate in these analyses.

Results for the poem task showed main effects of condition for the codings of mothers' verbalizations as being autonomy supportive versus controlling. Mothers in the high-pressure condition used more directives, did somewhat more taking over, and had a lower mean level of verbal autonomy support overall than those in the low-pressure condition. Mothers who had initially been rated by their children as having controlling styles in general displayed more controlling verbal behaviors (more taking over, somewhat more directives) and more controlling nonverbal behaviors (less available, more leading behavior) during the poem task. In addition, they were rated by observers as being more controlling in both their verbal and nonverbal behavior during the poem task.

Thus, for our poem task, when mothers were oriented toward the performance of their children they were more controlling verbally with their children. Interestingly, this task was a verbal task and the strongest effects were for verbal behavior. However, mothers' behavior was also highly dependent on the styles that they brought into the laboratory. This is not surprising because mothers and children have a history of working together and are likely to have established ways of interacting, especially on tasks similar to those they routinely do at home.

The results for our map task were a bit different. On this nonverbal task, there were also effects of our intervention on nonverbal behavior, but this time, there were both main effects and interactions. Mothers in the high-pressure condition took over more and gave the answers to their children more than mothers in the low-pressure condition. As in the poem task, individual differences in mothers' styles were highly predictive of their behavior; mothers whose children rated them as more autonomy supportive at home used fewer controlling verbal and nonverbal behaviors and were also rated as more autonomy supportive during the interactive tasks. Statistical interactions indicated that the effects of the manipulation were particularly striking for one group; the group that came in with controlling attitudes. In fact, our results showed that mothers with highly autonomy supportive attitudes were relatively unaffected by the manipulation, and, in some cases, the mothers high in autonomy supportive attitudes who were in the high-pressure condition were even more autonomy supportive during the task than were their counterparts in the low-pressure condition. Thus, mothers who had controlling styles and were subjected to the evaluation of the high-pressure condition were highly controlling. The other three groups were quite similar in their behavior.

Motivational Effects on Performance

Another set of analyses considered whether both the experimental condition and individual differences (i.e., mothers' styles) affected how the dyad performed on the tasks and, in particular, how the child performed when alone. For the poem, we coded whether the correct form was used and whether the lines rhymed as they were supposed to. For the map task, we determined whether all pieces of information (street, direction, cross streets) were used to give directions and also whether they were given in the correct order.

Results indicated that for the map task, holding constant child grades, children whose mothers both had controlling attitudes and were in the high-pressure condition showed poorer performance than those in the other three groups. Thus, the results parallel those for mother behavior. Children of mothers with controlling styles who were pressured were less likely to have internalized what they learned and thus less able to apply it on their own (Grolnick & Ryan, 1987). There were no effects for condition or for the condition by individual difference interaction on accuracy in the poem task, but there was an interaction effect on creativity (which was no longer significant when grades were controlled for). Children whose mothers came in with controlling attitudes and were assigned to the high-pressure condition wrote the least creative poems. Further, there was support for the idea that the effect of condition on performance was mediated by the mother's behavior—mothers in the high-pressusre condition behaved in a more controlling way and that, in turn, led to their children writing accurate but uncreative poems when they were alone.

In general, the results of our study show striking support for the idea that promoting parents' ego-involvement in their children's performance leads to the parents being more controlling, especially when they have controlling styles to begin with. The interaction result for the map task is reminiscent of the findings of Koestner, Bernieri, and Zuckerman (1992) which showed that more controlled individuals are less consistent in their attitudes and behavior than are more autonomous individuals. In our study, mothers who had controlling styles were especially vulnerable to the performance manipulation, whereas highly autonomy supportive mothers were invulnerable to our manipulation. Mothers who strongly endorse controlling children as a means of child rearing are likely to be control-oriented individuals. These results are also consistent with work by Bober and Grolnick (1995) showing that autonomous individuals are less swayed by inaccurate feedback about themselves, again showing that control-oriented individuals are more vulnerable and autonomous individuals less vulnerable to environmental contingencies. Thus, when academic or sports endeavors stress competition or evaluation, some parents will be more vulnerable to the effects of such pressures than others. The results also suggest that the effects of the environment on parents may differ according to the type of task in which they and their children are engaged.

Mothers' Experiences

A final set of findings concerned the mothers' experiences in the high- and low-pressure conditions. Striking was the fact that there were no differences between women in the two conditions in the amount of pressure they experienced while working with their children, in terms of their enjoyment of the task or their feelings of competence in working with their children. Why would this be so different from the pressure people feel when they are ego-involved in their own performance? Recall that both Ryan (1982) and Plant and Ryan (1985) found that when participants were ego-involved in their own performance they reported more feelings of pressure and tension and less enjoyment than when they were task-involved. What then is the difference between being ego-involved in your own performance versus that of your children? We suggest that when people are ego-involved in their own performance, they can pressure only themselves in an attempt to maintain their self-esteem. However, when parents or teachers are ego-involved in children's performance, they can push the children toward positive outcomes, thereby relieving their own pressure of evaluation. Thus, people can transform the evaluation they feel into behavior that is directed toward the children. By controlling the children, the mothers in the high-pressure condition may have inadvertently lessened their own pressure. It may not be nearly as aversive to be ego-involved in another's performance as in one's own performance because there is an outlet, albeit a counterproductive one.

Are Parents Especially Vulnerable to Being Ego-Involved?

In this last section, we present ideas based on evolutionary thinking. We ask the question, Are there built in "hooks" that make many parents especially vulnerable to acting in ego-involved and controlling ways with their children?

Of course, there are many ways in which the parent-child relationship is special when compared with various other relationships. Parents usually live with their children, have the primary responsibility for teaching their children how to live in the world, and know more about their children than do others. Importantly, children share 50% of their genes with each biological parent. And that, too, makes for a special situation.

We argue that indeed there are built in hooks. From the "gene's eye view," parents are invested in their children's welfare, in their offspring's surviving and reproducing. No doubt, evolution has selected for parents to be invested in their children. How else would it be possible for parents to make the personal sacrifices they make? Trivers (1974) coined the term "parental investment" to describe the resources parents provide to their offspring to increase the offspring's chance of surviving and hence of having reproductive success. Inherent in this concept is the idea that parents have only a finite amount of resources to invest in their offspring, themselves, and their potential future offspring. Humans use k-selection patterns, meaning we have low fertility rates, have fewer offspring than is biologically possible, and invest in a few highly competitive offspring. Species such as ours clearly differ from r-selected species, which evolved in highly unstable environments, have many offspring, and invest very little in each (Lovejoy, 1981).

How do we experience this push to put time, energy, and scarce resources into our offspring? Our experience is likely in the form of feelings. MacDonald

(1988) suggested that the human affectional system has evolved to keep family relationships close and to make sure parents invest in their children. MacDonald further suggested that the mechanism through which this occurs is a reward system in which parents feel intense love and caring for their children, making it positive for them to be together. Such feelings allow parents to invest time and energy and make sacrifices. A parallel system in children makes for mutual affection and closeness.

But is there a possibility of too much investment? The key to answering this question is to understand how high parental investment species such as ours determine how much and how to invest. Lovejoy (1981) suggested that although our selection is for high investment parenting, the system is also a flexible one in which the type of investment is dependent on cues in the environment. When cues suggest adverse conditions and competition for survival, there is especially high investment. If cues suggest optimal conditions and low competition, there is less investment. This would be highly adaptive in the environment in which humans evolved because a competitive, adverse environment might mean death for offspring and no reproduction. Thus, a very high parental investment in stressful times was adaptive in the environment of evolutionary adaptedness (EEA) because survival was on the line.

But our current environment is different from the EEA, and what might have been adaptive then may be less so today. If one imagines the cues parents encounter in Western society, it is likely that they are competitive, although survival is typically not at stake. Our schools and other institutions such as organized sports are set up as hierarchies with evaluation, social comparison, and "weeding out" a part of routine practices (Labaree, 1997). If parents pick up these cues, they may be likely to overinvest. This may lead to more controlling behavior than is adaptive. For while the use of these cues was adaptive in the EEA, today's "man-made" (non-survival oriented) competitive cues may lead to more control than is optimal in our current environment.

In the EEA, it would have been highly adaptive to have offspring who behaved closely in accord with parental behavior. This is another way in which genetic similarity may make for control. For the parent to have survived and reproduced, his or her behaviors had to have been successful in the environment. Assuming a relatively stable environment, offspring behaviors that were close to parental behaviors would be advantageous. It may therefore be expected that genes would persist that involve parents' attempting to maximize the likelihood of their offspring adhering to their behavioral examples and that result in the children's adhering to those examples. From the gene's viewpoint, psychological health per se is of no consequence. All that matters is successful reproduction. Thus, conservatism, in which parents attempt to channel children into their own paths, might be a vestige of our evolutionary heritage that is no longer adaptive in the current environment where flexible adjustment to environmental change is most adaptive.

We are just beginning to test aspects of this theory. One hypothesis is that parents who pick up competitive cues from the environment and see the world their children will inhabit as being harsh will likely be controlling with their children. This idea that cues of threat lead to controlling behavior does have support from work on threat and authoritarianism in the field of political psychology.

In 1973, Sales examined the effect of the Great Depression on conversion rates among church denominations, comparing the period from 1920 to 1929, a time of relative prosperity, with the Depression period from 1930 to 1939. Sales found that conversion rates from nonauthoritarian to authoritarian churches increased during the period of presumed societal threat, relative to the low-threat period. He then replicated this result for relatively good and bad economic years in Seattle. Doty, Peterson, and Winter (1991) more recently identified periods of relative high threat (1978-1982) and low threat (1983-1987) using indicators of income and the Consumer Price Index, as well as troubling events such as the disaster at Three Mile Island, the Soviet invasion of Afghanistan, and the seizure of the American Embassy in Tehran. These authors showed that societal measures of authoritarian syndrome, such as the purchase of attack dogs, cynicism, and acceptance of capital punishment, decreased from the high to the low threat periods.

Sales and Friend (1973) also looked at individual level effects. In two studies, participants were induced to succeed or fail on purported measures of intelligence and ability. Failure increased participants' level of authoritarianism, whereas success decreased it.

In a more complex model, Feldman and Stenner (1997) suggested that threat would not impact on authoritarianism directly (authoritarianism is a personality variable and thus presumed to be static) but rather would activate authoritarian *behavior* for individuals with the authoritarian tendency. Individuals with an authoritarian tendency (conformist child-rearing values) who perceived more economic and political threat were more ethnocentric and reported more punitive attitudes than those with a high authoritarian tendency who perceived low threat. There was no effect of threat on individuals with low authoritarian tendencies. In fact, if anything, low authoritarian individuals showed more liberal responses under higher threat. The results suggest that threat polarizes people, leading high-authoritarian individuals to behave in authoritarian ways but not having this effect on individuals low in authoritarianism.

In a recent pilot study (Grolnick & Gurland, 1999), we developed a questionnaire for parents asking them for their views about the world their children will inhabit in the future. Among the subscales are (1) concern about the future (e.g., "Thinking about kids today, it's scary to imagine what the world will be like for them in the future."); (2) harsh world (e.g., "Its getting harder and harder all the time to make a decent living."); and (3) perceived competition (e.g., "It's competitive out there, only some kids can make it."). We also measured parents' values for their children using Kohn's (1977) scale which asks parents to rank order values such as obedience and responsibility. Parents reported on their tendencies to use autonomy supportive versus controlling behaviors using the Parent

Attitude Scale and the Child Report of Parent Behavior Inventory (CRPBI; Schaefer, 1965). Parents also completed the General Causality Orientations Scale (Deci & Ryan, 1985).

We predicted that parents who were more concerned about the future and those who saw the world as more harsh and competitive would display more controlling attitudes and behavior than those who saw the world as less harsh and competitive and were less concerned. Preliminary data with 40 participants suggest some of the predicted relations. Parents who were more concerned about the future tended to be more likely to value obedience than those less concerned about the future. There were also marginally significant trends for parenting behavior with parents who were more concerned about the future reporting more psychological control and less autonomy support than parents who were less concerned. Finally, the results for the General Causality Orientations Scale are intriguing. Individuals high in the control orientation perceived more competition and perceived the world their children will inhabit as more harsh than those lower in this orientation.

The results provide some support for the idea that one of the reasons parents become controlling is that they experience threat for their children and, because they are invested in their children's performance, they tend to push them to achieve. In parents' minds, the push is perceived as something they almost have to do because they care about their children. The model of interaction between cues in our social contexts and parents' propensities to be invested suggests that the context in which parents find themselves may be a key to how their investment translates into behavior.

Summary and Conclusions

Autonomy supportive parenting is associated with children's self-regulation of behavior (Grolnick & Ryan, 1989) and emotion (Grolnick, Kurowski, McMenamy, Rivkin, & Bridges, 1998), as well as their achievement and adjustment (Grolnick, Deci, & Ryan, 1997). Thus, the identification of factors that facilitate autonomy supportive parenting is an important task. Among the issues we have recognized as making it difficult to provide autonomy supportive parenting are external factors such as stress and lack of support from others, as well as child factors such as the child being difficult to parent. Interestingly, these factors have also been found to undermine parents' involvement with their children. For example, parents who perceived their children as more difficult as well as those feeling less efficacious were less involved in their children's schooling than those seeing their children as easier and themselves as more effective as parents (Grolnick, Benjet, Kurowski, & Apostoleris, 1997). Stress and scarce resources were predictive of lower involvement for mothers of boys. Thus, arduous life circumstances and challenging child behavior may make it difficult to provide for children's needs more generally. Certainly such circumstances create a cycle whereby child difficulty leads to low involvement (Grolnick & Slowiaczek, 1994) which is likely to be of a controlling nature, and this in turn leads to greater difficulty.

A different dynamic, however, may occur with parents' ego involvement in their children's performance. When parents feel evaluated or feel their children are being evaluated, parents may become highly involved, but the type of involvement they provide is likely to be controlling. There is some evidence that, in some instances, high levels of controlling involvement may actually be less beneficial than lower levels of involvement (Weiss & Grolnick, 1991). The tendency toward ego-involvement and control may be at least in part a function of the competitive cues rampant in our culture that parents pick up and channel into control. Thus, well-meaning parents may become easily hooked into focusing on outcomes, pressuring their children, and undermining the very characteristics they wish to inculcate.

How can parents, teachers, and other adults responsible for socializing children refrain from falling into this trap? We suggest, first, through increased awareness of internal pressures to control. When individuals can identify such pressures, they can begin to ask themselves what stake they have in their children's performance. Do they see the children's behavior as reflecting upon themselves? Has the outcome become more important than the process? Such internal conversations can increase choicefulness about what parenting and teaching strategies to utilize. Second, we suggest identifying the cues in the environment that may be leading them to be ego involved. How is the activity structured so as to increase competition and threat? Is it possible to restructure or reinterpret these contingencies? Third, caretakers can support each other by discussing competitive feelings and fears. When parents understand that they are not alone in their worries about their children's futures, they may be better able to counter their own feelings of pressure. Such techniques can help parents to maintain autonomy supportive parenting in an environment that pulls for control, and this should in turn lead to positive effects for their children.

References

Almeida, D., & Galambos, N. (1991). Examining father involvement and the quality of father-adolescent relations. *Journal of Research on Adolescence, 11,* 155-172.

Amabile, T. (1983) *The social psychology of creativity.* New York: Springer-Verlag.

Ames, C., & Archer, J. (1988). Achievement goals in the classroom: Students' learning strategies and motivation processes. *Journal of Educational Psychology, 80,* 260-267.

Anderson, K. E., Lytton, H., & Romney, D. (1986). Mothers' interactions with normal and conduct disordered boys: Who affects whom? *Developmental Psychology, 22,* 604-609.

Bates, J. E. (1980). The concept of difficult temperament. *Merrill-Palmer Quarterly, 26,* 299-320.

Bell, R. Q. (1968). A reinterpretation of the direction of effects in studies of socialization. *Psychological Review, 75,* 81-95.

Bober, S., & Grolnick, W. S. (1995). Motivational factors related to differences in self-schemas. *Motivation and Emotion, 19,* 307-327.

Bronfenbrenner, U. (1986). Ecology of the family as a context for human development: Research perspectives. *Developmental Psychology, 22,* 723-742.

Buss, D. M. (1981). Predicting parent-child interaction from child's activity level. *Developmental Psychology, 17,* 59-65.

Conger, R. D., Ge, X., Elder, G. H., Lorenz, F. O., & Simons, R. L. (1994). Economic stress, coercive family process, and developmental problems of adolescents. *Child Development, 65,* 541-561.

Deci, E. L., Connell, J. P., & Ryan, R. M. (1989). Self-determination in a work organization. *Journal of Applied Psychology, 74,* 580-590.

Deci, E. L., Nezlek, J., & Sheinman, L. (1981). Characteristics of the rewarder and intrinsic motivation of the rewardee. *Journal of Personality and Social Psychology, 40,* 1-10.

Deci, E. L., & Ryan, R. M. (1985a). The general causality orientations scale: Self-determination in personality. *Journal of Research in Personality, 19,* 109-134.

Deci, E. L., & Ryan, R. M. (1985b). *Intrinsic motivation and self-determination in human behavior.* New York: Plenum.

Deci, E. L., Spiegel, N. H., Ryan, R. M., Koestner, R., & Kauffman, M. (1982). The effects of performance standards on teaching styles: The behavior of controlling teachers. *Journal of Educational Psychology, 74,* 852-859.

Diener, C. I., & Dweck, C. S. (1978). An analysis of learned helplessness: Continuous changes in performance, strategy, and achievement cognitions following failure. *Journal of Personality and Social Psychology, 36,* 451-462.

Dodge, K. A., Pettit, G. S., & Bates, J. E. (1994). Socialization mediators of the relation between socioeconomic status and child conduct problems. *Child Development, 65,* 649-665.

Doty, R. M., Peterson, B. E., & Winter, D. G. (1991). Threat and authoritarianism in the United States, 1978-1987. *Journal of Personality and Social Psychology, 61,* 629-640.

Dweck, D. S. (1975). The role of expectations and attributions in the alleviation of learned helplessness. *Journal of Personality and Social Psychology, 31,* 674-685.

Dweck, C. S., & Elliott, E. S. (1983). Achievement motivation. In P. H. Mussen (Gen. Ed.) & E. M. Hetherington (Vol. Ed.), *Handbook of child psychology: Vol. IV. Social and personality development* (pp. 643-691). New York: Wiley.

Feldman, S., & Stenner, K. (1997). Perceived threat and authoritarianism. *Political Psychology, 18,* 741-770.

Grolnick, W. S., Benjet, C., Kurowski, C., & Apostoleris, N. (1997). Predictors of parent involvement in children's schooling. *Journal of Educational Psychology, 89,* 1-11.

Grolnick, W. S., Deci, E. L., & Ryan, R. M. (1997). Internalization within the family: The self-determination theory perspective. In J. E. Grusec & L. Kuczynski (Eds.), *Parenting and children's internalization of values* (pp. 135-161). New York: Wiley.

Grolnick, W. S., & Gurland, S. T. (1999). *Threat and parenting.* Unpublished Manuscript, Clark University.

Grolnick, W. S., Gurland, S. T., DeCourcey, W., & Jacob, K. (in press). Antecedents and consequences of mothers' autonomy support: An experimental investigation. *Developmental Psychology.*

Grolnick, W. S., Kurowski, C. O., McMenamy, J. M., Rivkin, I., & Bridges, L. J. (1998). Mothers' strategies for regulating their toddlers' distress. *Infant Behavior and Development, 21,* 437-450.

Grolnick, W. S., & Ryan, R. M. (1987). Autonomy in children's learning: An experimental and individual difference investigation. *Journal of Personality and Social Psychology, 52,* 890-898.

Grolnick, W. S., & Ryan, R. M. (1989). Parent styles associated with children's self-regulation and competence in school. *Journal of Educational Psychology, 81,* 143-154.

Grolnick, W. S., Ryan, R. M., & Deci, E. L. (1991). The inner resources for school achievement: Motivational mediators of children's perceptions of their parents. *Journal of Educational Psychology, 83,* 508-517.

Grolnick, W. S., & Slowiaczek, M. L. (1994). Parents' involvement in children's schooling: A multidimensional conceptualization and motivational model. *Child Development, 65,* 237-252.

Grolnick, W. S., Weiss, L., McKenzie, L., & Wrightman, J. (1996). Contextual, cognitive, and adolescent factors associated with parenting in adolescence. *Journal of Youth and Adolescence, 25,* 33-54.

Jelsma, B. M. (1982). *Adult control behaviors: The interaction between orientation toward control in women and activity level of children.* Unpublished doctoral Dissertation, University of Rochester.

Kochanska, G. (1995). Children's temperament, mothers' discipline, and security of attachment: Multiple pathways to emerging internalization. *Child Development, 66,* 697-615.

Koestner, R., Bernieri, F., & Zuckerman, M. (1992). Self-regulation and consistency between attitudes, traits, and behaviors. *Personality and Social Psychology Bulletin, 18,* 52-59.

Kohn, M. L. (1977). *Class and conformity* (2nd Ed.). Chicago: University of Chicago Press.

Labaree, D. F. (1997). *How to succeed in school without really learning: The credentials race in American education.* New Haven: Yale University Press.

Lee, C. L., & Bates, J. E. (1985). Mother-child interaction at age two years and perceived difficult temperament. *Child Development, 56,* 1314-1325.

Longfellow, C., Zelkowitz, P., & Saunders, E. (1982). The quality of mother-child relationships. In D. Belle (Ed.), *Lives in stress: Women and depression* (pp. 163-176). Beverly Hills, CA: Sage.

Lovejoy, O. (1981). The origin of man. *Science, 211,* 341-350.

MacDonald, K. B. (1988). *Sociobiological perspectives on human development.* New York: Springer-Verlag.

Mahler, M. (1968). *On human symbiosis and the vicissitudes of individuation.* New York: International Universities Press.

McLoyd, V. C., Jayaratne, T. E., Ceballo, R, & Borquez, J. (1994). Unemployment and work interruption among African American single mothers: Effects of parenting and adolescent socioemotional functioning. *Child Development, 65,* 562-589.

McLoyd, V. C., & Wilson, L. (1991). The strain of living poor: Parenting, social support, and child mental health. In A. C. Huston (Ed.), *Children in poverty* (pp. 105-135). New York: Cambridge University Press.

Miller, A. (1981). *The drama of the gifted child*. New York: Basic Books.

Minuchin, S. (1974). *Families and family therapy*. Cambridge, MA: Harvard University Press.

Montemayor, R. (1982). The relationship between parent-adolescent conflict and the amount of time adolescents spend alone and with parents and peers. *Child Development, 13*, 1512-1519.

Patterson, G. R. (1982). *Coercive family processes*. Eugene, OR: Castalia Press.

Piuck, C. (1975). Child-rearing patterns in poverty. *American Journal of Psychotherapy, 29*, 485-502.

Plant, R. W., & Ryan, R. M. (1985). Intrinsic motivation and the effects of self-consciousness, self-awareness, and ego involvement: An investigation of internally controlling styles. *Journal of Personality, 53*, 435-449.

Rutter, M., & Quinton, D. (1984). Long-term follow-up of women institutionalized in childhood: Factors promoting good functioning in adult life. *British Journal of Developmental Psychology, 18*, 225-234.

Ryan, R. M. (1982). Control and information in the interpersonal sphere: An extension of cognitive evolution theory. *Journal of Personality and Social Psychology, 43*, 450-461.

Sales, S. M. (1973). Threat as a factor in authoritarianism: An analysis of archival data. *Journal of Personality and Social Psychology, 28*, 44-57.

Sales, S. M., & Friend, K. E. (1973). Success and failure as determinants of level of authoritarianism. *Behavioral Science, 18*, 163-172.

Schaefer, E. S. (1965). Children's reports of parental behavior: An inventory. *Child Development, 36*, 413-424.

Sherif, M., & Cantril, H. (1947). *The psychology of ego-involvements*. New York: Wiley.

Thomas, A., Chess, S., & Birch, H. G. (1968). *Temperament and behavior disorders in children*. New York: New York University Press.

Trivers, R. (1974). Parent-offspring conflict. *American Zoologist, 14*, 249-264.

Weiss, L. A., & Grolnick, W. S. (1991). *The roles of parental involvement and autonomy support in adolescent symptomatology*. Paper presented at biennial meeting of the Society for Research in Child Development, Seattle, WA.

Williams, G. C., Rodin, G. C., Ryan, R. M., Grolnick, W. S., & Deci, E. L. (1998). Autonomous regulation and adherence to medical regimens. *Health Psychology, 17*, 269-276.

Winch, G., & Grolnick, W. S. (1993). *Ego involvement, self-focus, and social interaction*. Unpublished manuscript, New York University.

9: Self-Determination Theory Applied to Educational Settings

Johnmarshall Reeve
University of Iowa

The utility of applying self-determination theory to educational settings is now evident. Two decades of empirical work support the following two conclusions: (1) autonomously-motivated students thrive in educational settings, and (2) students benefit when teachers support their autonomy. Further, the positive classroom outcomes experienced by autonomously-motivated students appear in both the academic and developmental domains.

The first conclusion essentially means that the quality of a student's motivation explains part of why he or she achieves highly, enjoys school, prefers optimal challenges, and generates creative products. To provide the evidence for this conclusion, researchers asked students to self-report their academic motivation, and they found that the degree to which their motivation was self-determined versus controlled predicted the outcomes listed on the left-hand side of Table 9-1. The second conclusion recognizes that the quality of a student's motivation depends, in part, on the quality of the student-teacher relationship (Eccles & Midgley, 1989). It essentially means that students achieve highly, learn conceptually, and stay in school in part because their teachers support their autonomy rather than control their behavior. The studies that provide evidence for this conclusion assessed (with a questionnaire) or manipulated (through an experiment) the teachers' interpersonal motivating styles and found that students benefited from autonomy-supportive teachers in the ways listed on the right-hand side of Table 9-1.

Author's note: I extend my gratitude to those colleagues who joined with me to carry out the research described in this chapter: Leah Arndt, Elizabeth Bolt, Yi Cai, Diane Hamm, Pat Hardre, Mafumi Omura, and Brad Sickenius. Please address all correspondence regarding this chapter to Johnmarshall Reeve, Division of Psychological and Quantitative Foundations, 361 Lindquist Center, University of Iowa, Iowa City, IA 52242. My e-mail address is johnmarshall-reeve@uiowa.edu.

How Students Benefit from Autonomous Motivation (left side) and from Teacher's Autonomy Support (right side)

Educational Benefits Shown By Autonomously-Motivated Students, Compared to Control-Motivated Students		Educational Benefits Shown by Students with Autonomy-Supportive Teachers, Compared to Students with Controlling Teachers	
Educational Benefit	Supportive Reference	Educational Benefit	Supportive Reference
Higher Academic Achievement	Miserandino, 1996 Flink et al., 1992	Higher Academic Achievement	Flink, Boggiano, & Barrett, 1990 Boggiano et al., 1993
Higher Perceived Competence	Ryan & Grolnick, 1986	Higher Perceived Competence	Deci, Schwartz et al., 1981 Ryan & Grolnick, 1986 Williams et al., 1994
More Positive Emotionality	Ryan & Connell, 1989 Garbarino, 1975 Ryan, 1982	More Positive Emotionality	Patrick et al., 1993
Higher Self-Worth	Ryan & Grolnick, 1986	Higher Self-Esteem	Deci, Schwartz et al., 1981 Deci, Nezlak, & Sheinman, 1981
Preference for Optimal Challenge	Shapira, 1976 Boggiano, Main, & Katz, 1988 Pittman et al., 1982	Greater Conceptual Understanding	Benware & Deci, 1984 Boggiano et al., 1993 Flink et al., 1990 Grolnick & Ryan, 1987
Pleasure from Optimal Challenge	Harter, 1974, 1978	Greater Flexibility in Thinking	McGraw & McCullers, 1979
Stronger Perceptions of Control	Boggiano & Barrett, 1985	More Active Information Processing	Grolnick & Ryan, 1987
Greater Creativity	Amabile, 1985	Greater Creativity	Koestner et al., 1984
Higher Rates of Retention	Vallerand & Bissonette, 1992	Higher Rates of Retention	Vallerand et al., 1997

Table 9.1

The utility of self-determination theory is that it explains *why* students benefit when teachers support their autonomy. Two premises central to the theory are that (a) different types of motivation exist (viz., autonomous and controlled), and (b) some types of motivation (viz., those that are autonomous) are associated with more positive educational and developmental benefits than are other types (viz., those that are controlled) (Deci & Ryan, 1991; Deci, Vallerand, Pelletier, & Ryan, 1991). Instead of arguing that motivation *per se* is the key resource that allows students to thrive in educational settings, research on self-determination theory shows that students benefit specifically from autonomous motivations (i.e., intrinsic motivation, identified regulation).

Autonomy Supportive Teaching

While it is now clear that students benefit from their relationships with autonomy-supportive teachers, it nonetheless remains a bit unclear as to how this actually works. My colleagues and I have been asking, for instance, just what are these autonomy-supportive teachers doing in the classroom from one moment to the next that their controlling counterparts are not doing? Are they listening more? Are they using directives less? Do they use rewards in different ways or for different purposes? This is a very practical question because if a teacher wanted to be more autonomy supportive with students, it is not yet clear just which teaching behaviors he or she should pursue. Once we pinpoint what autonomy-supportive teachers are doing, we can next seek to understand how students benefit from these sorts of behaviors. If listening is an autonomy supportive thing to do, then we can ask yet another question by trying to understand how a teacher's listening nurtures the sort of benefits listed in Table 9-1. To the extent that we can identify specific autonomy-supportive teaching behaviors and to the extent that we can understand why these behaviors benefit students, then we can pursue a third and practical concern. Namely, we can investigate the extent to which teachers can learn how to be autonomy supportive with students. These are the sort of questions that my colleagues and I have been trying to answer.

Autonomy-Supportive Teaching Behaviors

Which acts of teaching can be characterized as autonomy supportive, and which can be characterized as controlling? Researchers pursue this question in two different, but complementary, ways. First, the personality approach asks teachers to complete the Problems in Schools questionnaire to identify an interpersonal disposition toward autonomy support versus control (Reeve, Bolt, & Cai,

1999). Second, the social psychological approach exposes teachers to conditions that either do or do not pressure them toward a relatively controlling orientation (Deci, Spiegel, Ryan, Koestner, & Kauffman, 1982; Flink, Boggiano, & Barrett, 1990). Once autonomy supportive and controlling teachers are identified through either of these two means, researchers look for differences in the way autonomy-supportive and controlling teachers teach and motivate students.

Twenty-two possible behavioral differences between autonomy-supportive and controlling teachers appear in Table 9-2. The first column lists the results from a personality-based investigation while the second column lists the results from a social psychological investigation. Among the set of instructional behaviors included in these investigations, autonomy-supportive teachers distinguished themselves by listening more, spending less time holding instructional materials such as notes or books, giving students time for independent work, and giving fewer answers to the problems students face. Among the set of conversational statements, autonomy-supportive teachers distinguished themselves by avoiding directives, praising mastery, avoiding criticism, giving answers less often, responding to student-generated questions, and communicating statements rich in empathy and perspective-taking. Among the set of subjective impressions, autonomy-supportive teachers distinguished themselves by supporting intrinsic motivation, supporting internalizations, and coming across as less demanding or pressuring.

These findings allow us to begin to construct an understanding of what autonomy-supportive teachers are doing during student-teacher interactions. In essence, autonomy-supportive teachers are responsive (e.g., spend time listening), supportive (e.g., praise the quality of performance), flexible (e.g., give students time to work in their own way), and motivate through interest (e.g., support intrinsic motivation). Controlling teachers essentially take charge (e.g., hold the instructional materials, use directives/commands), shape students toward a right answer (e.g., give solutions), evaluate (e.g., criticize), and motivate through pressure (e.g., seem demanding and controlling).

How Students Benefit from Autonomy-Supportive Teaching Behaviors

Identifying what autonomy-supportive teachers do explains only half of the story in trying to understand the student benefits listed in Table 9-1. The other half concerns how these behaviors benefit students. In other words, it's interesting to know that autonomy-supportive teachers listen more and use directives less, but is not necessarily clear how or why students benefit from being listened to and how or why students suffer from being bossed.

According to self-determination theory, intrinsic motivation arises from the needs for self-determination and competence (Deci & Ryan, 1985). Knowing this, we designed a study in which we rated and scored the same set of behaviors

Teaching Behaviors Shown More Often by Autonomy-Supportive (AS > C) or by Controlling (C > AS) Teachers

	Results from Reeve *et al.* (1999).	Results from Deci *et al.* (1982).
Teacher's Instructional Behaviors		
Time spent talking	AS = C	AS < C
Time spent listening	AS > C	n/a
Time spent holding instructional materials	C > AS	n/a
Time given to student for independent work	AS > C	AS > C
Solutions Given	C > AS	C > AS
Teacher's Conversational Statements		
Directives/Commands	C > AS	C > AS
Should, Must, Have to Statements	AS = C	C > AS
Deadlines Statements	n/a	AS = C
Praises of Quality of Performance	AS > C	AS > C
Praises of Student	AS = C	C > AS
Encouragements	AS = C	n/a
Criticisms	n/a	C > AS
Hints Given	AS = C	AS = C
Solutions Given	C > AS	C > AS
Questions of What the Student Wants	AS > C	AS = C
Controlling Questions	AS = C	C > AS
Responses to Student-Generated Questions	AS > C	n/a
Self-disclosure Statements	AS = C	AS = C
Empathic, Perspective-taking Statements	AS > C	n/a
Raters' Subjective Impressions of Teacher's Style		
Supported Intrinsic Motivation	AS > C	AS > C
Supported Internalization	AS > C	n/a
Seemed Demanding and Controlling	C > AS	C > AS

Note. AS > C, autonomy-supportive teachers engaged in the behavior significantly more than did controlling teachers; C > AS, controlling teachers engaged in the behavior significantly more than did autonomy-supportive teachers; AS = C, this behavior showed no significant difference between autonomy-supportive and controlling teachers; n/a, this behavior was not assessed in the study.

Table 9.2

listed in Table 9-2 to see how each affected students' self-reports of self-determination and competence (Hamm & Reeve, 2002). Our hypothesis was that the functional significance of a truly autonomy-supportive behavior would be that it facilitated students' perceptions of self-determination and/or competence, just as the functional significance of a truly controlling behavior would be that it interfered with students' perceptions of self-determination and competence. We found that about half of the behaviors listed in Table 9-2 did indeed exert a significant influence on students' perceptions of self-determination or competence. We also found that what teachers did affected students' perceptions more than what teachers said.

As to the instructional behaviors (i.e., what the teacher did), students reported significantly higher perceptions of both self-determination and competence when teachers listened more, encouraged conversation, allocated time for independent work, and held the instructional materials less. As to the conversational statements (i.e., what the teacher said), students reported significantly higher perceptions of competence when their teachers provided hints but resisted giving answers. Students also felt more competent when teachers voiced perspective-ting statements. The rated subjective impressions were also important, as students felt more self-determined and more competent when teachers behaved in ways that supported their intrinsic motivation and valuing of what they were learning.

The story that emerges from these findings is an interesting one to tell. How a teacher teaches and motivates has a substantial and direct impact on how free and self-determining each student perceived himself or herself to be. Behaviors like listening and affording time for independent work nurtured autonomy, while behaviors like holding the instructional materials and teacher-dominated problem solving frustrated autonomy. How instruction affected perceived competence was through a more indirect route. Mostly, students felt competent when they performed well. In addition, students felt increasingly competent when teachers provided opportunities for independent work, opportunities to talk, timely hints, and perspective-taking statements; students felt increasingly incompetent when teachers hogged instructional materials, gave answers, and solved problems for the student.

Can Teachers Learn to Be Autonomy Supportive?

Having some confidence that we know what autonomy-supportive behaviors are and why they facilitate student motivation, we can now turn to practical matters and ask whether teachers can learn to be autonomy supportive with students. To find out, we prepared an informational booklet about self-determination and autonomy support and gave it to a group of preservice teachers. The booklets explained the concept of autonomy support, illustrated what it looks like in a classroom setting, summarized the benefits of autonomy support, and presented a couple of case studies so that readers could think about how to apply an autonomy-supportive style to student-teacher interactions. Other groups of preservice teachers received (using random assignment) informational booklets about other instructional strategies.

Results indicated that the preservice teachers did learn how to be autonomy supportive with students (Reeve, 1998), but their prior beliefs about the nature of motivation strongly affected how willing they were to accept the merits of an autonomy-supportive style. Preservice teachers with prior beliefs about motivation which were consistent with autonomy support conceptually agreed with the information, and they assimilated it rather easily. Preservice teachers with prior beliefs about motivation which were inconsistent with autonomy support initially disagreed with the information. Control-oriented preservice teachers who found the information to be a superior alternative to their pre-existing controlling motivational strategies experienced conceptual change and willingly adopted an autonomy supportive orientation. Control-oriented preservice teachers who found the information to be an inferior alternative to their pre-existing beliefs resisted conceptual change and maintained their commitment to a controlling orientation. So, preservice teachers can and do learn how to be autonomy supportive, but they experience enduring conceptual change only to the extent that they see autonomy support as a superior alternative to their pre-existing strategies.

Recognizing interest and disinterest in students. Supporting students' autonomy requires not only a respect and a valuing for students' intrinsic motivation and self-determination, but it also requires an array of interpersonal skills. These skills include taking the perspective of the students, acknowledging their feelings, providing rationale for requests, communicating with noncontrolling language, and so on (Deci, 1995; Deci, Eghrari, Patrick, & Leone, 1994). We have been particularly interested in the skill of being able to recognize when students are interested or disinterested in what they are doing. A few years ago, I visited elementary and high schools and tried a simple experiment. While students engaged themselves on worksheets, participated in group discussions, worked on computers, and visited interest areas, I asked each of them to tell me (on a questionnaire) how interested or disinterested he or she was at that particular moment on that particular activity. I also asked teachers to observe these students and estimate how interested or disinterested they thought each student was. Findings indicated that, although teachers were highly confident that they could tell who was and who was not interested, the teachers' interest estimates were in fact as likely to be wrong as they were to be right. In other words, estimating how interested students are during learning turns out to be difficult. Try it some time, and you will see what I mean.

We have been investigating precisely how people express interest through their nonverbal behavior (Reeve, 1993; Reeve & Nix, 1997), and we have learned several ways that people express interest during task engagements. For instance, the speed with which people move their hands while working on a manipulative task correlates highly with self-reported interest. (The idea is that the quicker the "hand speed," the greater the underlying desire to gain information/feedback from task exploration, experimentation, and mastery attempts.) In a recent investigation, we trained one group of preservice teachers to monitor students' "acts of exploration" as they watched students learning (Reeve, Arndt, & Omura, 2002). Teachers then estimated how interested or disinterested each student appeared to be. Compared to raters who received no such training (i.e., a control group), participants who closely monitored students' acts of exploration made significantly more accurate interest ratings. Thus, people can learn to recognize interest in others. In the classroom, this can be a handy skill, as it provides teachers with the critical feedback they need to diagnose whether or not the instruction they provide is interesting to students.

The concept of autonomy support. Pulling all this research together, a picture begins to emerge of what it means to be autonomy supportive in the classroom. In essence, autonomy support means teaching in ways that nurture students' intrinsic motivation and internalization processes. It also entails particular beliefs about motivation, a particular interpersonal orientation, and a set of interpersonal skills. As to beliefs about motivation, autonomy support begins by recognizing distinctions between types of motivation (viz., autonomous and controlled) and between teachers' ways of motivating students (viz., autonomy supportive and controlling) so as to appreciate the benefits of students' autonomous motivations sufficiently that one will seek ways to nurture them. As to one's interpersonal style of teaching, autonomy support requires a willingness to enter into relationships from the students' perspective to encourage initiative, nurture competence, and communicate in ways that are noncontrolling and information-rich. As to interpersonal skills, autonomy support involves acquiring talents such as perspective taking, acknowledging feelings, providing rationales for uninteresting lessons, recognizing interest in others, and so on.

This research supports two additional conclusions to supplement the two that introduced the chapter: (3) a teacher's style of motivating students is malleable, and (4) the theoretical concept of autonomy support informs classroom practice.

Conclusion #3 is wonderful news for educators. To the extent that teachers can learn to be autonomy supportive, they have under their control the means to promote for students the sort of educational benefits listed in Table 9-1. Our research suggests that any teacher interested in learning how to be autonomy supportive with students can do so. Conclusion #4 articulates the viability of putting an autonomy-supportive style into practice in educational settings, as it argues that the concept of autonomy support offers prescriptive advice to teachers interested in promoting students' active engagement and volition during learning. As encouraging as these two conclusions are, however, one question persistently dogs any effort to apply self-determination theory to educational settings. That question is, "If autonomy support is so great, then why are teachers so frequently controlling with their students?"

Why Are Teachers Often Controlling with Students?

Even though students benefit when teachers support their autonomy, teachers are nonetheless sometimes controlling with students. Its seems ironic, even

---

Eleven Reasons to Explain Why Teachers Are Sometimes Controlling With Students

1. Prevalence and popularity of behavior modification principles in teacher training programs.

2. Relative absence in these same teacher training programs of how to design instruction to promote student's autonomy.

3. Recognizing interest in others is difficult. So teachers, like everyone else, have a difficult time coordinating their instructional decisions with how interested/disinterested students are.

4. Teachers are themselves subjected to controlling, pressuring conditions within their jobs.

5. The more disengaged students are, the more they pull controlling behaviors out of the teacher.

6. Both parents and students adhere to the "maximal-operant" principle of motivation, which is basically the belief that "the larger the incentive, the greater the motivation."

7. Teachers sometimes underestimate students' abilities to motivate themselves.

8. Some teachers view motivation as a fixed trait in students. Accordingly, when motivation is low, controlling motivational strategies are used to overcome the perceived deficit.

9. The culture (U.S.) identifies teachers as powerful actors and students as relatively weak actors.

10. Both parents and students rate controlling teachers as significantly more competent than autonomy-supportive teachers.

11. Some teachers deeply and sincerely believe that researchers just don't really understand, as in, "If you tried that (i.e., autonomy support) in my classroom, chaos would break loose.

Table 9.3

contradictory, then, to realize that what teachers often practice is the opposite of what students benefit from. I have wondered why this is so, and my experiences, conversations, and research with teachers allows me to offer 11 reasons, which appear in Table 9-3.

Reasons 1-3 acknowledge the current state of affairs in preservice education, namely that education training programs do an admirable job of providing instruction in how to control students' behavior (i.e., courses in classroom management and behavior modification techniques) but a comparatively poor job in providing instruction in how to support students' autonomy. Programs do uphold intrinsic motivation as an important classroom aspiration, but preservice teachers are often left wondering, "OK, *how* do I promote autonomy—*what* would I do?" I hope the information in this chapter communicates some of that prescription (e.g., listen more, provide rationale for uninteresting but important lessons) and that the field as a whole will continue to focus on how to make learning more interesting and fun (Lepper & Cordova, 1992). Reason 3 suggests that if teachers cannot tell how interested students are, then they lack the information they need to adjust their instructional strategies around a theme of enhancing interest. In contrast, behavior modification strategies ask teachers to focus on easier-to-identify behaviors, such as whether or not students raise their hands, how many minutes of the day they are in or out of their seat, and so on. In short, pre-service and beginning teachers are more familiar with, and more skilled in, controlling motivational strategies than autonomy-supportive ones (e.g., Newby, 1991).

Reasons 4 and 5 acknowledge the circumstances of the profession. Demands on teachers such as performance standards, accountability pressures, curriculum priorities, deadlines, testing schedules, large class sizes, and urgent telephone calls from parents influence teachers to focus more and more on concrete performance outcomes and desired behaviors and less and less on nurturing initiative and promoting conceptual understanding. When pressures pile up, teachers often react by utilizing controlling strategies (Deci et al., 1982), largely because they assume that controlling strategies are the best way to maximize achievement outcomes (Boggiano, Barrett, Weiher, McClelland, & Lusk, 1987). Teachers also react in controlling ways when students are listless, irresponsible, and disengaged (Skinner & Belmont, 1993). That is, teachers often try to compensate and reverse student apathy by imposing relatively controlling and attention-getting limits and consequences.

Reasons 6-8 reflect widespread (but erroneous) beliefs about the nature of motivation that permeate the U.S. culture. People generally believe in the merits of extrinsic incentives as a means to cultivate rich and productive motivation in students; and people generally distrust the educational utility of student-owned motivational resources such as curiosity and intrinsic motivation (Boggiano et al., 1987; Hom, 1994). The belief in the "maximal-operant" principle of motivation facilitates a controlling style because it feeds the assumption that an absence of motivation is best countered by the presence of an incentive. Reason 8 acknowledges that some (but not all) teachers are "entity theorists" (Dweck, 1999) when it comes to understanding student motivation. As entity theorists, they see low student motivation as a fixed characteristic of some students that is best dealt with by creating extrinsic sources of motivation to overcome students' internal motivational deficits. The double-barreled implication that follows from reasons 6-8 is the following: If students show little or no autonomy, then how can a teacher be autonomy supportive? And what is wrong with using extrinsic incentives to get them motivated?

Reasons 9 and 10 pertain to what it means to be a teacher (or student) in the U. S. culture. In general, our culture expects a person in the role of a "teacher" to behave in relatively strong and influential ways and to enact behaviors such as "take control," "instruct," and "give directives" (i.e., behaviors consistent with the identity/role of a "teacher;" Heise, 1991). The culture expects a person in the role of a "student" to behave in ways that are relatively passive and compliant and to enact behaviors such as "listen," "observe," and "obey" (i.e., behaviors consistent with the identity/role of a "student;" Heise, 1991). These cultural expectations (and ideals) facilitate a relatively controlling orientation because if a teacher wants approval and positive ratings from parents, administrators, students, and peers, then he or she needs to enact more of the role of an instructor and less of the role of a facilitator (Boggiano, Flink, Shields, Seelbach, & Barrett, 1993).

Reason 11 concerns the common tendency to associate—or equate—high structure with a controlling style and low structure with an autonomy-supportive style. Structure is integral to a productive, smooth-running classroom, but autonomy support has little or nothing to do with a lack of structure. Optimal structure and high autonomy support can, and should, exist side-by-side in a mutually supportive way. It is to questions such as these—what is the relationship between structure and autonomy support?—that I turn next.

Five Additional Concerns and Questions

The utility of applying self-determination to educational settings has far-reaching implications. Here, I apply self-determination theory to five of the questions and concerns I hear most often from teachers and administrators.

What is the Relation between Autonomy Support and Structure?

Autonomy support revolves around giving students freedom to pursue their own agendas. Structure revolves around giving students clear expectations, optimal challenges, and timely and informative feedback as they attempt to make progress in living up to those expectations and challenges. Three relationships have been proposed to specify how autonomy support and structure relate both to one another and to student motivation. The first argues that the two are incompatible opposites, meaning that the act of supporting freedom is by definition the removal of structure. To endorse this view, autonomy support has to be miss-construed as permissiveness, neglect, independence, or a laissez-faire interaction style (i.e., the teacher lets students do whatever they want). Autonomy support is none of these things (Ryan, 1993), as it recognizes that all students depend on their teachers for information and guidance. This view simply misses the point of what it means to be autonomy supportive with students.

The second conceptualization argues for a curvilinear relationship between autonomy support and structure (deCharms, 1984). In a curvilinear relationship, student motivation suffers with both unstructured and rigidly structured classrooms while it thrives with moderate structure. That is, moderate structure is optimal structure. The problem with this curvilinear conceptualization, however, is that autonomy support ends up being defined by (or equated with) the provision of moderate structure. Autonomy support and structure are two different classroom elements which have different aims and different effects on students (Connell & Wellborn, 1991; Skinner, 1991). A third conceptualization is therefore needed, one that understands that autonomy support and structure exist as two independent contextual variables that can be complementary and mutually supportive (Connell & Wellborn, 1991). Teachers can provide little or much structure, and teachers can be controlling or autonomy supportive. Student motivation thrives under conditions in which teachers find ways to provide optimal structure and high autonomy support (Skinner & Belmont, 1993), as will be addressed in the discussion on engagement.

What Is Engagement; How Can It Be Facilitated?

Engagement refers to the intensity and emotional quality of students' involvement during learning (Connell & Wellborn, 1991; Skinner & Belmont, 1993; Wellborn, 1991). It features both behavioral and emotional aspects, such that an engaged student expresses not only high effort but also a positive emotional tone during that effort. Its opposite is disaffection, which means that students withhold effort, give up easily, do just enough to get by, feel burdened or pressured when they do try, and experience anxiety or even anger. The following indicate classroom engagement:

Behaviors During Learning	Emotions During Learning
• Attention	• Interest (vs. Boredom)
• Effort	• Enjoyment/Happiness
• Participation	• Enthusiasm
• Persistence	• (Lack of) Anxiety or Anger

Engagement is a useful concept for applying self-determination theory to educational settings because it provides teachers with an observable manifestation of the quality of a student's motivation. The motivations underlying engagement (i.e., intrinsic motivation and identified regulation) and the motivations underlying disaffection (i.e., external and introjected regulation) are not observable psychological events. Thus, engagement provides teachers with information they can more readily see and monitor than does motivation *per se*.

Engagement arises from experiences in which one's psychological needs for self-determination, competence, and relatedness are met (Connell & Wellborn, 1991; Skinner & Belmont, 1993; Skinner, Zimmer-Gembeck, & Connell, 1998). How teachers facilitate engagement therefore becomes a question of how they create classroom conditions to support and nurture students' needs for self-determination, competence, and relatedness. The teacher-created contextual element that nurtures students' need for self-determination is autonomy support; the contextual element that nurtures the need for competence is structure; and the contextual element that nurtures relatedness is interpersonal involvement.

The third element of an engagement-facilitating classroom climate, in addition to autonomy support and structure, is thus involvement. Involvement refers to the quality of the interpersonal relationship between a teacher and his or her students as well as the teacher's willingness to dedicate psychological resources (e.g., time, energy) to the students (e.g., expressing affection, enjoying spending time with students). Analyzing the conditions that foster engagement is important because it highlights the motivational significance not only of teacher-provided autonomy support but also of teacher-student relationships rich in optimal structure and warm involvement.

Intrinsic Motivation Is Fine, but Extrinsic Motivation Seems Necessary Too.

Few of my visits to schools pass without hearing a teacher say, in essence, that intrinsic motivation is fine and dandy but in the real-world of the classroom extrinsic motivation is also important. Teachers want information to aid them in their efforts to motivate students on tasks and lessons that are important but not necessarily intrinsically interesting (e.g., clean their desks, learn the periodic table). In other words, teachers want a theory of extrinsic motivation.

In self-determination theory, an analysis of extrinsic motivation revolves around the developmental process of internalization (Rigby, Deci, Patrick, & Ryan, 1992; Ryan, Connell, & Grolnick, 1992). Because students want satisfying interpersonal relationships and because they want to obtain esteemed positions in the social hierarchy, they voluntarily learn and internalize their culture's rules, skills, and values. It is through the process of internalization that extrinsic motivation enables self-determined engagement during important but uninteresting endeavors.

Three types of extrinsic motivation exist, and each type varies in how self-determined it is. In the list below, external regulation is not at all internalized or self-determined, introjected regulation is slightly internalized and only a bit self-determined, and identified regulation is highly internalized and largely self-determined:

External regulation: Motivation arises from and is dependent on the presence of environmental events such as rewards, pressures, and constraints ("I read this book so that I'll get a good grade on tomorrow's test.").

Introjected regulation: The student takes in—but does not truly accept—other people's rules or demands to think, feel, or behave in particular ways.

The internalized (but still pressure-inducing) demands of a teacher or parent actually regulate the student's behavior ("I should read this book, so I'll feel like a good student, even though I don't really see the point in it."). Often the student's feelings of worth are dependent on doing as he or she should.

Identified regulation: The student accepts the merits of a belief or behavior because he or she sees its importance or personal utility ("I'll read this book, because learning what it has to say will get me one step closer to an important goal of mine.").

Autonomy-supportive social contexts tend to promote identified regulatory styles in students, whereas controlling contexts tend to promote external and introjected regulatory styles. In other words, the type of internalization that occurs in autonomy-supportive classrooms tends to be identified in character resulting in greater self-determination, whereas the type of internalization that occurs in controlling classrooms tends to be nonexistent (i.e., external regulation) or less complete (i.e., introjected in character). Though more research needs to be done in this area, the specific qualities within an autonomy-supportive context that facilitate identified regulation appear to be the following: (1) providing students with a meaningful rationale as to why the task, lesson, or way of behaving is important or relevant to the child's well-being; (2) establishing an interpersonal relationship that emphasizes choice and flexibility rather than control and pressure; and (3) acknowledging and accepting the negative feelings associated with engaging arduous activities (d'Ailly, 1999; Deci, 1995; Deci et al., 1994; Reeve, Jang, Hardre, & Omura, 2002; Rigby et al., 1992; Ryan et al., 1992).

This line of research has practical utility because it provides classroom teachers with a viable alternative to extrinsic incentives on those tasks that teachers see as important but students see as uninteresting (see Reeve, 1996). To the extent that they feel confident in their ability to promote identified regulation in students, autonomy-supportive teachers will be prepared to motivate students on the full range of lessons and activities found in the school setting.

What Is Self-Determination and What Does It Feel Like?

Self-determination, or autonomy, is a theoretical concept (Deci & Ryan, 1987). It communicates an inner endorsement of one's action–the sense that an action is freely initiated and emanates from within one's self. But, calling self-determination a theoretical concept does not mean that it lacks practical utility or that it cannot be measured. In a couple of studies, we have placed participants into social contexts that we knew would affect their perceptions of self-determination, and while they learned under these conditions we measured various aspects of their subjective experience (Reeve, Nix, & Hamm, 2002). Our purpose in doing so was to identify self-determination's experiential qualities.

As shown in Figure 9-1, we found that the perception of self-determination revolved around three essential qualities–internal perceived locus of causality, volition, and perceived choice. Perceived locus of causality exists within a bipolar continuum that extends from internal to external and concerns the individual's belief that his or her behavior is initiated and regulated either by a personal (internal) or by an environmental (external) force. An internal perceived locus of causality reflects high self-determination (e.g., Because I was so interested, I read the book; deCharms, 1976; Deci & Ryan, 1985). Volition constitutes an unpressured willingness to engage in an activity. When volitional, the person feels free, but, when nonvolitional, he or she feels pressured (Deci, Ryan, & Williams, 1996). Perceived choice emanates from being afforded decision-making flexibility and opportunities to choose what to do (Zuckerman, Porac, Lathin, Smith, & Deci, 1978). These three qualities–or aspects of experience–capture the essence of what self-determination feels like. And, these qualities tell us how to measure people's experience of self-determination with a questionnaire (see the lower half of Figure 9-1). In addition, these findings inform teachers about what to focus on in the effort to promote students' sense of self-determination. That is, the potentially bewildering question of "How do I promote self-determination in students?" translates into the more straight-forward question of "How do I promote an internal locus of causality, a sense of volition, and a perception of choice?" These are the questions addressed in the next section.

What Can a Teacher Do to Support Autonomy in Students?

Supporting or promoting autonomy in others is not as straightforward as it might first appear to be. I say this because, at present, we know more about how to undermine and interfere with students' autonomy than we know about how to support and promote it (see Lepper & Cordova, 1992). For instance, imposing extraneous rewards (Lepper, Greene, & Nisbett, 1973), deadlines (Amabile, DeJong, & Lepper, 1976), and verbal directives (Boggiano et al., 1993) on students all effectively induce an external perceived locus of causality. And, telling students that their performances will be evaluated (Ryan, 1982), providing controlling performance feedback (Ryan, Mims, & Koestner, 1983), and introducing a competitive set that focuses on winning (Reeve & Deci, 1996) all effectively decrease volition. Similarly, assigning students tasks to perform creates a sense of obligation that works against the perception of choice (Zuckerman et al., 1978).

But what do we know about ways to increase students' sense of autonomy? The subjective experiences of an internal perceived locus of causality, high volition, and perceived choice are highly intertwined with one another, and in some ways it does not even make sense to talk about one of these qualities without also

Perceived Self-Determination

Internal Perceived Locus of Causality

Questionnaire Items
I felt like I was doing what I wanted to be doing.

I felt like I was doing what the teacher wanted me to be doing.*

I was pursuing my own goals, goals that were important to me.

I was pursuing the goals of the teacher, goals that were important only to the teacher, not me.*

Volition

Questionnaire Items
While doing this task, I felt a relaxed sense of personal freedom.

While I was doing this task, I felt pushed, forced, and pressured.*

During this task, I felt free.

During this task, I felt pressured.*

Perception of Choice

Questionnaire Items
I had a choice whether or not to engage and participate in this task.

I felt it was my own choice about what to do, when to do it, and whether to do anything at all.

I felt that I had control to decide what to do and whether to do it.

Throughout my participation, I had choices as to what I wanted to do.

* item is reversed scored.

Figure 9.1. Three Qualities within the Experience of Self-Determination

including the other two qualities in the conversation. But, exposing students to interesting and worthwhile tasks fosters an internal locus of causality (because felt interest and a sense of importance generates task engagement), promoting a "task" rather than an "ego" involvement cultivates a sense of volition (because it promotes freedom and diffuses pressure), and providing flexible interpersonal environments and opportunities to choose how, when, and whether to act facilitates the perception of choice (Cordova & Lepper, 1996; Schraw, Flowerday, & Reisetter, 1998; Swann & Pittman, 1977; Zuckerman et al., 1978).

Conclusion

In conclusion, applying self-determination theory to educational settings has proven to be a productive undertaking. The theory explains why autonomously-motivated students thrive, and it explains why students benefit when teachers support their autonomy. We have learned what autonomy-supportive teachers are doing from one moment to the next, and we have learned why these behaviors benefit students by articulating their effects on perceptions of self-determination and competence. We have further shown that one's motivating style is malleable, and that teachers can learn how to be more autonomy supportive with students. And, we have learned many of the reasons why teachers are sometimes controlling with their students (see Table 9-3). While the effort to learn how to integrate students' motivational resources such as self-determination into the school curriculum requires asking teachers to develop new skills and brave the waters of conceptual change, the benefits for students of doing so are many (see Table 9-1).

References

Amabile, T. M. (1985). Motivation and creativity: Effect of motivational orientation on creative writers. *Journal of Personality and Social Psychology, 48*, 393-399.

Amabile, T. M., DeJong, W., & Lepper, M. R. (1976). Effects of externally imposed deadlines on subsequent intrinsic motivation. *Journal of Personality and Social Psychology, 34*, 92-98.

Benware, C., & Deci, E. L. (1984). The quality of learning with an active versus passive motivational set. *American Educational Research Journal, 21*, 755-765.

Boggiano, A. K., & Barrett, M. (1985). Performance and motivational deficits of helplessness: The role of motivational orientations. *Journal of Personality and Social Psychology, 49*, 1753-1761.

Boggiano, A. K., Barrett, M., Weiher, A. W., McClelland, G. H., & Lusk, C. M. (1987). Use of the maximal-operant principle to motivate children's intrinsic interest. *Journal of Personality and Social Psychology, 53*, 866-879.

Boggiano, A. K., Flink, C., Shields, A., Seelbach, A., & Barrett, M. (1993). Use of techniques promoting students' self-determination: Effects on students' analytic problem-solving skills. *Motivation and Emotion, 17*, 319-336.

Boggiano, A. K., Main, D. S., & Katz, P. A. (1988). Children's preference for challenge: The role of perceived competence and control. *Journal of Personality and Social Psychology, 54*, 134-141.

Connell, J. P., & Wellborn, J. G. (1991). Competence, autonomy, and relatedness: A motivational analysis of self-esteem processes. In M. R. Gunnar & L. A. Sroufe (Eds.), *Self processes in development: Minnesota symposium on child psychology* (Vol. 23, pp. 167-216). Hillsdale, NJ: Lawrence Erlbaum.

Cordova, D. I., & Lepper, M. R. (1996). Intrinsic motivation and the process of learning: Beneficial effects of contextualization, personalization, and choice. *Journal of Educational Psychology, 88*, 715-730.

d'Ailly, H. (1999). *The effects of perceived autonomy on students' learning and interest.* Paper presented at the 107th annual conference of the American Psychological Association, Boston, MA.

deCharms, R. (1976). *Enhancing motivation: Change in the classroom.* New York: Irvington.

deCharms, R. (1984). Motivation enhancement in educational settings. In R. E. Ames & C. Ames (Eds.), *Research on motivation in education: Student motivation* (Vol. 1, pp. 275-310). San Diego, CA: Academic Press.

Deci, E. L. (1995). *Why we do what we do: The dynamics of personal autonomy.* New York: Penguin Books.

Deci, E. L., Eghrari, H., Patrick, B. C., & Leone, D. R. (1994). Facilitating internalization: The self-determination theory perspective. *Journal of Personality, 62*, 119-142.

Deci, E. L., Nezlek, J., & Sheinman, L. (1981). Characteristics of the rewarder and intrinsic motivation of the rewardee. *Journal of Personality and Social Psychology, 40*, 1-10.

Deci, E. L., & Ryan, R. M. (1985). *Intrinsic motivation and self-determination in human behavior.* New York: Plenum.

Deci, E. L., & Ryan, R. M. (1987). The support of autonomy and the control of behavior. *Journal of Personality and Social Psychology, 53*, 1024-1037.

Deci, E. L., & Ryan, R. M. (1991). A motivational approach to self: Integration in personality. In R. Dienstbier (Ed.), *Nebraska Symposium on Motivation: Perspectives on Motivation* (Vol. 38, pp. 237-288). Lincoln: University of Nebraska Press.

Deci, E. L., Ryan, R. M., & Williams, G. C. (1996). Need satisfaction and the self-regulation of learning. *Learning and Individual Differences, 8*, 165-183.

Deci, E. L., Schwartz, A. J., Sheinman, L., & Ryan, R. M. (1981). An instrument to assess adult's orientations toward control versus autonomy in children: Reflections on intrinsic motivation and perceived competence. *Journal of Educational Psychology, 73*, 642-650.

Deci, E. L., Spiegel, N. H., Ryan, R. M., Koestner, R., & Kauffman, M. (1982). Effects of performance standards on teaching styles: Behavior of controlling teachers. *Journal of Educational Psychology, 74*, 852-859.

Deci, E. L., Vallerand, R. J., Pelletier, L. G., & Ryan, R. M. (1991). Motivation in education: The self-determination perspective. *Educational Psychologist, 26*, 325-346.

Dweck, C. (1999). *Self-theories: Their role in motivation, personality, and development.* Philadelphia, PA: Psychology Press.

Eccles, J., & Midgley, C. (1989). Stage-environment fit: Developmentally appropriate classrooms for young adolescents. In C. Ames & R. Ames (Eds.), *Research on motivation in education: Goals and cognitions* (Vol. 3, pp. 139-186). New York: Academic Press.

Flink, C., Boggiano, A. K., & Barrett, M. (1990). Controlling teaching strategies: Undermining children's self-determination and performance. *Journal of Personality and Social Psychology, 59,* 916-924.

Flink, C., Boggiano, A. K., Main, D. S., Barrett, M., & Katz, P. A. (1992). Children's achievement-related behaviors: The role of extrinsic and intrinsic motivational orientations. In A. K. Boggiano & T. S. Pittman (Eds.), *Achievement and motivation: A social- developmental perspective* (pp. 189-214). New York: Cambridge University Press.

Garbarino, J. (1975). The impact of anticipated reward upon cross-aged tutoring. *Journal of Personality and Social Psychology, 32,* 421-428.

Grolnick, W. S., & Ryan, R. M. (1987). Autonomy in children's learning: An experimental and individual difference investigation. *Journal of Personality and Social Psychology, 52,* 890-898.

Hamm, D., & Reeve, J. (2002). *Teachers as resources and obstacles to students' intrinsic motivation.* Unpublished manuscript, Michigan State University.

Harter, S. (1974). Pleasure derived by children from cognitive challenge and mastery. *Child Development, 45,* 661-669.

Harter, S. (1978). Pleasure derived from optimal challenge and the effects of extrinsic rewards on children's difficulty level choices. *Child Development, 49,* 788-799.

Heise, D. R. (1991). *INTERACT 2: A computer program for studying cultural meanings and social interaction.* Department of Sociology, University of Indiana.

Hom, Jr., H. L. (1994). Can you predict the overjustification effect? *Teaching of Psychology, 21,* 36-37.

Koestner, R., Ryan, R. M., Bernieri, F., & Holt, K. (1984). Setting limits on children's behavior: The differential effects of controlling versus informational styles on intrinsic motivation and creativity. *Journal of Personality, 52,* 233-248.

Lepper, M. R., & Cordova, D. I. (1992). A desire to be taught: Instructional consequences of intrinsic motivation. *Motivation and Emotion, 16,* 187-208.

Lepper, M. R., Greene, D., & Nisbett, R. E. (1973). Undermining children's intrinsic interest with extrinsic rewards: A test of the "overjustification" hypothesis. *Journal of Personality and Social Psychology, 31,* 479-486.

McGraw, K. O., & McCullers, J. C. (1979). Evidence of a detrimental effect of extrinsic incentives on breaking a mental set. *Journal of Experimental Social Psychology, 15,* 285-294.

Miserandino, M. (1996). Children who do well in school: Individual differences in perceived competence and autonomy in above-average children. *Journal of Educational Psychology, 88,* 203-214.

Newby, T. J. (1991). Classroom motivation: Strategies of first-year teachers. *Journal of Educational Psychology, 83,* 195-200.

Patrick, B. C., Skinner, E. A., & Connell, J. P. (1993). What motivates children's behavior and emotion? Joint effects of perceived control and autonomy in the academic domain. *Journal of Personality and Social Psychology, 65,* 781-791.

Pittman, T. S., Emery, J., & Boggiano, A. K. (1982). Intrinsic and extrinsic motivational orientations: Reward induced changes in preference for complexity. *Journal of Personality and Social Psychology*, *42*, 789-797.

Reeve, J. (1993). The face of interest. *Motivation and Emotion*, *17*, 353-375.

Reeve, J. (1996). *Motivating others: Nurturing inner motivational resources*. Needham Heights, MA: Allyn & Bacon.

Reeve, J. (1998). Autonomy support as an interpersonal motivating style: Is it teachable? *Contemporary Educational Psychology*, *23*, 312-330.

Reeve, J., Arndt, L., & Omura, M. (2002). *Recognizing interest and disinterest in students*. Unpublished manuscript, University of Iowa.

Reeve, J., Bolt, E., & Cai, Y. (1999). Autonomy-supportive teachers: How they teach and motivate students. *Journal of Educational Psychology*, *91*, 537-548.

Reeve, J., & Deci, E. L. (1996). Elements of the competitive situation that affect intrinsic motivation. *Personality and Social Psychology Bulletin*, *22*, 24-33.

Reeve, J., Jang, H., Hardre, P., & Omura, M. (2002). *Providing a rationale for an uninteresting activity as a motivational strategy to support another person's self-determined extrinsic motivation*. Unpublished manuscript, University of Iowa.

Reeve, J., & Nix, G. (1997). Expressing intrinsic motivation through acts of exploration and facial displays of interest. *Motivation and Emotion*, *21*, 237-250.

Reeve, J., Nix, G., & Hamm, D. (2002). *The experience of self-determination in intrinsic motivation and the conundrum of choice*. Unpublished manuscript, University of Iowa.

Rigby, C. S., Deci, E. L., Patrick, B. P., & Ryan, R. M. (1992). Beyond the intrinsic-extrinsic dichotomy: Self-determination in motivation and learning. *Motivation and Emotion*, *16*, 165-185.

Ryan, R. M. (1982). Control and information in the intrapersonal sphere: An extension of cognitive evaluation theory. *Journal of Personality and Social Psychology*, *43*, 450-461.

Ryan, R. M. (1993). Agency and organization: Intrinsic motivation, autonomy, and the self in psychological development. In J. E. Jacobs (Ed.), *Nebraska symposium on motivation: Developmental perspectives on motivation* (Vol. 40, pp. 1-56). Lincoln: University of Nebraska Press.

Ryan, R. M., & Connell, J. P. (1989). Perceived locus of causality and internalization: Examining reasons for acting in two domains. *Journal of Personality and Social Psychology*, *57*, 749-761.

Ryan, R. M., Connell, J. P., & Grolnick, W. W. (1992). When achievement is *not* intrinsically motivated: A theory of internalization and self-regulation in school. In A. K. Boggiano & T. S. Pittman (Eds.), *Achievement and motivation: A social-developmental perspective* (pp. 167-188). New York: Cambridge University Press.

Ryan, R. M., & Grolnick, W. S. (1986). Origins and pawns in the classroom: Self-report and projective assessments of individual differences in children's perceptions. *Journal of Personality and Social Psychology*, *50*, 550-558.

Ryan, R. M., Mims, V., & Koestner, R. (1983). Relation of reward contingency and interpersonal context to intrinsic motivation: A review and test using cognitive evaluation theory. *Journal of Personality and Social Psychology*, *45*, 736-750.

Schraw, G., Flowerday, T., & Reisetter, M. F. (1998). The role of choice in reader engagement. *Journal of Educational Psychology*, *90*, 705-714.

Shapira, Z. (1976). Expectancy determinants of intrinsically motivated behavior. *Journal of Personality and Social Psychology*, *34*, 1235-1244.

Skinner, E. A. (1991). Development and perceived control: A dynamic model of action in context. In M. Gunnar & L. A. Sroufe (Eds.), *Minnesota Symposium on Child Psychology* (Vol. 23). Hillsdale, NJ: Lawrence Erlbaum.

Skinner, E. A., & Belmont, M. J. (1993). Motivation in the classroom: Reciprocal effects of teacher behavior and student engagement across the school year. *Journal of Educational Psychology, 85,* 571-581.

Skinner, E. A., Zimmer-Gembeck, M. J., & Connell, J. P. (1998). Individual differences and the development of perceived control. *Monographs of the Society for Research in Child Development, 63,* Serial No. 254.

Swann, W. B., & Pittman, T. S. (1977). Initiating play activity of children: The moderating influence of verbal cues on intrinsic motivation. *Child Development, 48,* 1128-1132.

Vallerand, R. J., & Bissonette, R. (1992). Intrinsic, extrinsic, and amotivational styles as predictors of behavior: A prospective study. *Journal of Personality, 60,* 599-620.

Vallerand, R. J., Fortier, M. S., & Guay, F. (1997). Self-determination and persistence in a real-life setting: Toward a motivational model of high school dropout. *Journal of Personality and Social Psychology, 72,* 1161-1176.

Wellborn, J. G. (1991). *Engaged and disaffected action: The conceptualization and measurement of motivation in the academic domain.* Unpublished doctoral dissertation, University of Rochester.

Williams, G. C., Wiener, M. W., Markakis, K. M., Reeve, J., & Deci, E. L. (1994). Medical students' motivation for internal medicine. *Journal of General Internal Medicine, 9,* 327-333.

Zuckerman, M., Porac, J., Lathin, D., Smith, R., & Deci, E. L. (1978). On the importance of self-determination for intrinsically-motivated behavior. *Personality and Social Psychology Bulletin, 4,* 443-446.

10: A Motivational Analysis of Self-Determination for Pro-Environmental Behaviors

Luc G. Pelletier
University of Ottawa

Environmental problems—air pollution, water pollution, the greenhouse effect, global climate change, depletion of the earth's ozone layer, the clearing of tropical rain forests, and others—are the result of human behavior (Gardner & Stern, 1996; McKenzie-Mohr, & Oskamp, 1995; Miller, 1994). The complexity of the environmental problems is further aggravated by growth in the world's population. It is estimated that the global population reached 1 billion in 1830. One hundred years later, by 1930, it had reached 2 billion. Sixty-five years later, in 1995, 5.6 billion people occupied the earth.

Although, predicting population growth is an inexact science, the United Nations Population Fund (1991) estimated that world population will be between 8 and 12 billion by 2050, and could be anywhere between 3.6 and 27 billion by 2150. The difference between the two projections, although vast, is a simple function of one child per woman. If fertility rates continue to drop until women have about two children each, which is a medium range projection, the population will stabilize at 10.8 billion. If the average is 2.6 children, the population will quadruple to 27 billion, but if the average falls to 1.6, the total could drop to 3.6 billion. Needless to say, this dramatic difference would have a huge effect in terms of competition for the world's increasingly scarce resources. Virtually all of the projected population increase by 2050 will occur in developing countries (primarily in Central and South America, in Africa, and in South Asia), as the population of the developed world (Australia, New Zealand, North America, Europe, and Northern Asia) is expected to fall, because women there continue to average fewer than two children each. Thus, the developing countries will experience the greatest press with respect to the scarce resources.

Interestingly, however, the population's impact on the environment is perhaps the most paradoxical aspect of the ecological problem. At present, countries in the developing world consume far fewer resources per capita than do the developed nations. Developed countries contain only 22% of the world's population, but as a result of their affluence, their technologies, and their industrialization, they consume 88% of the earth's natural resources and 73% of the energy resources, and they generate most of the air pollution and waste (Miller, 1994). As populations increase in the developing countries and industrialization continues, their global environmental impact should accelerate considerably. Consequently, the combined effects of population and technology on the earth's environment should accentuate many other threats to human, animal, and plant life such as air and water pollution, increased quantities of pesticides and toxins in food products, CFC (chlorofluorocarbons) causing depletion of the ozone layer, carbon dioxide and other gases causing the greenhouse effect, overuse of fossil fuels, that produce acid rain and lead to death of forests and lakes, destruction of forests by logging and subsistence agriculture, which leads to global climate changes, and extinction of thousands of species, which could create great danger of crop and human disease. In sum, the danger of humans' producing irreversible, harmful changes to the environment is grave and imminent.

Clearly if we are to have a sustainable future, substantial shifts in values, attitudes, and behavior must occur (McKenzie-Mohr & Oskamp, 1995). These shifts must involve individuals' learning new ways to meet their needs without compromising the ability of future generations to meet theirs (World Commission on Economic Development, 1987). In other words, it is becoming obvious that individuals are now facing the important challenge of adopting new environmentally responsible behaviors, maintaining those behaviors, and integrating them into their lifestyles.

Several theoretical perspectives have been proposed to better understand how these goals could be achieved (see Gardner & Stern, 1996; Geller, 1995; Stern, Young, & Druckman, 1992). One theoretical perspective of human motivation that has received a great deal of attention from researchers over the last decade and has implications for the issues of maintenance and integration of change is the theory of intrinsic motivation and self-determination proposed by Deci and Ryan (1985). This comprehensive theory holds the potential to contribute significantly to our understanding of the issues related to environmentally responsible behaviors for the following reasons. First, it distinguishes between different types of motivation that can have distinct impacts on the maintenance and integration of behaviors. Second, it presents clear hypotheses regarding the contextual as well as the interpersonal conditions that should hinder or facilitate individuals' motivation to adopt new behaviors. Third, it outlines various consequences (cognitive, affective, and behavioral) that are associated with the different types of motivation. And fourth, it addresses the issue of internalization—that is, the process by which changes that were initially reinforced by external sources (e.g., incentives or the approval of a significant other) become integrated within the individual to form a permanent part of his or her character.

This chapter presents the results of a program of research that focused on the application of self-determination theory (SDT) to environmentally responsible behaviors. Before turning to this program of research, a brief review is presented of research on the strategies and the key variables that have been derived from other approaches to promoting pro-environmental behaviors. Their limitations as they pertain to the issue of maintenance of behaviors and the issue of a sustainable future, are examined. The section following that presents the research supporting the validity of a scale designed to measure individuals' intrinsic motivation, four forms of regulation for extrinsic motivation (integrated, identified, introjected, and external regulation), and amotivation for environmental behaviors. Then, the next section presents a review of the evidence regarding the relations between the different types of motivation and various outcomes such as recycling, conservation of energy, environmental activism, and seeking out information about health risks. In the final section, we examine how individuals' perceptions of various environmental factors predict their levels of self-determination for environmental-friendly behaviors. Antecedents include variables such as satisfaction with the conditions of the environment and with government environmental policies, perceptions of competence towards environmental behaviors, and various sources of information such as the family, friends, children, and the government. The last section of the chapter presents final thoughts on this program of research.

Strategies for Promoting Pro-Environmental Behaviors: A Brief Review

In view of the seriousness and imminence of environmental threats, many social scientists and environmentalists have worked to find ways to instill environmental awareness and promote environmentally responsible behaviors. Most of the research has focused on two types of solutions or ways to encourage pro-environmental behaviors: (a) the use of programs of education, which attempt to encourage pro-environmental behaviors by giving people knowledge and by trying to change their attitudes about the environment; and (b) the use of government laws, behavioral intervention strategies, and incentives to encourage pro-environmental behaviors and discourage damaging behaviors.

Information about the Environment

Programs for environmental education typically have two types of agendas. First, they describe the nature and severity of the problem in an effort to change people's attitudes toward the environment. This is usually accomplished by trying to convince individuals that the problem is serious and important enough to justify their immediate action. Second, they outline the specific actions individuals can take to help solve the problem. The information provided about the seriousness of the situation is expected to serve as the motivation for becoming involved. The knowledge about the specific actions individuals should take to solve a problem is expected to foster a sense of competence in the individuals. Environmental information and perceptions of competence have been identified as prerequisites for environmentally conscious action (Arcury & Johnson, 1987). It seems logical to expect that people would need to possess factual information about the state of the environment and about the influence of human actions on the environment in order to start believing that it is important to do something to change the situation. It is also logical to believe that people must know what behaviors are important and feel competent to manifest these behaviors. These two factors, which constitute perceived control and perceived competence, are necessary, but not sufficient by themselves, to create a change of pro-environmental behaviors.

Recent statistics show that some individuals are more than ever concerned with the worsening condition of the environment (Angus Reid Group, 1992; Environment Canada, 1991). However, despite numerous environmental programs established mainly to provide the public with relevant information, it seems that the level of environmental knowledge about specific actions individuals should take remains low (Arcury & Johnson, 1987; Brothers, Fortner, & Mayer, 1991; Gigliotti, 1990) and even well-informed people often fail to act on their knowledge (Seligman, 1985). For example, Oskamp (1995) observed that, although all respondents surveyed indicated that their knowledge about the requirements of recycling was very high, only 40% of them recycled when they had access to a curbside recycling program. This number dropped to less than 10% when people indicated that they did not have access to a recycling program. Thus, although general environmental concern along with environmental knowledge and perceptions of competence appear to be necessary for environmental actions, these factors are still not sufficient to ensure a high level of pro-environmental behaviors.

Several studies have examined the effects of specific perceptions of environmental concern (e.g., degree of environmental threat) on pro-environmental behaviors. When specifically defined, environmental concern has usually been a significant mediating variable between individual characteristics (e.g., people's level of education) and environmental behaviors (Milbrath, 1984). It appears that the importance of environmental concern increases as a specific environmental threat is tied to a targeted environmental behavior (Chaiken & Stangor, 1987).

One class of specific environmental attitudes, namely, perception of health risks, has received some attention as a determinant of environmental behaviors. Perception of environmental health risks are generally found to generate strong public concern and to lead to social action and pro-environmental behaviors such as recycling (Gardner & Stern, 1996) and environmental activism (Séguin,

Pelletier, & Hunsley, 1998). However, educational efforts that increase perceptions of health risks (e.g., pollution by cars can increases the probability of having asthma) are unlikely to succeed if they require changing a behavior that individuals value, such as driving their cars (Oskamp, Harrington, Edwards, Sherwood, Okuda, & Swanson, 1991). It has also been observed that the relations between different types of environmental concerns and various behaviors were affected by self-efficacy or perceived control (Oskamp, 1995). In other words, although individuals may have information and be concerned about current environmental conditions, if they do not know what to do or they believe they can not change the situation, they are unlikely to engage in pro-environmental behaviors.

Educational approaches aimed at changing people's attitudes seem to be effective in promoting behavior primarily when the behaviors are relatively simple and easy. When protecting the environment requires great effort or expense, behaviors become unlikely unless interventions to reduce the external barriers are present. For example, depositing cans in curbside recycling bins or altering home thermostat settings, represent relatively simple and low-cost behaviors. As indicated before, Oskamp (1995) reported that 40% of citizens indicated that they were recycling when they had access to a curbside recycling program. This number dropped to less than 10% when citizens did not have access to a recycling program. Pelletier and Bellier (1999) observed similar results with citizens in different cities, some who had access to curbside recycling and others who did not. Interestingly, levels of recycling for individuals with curbside recycling dropped considerably when they were away from their homes or, for some other reason, did not have access to easy recycling. These results suggest that information about a specific behavior like recycling may lead to a positive attitude toward recycling and to more pro-environmental behaviors as long as these behaviors are not too costly or there are no barriers present.

Incentives

Researchers have often relied on incentives (or reinforcements) as a strategy for promoting pro-environmental behaviors (see Dwyer, Leeming, Cobern, Porter, & Jackson, 1993, or Geller, 1989, for literature reviews). Creating incentives is usually perceived as a powerful approach. Incentives can reduce the cost or the effort involved in following one's pro-environmental attitudes, and they can also make it attractive for a person who lacks such attitudes to engage in pro-environmental behaviors (e.g., to gain money for recycling tin cans). In addition, incentives can create barriers to actions that harm the environment (e.g., an increase in the cost of gasoline can be an incentive not to buy gas guzzling vehicles). According to this approach, because behavior is strongly dependent on the incentive structure, using incentives is an effective way to change behavior. But, do incentives really work?

Incentives seem to be most effective when aimed at organizations and decision makers. Such was the case when the increasing financial and political costs of waste disposal in landfills changed the incentives for the managers of municipal waste disposal programs and led many cities to sponsor recycling programs and other initiatives that made it easier for individuals to recycle. In most circumstances, incentives aimed at the general public have been less successful and have failed when significant barriers to action are part of a larger social system. For example, it is hard to conceive of incentives that would greatly reduce people's use of their automobiles. The geography of North American homes, workplaces, and shopping makes the shift to public transportation very inconvenient and time-consuming (Everett & Watson, 1987). Under some conditions, incentives can also have unintended consequences that are experienced as punishment (Gardner & Stern, 1996). For example, price increases for energy force low-income people to make hard choices between heating their homes in winter and buying food or clothing.

Incentives can lead to short-terms effects, but they can lose their appeal over time, making them inadequate for instilling long-term change (Geller, Winett, & Everett, 1982; Katzev & Johnson, 1984: Winett, Leckliter, Chinn, Stahl, & Love, 1985; Witmer & Geller, 1976). Several researchers (e.g., Aronson & Gonzales, 1990; DeYoung, 1986; Wang & Katzev, 1990; Witmer & Geller, 1976) observed that when incentives were discontinued responsible environmental behaviors returned to baseline levels. It seems that even when rewards do promote environmental behaviors, these behaviors persist only as long as the reward contingencies remain in effect.

In sum, research on environmental behaviors has typically examined whether educational programs designed to influence specific attitudes like environmental concern or satisfaction, as well as providing information about the current conditions of the environment, about health risks, or about the effect of specific behaviors, were related to pro-environmental behaviors. Although some of these variables did predict the target behaviors, individuals' levels of satisfaction or concern with the current environmental conditions appear not to be sufficient for action. Individuals must also believe that they know what to do and that their action can change the situation, otherwise they are unlikely to engage in pro-environmental behaviors. However, even though individuals feel that it is important to do something and they know what to do, the strategies that aim at changing people's attitudes and behaviors seem to be effective mainly with relatively simple or easy behaviors. When behaviors become more difficult or costly, the association between environmental attitudes, knowledge, and pro-environmental behaviors is considerably reduced.

As a complement to this first general strategy, many researchers have proposed using incentives to make it more attractive for people to engage in pro-environmental behaviors, to reduce the cost or effort involved in such behaviors, or to make the behaviors less difficult by removing some of the barriers for action. These strategies also have some serious limitations. First, it is not always possible to eliminate barriers when these barriers are part of the social system. Second, eliminating barriers (and using incentives) can be costly and difficult to maintain. Third, incentives can lead to short-term effects but lose their appeal over time. Fourth, they can promote target behaviors only as long as they are given to reinforce these behaviors; if they are discontinued, the behaviors returned to baseline levels. Overall, incentives can be successful on a short-term basis but are inadequate to instill much long-term change.

Self-Determination for Pro-Environmental Behaviors

In an attempt to address environmental problems and the threat to a sustainable future, the study of intrinsic motivation and self-determination was proposed as a means to gain insight into the regulation of enduring environmental behaviors (DeYoung, 1986; Pelletier, Tuson, Green-Demers, Noels, & Beaton, 1998). As a theoretical model, self-determination theory has received empirical support in a number of life domains such as education, interpersonal relationships, work, health, leisure, sports, and psychotherapy. In these various domains, SDT has been successfully employed to predict a variety of behaviors. Research has also isolated various antecedent variables that foster versus hinder self-determination. Thus, by examining similar antecedents in the environmental domain, it may be possible to specify ways of enhancing self-determination for pro-environmental behaviors and behavioral outcomes.

As a first step, such a program of research required a valid instrument to assess the full range of motives liable to underlie environmental actions. On the basis of SDT, we developed a new measure to assess motivation for pro-environmental behaviors, with one version for English-speaking populations, "The Motivation Towards the Environment Scale" (MTES; Pelletier et al., 1998) and one for French-speaking populations "l'Échelle de Motivation vis-à-vis les Comportements Écologiques" (EMCE; Green-Demers, Pelletier, & Legault, in press; Pelletier, Green-Demers, & Béland, 1997). By creating an instrument designed to assess the different types of motivation proposed by Deci and Ryan, we were hoping to lay the foundation for the study of self-determination for pro-environmental behaviors.

Why Are You Doing Things for the Environment?

The MTES comprises 24 items, distributed within 6 subscales (intrinsic motivation, extrinsic motivation in the form of integrated, identified, introjected, and external regulation, and amotivation). It thus measures the multiple types of motivation that fall along the self-determination continuum (Deci & Ryan, 1985). The items represent possible responses to the question, "Why are you doing things for the environment?"

The articles relating the results of the initial assessment of the psychometric properties of the MTES and EMCE offered encouraging support for the reliability and validity of the scales. The MTES was constructed prior to the EMCE, and its measurement characteristics were evaluated in the context of four independent studies (Pelletier et al., 1998). Results of exploratory and confirmatory factor analyses with more than 1200 participants, revealed that the MTES displayed a sound six-factor solution. Its construct validity was further substantiated by correlations with related environmental and psychological constructs (e.g., locus of control, perceived importance of environmental issues, and frequencies of environmental behaviors). Test-retest correlations and internal consistency values (Cronbach's alpha) indicated that the subscale scores were reliable. The French version, the EMCE, was created using the reversed parallel translation procedure proposed by Vallerand (1989). Its properties were assessed in two independent studies (Pelletier et al., 1997). The results of a confirmatory factor analysis yielded a sound factorial structure that was similar to the MTES. Also, the convergent validity of the scores of the EMCE subscales was supported by correlations with pertinent constructs. The subscales' scores exhibited adequate internal consistency values and test-retest correlations.

The MTES and the EMCE were designed to be formally identical. Nevertheless, given that respondents from different populations are likely to interpret questionnaire items in different ways, the psychometric equivalency was also assessed by testing for invariant factorial measurement across the English and French linguistic groups. The samples utilized in the development and validation of the English and French versions of this scale were compared anew to assess the replicability of the factorial structure of the MTES using the stringent test of formal invariance. The factor loadings and the factor covariance were generally invariant, which argued in favor of the metric equivalence of the MTES and EMCE. Finally, differences in latent means indicated that the English participants had higher intrinsic motivation, as well as higher integrated, identified, and introjected regulation than did the French participants. English participants displayed lower levels of external regulation as well. No differences were found in the latent means of the amotivation factor.

Research on the MTES and EMCE has followed the same sequence of scale development and validation procedures as those used in the domains of education (Vallerand, Blais, Brière, & Pelletier, 1989; Vallerand, Pelletier, Blais, Brière, Senécal, & Vallières, 1992, 1993) or sports (Pelletier, Fortier, Vallerand, Tuson, Brière, & Blais, 1995). They have a sound factor structure and adequate levels of internal consistency and temporal stability, and they are unrelated to social desirability. As suggested by Vallerand (1997), scores on each of the six subscales can be used separately or they can be combined into a global self-determination index (Blais, Sabourin, Boucher, & Vallerand, 1990; Grolnick & Ryan, 1987; Vallerand & Bissonnette, 1992; Vallerand, Fortier & Guay, 1998). The use of distinct scores for each subscale could be useful, for example, to identify which type of motivation is the best predictor of a specific pro-environmental behavior or to assess the impact of changes in government environmental policy on specific types of motivation. The use of a composite score obtained by giving weights to the motivational subscales according to their respective placement on the self-determination continuum, could be useful to identify individuals who are self-determined or non self-determined toward the environment. Individuals with different motivational profiles combined with the presence or the absence of a specific environmental program could then be used in a quasi-experiment to assess the impact of both individual differences and programs on a pro-environmental behavior (e.g., recycling). A global score of self-determination can also be useful when testing a parsimonious or integrative theoretical model that involves antecedents and consequences of autonomous versus controlled motivation. Finally, the intrinsic, integrated, and identified motivation subscales could be regrouped to form a global score of autonomous motivation, and the introjected, external regulation, and amotivation subscales could be regrouped to form a global score of non-self-determined motivation (Elliot & Sheldon, 1998; Sheldon & Elliot, 1998). The use of autonomous and controlled motivation could also be useful for examining antecedents and consequences of these two types of motivation, when one is interested in the concurrent relations of two global types of motivation to different environmental outcomes such as the frequency of a specific pro-environmental behavior or its maintenance.

In sum, the MTES and the EMCE seem to demonstrate very acceptable levels of reliability and validity. Because the constructs assessed by these scales can be related to both antecedents and consequences, they are key variables for elaborating theoretical models that address the complex relations among perceptions and concerns about the environment, types of motivation, and behaviors.

Motivation and Environmental Outcomes

Numerous studies have related the different types of motivation proposed by SDT to various types of outcomes. The types of motivational fall along a continuum of self-determination so it has been hypothesized that the consequences associated with the different types of motivation would vary as a function of their implied level of self-determination. Specifically, highly self-determined motivational subtypes were expected to lead to positive psychological and behavioral consequences. Conversely, low levels of self-determination were predicted to relate to negative psychological and behavioral consequences. Several studies, using different methodological strategies and performed in a variety of domains, offer support for this proposition. For instance, self-determined motivation has been associated with greater interest (Deci, 1992), more positive emotions (Brière & Vallerand, 1990), higher psychological well-being (Pelletier et al., 1995), and increased behavioral persistence (Vallerand, Fortier, & Guay, 1998; Vallerand & Bissonnette, 1992). In the context of the environment, we have investigated how the different types of motivation relate to specific pro-environmental behaviors (such as recycling, conserving energy, and purchasing specific products) and environmental activism. In addition, we have examined how the concept of self-determination relates to behaviors that have been made more easily accessible, behaviors for which barriers have been removed, and behaviors with different levels of difficulty. We have also examined how the concept of self-determination could play a role in people's pro-active behaviors such as educating themselves about environmental issues and searching for information about one of the most reliable predictors of pro-environmental behaviors, perceptions of health risks.

Pro-environmental behaviors. Given that pro-environmental behaviors can involve reusing products (e.g., the unused side of paper, paper or grocery bags, jars and containers for storing things), recycling (e.g., newspapers, aluminum cans, glass jars and bottles), purchasing environmentally friendly products (e.g., buying biodegradable products, items available in bulk, and products with less packaging), or conserving energy and resources (e.g., water, electricity, fuels), how do the different types of motivations assessed by our scales relate to these behaviors? Results indicate that self-determined motives (intrinsic motivation, integrated regulation, and identified regulation) display the highest correlations with the frequency of a variety of pro-environmental behaviors (Green-Demers, Pelletier, & Ménard, 1997; Pelletier, et al., 1998; Pelletier, et al, 1997). The magnitude of the correlations gradually decreases and becomes progressively more negative as the motivational types become less self-determined (introjected and external regulation, and amotivation). A similar pattern of results was observed between types of motivation and other self-reported pro-environmental behaviors, like participants' willingness to pay additional fees to sponsor a more intensive recycling program and whether or not they belong to an environmental group (Pelletier et al., 1998; Séguin, Pelletier, & Hunsley, 1999). Other studies using a global self-determination index (Green-Demers, et al., 1997; Séguin, Pelletier, & Hunsley, 1998, 1999; Pelletier, Green-Demers, & Béland, 1999; Pelletier & Tuson, 1999) indicated that high levels of self-determination toward the environment lead to higher levels of pro-environmental behaviors. In sum, like prior studies that have involved a great variety of behaviors in different life domains, the relationships between the different types of motivation postulated by SDT and pro-environmental behaviors generally vary as a function of their level of self-determination.

The difficulty of behavior. As mentioned before, environmentalists have proposed providing incentives to prompt different behaviors or overcome barriers (e.g., a pay-per-can refund system as an incentive to recycle) on reducing barriers directly by making the desired behaviors more accessible (e.g., providing a curb-side recycling program) . A thoughtful analysis of some of these strategies led us to believe, however, that they could have significant unintended consequences. First, the incentives could undermine people's initial motivation to act. Then, people would act only for the incentive and would likely require increasingly large incentives to maintain the behaviors they had done initially without incentives or with only small ones (Katzev & Johnson, 1987; DeYoung, 1993). Second, although direct strategies to reduce barriers have made some pro-environmental behaviors less difficult, they have made other behaviors appear more difficult by comparison. For example, individuals perceive recycling as easier when they have access to curbside recycling, but that leads them to perceive recycling as even more difficult when they are away from home and do not have easy access to recycling. These ideas lead us to explore the role of motivation in the prediction of pro-environmental behaviors of different difficulty levels and behaviors for which barriers have been removed. Second, how we have examined self-determined individuals, when compared to non self-determined individuals, behave in contexts where pro-environmental activities are easier versus more difficult.

Green-Demers et al. (1997) used the MTES along with self-reports of the perceived difficulty of environmental behaviors and the extent to which participants do these behaviors in order to evaluate the perceived level of difficulty of environmental behaviors as moderators of the relations between environmental self-determination and the occurrence of environmental behaviors. Three types of environmental behaviors were examined: Recycling, purchasing environmentally friendly products, and educating oneself about what can be done for the environment. It was hypothesized that the level of self-determination of environmental motivation would significantly predict the occurrence of environmental behaviors, and that the magnitude of the relationship between self-determination and environmental behaviors would increase as the level of perceived difficulty of the behaviors increased.

First, the authors established that the three groups of environmental behaviors differed significantly from one another in their perceived level of difficulty. Second, they examined correlations between MTES' motivational subtypes and frequency of environmental behaviors observing that self-determined types of motivation appeared to be stronger predictors of environmental behaviors as the difficulty of the environmental behaviors increased. Third, they examined whether the frequency of environmental behaviors was affected by the level of difficulty, the level of self-determination, and the additive combination of theses factors, observing that frequency of behaviors was higher when self-determination was higher and lower when behavioral difficulty was higher. However, the decrease in the frequency of behaviors caused by the behaviors' difficulty was less important when people were self-determined. Fourth, the relations between self-determination and easy, moderate, and difficult behaviors were estimated using structural equation modeling analyses. Results supported the proposed hypotheses. Self-determination was significantly related to environmental behaviors, and the magnitude of this relation significantly increased with each level of difficulty of the environmental behaviors (Green-Demers et al., 1997).

In a second study, Pelletier and Bellier (1999) examined the impact of the degree of self-determination and three levels of difficulty for recycling behavior on the amount of recycling. The investigators also examined the effect of self-determination and difficulty on the frequency of other environmental behaviors and on the strength of environmental attitudes (e.g., satisfaction with the environment, importance of the environment). Residents of three municipalities were randomly selected to participate in a survey on pro-environmental behaviors. In one of the municipalities, residents had access to curbside recycling (easy recycling). In the second municipality, residents had access to a recycling program, but had to carry their recyclables to one of the local municipal depots (moderate recycling). In the third municipality, residents did not have access to local municipal recycling, but could dispose of their recyclables by driving 20 minutes to the next municipality that had a recycling program (difficult recycling). Results revealed an interaction between the level of difficulty of recycling and the level of self-determination. For the easy recycling condition, the quantity of recycling was not significantly different for self-determined and non self-determined individuals. However, for the moderate condition, the amount of recycling for self-determined and non self-determined individuals became significantly different, although both groups recycled less than participants in the easy condition. In the difficult condition, the amount of recycling was also significantly different for self-determined and non self-determined individuals.

In other analyses, the authors compared the frequency of other pro-environmental behaviors and residents' environmental attitudes as a function of the level of difficulty of recycling and residents' levels of self-determination. Analyses revealed only a main effect for the level of self-determination. Self-determined residents in the three municipalities indicated higher frequencies for the other pro-environmental behaviors than nonself-determined residents. Apparently, making recycling easier or accessible did not have a transferable effect on other pro-environmental activities. Examination of the effects of self-determination and difficulty on perception of satisfaction with the environmental conditions, satisfaction with government environmental policy, and the importance of the environment, also revealed similar patterns. Self-determined residents indicated that they were less satisfied with the current environmental conditions and the government environmental policy, and that they considered the ecological situation more important than nonself-determined individuals. These perceptions did not differ significantly as a function of the level of difficulty of recycling behaviors across the three settings (Pelletier & Bellier, 1999).

These studies suggest that pro-environmental behaviors could be encouraged by either making recycling easier or by fostering people's self-determination with respect to the environment. Although it is possible to decrease the difficulty of an environmental behavior and thereby increase its occurrence, programs like curbside recycling could be costly to implement and could become costly to maintain. Moreover, it seems that this type of program does not necessarily increase people's awareness or concern toward the environment. As a consequence, there is no guarantee that the behavior will be maintained if the program is discontinued, or if the person is on holiday or away from home. On the other hand, behaviors performed for self-determined reasons do seem to have a better chance of becoming more frequent and being maintained once they have been developed. As the behaviors become more integrated in the person's self-system and lifestyle, the negative impact of the behavior's perceived difficulty should diminish. It is difficult at this point in time to speculate on how to facilitate or develop self-determination toward the environment and how expensive it would be to do so. First, it is necessary to examine the antecedent conditions that promote different levels of self-determination for the environment, an issue that will be addressed later on in the chapter.

The perception of health risks. As noted earlier, one class of specific determinants of pro-environmental behaviors that has received some attention and has appeared to be an important predictor of environmental behaviors, is perceptions of health risks. Research on perceptions of health risks developed largely in reaction to the way the concept of health risks had been treated by risk managers such engineers and by politicians (Slovic, Fischhoff, & Lichtenstein, 1980). Those groups tend to equate the risk of a technology (such as a nuclear power plant or the release of chemicals in the air by an industry) with the probable number of human deaths the technology can directly or indirectly cause. Damage to ecosystems and to nonhuman life is usually overlooked. A technology is judged acceptable to society based on whether the technology's benefits (e.g., the electricity generated), usually measured in dollars, outweigh the risks for human life and the costs associated with the management of the industry. If the benefits exceed the risks and the costs, the technology is perceived as relatively acceptable to society. If not, it is expected that stricter government regulations (or in some cases, industry self-regulations) will lower risk enough for the technology to be acceptable.

In contrast, perceptions of health risks in the general public, while also influenced by the number of human deaths a technology can cause, are based on a broader definition of risk. Among the characteristics to which the public also pays attention are the degree of disagreement in the scientific community about the risks of the technology, the degree to which the technology can kill many people in a single accident or can affect future generations, how the technology affects quality of life, what damage it causes to ecosystems and nonhuman forms of life, and whether the risks are equitably and voluntarily distributed among those who reap its benefits (Gardner & Stern, 1996). The differences between the definitions of risks and acceptability used by the public versus the government and industry can lead to significant mistrust or miscommunication among the different groups. The differences in definition can, for example, lead government and industry to view the public as alarmist and, at the same time, lead the public to view government and industry as untrustworthy and driven only by financial factors.

Individuals' perceptions of health risks have been found to be affected by the specific information about health risks they obtain from the media, government agencies, activist organizations, public groups, or peers (Kasperson, Renn, Slovic, Brown, Emel, Goble, Kasperson, & Ratick, 1988; Renn, Burns, Kasperson, Kasperson, & Slovic, 1992). In addition, these researchers have suggested that the characteristics of the sources of information (e.g., frequency of information given, trustworthiness, credibility, impartiality) could either amplify or attenuate the perceptions of environmental health risks and consequently lead to either more or less pro-environmental behavior. The more confidence people have in a particular source of information on environmental health risks, the more they should perceive health risks in the environment and the more they should manifest pro-environmental behaviors.

Self-determination, health risks, and behavior. Séguin, Pelletier, and Hunsley (1998) tested a model of environmental activism in which the contributions of self-determination for the environment and perceptions of various environmental health risks were specified. Data were obtained from a survey mailed to 750 residents of Eastern Ontario. Participants completed the MTES, as well as measures of perceptions of problems in the local environment, perceptions of health risks related to the environmental conditions, information they were obtaining from different sources (e.g., university scientists, medical doctors, environmental groups, government officials), and their perceptions of the level of responsibility of various organizations (e.g., municipal or provincial government, private industry) for preventing health risks. The level of activism was measured by a 6-item scale representing behaviors related to environmental activism (e.g., participation in events organized by ecological groups, financial support to these groups, circulation of petitions, writing letters to industries that manufacture harmful products). The model was tested by means of recursive path analyses.

The authors observed that the more individuals were self-determined toward the environment, the more they were attentive to information about health risks, to problems in their local environment, and to the responsibility of different organizations to prevent health risks. In turn, the more individuals were sensitive to information about environmental health risks and were aware of possible problems in their local environments, the higher was their level of perceived health risks. Interestingly, the more individuals perceived that various organizations had responsibilities to prevent health risks in the environment, the higher were their perceptions of risks to their health (an issue that is discussed in more detail in the next section). Finally, the more individuals perceived health risks in the environment, the more they indicated being engaged in environmental activism.

An important aspect of these findings pertains to the role of self-determined motivation as a factor leading individuals to be more proactive and to seek out information on environmental health risks, the condition of their local environment, and the organizations responsible to prevent health risks in the environment. These results suggest that self-determined motivation may represent more than a reliable predictor of pro-environmental behaviors. Self-determined motivation may also be a predictor of the processes leading individuals to be more active toward their environment and to take steps to prevent damage to their health or the environment (Séguin et al., 1998).

In a second study Séguin et al. (1999) tested a more elaborate model of the relations among motivation toward the environment, perceptions of health risks, the origin of the information on health risks, and pro-environmental behaviors. Participants completed a survey about their perceptions of more than 20 environmental health risks, the extent to which they were seeking information on health risks from different sources, their levels of confidence in these sources, the MTES, and the frequency of pro-environmental behaviors.

The sources of information on health risks included federal government agencies, provincial governments, public interest groups, environmental groups, the media, and industry. Past research had shown that people have much more confidence in environmentalists, public groups, or scientists as information sources on environmental health risks than they do in municipal or provincial governments (i.e., regional governments), or media sources (Ostman & Parker, 1986; Soden, 1995). Federal government agencies such as Health and Welfare Canada, are usually more trusted as sources of information on environmental health hazards than are regional governments. These varying degrees of confidence in different sources of information could be related to the type of information given, the particular mandate of each one of those sources, and how successful they are at fulfilling their respective mandate. For example, environmental groups ordinarily have the mandate to produce and disseminate information about the possible and actual environmental health risks (Soden, 1995). Federal government agencies, such as Environment Canada or Health and Welfare Canada, ordinarily have the mandate to inform people about how to deal with possible environmental health hazards (Soden, 1995). Regional governments ordinarily have the mandate to prevent environmental health risks. Whereas the first two sources of information on environmental health risks are usually able to fulfill their mandate, it is often believed that regional governments do not always fulfill their obligation toward public safety and health. Over time, regional governments have tended to lose the trust of the public, perhaps because they have not been able to deal effectively with environmental issues, even if they routinely express a strong commitment toward risk communication and prevention (Chess & Salomone, 1992; Soden, 1995). Because of the different degrees of trust in various government agencies and public groups, information from regional governments was not expected to be strongly associated with perceived environmental health risks, whereas information from federal government agencies and public groups was expected to be more strongly associated with perceived environmental health risks.

Séguin et al. (1999) observed that self-determination toward the environment was a significant predictor of both environmental behaviors and the seeking of information on environmental health risks. More specifically, self-determination toward the environment was associated with the amount of information individuals obtained from various sources of information on health risks (federal government agencies, regional governments, and public groups), and the amount of information people received was positively associated with their confidence in these sources of information. In turn, the level of confidence in the different sources of information was a significant predictor of individuals' perceptions of environmental health risks and these perceptions were predictors of environmental behaviors. Because of the possible lack of confidence individuals had in regional governments and industry as a source of information on health risks, these two sources of information did not predict the level of perceived health risks and consequently did not contribute to the prediction of pro-environmental behaviors. One final note, self-determination toward the environment was a much stronger predictor of pro-environmental behaviors than perceptions of health risks (twice as strong) even after controlling for the effect of motivation on the search for information on health risks.

In sum, the results of our studies reveal that people are not only engaging in pro-environmental behaviors for different reasons, but it appears that these reasons (used individually or globally as an index of people's levels of self-determination) are related to various consequences. Consistent with self-determination theory, the more individuals indicate that they are self-determined toward the environment, the more they engage in pro-environmental behaviors, mild activism, and more difficult behaviors, and the more they seek out information about health risks. Thus, our studies seem to indicate that self-determination represents a useful predictor of pro-environmental behaviors. Given the consequences linked to a more self-determined profile of motivation, it becomes worthwhile to investigate possible factors that could either enhance or possibly impair the development of this motivational orientation. In the next section, we turn our attention to studies that have examined the determinants of environmental motivation.

Social and Contextual Influences on Motivation

Studies on social and contextual factors in the environmental domain have typically examined how strategies for providing specific knowledge and affecting people's attitudes about the environment (e.g., satisfaction, importance, concern, or other perceptions about the environment) are associated with their pro-environmental behaviors. In most of these studies, motivation was not directly measured but was inferred from participants' behaviors. Participants were considered motivated if the frequency or the intensity of their behaviors increased in the presence of the social or contextual factor. Although, it may be acceptable to infer motivation in some circumstances, it is nevertheless important to distinguish whether motivated actions are self-determined or are controlled by some interpersonal or intrapersonal force. As discussed earlier, the important point about this distinction is that the regulatory processes of these types of motivations are different, so qualities of behavior such as maintenance, persistence, or integration in one's lifestyle, are expected to be different. In our research, we focused on strategies for providing knowledge and influencing attitudes about the environment to examine how these typical factors used in environmental research might be related to environmental self-determination.

We were also interested in how aspects of the social context, such as the behavior of others, facilitate a person's perceptions of competence, autonomy, and relatedness. According to self-determination theory, these factors are important because they relate to fundamental human needs that individuals seek to satisfy. When social or interpersonal behaviors of others are perceived to provide structure and foster competence, people will tend to experience a sense of interacting effectively with the environment and efficiently producing desired outcomes and preventing undesired events. When individuals experience others as providing support for their autonomy, they will tend to engage in activities of their own choosing and they will experience being the origin of their action. Finally, when they perceive others in their social context as being concerned and interested in them, they feel a greater sense of connectedness to others. In turn, when people experience satisfaction of these three needs, their intrinsic motivation and self-determined forms of motivation will be enhanced.

With respect to the environment, critical social-contextual factors include not only organizational behaviors, such as the government's approach to implementation of environmental programs and strategies, but also the behaviors of people in a relatively close social environment (e.g., a spouse, friends, children, educators) that could represent a daily source of influence on motivation towards pro-environmental behaviors. The study of these behaviors could have interesting implications for prediction of self-determination for pro-environmental behaviors, for understanding the interpersonal as well as global factors (e.g. government regulations) that could foster self-determination, and for determining the best strategies that could be used to implement government environmental policies.

Influencing people's attitudes and beliefs about the environment. As discussed earlier, strategies targeting people's attitudes and beliefs about the environment usually involve both providing knowledge about the seriousness of the situation as a reason or motivation for becoming involved and outlining specific actions that individuals can take to help solve the problem. Describing the nature and the severity of a problem in an informational, nonpressuring way may make people more conscious about the situation and affects their environmental attitudes or beliefs. Similarly, providing information about specific actions to solve a problem can foster a sense of competence in individuals. As a consequence, the individuals are expected to become more involved in pro-environmental behaviors. However, little attention has been paid to developing the indicators of residents' perceptions of the degradation of ecosystems and their perceptions of environmental quality, which would be necessary for examining these issues empirically. As we will see below, these indicators can represent an assessment of individuals' concern about the environment, their willingness to change their environmental behaviors, and/or the extent to which they feel helpless or hopeless about their abilities to have a positive impact on the environment (Cone & Hayes, 1980). In other words, they can represent important determinants of individuals' motivation.

To examine these issues, we surveyed more than 2,000 adult residents of different municipalities in Eastern Ontario and Western Quebec (Pelletier, Hunsley, Green-Demers, & Legault, 1996). Participants completed surveys designed to assess a broad spectrum of environmentally relevant variables, ranging from their satisfaction with their local environment to their perceptions of government policies dealing with the environment. In particular, we focused on critical variables such as priorities for environmental planning, environmental concerns, perceptions of health risks, satisfaction with the environment and with environmental policies, and views of government policies. Our main goals for the surveys were (1) to determine, among various populations, perceptions of the current environmental quality (including water, land, and air), the perceived importance of regional environmental resources (e.g., rivers, lakes, forests), and the level of satisfaction with environmental policies and practices; (2) to relate these perceptions to motivation for pro-environmental behaviors and to the extent to which individuals adopt behaviors for environmental protection; and (3) to use the data to begin identifying priorities for public policy, both in terms of the nature of the policies and the manner in which such policies could be implemented (a subject that will not be discussed here).

Considering our results (Pelletier, Hunsley, et al., 1996), it was abundantly clear that the participants were very concerned about the health of the environment in which they live and work. Participants felt that addressing significant environmental issues should be a priority. As reflected by measures of "Importance of Environmental Issues" and "Satisfaction with Local Environmental Conditions" (Pelletier, Blanchard, & Legault, 1996; Pelletier, Legault, & Tuson, 1996) participants indicated that they considered it important to do something about the current local environmental situation and that they were very dissatisfied with the current state of the environment. Importantly, our data also suggested that survey participants were committed to improving their environment and that they felt they do indeed possess some of the requisite abilities for rehabilitating their ecosystem. Residents reported that they felt they could contribute to the improvement of their environment and that they were taking a number of meaningful steps to do so. Air and water pollution from industries were rated as the two most important environmental issues. Participants were very concerned about the impact of such pollution on the quality of their drinking water, the contamination of game fish, and the advisability of using local streams and rivers for leisure activities.

Survey respondents rated the extent to which they were concerned about 21 different potential environmentally related health risks. Perhaps reflecting recent and ongoing government information campaigns, residents rated the depletion of the ozone layer and chemical pollution in the environment as the most important health risks. Risks from nuclear wastes and from nuclear power plants were ranked in ninth and sixteenth positions, respectively. As nuclear energy hazards are usually perceived as the number one environmental hazard by the general population (Slovic, 1993), it is informative to examine the potential health risks that received higher rankings from the participants. Consistent with ratings of concern about local environmental issues, industrial and agricultural pollution (for example, mercury in fish, PCBs, pesticides in food) were perceived as greater risks to health than were nuclear wastes (Pelletier, Hunsley, et al., 1996).

Pelletier and Tuson (1999) used structural equation modeling to examine how citizens' levels of satisfaction about environmental conditions and government environmental policies, competence for environmental behaviors, and concern about the environment, related to motivation towards pro-environmental behaviors, and, in turn, the frequency of these behaviors. It was hypothesized that self-determination for pro-environmental behaviors would mediate the relationships between the antecedent variables and the frequency of pro-environmental behaviors. Results supported the hypothesized model. The more people were dissatisfied with the environmental conditions and with government environmental policies, and the more they felt competent towards environmental behaviors, the more they were concerned about the environment. Higher levels of concern and competence were associated with higher levels of self-determination for environmental behaviors, which in turn, were associated with higher levels of pro-environmental behaviors (recycling, conserving energy, purchasing environmentally-friendly products, searching for information on the environment).

A central aspect of this study—an aspect typically neglected in empirical work linking concern about the environment to pro-environmental behaviors—was the mediational role of self-determination. As predicted, self-determined motivation was the mediating mechanism responsible for the relations between two environmental antecedents, namely concern and competence, and pro-environmental behaviors. Most of the contemporary research on motivation for pro-environmental behaviors has proposed that individuals are expected to become more involved in pro-environmental behaviors as a result of the combined effect of being aware of the severity of the environmental situation and the development of a sense of competence for specific actions that could solve a problem. The study by Pelletier and Tuson (1999), however, indicates that when self-determined motivation is considered, it serves the role of proximal mediator of the relationship between these two antecedent variables and pro-environmental behaviors. In other words, the combined effect of environmental concern and competence does not necessarily lead to more pro-environmental behaviors. They may be indirectly associated with pro-environmental behaviors because they promote self-determined motivation toward the environment.

Support for autonomy, competence, and relatedness. Deci and Ryan (1991) contend that people's motivation and self-determination are affected by their perceived levels of competence and agency. Events that boost these feelings are hypothesized to lead to gains in self-determination, while events that undermine these feelings are expected to thwart self-determination. Substantial research results support these theoretical postulates (see Deci & Ryan, 1987, 1991, for reviews). For example, the support of one's autonomy, the provision of a rationale for requested activities, and constructive feedback have all been associated with increases in self-determination (Deci, Eghari, Patrick, & Leone, 1994; Deci & Ryan, 1987). Conversely, threats, surveillance, and feedback that promote feelings of incompetence have systematically been related to losses in self-determination (Deci & Ryan, 1987). Of all social factors, interpersonal behaviors have been among the most extensively studied. The term "interpersonal behaviors" describes the quality of behavior of a significant other (parent, teacher, etc.) as it affects the target person's need satisfaction. Typically, this construct refers to an interaction between two individuals. However, in the environmental domain, it seemed plausible that people are in a position to react to messages coming from two types of social contexts, one created by the immediate social surrounding (e.g., family and friends) and the other by the government. It is hereby postulated that messages coming from an institution such as the government could be perceived as supporting basic psychological needs and could have an impact on people's self-determination. We have examined both sources of influence. Consider first the influence of government environmental policies.

Pelletier, Green-Demers, and Béland (1999) conducted two studies to examine how people's perceptions of the government's style of presenting policies affect their motivation toward pro-environmental behaviors. In a first study the researchers developed and validated a new scale (the Government Style Questionnaire; GSQ) pertaining to the implementation of environmental programs and policies. The GSQ measured three dimensions, namely autonomy support of citizens by the government (e.g., "I feel that the government respects the public's opinion concerning environmental issues"), government's use of pressure and control regarding environmental issues (e.g., "I think the government puts a lot of pressure on people and organizations to adopt pro-environmental behaviors"), and informational support of citizens by the government ("Information concerning what I can do to help the environment is easily accessible through the programs provided by the government"). Results of the first study supported the structure of the scale and its psychometric properties (internal consistency and construct validity).

In a second study, 270 residents of the Ottawa region completed a questionnaire containing the GSQ, the MTES, and measures of pro-environmental behaviors (the questionnaire also included measures of Social Political Control, Social Criticism, Satisfaction toward the Environment and toward Environmental Policies to further examine the construct validity of the GSQ). The structure of the scale was verified using a confirmatory factor analysis and the relations between the dimensions of the GSQ and the subscales of the MTES were examined. It is interesting to note that the means of the three subscales of the GSQ were relatively low (all below the middle point of the Likert scale). Participants indicated that they perceived the government (and the government policies) as noninformational and not very autonomy supportive. Interestingly, participants also indicated that they perceived the government as not being very controlling, especially toward industry. Perhaps not surprisingly, associations between GSQ subscales and MTES subscales were quite low. The highest relations appeared between each of the GSQ subscales and external regulation. However, relationships between MTES subscales and pro-environmental behaviors were strong and similar to the ones observed in prior studies. Briefly, it appears that participants were making distinctions among three aspects of government style toward the environment, but they perceived the government as being relatively low on all three communication styles. This situation could be characterized as "laissez-faire" or indifference, a type of climate, according to Deci and Ryan (1985), that should not have a positive impact on motivation. More research is needed to further establish the GSQ' validity and to determine more clearly how government's involvement (or indifference) affects citizens' motivation.

In light of these findings, it became particularly relevant to expand our examination of factors influencing the development and evolution of self-determined motivation for pro-environmental behaviors. In a next step, we turned our attention to whether people's perceptions of the interpersonal climate would influence their environmental motivation (Pelletier, Legault, & Green-Demers, 1999). Because no scales were available, individuals from different backgrounds were interviewed to create a pool of perceptions regarding the interpersonal climate likely to influence their environmental motivation and behaviors. These perceptions were worded to reflect five dimensions (1) autonomy support, (2) information, (3) pressure, (4) involvement, and (5) indifference. Then, subjects were asked to evaluate the extent to which different categories of people (e.g., friends, professors, colleagues, children, relatives) influence them with respect to the environment. Subjects were also asked to identify which category of people had the highest impact on them in this respect and to refer to that group while answering the items of the scale.

In two studies, a sample of 224 randomly selected residents of Eastern Ontario and a second sample of 385 randomly selected residents of the Ottawa region completed a mail survey that included the Interpersonal Climate Scale, the MTES, the Environmental Satisfaction Scale, measures of perceived competence for environmental behaviors, perceived environmental importance, and frequency of pro-environmental behaviors. Results with the first sample supported the factor structure of the scale and revealed satisfactory levels of internal consistency. The construct validity of the scale was supported by significant relations between the different dimensions of the scale and relevant environmental (satisfaction, importance, competence) and behavioral variables, as well as motivational subtypes. Specifically, while the positive dimensions of social climate (involvement, information, autonomy support) displayed higher correlations with self-determined types of motivation, the negative dimensions of social climate (indifference and pressure) were mostly correlated with the non self-determined types of motivation (Pelletier, Legault, & Green-Demers, 1999).

The factorial structure obtained with the first sample was cross-validated with the second sample using confirmatory factor analysis, thus, offering strong support for the factorial structure of the Social Climate Scale. A structural equation model was also built to illustrate the relations between the dimensions of the scale, the environmental constructs, and the self-determination index. Results showed that involvement and autonomy support were positively related to self-determination, though indirectly through the mediating action of importance and competence respectively. Information was positively related to self-determination while pressure was negatively related to the same variable. Finally, indifference was directly and negatively related to self-determination, as well as positively related to satisfaction with the current state of the environment which was in turn negatively related to self-determination. In sum, contrary to the first study on the relations between government style for the regulation of environmental polices and motivation for pro-environmental behaviors, the second study on the relationships between the interpersonal climate of close associates and motivation indicated that people's motivation for pro-environmental behaviors was affected by the ways individuals around them express concern about the environment.

Interestingly, results with both samples indicated that children represented the most important source of influence on participants' motivation (followed by spouses and friends). In a recent study, Legault and Pelletier (2000) hypothesized that children, especially children who were involved in schools where environmental studies were included in the curriculum, would be more informed, more conscious about the environmental situation, and more involved. As a consequence, the members of their families should become more aware of the situation and more involved. Results showed that the more children were involved in an environmental education program, the more family members were getting information and were aware of the environmental situation, and the less satisfied they were with the environmental condition. As a consequence, they indicated being more involved in some pro-environmental behaviors (like recycling and conserving energy) and having lower levels of non self-determined motives.

Although these initial results on the influence of the social climate on people's environmental motivation are exploratory, they are encouraging. It seems that people in one's social network (in comparison with government's influence) represent the principal source of influence on one's attitudes and behaviors. Thus, it might be profitable to take social climate into account in the promotion of pro-environmental behaviors. Additional research is necessary to further validate the current findings and to expand them. It is our hope that the study of the influence of social climate on people's environmental motivation will yield insights regarding the processes by which pro-environmental attitudes and behaviors can be promoted. One strategy in particular, the possibility of including environmental issues in school curricula, represents a promising way to sensitize individuals to environmental issues. It represents not only an indirect source of influence on adults' motivation and behavior, but also a way to develop environmental behaviors that could be integrated into the lifestyle of young individuals. In this way, it could help promote a sustainable future.

Conclusion

The integration of environmentally responsible behaviors into people's lifestyle represents an important issue for the preservation of the environment and the promotion of a sustainable future. Self-determination theory offers an interesting framework for understanding the social factors that could lead to or interfere with such behaviors. The purpose of this chapter was to review the results of a program of research that focused on the application of SDT to environmentally responsible behaviors. Research supports the validity of a scale designed to measure individuals' motivation for environmental behaviors. Consistent with SDT, the different forms of motivation fall along a self-determination continuum and the level of self-determination of environmental motivation predicts the occurrence of a variety of outcomes (recycling, conservation of energy, environmental activism, search for information about health risks) and behaviors of different difficulty levels. We have examined how different antecedent variables (e.g., satisfaction with the environment, perceived competence, family, friends, children, and government policies) predicted levels of self-determination. It appears that self-determination represents an important mediational variable between people's satisfaction, importance, and perceived competence toward the environment and pro-environmental behaviors. The use of regulations by the government to implement environmental policies seems to encourage mainly non self-determined forms of motivation. However, people around us (especially children and spouses) represent the main sources of influence on individuals' motivation for pro-environmental behaviors. The education of children, and in particular the development of environmental education programs, may be critical for the future. By using the school system to educate our children about environmental issues we may instill in them pro-environmental behaviors that will become part of their lifestyle. We may also create hundreds of thousand of pro-environmentalists or activists who could take important information into their homes. These children may then become a critical source of information for other members of the family.

An important limitation of the studies described in this chapter concerns their correlational nature. Although structural equation modeling and path analyses indicated that our data supported models consistent with SDT, experimental methodologies are required to demonstrate causality. Future research should aim to identify strategies that could foster self-determination towards environmental behaviors. Such research could be guided by the growing body of research addressing the determinants of motivational orientations such as the degree to which friends, relatives, or policy-makers encourage people to initiate and make their own choices rather than apply pressure to control their behavior, or the degree to which they provide constructive feedback about people's competence. Along these lines, research on management and conservation behaviors could examine how helping people understand the nature of environmental problems, as opposed to using coercive techniques (e.g. social pressure, punishment, or taxes), might help them to carry out these environmental behaviors.

The MTES could also be used at different points in time in order to better understand the motivational changes produced by the provision of new government policies, and by varying the ways these policies are implemented. In a first step, the effects on self-determination of different governmental strategies (e.g., relying on material incentives or social pressure, versus providing choices or more information on how to behave) could be assessed. In a second step, changes in self-determination levels could be examined as a function of the different strategies used and could be linked to the integration and maintenance of environmental behaviors into people's lifestyles. Further research on these issues is needed to augment our knowledge of the relations between motivational orientations and the maintenance of environmental behaviors.

In sum, self-determination theory holds some interesting possibilities for applied interventions concerning the environment. It is our hope that the program of research on the promotion versus inhibition of autonomous motives for the environment will contribute to a better understanding of the interaction between real-life environments, motivation, and the integration of environmentally-conscious behaviors into people's lifestyles.

References

Angus Reid Group. (1992). *Canadians and the Environment, 1992.* Vancouver, B. C.: Angus Reid Group.

Arcury, T. A., & Johnson, T. P. (1987). Public environmental knowledge: A statewide survey. *Journal of Environmental Education, 18*, 31-37.

Aronson, E., & Gonzales, M. H. (1990). Alternative social influence processes applied to energy conservation. In J. Edwards, R. S. Tindale, L. Heath, & E. J. Posavac (Eds.), *Social influence processes and prevention* (pp.301-325). New York: Plenum Press.

Blais, M. R., Sabourin, S., Boucher. C., & Vallerand, R. J. (1990). Towards a motivational model of couple happiness. *Journal of Personality and Social Psychology*, *59*, 1021-1031.

Brière, N. M., & Vallerand, R. J. (1990). Effect of private self-consciousness and success outcome on causal dimensions, *Journal of Social Psychology*, *130*, 325-332.

Brothers, C. C., Fortner, R. W., & Mayer, V. J. (1991). The impact of television news on public environmental knowledge. *Journal of Environmental Education*, *22*, 22-29.

Chaiken, S., & Stangor, C. (1987). Attitudes and attitude change. *Annual Review of Psychology*, *38*, 575-630.

Chess, C., & Salomone, K. L. (1992). Rhetoric and reality: Risk communication in federal government agencies. *Journal of Environmental Education*, *23*, 28-33.

Cone, J. D., & Hayes, S. C. (1980). *Environmental problems/behavioral solutions*. Monterey, CA: Brooks/Cole.

Deci, E. L. (1992). The relation of interest to the motivation of behavior: A self-determination theory perspective. In A. Renninger, S. Hidi, & A. Krapp (Eds.), *Interest in learning and development* (pp.43-70). Hillsdale, NJ: Erlbaum.

Deci, E. L., Eghari, H., Patrick, B. C., & Leone, D. R. (1994). Facilitating internalization: The self-determination theory perspective. *Journal of Personality*, *62*, 119-142.

Deci, E. L., & Ryan, R. M. (1985). *Intrinsic motivation and self-determination in human behavior*. New York: Plenum Press.

Deci, E. L., & Ryan, R. M. (1987). The support of autonomy and the control of behavior. *Journal of Personality and Social Psychology*, *53*, 1024-1037.

Deci, E. L., & Ryan, R. M. (1991). A motivational approach to self: Integration in personality. In R. Dienstbier (Ed.), *Nebraska Symposium on Motivation: Vol. 38. Perspectives on Motivation*. Lincoln, NE: University of Nebraska Press.

DeYoung, R. (1986). Encouraging environmentally appropriate behavior: The role of intrinsic motivation. *Journal of Environmental Systems*, *15*, 281-292.

DeYoung, R. (1993). Changing behavior and making it stick: The conceptualization and management of conservation behavior. *Environment and Behavior*, *25*, 485-505.

Dwyer, W. O., Leeming, F. C., Cobern, M. K., Porter, B. E., & Jackson, J. M. (1993). Critical review of behavioral interventions to preserve the environment - Research since 1980. *Environment and Behavior*, *25*, 275-321.

Elliot, A. J., & Sheldon, K. M. (1998). Avoidance personal goals and the personality-illness relationship. *Journal of Personality and Social Psychology*, *75*, 1282-1299.

Environment Canada. (1991). *National Report of Canada* (Catalogue number EN 21-17/1991S). Ottawa, Canada: Ministry of Supply and Services.

Everett, P., & Watson, B. (1987). Psychological contributions to transportation. In D. Stokols & I. Altman (Eds.), *Handbook of Environmental Psychology*. New York: Wiley.

Gardner, G. T., & Stern, P. C. (1996). *Environmental problems and human behavior*. Needham Heights: Allyn & Bacon.

Geller, E. S. (1989). Applied behavior analysis and social marketing: An integration for environmental preservation. *Journal of Social Issues*, *45*, 17-36.

Geller, E. S. (1995). Integrating behaviorism and humanism for environmental protection. *Journal of Social Issues*, *51*, 179-195.

Geller, E. S., Winett, R. A., & Everett, P. B. (1982). *Preserving the environment: New strategies for behavior change*. Elmsford, NY: Pergamon.

Gigliotti, L. M. (1990). Environmental education: What went wrong? What can be done? *Journal of Environmental Education, 22*, 9-12.

Green-Demers, I., Pelletier, L. G., & Legault, L. (in press). Factorial invariance of the Motivation Towards the Environment Scale (MTES) across samples of francophone and anglophone Canadians. *Social Indicators Research*.

Green-Demers, I., Pelletier, L. G., & Ménard, S. (1997). The impact of behavioral difficulty on the saliency of the association between self-determined motivation and environmental behaviors. *Canadian Journal of Behavioral Sciences, 29*, 157-166.

Grolnick, W. S., & Ryan, R. M. (1987). Autonomy in children's learning: An experimental and individual difference investigation. *Journal of Personality and Social Psychology, 52*, 890-898.

Kasperson, R. E., Renn, O., Slovic, P., Brown, H. S., Emel, J., Goble, R., Kasperson, J. X., & Ratick, S. (1988). The social amplification of risk: A conceptual framework. *Risk Analysis, 8*, 177-187.

Katzev R. D., & Johnson, T. (1984). Comparing the effects of monetary incentives and foot-in-the-door strategies in promoting residential electricity conservation. *Journal of Applied Social Psychology, 14*, 12-27.

Legault, L., & Pelletier, L. G. (2000). Assessment of an educational environmental program's impact on students' and their parents' attitudes motivation, and behaviors. *Canadian Journal of Behavioural Science, 32*, 243-250.

McKenzie-Mohr, D., & Oskamp, S. (1995). Psychology and Sustain capacity: An Introduction. *Journal of Social Issues, 51*, 1-14.

Milbrath, L. W. (1984). *Environmentalists: Vanguard for a new society*. Albany: SUNY Press.

Miller, Jr., G. T. (1994). *Living in the environment (8th edition)*. Belmont, CA: Wadsworth Publishing Co.

Oskamp, S. (1995). Resource Conservation and Recycling: Behavior and Policy. *Journal of Social Issues, 51*, 157-177.

Oskamp, S., Harrington, M.J., Edwards, T.C., Sherwood, D.L., Okuda, S.M., & Swanson, D.C. (1991). Factors influencing household recycling behavior. *Environment and Behavior, 23*, 494-519.

Ostman, R. E., & Parker, J. L. (1986). A public's environmental information sources and evaluations of mass media. *Journal of Environmental Education, 18*, 9-17.

Pelletier, L. G., & Bellier, P. (1999). *How difficult is it to recycle? Self-determination and the level of difficulty of recycling behaviors*. Manuscript in preparation, University of Ottawa.

Pelletier, L. G., Blanchard, C., & Legault, L. M. (1996). Traduction et validation d'une échelle sur la satisfaction vis-à-vis les conditions de l'environnement et les politiques gouvernementales. (Translation and validation of a scale on satisfaction towards the environmental conditions and govermental policies). *Science et Comportement, 25*, 239-253.

Pelletier, L. G., Fortier, M. S., Vallerand, R. J., Tuson, K. M., Brière, N. M., & Blais, M. R. (1995). Toward a new measure of intrinsic motivation, extrinsic motivation, and amotivation in sports: The Sport Motivation Scale (SMS). *Journal of Sport and Exercise Psychology, 17*, 35-54.

Pelletier, L. G., Green-Demers, I., & Béland, A. (1997). Pourquoi effectuez-vous des comportements écologiques? Validation en langue française de l'Échelle de Motivation vis-à-vis les Comportements Écologiques (why do you adopt environmental behaviors? Validation in French of the Motivation Toward the Environment Scale). *Revue Canadienne des Sciences du Comportement, 29*, 145-156.

Pelletier, L. G., Green-Demers, I., & Béland, A. (1999). *Government style, citizens' motivation, and pro-environmental behaviors.* Unpublished manuscript. University of Ottawa.

Pelletier, L. G., Hunsley, J., Green-Demers, I., & Legault, L. (1996). Environmental concerns, challenges, and commitments: The Environmental Attitude and Perceptions Survey. In R.D. Needham & N. Novakowski (Eds.), *Sharing knowledge, linking sciences: An international conference at the St-Lawrence ecosystem. Conference proceedings (*pp. 503-514).

Pelletier, L. G., Legault, L., & Green-Demers, I. (1999). *Interpersonal climate, motivation, and pro-environmental behaviors.* Unpublished manuscript, University of Ottawa.

Pelletier, L. G., Legault, L. R., & Tuson, K. M. (1996). The Environment Satisfaction Scale: A Measure of Satisfaction with local environmental conditions and government environmental policies. *Environment and Behavior, 28*, 5-26.

Pelletier, L. G., & Tuson, K. M. (1999). *On the prediction of environmentally conscious behaviors: The role of environmental satisfaction, importance, competence, and motivation.* Manuscript submitted for publication, University of Ottawa.

Pelletier, L. G., Tuson, K. M., Green-Demers, I., Noels, K., & Beaton, A. M. (1998). Why are you doing things for the environment? - The Motivation Toward the Environmental Scale (MTES). *Journal of Applied Social Psychology, 28*, 437-468..

Pelletier, L. G., Vallerand, R. J., Green-Demers, I., Blais, M. R., & Brière, N. M. (1995). Loisirs et santé mentale: les relations entre la motivation pour la pratique des loisirs et le bien-être psychologique [Leisure and mental health: Relationships between leisure motivation and psychological well-being]. *Canadian Journal of Behavioral Sciences, 27*, 140-156.

Renn, O., Burns, W. J., Kasperson, J. X., Kasperson, R. E., & Slovic, P. (1992). The social amplification of risk: Theoretical foundations and empirical applications. *Journal of Social Issues, 48*, 137-160.

Séguin, C., Pelletier, L. G., & Hunsley, J. (1998). Toward a model of environmental activism. *Environment and Behavior, 30*, 628-652.

Séguin, C., Pelletier, L. G., & Hunsley, J. (1999). Predicting environmental behaviors: The influence of self-determination and information about environmental health risks. *Journal of Applied Social Psychology, 29*, 1582-1604.

Seligman, C. (1985). Information and energy conservation. *Marriage and Family Review, 9*, 135-149.

Sheldon, K. M., & Elliot, A. J. (1998). Not all personal goals are personal: Comparing autonomous and controlled reasons for goals as predictors of effort and attainment. *Personality and Social Psychology Bulletin, 24*, 546-557.

Slovic, P. (1993). Perceptions of environmental hazards: Psychological perspectives. In T. Gärling & R. Golledge (Eds.), *Behavior and environment: Psychological and geograp hical approaches.* Holland: Elsevier Science Publishers.

Slovic, P., Fischhoff, B., & Lichtenstein, S. (1980). Facts and fears: Understanding perceived risk. In R. C. Schwing & W. A. Albers (Eds.), *Societal risk assessment: How safe is safe enough?* New York: Plenum.

Soden, D. L. (1995). Trust in sources of technical information. *Journal of Environmental Education, 26(2),* 16-20.

Stern, P., Young, O., & Druckman, D. (Eds.). (1992). *Global environmental chane: Understanding the human dimensions*. Washington, DC: National Academy Press.

United Nations Population Fund. (1991). *Population, resources and the environment: The critical challenges*. New York: Author.

Vallerand, R. J. (1989). Vers une méthodologie de validation trans-culturelle de questionnaires psychologiques: Implications pour la recherche en langue française. *Psychologie Canadienne, 30*, 662-680.

Vallerand, R. J. (1997). Toward a hierarchical model of intrinsic and extrinsic motivation. In M. P. Zanna (Ed.), *Advances in Experimental Social Psychology* (vol. , pp. 271-360). New York: Academic Press.

Vallerand R. J., & Bissonnette, R. (1992). Intrinsic, extrinsic, and amotivational styles as predictors of behavior: A prospective study. *Journal of Personality, 60*, 599-620.

Vallerand, R. J., Blais, M. R., Brière, N. M., & Pelletier, L. G. (1989). Construction et validation de l'échelle de motivation en éducation (EME). *Revue Canadienne des Sciences du Comportement, 21*, 323-349.

Vallerand, R. J., & Fortier, M., & Guay, F. (1998). Self-determination and persistence in a real-life setting: Toward a motivational model of high school drop out. *Journal of Personality and Social Psychology,*

Vallerand, R. J., Pelletier, L. G., Blais, M. R., Brière, N. M., Sénécal, C., & Vallières, E. F. (1992). The academic motivation scale: A measure of intrinsic, extrinsic, and amotivation in education. *Educational and Psychological Measurement, 52*, 1003-1017.

Vallerand, R. J., Pelletier, L. G., Blais, M. R., Brière, N. M., Sénécal, C., & Vallières, E. F. (1993). On the assessment of intrinsic, extrinsic, and amotivation in education: Evidence on the concurrent and construct validity of the Academic Motivation Scale. *Educational and Psychological Measurement, 53*, 159-172.

Wang, T. H., & Katzev, R. (1990). Group commitment and resource conservation: Two field experiments on promoting recycling. *Journal of Applied Social Psychology, 20*, 265-275.

Winett, R. A., Leckliter, I. N., Chinn, D. E., Stahl, B., & Love, S. Q. (1985). Effects of television modeling on residential energy conservation. *Journal of Applied Behavior Analyses, 18*, 33-44.

Witmer, J. F., & Geller, E. S. (1976). Facilitating paper recycling: Effects of prompts, raffles, and contests. *Journal of Applied Behavior Analysis, 9*, 315-322.

World Commission on Economic Development. (1987). *Our common future*. New York: Oxford University Press.

11: Improving Patients' Health Through Supporting the Autonomy of Patients and Providers

Geoffrey C. Williams
University of Rochester

> *"Diseases are of two types: those we develop inadvertently, and those we bring on ourselves by failure to practice preventive measures. Preventable illness makes up approximately 70% of the burden of illness and associated costs."*
> C. E. Koop (1995)

Strengths of the U.S. health-care system have resulted largely from biomedical research leading to development of effective treatments for acute diseases and from epidemiological research leading to identification of the risks and benefits of health-related behaviors. These strengths, however, also reveal the weakness of the health-care system, as alluded to by Koop (1995). Specifically, because the focus has been on dramatic interventions for diseases developed inadvertently and on end-stage treatment of diseases that resulted from unhealthy behavior, remarkably little attention has been given to preventive health-care and to facilitating change of the high-risk behaviors, such as smoking, eating unhealthy diets, not exercising, and excessive drinking, that lead to or exacerbate disease.

To understand the magnitude of the problem, consider that, of the roughly two million American deaths in 1990, 860,000 were brought on by tobacco use, diet and activity patterns, alcohol abuse, and preventable infections such as HIV (McGinnis, & Foege, 1993). In other words, 43% of American deaths during that year were premature and resulted from people's behaviors in these four domains. In fact, the behavior of smoking was itself responsible for 19% of all American deaths. It seems that an amazing number of people are bringing about their own morbidity and mortality by behaving in unhealthy ways.

A related problem that also troubles health-care practitioners is that many people fail to adhere to medical regimens. A review of evidence suggests that patients take an average of about 50% of their prescribed medication (Haynes, McKibbon, & Kanani, 1996; Rudd, Byyny, Zachary, LoVerde, Mitchell, Titus, & Marshal, 1988; Sackett & Snow, 1979; Stephenson, Rowe, Haynes, Macharia, &

Leon, 1993) and that fully half of all patients who are prescribed medications for two weeks or longer take a level of the medication that is below what is necessary for it to be effective (Dwyer, Levy, & Menander, 1986; Epstein & Cluss, 1982).

Practitioners thus face a daunting challenge in dealing with patients concerning how they behave—that is, taking their medications, refraining from unhealthy behaviors such as smoking, engaging in healthy behaviors such as exercising, undergoing preventive procedures such as screening mammography, and, indeed, even showing up for scheduled medical appointments.

Clearly, having patients be more motivated to behave in ways that would improve the length and quality of their lives would be of great benefit not only to the patients themselves but also to the medical profession as a whole. However, although the importance of patients' behavior change is now widely understood, there has until recently been relatively little research on the psychological processes through which healthy behavior change occurs and on the means through which providers can facilitate these change processes. Furthermore, even the research-based knowledge that is now available about facilitating behavior change is seldom put into practice by clinicians as the health-care system remains focused on treating patients' acute illnesses. Thus, the problem resides not only in patients' lack of motivation for behaving healthily but also in the practitioners' lack of motivation to attend to their patients' needs for prevention and chronic disease management.

Consider the example of patients' smoking. Research has identified clear and beneficial counseling and pharmacologic interventions for promotion of smoking cessation, yet studies indicate that the rate at which smokers are counseled to quit by their physicians is below 30% (Thorndike, Rigotti, Stafford, & Singer, 1998). Similarly, although effective treatment exist for coronary artery disease, well over half of post-MI (heart attack) patients do not use beta blockers and aspirin and fail to reach the standards for cholesterol lowering (Pearson & Peters, 1997). A comparable percentage of patients with hypertension fail to reach the recommended blood pressure levels of 140/90 (Joint National Committee on Prevention, 1997) in spite of the fact that there are effective treatments that could be prescribed and could be carried out by the patients. These dismal statistics, no doubt, are in part a function of the providers' not being motivated to address the issues adequately and in part a function of the patients' not being motivated to carry out the needed behavior change.

In sum, a clear gap exists between our collective knowledge of life enhancing and life extending treatments and the implementation of these treatments by both providers and patients. Although some of this gap may be explained by lack of physician knowledge, it is probable that much more of the problem lies iphysicians' not putting their knowledge into effective practice and by patients' failing to carry through with the treatment regimens that are recommended.

Medical Education

In line with practice patterns, medical educators continue to focus on training practitioners to do dramatic interventions for acute diseases and virtually ignore how practitioners could facilitate patients' behaving in healthier ways. In fact, just as relatively little research attention had, until recently, been given to how providers can facilitate behavior change, even less has been given to how to train providers to enact the methods that are increasingly being shown to be effective in facilitating prevention and promoting change of high risk behaviors.

In this chapter, we use self-determination theory (Deci & Ryan, 1985b; Ryan & Deci, 2000) to address the issues of how medical providers can facilitate patients' motivation to behave in healthier ways, and how medical educators can facilitate the motivation of both future and current medical practitioners to address the issues necessary to promote prevention and behavior change. The focus of the chapter is on physicians' reliable, self-directed implementation of relevant knowledge using an interpersonal style that in turn increases the likelihood of patients' carrying out recommendations that could improve their health.

Self-Determination Theory

Self-determination theory (SDT), as noted in other chapters of this volume, proposes that humans have three innate psychological needs—namely, those for autonomy, competence, and relatedness to others. Autonomy is defined as the degree to which individuals feel volitional and responsible for the initiation of their behavior. Competence concerns the degree to which they feel able to achieve their goals and desired outcomes. Relatedness is defined as the extent to which they feel connected to others in a warm, positive, interpersonal manner. The theory maintains that supports for these needs by the social environment will enhance individuals' psychological growth and adjustment, and both their mental and physical health.

Central to SDT is the distinction between autonomous and controlled behaviors, which are two types of motivated behaviors that involve different reasons for behaving (Ryan & Connell, 1989). To be autonomous means to act with a full sense of volition and choice because the activity is interesting or personally important, whereas to be controlled means to act with the feeling of pressure because of a coercive demand or a seductive offer. The theory suggests that people will tend to be more autonomous, relative to controlled, when they experience greater fulfillment of the three psychological needs.

The distinction between autonomous and controlled motivation represents a continuum rather than a dichotomy, and as such any action can be characterized in terms of the degree to which it is autonomous versus controlled. The degree to which behaviors are autonomous is thus predicted to be a function of the degree to which people are able to experience basic need satisfaction while engaging in the behaviors. In the research herein reviewed, the focus is on the extent to which people experience a specific behavior such as stopping smoking or lowering their fat intake as being freely chosen (i.e., as being autonomous) versus being pressured by some interpersonal or intrapsychic force (i.e., being controlled), and on the antecedents and consequences of those behaviors being more autonomous versus controlled.

Autonomy Is Not Independence

Frequently, in discussion of patient autonomy, the concept of autonomy is confused with that of independence. To be autonomous means to feel volitional or willing to engage in a behavior, whereas to be independent means to act without reference to or support from another (Ryan, 1993; Ryan & Lynch, 1989). People would be autonomous in stopping smoking or undergoing angioplasty if they did those actions with a sense of choice and personal endorsement. In making a decision to change a behavior or undergo a procedure, patients often want and need advice and support from their physicians; they seldom want to decide or act in a wholly independent way. Thus, being volitional does not necessarily mean that people act independently of others—notably, of their providers—it simply means that they experience a full sense of volition in proceeding with a behavior or treatment.

Accordingly, for a provider to support patients' autonomy does not mean abandoning the patients to act or decide for themselves. Patients can be autonomous while relying on their providers, and it is important for providers to be sensitive to how much advice and support the patients want. As well as needing to feel autonomous, people need to feel related to others, and patients' feeling related to and supported by their providers is an important element in the patients' feeling able to act autonomously. If providers abandon the patients, while claiming to be supporting their autonomy, the providers are demanding that the patients be independent and are failing to support the patients' autonomy. Similarly, in the realm of medical education, students typically want to feel like they can rely on their instructors to support their autonomous learning.

Internalization: Becoming More Autonomous

According to SDT, self-regulation develops and people become autonomous through the processes of internalization. Internalization involves converting external regulatory processes into internal regulatory processes (Schafer, 1968); however, within SDT there are two types of internalization, namely introjection and integration. *Introjection* is a kind of partial internalization in which regulations are taken in by people but are not really accepted as their own. *Integration*, on the other hand, is a much fuller internalization in which people identify with the importance of the behavior and synthesize its regulatory process with other aspects of their self. As such, they will have more fully accepted the regulation as their own.

Through internalization, a patient or a student can take in regulations that initially resided in the urgings of the patient's doctor or the student's teacher. Insofar as the regulation is merely introjected, people will tend to use it to coerce themselves into action—for example with threats of guilt or shame—and as such the behavior will continue to be controlled even though the source of control is now within the person. Thus, when the form of internalization is introjection, the person will not be autonomous in carrying out the behavior (Deci & Ryan, 1991), and so less persistence and less positive health-care outcomes are predicted. In contrast, with integration, the person will be autonomous in carrying out the behavior. Because the regulation has been integrated into individuals' sense of self, they will feel volitional in carrying out the behavior, so more positive outcomes would be expected.

The phenomenon of initially external regulations being internalized occurs in health-care all the time. Frequently, when patients get diagnosed with a common illness such as having an elevated cholesterol (hyperlipidemia), they demonstrate little interest in performing appropriate behaviors like reducing their fat intake, exercising regularly, losing weight if they are obese, or taking their medication. Similar events occur around the diagnosis of heart disease and diabetes. For better health outcomes, the patients must assume responsibility for these regulatory functions. Internalization is the general process through which that happens, and integration is the optimal form of internalization.

When the process of internalization fails altogether, it is likely that patients will not even carry out the treatment behaviors and thus will experience increased morbidity and mortality. As well, the health-care system will encounter greater costs both in trying to get the patients to comply with the regimens and in caring for them as they develop diseases such as strokes, renal failure, and coronary artery disease.

In terms of medical education, internalization is in evidence as trainees' learn about disease processes and corresponding treatment options. As these treatments are presented to the students, if the students feel controlled in their learning and carrying out the procedures, it is predicted that they will be less likely to internalize the material and thus will be less likely to use it effectively. Because the half-life of medical education (the time it takes for 50% of the current treatment recommendations to become outdated) is estimated to be about 4 years, practicing physicians must regularly internalize new or changed treatments into their everyday practice. Thus, internalization is an important process throughout physicians' careers, and if they have not begun the process effectively during medical training it is likely that they will continue to be less effective as their careers progress.

Facilitating Internalization by Supporting Autonomy

Differentiating the autonomous versus controlled regulatory processes is important, at least in part, because it is possible to identify factors in health-care climates and learning climates that facilitate versus undermine internalization and integration. More specifically, if climates support the fulfillment of patients' or students' basic needs for competence, autonomy, and relatedness, those individuals will be more likely to internalize and integrate the material being presented. Treatment climates that are cold and controlling are predicted to result in incomplete internalization of regulations, and thus in less maintained behavior change, less health status improvement, and greater health-care costs. Similarly, when learning climates are not supportive of the students' needs, less internalization of the important learnings is expected. In contrast, interpersonal environments that support the patients' and learners' needs for autonomy, competence, and relatedness are predicted to facilitate greater internalization, resulting in more behavior change and its maintenance, which in turn will lead to improved health outcomes or learning outcomes.

The concept of *autonomy support* describes an interpersonal climate in which authority figures such as physicians (or teachers) take the perspectives of the patients (or students) into account, provide relevant information and opportunities for choice, and encourage the patients (or students) to accept more responsibility for their health (or learning) behaviors. Autonomy support also entails practitioners' (or instructors) interacting more meaningfully with the patients (or students) by asking what the patients (or students) want to achieve, listening and encouraging questions, providing understandable and satisfying replies to the patients' (or students') questions, and suspending judgement while soliciting the opinions and histories of past behaviors. An autonomy supportive orientation minimizes the use of pressure and control.

In contrast, practitioners who are more *controlling* tend to pressure their patients with rewards, punishments, or judgmental evaluations. Because studies have indicated that practitioners in traditional medical encounters tend to be quite controlling (Beckman & Frankel, 1984; Kaplan, Greenfield, & Ware, 1989; Marvel, Epstein, Flowers, & Beckman 1999), research on the effects of autonomy supportive versus controlling health-care climates is highly pertinent. Similarly, traditional medical education has been found to be highly controlling (Becker, Geer, Hughes, & Strauss, 1966; Bosk, 1979; McMurray, Schwartz, Genero, & Linzer, 1993), so past research concerning the effects of autonomy supportive versus controlling learning environments at various levels of education on students' autonomous motivation to learn is also very important (Deci, Ryan, & Williams, 1996; Reeve, Bolt, & Cai, 1999).

Elements of autonomy support. A laboratory experiment by Deci, Eghrari, Patrick, and Leone (1994) examined specific elements of an interpersonal context that constitute autonomy support and thus facilitate internalization and integration. They isolated three important elements of supporting autonomy; namely, providing a meaningful rationale for why a behavior is being recommended so individuals will understand the personal importance of the activity for themselves; acknowledging people's feelings and perspectives so they will feel understood; and using an interpersonal style that emphasizes choice and minimizes control so the individuals will not feel pressured to behave. Results of this experiment indicated that the three facilitating factors lead to greater internalization and integration. Although the experiment was not done in a medical setting, it nonetheless suggests that when health-care practitioners and medical educators acknowledge their patients' or students' perspectives, provide meaningful rationales for suggested behaviors, and provide choice while minimizing pressures and controls, it is likely that patients and students will evidence greater internalization and integration of pertinent regulations and feel more autonomous and competent in carrying them out.

Causality orientations. Although SDT emphasizes that the health-care (or educational) climate's being autonomy supportive will facilitate autonomous motivation for specific health-care or educational behaviors, the theory also proposes that enduring personality factors concerning people's orientations toward causality (Deci & Ryan, 1985a) affect their autonomy with respect to the particular behavior.

The autonomous causality orientation, assessed with the General Causality Orientations Scale concerns people's general tendency to orient toward autonomy support in the social environment and to be more self-determined. This involves being more aware of their own needs and feelings and experiencing a greater sense of choice in the regulation of their behavior. Previous research has shown that people high on the general autonomy orientation tend to be more autonomous in enacting specific health-relevant and learning behaviors.

The Self-Determination Model

From the various propositions, an interesting picture begins to emerge for medical education, a picture in which learning environments that are controlling tend to produce practitioners who provide care for their patients in a controlling manner, which is expected, in turn, to lead to less effective treatment. Pressures and controls in the medical practice environment—for example, time and reimbursement demands—are expected also to further diminish practitioners feelings of autonomy and their capacity to provide autonomy support for their patients.

In essence, this overall picture can be represented in two self-determination models: one that relates providers' interpersonal style to patients' motivation, behavior change, and health; and the other that relates medical educators' interpersonal style to students' motivation for learning and subsequent treatment of patients.

Figure 11-1 presents the elements of the SDT health-care model, as it pertains to patients. Figure 11-2, which appears later in the chapter, presents the model as it relates to providers acquiring effective practice techniques. The practical importance of this pair of models is that autonomous motivation in both patients and providers is expected to yield long-term persistence for patients and practitioners, repeated efforts to effect behavior change, and the energy necessary to maintain behavior change long enough for important outcomes to accrue.

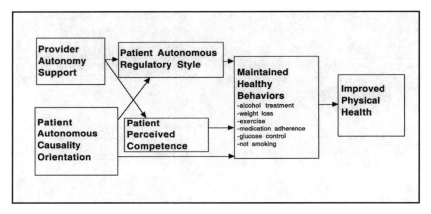

Figure 11.1. Self-Determination Model of Patients' Motivation, Behavior, and Health

Research on Aspects of the SDT Model of Physical Health

During the past decade we have been engaged in a program of studies testing various aspects of the self-determination model with respect to various health-related behaviors. In each case, providers' support for patients' autonomy has been related to autonomous motivation, and that in turn has been used to predict patient behavior. In some of the studies, patients' perceived competence for the requisite behavior change has also been assessed because SDT proposes that perceived competence, as well as autonomous motivation, is necessary for effective behavior change. Also, in some studies, the relation between patient behavior and specific physiological outcomes has been examined, and, in some, patients' general autonomy orientation has been used as a predictor of autonomous motivation for the target behavior.

We have tested the general hypothesis that provider autonomy support and patients' general orientation toward autonomy will predict the patients' being more autonomously motivated (and feeling more competent) to carry out the healthy behavior. In turn, autonomous motivation (and perceived competence) are hypothesized to predict maintained behavior change and positive health outcomes.

Assessing Motivation and Treatment Contexts

Autonomous and controlled motivations for participating in treatment or behaving in a healthy way are assessed with the Treatment Self-Regulation Questionnaire (TSRQ), which uses an approach to assessing motivation developed by Ryan and Connell (1989) and provides a reflection of the extent to which people engage in healthy behaviors for their own personal reasons versus because they feel pressured to do so. Perceived competence is measured with a four-item Perceived Competence Scale (PCS), which reflects how able the individuals feel to carry out the treatment regimen or change the target behavior. Each of these scales is adapted to the treatment goal or behavior being studied, so in cases of smoking cessation the questions all pertain to that behavior, whereas with exercise the questions are essentially the same but they are asked in terms of exercising regularly rather than in terms of stopping smoking.

Autonomy supportiveness of the provider is assessed with the Health-care Climate Questionnaire (HCCQ), which can be used either with patients' reporting their perceptions of provider autonomy support or with trained observers' responding to the same items to report their perceptions of the providers. Finally, trained observers can also rate the extent to which patients are actively involved in their meetings with the clinicians. Although being actively involved during a consultation with the provider is not the same thing as being autonomously motivated to carry out the treatment regimen or behave in a healthier way, the two concepts do tend to be related.

Studies of Patient Motivation in Health Care

Aspects of the self-determination model have been specifically tested in studies of individuals attending an alcohol treatment program, morbidly obese patients participating in a very-low-calorie weight-loss program, adult outpatients adhering to medication prescriptions, patients with diabetes controlling their blood-sugar levels, and both adolescents' and adults' motivation for smoking reduction. These studies are all longitudinal both because it takes time for the internalization and integration of a behavior-change regulation to be accomplished and because important health benefits tend to accrue only after changes have been maintained for a significant period of time.

Alcohol treatment. Ryan, Plant, and O'Malley (1995) used the TSRQ with individuals who entered an alcohol-treatment program, some of whom were mandated to be there. Outcomes for the eight-week program were attendance during the program and clinicians' ratings of how involved each participant was in the treatment program. Results indicated that participants who reported more internalized motivation for being in treatment attended treatment more regularly and were rated by their counselors as being more involved in the treatment. In this study, controlled motivation also contributed to prediction of attendance, although people high in controlled motivation who were low in the more autonomous type of motivation attended poorly and were not very engaged in the treatment. Thus, having high autonomous motivation was important for treatment success, but having some external motivation in addition to the autonomous motivation also helped.

A weight-loss program. Another relevant study involved severely obese patients participating in a 26-week medically supervised, very-low-calorie, weight-loss program (Williams, Grow, Freedman, Ryan, & Deci, 1996). All patients in this study were about twice their "healthy body weight." Because the program does have some potentially negative health consequences, patients are admitted only if they are so obese that the risks associated with their obesity out-weigh the risks of the diet. In addition to following the diet, which involved only the liquid diet for 3 months and then gradually introduced healthy portions of regular food, patients attended weekly meetings at which they consulted a doctor or nurse and met in a group counseling session intended as a support group for participants. Nutritionists and exercise physiologists attended some of the meetings to consult with the patients.

A few weeks into the program, patients completed the TSRQ, indicating the degrees to which their reasons for following the program guidelines for diet and exercise were autonomous and controlled. Then, at the end of the six-month program their attendance at the weekly program meetings and their change in body mass index (BMI) over the period of the program was tabulated. BMI is closely correlated with weight but allows for adjustment due to frame size and is considered the more appropriate measure in studies of obesity. Finally, at a two-year follow-up, their long-term change in BMI was assessed, as was the amount they exercised regularly, as indicators of the degree to which the healthy behaviors were maintained after the program had ended.

Results of the study revealed that patients who reported more autonomous reasons for program participation attended more regularly and in turn evidenced greater reduction of body mass index during the six months of the program. Controlled motivation was unrelated to the outcomes. Even more importantly, the extent to which patients' reasons for participation were autonomous was a positive predictor both of the amount they exercised at two-year follow up and of their maintained reduction in BMI over that same time period. It appears that when patients are autonomous in their motivation for participating in a weight-loss program, the outcomes are substantially more likely to be positive than when their motivation is controlled.

Participants in this study also provided their perceptions of their providers' autonomy supportiveness using the HCCQ. Analyses revealed that perceived autonomy supportiveness predicted autonomous regulation, attendance in the program, and long-term reduction in body mass index. As predicted by the SDT model, the relationships between autonomy support and both attendance and long-term change were mediated by autonomous regulation. Thus, this study provided considerable support for the self-determination model of health-behavior change.

Medication adherence. Williams, Rodin, Ryan, Grolnick, and Deci (1998) did a study of medication adherence that also supported SDT. One hundred and twenty-six patients who had been prescribed long-term medication participated in the study, and adherence was assessed with both self-reports of medication taking and a two-week pill count. Analyses revealed that patients' autonomous motivation—that is, the internalization of the value and regulation of medication taking—was a strong positive predictor of adherence, whereas controlled regulation was unrelated to medication taking.

Interestingly, in this study physicians were asked to predict which patients would adhere to their prescriptions, and analysis revealed that physician predictions were unrelated to actual adherence. This point is an important one because it suggests that people can look just as motivated whether their motivation is autonomous or controlled, and the physicians were probably using any overt sign of motivation to make their predictions. However, these and other results suggest that it is only when that motivation is autonomous that positive consequences such as maintained adherence are likely to be manifest.

In this study of medication adherence, patients also rated the extent to which their physicians were autonomy supportive. Results showed that perceptions of physicians' being more autonomy supportive were associated with their patients' being more autonomously regulated in taking their medications. Autonomy support also predicted greater adherence, and path analyses showed that, as expected, autonomous regulation mediated the relationship between autonomy support and medication adherence.

By providing insight into why people take their medications and by identifying a potential relationship between patients' perception of the health-care climate and the patients' reliable use of medication, these results could help patients maximize their treatment benefits for a wide range of chronic diseases including hypertension, HIV, tuberculosis, depression, anxiety, congestive heart failure, hyperlipidemia, and osteoporosis, all of which cause a great deal of suffering for those with the diseases. In the cases of HIV and tuberculosis, strict adherence to medications can also reduce the public's risk of the spread of resistant organisms in the community. Finally, with more accurate assessment of adherence, practitioners can avoid unnecessary prescriptions of the higher doses or stronger medications that can lead to greater side effects for the patient.

Glucose control. A recent study of patients with diabetes (Williams, Freedman, & Deci, 1998) explored the relation between autonomous regulation and patients' average glucose control as reflected in the physiological measure of glycosylated hemoglobin (HbA1c). A higher HbA1c has been firmly linked to the long-term diabetes consequences of kidney failure (nephropathy), numbness in hands and feet (neuropathy), and damage to the eyes (retinopathy) including blindness (DCCT, 1993). Thus, a low HbA1c represents an excellent proximal endpoint of health status.

In the Williams, Freedman, and Deci, (1998) study, 126 patients completed the TSRQ and the PCS, and a factor analysis indicated that the constructs of autonomous motivation, controlled motivation, and perceived competence were separate factors. Patients' HbA1c levels were obtained from blood samples at the beginning of the 12-month period and again at the end. Finally, patients' perceptions of the degree to which their providers were autonomy supportive were assessed 4 months into the year-long period.

Analyses revealed that patients who experienced their providers as more autonomy supportive were more able to lower their glucose levels over the 12-month period than those who experienced the providers as more controlling. Further, those patients who experienced their providers as more autonomy supportive became more autonomous in their motivation for maintaining a healthy diet and exercising regularly. As they became more autonomous they also experienced themselves as more competent to adhere to their diets and exercise regimens, and these increases in perceived competence predicted decreases in glucose level. In other words, autonomy supportive providers tended to promote more positive health outcomes and these outcomes appear to have come about because the providers' autonomy support facilitated the patients' becoming more autonomously motivated and feeling more competent. As in the medication-adherence and weight-loss studies, controlled motivation did not predict medical outcomes. In short, autonomous motivation and perceived competence for the goal of better glucose control were predictive of an important, long-term physiologic indicator of health for patients with diabetes, and these patient characteristics were facilitated by the autonomy support of providers.

Adolescent smoking. In a study of adolescents (both smokers and nonsmokers) attending a suburban high school, Williams, Cox, Kouides, and Deci (1999), assessed the students' intensity and frequency of smoking at baseline and again 4 months later. (The rate for nonsmokers was, of course, 0 cigarettes per day.) The autonomous and controlled reasons for why all of the students would not smoke were also assessed at these two points in time.

This study was designed to test whether the communication style used by a presenter of information about smoking would effect the students' autonomous motivation for not smoking and in turn their actual smoking behavior. Therefore, following baseline assessment, the students were randomized to receive one of two 20-minute presentations about smoking, one of which was done with an autonomy supportive style, focusing on the students' making a clear choice for themselves about whether or not to smoke, and the other of which was done with a controlling style, where the students were told they should not smoke because of the terrible risks for contracting and dying from smoking related diseases such as lung cancer, emphysema, and heart disease. Following the presentation, students rated the degree to which their presenter had been autonomy supportive.

Students who experienced the presenter as more autonomy supportive reported greater autonomous motivation for not smoking. Further, the students' autonomous reasons for not smoking significantly predicted a reduction in their frequency and intensity of smoking. Although the two interventions did not have a significantly different effect of smoking reduction over the four months, there was nonetheless evidence that autonomy support is important for promoting autonomous motivation and healthy behavior change.

Adolescence is an important developmental stage where issues of autonomy, relationships, and competence are all changing. The results indicate that further investigation of smoking interventions that invite the adolescent to consider both sides of their decision about whether or not to smoke may be important for helping the teens not smoke.

Long-term smokers face a 50% probability of dying prematurely from a smoking related disease. However, if a smoker abstains from smoking for 12 months, that probability is substantially reduced (US DHHS, 1990). After 10 to 15 years of abstinence, mortality rates for former smokers return to those for nonsmokers. Given these statistics, and because smoking rates of high school students had risen to nearly 40% in 1999 from 28% in 1992, further research of this sort on promoting smoking abstinence and cessation among teens is indeed important.

Adult smoking cessation. Two related studies have examined the motivational processes of smoking cessation among adult smokers. One (Williams, Gagne, Ryan, & Deci, 2002) tested the self-determination model with respect to smoking cessation. In it, 27 community physicians counseled their smokers to quit using the NCI Guidelines presented in either a relatively autonomy supportive or a more controlling manner. Smoking cessation was assessed at 6, 12, and 30 months using self-reports of cessation validated by carbon monoxide testing. An index of continuous cessation was created from the three points in time. The degree of physician autonomy support was rated by research assistants from audio-taped recordings. Patient demographics, perceived competence, and autonomous motivation for quitting were assessed by questionnaires.

Structural equation modeling was used to test the SDT model, confirming that the average ratings of physicians using the autonomy supportive approach were significantly more autonomy supportive than the those of physicians using the controlling approach. Further, the rated autonomy support of the counselling interaction predicted patients' autonomous motivation for stopping smoking. Finally, both autonomous motivation and perceived competence independently predicted continuous abstinence. Thus, the self-determination model for maintained smoking cessation did receive support from the analyses.

In an examination of other data from this study (Williams & Deci, 2001), the concept of patient activation introduced by Kaplan, Greenfield, and Ware (1989) was the focus. These researchers had found that if a research assistant met with patients for a relatively brief period just before the patients had an appointment with their physicians, and if they spent that time reviewing the patients' charts and having the patients formulate questions to ask their doctors during the visit, the patients were indeed more active in the meetings with their doctors and their degree of activation positively predicted long term health consequences.

Williams and Deci (2001) hypothesized that if doctors were more autonomy supportive during the meeting, that in itself might activate patients just as having an assistant meet with them first had done in the Kaplan et al. (1989) study, and that this patient activation should have positive health effects for the patients. Thus, Williams and Deci had trained raters rate the degree to which the patients were active in the interchange with their doctors, expecting that patients would be more active in meetings where the doctors who counselled them about smoking cessation used an autonomy supportive approach than in meetings where the doctors used a more controlling approach. Rated activation of the patients during the counselling session was in turn predicted to result in better maintained cessation rates.

As predicted, in the experimental condition where doctors were to use an autonomy supportive approach, patients were significantly more active in their engagement with the doctor, and their degree of activation did indeed predict their biochemically validated quit rates.

Summary. When taken together, these studies indicate that only when patients' motivation for health-related behavior change is primarily autonomous are they likely to ongoingly engage in their healthy behaviors, including adhering to prescriptions, attending treatment programs, losing weight, exercising, and not smoking. These maintained behaviors were in turn related to better health or lower health risks, as evidenced for example in lower levels of glycosylated hemoglobin. Thus, autonomous motivation, supplemented by perceived competence, appear to be important predictors of physical health. Finally, the studies showed repeatedly that when providers were autonomy supportive, patients became more autonomously motivated and felt more competent, and in turn they behaved in healthier ways. So it seems that in fact health-care providers can indeed have an important effect on patients' health by relating to them in ways that promote their autonomous motivation and perceived competence.

Supporting autonomous regulation. Being autonomy supportive refers to the provision of choice, the encouragement of self-initiation, and the acknowledgment of patients' perspectives; whereas, being controlling refers to pressuring patients to think, feel, or behave in specific ways. Providers who are autonomy supportive do not emphasize and rely on their authority as experts, but instead they take the patients' perspectives and are sensitive to the patients' needs so they can provide supports not only for autonomy but also for competence and relatedness when that is appropriate for the patients' condition.

Because being autonomy supportive involves taking a patient's perspective, it will necessitate understanding the patient's reasons for engaging in unhealthy behaviors or failing to engage in healthy ones. It is important for providers to accept these reasons and not to pressure the patient to change. Instead, by making relevant information available to the patient in a style that allows the patient to consider it without feeling forced and by encouraging the patient to take responsibility for his or her own behavior, providers can respect and accept a patient's decision while at the same time having a positive influence on the patient's health outcomes.

Other Health Care Studies

A number of studies have been done in other laboratories that have examined health-care issues in a way that is relevant to the SDT model. They have used varied approaches and methods, and will now be very briefly summarized.

A study conducted in a home for the aged revealed that the residents' perceptions of the staff's being autonomy supportive was positively predictive of the residents' vitality, perceived well-being, and life satisfaction (Kasser & Ryan, 1999).

A review of 32 studies of brief interventions for problem drinkers (Bien, Miller, & Tonigan, 1993) isolated common elements of successful interventions, and among the most important elements identified were giving nonevaluative feedback, providing choice, encouraging patients to take responsibility, and being empathic, all of which are central features of an autonomy supportive style of providing health-care.

Harackiewicz, Sansone, Blair, Epstein, and Manderlink (1987) studied smokers who were randomly assigned to various self-help treatment conditions including an intrinsic (i.e., autonomy oriented) self-help condition, in which the importance of one's own initiations and efforts was highlighted. Results showed that subjects in this autonomy-supporting, self-help condition remained abstinent longer than those in the two more controlling conditions or in the comparison group.

Another study of self-help smoking cessation programs (Curry, Wagner, & Grothaus, 1991) involved participants being assigned to one of four groups: an intrinsic, personalized-feedback (i.e., autonomy-supportive) group; an extrinsic, financial-incentive group; an intrinsic plus extrinsic group; and a comparison group. Results of the study indicated that the autonomy-supportive condition yielded the best continuous abstinence measured at 3 and 12 months (biochemically confirmed).

Other relevant studies of behavior change have explored the effects of providers using different styles of counseling patients. For example, Ockene et al., (1991) had physicians vary their style of counseling patients for smoking cessation and found that using a more patient-centered (i.e., autonomy supportive) style resulted in more positive attitudes toward the physicians and greater abstinence at a six-month follow up than did a more directive (i.e., controlling) style.

Miller, Benefield, and Tonigan (1993) found that when providers were patient-centered (rather than controlling and confrontational) in counseling problem drinkers, their patients were less resistant and drank less alcohol at one year follow up. A meta-analysis of smoking cessation studies conducted for the Agency for Health-care Policy and Research by Fiore et al. (1996) revealed that when practitioners provided what they have called "intra-treatment social support" (which appears very similar to autonomy support), smokers were almost twice as likely to not be smoking 5 months later than when this interpersonal support is not given.

Finally, Langer and Rodin (1976) found that supporting the autonomy of institutionalized elderly patients by providing them control over aspects of their lives and encouraging them to be more self-initiating and accepting of responsibility led to enhanced physical and psychological well-being and lowered mortality.

Promoting Autonomy Support in Health-Care Providers

Because research results have repeatedly indicated that providers' being autonomy supportive has positive behavior-change and health consequences, we have also been exploring the issue of how to teach providers to be more autonomy supportive. This work has been conducted in medical schools and has extended previous work that had been done in other educational settings. Previous work had reliably found that autonomy support by teachers was associated with greater internalization and autonomous motivation for learning among students in public schools (Deci, Schwartz, Sheinman, & Ryan, 1981) and at university (Black & Deci, 2000).

Williams and Deci (1996) used interviewing courses for second year medical students at two university medical centers as the setting to examine issues of autonomy support in medical education. Autonomy support by instructors was hypothesized to lead to greater autonomous motivation on the part of the students; student autonomy was predicted to increase the likelihood that the students would internalize the biopsychosocial values that were extant in the course;

and internalization of biopsychosocial values (see Engel, 1977) was expected to lead these doctors-in-training to be more autonomy supportive with patients.

At each university, several instructors taught the course, and students were asked to rate the degree to which their instructor was autonomy supportive using a Learning Climate Questionnaire (adapted from the Health-Care Climate Questionnaire). The students' reasons for attending the course and their psychosocial values were measured at the beginning and the end of the six month course using the Learning Self-Regulation Questionnaire (adapted from the Treatment Self-Regulation Questionnaire). Results of the study indicate that students who had perceived their instructors as autonomy supportive, relative to those who perceived their instructors as controlling, attended the course more regularly, became more autonomous in the reasons they gave for why they attended class, and in turn developed stronger psychosocial values that persisted over a two-year period.

The study further yielded the important finding that students who became more autonomously motivated and evidenced greater internalization of psychosocial values during their second-year interviewing course subsequently used a more autonomy-supportive approach in their third year when counseling simulated patients about changing cardiovascular risk behaviors. It seems, therefore, that medical school instructors' being autonomy supportive in their style of teaching medical interviewing leads medical students to become more biopsychosocially oriented and to relate to patients in more autonomy supportive ways.

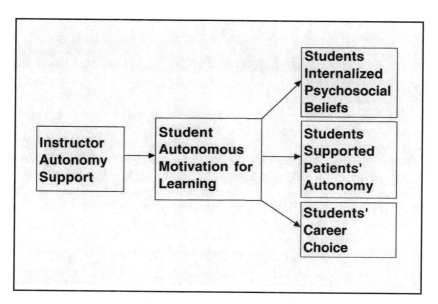

Figure 11.2. Self-Determination Model for Medical Education

That, in turn, as has been argued throughout, leads patients to behave in more autonomous and healthy ways. The relations of instructor orientation to student motivation and internalization are shown in Figure 11.2.

Two related studies (Williams, Wiener, Markakis, Reeve, & Deci, 1994; Williams, Saizow, Ross, & Deci, 1997) showed that students tended to select a residency in a subspecialty where they had perceived their instructors to be more autonomy supportive. Structural Equation Modeling indicated that the autonomy-supportive instructors facilitated students' developing interest in the content they were teaching and feeling more autonomous while learning the material, and that in turn increased the likelihood of the students' pursuing it as a career. Although these studies do not provide any information about how the students will practice medicine, they nonetheless highlight the importance of the concept of autonomy supportive teaching for predicting the medical students' subsequent behavior. The results of these studies are also summarized in the SDT model of medical education presented in Figure 11.2.

Conclusions

The closely related issues of adherence and maintained behavior change represent a major challenge to the health-care field with respect to prevention, well being, and health outcomes. It appears from this research that patients will be more likely to adhere and maintain healthy behaviors if they have integrated the regulation for those behaviors and are thus more autonomously motivated to carry them out. The research now indicates that such internalization is more likely to occur in health-care climates that are supportive of patients' autonomy. Research has also shown that when medical school instructors are more autonomy supportive in their teaching, students become more biopsychosocially oriented and are accordingly more autonomy supportive of their patients, which of course would be expected to lead to more positive health consequences.

Taken together, the parallel results from the health-care and health-education studies suggest that there are wide ranging advantages to being autonomy supportive. When medical educators and health-care practitioners are autonomy supportive, their students and patients are likely to become more autonomous and competent, which in turn leads to a variety of positive outcomes. In education, autonomous self-regulation has been associated with enhanced learning and better adjustment, and in medical care, it has been associated with maintained behavior change, more positive health status, and better mental health (Deci, Ryan, & Williams, 1996).

By impacting the orientation of practitioners-in-training, it seems possible to have the kind of impact on health delivery that will result in patients' behaving more responsibly and thus realizing better health. Not only is motivation expected to improve health by leading patients to use their medications in ways known to ameliorate disease, but also through encouraging patients' use of preventive procedures and change of health-risk behaviors. Thus, it appears that applying self-determination theory to practitioner and patient behavior could help to reduce the gap that exists between what is known to improve patients' health and what is actually done in practice.

References

Becker, H. S., Geer, B., Hughes, E. C., & Strauss, A. L. (1966). *Boys in White: Student Culture in Medical School.* Chicago: University of Chicago Press.

Beckman, H., & Frankel, R. (1984). The impact of physician behavior on the collection of data. *Annals of Internal Medicine, 101, 5*, 692-696.

Bien, T., Miller, W., & Tonigan, J. (1993). Brief interventions for alcohol problems: A review. *Addiction, 88*, 315-336.

Black, A. E., & Deci, E. L. (2000). The effects of student self-regulation and instructor autonomy support on learning in a college-level natural science course: A self-determination theory perspective. *Science Education, 84*, 740-756.

Bosk, C. L. (1979). *Forgive and Remember.* Chicago: University of Chicago Press.

Curry, S. J., Wagner, E. H., & Grothaus, L. C. (1991). Evaluation of intrinsic and extrinsic interventions with a self-help cessation program. *Journal of Consulting and Clinical and Social Psychology, 59*, 318-324.

DCCT (Diabetes Control and Complications Trial Research Group). (1993). The effect of intensive treatment of diabetes on the development and progression of long-term complications in insulin-dependent diabetes mellitus. *New England Journal of Medicine, 329*, 977-986.

Deci, E. L., Eghrari, H., Patrick, B. C., & Leone, D. (1994). Facilitating internalization: The self-determination theory perspective. *Journal of Personality, 62*, 119-142.

Deci, E. L., & Ryan, R. M. (1985). The general causality orientations scale: Self-determination in personality. *Journal of Research in Personality, 19*, 109-134.

Deci, E. L., & Ryan, R. M. (1985b). *Intrinsic motivation and self-determination in human behavior.* New York: Plenum.

Deci, E. L., & Ryan, R. M. (1991). A motivational approach to self: Integration in personality. In R. Dienstbier (Ed.), *Nebraska symposium on motivation: Vol. 38. Perspectives on motivation* (pp. 237-288). Lincoln, NE: University of Nebraska Press.

Deci, E. L., Ryan, R. M., & Williams, G. C. (1996). Need satisfaction and the self-regulation of learning. *Learning and Individual Differences, 8*, 165-83.

Deci, E. L., Schwartz, A. J., Sheinman, L., & Ryan, R. M. (1981). An instrument to assess adults' orientations toward control versus autonomy with children: Reflections on intrinsic motivation and perceived competence. *Journal of Educational Psychology, 73*, 642- 650.

Dwyer, M. S., Levy R. A., & Menander, K. B. (1986). Improving medication compliance through the use of modern dosage forms. *Journal of Pharmacology and Technology, July/August*, 166-170.

Engel, G. L. (1977). The need for a new medical model: A challenge for biomedicine. *Science, 196*, 129-136.

Epstein, L. H., & Cluss, P. A. (1982). A behavioral medicine perspective on adherence to long-term medical regimens. *Journal of Consulting and Clinical Psychology, 50*, 950-971.

Fiore, M. C., Bailey, W. C., Cohen, S. C., et al. (April, 1996). *Smoking Cessation: Clinical Practice Guideline No. 18.* Rockville, MD: Agency for Health-care Policy and Research; Publication No. 96-0692.

Harackiewicz, J. M., Sansone, C., Blair, L. W., Epstein, J. A., & Manderlink, G. (1987). Attributional processes in behavior change and maintenance: Smoking cessation and continued abstinence. *Journal of Consulting and Clinical Psychology, 55*, 372-378.

Haynes, R. B., McKibbon, K. A., & Kanani, R. (1996). Systematic review of randomized trials of interventions to assist patients to follow prescriptions for medications. *Lancet, 348* 383-386.

Joint National Committee on Prevention, Sixth Report: Detection, Evaluation, and Treatment of High Blood Pressure. (1997). *Archives of Internal Medicine, 157,* 2413-2446.

Kaplan, S. H., Greenfield, S., & Ware, J. E. (1989). Assessing the effects of physician-patient interactions on the outcomes of chronic disease. *Medical Care, 27*, S110-S127.

Kasser, V. G., & Ryan, R. M. (1999). The relation of psychological needs for autonomy and relatedness to vitality, well being, and mortality in a nursing home. *Journal of Applied Social Psychology, 29*, 935-954.

Koop, C. E. (1995). Editorial: A personal role in Health-care Reform. *American Journal of Public Health, 85(6):* 759-760.

Langer, E. J., & Rodin, J. (1976). The effects of choice and personal responsibility for the aged: A field experiment in an institutional setting. *Journal of Personality and Social Psychology, 34*, 191-198.

Marvel, K. M., Epstein, R. M., Flowers, K., & Beckman, H.B. (1999). Soliciting the patients' agenda: Have we improved? *Journal of the American Medical Association, 281*, 283-287.

McGinnis, M. J., & Foege, W. H. (1993). Actual causes of death in the United States. *Journal of the American Medical Association, 270(18):* 2207-2212.

McMurray, J. E., Schwartz, M. D., Genero, N. P., & Linzer, M. (1993). The attractiveness of internal medicine: a qualitative analysis of the experiences of female and male medical students. Society of General Medicine Task force on Career Choice in Internal Medicine. *Annals of Internal Medicine, 119*, 812-8.

Miller, W. R., Benefield, R. G., & Tonigan, J. S. (1993). Enhancing motivation for change in problem drinking: A controlled comparison of two therapist styles. *Journal of Consulting and Clinical Psychology, 61*, 455-461.

Ockene, J. K., Kristeller, J., Goldberg, R., Amick, T. L., Pekow, P. S., Hosmer, D., Quirk, M., & Kalan, K. (1991). Increasing the efficacy of physician delivered smoking interventions: A randomized clinical trial. *Journal of General Internal Medicine, 6*, 1-8.

Pearson, T. A., & Peters, T. D. (1997). The treatment gap in coronary artery disease and heart failure: Community standards and the post-discharge patient. *American Journal of Cardiology, 80(8B):* 45H-52H.

Reeve, J., Bolt, E., & Cai, Y. (1999). Autonomy-supportive teachers: How they teach and motivate students. *Journal of Educational Psychology, 91*, 537-548.

Rudd, P., Byyny, R. L., Zachary, V., LoVerde, M. E., Mitchell, W. D., Titus, C., & Marshall, G. (1988). Pill count measures of compliance in a drug trial. *Cardiology, 80(suppl 1)*, 2-10.

Ryan, R. M. (1993). Agency and organization: Intrinsic motivation, autonomy and the self in psychological development. In J. Jacobs (Ed.), *Nebraska symposium on motivation: Developmental perspectives on motivation* (Vol. 40, pp. 1-56). Lincoln, NE: University of Nebraska Press.

Ryan, R. M., & Connell, J. P. (1989). Perceived locus of causality and internalization: Examining reasons for acting in two domains. *Journal of Personality and Social Psychology, 57*, 749-761.

Ryan, R. M., & Deci, E. L. (2000). Self-determination theory and the facilitation of intrinsic motivation, social development, and well-being. *American Psychologist.*

Ryan, R. M., & Lynch, J. (1989). Emotional autonomy versus detachment: Revisiting the vicissitudes of adolescence and young adulthood. *Child Development, 60*, 340-356.

Ryan, R. M., Plant, R. W., & O'Malley, S. (1995). Initial motivations for alcohol treatment: Relations with patient characteristics, treatment involvement and dropout. *Addictive Behaviors, 20*, 279-297.

Sackett, D. L., & Snow, J. C. (1979). The magnitude of compliance and noncompliance. In R. B. Haynes, D. W. Taylor, & D. L. Sackett (Eds.), *Compliance in Health-care* (pp. 11-22). Baltimore, MD: Johns Hopkins University Press.

Schafer, R. (1968). *Aspects of internalization.* New York: International Universities Press.

Stephenson, B. J., Rowe, B. H., Haynes, R. B., Macharia, W. M., & Leon, G. (1993). Is the patient taking the treatment as prescribed? *Journal of the American Medical Association, 269*, 2779-2781.

Thorndike, A. N., Rigotti, N. A., Stafford, R. S., & Singer, D. E. (1998). National patterns in the treatment of smokers by physicians. *Journal of the American Medical Association, 279*, 604-608.

US DHHS (Department of Health and Human Services). (1990). *The health benefits of smoking cessation: a report of the Surgeon General.* Atlanta (GA): US DHHS, Public Health Service, Centers for Disease Control, Center for Chronic Disease Prevention and Health Promotion, Office on smoking and health. DHHS Publication No. (CDC) 90-8416.

Williams, G. C., Cox, E. M., Kouides, R., & Deci, E. L. (1999). Presenting the facts about smoking to adolescents: The effects of an autonomy supportive style. *Archives of Pediatrics and Adolescent Medicine, 153*, 959-964.

Williams G. C., & Deci, E. L. (1996). Internalization of biopsychosocial values by medical students: A test of self-determination theory. *Journal of Personality and Social Psychology, 70*, 767-79.

Williams, G. C., & Deci, E. L. (2001). Activating patients for smoking cessation through physician autonomy support. *Medical Care, 39*, 813-823.

Williams, G. C., Freedman, Z. R., & Deci, E. L. (1998). Supporting autonomy to motivate patients with diabetes for glucose control. *Diabetes Care, 2*, 1644-1651.

Williams, G. C., Gagne, M., Ryan, R. M., & Deci, E. L. (2002). Facilitating autonomous motivation for smoking cessation. *Health Psychology, 21*, 40-50.

Williams, G. C., Grow, V. M., Freedman, Z. R., Ryan, R. M., & Deci, E. L. (1996). Motivational predictors of weight loss and weight-loss maintenance. *Journal of Personality and Social Psychology, 70*, 115-126.

Williams, G. C., Rodin, G. C., Ryan, R. M., Grolnick, W. S., & Deci, E. L. (1998). Autonomous regulation and long-term medication adherence in adult outpatients. *Health Psychology, 17*, 269-276.

Williams, G. C., Saizow, R., Ross, L., & Deci, E. L. (1997). Motivation underlying career choice for internal medicine and surgery. *Social Science and Medicine, 45*, 1705-1713.

Williams, G. C., Wiener, M. W., Markakis, K. M., Reeve, J., & Deci, E. L. (1994). Medical students' motivation for internal medicine. *Journal of General Internal Medicine, 9*, 327-333.

12: Intrinsic Need Satisfaction in Organizations: A Motivational Basis of Success in For-Profit and Not-for-Profit Settings

Paul P. Baard
Fordham University

Books on organizational leadership continue to be among the best-sellers in the business sector ("Business Week Best-Sellers," 1999) and, increasingly, the topic appears to be of interest to those who lead houses of worship ("CBA Best Sellers," 1999). Leaders in both the for-profit and not-for-profit domains are faced with significant, new challenges in dealing with their constituents. Corporate America finds itself experiencing prolonged, high-employment levels, making retention of employees difficult as demand for workers often exceeds supply. Traditional reliance upon financial incentives has led to ever more complex strategies for compensating workers in a time of relative prosperity (e.g., Dolmat-Connell, 1999). Mergers of corporations have resulted in undermining any sense of loyalty among employees (Brockner, 1992). Leaders of religious institutions have discovered that many people no longer follow the tradition of attending the house of worship in which they were raised, and some no longer attend any religious services (Barna, 1999). Church attendance and giving levels are greatly depressed relative to those of only a generation ago (Ronsvalle & Ronsvalle, 1998). Church shopping is the norm for those choosing to affiliate at all, and gaining commitments for time from volunteers is even tougher in today's typical two-wage-earner household (Barna, 1999).

Leadership gurus from the business and church sectors often propose dramatic solutions, from reengineering corporations (Hammer & Champy, 1993) to reinventing churches (Warren, 1995) as a way of solving the daunting challenges facing those organizations. But these types of restructuring approaches typically require major organizational upheaval, something many leaders find themselves either disinclined or unable to do. An alternative tactic is to focus on the individuals in an organization and on how management of the organization can facilitate more effective involvement of these individuals.

One concern that cuts across all domains of leadership is the motivation of those who are led. In such diverse fields as education and athletic competition, teachers, and coaches seek to "motivate" their charges. This inclination is true also in the worlds of business and religion. Managers try different methods of incentives or fear to get more productivity out of their subordinates. Pastors attempt to cajole greater commitment from parishioners, including increased attendance, giving, and serving. Often they employ techniques such as public recognition of contributors, an appeal to feelings of guilt, etc. However, there is a burgeoning literature suggesting that the use of incentives and attempts to cajole may be experienced by employees or parishioners as controlling or pressuring and that such attempts to manipulate people have a significant downside (see, e.g., Kohn, 1993).

This chapter reports on two studies applying self-determination theory (SDT) to organizations. It differentiates types of motivation and then identifies institutional structures and leadership behaviors that tend to enhance the different types of motivation in those who are led. Illustrations are offered from the for-profit (a business corporation) and not-for-profit (a Christian church) sectors.

Types of Motivation

Several different types of motivation are evident in daily living. The following describes these motivations as they appear in the worlds of work and worship.

Intrinsic motivation is the ". . . inherent tendency to seek out novelty and challenges, to extend and exercise one's capacities, to explore, and to learn" (Ryan & Deci, 2000). It is the energy behind taking on optimal challenges to one's current knowledge or skill. When one is intrinsically motivated for an activity, there is not a preoccupying concern with the possibility of attaining a reward other than the satisfaction of doing the activity itself, nor is there a worry about avoiding a potential punishment for not doing it well enough. Intrinsic motivation has been associated with greater performance, more persistence, and higher levels of satisfaction and creativity (Deci & Ryan, 1991). People involved in endeavors due to this type of self-motivation experience heightened vitality and general well-being (Ryan & Deci, 2000).

When intrinsically motivated, people are autonomous because the motivation and direction of their behavior comes from them. It is the type of motivation many people experience when they are engaged, for example, in a hobby or sport. The activity itself provides inherent satisfaction and reward. This type of motivation is less likely to be found in the workplace, where everyone has some level of concern for such things as compensation and recognition, but there are times when even work possesses many of the characteristics that prompt intrinsic motivation. Being given a particularly exciting assignment, with no undue pressure to succeed, can be challenging and carry with it a satisfaction that is distinctly enjoyable.

In the world of church participation there can certainly be opportunities for the experience of intrinsic motivation, opportunities where one might say "I find this really fulfilling." A joyous wedding cebration, a somber but moving memorial service, or a particularly compelling Sunday worship service might, for example, be experienced as intrinsically satisfying by participants.

Extrinsic motivation describes doing an activity with a focus on some separable outcome, rather than engaging in it for its inherent satisfaction. Typical examples from everyday life include undertaking a task out of a desire to gain a reward or recognition, or to avoid ill consequence such as punishment or guilt. Extrinsic motivation falls along a continuum from being pressured and controlled by the separable outcomes to being relatively self-determined in pursuing them. When extrinsic motivation is of the controlled type, it is associated with feelings of anxiety and pressure and has been linked with less long-term persistence (Deci & Ryan, 1985b). When extrinsic motivation is more self-regulated, it shares with intrinsic motivation the quality of being autonomous. In fact, within SDT, intrinsic motivation and self-regulated extrinsic motivation represent the two types of autonomous motivation. In contrast, when motivation is either fully external, as when a behavior is engaged in only for a reward or to avoid a punishment, or is within the person in the form of self-demands that are buttressed by internal sanctions such as guilt, people experience their behavior as being controlled rather than autonomous.

The employee characterized by external motivation is sometimes identified as a "You get what you pay for with him"-type of person. With each assignment, this individual's focus will be almost exclusively on "What is in it for me?" or "What reward can I expect?" Most employees will not be so exclusively focused on rewards, but they will to differing degrees be influenced by the various incentives offered by their companies.

At church, those who attend largely out of a compulsion to do what they "should" do, often more a reflection of their controlling upbringing than a freely held belief, are also extrinsically motivated in a controlling way. They may fear ill consequences—from social disapproval to eternal damnation—for not going to church, giving money, volunteering time, etc. Churches engage this extrinsic motivation when they offer incentives to contribute, such as having one's name appear on a prestigious list of donors, and when they use door prizes and other gimmicks to induce giving. Also, preaching which is done with a shaming style will incline the listener toward this less desirable, more pressured state of motivation.

While those operating out of these kinds of pressured extrinsic motivation can be productive because incentives often work in the short-term, the psychological dynamics involved with such motivation are potentially undermining of a continuance and a full involvement with the task or relationship. Indeed, the introduction of extrinsic variables to what had once been an intrinsically satisfying activity has been found, under some circumstances, to lead to amotivation toward that activity (Deci, 1971).

Amotivation describes a sense of futility in an engagement, with the individual not valuing the activity, not feeling capable of doing it, or not expecting to achieve a desired outcome for having done it (Deci & Ryan, 1985b). Amotivation leaves a person participating at only a minimal level, if at all. The dramatic downsizing in corporate America throughout the nineties seems to have undermined a sense of purposefulness in many employees. Working hard and loyally for an employer have come to be viewed as having little to do with one's advancing or even retaining a career in the organization. If age and earnings correlate negatively with the probability of retention, what can a person realistically do about either?   Reduced workforces result in more work and less perceived job security for those remaining, leading to "survivor's syndrome" (Brockner, 1992), a state of disengagement or amotivation.

In the context of houses of worship, an amotivated condition can come about when church beliefs and rituals are communicated in a manner leaving a congregant feeling incapable of satisfactorily meeting standards for behavior, and even thought. Similarly, when participants feel coerced into volunteering or contributing, a tendency to avoid such persuasive circumstances can develop. Or a member might simply come to view the church in an amotivated manner if the focus is consistently perceived as irrelevant to one's life-values and goals. This appears to be the dynamic behind the massive dropout of adolescents being experienced by many churches (Baard & Aridas, 1999).

Self-regulated extrinsic motivation describes a state in which one engages in an activity or relationship primarily to attain some separable outcome but still has a clear sense of volition (Ryan & Deci, 2000). Nearly everyone goes to work to earn a living. But when given sufficient control over how a job gets done—being empowered, in contemporary managerial jargon—the motivational experience contains many elements associated with intrinsic or self-motivation. In such situations, if the rewards are not made overly salient in an attempt to motivate or control people, the people may be self-determined even though they are working for extrinsic rewards. The experiences and consequences of this self-regulated extrinsically-motivated behavior can approximate those of intrinsic motivation and accordingly increase the likelihood of positive outcomes.

In the church experience, one might choose to be involved in a house of worship because parents and local culture have emphasized that "It is the right thing to do." A higher level of autonomy would be experienced if the person arrived at that position as a result of a reflectively-held belief that such a religious relationship is consistent with his or her own faith (e.g., "Because I believe in God, I want to go and worship Him each week"). The person will have personally identified with the value, and this internalized belief would differ from one that is only introjected—that is, one which would have the person feeling coerced to go to church out of an "ingested" or inherited standard (Ryan, Rigby, & King, 1993).

Self-Determination Theory

According to self-determination theory (Ryan & Deci, 2000), opportunities to satisfy three innate, psychological needs will facilitate self-motivation (i.e., intrinsic and self-regulated extrinsic motivation that results from full internalization of extant values and regulatory processes). In such cases, there will be more effective functioning and better adjustment because need satisfaction provides the necessary nutriments for human growth and development (Ryan, 1995). Thwarted satisfaction of those needs undermines self-motivation, leads to external motivation or amotivation, and results in maladaptive consequences (Baard, 1994; Ryan, Sheldon, Kasser, & Deci 1996; Sheldon, Ryan, & Reis 1996).

The basic needs identified by SDT, which were deduced using the empirical process, are those for: *autonomy*, which concerns experiencing choice and feeling like the initiator of one's actions (deCharms, 1968; Deci, 1975); *competence*, which concerns succeeding at optimally challenging tasks and being able to attain desired outcomes (White, 1959); and *relatedness*, which concerns establishing a sense of mutual respect and reliance with others (Baumeister & Leary, 1995). These needs appear to be essential for facilitating optimal functioning of the natural propensities for growth and integration, as well as for constructive social development and personal well-being (Ryan & Deci, 2000).

The studies described below applied this general hypothesis in the domains of work and church participation. Principles derived from this and related research are presented in the form of organizational and managerial behaviors found to either support or frustrate the satisfaction of these intrinsic needs. SDT thus "concerns itself with the conditions that elicit and sustain, versus subdue and diminish, one's innate propensity toward mastery, spontaneous interest and exploration" (Ryan & Deci, 2000). A further explication of these innate needs appears in the respective application sections below.

The concept of need satisfaction is particularly useful in organizational theory in that it has substantial heuristic utility for delineating dimensions of the environment that would be expected, a priori, to lead to positive versus negative endeavor-related outcomes. Aspects of the environment likely to allow need satisfaction were predicted to yield positive outcomes, whereas those likely to thwart need satisfaction were predicted to yield negative outcomes. The motivational consequences on employees of the behavior of those in leadership positions has been a focus of the application of SDT because such individuals are a crucial part of employees' environments (e.g., Ilardi, Leone, Kasser, & Ryan, 1993; Kasser, Davey, & Ryan, 1992).

SDT and Work: A Field Study

The field of management has devoted considerable attention to need theories such as those of Murray (1938), Maslow (1943), and McClelland (1985). This often has led to organizational attempts to assess the strength of the "needs" in job applicants or those considered for promotion (see, e.g., Keyser & Sweetland, 1994). Such an approach, however, reduces the concept of needs to "learned wants" or desires because, if something were truly an innate need, it would exist in everyone, and a desire would certainly not be considered a need if it were detrimental or harmful (Kasser & Ryan, 1996). In fact, from the SDT perspective, a desire is considered a need only if it can be shown empirically that satisfaction of the desire is associated with people's growth and health.

Numerous studies have shown that what are called autonomy-supportive contexts promote self-motivation (Deci, Schwartz, Sheinman & Ryan, 1981; Grolnick & Ryan, 1989), satisfaction (Deci, Connell, & Ryan, 1989), and better performance in various settings (Benware & Deci, 1984; Koestner, Ryan, Bernieri, & Holt, 1984). Empowering managers are those who afford their subordinates significant influence in how the work gets done, allowing greater satisfaction of the subordinates' innate needs for autonomy, competence, and relatedness. In a parallel fashion, thwarted satisfaction of those needs will undermine motivation and have maladaptive consequences (Baard, 1994; Ryan et al., 1996; Sheldon et al., 1996). SDT's view of needs in terms of nutrients essential for survival, growth, and integrity of the individual (Ryan et al., 1996) shifts the focus from getting the right person in a job to presenting an environment for all employees in which they have the opportunity to get their intrinsic needs met and thus to do well.

Matters of concern to organizations such as performance and psychological adjustment were hypothesized to be positively related to need satisfaction.

Research Methodology

The study (Baard, Deci, & Ryan, 2000) took place in a major investment banking firm. Since this was a company-endorsed project, conducted on the firm's premises during the workday, a high response rate was achieved—495 employees (approximately 79% of its home office personnel) submitted complete data for the 16-pages of questions.

Among the instruments incorporated in the respondents' survey booklet were the Need Satisfaction Index-Work (NSI-W), a 23-item scale, with a 7-point Likert-like response format, which assesses the extent to which employees experience satisfaction of their three intrinsic psychological needs—for self-determination, competence, and relatedness—on their job (Leone, 1995). Sample statements about which employees were asked to express their agreement/disagreement appear in Table 12-1.

Sample Items from Need Satisfaction Index: Work

Autonomy
—I feel like I can make a lot of inputs to deciding how my job gets done.
—I feel pressured at work. (Reverse score.)

Competence
—I enjoy the challenges my work provides.
—When I am working, I often do not feel very capable. (Reverse score.)

Relatedness
—I get along with people at work.
—There are not many people at work that I am close to. (Reverse score.)

Table 12.1

The General Causality Orientations Scale (GCOS; Deci & Ryan, 1985a) presents different vignettes about problems or situations that arise in life (e.g., the opportunity to take a new job) and was used to assess the individual difference variable of workers' autonomy orientations. Additionally, perceived autonomy support by one's supervisor was measured with the Work Climate Questionnaire (WCQ). The WCQ is a 15-item scale that assesses participants' perceptions of the degree to which they experience their managers as autonomy supportive (Williams, Grow, Freedman, Ryan, & Deci, 1996). Both the autonomy orientations of employees and the autonomy supportiveness of managers were expected to positively predict need satisfaction of the employees.

Self-reported annual performance evaluation ratings served as the dependent variable "Performance." A three-point scale was used to assess each person's over-all performance. A comparison made for one large work group's self-reported ratings with the Human Resources records for that unit revealed almost identical proportions of the three rating levels between the sample and the representative full work unit, thus suggesting that the self-reports were veridical.

To assess psychological well-being or adjustment, 14 items related to anxiety and somatization from the General Health Questionnaire (Goldberg & Hillier,

1979) were combined (each score was reversed), along with a 7-item vitality scale (Ryan & Frederick, 1997). Intrinsic need satisfaction was expected to positively predict both performance and adjustment.

Findings

Results of the study provided additional support for the relevance of self-determination theory to motivation in the workplace. As expected, intrinsic need satisfaction significantly predicted both work performance and adjustment. Further, the managers' being perceived as more autonomy supportive and subordinates' having a stronger autonomy orientation were related to the subordinates' experiences of greater intrinsic need satisfaction. An overall test (using LISREL) of SDT's need-satisfaction model of performance and adjustment at work provided excellent support for the model (Baard, Deci, & Ryan, 2000).

Implications for Business Practices

As described, SDT studies of the workplace measure the degree to which subordinates reported their intrinsic needs being met in their work environment. Of particular concern are the daily experiences of workers interacting with those in authority over them. A review of these opportunities for motivational impact follows.

Autonomy

The need for autonomy is about sensing some level of control and choice about the work one is doing. It is not about managers' being permissive or neglectful, but rather about subordinates' having influence in the workplace. "Empowerment" is the management cliché often used to connote this notion of shared responsibility in how work gets done.

From this concept of the need for autonomy come some specific organizational and managerial behaviors that are found to help satisfy this need. The Saturn Corporation, a unit of General Motors Corporation, incorporated some novel ideas as it established itself in the late 1980s (Gwynne, 1990). These innovations are consistent with principles identified by SDT.

Several practices were directed at worker autonomy. Because it would be a unionized work force (as is true for production-line workers throughout General Motors), Saturn decided to minimize union resistance by building a staff from current GM employees who wished to join in on the building of "a different kind of car" by a "different kind of company" (O'Toole, 1996). General Motors was determined to match the quality Japanese car makers had achieved, resulting in their acquiring a significant portion of the U.S. passenger-car market. The new Saturn plant would be in Spring Hill, Tennessee, far from the assembly lines and corporate culture of Detroit-area facilities. The initial staffing would consist of UAW volunteers who would leave their established places of work and their earned seniority at other GM plants to partake in this new venture. So even the decision to work at this new plant was an entirely autonomous one.

Managerial Behaviors that Support Autonomy

1. Optimize subordinate's control/influence

   —over how his or her work gets done, bonus is structured, goals are set, etc.

2. Ameliorate internal and external pressures

   —rather than simply passing it on from your own superordinates, clients, etc.

3. Reduce or eliminate excessive rules

   —making certain that outdated organizational policies do not impede performance.

4. Allow self-selection for tasks

   —whenever possible.

5. Permit failure
   —when feasible (the absence of the permission to fail connotes rigid bound aries of behavior and eliminates a possible learning process).

6. Take subordinate's perspective, at least initially, even if you believe it to be inaccurate

   —trying to understand it before you begin to explain your reality.

7. Provide feedback in a non-controlling manner

   —so that your subordinate does not feel pressured into a position.

8. Choose an assertive communication style

   —rather than using controlling (aggressive) language.

9. Avoid manipulative incentive systems

   —using rewards as affirmation of work done well, rather than a means to get more.

Table 12.2

A second autonomy-supportive step by Saturn was the inclusion of workers in nearly all decisions, from how a bonus system would work to which advertising agency would handle the car's introductory promotion campaign. This inclusiveness was most unusual in the antagonistic "labor versus management" world of auto manufacturing in the United States (O'Toole, 1996).

Perhaps the most significant support for autonomy, however, was a more subtle one. At each work station along the assembly line hung a cord with a blue handle at its end, above head-level but within reach. Every worker was empowered to pull that cord and stop the entire production line if he or she detected a systemic problem. For example, if someone assigned to the tire-mounting unit noted an axle slightly pitched, that worker would normally tag the car and a correction would be made at some point down the line. However, if a Saturn worker saw the next car with the same problem, he or she could stop production. This is a significant responsibility for line workers, most of whom have limited education and have never been given this level of authority in their careers. While the need to pull the lever is not frequent, it is the knowledge that they *could* do so which would support a sense of autonomy in this environment. Company reports indicate that any managerial fears that this would be misused by these UAW members were soon dispelled as workers handled this delegation of authority responsibly.

While there are many organizational means for either supporting or frustrating the need for autonomy, the research suggests day-to-day experiences with one's immediate supervisor can help ameliorate even a relatively controlling atmosphere (Baard, Deci, & Ryan, 2000). Table 12-2 identifies some of these means.

Competence

The need for competence is about growing and experiencing challenge to one's current abilities or knowledge. In the world of work, this does not necessarily entail having exciting new things to do each day. Much of one's work, whether it is building a car, maintaining a home, teaching a class, or seeing patients in a clinic involves routine chores and tasks. The competence need expresses itself in a desire to have some growth experience over a reasonable period of time.

Saturn Motors Corporation built such possibilities into its modus operandi. All employees would spend five percent of their time in training. This had to be an intriguing proposition for a UAW member accustomed to physically demanding labor throughout his or her 40-hour work week. Training to do one's specific job could be expected, but then what? Becoming acquainted with other functions along the assembly line would be a natural progression. Yet all of that would take only months at an average of two hours per week. What then? Saturn had in mind providing its employees opportunities to learn many practical life-skills, completely unrelated to building good cars. This would allow workers to keep growing throughout their careers. Thus, one of their intrinsic needs would be met by employer Saturn.

Another Saturn policy that clearly addresses the competence need is the provision to workers of the best equipment. This was made easier, of course, in that the entire physical facility in Spring Hill, Tennessee was new, so managers could take advantage of things learned in the decades since many of the production plants of the Detroit-area were built. There would also be fewer work rules; for example, the assembly-line person could actually go and get his or her own replacement tool and not be required to submit a request and wait for the item to be delivered. Workers would have the satisfaction of getting more work done. And each work unit would be entrusted with picking its own suppliers, even of significant components of the vehicles it was assembling.

Managerial Behaviors that Support Competence

1. Train, prepare, and support subordinates

    —so their probability of success is maximized.

2. Remove barriers to efficient performance

    —including physical (e.g., air quality) and procedural (e.g., gratuitous rules).

3. Agree on achievable goals

    —ones that are discussed and agreed upon, rather than imposed on, subordinate employees.

4. Help subordinates determine reasonable ambitions

    —to improve probability of subordinates' career successes.

5. Provide optimal challenges

    —by delegating interesting assignments and tasks that develop new skills.

6. Allow feedback to occur regularly

    —so that timely corrections can be made.

7. Keep critical comments in perspective

    —not offering too much negative feedback at once.

8. Encourage self-discovery of errors

    —allowing the person time to address them on his or her own whenever possible.

Table 12.3

We see then that, regardless of organizational policies or procedures, people's need for competence can often be addressed day-to-day by their supervisors or managers. Another example of this need being met was giving a receptionist, usually charged only with greeting visitors and performing light clerical tasks, the responsibility for arranging production of photo identification tags for new employees. Although this task may not be experienced as a challenge by some people, it does add responsibility to the receptionist's job, is important to the company, and could provide the receptionist with a greater sense of competence. At a higher organizational level, allowing a middle-level executive the opportunity to develop the business plan for his or her work unit is another example of growth enhancement. Some frequently-occurring opportunities for those in supervisory positions to support the competence need in their subordinates appear in Table 12-3.

Relatedness

Experiencing mutual reliance and respect is at the heart of the relatedness need. It is about feeling connected, sharing a mutual goal, and being in a relationship for the long haul. The downsizings which persist in corporate America are an obvious threat to the satisfaction of this innate need. Although not even the chief executive officer of a company can say with absolute assurance that there will be no future layoffs, managers can endeavor to express care for and to employees when a downsizing occurs (Brockner, 1992).

Organizational procedures can provide an institutional opportunity to support the need for relatedness. Saturn Motors Corporation built in some ideas that were not only novel but also provocative to the automotive industry at the time (O'Toole, 1996). Each work unit would be responsible for hiring its own members. Because a new culture of quality and efficient work was a core value at Saturn, on-line workers interviewed and selected new members of their team to help insure the team's effective performance. In this way the team was able to communicate its belief in a new attitude toward work. Calling in sick on Mondays would not be this culture's norm. And because group members selected future co-workers, peer acceptance and support began Day One for the new hire.

The practice of job rotation was introduced, with members of work units changing roles every so often. This tended to create greater empathy and respect for a colleague's work. In addition, the heads of labor and of management had offices immediately adjacent to one another, visually and practically lessening a "them versus us" orientation and providing a setting for easy sharing of information. Their daily exchanges communicated a "togetherness" people system to the organization (O'Toole, 1996).

Managerial Behaviors that Support Relatedness

1. Hold regular meetings

    —so that you are easily accessible even to those somewhat timid.

2. Set reward structures that support cooperation

    —and do not encourage competition between individuals or teams.

3. Avoid triangulation

    —do not speak negatively about a party not present.

4. Share information whenever feasible

    —trusting your associates to keep certain matters confidential.

5. Conduct team-building exercises when appropriate

    —which need not be dramatic to be effective.

Table 12.4

While "team building" became a management buzzword in the '90s, it was often undermined by divisive organizational practices such as internally-competitive bonus systems. Yet despite such policies, daily interactive opportunities afford the insightful manager a chance to satisfy the relatedness needs of subordinates (see Table 12-4).

SDT and Worship: A Field Study

There are an estimated 367,000 religious organizations in the United States. Most of these continue to endure relatively low levels of financial support, and their membership levels are plateauing or declining despite population growth (Bedell, 1996). A carefully-controlled field study placed weekly attendance rates at only about 25% of congregants (Hadaway, Marler, & Chaves, 1993). This statistic, confirmed by individual congregational data (Malphurs, 1999), contradicted what had been conventional wisdom placing attendance levels at consistently above 40%. The latter inflated figure, reported nearly annually by such polling firms as Gallup and Barna Research (e.g., Barna, 1999), hid the problem most local pastors knew too well. Membership itself is also in decline (Malphurs, 1999;

Woodward, 1993). Associated with this lack of involvement is not only the relative failure to fulfill a church's mission of developing human spirituality, but also a reduced capacity to fund benevolence programs, such as caring for the needy. Contributions to religious groups, as a percent of household income, are down markedly from their highs of only a generation ago (Ronsvalle & Ronsvalle, 1996).

Much of what is written about the fate of houses of worship takes a sociological perspective, examining demographic trends, denominational popularity, etc. By contrast, SDT—emanating from the discipline of psychology—identifies conditions under which members are likely to experience intrinsic motivation with respect to their church involvement. Certain congregations, despite being affiliated with denominations in severe decline, are experiencing dramatic growth (Malphurs, 1999). SDT hypothesizes that when members' needs for competence, autonomy, and relatedness are met within the church setting, those churches will experience higher levels of growth, attendance, and contributions than churches not doing as well at meeting these basic needs in their members.

Research Methodology

In the church growth study (Baard, 1994), preliminary meetings explaining the purpose of the research were held with the pastors of three churches of differing denominations. These leaders were asked to endorse the research from their pulpits and/or in their weekly bulletins announcing church activities. On the research date, prospective survey participants were handed a packet of materials, including an explanatory letter assuring confidentiality, a two-page survey, and a stamped return envelop. The sample cooperation level was at least 50% for each of the surveyed churches.

One instrument used was the Needs Satisfaction Index-Church (Ryan & Baard, 1997), patterned after the NSI-Work questionnaire. Sample items appear in Table 12-5. The Christian Religious Internalization Scale (CRIS) was also included in the survey. The CRIS is a 12-item measure with Likert-like scales designed to assess the degree to which participation in religious activities is autonomous or self-motivated versus controlled (Ryan, Rigby, & King, 1993).

Findings

Results of the study provided support for the relevance of SDT to motivation in the church domain. Attendance, giving, and growth levels of the churches were all related to the satisfaction levels of attendees' needs for competence, autonomy, and relatedness in their church experiences (Baard, 1994).

Sample Items from Need Satisfaction Index: Church

Autonomy

—My church is really open to suggestions from its members.

—I feel pressured at church. (Reverse score.)

Competence

—I don't think the sermons I hear at my church are very stimulating. (Reverse score.)

—I've been able to learn interesting new things at church.

Relatedness

—People at church are pretty friendly toward me.

—There are not many people at work that I am close to. (Reverse score.)

Table 12.5

Findings included a similar pattern within each church regarding the self-motivation of behaviors, and the church that had the highest scores for meeting members' intrinsic needs also had the highest mean level of self-motivated behavior, which was associated with greater enjoyment of the religious experience (Ryan et al., 1993).

Implications for Church Practices

In 1980, an ambitious seminary graduate, Rev. Rick Warren, set out to start a church from scratch on the West Coast in an area where a young, growing population seemed uninterested in organized religion. By introducing some innovative ideas for a house of worship, Saddleback Community Church in Orange County, California has enjoyed dramatic and persistent growth. From an initial membership of two (the pastor and his wife), weekly attendance grew to over 14,000 people (Warren, 1995). Practices implemented by this church leader with respect to empowerment, growth, and connectedness can be readily identified as consistent with SDT. While some denominations are more hierarchically structured and thus less institutionally empowering than others, what a pastor does at the congregational level can ameliorate the potentially damaging effects of hier-archy on congregational members. The following identifies some of the things Saddleback does as an organization. Also listed are some means with which most local church leaders can satisfy the innate psychological needs identified by SDT.

Autonomy

Church leaders can note that SDT's assertion of an innate need for autono-my is consistent with Scripture's depiction of humanity's being given self-deter-mination at its very origin, as depicted in Genesis 2:16 (*NIV Study Bible*, 1985). In church involvement, autonomy is about experiencing choice—about not feeling pressured. Saddleback's pastor makes a practice of empowering people, allowing members with an idea for a ministry to begin putting it in place, so long as it does not violate the church's stated principles. The church provides support as need-ed. Participation in small spiritual growth groups is encouraged, yet no pressure is put on members to do so. Similarly, when a particular financial need arises, the congregation is merely informed, and members are left to make their own deci-sion regarding increased giving. As to preaching, Warren declares "People need fewer 'ought-to' sermons, and more 'how-to' sermons" (Warren, 1995, p. 229).

Any pastor or local church leader can make it a daily practice to work toward meeting parishioners' needs for self-determination. A few examples appear in Table 12-6.

Church Leader Behaviors that Support Autonomy

1. Offer a say in parish activities

    —including an occasional questionnaire in weekly bulletin soliciting input for sermon topics, song selections, ministry needs.

2. Invite rather than pressure

    —resisting a "should" orientation in sermons; taking a more inviting, less-pressuring approach to instruction in godly living.

3. Permit freedom of expression

    —do not confuse an individual's expressed disagreement with a church policy with actual defiance of it.

4. Acknowledge contributions without a "hook"

    —avoiding public lists of contributors as a means to subtly pressure people to look good by giving.

Table 12.6

Competence

Genesis 1:26-28 depicts humanity being given responsibility over all the earth and its creatures (*NIV Study Bible*, 1985). In the religious context, competence can be viewed as a challenge to growth in a spiritual sense. New knowledge as well as opportunities to serve are salient variables in the church experience. The innate need for competence can be satisfied in a church involvement by learning new things of a theological nature, growing in one's relationship with God, or contributing to the congregation's work.

The Saddleback Church endeavors to have its people mature in their faith by offering a series of formal learning opportunities organized to take a person from an initial introduction to the Christian faith through actually becoming lay ministers (Warren, 1995). Each is able to progress at his or her own pace, attending courses as time and interest permit. Weekly sermons are well-prepared, designed to promote mastery, over time, of many theological issues. Principles of faith are consistently related to matters of daily living. An ultimate goal of the church's educational programs is to equip each member to conduct his or her own ministry with competence.

At the local congregation level, priests, ministers, and lay leaders can take into account the importance of members' satisfying their need for competence. Illustrations of possible initiatives appear in Table 12-7.

Church Leader Behaviors that Support Competence

1. Deliver quality sermons

    —making certain preparation is sufficient for this primary learning opportunity each week, and that insights offered are neither too obvious nor too esoteric.

2. Set achievable goals

    —acknowledging "all fall short" of living a godly life, the pastor included.

3. Use parishioners' talents

    —making access to committees and ministries known to all.

4. Extend opportunities for further growth

    —scheduling learning events such as Bible studies at convenient times so that working people and those with evening responsibilities can participate.

Table 12.7

Relatedness

The idea of people being designed to be in relationship with others first appears in the Bible in Genesis 2:18 (*New International Version Study Bible*, 1985). Houses of worship would certainly seem to offer natural occasions to satisfy one's need for relatedness—to feel connected with others. Ironically, this is not the experience of many (Warren, 1995). Cliques and organizational exclusion often greet visitors to churches. Saddleback worked hard to make itself inviting to a first-time visitor and very supportive for on-going members. Ushering efforts begin out in the parking lots, as visitors are assisted in locating a space and getting a golf-cart ride from remote spaces and are made to feel genuinely welcome. Sunday services are designed so that even the most unchurched person will not feel lost or put off by strange liturgical practices. For example, because Saddleback's research revealed new attendees are often reluctant to sing aloud, the church shifted it's emphasis toward less participative singing and more hymns being performed.

Informal, pot-luck dinners and gatherings provide ample opportunities for families and singles alike to form and maintain church-based relationships. Weekly encounters at any church provide opportunities for pastors to facilitate fulfillment of people's relatedness need (examples appear in Table 12-8).

Church Leader Behaviors that Support Relatedness

1. Promote connection at services

    —having people greet those sitting nearby at some point; replacing immediate conversation with familiar others with an intentional outreach first.

2. Greet each person upon entry and exit

    —making visitors a priority, encouraging members with church business questions to wait.

3. Build a sense of family

    —including social information items such as births and illnesses in the church bulletin.

4. Create a shared, emotional experience

    —encouraging the singing of songs at the Sunday worship service if members are comfortable doing that.

Table 12.8

Conclusion

SDT presents guidelines for a systemic means of accomplishing many of the outcomes leaders pursue across a range of human involvements. It offers a distinct approach in management theory explaining how work organizations as well as individuals at any level of leadership can do things that promote self-motivating experiences in employees. A body of empirical research has established that support of the three innate psychological needs leads to greater enjoyment and participation, better performance, and reduced stress in a variety of settings. By contrast, thwarted satisfaction of these needs has maladaptive consequences. Similarly, in houses of worship, members can either become more fully engaged or be put off by their salient motivational experiences, which in turn are dependent upon a leader's and/or a church's practices.

Leaders face daily choices of whether to empower or control, to offer helpful feedback or blame, to promote cooperation or competition. Their choices have motivational consequences ranging from the quantity and quality of the work that gets done, to the well-being of those who do it.

References

Baard, P. P. (1994). A motivational basis for consulting with not-for-profit organizations: A study of church growth and participation. *Consulting Psychology Journal, 46* (3), 19-31.

Baard, P. P. & Aridas, C. (2001). *Motivating your church: How any leader can ignite intrinsic motivation and growth.* New York: Crossroad.

Baard, P. P., Deci, E. L., & Ryan, R. M. (2000). *Intrinsic need satisfaction: A motivational basis of performance and well-being in two work settings.* Fordham University, Unpublished manuscript.

Barna, G. (1999, March 8). *News Release: Attendance at church services.* Available from Barna Research Group, Ltd., 5528 Everglades Street, Ventura, CA 93003.

Baumeister, R., & Leary, M. R. (1995). The need to belong: Desire for interpersonal attachments as a fundamental human motivation. *Psychological Bulletin, 117,* 497-529.

Bedell, K. B. (Ed.), (1996). *Yearbook of American & Canadian Churches.* Nashville: Abingdon Press.

Beneware, C., & Deci, E. L. (1984). Quality of learning with an active versus passive motivational set. *American Educational Research Journal, 21,* 755-765.

Brockner, J. (1992). Managing the effects of layoffs on survivors. *California Management Review, 34* (2), 9-28.

Business Week Best Seller List. (1999, August 6). *Business Week,* p. 16.

CBA Best Sellers. (1999, August). *Christian Booksellers Marketplace,* p. 102.

deCharms, R. (1976). *Enhancing motivation: Change in the classroom.* New York: Irvington.

Deci, E. L. (1971). Effects of externally mediated rewards on intrinsic motivation. *Journal of Personality and Social Psychology, 18,* 105-115.

Deci, E. L. (1975). *Intrinsic motivation.* New York: Plenum.

Deci, E. L., Connell, J. P., & Ryan, R. M. (1989). Self-determination in a work organization. *Journal of Applied Psychology, 74,* 580-590.

Deci, E. L., & Ryan, R. M. (1985a). The general causality orientations scale: Self-determination in personality. *Journal of Research in Personality, 19,* 109-134.

Deci, E. L., & Ryan, R. M. (1985b). *Intrinsic motivation and self-determination in human behavior.* New York: Plenum.

Deci, E. L., & Ryan, R. M. (1991). A motivational approach to integration of self: Integration in personality. In R. Dienstbier (Ed.), *Nebraska Symposium on Motivation: Vol. 38, Perspectives on motivation* (pp. 237-288). Lincoln, NE: University of Nebraska Press.

Deci, E. L., Schwartz, A. J., Sheinman, L., & Ryan, R. M. (1981). An instrument to assess adults' orientations toward control versus autonomy with children: Reflections on intrinsic motivation and perceived competence. *Journal of Educational Psychology, 73,* 642-650.

Dolmat-Connell, J. (1999, March/April). Developing a reward strategy that delivers shareholder and employee value. *Compensation and Benefits Review,* pp. 46-53.

Goldberg, D. P., & Hillier, V. F. (1979). A scaled version of the General Health Questionnaire. *Psychological Medicine, 9,* 139-145.

Grolnick, W. S., & Ryan, R. M. (1989). Parent styles associated with children's self-regulation and competence in school. *Journal of Educational Psychology, 81,* 143-154.

Gwynne, S. C. (1990, October 29). The right stuff. *Time,* pp. 74-84.

Hadaway, C. K., Marler, P. L., & Chaves, M. (1993). What the polls don't show: A closer look at U.S. church attendance. *American Sociological Review, 50,* 741-752.

Hamner, M., & Champy, J. (1993). *Reengineering the corporation.* New York: Harper Collins.

Ilardi, B. C., Leone, D., Kasser, T., & Ryan, R. M. (1993). Employee and supervisor ratings of motivation: Main effects and discrepancies associated with job satisfaction and adjustment in a factory setting. *Journal of Applied Social Psychology, 23,* 1789-1805.

Kasser, T., & Ryan, R. M. (1996). Further examining the American dream: Differential correlates of intrinsic and extrinsic goals. *Personality and Social Psychology Bulletin, 22,* 80-87.

Kasser, T., Davey, J., & Ryan, R. M. (1992). Motivation and employee-supervisor discrepancies in a psychiatric vocational rehabilitation setting. *Rehabilitation Psychology, 37,* 175-187.

Keyser, D. J., and Sweetland, R. C. (Eds.), (1994). *Test Critiques-Volume X.* Austin, TX: Pro-ed.

Koestner, R., Ryan, R. M., Bernieri, F., & Holt, K. (1984). Setting limits on children's behavior: The differential effects of controlling versus informational styles on intrinsic motivation and creativity. *Journal of Personality, 52,* 233-248.

Kohn, A. (1993). *Punished by rewards.* New York: Houghton Mifflin.

Leone, D. (1995). *The relation of work climate, higher order need satisfaction, need salience, and causality orientations to work, engagement, psychological adjustment, and job satisfaction.* Unpublished doctoral dissertation, University of Rochester.

Malphurs, A. (1999). *Advanced strategic planning.* Grand Rapids, MI: Baker Books.

Maslow, A. H. (1943). A theory of human motivation. *Psychological Review, 50,* 370-396.

McClelland, D. C. (1985). *Human motivation.* Glenview, IL: Scott Foresman.

Murray, H. A. (1938). *Explorations in personality*. New York: Oxford University Press.

New International Version Study Bible. (1985). Grand Rapids, MI: Zondervan.

O'Toole, J. (1996). *Forming the future: Lessons from the Saturn Corporation*. Cambridge, MA: Blackwell.

Ronsvalle, J. L., & Ronsvalle, S. (1998). *The state of church giving through 1996*. Champaign, IL: empty tomb, inc.

Ryan, R. M. (1995). Psychological needs and the facilitation of integrative processes. *Journal of Personality, 63*, 397-427.

Ryan, R. M., & Baard, P. P. (1997). The motivation needs index for church. In *HaPI and Psychosocial Instruments*. Pittsburgh, PA: Behavioral Measurement Database Services.

Ryan, R. M., & Deci, E. L. (2000). Self-determination theory and the facilitation of intrinsic motivation, social development, and well-being. *American Psychologist, 55*.

Ryan, R. M., & Frederick, C. M. (1997). On energy, personality and health: Subjective vitality as a dynamic reflection of well-being. *Journal of Personality, 65*, 529-565.

Ryan, R. M., Rigby, S., & King, K. (1993). Two types of religious internalization and their relations to religious orientations and mental health. *Journal of Personality and Social Psychology, 65* (3), 586-596.

Ryan, R. M., Sheldon, K. M., Kasser, T., & Deci, E. L. (1996). All goals are not created equal: An organismic perspective on the nature of goals and their regulation. In P.M. Gollwitzer & J.A. Bargh (Eds.), *The psychology of action: Linking cognition and motivation to behavior* (pp. 7-26). New York: Guilford.

Sheldon, K. M., Ryan, R. M., & Reis, H. T.(1996). What makes for a good day? Competence and autonomy in the day and in the person. *Personality and Social Psychology Bulletin, 22*, 1270-1279.

Warren, R. (1995). *The Purpose-Driven Church*. Grand Rapids, MI: Zondervan.

White, R. W. (1959). Motivation reconsidered: The concept of competence. *Psychological Review, 66*, 297-333.

Williams, G. C., Grow, V. M., Freedman, Z. R., Ryan, R. M., & Deci, E. L. (1996). Motivational predictors of weight loss and weight-loss maintenance. *Journal of Personality and Social Psychology, 70*, 115-126.

Woodward, K. L. (1993, August 9). Dead-end for the Mainline? *Newsweek*, pp. 46-48.

13: Self-Determination Theory and Participation Motivation Research in the Sport and Exercise Domain

Christina M. Frederick-Recascino
Embry-Riddle Aeronautical University

Motivation in the sport and exercise domain was an early topic of interest to sport psychologists. Even in the first sport psychology textbooks, motivation was a primary area of study and was given at least a chapter or more (Harris, 1973; Alderman, 1974). Typically, motivation in sport has been discussed in terms of both participation motivation and achievement motivation. Those individuals who focused on achievement tended to use Atkinson's (1974) cognitive framework based on McClelland's (1961) concept of need for achievement, although more recently some (e.g., Wong & Bridges, 1995) have applied Harter's competence motivation theory (Harter, 1981;1978). In contrast, researchers in the domain of participation motivation have been more diverse and atheoretical in focus, and their studies have included a wide spectrum of age groups and sports (Gill, Gross & Huddleston, 1983; Gould, Feltz & Weiss, 1985; McGuire & Cook, 1983).

During the 1990's there was substantial interest in the study of participation motivation (Duda, Chi, Newton, Walling & Catley, 1995; George & Feltz, 1995; Kerr, 1997; Roberts & Treasure, 1995), and this chapter focuses on this newer work in participation motivation for sport and exercise. The chapter will, first, present an overview of theories used in understanding participation motivation, with primary attention devoted to self-determination theory. Second, the chapter discusses the research using self-determination theory and the contribution of this research for understanding sport participation. Last, suggestions will be made about the future of participation motivation research as the new millennium begins.

The author acknowledges the continued contribution of Richard M. Ryan and Craig Morrison to this work, as well as the editorial assistance of Bonny Bryan.

Theoretical Approaches to the Study of Participation Motivation in Sport

During the 1990's, primary attention was paid to linking participation motivation research to theory. These efforts took several directions, but two of the most popular theoretical perspectives for research generation were self-efficacy and goal perspective theories.

Self-efficacy and sport motivation. Self-efficacy theory is a framework for understanding human behavior which uses a socio-cognitive approach (Bandura, 1986). Within this theory, efficacy can be defined as a person's belief in his or her ability and capacity to enact goal-directed behaviors within a domain of activity. An individual develops efficacy expectations via a number of sources including past performance, physiological states, vicarious experiences related to an activity, and verbal persuasion cues (Feltz, 1988). The individual then uses his or her efficacy expectations to initiate, engage, and persist in a given activity (Feltz 1992). In sport, high efficacy expectations are theorized to motivate greater initial engagement in an activity, as well as promote repeated experiences with that activity.

The goals approach. Another popular theoretical framework for understanding motivation for sport and exercise is the goals approach (Duda, 1992; Nicholls, 1984, 1989). As in self-efficacy theory, the goals approach places primary emphasis on perceptions of competence. Toward the overall end of developing competence, an individual can assume one of two different orientations – a task or ego orientation. A task orientation, also labeled a mastery-goal orientation, focuses on the process of initiating challenging activities, exerting effort within an activity, and persisting at the activity (Ames, 1992; Duda, 1992). Task orientation has been related to intrinsic motivation for an activity (e.g., Dweck, 1985). On the other hand, an ego orientation, also referred to as a performance-goal orientation, involves a focus on performance evaluations. When operating under an ego orientation, a comparative process of self-worth is developed wherein one's feelings of competence and worth are based on successful completion of tasks in comparison to other individuals' performance on those same tasks.

Within the domain of sport or physical activity, it is hypothesized that when initial attraction to a sport or exercise activity involves a mastery-goal orientation, rather than a performance-goal orientation, the orientation will facilitate learning new skills related to the sport or activity (Dweck, 1986). A task or mastery orientation has also been favorably linked to higher participation motivation (White & Duda, 1994; Williams & Gill, 1995), greater perceptions of competence (Williams, 1991), and more adaptive attributions about success or failure (Newton & Duda, 1993).

Self-Determination Theory and Sport Participation

The theories discussed so far have contributed in significant ways to understanding sport motivation. However, their cognitive emphasis and their central focus on competence or efficacy has limited their discussion of other important factors that initiate motivated behavior. Self-determination theory (SDT), in contrast, provides a more comprehensive framework by considering issues of autonomy and relatedness, as well as those of competence, in predicting sport and exercise participation. More specifically, SDT begins with the premise that there are three primary, psychology needs that motivate human behavior across domains (Deci, 1980; Deci & Ryan, 1985; Deci & Ryan, 1991). These needs are aonomy, competence, and relatedness to others. As individuals, we seek support for these needs in order to have a healthy psychological environment within which to exist. In the participation motivation literature, most empirical focus has been on the needs for autonomy and competence because satisfaction of these needs has reliably been shown to be necessary for intrinsically motivated behavior. Still, relatedness can play an important role in promoting participation motivation, especially for less interesting activities.

When individuals are in a state of intrinsic motivation, they experience choicefulness in their behavior, thereby fulfilling their need for autonomy. Additionally, they are at a level of optimal challenge, which fulfills their competence need. A state of intrinsic motivation is associated with feelings of satisfaction, enjoyment, competence, and the desire to persist at the activity. Sport and exercise for many individuals provide domains in which intrinsic motivation is frequently present. Experiencing "flow," or being in "the zone," widely discussed in athletic experience (Csikszentmihalyi, 1990, 1975) is understood in self-determination theory as representing the heightened awareness and feelings of well-being associated with intrinsic motivation.

On the other hand, when one fails to experience optimal challenge and autonomy, a state of extrinsic control is necessary if participation is to occur (Deci & Ryan, 1985; Ryan & Connell, 1989; Ryan, Koestner & Deci, 1991). In sport, motives reflecting pressure to participate and those resulting from the need for status or approval are reflective of an extrinsic motivational orientation. Here, people are not motivated by enjoyment of the activity itself, but instead see the activity as a means to some other end.

When examining sport and exercise motivation using self-determination theory, some researchers have focused on which motives and psychological needs prompt participation (autonomy, competence, or relatedness) and others have focused on factors that influence a person's level of intrinsic motivation versus extrinsic control for an activity. The latter body of significant research is typically discussed using the subtheory of SDT referred to as cognitive evaluation theory (Deci & Ryan, 1985; Frederick & Ryan, 1995; Ryan, Vallerand, & Deci, 1984). Because participation motivation is the focus of the present chapter, the research that has been dedicated to determining how factors such as rewards, feedback, and competition enhance or undermine intrinsic motivation, is not addressed further here.

SDT's Contributions to Understanding Sport Motivation

Three recent efforts have been made to develop scales to measure participation motivation, using the SDT framework. Two of these (Goudas, Biddle, & Fox, 1994; Pelletier, Fortier, Vallerand, Tuson, Briere, & Blais, 1995) used a model of motivation based in the concept of perceived locus of causality (PLOC: Ryan & Connell, 1989). This model involves the concepts of intrinsic motivation as well as different types of extrinsic motivation. More specifically, it suggests that there are four different types of regulation that can underlie activities that are not intrinsically motivated. These types of regulation can be placed along a continuum that specifies the degree to which the type of regulation represents autonomy. At the least autonomous end of the continuum is externally regulated behavior, which is behavior that is entirely controlled by external contingencies. In order for an individual to move toward self-determination with respect to such a behavior, regulation of the activity must be internalized. The first level of internalization is referred to as *introjected regulation*. At this level, which can be thought of as partial internalization, the individual regulates his or her behavior in order to gain social approval or avoid disapproval, or to gain self-worth or avoid self-disparagement. At the next level of self-regulation, which involves a fuller internalization, the individual moves from seeking social approval into more self-determined motives, based in perceptions of the value, benefits, and importance of a behavior to one's self. This level of regulation is referred to as *identified regulation*. At the last and most self-determined level of regulation, *integrated regulation*, the individual develops organization and correspondence among values, attitudes, and regulations across various behavioral domains, thus creating a sense of congruence in one's self and actions (Deci & Ryan, 1991).

Research within this framework has occurred across a variety of domains, including education/academics (Grolnick & Ryan, 1987, 1989; Grolnick, Ryan, & Deci, 1991; Ryan & Connell, 1989; Vallerand, Blais, Briere, & Pelletier, 1989), religion (Ryan, Rigby & King, 1993), marital relations (Blais, Sabourin, Boucher, & Vallerand, 1990), health care (Ryan, Plant, & O'Malley, 1995) and work (Deci, Connell & Ryan, 1989). Based on knowledge derived from these various domains, predictions were made about how the type of motivation individuals have toward sport and physical activity influences such outcomes as adherence, emotion, and well-being. It has been predicted that individuals who participate in sport or exercise for intrinsic motives or for well-internalized extrinsic reasons would experience higher levels of positive affect, increased perceptions of satisfaction and competence, and persist at the activity longer. Less well internalized extrinsic motivation was expected to relate to lower levels of positive affect, less self-reported satisfaction and competence, and lower reports of adherence to the activity.

Across studies in all these domains, research results clearly indicate that level of internalization (i.e., the degree of autonomy) does influence affect and behavior within each domain. More specifically, levels of internalization that represent greater self-determination (i.e., identified and integrated regulation), like intrinsic motivation, are associated with positive affect, as well as greater achievement, persistence, effort expenditure, and well-being. On the other hand, external and introjected regulatory styles are associated with higher levels of anxiety and less activity persistence. For example, results from the Ryan & Connell (1989) study indicated that a higher level of internalization (identified or integrated regulation) related positively to higher levels of school enjoyment, effort in school, empathy and social connectedness to others. Likewise, Blais et al. (1990) found greater marital adjustment to be associated with higher levels of internalization of motives for living with one's spouse, while lower levels of marital adjustment were associated with external and introjected levels of internalization.

Perceived Locus of Causality and Sport

As noted, research using the PLOC approach to address issues of motivation within the sport and exercise domain have employed two scales. One, a short version of the Perceived Locus of Causality Scale, was developed by Goudas, et al., (1994). This scale, which was created for use with children, measures level of self-regulation and amotivation with regard to physical education classes. Using the Perceived Locus of Causality Scale for children, Goudas et al., (1994) and Chatzisarantis and Biddle (1996) have shown greater internalization of motivation for physical education classes to be positively related to greater intent to exercise during leisure hours.

The other assessment tool that uses the PLOC approach is the Sport Motivation Scale (SMS: Pelletier et al., 1995). This scale is a 28-item self-report scale with seven subscales. Three subscales assess the types of intrinsic motivation for sport: intrinsic motivation to learn, intrinsic motivation to accomplish things, and intrinsic motivation to experience stimulation. Three subscales assess the levels of extrinsic regulation: external, introjected, and identified regulation. The seventh subscale provides a measure of amotivation. Results of initial work in sport and exercise with the SMS indicate outcomes similar to those found within other domains (Pelletier et al., 1995). Amotivation was found to be negatively correlated with perceived competence and effort, while showing a positive correlation with distraction. In contrast, all three types of intrinsic motivation as well as identified regulation were positively related to perceived competence and effort and negatively related to distraction. The SMS has also been used to study other aspects of behavior within the sport domain, including gender and sport-related differences in motivation (Chantal, Guay, Dobreva-Martinova, & Vallerand, 1996; Fortier, Vallerand, Briere, & Provencher, 1995; Losier & Vallerand, 1994; Vallerand & Losier, 1994).

Participation Motivation

The third scale to be developed using self-determination theory as a starting point for the study of sport motivation is focused on different types of motives for participation rather than on the PLOC-based regulatory styles. The initial Motivation for Physical Activities Measure (MPAM: Frederick, 1991; Frederick & Ryan, 1993) and its revision (MPAM-Revised: Ryan, Frederick, Lepes, Rubio & Sheldon, 1997) examine specific outcome-oriented goals that motivate sport or exercise behaviors. These goals are then organized and discussed in terms of the types of motivation they reflect or the basic psychological needs they most closely address.

The MPAM-R is a 30-item, self-report scale that assesses five types of adult, participation motivation: interest/enjoyment motives (e.g., "Because it is fun"), competence motives (e.g., "Because I like engaging in activities that physically challenge me"), fitness motives (e.g., "Because I want to be physically fit"), appearance-based motives (e.g., "Because I want to define my muscles so I look better"), and social motives (e.g., "Because I want to be with my friends"). Of these five, interest/enjoyment and competence motives reflect intrinsic motivation toward physical activity, whereas appearance-based motives are extrinsic in nature, tending to reflect introjected regulation, and fitness motives reflect the relatively autonomous form of motivation represented in identified regulation. Social motives reflect the need for relatedness.

The MPAM-R has been used to relate participation motives to adherence variables, emotional attitudes associated with sport, and personality characteristics of participants (Frederick & Morrison, 1996; Frederick, Morrison, & Manning, 1996; Ryan, et al., 1997). The remaining pages of this chapter are devoted to examining theory and research addressing these individual differences using the MPAM-R.

Activity-Related Differences in Goals: The Different Motives behind Sport and Exercise

Because the focus of the MPAM approach is on people's goals in engaging in an activity, it can be applied to the issue of why people differentially participate in different physical activities. Theoretically, a focus on outcomes related to sport that are different from the enjoyment of the sport itself (e.g., winning, losing weight, or increasing a player's salary) would indicate an extrinsic motivational orientation toward sport. On the other hand, sports or exercise activities that emphasize immersion in the experience of the activity, or that focus on process goals, seem to be more congruent with an intrinsic motivational orientation. When participants are attuned to the experience, rather than to outcomes, they are likely to feel enjoyment and seek out personal challenges without fear of failure (Deci & Ryan, 1985; Duda et al., 1995).

One focus of research using the MPAM approach has been to examine whether individuals show motivational differences based on the type of sport or exercise activity in which they are engaged. Are there certain types of sport for which an extrinsic focus might be more prevalent and other types where an intrinsic orientation may prevail? For example, participation in activities that are frequently used to increase attractiveness or lose weight and tend to be experienced as repetitive and boring (e.g. stairclimbing, walking on a treadmill) may result from extrinsic motivation. In contrast, exercise or sport activities that are freely chosen, provide challenge, and allow participants to focus on the activity may be conducive to intrinsic participation motivation. As examples of this type of research, Frederick (1991) and Frederick and Ryan (1993) divided respondents into two sport groups: fitness activity participants (e.g., weightlifters, aerobic class participants), and individual sport participants (e.g., tennis players, martial arts participants). Comparing these groups it was found that individual sport participants showed significantly higher interest and competence motivation, and significantly lower appearance motivation, than fitness activity participants. These results indicated that individual sport participants focused more on engagement in their activity, a quality characteristic of an intrinsic orientation. In contrast, fitness group individuals used their activity as a means to reach their goal of becoming more attractive or fit. This type of motivation is more likely to be found at an introjected or identified level of regulation.

Ryan et al. (1997) compared motivational differences in two different exercise groups. The first group included members of an aerobics class and the second consisted of participants in a Tae Kwon Do class. Types of motivation for each activity were contrasted using the MPAM-R. Results of this comparison indicated that participants in the aerobics class had significantly higher body-related motives than did the Tae Kwon Do participants. On the other hand, Tae Kwon Do participants showed higher levels of enjoyment and competence motives than did the aerobics' participants. These findings substantiate those shown in the previous studies discussed above.

Participants in a more recent study (Frederick, 1999) showed a similar pattern of motivational differences based on activity type. In this sample, two activity groupings were created: a sport group (consisting of individual and team sport participants), and a fitness activity group. Mean differences between these groups were examined on the MPAM-R subscales. Consistent with the Frederick and Ryan (1993) work, results indicated that the sport group showed higher levels of interest/enjoyment and competence motivation than did fitness activity participants.

In the case of variations in motivational orientation by activity type, theory and research are consistent. Participants engaged in activities associated with a focus on physical appearance show higher levels of extrinsic motivation than participants in other sport or exercise activities. Namely, activities such as aerobic dance classes, body building and fitness center workouts may appeal to a different type of participant who shows less self-determination with respect to their participation. In contrast, participants who focus more on the experience of engaging in the activity, such as those in individual sports, tend to have higher levels of self-determination toward their activity.

Gender Differences in Participation Motivation

One of the first areas of inquiry using the MPAM was an examination of gender differences in participation motivation (Frederick, 1991). Although, self-determination theory hypothesizes the same underlying psychological needs for men and women, societal influences can contribute to greater salience of specific motives for each gender.

Early research using the MPAM found that gender differences existed for competence and body-related types of motivation (Frederick, 1991). Men showed significantly higher competence motivation than women, reflective of the traditional emphasis placed on men to be competent and dominant in domains of life judged to be related to male behaviors (e.g., work, sports, mechanical ability). On the other hand, in motivation related to physical attractiveness and appearance women showed higher scores (Frederick, 1991). This result was also not surprising and likely related to traditional pressures placed on women in American society to adhere to norms for attractiveness. Also using the MPAM, results of the Frederick and Ryan (1993) study showed a similar pattern of results. Although in this sample, there were no gender differences in competence motivation, women did show significantly higher scores for body-related motivation than did men.

In two more recent samples in which the MPAM-R was used to assess participation motivation, sex differences in motives occurred in both samples. In a study designed primarily to examine the relations between motivation and exercise, Frederick, Morrison, and Manning (1996) found differences in body-appearance and fitness motives with women showing higher scores than men on both of these dimensions. No gender differences were shown for interest/enjoyment, competence, or social motives. In Frederick and Morrison's (1996) study, which related social physique anxiety to motivation, gender differences in motivation were also apparent. Identical to the Frederick, Morrison, and Manning (1996) study, results indicated that women reported higher levels of body-appearance and fitness motivation. Again, no gender differences were found for interest/enjoyment, competence, or social motives.

Overall, the conclusion can be drawn that women evidence more appearance and fitness-related motivation than do their male counterparts. This is not surprising in a society that endorses stringent standards of physical beauty for its female members. What should also be noted is that recent studies have not found the same difference in competence motivation between sexes that was evidenced in the original MPAM work. While initial studies indicated that competent women athletes were viewed as less desirable role models than competent male athletes (Griffin, 1973), later research shows no such effects (Brown, 1988; Kingsley, Brown, & Seibert, 1977; Vickers, Lashuk, & Taerum, 1980;). Female sport and exercise participants may now feel that it is more acceptable to express their desires to achieve and become competent as motivating factors in their participation, without experiencing social stigma.

Motivation Across Age Groups

Research within the sport and exercise domain has found age-related differences in motivation. In studies involving youths (Buonamano, Cei, & Mussino, 1995; Gill, Gross, and Huddleston, 1983; Klint and Weiss, 1987; Sapp and Haubenstricker, 1978; Whitehead, 1995) evidence suggests that intrinsic motives, such as fun, enjoyment, skill development, and challenge, supersede other motives in explaining their sport participation. Research with young and middle-aged adults, however, indicates that a more diverse set of motives drives these older sport and exercise participants (Biddle and Bailey, 1985; Gill, Williams, Dowd, Beaudoin, and Martin, 1996; Mathes and Battista, 1985; Summers et al., 1983, 1982). Adults, while maintaining aspects of intrinsic motivation, have other motives for their participation in physical activity. These additional motives tend to reflect a more extrinsic orientation and include fitness motivation, stress release, and weight control.

Within self-determination theory, as studied using the MPAM, age has been a relatively neglected variable of interest. Predictions within the theory tend to correspond with results from the studies discussed above. It is in the area of play and physical activity that children may first experience and test their levels of competence and autonomy. With age and the development of cognitive ability would come the experience and recognition of outside pressures as determinants of behavior within the realm of play or physical activity, and extrinsic motivations might become quite prevalent for participation in various types of exercise and sport by young and middle-aged adults.

On the other end of the age spectrum is the question of motivation for sport and exercise in older adults. Although older adults are living longer and are in better physical condition than in previous generations (Horn & Meer, 1987; Kolata, 1996), they also tend to engage in regular physical exercise less than younger individuals (Leventhal, Prohaska, & Hirschman, 1985). Thus, for older adults, overall motivation for exercise appears to decline as these individuals age, but for those older adults who do exercise regularly, the nature of their motivations toward exercise is still unknown.

In recent study (Frederick, 1999), age-related differences in adult motivation were assessed for individuals between 18 and 51 years of age. Correlations among age and the five MPAM-R factors showed that age correlated significantly and negatively with interest, competence, appearance, and social motives. Age was not correlated with fitness motives. These results would indicate that with an increase in age comes a decrease in both intrinsic and extrinsic motivates. However, further data need to be collected with a larger age range to truly assess motivational changes for sport and exercise across all age groups.

Motivation and Adherence

Perhaps one of the most important and compelling reasons for studying motivation in the sport and exercise domain is the desire to link motivation with adherence. In fields such as education, self-determined motivation has been found to relate positively with persistence (Deci & Ryan, 1985). If this relation between motivation and adherence also exists for sport and exercise behavior, then it could be a key to promoting health in the general population.

Frederick (1991) and Frederick and Ryan (1993) found clear relations between participation motivation and self-reports of adherence in exercise. Interest/enjoyment and competence motives were positively related to the numbers of hours per week one exercised. In contrast, although body-related motivation (an extrinsic orientation) was positively related to days per week of exercise, it was negatively related to hours per week of exercise, self-reported length of participation in the current activity and estimated length of future participation. This suggests, then, that overall the motives affiliated with intrinsic motivation yielded greater adherence than those more extrinsically focused.

Ryan et al. (1997) found comparable results in the initial MPAM studies. In this work, Tae Kwon Do participants showed greater adherence to their activity than did aerobics class participants. Analyses examining the role of motivation in predicting adherence found that these differences in adherence were explained by the greater interest/enjoyment motivation expressed by the Tae Kwon Do participants. A second sample examined in the Ryan et al. study indicated that long-term adherence at a fitness center was associated with interest/enjoyment, competence, and social motives, but was unrelated to appearance or fitness motives.

Together, the studies showed links between motivational orientation toward exercise and adherence-related variables, which are in line with SDT. Interest/enjoyment and competence motivations for sport and exercise are intrinsic in nature (Frederick & Ryan, 1993), and individuals experiencing this type of motivation may enter a state of absorption in an activity for which time becomes irrelevant. This state, similar to flow (Csikszentmihalyi, 1975, 1990), could easily explain the relationship between intrinsic participation motives and increased levels of adherence.

Individuals who exercise for extrinsic reasons, however, have a different motivational experience. Extrinsic motivation, such as the body-image motive, tends to be characterized by a sense of control, guilt, and pressure to participate (Deci & Ryan, 1985). Exercisers who are oriented in this manner, may feel a push to exercise a set number of days per week to meet fitness requirements, but they do not persist for long on each of those visits to the gym. An example of such a person might be the exerciser who goes to the gym three days a week, does a compulsory 20 minute workout, and then leaves.

In addition, participants who have a higher extrinsic orientation report less persistence in the duration (in months or years) of their exercise regimen and do not foresee themselves persisting at this activity into the future (Frederick, 1991). Although these individuals may, at present, be ritualistic in their participation, their self-reported attitudes about their participation may not bode well for their long-term physical health.

Findings from Frederick (1999) were relatively consistent with the results just discussed. In that study, both interest/enjoyment motivation and competence motivation were positively correlated with both hours per week of exercise and days per week of exercise. By contrast, the two extrinsically based motives, appearance and fitness, were uncorrelated with days per week or hours per week of exercise. Frederick (1999) also found social motivation to be positively correlated with both hours per week of exercise and days per week of exercise.

Overall, the work relating motivation to adherence is important for its implications regarding health and fitness. Recent estimates indicate 31% of the adult male population and 24% of the adult female population in the United States are overweight (National Research Council, 1989). In addition, cardiovascular disease and heart attacks account for 38% of the deaths in this country (USDHHS, 1992). One proven way to help maintain a lower body weight, lower blood pressure, and lower risk of coronary heart disease is through regular physical activity (Bernard & Krupat, 1994). Results of work with the MPAM-R suggests that exercise and activity settings that foster an intrinsic, and perhaps social, motivational orientation would help promote greater engagement in, and adherence to, physical activity.

Motivation, Emotion, and Well-being in Physical Activity

Motivation, emotion, and personality have often been studied together within self-determination theory (Deci & Ryan, 1985; Ryan, Connell, & Plant, 1990; Ryan & Frederick, 1997). Typically, an intrinsic orientation and the more autonomous forms of extrinsic motivation have been associated with expression of positive affect and healthy personality, whereas the less autonomous forms of extrinsic motivation have been associated with negative affective states such as feeling frustrated, tense, pressured, or controlled, as well as with less positive personality factors, such as low self-esteem.

Frederick and Ryan (1993) found some significant correlations between exercise motivation and aspects of emotion and well-being that were consistent with previous work. For example, interest/enjoyment and competence motives were positively related to feelings of satisfaction about one's chosen activity. Body-related motives were negatively related to body appearance self-esteem and global self-esteem and were positively related to anxiety and depression. A later study (Frederick & Morrison, 1996) showed that high body appearance motivation related positively to anxiety about one's physique.

In Frederick, Morrison and Manning (1996), mediational analyses were performed to relate exercise motivation to exercise-related emotion (e.g., exercise fulfillment and satisfaction) and, in turn, to outcomes associated with participation, such as hours per week of participation and perceived competence. The results were only partially successful in delineating these relationships. For men, interest/enjoyment motives positively predicted hours per week of exercise, and this relation was mediated through exercise fulfillment. For women, both interest/enjoyment motivation and self-development motivation predicted perceived competence, and this was also mediated by feelings of exercise fulfillment.

When the results of these studies are examined as a whole, tentative conclusions can be drawn about the relations among participation motivation, emotion, and both behavioral and perceptual outcomes in the domain of physical activity. In some cases, the relations between participation motivation and emotion were direct, and in turn predicted levels of adherence, perceived competence, and satisfaction. Thus, the results suggest motivation does have important relations with emotional functioning and adherence in the realm of sport and exercise, but greater thought and study is needed. What will be important in the future are studies using more sophisticated modeling techniques, which contribute new understanding about how motivational factors, personality, emotion, and adherence variables combine to explain participation in various kinds of physical activities for variously aged participants.

Conclusion

Throughout this chapter, the relationship between self-determination theory and sport motivation has been discussed. Research using the MPAM approach developed out of SDT has delineated the relations between both intrinsic and extrinsic motives and a variety of factors such as activity differences, gender, age, adherence, personality variables, and emotion. In sport and exercise, as in other contexts, the importance of creating an environment that allows intrinsic motivation to flourish cannot be underestimated. Interest/enjoyment and competence motives within the physical activity domain were typically found to relate positively to elements of adherence, personality and emotion. In addition, the distinction between intrinsic and extrinsic aspects of participation were found relevant in explaining age and activity-related differences in participation.

Although much work has already been done using SDT to explore sport motivation, there are old roads that need to be re-traveled and new ones that need to be built. More sophisticated modeling and measurement strategies need to be pursued for examining the relations among sport and exercise motivation, personality, and emotion. Likewise, an in-depth longitudinal study of the emergence of age-related changes and gender differences in motivation would be of benefit in this area.

New work can be started in a number of areas. Two distinct approaches have been developed to study participation motivation within the context of self-determination theory. The first approach uses a self-regulation framework, and measurement scales such as the SMS (Pelletier et al, 1995) and Perceived Locus of Causality Scale for sports (Goudas, Biddle & Fox, 1994). Using the SMS along with the MPAM-R would allow participation motives to be related directly to the types of motivation enumerated by SDT rather than indirectly related as has been done so far (Frederick & Ryan, 1993; Ryan, et al, 1997). A promising avenue of research would examine not only how the SMS and the MPAM-R relate to one another, but also how they could be used together to investigate motivational issues in sport and exercise.

The interest/enjoyment scale of the MPAM-R is expected to relate positively to all three intrinsic motivation dimensions of the SMS, but most strongly with the stimulation dimension. The competence factor of the MPAM-R should correlate strongly with the two SMS intrinsic dimensions of knowledge and accomplishment. The appearance subscale of the MPAM is predicted to correlate positively with introjected and external levels of regulation, while the fitness subscale should correlate most strongly with the identified level of regulation, but may also be related to introjected regulation. It is unclear how social motivation would relate to self-regulatory styles. However, study of the relationship between social motivation in sport and self-regulation could open up another area of inquiry.

Assessment of changes in motivation over time is another line of inquiry that needs to be addressed. No published study has yet considered questions surrounding positive longitudinal changes in sport motivation. How does an individual become more autonomous in motivational orientation for sport and exercise, and what contexts foster or hinder such changes? It is reasonable to assume that, as fitness participants levels and skills increase, personal motivational changes could occur, which would then alter sport and exercise behavior. To further understand the motivational process in sport, it is crucial to move from a cross-sectional to a longitudinal approach to research. A recent study (B. Jensen, personal communication, April 10, 1999) has begun to address some of these issues. This in-progress work assesses exercise motives using the MPAM-R across a six-month period in order to relate motivation to self-efficacy and adherence.

Finally, relatedness issues in sport motivation need to be addressed more fully. Beginning with the MPAM-R, social motivation and its correlates are being examined. However, the focus of SDT within sport has almost exclusively been on examination of issues related to autonomy and competence, rather than social issues of relatedness. Beyond the limited work done with the MPAM-R, little is known about the workings of social participation motives in the sport context. It is possible, for example, that relatedness could be involved in both extrinsic and extrinsic aspects of participation motivation.

It can be said, in conclusion, that the future of motivation research within the domain of sport and exercise is bright and growing brighter all the time. Self-determination theory can be used as a unifying approach for the study and understanding of sport motivation issues, and current research using SDT shows potential for understanding and intervening in the motivational context to effect positive changes in the health and well-being of the population.

References

Alderman, R. B. (1974). Psychological behavior in sport. Philadelphia, Pennsylvania: W. B. Saunders Company.

Ames, C. (1992). Achievement goals, motivational climate, and motivational processes. In G. C. Roberts, *Motivation in sport and exercise* (pp. 57-92). Champaign, IL: Human Kinetics Books.

Atkinson, J. W. (1974). The mainstream of achievement-oriented activity. In J. W. Atkinson J. W. & J. O. Raynor (Eds.), *Motivation and achievement* (pp.13-41). New York: Halstead.

Bandura, A. (1986). *Social foundations of thought and action: A social cognitive theory.* Englewood Cliffs, NJ: Prentice-Hall.

Bernard, L. C., & Krupat, E. (1994). *Health psychology biopsychosocial factors in health and illness.* Orlando, FL: Harcourt Brace College Publishers.

Biddle, S., & Bailey, C. (1985). Motives toward participation and attitudes toward physical activity of adult participants in fitness programs. *Perceptual and Motor Skills, 61,* 831-834.

Blais, M. R., Sabourin, S., Boucher, C., & Vallerand, R. J. (1990). Toward a motivational model of couple happiness. *Journal of Personality and Social Psychology, 59,* 1021-1031.

Brown, B. (1988). Study: Girls find activities for a lifetime. *USA Today,* June 8, 9C.

Buonamano, R., Cei, A., & Mussino, A. (1995). Participation motivation in Italian youth sport. *Sport Psychologist, 9,* 265-281.

Chantal, Y., Guay, F., Dobreva-Martinova, T., & Vallerand, R. (1996). Motivation and elite performance: An exploratory investigation with Bulgarian athletes. *International Journal of Sport Psychology, 27,* 173-182.

Chatzisarantis, N., & Biddle, S. (1996). *A self-determination theory approach to the study of intentions and the intention-behaviour relationship in children's physical activity.* University of Exeter, UK, Unpublished Manuscript.

Csikszentmihalyi, M. (1975). *Beyond boredom and anxiety.* San Francisco: Jossey-Bass.

Csikszentmihalyi, M. (1990). *Flow: The psychology of optimal experience.* New York: HarperCollins.

Deci, E. L. (1980). *The psychology of self-determination.* Lexington, MA: Lexington Books.

Deci, E. L., Connell, J. P., & Ryan, R. M. (1989). Self-determination in a work organization. *Journal of Applied Psychology, 74,* 580-590.

Deci, E. L., & Ryan, R. M. (1985). *Intrinsic motivation and self-determination in human behavior.* New York: Plenum.

Deci, E. L., & Ryan, R. M. (1991). A motivational approach to self: Integration in personality. In R. Dienstbier (Ed.), *Nebraska symposium on motivation 1990: Perspectives on motivation* (pp. 237-288). Lincoln: University of Nebraska Press.

Duda, J. (1992). Motivation in sport settings: A goal perspective approach. In G.C. Roberts (Ed.), *Motivation in sport and exercise* (pp. 57-92). Champaign, IL: Human Kinetics Books.

Duda, J. L., Chi, L., Newton, M. L.,Walling, M. D., & Catley, D. (1995). Task and ego orientation and intrinsic motivation in sport. *International Journal of Sport Psychology, 26,* 40-63.

Dweck, C. S. (1985). Intrinsic motivation, perceived control, and self-evaluation maintenance: An achievement goal analysis. In C. Ames & R. E. Ames (Eds.), *Research on motivation and education: The classroom milieu.* New York: Academic Press.

Dweck, C. S. (1986). Motivational processes affecting learning. *American Psychologist, 41,* 1040-1048.

Feltz, D. (1988). Gender differences in the causal elements of self-efficacy on a high avoidance motor task. *Journal of Sport Psychology, 10,* 151-166.

Feltz, D. (1992). Understanding motivation in sport: A self-efficacy perspective. In G.C. Roberts (Ed.), *Motivation in sport and exercise* (pp. 93-106). Champaign, IL: Human Kinetics Books.

Fortier, M. S., Vallerand, R. J., Briere, N. M., & Provencher, P. J. (1995). Competitive and recreational sport structures and gender: A test of their relationship with sport motivation. *International Journal of Sport Psychology, 26,* 24-39.

Frederick, C. M. (1991). *An investigation of the relationship among participation motives, level of participation, and psychological outcomes in the domain of physical activity.* Unpublished doctoral dissertation, University of Rochester.

Frederick, C. M. (1999, April). *Measuring participation motivation in sport: The MPAM approach.* Paper presented at the First International Conference on Self-Determination Theory. Rochester, New York.

Frederick, C. M., & Morrison, C. S. (1996). Social physique anxiety: Personality constructs, motivations, exercise attitudes, and behaviors. *Perceptual and Motor Skills, 82,* 963-972.

Frederick, C. M., Morrison, C. S., & Manning, T. (1996). Motivation to participate, exercise affect, and outcome behaviors toward physical activity. *Perceptual Motor Skills, 82,*691-701.

Frederick, C. M., & Ryan, R. M. (1993). Differences in motivation for sport and exercise and their relations with participation and mental health. *Journal of Sport Behavior, 16,* 124-146.

Frederick, C. M., & Ryan, R. M. (1995). Self-determination in sport: A review using cognitive evaluation theory. *International Journal of Sport Psychology*, *26*, 5-23.

George, T. R., & Feltz, D. L. (1995). Motivation in sport from a collective efficacy perspective. *International Journal of Sport Psychology*, *26*, 98-116.

Gill, D. L., Gross, J. B., & Huddleston, S. (1983). Participation motivation in youth sports. *International Journal of Sport Psychology*, *14*, 1-14.

Gill, D. L., Williams, L., Dowd, D. A., Beaudoin, C. M., & Martin, J. J. (1996). Competitive orientations and motives of adult sport and exercise participants. *Journal of Sport Behavior*, *19*, 307-318.

Goudas, M., Biddle, S., & Fox, K. (1994). Perceived locus of causality, goal orientations and perceived competence in school physical education classes. *British Journal of Educational Psychology*, *64*, 453-463.

Gould, D., Feltz, D., & Weiss, M. (1985). Motives for participating in competitive youth swimming. *International Journal of Sport Psychology*, *16*, 126-140.

Griffin, P. (1973). What's a nice girl like you doing in a profession like this? *Quest*, *19*, 96-101.

Grolnick, W. S., & Ryan, R. M. (1987). Autonomy in children's learning: An experimental and individual difference investigation. *Journal of Personality and Social Psychology*, *52*, 890-898.

Grolnick, W. S., & Ryan, R. M. (1989). Parent styles associated with children's self-regulation and competence in school. *Journal of Educational Psychology*, *81*, 143-154.

Grolnick, W. S., Ryan, R. M., & Deci, E. L. (1991). The inner resources for school performance: Motivational mediators of children's perceptions of their parents. *Journal of Educational Psychology*, *83*, 508-517.

Harris, D. (1973). Involvement in sport: A somatopsychic rationale for physical activity. Philadelphia, PA: Lea & Febiger.

Harter, S. (1978). Effectance motivation reconsidered: Towards a developmental model. *Human Development*, *21*, 34-64.

Harter, S. (1981). A model of intrinsic mastery motivation in children: Individual differences and developmental change. In A. Collins (Ed.), *Minnesota symposium on child psychology* (Vol 14, pp. 215-255). Hillsdale, NJ: Erlbaum.

Horn, J. C., & Meer, J. (1987, May). The vintage years. *Psychology Today*, pp. 76-84, 89-90.

Kolata, G. (1996). New era of robust elderly belies the fears of scientists. *New York Times*, February 27, A1, C3.

Kerr, J. H. (1997). *Motivation and emotion in sport reversal theory*. East Sussex, UK: Psychology Press Ltd.

Kingsley, J., Brown, F., & Seibert, M. (1977). Social acceptance of female athletes by college women, *Research Quarterly*, *48*, 727-733.

Klint, K., & Weiss, M. (1987). Perceived competence and motives for participating in youth sports: A test of Harter's competence motivation theory. *Journal of Sport Psychology*, *9*, 55-65.

Leventhal, H., Prohaska, T. R., & Hirschman, R. S. (1985). Preventive health behavior across the lifespan. In J. C. Rosen & L. J. Solomon (Eds.), *Prevention in health psychology*. Hanover, New Hampshire: University Press of New England.

Losier, G. F., & Vallerand, R. J. (1994). The temporal relationship between perceived competence and self-determined motivation. *Journal of Social Psychology*, *134*, 793-801.

Mathes, S., & Battista, R. (1985). College men's and women's motives for participation in physical activity. *Perceptual and Motor Skills, 61,* 719-726.

McClelland, D. (1961). *The achieving society.* New York: Free Press.

McGuire, R. T., & Cook, D. L. (1983). The influence of others and the decision to participate in youth sports. *Journal of Sport Behavior, 6,* 9-15.

National Research Council (1989). *Diet and health: Implications for reducing chronic disease risk.* Washington, DC: Government Printing Office.

Newton, M. L., & Duda, J. L. (1993). Elite adolescent athletes' achievement goal and beliefs concerning success in tennis. *Journal of Sport and Exercise Psychology, 15,* 437-448.

Nicholls, J. G. (1984). Achievement motivation: Conceptions of ability, subjective experience, task choice, and performance. *Psychological Review, 91,* 328-346.

Nicholls, J. G. (1989). *The competitive ethos and democratic education.* Cambridge, MA: Harvard University Press.

Pelletier, L. G., Fortier, M. S., Vallerand, R. J., Tuson, K. M., Briere, N. M., & Blais, M. R. (1995). Toward a new measure of intrinsic motivation, extrinsic motivation, and amotivation in sports: The sport motivation scale (SMS). *Journal of Sport and Exercise Psychology, 17,* 35-53.

Roberts, G. C., & Treasure, D. C. (1995). Achievement goals, motivational climate, and achievement strategies and behaviors in sport. *International Journal of Sport Psychology, 26,* 64-80.

Ryan, R. M., & Connell, J. P. (1989). Perceived locus of causality and internalization: Examining reasons for acting in two domains. *Journal of Personality and Social Psychology, 57,* 749-761.

Ryan, R. M., Connell, J. P., & Plant, R. W. (1990). Emotions in non-directed text learning. *Learning and Individual Differences, 2,* 1-17.

Ryan, R. M., & Frederick, C. M. (1997). On energy, personality, and health: Subjective vitality as a dynamic reflection of well-being. *Journal of Personality, 65,* 529-564.

Ryan, R. M., Frederick, C. M., Lepes, D., Rubio, N., & Sheldon, K. (1997). Intrinsic motivation and exercise adherence. *International Journal of Sport Psychology, 28,* 335-354.

Ryan, R. M., Koestner, R., & Deci, E. L. (1991). Varied forms of persistence: When free-choice behavior is not intrinsically motivated. *Motivation and Emotion, 15,* 185-205.

Ryan, R. M., Plant, R. W., & O'Malley, S. (1995). Initial motivations for alcohol treatments: Relations with patient characteristics, treatment involvement, and dropout. *Addictive Behaviors, 20,* 279-297.

Ryan, R. M., Rigby, S., & King, K. (1993). Two types of religious internalization and their relations to religious orientations and mental health. *Journal of Personality and Social Psychology, 65,* 586-596.

Ryan, R. M., Vallerand, R., & Deci, E. L. (1984). Intrinsic motivation in sport: A cognitive evaluation theory interpretation. In W. F. Straub & J. M. Williams (Eds.), *Cognitive Sport Psychology,* pp 231-241. Lansing, NY: Sport Science Associates.

Sapp, M., & Haubenstricker, J. (1978). *Motivation for joining and reasons for not continuing in youth sports programs in Michigan.* Paper presented at the American Alliance for Health, Physical Education, Recreation and Dance National Conference , Kansas City, Missouri, April 7, 1978.

Summers, J., Machin, V., & Sargent, G. (1983). Psychosocial factors related to marathon running. *Journal of Sport Psychology, 5,* 314-331.

Summers, J., Sargent, G., Levey, A, & Murray, K. (1982). Middle-aged , non-elite marathon runners: A profile. *Perceptual and Motor Skills, 54,* 963-969.

USDHHS (1992). *Healthy people 2000: National health promotion and disease prevention objectives* (Publication No. PHS 91-50213). Washington, DC: U.S. Government Printing Office.

Vallerand, R. J., Blais, M. R., Briere, N. M., & Pelletier, L. G. (1989). Construction et validation de l'echelle de motivation en education (EME). *Canadian Journal of Behavioral Sciences, 21,* 323-349.

Vallerand, R. J., & Losier, G. F. (1994). Self-determined motivation and sportsmanship orientations: An assessment of their temporal relationship. *Journal of Sport and Exercise Psychology, 16,* 229-245.

Vickers, J., Lashuk, M., & Taerum, T. (1980). Differences in attitude toward the concepts "male", "female", "male athlete" and "female athlete". *Research Quarterly for Exercise and Sport, 51,* 407-416.

White, S. A., & Duda, J. L. (1994). The relationship of gender, level of sport involvement, and participation motivation to task and ego orientation. *International Journal of Sport Psychology, 25,* 4-18.

Whitehead, J. (1995). Multiple achievement orientations and participation in youth sport: A cultural and developmental perspective. *International Journal of Sport Psychology, 26,* 431-452.

Williams, L. (1991). *Goal orientations and an athlete's sources and interpretations of competence information.* Unpublished Master's Thesis, University of Oregon, Eugene.

Williams, L., & Gill, D. L. (1995). The role of perceived competence in the motivation of physical activity. *Journal of Sport and Exercise Psychology, 17,* 363-378.

Wong, E. H., & Bridges, L. J. (1995). A model of motivational orientation for youth sport: some preliminary work. *Adolescence, 30,* 437-449.

PART IV

❖ ❖ ❖

RELATED VIEWPOINTS

14: Self-Determination, Coping, and Development

Ellen Skinner
Kathleen Edge
Portland State University

> *"Don't follow me, follow you."*
> Nietzsche

All people's lives include obstacles, troubles, failures, and loss. How people deal with adversity—how they cope—influences the impact these events have on them, not only in terms of momentary emotional states or the resolution of specific stressful episodes, but also cumulatively in their long-term mental and physical health. Because coping is so central to processes of adjustment and thriving, much research has been devoted to analyzing the factors that allow people to cope more adaptively.

From that body of research, consensus has emerged that two factors are central in shaping how people cope. They are a sense of control and social support. Research across the lifespan shows that a person's sense of control over desired and undesired outcomes is a powerful ally in times of stress (Folkman, 1984). People who are convinced of their own efficacy at overcoming obstacles are more likely to appraise failures and stressors as challenges, to cope using problem-solving and strategizing, and to persevere and remain optimistic in the face of obstacles. In contrast, people who believe themselves to be incompetent tend to panic and show confusion when faced with setbacks, to become pessimistic and doubting, to ruminate and lose concentration, to escape the stressor if possible, and to

We express our gratitude to the Motivation Research Group, especially James Connell, Edward Deci, Thomas Kindermann, and Richard Ryan. We would especially like to acknowledge James Wellborn for his earlier work on conceptualization and measures of coping. We thank Teresa Young, Tatiana Snyder, Carrie Furrer, Linda Newton-Curtis, Annie Torres, Joni Jannsen, and Elizabeth Vale for their work on earlier drafts of the manuscript. We acknowledge support from the W. T. Grant Foundation and from the National Institute of Child Health and Human Development (HD19914).

expect the worst about future stressful encounters (Bandura, 1997; Compas, Banez, Malcarne, & Worsham, 1991; Dweck, 1999; Flammer, 1995; Folkman, 1984; Forsythe & Compas, 1987; Peterson, Maier, & Seligman, 1993; Skinner, 1995; Weiner, 1986).

The second major predictor of coping is social support. People who have close, loving relationships fare better during stress than individuals who are more socially isolated or who have conflictual personal relationships. Social support has been shown to act as a buffer against psychological distress and has been linked to such positive outcomes as lower rates of depression, decreased loneliness, and a more positive self-image (Cohen, Sherrod, & Clark, 1986; Lepore, 1992; Pierce, Sarason, & Sarason, 1991, 1996; Reis & Franks, 1994; Sarason et al., 1991; Windle, 1992). Attachment theory suggests that the proximal predictors of coping are individuals' *experiences* of social relationships as supportive (Bretherton, 1985) and points out that close relationships can therefore either promote or undermine coping, depending on how they are experienced. Although the connections among attachment, social support, and control are not completely clarified, their importance to coping is nevertheless documented by decades of research.

The goal of this chapter is to argue that there is an important set of psychological processes, in addition to those captured by attachment and perceived control, that are central to the study of coping—namely, processes of autonomy. *Autonomy* refers to the need to express one's authentic self and to experience that self as the source of action. It is hypothesized to underlie processes of self-determination (Deci & Ryan, 1985b, 1987, 1991, 1995). At the present time, the contribution of autonomy to the study of stress and coping is not fully realized. However, we review research on self-determination as well as on infancy, temperament, volition, self-regulation, and aging that points to the critical functions of autonomy during stressful transactions with the environment.

Throughout the chapter, we also emphasize that processes of coping reciprocally shape autonomy. Coping episodes in which goals are blocked or in which competing goals cannot be met, mark transactions of potential significance to the development of autonomy. We argue that the contributions of stress and coping to the study of autonomy have not yet been fully explored, and we hold that a focus on self-determination and coping can be mutually informative, potentially adding richness to conceptualizations and research in both areas.

Overview of the Chapter

We begin by providing background from self-determination theory about autonomy as a fundamental human need, about the self-system processes connected to autonomy, and about the social contexts that support versus undermine their development. The majority of the chapter focuses on the role of autonomy in coping. Specifically, we argue that the self-systems and social supports connected with autonomy are primary determinants of how people deal with stress, that a focus on autonomy reveals several ways of coping that are not often distinguished in current taxonomies of coping, that autonomy plays a critical role in moment-to-moment coping interactions, and that constructs of autonomy are useful in characterizing the long-term regulatory capacities and relationship qualities that link coping to development.

also show how the addition of autonomy to the current focus on social support and control can clarify several issues in the coping area, including the role of secondary control, the adaptiveness of approach versus avoidance coping, and intentionality in coping. Although our arguments emphasize that autonomy matters to coping, we also wish to highlight the reciprocal connection, namely, that coping matters to autonomy. More specifically, coping marks the site of transactions that influence the development of the self-system processes and relationship qualities associated with autonomy. Because our goal is to *add* autonomy to conceptualizations of coping and not to replace constructs of social support, attachment, efficacy, or control, we begin by describing a motivational model which incorporates work from all these areas.

The Motivational Model

The motivational model is an action-theoretical account of motivation, and its goal is to provide a framework for explaining psychological sources of energized and directed action. The basic model, depicted graphically in Figure 14-1, integrates work on attachment, perceived control, and self-determination. It does so by assuming that each reflects the study of a basic psychological need—namely, the needs for relatedness, competence, and autonomy (Connell, 1990; Connell & Wellborn, 1991; Deci & Ryan, 1985b, 2000; Skinner, 1991). This assumption is shared by researchers from many areas, as can be seen in numerous chapters within the current volume.

According to the model, social contexts within different enterprises (e.g., family, work, daycare, school) differentially provide people with opportunities to fulfill their fundamental psychological needs. From these experiences, individuals construct and revise self-system processes organized around relatedness, competence, and autonomy. These self-system processes in turn guide people's participation in the activities of the enterprise, including their coping.

Central to this model is the notion of "patterns of action." *Engaged* versus *disaffected* patterns of action are primary consequences of motivational processes (Wellborn, 1991). Ongoing engagement refers to active, goal-directed, flexible, constructive, persistent, focused interactions with the social and physical envi-

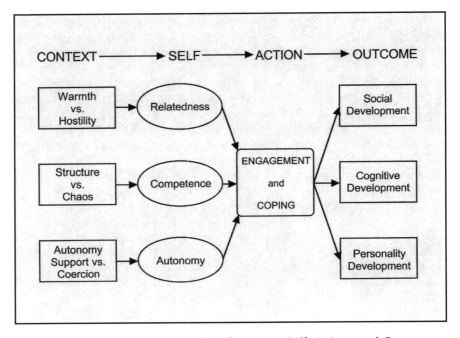

Figure 14.1. A Motivational Model of Context, Self, Action, and Outcomes.

ronments. In contrast, patterns of action are described as disaffected when individuals are emotionally alienated or behaviorally disengaged from participation in an enterprise. Coping describes patterns of action when ongoing engagement encounters resistance or is disrupted. Energetic resources (effort, executive capacity, ego resources) are required to regulate actions. Action regulation under stress is considered "coping." Engagement and coping are critical mechanisms through which motivational processes influence the quality of self-systems and social relationships and, over time, shape development.

Relatedness and Competence as Fundamental Psychological Needs

Within the literatures on attachment and control, it is not particularly controversial to assert that infants are born with psychological needs, that is, with a predisposition to be attracted to, interested in, and responsive to certain kinds of stimulation or experiences. It is assumed that motivational proclivities are based in physiology and that they are evolutionarily adaptive, in that they predispose infants (and people in general) to attend and respond to certain important classes of interactions with the social and physical environments (Barrett & Campos, 1991).

The attachment perspective is founded on the assumption that normal infants are born with the capacity and desire to detect, seek out, initiate, and take pleasure from interactions with social partners and to protest and defend against separation (Ainsworth, 1979; Bowlby, 1969, 1973; Papousek & Papousek, 1980). In the attachment area, it is assumed that infants' cries and clinging (and caregiver comforting and protection) are part of a mutually adaptive system that is physiologically-based and that directs attention, behavior, and emotion. In the motivational model, the need to experience oneself as connected to other people, as belonging, is referred to as *relatedness*. The "need to belong" has been documented across the lifespan (Baldwin, 1992; Baumeister & Leary, 1995; Weiner, 1991).

Competence refers to the need to experience oneself as effective in one's interactions with the social and physical environments. It is hypothesized to underlie processes of control (Bandura, 1997; Peterson et al., 1993; Weiner, 1986). Within work on perceived control, a group of theorists argue that infants are born with the capacity and desire to create effects in the environment. This "human tendency" has been referred to as effectance motivation (Harter, 1978; White, 1959) or competence motivation (Koestner & McClelland, 1990). Research has demonstrated that infants are innately willing and able to detect, initiate, operate, prolong, and enjoy contingent interactions and that they show distress and frustration when faced with noncontingency (Watson, 1966; Watson & Ramey, 1972). The psychophysiological basis of reactions to noncontingency has been documented (Gunnar, 1980) and provides one explanation for why prolonged exposure to noncontingency is stressful and can compromise immune system functioning (Seligman, 1975). These effects have also been documented across the lifespan (J. Heckhausen & Schulz, 1995; Skinner, 1995). A goal of the motivational model is to bring together the consideration of both of these needs simultaneously and to posit the inclusion of a somewhat more controversial third fundamental psychological need—that for autonomy.

Autonomy as a Fundamental Psychological Need

A basic tenet of self-determination theory is that all people intrinsically desire to be autonomous, that is, they innately desire to act according to their genuine desires and preferences, to show courses of action that reflect their true selves, and to experience themselves as the source of their own actions (deCharms, 1968; Deci & Ryan, 1985b, 1991, 2000). It is clear that, from birth, infants are able to vigorously express and defend their states, actions, desires, and preferences, and that they protest restraint and pressure to act counter to their desires. Stated colloquially, infants do not need to be told "No, tell me what you really want."

An autonomy perspective highlights the implications of these intrinsic abilities and motivations, pointing out that infants are born with the capacity and will to be autonomous. That is, all infants come with genuine preferences, desires, and wants, and they are innately able and motivated to recognize them and to show actions that express them. In fact, these patterns of expression are clear enough to allow experienced caregivers to respond to infants' actions appropriately, that is, in concert with infants' actual desires. Social interactions in which caregivers respond appropriately to infants' expressed wants and desires are psychologically and physiologically beneficial to infants, contributing to the development of intentionality, expressiveness, and personality (Zeedyk, 1996).

The assumption that normal humans come with the need for self-determination does not preclude individual differences in corresponding inborn capacities and desires. For example, individual differences in emotional expressiveness and resistance to demands have been studied in work on temperament and emotion regulation (Calkins, 1994). Individual differences in expressions of autonomy are also influenced by the characteristics of the different social contexts in which children and adults function and develop.

The Construction of Self-system Processes Associated with Autonomy

Like researchers in the areas of self-determination, we believe that people are inherently expressive and volitional. In addition, and in keeping with work from many areas, we assume that individuals act on the motivations provided by psychological needs in social contexts that are differentially responsive to them (Connell & Wellborn, 1991; Deci & Ryan, 1985b; Grolnick & Ryan, 1989; Skinner, 1995). During these social interactions, people experience themselves as differentially related, competent, and autonomous.

From these experiences, individuals cumulatively construct and revise views of themselves and their social/physical worlds, referred to as *self-system processes* (Connell & Wellborn, 1991). These beliefs are not momentary self-perceptions. They are relatively durable convictions about the nature of the self and the world. Because self-system processes guide participation in and interpretation of subsequent social   interactions, they help create compelling experiences of "apparent reality" (Fridja, 1988).

For autonomy, self-system processes have been studied as autonomy or goal orientations (deCharms, 1968; Deci & Ryan, 1985b, 1991; Dweck, 1991; Kuhl, 1987; Ryan & Connell, 1989), and contain views about the self as genuine (versus inauthentic) and about the environment as encouraging open expression of genuine preferences (versus being coercive). Based on a history of experience with differential autonomy support versus coercion, people develop an orientation toward their own goals and actions, which becomes a critical individual difference factor shaping their motivation and participation. These orientations have been described and measured in a variety of ways, including origin versus pawn (deCharms, 1968); intrinsic versus extrinsic orientations (Harter, 1978); learning versus performance goals (Dweck, 1999; Dweck & Leggett, 1988); and self-regulatory styles (including external, introjected, identified, and intrinsic regulation; Ryan & Connell, 1989).

Social Contexts and the Construction of Self-system Processes

The model attempts to describe how social and physical contexts provide people with opportunities to fulfill their needs (Connell & Wellborn, 1991; Deci & Ryan, 1985b; Grolnick & Ryan, 1989; Skinner, 1995). Accordingly, people are given opportunities to experience themselves as related and belonging when they interact with social partners who love them, who are involved and emotionally available, and who express affection, warmth, caring, and nurturance. When social partners are hostile or neglectful, individuals experience themselves as unlovable and the context as unavailable or untrustworthy (Ainsworth, 1979; Lamb & Easterbrooks, 1981). People accumulate experiences of competence when they interact with contexts that respond to them, and that are structured, predictable, contingent, and consistent. When contexts, partners, or activities are noncontingent, uncontrollable, or chaotic, people will come to experience themselves as incompetent (Bandura, 1981; Carton & Nowicki, 1994; Gunnar, 1980; Schneewind, 1995; Skinner, Zimmer-Gembeck, & Connell, 1998; Suomi, 1980).

Support of autonomy. Opportunities to experience oneself as *autonomous* are facilitated by contexts that are autonomy supportive (Deci & Ryan, 1987, 1991; Grolnick & Ryan, 1989; Reeve, Bolt, & Cai, 1999; Ryan, 1982; Ryan & Solky, 1996). Adults and children experience themselves as autonomous when they interact with social partners or institutions who respect and defer to them, allowing them freedom of expression and action, and encouraging them to attend to, accept, and value their inner states, preferences, and desires.

Definitions of autonomy support, for example in parenting, tend to focus on the absence of psychological control or coercion (Barber, 1996). However, support for autonomy extends beyond allowing an individual freedom of choice and expression, to providing genuine respect and deference and encouraging individuals to actively discover, explore, and articulate their own views, goals, and preferences. Autonomy support characterizes interactions in which people are expected to express their views and opinions and in which these are given weight in decision-making and problem-solving. Social partners can participate actively in this process through attempts to help the individual become aware of, reflect on, and express his or her true feelings, intentions, and desires. This is especially important with children and in situations when feelings are opaque or confusing. Explanations that are accurate and that validate the person's perspective can provide the person insight into his or her own goals and personality (for reviews, see Barber, 1996; Deci & Ryan, 2000; Reeve et al., 1999).

Autonomy supportive contexts can be distinguished from "permissive" contexts on several grounds. A permissive style, often used to refer to styles of parenting, describes a warm but laissez faire approach to interactions, which sometimes implies lax discipline, few maturity demands, benign neglect, or low structure (Baumrind, 1971, 1977). Autonomy support includes the freedom from coercion implied by such an interaction style; however, an autonomy supportive context is considered to be more involved and active in facilitating the development of individuality. The goal of autonomy supportive partners is not to leave the person alone, but to actively participate in interactions in which the individual discovers and expresses his or her true self.

Coercion. The opposite of autonomy support is coercion or controlling social conditions (Deci & Ryan, 1985b, 1991; Ryan, 1982; Ryan & Solky, 1996). When social partners or contexts are coercive, pressuring, or controlling, individuals experience themselves as "pawns" (deCharms, 1968). Coercion can be conveyed through many channels. The most obvious is direct exertion of force, through threats, intimidation, or emotional blackmail. However, social contexts can also be coercive if they are characterized by excessive rules, rigid prescriptions of behavior, or demands for conformity. A social partner's strong emotion, such as intense anger or anxiety, can deflect an individual away from a genuinely desired course of action. Even well-intentioned social contexts can be coercive if they are overprotective, intrusively helpful, or insistently directive. These contextual features tend to focus people on what "should" be happening and away from their intrinsic involvement in tasks or activities (Dweck, 1999; Ryan, 1982).

A critical issue in defining the nature of coercive contexts is the distinction between "informational" and "controlling" responses to one's actions (Ryan, 1982). Many kinds of social reactions, such as praise, feedback, rewards, or evaluations, cannot be classified a priori as autonomy supportive or coercive. For example, not all praise can be considered autonomy supportive nor all rewards coercive. Instead, it depends on the quality of the reactions, specifically whether the social response provides (or is experienced as providing) information that would be helpful to improved performance (informational) or, alternatively, exerts pressure to engage in certain actions (coercive). Social feedback can be "purely" informational when it contains no pressure to carry out specific actions or it can be "purely" coercive if it contains only an imperative and no information; and, of course, some reactions contain both information and pressure.

However, it has been possible to distinguish empirically the features of social messages that make them more coercive (including linguistic features like "should" or "must") from those that make them more informative (specific descriptions of actions and their consequences), and these features have been linked in the expected manner to individuals' perceptions of autonomy support and to their autonomous action (Deci & Ryan, 1985b; Deci, Eghrari, Patrick, & Leone, 1994; Deci, Koestner, & Ryan, 1999; Reeve et al., 1999). Theoretically, informational feedback can be seen as part of structure, which supports experiences of competence. Empirical studies document the effect of informational contexts on perceptions of competence and control (Deci & Ryan, 1985b; Deci et al., 1999). According to the model, autonomy support versus coercion, along with provision of warmth/involvement versus hostility, and structure versus chaos, are contextual supports that provide opportunities for individuals to fulfill their psychological needs (see Figure 14-1).

A Motivational Model of Stress and Coping

The motivational model has been used as a springboard for addressing basic issues in stress and coping, such as: What kinds of experiences are objectively and universally stressful? What are the contents of appraisals of challenge and threat? Why are behavioral and emotional reactions to stress so powerful and compelling? What kind(s) of coping are adaptive? What kinds of personal and social resources can support adaptive coping? (Skinner & Wellborn, 1994, 1997; Skinner & Edge, 1998, in press).

The assumption of fundamental psychological needs adds *content* to theories of coping. It provides an explanation for why certain experiences are objectively stressful: because they challenge or threaten universal human needs. The model suggests that appraisals of situations as challenges or threats to the three needs are key mechanisms by which objective stressors trigger energized and compelling emotional and behavioral reactions. It explains why self-system processes, such as perceived control and feelings of connectedness to others, exert such powerful effects during times of stress: because they shape the "apparent reality" of objective events. It also suggests that social contexts which support the three needs can have positive effects on appraisals and coping as well. Two interesting implications from the motivational model are the definition of coping as "action regulation under stress" and the suggestion that ways of coping may be organized as "families" around the three needs.

Coping as Action Regulation

When coping is thought of as action regulation under stress, it implies that coping is based on *action tendencies*. These are flexible motor programs that include behavior, emotion, and orientation responses (Barrett & Campos, 1991; Campos, Mumme, Kermoian, & Campos, 1994; Fridja, 1987, 1988). Action tendencies are not reflexes; however, they are compelling, automatized predispositions to act. They are experienced as "urges" or "desires," and are redundantly energized and directed by behavior, emotion, and orientation.

Action tendencies are goal directed and effortful (in that they require energetic resources) but are not usually voluntary, in the sense of being under conscious control (cf., Compas, Connor, Osowiecki, & Welch, 1997). According to this reasoning, when a man feels pressured, he doesn't "decide" to lash out; he "finds himself" digging his heels in. This holds not only for maladaptive but also for adaptive responses to stress. For example, when a girl appraises a problem as challenging, she doesn't "decide" to problem solve; her attention and interest are "captured" by the problematic interaction.

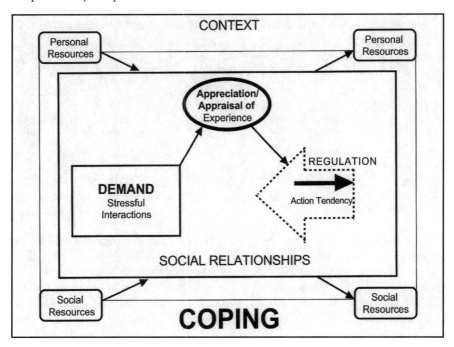

Figure 14.2. A Depiction of Coping as Action Regulation under Stress.

In keeping with action theory and functionalist theories of emotion, we hold that action tendencies are triggered by an appreciation of the significance of an interaction for an individual's well-being (Barrett & Campos, 1991; Campos et al., 1994; Fridja, 1987, 1988). We view individuals' appraisals of challenges and threats to the three needs as prototypical examples of the kinds of appreciations that trigger action tendencies. It is these action tendencies that are the targets of people's regulation under stress. As depicted in Figure 14-2, coping can be seen as an action tendency (represented by the smaller dark arrow), triggered by an appraisal and shaped by a regulation (represented by the larger dashed arrow), that is embedded in a specific context and a set of social relationships. It can be noted that the arrows representing the action tendency and the regulation are pointed in opposite directions in Figure 14-2. This suggests that, in this example, the function of the regulation is not to boost the action tendency (as would be suggested by arrows pointing in the same direction), but to redirect it. Many alternative combinations of action tendency and regulation are also possible.

Six Families of Coping

The motivational model was useful in identifying and organizing categories of coping. Three concepts were particularly important in this endeavor: the notion of "families" of ways of coping, the concept of action tendencies, and the three self-system processes. The notion of families allows multiple manifestly different ways of coping to be considered part of the same family based on common underlying characteristics. For example, such diverse ways of coping as reading about a disease, joining a support group, seeking advice from a friend, and watching a peer group could be classified as belonging to the family of coping characterized as "information-seeking." This scheme acknowledges that ways of coping can be infinitely adapted according to the specifics of a stressful encounter—demands, contexts, personalities, and developmental levels—without requiring an infinite number of categories to meaningfully capture them.

The concept of "action tendencies" was useful in specifying the criteria for family membership, namely, the underlying root action tendency: All members of a family have in common the underlying urge or desire triggered by a particular appraisal of the stressful encounter, and the prototypical pattern of behavior, emotion, and orientation which characterizes that action tendency. They take their *specific* form from the developmental capacities and the situational possibilities available during the stressful episode (Skinner, Edge, Altman, & Sherwood, 2002). For example, if the root action tendency in response to an appraisal of coercion is aggression, then that action tendency will be implemented directly (i.e., expressed as coping) only if certain developmental capacities are present (e.g., after a child can intentionally hit), and only in certain contexts (e.g., ones that allow the child to aggress). With social partners against whom the child is not allowed to aggress (e.g., the teacher), the child will have to express the action tendency of fighting indirectly, through oppositional behavior, displaced aggression, or fantasy. Or an uncoordinated infant may "fight" through temper tantrums.

The three self-system processes were used to identify six families of coping (see Figure 14-3). For each of the self-systems, one family is organized around the root action tendency triggered by an appraisal of obstacles as a *challenge* to that need and one is organized around the root action tendency triggered by an appraisal of *threat*. These six families are depicted in Figure 14-3, along with the corresponding behavior, emotion, and orientation. For example, when an obstacle is appraised as resistance, that is, as a challenge to autonomy, then this triggers the root action tendency of defense, which is characterized by behavior that

Psychological Need	Environmental Event/ Appraisal	Action Tendency	Behavior	Emotion	Orientation	
Relatedness	Separation	Seek proximity	Go to other	Yearning	Make contact	Away (to other)
	Loss	Freeze	Hold still	Shock	Disappear	Toward (inward)
Competence	Novelty	Observe	Study	Interest	Discover	Toward (object)
	Chaos	Flee	Run away	Fear	Escape	Away (outward)
Autonomy	Resistance	Defend	Stand firm	Indignation	Protect	Away (to obstacle)
	Coercion	Fight	Move toward obstacle	Anger	Attack	Toward (to object)

Figure 14.3. Ways of Coping and Their Root Action Tendencies.

stands firm, the emotion of indignation, and an orientation toward protecting the desired goal. In contrast, an appraisal of a stressful encounter as coercion, that is, as a threat to autonomy, triggers an action tendency that can be labeled as "fight," characterized by a prototypical pattern of behavior (moving toward the obstacle), emotion (anger), and orientation (attacking the source of coercion).

Development of Coping Capacity

This conceptualization of coping makes clear that "stress" is not inherently damaging to people, even children, and that the primary function of coping is not simply to shield people from stressful experiences (Compas, 1993; Weisz, 1993). Coping can function to prolong constructive interactions as well as to escalate stress. If demands are a true threat and overwhelm a person, then the person becomes confused, isolated, or rebellious, and these experiences are counterproductive. However, if situations are experienced as challenging, they can contribute to development.

In fact, stress and challenges are necessary conditions for the construction of children's self-system processes and their close relationships. For example, it is precisely by dealing with situations in which goals are blocked or in conflict with the goals of others that people develop autonomy. During prolonged negotiations with environmental demands, people learn about their own genuine goals and preferences and learn how to respect and influence those of others. They learn how to coordinate and balance conflicting goals, for example, how to shape short-term actions in service of long-term goals (Metcalfe & Mischel, 1999). Such conflicts, negotiations, and concessions characterize the very processes of internalization, through which originally extrinsic goals become integrated with the true self and hence autonomously regulated (Deci & Ryan, 1991; Kochanska, 1995; Ryan, 1993). Constructive coping interactions are key loci of development, representing opportunities for people to discover and expand their own capacities and to learn about and shape the affordances of the physical and social environment.

Autonomy as Central to Coping

It is relatively easy to map concepts from the areas of control and attachment onto fundamental issues in coping. For example, work on control, efficacy, and helplessness (Compas, 1987; Dweck & Wortman, 1982; Skinner, 1995) holds that "uncontrollability" is an objective stressor that universally places significant demands on people. This perspective suggests that a sense of efficacy is a critical psychological resource in dealing with uncontrollable situations, because it affects whether such events will be appraised as challenges to competence and so coped with though problem-solving, strategizing, and information-seeking, or, alternatively, will be appraised as threats and so lead to confusion, helplessness, or escape (Dweck, 1999; Peterson et al., 1993).

Likewise, it is relatively easy to see how the tenets of attachment theory can inform work on coping (Compas, 1987; Skinner & Wellborn, 1994). According to an attachment perspective (Ainsworth, 1979; Bowlby, 1969, 1973), separation is objectively demanding, personal resources are appraisals of availability of attachment figures in times of distress, and social resources include a secure attachment. Appraisals of stressful situations as a challenge to relatedness are likely to trigger proximity-seeking and self-reliance, whereas appraisals of stressful encounters as threats trigger social isolation or excessive dependency.

Compared to work on attachment and control, much less has been written and studied about the connection between coping and autonomy. Nevertheless, self-determination theory can provide a complementary set of answers to fundamental questions of coping. This perspective suggests that a class of universally stressful events are ones that are objectively *coercive*; an important psychological resource for dealing with demands is a *sense of autonomy;* and *autonomy support* is an important social resource. These resources increase the likelihood that objective stressors will be appraised as challenges rather than as threats to autonomy. Self-determination theory also suggests that several important *ways of coping* (patterns of action regulation) are organized around the need for autonomy. Since these propositions are rarely considered in research on coping, each of them is analyzed in more detail below.

Coercion as an Objective Stressor

Current theories of stress and coping tend to back away from the notion of "universal stressors." That is, for the most part, conceptualizations decline to identify any particular experience or class of experiences as objectively demanding to all people. Instead, stress is described as transactional, that is, as shaped jointly by environmental demands, individuals' appraisals, and personal and social resources (Lazarus & Folkman, 1984). The only two conditions that have come close to being considered universally stressful are noncontingency (Seligman, 1975) or loss of control (Miller, 1979) and social deprivation (Baumeister & Leary, 1995; Stroebe, Stroebe, Abakoumkin, & Schut, 1996) or loss of an attachment figure (Ainsworth, 1979; Bowlby, 1969, 1973).

The consideration of actual loss of control and actual loss of attachment figures as universally stressful has been useful in analyzing a wide variety of life events for their objective demand characteristics and for the kinds of distress and coping they tend to elicit. For example, the centrality of loss of attachment figures has informed work on maternal deprivation (Rutter, 1979), bereavement (Bonanno & Kaltman, 1999), and dealing with social losses during normative aging (Carstensen, 1998). Other work focuses on the objective controllability of stressors. For example, it has been suggested that traumatic events such as life-threatening illness, divorce, natural disasters, violent crime, abuse, and even aging, are stressful at least in part because they entail objective losses of competence and control. The extent of the objective loss of control turns out to be a good indicator of many sequelae of the event, including subjective experiences of loss of control, emotional distress, behavioral disorganization, and the kinds of coping evinced (Band & Weisz, 1988; Compas et al., 1991; Folkman, 1984; Forsythe & Compas, 1987; Weisz, 1993).

The motivational model underscores the universal stressfulness of both loss of attachment figures and loss of control. It posits that these are direct assaults on fundamental human needs, and that all people are psychologically and physiologically predisposed to register their stressfulness. In addition, the model posits a third class of universally stressful experiences: coercion or loss of freedom. These experiences are also considered to thwart a universal human need, in this case, for autonomy. However, in analyses of life events, coercion is rarely mentioned as a source of stress. Further, many of the life events described as entailing losses of or threats to control or attachment relationships, also contain coercive features and the coerciveness of these experiences may add to or even outweigh the effects of other losses or threats.

Coercive crimes. Once the concept of coercion is articulated, it is relatively easy to identify some classes of life events that are stressful primarily because they are coercive. For example, violent crimes, such as robbery or rape, are defined by the very coerciveness of the acts. The same activities performed consensually do not involve violence and are not even considered crimes. That is not to say that victimization never entails loss of control or threats to relationships, but only to emphasize that such incidents *always* include the experience of overwhelming coercion and violation of will.

Coercive medical conditions. Another clear illustration of the importance (and neglect) of the characteristic of coercion can be drawn from work on coping with life-threatening illness. Research on coping with medical conditions often focuses almost exclusively on the controllability of the disease, sometimes even classifying and studying conditions separately according to the extent to which symptoms or diseases respond to treatment. We argue that an additional dimension is critical in determining the stressfulness of a medical condition, namely, its coerciveness, defined as the extent to which it prevents people from showing the actions they desire. For example, diseases that interfere with activities of daily living or are disabling may or may not respond to treatment, but they are coercive. They prevent people from doing what they want to do (such as playing tennis) and they also pressure people into doing things that they do not want to do (such as staying in bed). Effective treatments may not only restore control but may also reduce the coerciveness of symptoms.

It should be noted, however, that treatments can themselves be coercive. They can involve submitting to diagnostic procedures or regimens that are painful or invasive. They can include taking medications with harmful side effects or participating in therapies that are painful or boring. They can also include adding undesired or refraining from desired activities. In most cases, the stressfulness of both medical conditions and their treatments can be appreciated, not only in terms of loss of control, but also with reference to coercion.

Coerciveness in life events. We believe that it is useful to evaluate *all* stressful life events in terms of their coerciveness. For some events, like victimization, abuse, or disease, issues of coercion may be a defining feature. For others, a consideration of coercion may add depth to an understanding of the psychological demands presented by an event. For example, the stressfulness of bereavement and divorce may be characterized primarily in terms of losses of or threats to attachment relationships. However, loss of a partner may also be coercive if it forces the remaining partner into new roles and actions. Divorce may be more coercive (and hence more upsetting) if the target individual (partner or child) does not want it and it occurs against his or her will. Likewise, a dominant theme in aging may be loss of competencies and loss of relationships. However, freedom may also be lost, as a result of or in addition to these other losses. Analysis of the coerciveness of life events can provide insight into subjective experiences and reactions to these events, as well as suggesting interventions to ameliorate or buffer their effects.

Coercion versus loss of control. Part of the problem with characterizing experiences in terms of their coerciveness is the difficulty in distinguishing coercion from loss of control (Skinner, 1996). Some of this confusion is terminological. For example, work on control has adopted concepts like "decision control" (Averill, 1973) and "secondary control" (J. Heckhausen & Schulz, 1995) to refer to processes that typically have been dealt with in theories of self-determination. At the same time, self-determination theorists have used terms like "locus of causality" (deCharms, 1968) and characterize conditions, contexts, and events that thwart autonomy as "controlling" (Ryan, 1982).

Conceptually, however, the difference is clear (deCharms, 1981). Loss of control refers to the loss or absence of action-outcome contingencies, as described by terms like noncontingency, unpredictability, and (our preferred umbrella concept) chaos. Chaotic contexts prevent people from being effective or masterful, and from producing desired or preventing undesired outcomes. They either prevent people from figuring out what to do to get what they want or they block people from obtaining the competencies to do it. In some general way, chaos can be thought of as similar to "anarchy" (and can be contrasted to the rule of law).

In contrast, coercion refers to loss of freedom, or resistance to showing the actions of one's choice, as described by terms like pressure, force, interference, manipulation, or intrusiveness. Coercive contexts prevent people from being genuine and authentic, from expressing the actions that reflect their actual preferences and desires. In simple terms, they prevent people from being true to themselves. Coercion can be thought of as similar to a "totalitarian" system (and can be contrasted with democracy).

Contexts can be very structured in that they are contingent and predictable, but if they also contain pressure to produce particular outcomes or if only certain classes of (undesired) actions are effective, they can also be very coercive. Many life events and many contexts (such as work places, families, and schools) can be characterized by this combination of conditions. For example, parental approval may be contingent on a child's conformity to parental desires (Kamins & Dweck, 1999; Mueller & Dweck, 1998), or evaluations of teachers may be linked to the performance of their students (Deci, Spiegel, Ryan, Koestner, & Kauffman, 1982). Even though such contexts are high on opportunities to control outcomes, they are still stressful because of their negative effects on autonomy. And, of course, contexts that are both chaotic *and* coercive should be more stressful than contexts that exhibit only one of these characteristics.

Self-system Processes of Autonomy as Motivational Determinants of Coping

Adaptive self-system processes are hypothesized to act as key personal resources during stressful interactions. At the most general level, they contribute, along with objective events (including the actions of social partners), to an orientation toward the stressful transaction. They create "head sets" about what is at stake in stressful interactions, influencing what people focus on as they cope. These are reflected in appraisals of the meaning of internal and external demands (Lazarus & Folkman, 1984), including, for example, what is attended to, how interactions are interpreted, estimations of their potential impact on current well-being and future goals, and views about the role of the self and others in dealing with the stressful situation.

Each of the self-system processes shapes appraisals that trigger corresponding families of coping. The families of coping associated with competence and relatedness, namely, problem-solving and support-seeking, respectively, have been studied fairly thoroughly and appear in almost all typologies of ways of coping (Ryan-Wenger, 1992; Skinner & Wellborn, 1994). Moreover, the self-system processes of competence and relatedness have often been included in studies of coping and have been found to predict their designated ways of coping. For example, perceived control is a robust predictor of problem-solving, active, and approach coping in children (Compas et al., 1991; Kliewer, 1991) and across the lifespan (Skinner, 1995). And studies that examine coping as a function of attachment status have found that children with secure attachments (relative to children who are insecurely attached) show more active, approach, and support-seeking coping (Armsden & Greenberg; 1987; Nachmias, Gunnar, Mangelsdorf, Parritz, & Buss, 1996; Shulman, 1987; Skinner & Edge, in press; Skinner & Snyder, 1999).

Compared to studies on perceived control and attachment status, almost no research has explored the effects of the third self-system process, namely, perceived autonomy. Furthermore, the ways of coping associated with autonomy are often missing from taxonomies of coping, or if they appear, their links to autonomy are not explicit. Hence, the next sections focus on autonomy as a personal resource in coping and on the families of coping organized around it.

Perceived autonomy. Usually labeled autonomy orientations, these self-system beliefs refer to the extent to which one has access to one's genuine preferences and goals and the extent to which one expects the social context to respect, value, and defer to one's own agenda (Deci & Ryan, 1985b; Ryan & Connell, 1989). A person with an autonomous orientation can form and express robust goals and intentions that reflect his or her actual preferences. Moreover, an autonomous orientation includes the psychological freedom to act on those preferences and goals. In response to environmental or intrapsychic pressures, these expectations and capacities are a basis for open and flexible action, allowing the individual to "stay in touch with" the hierarchy of his or her genuine priorities, and not to lose sight of them while negotiating environmental or internal demands.

Individuals with low perceived autonomy have poor access to their actual preferences and generally expect that others will try to pressure and coerce them. Hence, environmental events tend to be appraised as coercive and social partners' intentions as hostile (Graham, Hudley, & Williams, 1992). In response to stress, such an orientation creates a great deal of pressure, which, when channeled externally, produces an "external" style of regulation in which the individual experiences the source of his or her action as originating in the external environment (Deci & Ryan, 1985a; Ryan & Connell, 1989). Pressure can also be "introjected," or channeled internally, in which the person takes on the coercive functions of the external demands and pressures the self to act accordingly (Deci & Ryan, 1985b; Ryan & Connell, 1989). Both of these styles of regulation are considered nonautonomous, in that they are reactive and not willfully deployed.

They can be contrasted with two more autonomous styles of responding. The first reflects regulations that were once externally imposed but have subsequently been willingly endorsed and autonomously internalized. It is labeled "integrated" to reflect the fact that these goals have been harmoniously combined with existing self structures. The second style is labeled "intrinsic." It describes a source of energy and direction for activities that are spontaneously enjoyable, like activities of learning, self-expression, and social interaction. Because these activities are inherently pleasurable, willingness to participate in them does not have to be recruited and then internalized. However, it should be noted that their regulation will remain "intrinsic" only so long as other coercive elements, such as judgement and evaluation, are not superimposed upon them. To illustrate the flavor of these orientations, Table 14-1 includes items used to tap them during childhood and adulthood.

Causality Orientation Scale (Deci & Ryan, 1985a)

You have been offered a new position in a company and the first question that comes to your mind is, "I wonder if the new work will be interesting?" (+)

A close (same sex) friend of yours has been moody lately and a couple of times has become very angry with you for "nothing." Your approach to handling this would be to share your observations with your friend and try to find out what is going on for him or her. (+)

Self-Regulation Scale - Academic (Ryan & Connell, 1989)

The reason I do my classwork is that I want to learn new things. (+)

The reason I try to answer hard questions in class is so I will know if I am right or wrong. (+)

Parenting Sense of Autonomy (Skinner & Regan, 1992)

When I'm with my kids, there's nothing else I'd rather be doing. (+)

I wish I didn't feel so trapped by parenting duties. (-)

I look forward to being with my children. (+)

I feel that parenting runs my entire life. (-)

Perceived Academic Self-determination (Vallerand, Pelletier, Blais, Brière, Senécal, & Vallières, 1993)

At school, I feel like I am in prison. (-)

I go to school out of personal choice. (+)

Table 14.1. Sample Items Tapping Self-system Processes Connected with Autonomy.

Ways of Coping Organized around Autonomy

Compared to the families of coping connected to relatedness and competence, very little has been written or studied about the families of coping associated with autonomy. We argue that, in general, the action tendencies triggered by interactions that tax autonomy are organized around concession and defense. Concession and defense can be either autonomous or nonautonomous. Appraisals of environmental demands as threats to autonomy lead to reactive (nonautonomous) action tendencies, whereas appraisals of demands as challenges to autonomy trigger action tendencies that are self-determined.

Figure 14-4 depicts our current thinking about the autonomous and nonautonomous modes of concession and defense, along with some of the behaviors, emotions, and orientations that characterize them. For defense, we label the nonautonomous family of ways of coping "opposition;" for concession, it is labeled "perseveration." The autonomous form of defense is labeled "negotiation" and the autonomous form of concession is "accommodation." In the next four sections, we describe each way of coping in more detail and mention research that has touched on similar concepts.

	CONCESSION	DEFENSE
A U T O N O M O U S	**Challenge to SELF** Implement AUTHENTIC Action **Accommodation** Cooperation Concession Acquiesce Defer Acceptance Good will Commitment Conviction Endorsement	**Challenge to CONTEXT** Promote AUTONOMY SUPPORT **Negotiation** Blamelessness Taking other's perspective Good will Decision-making Goal-setting Priority-setting
N O N A U T O N O M O U S	**Threat to SELF** Promote COERCION **Perseveration** Compliance Conformity Rigidity Submission Self-blame Urgency Compulsion Obsession Rumination Intrusive thoughts	**Threat to CONTEXT** Reduce Opportunities for AUTONOMOUS Action **Opposition** Aggression Projection Blame others Venting Explosion Anger Reactance Revenge

Note. Within each column, the way of coping in bold is the most common label for that family of ways of coping.

Figure 14.4. Families of Coping Associated with Autonomy.

Opposition. "Oppositional" coping is considered a nonautonomous reaction to demands because its goal is taken from outside the self—that is, it is completely determined by the environmental demand, specifically, by the *opposite* of the demand. Within the coping area, this pattern of responding to stress has been given labels reflecting its anger, rigidity, and opposition, such as "externalizing," "venting," and "projection." Defiance, reactance, rebellion, explosion, projection, blaming others, venting, and revenge have in common that they are patterns of action recruited to *oppose* someone else's goals. Hence, we label this pattern of coping as "opposition." These behaviors have been observed, for example, as part of escalating cycles of parent-child coercion (Kochanska, 1995, 1997; Patterson & Bank, 1989) and have been studied as psychological reactance (Brehm, 1966).

Oppositional reactions usually have serious social consequences. Oppositional behavior tends to provoke escalated demands, even from initially benign social partners (Dodge, 1991; Graham, 1998; Parpal & Maccoby, 1985). A less obvious consequence is that, in his or her push toward defiance, the person forgoes the opportunity to form or defend an autonomous goal (Deci & Ryan, 1985b). This interferes with any attempts to create a scenario in which that goal can be realized. The individual also learns little about the actual goals of social partners or how to coordinate them with his or her own goals.

Perseveration. The nonautonomous form of concession is "perseverance" or rigid compliance. Perseveration, and its variations, including compliance, conformity, or submission, are based on an introjected style of regulation in which the individual, in response to environmental demands, is subjected to strong internal pressures to submit. This pattern of engagement can be distinguished from willing cooperation and problem-solving because of its rigid and urgent quality and because it lacks flexibility and responsiveness to external and internal feedback. The pressured and anxious quality of engagement, in addition to dampening enjoyment and draining energetic resources, also blocks access to cognitive and social resources, and interferes with hypothesis-testing and strategizing, thereby short-circuiting learning.

Most important for autonomy, perseveration is coercive and does not allow the individual the psychological freedom to alter, refocus, or relinquish goals. Several researchers have suggested that this pattern of action constitutes a risk factor for depression and hopelessness (Brandtstädter, 1999; Nolen-Hoeksma, 1998). Perseveration may reflect the inability to disengage from goals that are no longer feasible or that interfere with other more important goals. Prolonged pursuit of unattainable goals, such as remaining young, creates the experience of helplessness. Prolonged pursuit of the wrong goals, such as image or money, means that healthier goals are less likely to be attained (Kasser & Ryan, 1993). Moreover, if social partners come to see that these goals are not feasible or genuinely important, perseveration may also erode social support.

Negotiation. The more positive patterns of responding connected to autonomy have been studied less or have been incorporated into an amalgam of "positive" or "approach" coping that includes problem-solving. We believe it is important to differentiate and specifically study forms of autonomous defense and concession. The autonomous form of defense is "negotiation." Defense of high priority goals, because it is autonomous, differs from opposition in that negotiation is flexible, open, creative, and responsive to new information. The primary orientation is not toward foiling an opponent but toward creating a scenario in which all genuine high priority goals can be met. Processes of social negotiation do not result in "winning," they allow the individual to achieve high priority goals and to concede to high priority goals of others.

Similarly, processes of "internal negotiation" do not result in "self-sacrifice;" they allow individuals to articulate, prioritize, and coordinate their own multiple important goals. Negotiations during stressful encounters are, in turn, key experiences in which to learn about the values of the self and others, as well as to experience others as flexible negotiators. In such interactions, individuals discover and create hierarchies of goals and are able to integrate their goals meaningfully with those of others (individuals, organizations, or societies).

Accommodation. Accommodation has been described as a major mode of coping in work focusing on the challenges of successful aging (Brandtstädter & Renner, 1990; Brandtstädter, Wentura, & Greve, 1993; Brandtstädter, Wentura, & Rothermund, 1999). Accommodation reflects a pattern of "willing submission" or "committed compliance" (Kochanska & Aksan, 1995) and results from integrated regulation (Ryan & Connell, 1989). Accommodation implies a quality of concession that is above and beyond grudging acceptance or foot-dragging compliance. It emphasizes flexibility, openness, cooperation, and "good will." It is autonomous in that it reflects genuine acceptance, authentic endorsement, and personal conviction.

As studied under the misleading label "secondary control" (J. Heckhausen & Schulz, 1995), accommodation has been shown to be a critical part of adaptation to uncontrollable or unavoidable events. Stated colloquially, accommodative processes allow people to act according to the maxim: "If you can't get out of it, get into it." These are processes that allow people to move beyond self-pity, bitterness, and recrimination to an orientation of acceptance of current constraints, whatever their source. In general, they allow a person to stop focusing on the past and assigning blame and to begin focusing on the future and accepting responsibility (Brickman et al, 1982). Accommodation allows creation of fresh perspectives, such as by focusing on the positive or carrying out downward social comparisons. This frees resources for action and allows the emergence of new goals, which are not only genuine but are also constructive and attainable. The emergence of revised goal hierarchies is a hallmark of adjustment after loss. It is a turning point in the decision to let the past stay in the past and to move on.

Autonomy Support as a Characteristic of the Social Context

An important function of autonomy support in the social context, and not just during times of stress, is to contribute to the development of an autonomous orientation in the people who function there (Ryan & Solky, 1996). Whether referring to a society, an organization, an institution, a family, or a dyadic partnership, social contexts that provide people opportunities to realize their genuine goals and preferences will promote in people the accumulation of personal resources described as perceived autonomy.

Important determinants of how supportive social partners and contexts will be are the actions of individuals themselves, some of which are captured in the ways of coping just described. For example, when individuals clearly express their preferences and negotiate for solutions, social partners are more likely to defer to their wishes. When individuals willingly cooperate, it is easier for partners to willingly cooperate as well. When people actively and enthusiastically problem solve about how to meet the goals of all parties involved, social partners are more likely to suggest compromises and to concede low priority goals.

Unfortunately, less adaptive ways of coping are likely to provoke less supportive reactions from social partners. For example, when people simply conform, it is difficult for partners to discern that they are experiencing pressure. When, in reaction to resistance, individuals submit very quickly, social contexts are likely to overestimate their agreement, thus forfeiting the individuals' opportunities to negotiate. On the other hand, when individuals react to demands with defiance, social contexts are likely to become more coercive (Patterson & Bank, 1989) or to simply withdraw their support (Tennen & Affleck, 1990). These patterns of person-context interaction suggest cycles that maintain or amplify individual's ways of coping and context support (or lack of support) over time.

Research on Autonomy and Coping

In our own work on children's coping in the academic domain, we have begun to explore the connections among perceived autonomy, autonomy support, and children's coping. The work began with the assessment of the four families of coping associated with autonomy as responses to failures and setbacks in school (Skinner & Wellborn, 1994, 1997). The assessment of opposition and accommodation and their characteristic behaviors, emotions, and orientations were relatively straightforward. However, because of the power relations in the classroom, ways of coping that belong to the family of "negotiation" were more difficult to assess; and in general are rarely seen or reported in the classroom context, even in open-ended interviews with children (Skinner, Altman, & Sherwood, 1991).

In the first set of studies, we concentrated on two ways of coping: accommodation and opposition. A few previous studies had shown a correlation between children's perceived autonomy (assessed with the Relative Autonomy Index or RAI; Ryan & Connell, 1989) and two related ways of coping, positive coping (problem-solving and self-comforting) and projection (blaming others) (Wellborn, Mellor-Crummey, Connell, & Skinner, 1989). Unique effects of perceived autonomy were found on these two ways of coping, over and above the significant effects of perceived competence and relatedness.

In our longitudinal study of about 1600 elementary school children in grades three through seven (see Skinner et al., 1998, for details), we also found that children's perceived autonomy (as indexed by scores on the RAI) was a significant predictor of both accommodation and oppositional coping, even after controlling for the significant effects of relatedness and competence. Most importantly, we tested a model of context, self, and action. In this model, children's experiences of parental autonomy support versus coercion were examined as predictors of children's perceived autonomy which in turn predicted their accommodation and opposition coping. This model was found it to be a good fit with self-report data (Skinner & Edge, in press).

Moreover, we examined children's perceived autonomy as a predictor of *changes* in children's coping over the school year. As expected, children's perceived autonomy in the fall predicted changes in their coping from fall to spring of the school year, in spite of relatively high interindividual stability in children's ways of coping over time (Skinner & Edge, in press; Skinner & Snyder, 1999). Parent reports of parenting also predicted children's ways of coping; an especially strong connection was found between coercive parenting and children's oppositional coping in school (Skinner & Snyder, 1999).

Reciprocal feedback effects were also examined, in which children's coping was used to predict changes in parenting over the school year. As expected, children's ways of coping in the fall were significant predictors of changes in their experiences of parent action from fall to spring. Children who showed more accommodative coping in the fall experienced their parents as becoming more autonomy supportive from fall to spring of the school year, whereas children who coped through opposition reported that their parents became more coercive over the same time period (Skinner & Edge, in press).

Recent analyses are examining the relations between different styles of self-regulation (external, introjected, identified, and intrinsic) and different ways of coping in school. Analyses focused on the four ways of emotion regulation as markers of the four families of coping, with accepting responsibility as a marker of accommodation, blamelessness as a marker of negotiation, self-blame as a marker of perseveration, and projection as a marker of opposition (see Skinner & Wellborn, 1994, 1997, for a more detailed discussion of regulation of emotion and ways of coping). We found that, as predicted, accommodation and negotiation coping were both correlated positively with the two more autonomous forms of regulation, namely, identified and intrinsic regulation. The nonautonomous ways of coping were, as predicted, correlated with the nonautonomous regulatory styles: Perseveration was strongly related to an introjected style of regulation and opposition was correlated with external regulation.

A final set of analyses examined the effects of perceived autonomy on each way of coping, over and above the effects of perceived competence and relatedness. For each way of coping, perceived competence and relatedness were entered as a block, and then the designated style of self-regulation was entered. Of interest was whether perceived autonomy significantly increased the prediction of its way of coping. For all four ways of coping, perceived autonomy did make a significant unique contribution to its way of coping over and above the (significant) effects of the other self-system processes. The results of these analyses provide initial empirical support for the connections among perceived autonomy, autonomy support, and coping suggested by the motivational model. The data were consistent with the notion that parental autonomy support contributes to children's academic autonomy orientations, which in turn shapes how they cope with challenges and problems in school; as well as the possibility that the ways in which children cope have a reciprocal effect on how their parents deal with them.

The Functions of Autonomy During Actual Stressful Episodes

What does the model's definition of coping, namely, action regulation under stress, imply about the functions of autonomy and autonomy support during interactions when people are distressed? The model suggests that autonomy, like the other self-system processes, can supply key motivational resources in times of stress, acting as a source of energy and direction for behavior, emotion, and orientation. When people have access to motivational resources, the regulation of their action is more adaptive, by which we mean more organized and coherent, more flexible and open to internal and external information, and more constructive and prosocial. This quality of regulation allows a course of action to be implemented which is effective in service of one's own genuine high priority goals and the high priority goals of important social partners, even when demands tax or exceed an individual's resources. (For reviews of the concept of regulation in coping, see Barrett & Campos, 1991; Block & Block, 1980; Carver & Scheier, 1998; Eisenberg, Fabes, & Guthrie, 1997; Rossman, 1992; Skinner, 1999).

In specific situations, adaptive self-system processes improve coping by reducing objective demands, by leading people to appraise stressful interactions as challenges, by triggering adaptive action tendencies, and by boosting the quality of their regulation. When maladaptive self-system processes are applied to a stressful interaction, they can undermine coping by increasing objective demands, by escalating the experience of threat, by triggering maladaptive action tendencies, or by interfering with regulatory efforts. In the following sections, we consider autonomy and autonomy support as potential motivational resources for coping.

Autonomy as an Asset or Liability during Actual Coping Episodes

During stressful interactions, the self-system processes connected to autonomy can serve as a source of energy and as a personal "compass." Perceived autonomy functions as a set of guides for potential action and as a source of energy for regulation. In general, a sense of autonomy allows individuals to maintain access to their genuine goals and preferences (basically convictions about the limits of what they will and will not do) as well as to maintain the expectation that interaction partners (including people, events, and institutions) respect those goals. Taken together, these contribute to the experience of having genuine choices. This capacity can be stabilizing during stressful transactions.

Appraisals and experiences of stress. As a first line of defense, a sense of autonomy shapes the experience of stress. When events or people actually are objectively coercive (that is, when they really are attempting to pressure an individual's actions), people with a sense of autonomy experience these events as *less* coercive. That is, they appraise them more as a challenge than as a threat to autonomy. This does not imply that they are unaware that events or social partners are exerting force. However, an autonomous orientation creates a kind of buffer around those events, within which the individual maintains the psychological space to willfully decide how to respond to external pressure. For example, he or she assumes that the forces are not acting malevolently but instead are acting out of their own high priority goals. The individual further assumes that, when social partners realize they are trespassing on the individual's rights, they will be willing to readjust their demands. In general, people who are high on autonomy tend to view coercive events, not as demands, but as "requests." Even when coerced, they are able to maintain the sense that there is a piece of themselves that is indomitable.

The buffering effects of an autonomous orientation can be contrasted with the amplifying effects of a nonautonomous head set. This general orientation, in which people have difficulty maintaining access to their own genuine goals and at the same time expect the social context to be intentionally coercive, makes stress more stressful. Even minor requests are experienced as demands and can create enormous intrapsychic pressure. All demands are escalated to imperatives and, as a result, the hierarchy of genuine preferences held by the self and by the external environment is disguised. With no psychological space to actively decide how to respond, the person can experience demands as overwhelming.

Action tendencies. Appraisals of events as challenges or threats to autonomy trigger corresponding action tendencies. The experience of demands as a challenge can lead to accommodation or to negotiation, depending on the extent to which the demands impinge on high priority goals, and it would not be unusual to move flexibly between these two action tendencies. In stressful situations, their effects are synergistically positive. Concession of low priority goals allows more resources to be devoted to the defense of high priority goals; more achievement of high priority goals allows more good will to be channeled into concession. Defense of high priority goals is unambivalent, and the self is less likely to feel threatened that it will be overrun by demands.

A sense of autonomy can be helpful even when people are (or anticipate being) forced into acting against their will. Processes of autonomy can keep these experiences of involuntary submission from becoming overwhelming by accepting constraints and re-exerting the will. The act of *deciding* to submit to painful medical procedures, or of *deciding* that a disability will not curb certain desired activities, or of *deciding* that a crime will not continue to exert coercive effects (e.g., by keeping one at home), are exertions of autonomy.

In contrast, the appraisal of events as threats to autonomy tends to trigger the action tendency of opposition. When this response is socially or personally unacceptable, it may be overridden by rigid compliance, in which intrapsychic pressures force the self to submit. Neither opposition nor perseveration are autonomous or volitional and they have synergistic negative effects. The pressure created by submission escalates the experience of coercion, which makes it more likely that an explosion will occur. The rigidity and non-responsiveness of these two forms of coping seal the individual off from communication with the external (or internal) world, for example, from signals that certain demands reflect high priorities and that others can be downgraded in importance. These forms of coping rob action of its flexibility, making it less likely that the true goals of the individual will be accomplished.

Energetic resources for regulation. By definition, coping regulations take place during interactions that tax or exceed a person's resources. Volitional models of self-regulation (e.g., H. Heckhausen, 1991; H. Heckhausen & Kuhl, 1985; Kuhl, 1986) point out that one effect of stress can be to block an individual's access to his or her own personal capacities (cognitive, motivational, volitional) for adaptive action. Access can be blocked by anything that uses up energetic resources, such as intense emotions, cognitive ruminations, competing action tendencies, or attentional distracters.

Perceived autonomy can aid in regulation by helping a person reestablish or maintain access to his or her own personal resources. It does so because coping that is self-determined requires fewer regulatory resources compared to nonautonomous forms of coping. This is true for two reasons. First, autonomous action tendencies originate from the true self and bring their own psychic energy.

During autonomous (intrinsic or integrated) regulation, in which the true self is experienced as the source of action, action tendencies (behaviors, emotions, and orientations) work in a synergistic fashion, and executive or ego energy is available for engagement without being used for self-awareness or conscious control (Kuhl, 1984).

Second, autonomous forms of coping, like accommodation and negotiation, are recognized by both the self and the social context as more adaptive. Hence, they are less likely to need to be intentionally regulated, that is, deflected or halted. For the most part, during stressful transactions, these action tendencies need only to be boosted, supported, or focused. Such boosting requires relatively few regulatory resources. However, even when these action tendencies do need to be regulated, it is relatively easy to do so, because they are flexible and open to new information.

In contrast, the action tendencies triggered by appraisals of stressful transactions as threats to autonomy require more regulatory resources. First, the expression of the action tendencies themselves involves intense affect. Specifically, perseveration includes intense anxiety, and opposition is characterized by intense anger. These emotions and their accompanying ruminations use up energetic resources, and block access to other cognitive and motivational processes. The force and focus of these nonautonomous action tendencies also interferes with the consideration of alternative, potentially more adaptive, action tendencies.

Second, action tendencies like perseveration and opposition, are likely to be viewed by the self and social partners as undesirable. Hence, they often become targets of regulation, that is, of active attempts to intentionally tone them down, or to contain and disguise them. These regulatory efforts are difficult because both perseveration and opposition are rigid and not particularly open to information from internal or external sources. As a result, the nonautonomous forms of coping require a great deal of energetic resources. It is common for a person to have to concentrate all his or her effort on derailing these action tendencies before the person even has the option of accessing their cognitive resources or consulting with themselves or others about alternative courses of action. The phrase "I was beside myself" is an apt description of the experience when a nonautonomous action tendency is in charge of coping.

Autonomy Support versus Coercion in Stressful Interactions

From the motivational model, shown in Figure 14-5, comes the idea that social contexts can promote (versus undermine) coping by the extent to which they bring warmth, structure, and autonomy support (versus hostility, chaos, and coercion) to stressful interactions. A common example of autonomy support during a stressful interaction is when a parent validates a child's feelings. Simply by accurately acknowledging a child's experience, for example, during a painful medical procedure or during a child's adjustment to a new context, a parent may reduce the child's distress enough that the child has access to energetic resources sufficient to successfully regulate his or her own action tendencies (e.g., emotional upset or the desire to leave or resist).

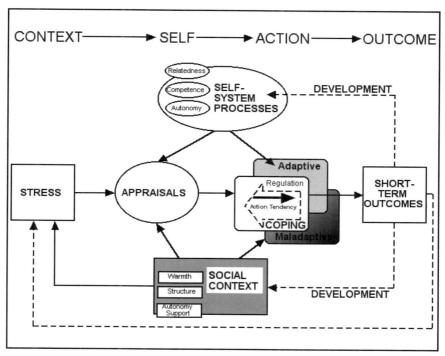

Figure 14.5. A Process Model of Coping.

When social partners add motivational resources to an interaction, they improve coping through precisely the same means as does the person, that is, by reducing demands, by promoting appraisals of challenge, and by helping the person maintain or gain access to personal resources for regulation. Social partners can reduce coercion by creating or negotiating some breathing room around a stressful event for more active decision-making. Social partners can promote appraisals that acknowledge the target person's true feelings and experiences and that are not judgmental or prescriptive about reactions to stress. They can remind or reflect on the person's own goal hierarchy and help distinguish high from low priority goals.

During coping, social partners who wish to support autonomy can actively encourage selective and choiceful concession and negotiation. Concession can be facilitated by pointing out the reasons for going along and by highlighting the connection between current cooperation and long-term goals. Social partners can support "negotiation" even with seemingly fixed events, such as disability or disease, essentially helping people distinguish the actions that must be conceded from the goals which can still be met. Especially useful may be helping people untangle higher-order goals from their lower-order instantiation. For example, even if walking is no longer possible, people may still be able to be mobile, independent, and social. Or, even if biological children are not an option, people can still have a role in nurturing the young.

Unfortunately, social contexts can also bring coercion to stressful transactions, thereby interfering with adaptive coping. People can insist that there is only one correct course of action or can demand certain reactions to events. Social partners can add coercion by falling apart themselves and demanding care from the target individual. Social contexts can influence appraisals, for example, by emphasizing the coercive features of the experience or by focusing on the negative consequences of noncompliance. They can help trigger maladaptive action tendencies. For example, when social partners become demanding, the person may begin to feel coerced and become angry and oppositional. These competing action tendencies interfere with regulation.

Autonomy as a Quality of Regulatory Capacity and of Relationships

People's self-system processes and social relationships shape their coping, both in specific situations and cumulatively over time. At the same time, however, coping feeds back into these processes. A primary function of constructive coping episodes is to provide opportunities for the development of adaptive self-system processes and social relationships. These function as short-term personal and social resources for coping. These resources, because they propel and sustain constructive engagement with the social and physical environment, contribute to the development of people's long-term coping capacity and to the qualities of their relationships.

Development of autonomy. In terms of autonomy, an important function of dealing constructively with adversity is allowing people to discover and elaborate their "true selves" and to learn how to articulate, coordinate, and defend the life values that are genuinely important to them. More specifically, stressful situations, in which all desired goals are not available, are opportunities to learn about the self and about priorities. Losses can lead to the realization of what is really important. Adversity may inspire people to create and maintain a course of action that is more congruent with their genuine desires and preferences. They may become less interested in societal or other external definitions of success and more resolved to build a life congruent with their own values and priorities.

Challenges provide opportunities for the development of capacities needed to exercise autonomy. These can be recognized in childhood as the development of autonomous regulation (Ryan, 1993) or conscience (Kochanska, 1993). These capacities suggest that prosocial goals and habits of effectiveness have been harmoniously integrated into the value hierarchy of the self. These capacities not only facilitate social relationships and achievements; they are also the basis from which children learn to "deploy themselves" in service of their own goals (Kuhl & Fuhrmann, 1998). These capacities continue to develop throughout the lifespan (Brandtstädter et al., 1999). They include the construction of rich and flexible goal hierarchies, the ability to make choices that are in one's own genuine self-interest, and to be steadfast in following paths that allow one to realize one's own goals.

Autonomous relationships. Processes of concession and negotiation during constructive coping also contribute to the development of mutually autonomous relationships (Butzel & Ryan, 1997). Identification of high-priority goals is a process of discovery, not only about the self, but about the social context as well. Within constructive social interactions, these processes allow people to identify goals that are commonly shared as well as goals that diverge. Mutual respect for divergent goals creates an atmosphere in which problem-solving can ensue to coordinate or sequence multiple goals. Autonomous concession of less important goals creates good will in social partners which can then motivate complementary concessions from the other person. Creation of genuine goal hierarchies for dyads, families, groups, or institutions provides a solid base for autonomous joint decision-making during stress.

These relationship qualities also allow dyads and social groups to be differentially constructive and flexible in stressful situations. Adaptive dyads (or social groups) are ones that can work together to articulate what each member really wants in an interaction and can generate several effective strategies that allow high-priority goals to be met. When dyads or groups are characterized by a history of rigid rule following or one-sided authority, adaptive action in the face of stress is blocked. Relationship qualities reflect a history of experiences that shape the self-systems of all participants, and so contribute to appraisals of each others' intentions (for example, as genuine vs. manipulative) and trigger adaptive or maladaptive joint action tendencies (such as cooperation vs. power struggles). These appraisals and action tendencies can facilitate or constrain adaptive coping when people are distressed.

Conclusions

The goal of this chapter was to make a case for the centrality of self-determination to coping. We argue that constructs, principles, and assessments of autonomy can contribute to the conceptualization and empirical study of many facets of the coping process. Autonomy-related concepts can be used to explain why certain classes of events are stressful, to identify ways of coping that have been largely ignored up to now, to describe a set of personal and social resources that support coping, to suggest mechanisms by which the self and social partners can promote or hinder coping in moment-to-moment stressful transactions, and to characterize the kinds of regulatory capacities and social relationships that both shape and are shaped by coping episodes.

Adding autonomy to research on coping processes should complement, without detracting from, the personal and social resources emphasized in work on perceived control, social support, and attachment. Beyond their additive effects, however, theories of self-determination can help create a platform from which to reconsider issues faced by the field of coping as a whole. In closing, we mention three, namely, intentionality in coping, secondary control, and the adaptiveness of approach versus avoidance coping.

Intentionality in coping. Theories of self-determination, because they focus on the will, bring the questions and terminology of volition to conceptualizations of coping (Skinner, 1999). Some theorists have suggested that only stress reactions with certain qualities of volition qualify as coping. For example, Compas et al. (1997) have argued that only effortful and voluntary reactions to stress should be considered coping and they have classified certain ways of coping according to such criteria.

Theories of self-determination and volition make clear that no action (and by implication, no way of coping) can be classified *a priori* as effortful or voluntary. Most actions (except reflexes) are available to many different levels of volition, for example, automatic action tendencies, effortful action regulation, intentional action regulation, and autonomous regulation. Such dimensions may be useful for distinguishing *within* a family of action tendencies or coping categories. However, voluntary versus involuntary is not a good dimension for distinguishing *between* ways of coping and so is not useful as a higher-order dimension upon which to build taxonomies of coping.

Secondary control. A whole set of processes by which people come to terms with losses have entered the fields of control and coping under the label of "secondary control." Originally described by Rothbaum, Weisz, and Snyder (1982) and recently elaborated by J. Heckhausen and Schulz (1995), these processes are contrasted with primary control, which refers to active attempts to change the state of the world in line with one's wishes. Secondary control, which refers to attempts to bring oneself in line with the state of the world, consists mostly of psychological processes that promote constructive disengagement from goals that are no longer attainable. When looked at from the perspective of control, these are considered "secondary," and recent discussions have emphasized the evolutionary and adaptive primacy of primary control (J. Heckhausen & Schulz, 1994). Indeed, experiences of primary control are necessary for the development of a sense of competence and control and for the capacity to implement effective action.

Nevertheless, we argue that, although processes described as secondary control are useful in dealing with loss of control, that is not their most important function. When the criteria of *effective* action is broadened to focus instead on *adaptive* action, then it becomes clear that "secondary control" processes are actually *primary* in the service of autonomy. They refer to processes by which goals, intentions, and plans are constructed and revised. Lack of controllability is one condition which requires reconsideration of goal pursuit, but it is only one condition. People can disengage from goals that are objectively attainable because they are too costly, because they interfere with one's own higher-priority goals, or because they compromise the interests of other people or groups.

These processes are better referred to using terms such as "flexible goal pursuit," "accommodation" (Brandtstädter & Renner, 1990), or autonomous regulation (Deci & Ryan, 1985b). The term "secondary control" is misleading; it represents a myopic focus on control and obscures the connection between these processes and autonomy. It is noteworthy that recently developed measures of "assimilation" (primary control) and accommodation find them to be independent constructs, and further find that the negative pole of assimilation is helplessness, whereas the negative pole of accommodation is "rigid perseveration" (Brandtstädter & Renner, 1990). It is also interesting that studies examining the effects of secondary control have used measures of accommodation to tap these processes (J. Heckhausen, 1997).

Approach versus avoidance coping. Discussions of overarching dimensions of coping have long included debates about whether, in times of stress, it is better to approach or avoid stressful transactions (Roth & Cohen, 1986). Although most discussions conclude that both strategies are important, at least in theory, the majority of studies find that approach coping is more adaptive, in the sense of showing stronger associations with positive antecedents and outcomes. A main reason for this finding is that approach coping usually consists of problem-solving and strategizing whereas avoidance coping usually refers to escape.

Work on autonomy emphasizes that both engagement and disengagement, just like concession and defense, can be adaptive or maladaptive depending on the qualities with which they are implemented. Perseveration as a form of rigid engagement is a kind of approach coping, but it is not adaptive. Autonomously deciding to relinquish certain goals is a form of avoidance coping that is also adaptive, in that it frees up resources for higher priority or attainable goals. This analysis implies that it is not approach or avoidance *per se* that makes the coping more or less adaptive. Instead it is the extent to which the patterns of action are flexible, organized, and constructive.

In sum, many researchers working in the area of coping have pointed out the need for conceptualizations and studies of coping that reflect the depth and complexity of adaptive processes (Compas, 1998; Lazarus, 1993). Theories of perceived control, attachment, and social support have brought important insights and assessments to research on coping. The central thesis of this chapter is that the large body of theory and research on self-determination can further enrich work on coping. As integrated and organized by the motivational model, these theories view the self and its social relationships as key assets or liabilities during coping, shaping appraisals, action tendencies, and patterns of regulation during stressful transactions with the social and physical environments.

The model points out, however, that coping is not just the beneficiary of relatedness, competence, and autonomy. At the same time, coping is also a catalyst critical to their development. Patterns of coping, like negotiation and opposition, elicit reactions from the context that set in motion cycles of person-context interactions, which shape the self-system beliefs and social relationships which gave rise to them. Cumulatively, and over time, these processes of interaction contribute to cycles of coping and context reactions that promote (or undermine) the development of regulatory capacities and relationship qualities. We hope that some of the arguments presented in this chapter may encourage researchers to pursue the study of the dynamics among self-determination, coping, and development.

References

Ainsworth, M. D. S. (1979). Infant-mother attachment. *American Psychologist, 34,* 932-937.

Armsden, C. C., & Greenberg, M. T. (1987). The inventory of parent and peer attachment: Individual differences and their relationship to psychological well-being in adolescence. *Journal of Youth and Adolescence, 16,* 427-454.

Averill, J. R. (1973). Personal control over aversive stimuli and its relationship to stress. *Psychological Bulletin, 80*(4), 286-303.

Baldwin, M. W. (1992). Relational schemas and the processing of social information. *Psychological Bulletin, 112*(461-484).

Band, E. B., & Weisz, J. R. (1988). How to feel better when it feels bad: Children's perspectives on coping with everyday stress. *Developmental Psychology, 24,* 247-253.

Bandura, A. (1981). Self-referent thought: A developmental analysis of self-efficacy. In J. H. Flavell & L. Ross (Eds.), *Social cognitive development: Frontiers and possible futures* (pp. 200-239). Cambridge, UK: Cambridge University Press.

Bandura, A. (1997). *Self-efficacy: The exercise of control.* New York: Freeman.

Barber, B. K. (1996). Parental psychological control: Revisiting a neglected construct. *Child Development, 67,* 3296-3319.

Barrett, K. C., & Campos, J. J. (1991). A diacritical function approach to emotions and coping. In E. M. Cummings, A. L. Greene, & K. H. Karraker (Eds.) *Lifespan developmental psychology: Perspectives on stress and coping* (pp. 21-41). Hillsdale, NJ: Erlbaum.

Baumeister, R. F., & Leary, M. R. (1995). The need to belong: Desire for interpersonal attachments as a fundamental human motivation. *Psychological Bulletin, 117,* 497-529.

Baumrind, D. (1971). Current patterns of parental authority. *Developmental Psychology Monographs, 4,* (Serial No. 1, Pt. 2), 1-102.

Baumrind, D. (1977). *Socialization determinants of personal agency.* Paper presented at the Biennial Meeting of the Society for Research in Child Development, New Orleans.

Block, J. H., & Block, J. (1980). The role of ego-control and ego-resiliency in the organization of behavior. In W. A. Collins (Ed.), *Minnesota Symposium on Child Psychology: Vol. 13. Development of cognition, affect, and social relations* (pp. 39-101). Hillsdale, NJ: Erlbaum.

Bonanno, G. A., & Kaltman, S. (1999). Toward an integrative perspective on bereavement. *Psychological Bulletin, 125*, 760-776.

Bowlby, J. (1969 and 1973). *Attachment and loss* (Vols. 1 and 2). New York: Basic Books.

Brandtstädter, J. (1999). Intentional self-development: Intentionality and action in development. In L. J. Crockett (Ed.), *Nebraska Symposium on Motivation: Motivation, agency, and the life course* (pp. xx-xx). Lincoln, NB: University of Nebraska Press.

Brandtstädter, J., & Renner, G. (1990). Tenacious goal pursuit and flexible goal adjustment: Explication and age-related analysis of assimilative and accommodative strategies of coping. *Psychology and Aging, 5*(1), 58-67.

Brandtstädter, J., Wentura, D., & Greve, W. (1993). Adaptive resources of the aging self: Outlines of an emergent perspective. *International Journal of Behavioral Development, 16*(2), 323-349.

Brandtstädter, J., Wentura, D., & Rothermund, K. (1999). Intentional self-development through adulthood and later life: Tenacious pursuit and flexible adjustment of goals. In J. Brandtstädter & R. M. Lerner (Eds.), *Action and self-development : Theory and research though the lifespan* (pp. 373-400). Thousand Oaks, CA: Sage.

Brehm, J. W. (1966). *A theory of psychological reactance.* San Diego, CA: Academic Press.

Bretherton, I. (1985). Attachment theory: Retrospect and prospect. In I. Bretherton & E. Waters (Eds.), Growing points in attachment theory and research. *Monographs of the Society for Research in Child Development, 50* (1-2, Serial No. 209).

Brickman, P., Rabinowitz, V. C., Karuza, J., Jr., Coates, D., Cohn, E., & Kidder, L. (1982). Models of helping and coping. *American Psychologist, 37*, 368-384.

Butzel, J. S., & Ryan, R. M. (1997). The dynamics of volitional reliance: A motivational perspective on dependence, independence, and social support. In G. R. Pierce, B. Lakey, I. G. Sarason, & B. R. Sarason (Eds.), *Sourcebook of social support and personality.* New York: Plenum Press.

Calkins, S. D. (1994) Origins and outcomes of individual differences in emotion regulation. In N. A. Fox (Ed.), *Monographs of the Society for Research in Child Development, 59*, 53-72.

Campos, J. J., Mumme, D. L., Kermoian, R., & Campos, R. G. (1994). A functionalist perspective on the nature of emotion. *Monographs of the Society for Research in Child Development, 59*, 284-303.

Carstensen, L. (1998). A lifespan approach to social motivation. In J. Heckhausen & C. Dweck (Eds.), *Motivation and self-regulation across the life span* (pp. 341 - 364). Cambridge, UK: Cambridge University Press.

Carton, J. S., & Nowicki, S. (1994). Antecedents of individual differences in locus of control of reinforcement: A critical review. *Genetic, Social, and General Psychology Monographs, 120*, 31- 81.

Carver, C. S., & Scheier, M. F. (1998). *On the self-regulation of behavior.* Cambridge, UK: Cambridge University Press.

Cohen, S., Sherrod, D. R., & Clark, M. S. (1986). Social skills and the stress-protective role of social support. *Journal of Personality and Social Psychology, 50*, 963-973.

Compas, B. E. (1987). Coping with stress during childhood and adolescence. *Psychological Bulletin, 101*, 393-403.

Compas, B. E. (1993, April). *An analysis of "good" stress and coping in adolescence.* Paper presented at the 60th meeting of the Society for Research in Child Development, New Orleans.

Compas, B. E. (1998). An agenda for coping research and theory: Basic and applied developmental issues. *International Journal of Behavioral Development, 22,* 231-237.

Compas, B. E., Banez, G. A., Malcarne, V., & Worsham, N. (1991). Perceived control and coping with stress: A developmental perspective. *Journal of Social Issues, 47*(4), 23-34.

Compas, B. E., Connor, J., Osowiecki, D., & Welch, A. (1997). Effortful and involuntary responses to stress: Implications for coping with chronic stress. In B. J. Gottlieb (Ed.), *Coping with chronic stress.* New York: Plenum Press.

Connell, J. P. (1990). Context, self, and action: A motivational analysis of self-system processes across the lifespan. In D. Cicchetti & M. Beeghly (Eds.), *The self in transition: From infancy to childhood* (pp. 61-97). Chicago: University of Chicago Press.

Connell, J. P., & Wellborn, J. G. (1991). Competence, autonomy and relatedness: A motivational analysis of self-system processes. In M. Gunnar & L. A. Sroufe (Eds.), *Minnesota Symposium on Child Psychology* (Vol. 23, pp. 43-77). Chicago: University of Chicago Press.

deCharms, R. (1968). *Personal causation.* New York: Academic Press.

deCharms, R. (1981). Personal causation and locus of control: Two different traditions and two uncorrelated constructs. In H. Lefcourt (Ed.), *Research with the locus of control construct, Vol. 1.* (pp. 337-358). San Diego, CA: Academic Press.

Deci, E. L., Eghrari, H., Patrick, B. C., & Leone, D. R. (1994). Facilitating internalization: The self-determination theory perspective. *Journal of Personality, 62,* 119-142.

Deci, E. L., Koestner, R., & Ryan, R. M. (1999). A meta-analytic review of experiments examining the effects of extrinsic rewards on intrinsic motivation. *Psychological Bulletin, 125,* 627-668.

Deci, E. L., & Ryan, R. M. (1985a). The general causality orientation scale: Self-determination in personality. *Journal of Research in Personality, 19,* 109-134.

Deci, E. L., & Ryan, R. M. (1985b). *Intrinsic motivation and self-determination in human behavior.* New York: Plenum Press.

Deci, E. L., & Ryan, R. M. (1987). The support of autonomy and the control of behavior. *Journal of Personality and Social Psychology, 53,* 1024-1037.

Deci, E. L., & Ryan, R. M. (1991). A motivational approach to self: Integration in personality. In R. Dienstbier (Ed.), *Nebraska Symposium on Motivation: Vol. 38. Perspectives on motivation* (pp. 237-288). Lincoln: University of Nebraska Press.

Deci, E. L., & Ryan, R. M. (1995). Human autonomy: The basis for true self-esteem. In M. Kernis (Ed.), *Efficacy, agency, and self-esteem* (pp. 31-49). New York: Plenum.

Deci, E. L., & Ryan, R. M. (2000). The "what" and "why" of goal pursuits: Human needs and the self-determination of behavior. *Psychological Inquiry, 11,* 227-268.

Deci, E. L., Spiegel, N. H., Ryan, R. M., Koestner, R., & Kauffman, M. (1982). Effects of performance standards on teaching styles: Behavior of controlling teachers. *Journal of Educational Psychology, 74,* 852-859.

Dodge, K. A. (1991). Emotion and social information processing. In J. Garber & K. Dodge (Eds.), *The development of emotion regulation and dysregulation* (pp. 177-181). New York: Cambridge University Press.

Dweck, C. S. (1991). Self-theories and goals: Their role in motivation, personality, and development. In R. A. Dienstbier (Ed.), *Perspectives on motivation: Nebraska Symposium on Motivation* (Vol. 38). Lincoln: University of Nebraska Press.

Dweck, C. S. (1999). *Self-theories: Their role in motivation, personality, and development.* Philadelphia, PA: Psychology Press.

Dweck, C. S., & Leggett, E. L. (1988). A social-cognitive approach to motivation and personality. *Psychological Review, 95,* 256-273.

Dweck, C. S., & Wortman, C. B. (1982). Learned helplessness, anxiety, and achievement motivation: Neglected parallels in cognitive, affective, and coping responses. In H. W. Krohne & L. Laux (Eds.), *Achievement, stress, and anxiety* (pp. 93-125). New York: Hemisphere Publishing.

Eisenberg, N. Fabes, R. A., & Guthrie, I. (1997). Coping with stress: The roles of regulation and development. In S. A. Wolchik & I. N. Sandler (Eds.), *Handbook of children's coping : Linking theory, research , and intervention* (pp. 41-70). New York: Plenum Press.

Flammer, A. (1995). Developmental analysis of control beliefs. In A. Bandura (Ed.), *Self-efficacy in changing societies* (pp. 69-113). New York: Cambridge University Press.

Folkman, S. (1984). Personal control and stress and coping processes: A theoretical analysis. *Journal of Personality and Social Psychology, 46*(4), 839-852.

Forsythe, C. J., & Compas, B. E. (1987). Interaction of cognitive appraisals of stressful events and coping: Testing the goodness of fit hypothesis. *Cognitive Therapy and Research, 11*(4), 473-485.

Fridja, N. H. (1987). Emotions, cognitive structure, and action tendency. *Cognition and Emotion, 1,* 115-144.

Fridja, N. H. (1988). The laws of emotion. *American Psychologist, 43,* 349-358.

Graham, S. (1998). Social motivation and perceived responsibility in others: Attributions and behaviors of African-American boys. In J. Heckhausen & C. Dweck (Eds.), *Motivation and self-regulation across the life span* (pp. 137-158). Cambridge, UK: Cambridge University Press.

Graham, S., Hudley, C., & Williams, E. (1992). Attributional and emotional determinants of aggression among African American and Latino early adolescents. *Developmental Psychology, 31,* 274-284.

Grolnick, W. S., & Ryan, R. M. (1989). Parent styles associated with children's self-regulation and competence: A social contextual perspective. *Journal of Educational Psychology, 81,* 143-154.

Gunnar, M. R. (1980). Contingent stimulation: A review of its role in early development. In S. Levine & H. Ursin (Eds.), *Coping and health* (pp. 101-119). New York: Plenum.

Harter, S. (1978). Effectance motivation reconsidered: Toward a developmental model. *Human Development, 21,* 36-64.

Heckhausen, H. (1991). *Motivation and action* (Peter K. Leppmann, Trans.). Berlin: Springer-Verlag.

Heckhausen, H., & Kuhl, J. (1985). From wishes to action: The dead ends and short cuts on the long way to action. In M. Frese & J. Sabini (Eds.), *Goal-directed behavior: Psychological theory and research on action* (pp. 134-160). Hillsdale, NJ: Erlbaum.

Heckhausen, J. (1997). Developmental regulation across adulthood: Primary and secondary control of age-related challenges. *Developmental Psychology, 33,* 176-187.

Heckhausen, J., & Schulz, R. (1994). *Primacy of primary control as a universal feature of human behavior.* Paper presented at the 13th Biennial Meeting of the International society for the Study of Behavioural Development, Amsterdam.

Heckhausen, J., & Schulz, R. (1995). A lifespan theory of control. *Psychological Review, 102,* 284-304.

Kamins, M. L., & Dweck, C. S. (1999). Person versus process praise and criticism: Implications for contingent self-worth and coping. *Developmental Psychology, 35,* 835-847.

Kasser, T., & Ryan, R. M. (1993). A dark side of the American dream: Correlates of financial success as a central life aspiration. *Journal of Personality and Social Psychology, 65,* 410-422.

Kliewer, W. (1991). Coping in middle childhood: Relations to competence, type a behavior, monitoring, blunting and locus of control. *Developmental Psychology, 27*(4), 689-697.

Kochanska, G. (1993). Toward a synthesis of parental socialization and child temperament in early development of conscience. *Child Development, 64,* 325-347.

Kochanska, G. (1995). Children's temperament, mother's discipline, and security of attachment: Multiple pathways to emerging internalization. *Child Development, 66,* 597-615.

Kochanska, G. (1997). Mutually responsive orientation between mothers and their young children: Implications for early socialization. *Child Development, 68,* 94-112.

Kochanska, G., & Aksan, N. (1995). Mother-child mutually positive affect, the quality of child compliance to requests and prohibitions, and maternal control as correlates of early internalization. *Child Development, 66,* 236-254.

Koestner, R., & McClelland, D. C. (1990). Perspectives on competence motivation. In L. A. Pervin (Ed.), *Handbook of personality: Theory and research* (pp. 527-548). New York: Guilford Press.

Kuhl, J. (1984). Volitional aspects of achievement motivation and learned helplessness: Toward a comprehensive theory of action control. In B. A. Maher & W. A. Maher (Eds.), *Progress in experimental personalities research* (pp. 99-171). New York: Academic Press.

Kuhl, J. (1986). Aging and models of control: The hidden costs of wisdom. In M. M. Baltes & P. B. Baltes (Eds.), *The psychology of control and aging* (pp. 1-33). Hillsdale, NJ: Erlbaum.

Kuhl, J. (1987). Action control: The maintenance of motivational states. In F. Halisch & J. Kuhl (Eds.), *Motivation, intention, and volition* (pp. 279-291). New York: Springer

Kuhl, J., & Fuhrmann, A. (1998). Decomposing self-regulation and self-control: The Volitional Components Inventory. In J. Heckhausen & C. S. Dweck (Eds.), *Motivation and self-regulation across the life span* (pp. 15-49). Cambridge, UK: Cambridge University Press.

Lamb, M. E., & Easterbrooks, M. A. (1981). Individual differences in parental sensitivity: Some thoughts about origins, components, and consequences. In M. E. Lamb & L. R. Sherrod (Eds.), *Infant social cognition: Empirical and theoretical considerations* (pp. 127-153). Hillsdale, NJ: Erlbaum.

Lazarus, R. S. (1993). Coping theory and research: Past, present, and future. *Psychosomatic Medicine, 55,* 234-247.

Lazarus, R. S., & Folkman, S. (1984). *Stress, appraisal, and coping.* New York: Springer.

Lepore, S. J. (1992). Social conflict, social support, and psychological distress: Evidence of cross-domain buffering effects. *Journal of Personality and Social Psychology, 63,* 857-867.

Metcalfe, J., & Mischel, W. (1999). A hot/cool-system analysis of delay of gratification: Dynamics of willpower. *Psychological Review, 106,* 3-19.

Miller, S. M. (1979). Controllability and human stress: Method, evidence and theory. *Behavior Research and Theory, 17,* 287-304.

Mueller, C. M., & Dweck, C. S. (1998). Praise for intelligence can undermine children's motivation and performance. *Journal of Personality and Social Psychology, 75,* 33-52.

Nachmias, M., Gunnar, M., Mangelsdorf, S., Parritz, R. H., & Buss, K. (1996). Behavioral inhibition and stress reactivity: The moderating role of attachment security. *Child Development, 67,* 508-522.

Nolen-Hoeksma, S. (1998). Ruminative coping with depression. In J. Heckhausen & C. S. Dweck (Eds.), *Motivation and self-regulation across the life span* (pp. 237-256). Cambridge, UK: Cambridge University Press.

Papousek, H., & Papousek, M. (1980). Early ontogeny of human social interaction: Its biological roots and social dimensions. In M. von Cranach, K. Foppa, W. Lepenies, & D. Ploog (Eds.), *Human ethology: Claims and limits of a new discipline*. Cambridge: Cambridge University Press.

Parpal, M., & Maccoby, E. E. (1985). Maternal responsiveness and subsequent child compliance. *Child Development, 56,* 1326-1334.

Patterson, G., & Bank, L. (1989). Some amplifying mechanisms for pathologic processes in families. In M. R. Gunnar & E. Thelen (Eds.), *Systems and development. The Minnesota Symposium on Child Psychology, (Vol. 22)* (pp. 167-209). Hillsdale, NJ: Erlbaum.

Peterson, C., Maier, S. F., & Seligman, M. E. P. (1993). *Learned helplessness: A theory for the age of personal control.* New York: Oxford University Press.

Pierce, G. R., Sarason, B. R., & Sarason, I. G. (1991). General and relationship-based perceptions of social support: Are two constructs better than one? *Journal of Personality and Social Psychology, 61,* 1028-1039.

Pierce, G. R., Sarason, B. R., & Sarason, I. G. (Eds.) (1996). *Handbook of social support and the family.* New York: Plenum Press.

Reeve, J., Bolt, E., & Cai, Y. (1999). Autonomy supportive teachers: How they teach and motivate students. *Journal of Educational Psychology, 91,* 537-548.

Reis, H. T., & Franks, P. (1994). The role of intimacy and social support in health outcomes: Two processes or one? *Personal Relationships, 1,* 185-197.

Rossman, B. B. R. (1992). School-aged children's perceptions of coping with distress: Strategies for emotion regulation and the moderation of adjustment. *Journal of Child Psychiatry, 33,* 1373-1397.

Roth, S. & Cohen, L. (1986). Approach, avoidance, and coping with stress. *American Psychologist, 41,* 813-819.

Rothbaum, F., Weisz, J. R., & Snyder, S. S. (1982). Changing the world and changing the self: A two-process model of perceived control. *Journal of Personality and Social Psychology, 42*(1), 5-37.

Rutter, M. (1979). Maternal deprivation. *Child Development, 50,* 283-294.

Ryan, R. M. (1982). Control and information in the intrapersonal sphere: An extension of cognitive evaluation theory. *Journal of Personality and Social Psychology, 43,* 450-461.

Ryan, R. M. (1993). Agency and organization: Intrinsic motivation, autonomy and the self in psychological development. IN J. Jacobs (Ed.), *Nebraska symposium on motivation: Developmental perspectives on motivation, Vol. 40* (pp. 1-56). Lincoln: University of Nebraska Press.

Ryan, R. M., & Connell, J. P. (1989). Perceived locus of causality and internalization: Examining reasons for acting in two domains. *Journal of Personality and Social Psychology, 57,* 749-761.

Ryan, R. M., & Solky, J. A. (1996). What is supportive about social support? On the psychological needs for autonomy and relatedness. In G. R. Pierce, B. R. Sarason, & I. G. Sarason (Eds.), *Handbook of social support and the family* (pp. 249-267). New York: Plenum Press.

Ryan-Wenger, N. M. (1992). A taxonomy of children's coping strategies: A step toward theory development. *American Journal of Orthopsychiatry, 62,* 256-263.

Sarason, B. R., Pierce, G. R., Shearin, E. N., Sarason, I. G., Waltz, J. A., & Poppe, L. (1991). Perceived social support and working models of self and actual others. *Journal of Personality and Social Psychology, 60,* 273-287.

Schneewind, K. A. (1995). Impact of family processes on control beliefs. In A. Bandura (Ed.), *Self-efficacy in changing societies* (pp. 114-148). New York: Cambridge University Press.

Seligman, M. E. P. (1975). *Helplessness: On depression, development, and death.* San Francisco: Freeman.

Shulman, S. (1987). Adolescent coping style as a function of perceived family climate. *Journal of Adolescent Research,, 2,* 367-381.

Skinner, E. A. (1991). Development and perceived control: A dynamic model of action in context. In M. Gunnar & L. A. Sroufe (Eds.), *Minnesota Symposium on Child Psychology* (Vol. 23, pp. 167-216). Hillsdale, NJ: Erlbaum.

Skinner, E. A. (1995). *Perceived control, motivation, and coping.* Newbury Park, CA: Sage Publications.

Skinner, E. A. (1996). A guide to constructs of control. *Journal of Personality and Social Psychology, 71,* 549 -570.

Skinner, E. A. (1999). Action regulation, coping, and development. In J. Brandtstadter & R. M. Lerner (Eds.), *Action and self-development: Theory and research through the lifespan* (pp. 465-503). Thousands Oaks, CA: Sage.

Skinner, E. A., Altman, J., & Sherwood, H. (1991, July). *An analysis of open-ended interview of children's coping in the domains of academics and friendship.* Paper presented at the Biennial Meetings of the International Society for the Study of Behavioral Development. Minneapolis, MN.

Skinner, E. A., & Edge, K. (1998). Reflections on coping and development across the lifespan. *International Journal for the Study of Behavioral Development, 22,* 357-366.

Skinner, E. A., & Edge, K. (in press). Parenting, motivation, and the development of coping. In L. J. Crockett (Ed.), *Nebraska Symposium on Motivation: Motivation, agency, and the life course* (pp. xx-xx). Lincoln NB: University of Nebraska Press.

Skinner, E. A., Edge, K., Altman, J., & Sherwood, H. (2002). *Searching for the structure of coping.* Unpublished manuscript, Portland State University.

Skinner, E. A., & Regan, C. (1992). *Parenting sense of autonomy.* Technical Report, University of Rochester, Rochester, NY.

Skinner, E. A., & Snyder, T. (April 1999). *Parenting, motivation, and children's coping: Empirical analyses.* Poster presented at the Biennial Meetings of the Society for Research in Child Development, Albuquerque, NM.

Skinner, E. A., & Wellborn, J. G. (1994). Coping during childhood and adolescence: A motivational perspective. In D. Featherman, R. Lerner, & M. Perlmutter (Eds.) *Lifespan development and behavior,* Vol. 12 (pp. 91-133). Hillsdale, NJ: Erlbaum.

Skinner, E. A., & Wellborn, J. G. (1997). Children's coping in the academic domain. In S. A. Wolchik & I. N. Sandler (Eds.), *Handbook of children's coping with common stressors: Linking theory and intervention* (pp. 387 - 422). New York: Plenum Press.

Skinner, E. A., Zimmer-Gembeck, M. J., & Connell, J. P. (1998). Individual differences and the development of perceived control. In the *Monographs of the Society for Research in Child Development,* whole no. 204.

Stroebe, W., Stroebe, M., Abakoumkin, G., & Schut, H. (1996). The role of loneliness and social support in adjustment to loss: A test of attachment versus stress theory. *Journal of Personality and Social Psychology, 70,* 1241-1249.

Suomi, S. J. (1980). Contingency, perception, and social development. In L. R. Sherrod & M. E. Lamb (Eds.), *Infant social cognition: Empirical and theoretical considerations.* Hillsdale, N. J.: Erlbaum.

Tennen, H., & Affleck, G. (1990). Blaming others for threatening events. *Psychological Bulletin, 108,* 209-232.

Vallerand, R. J., Pelletier, L. G., Blais, M. R., Brière, N. M., Senécal, C., & Vallières, E. F. (1993). On the assessment of intrinsic, extrinsic, and amotivation in education: Evidence on the concurrent and construct validity of the Academic Motivation Scale. *Educational and Psychological Measurement, 53,* 159-172.

Watson, J. S. (1966). The development and generalization of "contingency awareness" in early infancy: Some hypotheses. *Merrill-Palmer Quarterly, 12,* 123-135.

Watson, J. S., & Ramey, C. T. (1972). Reactions to response-contingent stimulation in early infancy. *Merrill-Palmer Quarterly, 18,* 219-227.

Weiner, B. (1986). *An attributional theory of motivation and emotion.* New York: Springer-Verlag.

Weiner, B. (1991). Metaphors in motivation and attribution. *American Psychologist, 46*(9), 921-930.

Weisz, J. (1993, April). *An analysis of "good" stress and coping in middle childhood.* Paper presented at the 60th meeting of the Society for Research in Child Development, New Orleans.

Wellborn, J. G. (1991). *Engaged and disaffected action: The conceptualization and measurement of motivation in the academic domain.* Unpublished doctoral dissertation, University of Rochester, New York.

Wellborn, J. G., Mellor-Crummey, C. A., Connell, J. P., & Skinner, E. A. (1990, August). *A motivational perspective on children's coping in the academic and social domains.* Paper presented at the American Psychological Association, New Orleans, LA.

White, R. W. (1959). Motivation reconsidered: The concept of competence. *Psychological Review, 66,* 297-333.

Windle, M. (1992). Temperament and social support in adolescence: Interrelationships with depressive symptoms and delinquent behaviors. *Journal of Youth and Adolescence, 21,* 1-21.

Zeedyk, M. S. (1996). Developmental accounts of intentionality: Toward integration. *Developmental Review, 16,* 416-461.

15: Distinguishing Between Secure and Fragile Forms of High Self-Esteem

Michael H. Kernis[1]
Andrew W. Paradise
University of Georgia

To have high self-esteem is a good thing. Until recently, this simple assertion has gone virtually unchallenged. After all, what could be bad about liking oneself and feeling like a valuable and worthwhile individual? Although it is highly appealing to characterize high self-esteem in unequivocally positive terms, recent theory and evidence suggest that this characterization is not necessarily true. In fact, there appear to be multiple forms of high self-esteem that vary in how closely they mirror healthy, optimal psychological functioning. In this chapter, we distinguish among these various forms of high self-esteem and describe their implications for mental health and well-being. In so doing, we draw on a number of constructs and insights offered by Self-Determination Theory (e.g., Deci & Ryan, 1985; 1987; 1991; 1995; Ryan, 1993).

Contrasting Perspectives on The Essence of High Self-Esteem

Currently, there exist two broad perspectives on what it means to possess high self-esteem. One perspective characterizes high self-esteem as reflecting positive feelings of self-worth that are well-anchored and secure, and that are positively associated with a wide range of psychological health and well-being indices. Its roots lie in the writings and research of clinical and personality psychologists with humanistic inclinations (e.g., Rogers, 1951; 1959). From this vantage point, high self-esteem individuals are people who like, value, and accept themselves, "warts and all." They do not feel a need to be superior to others, but instead are satisfied with being on an "equal plane with others" (Rosenberg,

1. Preparation of this chapter and a portion of the research reported herein were supported by a grant from the National Science Foundation (SBR-9618882).

1965). Attempts to bolster their feelings of worth through self-promoting or self-protective strategies are rare, given that their feelings of self-worth are not easily challenged. In other words, they typically experience everyday positive and negative outcomes in ways that do not implicate their global feelings of worth or value. Throughout this chapter, we refer to this perspective as describing *secure* high self-esteem.

The other, contrasting, perspective characterizes high self-esteem as reflecting positive feelings of self-worth that seemingly are fragile and vulnerable to threat, inasmuch as they are associated with many different types of self-protective or self-enhancement strategies. We refer to this perspective as describing *fragile* high self-esteem. Although this type of high self-esteem has been recognized for some time (e.g., Horney, 1950), empirical support for it has been accumulating only relatively recently. For example, research has shown that high self-esteem individuals may take great pride in their successes ("I am brilliant"), yet deny any involvement in their failures ("That test was stupid") (Fitch, 1970), that they derogate individuals who pose threats to their (or their group's) sense of value and worth (Crocker, Thompson, McGraw, & Ingermane, 1987), and that they create obstacles to successful performance so that their competencies will seem especially noteworthy should they subsequently succeed anyway (Tice, 1991). Some researchers have taken findings such as these to mean that high self-esteem individuals are especially caught up in how they feel about themselves and that they will do whatever it takes to bolster, maintain, and enhance these self-feelings. In fact, a few researchers appear to have dismissed the existence of *secure* high self-esteem (e.g., Baumeister, Tice, & Hutton, 1989), claiming instead that high self-esteem reflects an aggressively self-enhancing presentational style.

We take exception to this dismissal and instead argue that both *secure* and *fragile* high self-esteem exist. To acknowledge their existence, however, raises the thorny issue of how to determine which form is operative. Traditional measures of self-esteem by themselves are not particularly helpful in this regard. Take, for example, Rosenberg's (1965) Self-esteem Scale, one of the most widely used and well-validated measures of self-esteem (Blascovich & Tomaka, 1991). Respondents indicate their extent of agreement to such statements as: "I feel that I have a number of good qualities"; "I feel that I am a person of worth, at least on an equal basis with others;" "I feel that I do not have much to be proud of" (reverse scored). High self-esteem is reflected by strong agreement to the first two items and strong disagreement to the last one. However, based on these responses alone, there is no way to know if the person's high self-esteem is *secure* or *fragile*. Additional factors must be taken into account. In fact, recent theory and evidence suggest that there are at least four different ways to distinguish between *secure* and *fragile* high self-esteem. Each of these ways relies on theoretical concepts that focus on distinctions between various kinds of self-esteem. The remainder of this chapter is devoted to describing these theoretical concepts and the implications they have for distinguishing secure from fragile high self-esteem. We present relevant empirical work as well, much of which is very recent.

Is the Person Lying?

One way to distinguish *secure* from *fragile* high self-esteem is to determine whether respondents misrepresented their self-feelings when completing the self-esteem measure. Some people, out of immense dires to be accepted by others, are unwilling to admit to possessing negative self-feelings. These individuals are so afraid that others will reject them if they admit to the negative self-feelings they actually feel that they present their self-feelings positively (though falsely) on the self-esteem measure. Dubbed *defensive* high self-esteem (Horney, 1950; Schneider & Turkat, 1975), it is thought to trigger heightened efforts to undermine self-threatening information and to magnify the portrayal of personal strengths unrelated to the content of the threat (Schneider & Turkat, 1975). Qualities such as these suggest that *defensive* high self-esteem is one manifestation of *fragile* high self-esteem.

In contrast, *genuine* high self-esteem reflects the honest reporting of one's inner positive self-feelings. When confronted with threatening information, genuine high self-esteem individuals do not react particularly strongly, by, for example, magnifying the positivity of their other personal qualities. Without the strong concerns about social acceptance that characterize their defensive counterparts, genuine high self-esteem persons are less threatened by negative evaluative information. Genuine high self-esteem is thus considered one manifestation of *secure* high self-esteem.

Defensive and genuine high self-esteem traditionally have been distinguished by individuals' responses to measures of socially desirable responding (e.g., the Crowne-Marlowe Social Desirability Scale; Crowne & Marlowe, 1960). Socially desirable responding is the pervasive tendency to endorse as self-descriptive highly positive, yet extremely uncommon, statements pertaining to one's behaviors or attitudes, and to reject as self-descriptive distasteful, yet highly common, behavioral or attitudinal statements. High self-esteem coupled with a high social desirability score presumably reflects defensive high self-esteem given the person's pronounced unwillingness to admit to unflattering characteristics that he or she is likely to possess. In contrast, high self-esteem coupled with a low social desirability score presumably reflects genuine high self-esteem given that the person has shown little tendency to hide negative characteristics from others.

Though genuine and defensive high self-esteem are conceptually appealing constructs that have been around for over fifty years, they have not generated a large body of empirical findings. The research that does exist, however, has produced findings supporting the distinction (see for example, Schneider & Turkat, 1975). One potential direction for future research would be to isolate the implications for self-esteem processes of the self-deception and impression management components of socially desirable responding (Paulhus, 1991). For our present purposes, we merely point out that research and theory on the distinction between defensive and genuine high self-esteem suggest one way to distinguish *fragile* from *secure* forms of high self-esteem.

Do the Person's Conscious and Nonconscious Feelings of Self-Worth Match?

A second way to distinguish *secure* from *fragile* high self-esteem involves a consideration of both conscious and nonconscious feelings of self-worth. Specifically, some high self-esteem individuals may report favorable feelings of self-worth, yet simultaneously hold negative self-feelings that they are unaware of (rather than just being unwilling to report, as in defensive high self-esteem). The idea that people may possess feelings of self-worth of which they are not aware is also not a new one. However, it is only in recent years that it has received substantive attention, due in part to the advent of sophisticated methodologies that may have allowed for its examination.

Epstein and Morling (1995) discuss these dual self-esteem components within the framework of Cognitive Experiential Self Theory (CEST), which holds that people possess two separate, but interacting, psychological systems. One system, referred to as the cognitive or rational system, operates at the conscious level according to linguistic and logical principles. Explicit self-esteem resides in the cognitive/rational system, reflecting the feelings of self-worth that people are conscious of possessing. It can be measured by standard self-esteem scales like the Rosenberg measure. The second system, called the experiential system, operates at the nonconscious level, guided in large part by significant affective experiences and heuristic principles. Implicit self-esteem resides in the experiential system, reflecting feelings of self-worth that are nonconscious but that nonetheless can "seep through" to affect peoples' thoughts, emotions, and behaviors. Implicit self-esteem cannot be assessed by directly asking people how they feel about themselves.

Epstein and Morling suggest that when people possess high explicit self-esteem, but low implicit self-esteem, they will often react very defensively to potentially negative evaluative information. This prediction mirrors the one made for defensive high self-esteem individuals. Specifically, people who report high self-esteem, but who simultaneously hold low self-esteem that they are either unwilling (defensive) or unable (implicit) to admit to, are hypothesized to be easily threatened by negative self-relevant information. High explicit self-esteem that is coupled with low implicit self-esteem is *fragile* and so may relate to defensive and self-aggrandizing strategies even in the absence of explicit threat. In contrast, when explicit and implicit self-esteem both are favorable, one's high self-esteem is *secure*, making it less necessary to defend against real or imagined threats or to flaunt one's strengths.

A variety of approaches can be used to examine implicit self-esteem and its implications for psychological functioning. One approach developed by Greenwald and colleagues (e.g., Farnham, Greenwald, & Banaji, 1999) involves the use of reaction time methods to assess the strength of associative links between self defining terms and various positive and negative stimuli. The greater the relative strength of positive-self associations to negative-self associations, the higher one's implicit self-esteem (for a review of this work, see Farnham et al., 1999). An alternative approach is to situationally activate implicit self-esteem by exposing people to positive or negative self-esteem relevant stimuli (e.g., words such as worthless, capable, likeable, insecure) at speeds too fast to be consciously recognized. Abend, Kernis, and Hampton (2000) recently employed this strategy to examine whether discrepant explicit/implicit self-esteem increases self-serving responding among college students. In the first of two laboratory sessions, participants completed Rosenberg's (1965) self-esteem scale (explicit self-esteem) and a "background survey" in which they indicated whether or not a wide range of characteristics were self-descriptive (e.g., I have a close relationship with my mother; I have good social skills; I am a leader; I regularly read books for pleasure).

Approximately one to two weeks later, participants returned to the lab to perform several different tasks. The first task was described as a "visual perception task", but, in actuality, it was designed to situationally activate either positive or negative implicit self-esteem. Participants were seated in front of a computer screen, and a series of self-relevant words were flashed on the screen. The words were presented at a rate too fast to be read and were followed immediately by a mask of random letters. The participants' task was to indicate whether each flash appeared to the left or the right of a fixation point in the center of the screen (which consisted of the words " I AM"). Depending on the condition, the flashed self-relevant words were either all positive (e.g., capable, talented, likable, worthwhile) or all negative (e.g., cruel, insecure, worthless, inconsiderate). The positive ones were primes for high implicit self-esteem and the negative ones were primes for low implicit self-esteem. Following an intervening task, participants read a description of a fictitious college student and then rated the extent to which various attributes contributed to her successful graduation from college. These were the same attributes that participants had, during the earlier session, indicated were or were not self-descriptive. A measure of self-serving responding was created by computing the average importance rating of attributes for successful graduation that the participant previously deemed non-self-descriptive and subtracting it from the average importance rating given to self-descriptive attributes. Computed this way, higher scores reflect the self-serving judgment that successful college performance depends more on those attributes one possesses than on those attributes one does not possess. This task has been used to assess self-serving responses by Dunning and his colleagues in a number of studies (e.g., Dunning, Leuenberger, & Sherman, 1995).

As anticipated by Epstein and Morling's theorizing, self-serving responses were greater among those high self-esteem individuals who were presented with negative self-relevant words (high explicit/low implicit self-esteem) than among those who were presented with positive self-relevant words (high explicit/high implicit self-esteem). In other words, those representing high fragile self-esteem were more self serving that those representing high secure self-esteem. Interestingly, low explicit/high implicit self-esteem also related to more self-serving responses than did low explicit/low implicit self-esteem. To our knowledge, these findings represent the first demonstration that discrepant explicit/implicit self-esteem heightens self-serving responses. Although we are excited about their potential implications, much more work needs to be done. Still, they provide initial empirical support for the assertion that some instances of *fragile* high self-esteem may reflect high explicit self-esteem that coexists with low implicit self-esteem.

Is the Person's Self-esteem Dependent Upon Certain Outcomes?

To this point, we have not discussed insights that Self-Determination Theory (SDT) provides in distinguishing between *fragile* and *secure* high self-esteem. In this section, we begin to do so by focusing directly on Deci and Ryan's (1995) distinction between contingent and true high self-esteem. In their words, "Contingent self-esteem refers to feelings about oneself that result from — indeed, are dependent on — matching some standard of excellence or living up to some interpersonal or intrapsychic expectations (p. 32)." For someone with contingent high self-esteem, preoccupations with one's standings on specific evaluative dimensions (e.g., How smart am I?) and how one is viewed by others (Do people think I am attractive?), together with engaging in a continual process of setting and meeting evaluative standards for validational purposes, constitute the *sin qua non* of everyday life.

In other words, contingent self-esteem involves a highly ego-involved form of self-regulation in which one's behaviors and outcomes are linked directly to self- and other-based (dis)approval (Deci & Ryan, 1995). A poor performance is not merely a poor performance inasmuch as it is likely to trigger feelings of incompetence, shame, and worthlessness. Deci and Ryan pointed out that people with contingent high self-esteem will go to great lengths to avoid such painful experiences, even if it means distorting one's performance or derogating the source of negative feedback. Conversely, good performances validate contingent-high-self-esteem people's feelings of overall value and worth, so such experiences are eagerly sought and may, in the extreme, even be fabricated.

High self-esteem that is contingent is *fragile*, because it remains high only as long as one is successful at satisfying relevant criteria. If one is continually successful, high self-esteem may appear to be secure and well-anchored. As Deci and Ryan emphasized, however, it is not secure, because the need for continual validation drives the person to attain more and more successes. And, should these successes cease, the person's self-esteem may plummet. The self-regulatory processes that are associated with contingent self-esteem are especially powerful precisely because they involve the linking of behaviors and outcomes to self- and other-based demands and (dis)approval (Deci & Ryan, 1995).

In contrast, true high self-esteem reflects feelings of self-worth that are well-anchored and secure, that do not depend upon the attainment of specific outcomes, and that do not require continual validation. According to Deci and Ryan (1995), true high self-esteem develops when one's actions are self-determined and congruent with one's inner, core self, rather than a reflection of externally-imposed or internally-based demands. Activities are chosen and goals are undertaken because they are of interest and importance. Furthermore, relationships with others are characterized by mutual acceptance, intimacy, and understanding (e.g., Ryan, 1993).

True high self-esteem is not "earned," nor can it be "taken away." Doing well is valued because it signifies effective expression of one's core values and interests and it is this effective expression that is valued, not high self-esteem per se. Directly pursuing high self-esteem reflects contingent, not true, high self-esteem. Conversely, individuals with true high self-esteem do not interpret poor performance as indicative of their incompetence or worthlessness. Instead, poor performance is used nondefensively as a source of information to guide one's future behavior. This does not mean that people with true high self-esteem react unemotionally to poor performances. As Deci and Ryan (1995) noted, they may feel disappointed and perhaps somewhat sad or irritated, but they are unlikely to feel devastated or enraged, the latter set of feelings being more likely when one's self-esteem is invested in the outcome.

Building upon Deci and Ryan's framework, Crocker and Wolfe (2001) provide evidence that there are individual differences in what criteria people with contingent high self-esteem feel they must satisfy to maintain their positive self-feelings. For some people, academic competence is most critical, whereas for others, it is how socially accepted they are. Other major categories of contingencies, each having its own criteria to be met, include one's physical appearance, God's love, power, and self-reliance. Initial empirical efforts to assess individual differences in the strength of these various contingencies have been very encouraging (see Crocker & Wolfe, 1998). We see great potential value in determining the precise nature of individuals' self-esteem contingencies. For our present purposes, however, the specific content of one's contingencies is less important than whether contingencies per se are operative.

Paradise and Kernis (1999) examined the role of contingent self-esteem in predicting the intensity of anger aroused by an ego-threat. We reasoned that people with highly contingent self-esteem would be easily threatened by an insulting evaluation and would deal with this threat by becoming especially angry and hostile. To test this hypothesis, we developed a measure of contingent self-esteem (The Contingent Self-Esteem Scale; Paradise & Kernis, 1999), which consists of 15 items, each rated on 5-point Likert scales (ranging from "Not at all like me" to "Very much like me"). Sample items include "An important measure of my worth is how well I perform up to the standards that other people have set for me" and "Even in the face of failure, my feelings of self-worth remain unaffected" (reverse-scored). The scale is internally consistent (alpha = .85) and shows considerable test-retest reliability (r = .77).

Participants were undergraduate women whose self-esteem level, contingent self-esteem, and stability of self-esteem (another reflection of fragile self-esteem, to be discussed in the next section) were assessed first. Next, they participated in a laboratory session in which their "presentational skills" were rated ostensibly by an unseen observer in another room. Through random assignment, some women received an evaluation that contained highly insulting statements about their appearance and mannerisms, whereas other women received a generally positive evaluation. Following receipt of the evaluation, they indicated how angry and hostile they felt (using a modified version of a state hostility measure employed by Anderson, Anderson, & DeNeve, 1995). The results indicated that, as anticipated, the more contingent the women's self-esteem, the more intense their anger in response to the insulting treatment. This effect occurred after controlling for the effect of self-esteem level, supporting the notion that contingent self-esteem reflects a form of fragile self-esteem that is associated with heightened vulnerability and reactivity to self-esteem threats.

Several weeks later, participants also completed the Anger Response Inventory (ARI; Tangney et al., 1996), a self-report instrument that taps various aspects of the experience and expression of anger, including anger intensity, intentions for expressing anger, and tendencies to engage in physical or verbal aggression. In line with the laboratory findings, there was a marginally significant positive relation between the degree of women's contingent self-esteem and the intensity of anger they indicated they would experience in response to scenarios depicting various daily events. Additionally, the more contingent the women's self-esteem, the more malevolent their intentions for expressing their anger (i.e., they wanted to get back at or hurt the instigator), and the greater their desire to "let off steam." However, rather than attack the instigator directly, highly contingent self-esteem women, relative to women with less contingent self-esteem, were more likely to focus their anger inward and stew about it, chastise themselves for not doing anything, and lash out at innocent others and things (i.e., displaced verbal, or indirect, aggression).

In sum, recent research and theory offer encouraging support for the construct of contingent self-esteem, its assessment, and its implications for distinguishing between fragile and secure self-esteem. At least two measurement instruments are available (Crocker & Wolfe, 2001; Paradise & Kernis, 1999), which hopefully will facilitate the conduct of additional research. SDT, in addition to offering the construct of contingent self-esteem, has a number of other implications for fragile and secure high self-esteem. We continue our discussion of these implications in the following section.

Do the Person's Current, Contextually-Based Feelings of Self-Worth Fluctuate?

A fourth way to distinguish between *secure* and *fragile* high self-esteem is based on the extent to which a person's current feelings of self-worth fluctuate across time and situations. These short-term fluctuations in one's *immediate, contextually-based* feelings of self-worth reflect the degree to which one's self-esteem is unstable; the greater the magnitude of fluctuations, the more unstable one's self-esteem. Stability of self-esteem is conceptualized as being distinct from self-esteem level, with the latter reflecting the positivity of one's *typical* or *general* feelings of self-worth (for reviews, see Greenier, Kernis, & Waschull, 1995; Kernis, 1993; Kernis & Waschull, 1995).

Consider Jaime who reports that she typically holds highly positive feelings of self-worth. However, when she is asked on multiple occasions over a period of 5-7 days, "how do you feel about yourself at this moment," her answers vary considerably from "I like myself a lot" to "I am very unhappy with myself and I feel pretty useless." Cheryl also reports that she typically holds highly positive feelings of self-worth. In contrast to Jaime, however, Cheryl's repeated responses to the question "how do you feel at this moment?" remain essentially the same (I like myself a lot). Whereas Jaime's high self-esteem is *unstable* (i.e., her current feelings of self-worth substantially fluctuate across time), Cheryl's high self-esteem is *stable* (i.e., her current feelings of self-worth remain constant). This example admittedly is oversimplified. We offer it merely to illustrate that although two people may have a high *level* of self-esteem, they can differ very much in the *stability* of their self-esteem.

Considerable research supports the usefulness of distinguishing among high self-esteem individuals on the basis of how much their immediate feelings of self-worth fluctuate (e.g., Kernis, Cornell, Sun, Berry, & Harlow, 1993; for summaries, see Greenier, Kernis, & Waschull, 1995; Kernis & Waschull, 1995). Stable high self-esteem individuals have positive, well- anchored feelings of self-worth that are little affected by specific evaluative events. In contrast, unstable high self-esteem individuals possess positive, yet fragile and vulnerable, feelings of self-worth that are influenced by evaluative events that are internally generated (e.g., reflecting on one's earlier interactions with others) or are externally provided (e.g., a positive evaluation).

A core characteristic of people with fragile self-esteem is that they react very strongly to events that they view as self-esteem relevant; in fact, they may even see self-esteem relevance in cases where it does not exist. As in Deci and Ryan's conceptualization of contingent high self-esteem, people with unstable high self-esteem are thought to be highly ego-involved in their everyday activities. Elsewhere, we (Greenier et al., 1999; Kernis, Greenier, Herlocker, Whisenhunt, & Abend, 1997) have portrayed this heightened ego-involvement as an "evaluative set" consisting of several interlocking components. First, an *attentional* component involves "zeroing in" on information or events that have potentially self-evaluative implications. Second, a *bias* component involves interpreting ambiguously or nonself-esteem relevant events as self-esteem relevant. Finally, a *generalization* component involves linking one's immediate global feelings of self-worth to specific outcomes and events (e.g., a poor math performance is taken to reflect low overall intelligence and worth). Each of these components may operate outside of one's awareness or be consciously and deliberately invoked. We turn to some recent studies that are relevant to this evaluative set.

Depressive symptoms. Kernis et al. (1998) examined how stability and level of self-esteem relate to increases in depressive symptoms that may occur when people's lives are full of daily hassles (e.g., not having enough time to do things, money shortages, and interpersonal conflicts). Depressive symptoms were measured twice, separated by an interval of about four weeks. A measure of daily hassles (Kanner, Coyne, Schaefer, & Lazarus, 1981) was administered along with the second depression assessment and participants indicated the severity of hassles that they experienced during the intervening time period. With respect to self-esteem stability, increases in depressive symptoms were most apparent among individuals who reported experiencing considerable daily hassles *and* whose self-esteem was *unstable* (i.e., a self-esteem stability x hassles interaction). In contrast, self-esteem level did not predict increases in depressive symptoms, either alone or interacting with the degree of hassles people reported experiencing (for conceptually similar findings, see also Butler, Hokanson, & Flynn, 1994; Roberts & Monroe, 1992).

Additional findings linked unstable self-esteem to the tendency to overgeneralize the negative implications of failure (i.e., when specific failures activate global feelings of incompetence; Carver & Ganellen, 1983). As was the case for self-esteem stability, the overgeneralizing tendency also interacted with daily hassles in predicting increases in depressive symptoms. Specifically, increases in depressive symptoms among individuals who experienced considerable daily hassles were especially apparent among high overgeneralizers. When self-esteem stability and overgeneralization were entered in regression models along with daily hassles to predict depressive-symptom change, the overgeneralization x hassles interaction became nonsignificant, but the self-esteem stability x hassles interaction remained significant. One interpretation of these findings is that the tendency to overgeneralize the implications of negative events is associated with increases in depressive symptoms only to the extent that it results in short-term shifts in feelings of self-worth (for a similar view, see Kuiper's self-worth contingency model of depression; Kuiper & Olinger, 1986). In other words, short-term self-esteem fluctuations may account for why overgeneralizing tendencies are associated with heightened depressive symptoms in the face of aversive daily events (for a more extensive discussion, see Kernis et al., 1998). Although somewhat speculative, this interpretation suggests one implication of the "evaluative set" that is particularly deserving of further attention.

Reactivity to daily events. Everyday positive and negative events also have a greater impact on the immediate self-feelings of people with unstable as compared to stable self-esteem. Greenier et al. (1999) had college students provide daily descriptions of their most positive and negative experiences on Monday through Thursday for two weeks. For each event, participants indicated the extent to which it made them feel better or worse about themselves. The more unstable individuals' self-esteem, the worse they reported feeling in response to negative events and the better they reported feeling in response to positive events.

Interestingly, independent "uninvolved" coders rated the negative (but not the positive) events reported by unstable self-esteem individuals as more self-esteem relevant than the negative events reported by stable self-esteem individuals. These ratings may indicate that unstable, as compared to stable, self-esteem individuals have a greater preponderance of negative self-esteem relevant events in their lives. Alternatively, the ratings may indicate that unstable self-esteem individuals have a heightened tendency to *attend* to negative events that are self-esteem relevant or to *bias* their event descriptions to emphasize aspects potentially implicating self-esteem concerns. Stated differently, the ratings made by these coders may either reflect "objective" differences in the actual events reported or "subjective" differences associated with the way the particular events were attended to and described (i.e., components of the evaluative set described earlier). Space precludes a more extended discussion of these issues here (interested readers should consult Greenier et al., 1999).

Intrinsic motivation and reasons for anger. As discussed in SDT (e.g., Deci & Ryan, 1985; 1987) and as shown in past research (e.g., Ryan, 1982), situational factors that emphasize the link between specific outcomes and one's self-esteem (i.e., that are highly ego-involving) often undermine intrinsic motivation and the desire to take on challenges and instead promote a safer, more cautious self-esteem protective route to positive outcomes. It follows, then, that if unstable self-esteem reflects a heightened tendency to be ego-involved, it should relate to lower levels of intrinsic motivation in the classroom.

To test this prediction, Waschull and Kernis (1996) had fifth grade children from several schools complete Harter's (1981) Intrinsic vs. Extrinsic Orientation in the Classroom Scale, the global self-worth subscale of Harter's Perceived Competence Scale for Children to measure self-esteem level, and a modified version of the global self-worth subscale (reworded to reflect current self-esteem) twice daily for one week to measure self-esteem stability. Importantly, regression analyses controlling for self-esteem level showed that unstable self-esteem independently predicted lower Preference for Challenge (PfC; Does the child prefer challenging tasks or those that are easy?) and lower Curiosity/Interest scores (CI; Is the child motivated by curiosity or to get good grades and please the teacher?). Compared to children with stable self-esteem, then, children with unstable self-esteem reported a relatively more cautious or strategic self-esteem focused orientation toward learning, rather than an intrinsic orientation toward learning for learning's sake.

In another facet of this study, Waschull and Kernis examined whether stability of self-esteem related to children's reasons for becoming angry at their peers. Five hypothetical scenarios depicting aversive interpersonal events were constructed, each of which constituted an instrumental goal blockage as well as a potential self-esteem threat (e.g., a peer jumping in front of the child in a water fountain line). A heightened tendency to attend to the self-evaluative implications of events was revealed in the responses of children with unstable self-esteem. Specifically, compared to children with stable self-esteem, children with unstable self-esteem reported that they would be more likely to get angry because of the scenarios' self-esteem threatening aspects. Once again, this effect emerged independently of children's self-esteem level.

Self-regulation of everyday goals. The findings discussed so far provide convergent, albeit indirect, evidence that unstable self-esteem is linked to a heightened tendency to be ego-involved in everyday events and, by extension, to the possession of an "evaluative set." Additional evidence comes from a recent study (Kernis, Paradise, Whitaker, Wheatman, & Goldman, 2000) that focused on the ways that people regulate their everyday, recurrent goals, referred to as personal strivings (Emmons, 1986).

In their discussion of *self-regulatory styles,* Ryan and Connell (1989) proposed that people engage in goal-directed activities for reasons that reflect varying degrees of choicefulness, self-determination, and integration with one's core self. *External* regulation reflects the absence of self-determination inasmuch as the impetus for action is external to the actor (e.g., another person's request that is tied implicitly or explicitly to reward or punishment). *Introjected* regulation involves the direct application of affective and self-esteem contingencies to motivate oneself (Ryan, Rigby, & King, 1993). Gaining the approval of self and others promotes behaviors that "are performed because one 'should' do them, or because not doing so might engender anxiety, guilt, or loss of self-esteem" (1993, p. 587). Introjected regulation goes hand in hand with heightened ego-involvement and, as such, involves only minimal self-determination. Considerably more self-determination is present in *identified* regulation, which involves the individual personally and freely identifying with the activity's importance for his or her functioning and growth. *Intrinsic* regulation is the prototypical form of self-determined regulation in that activities are chosen purely for the pleasure and enjoyment they provide.

SDT (e.g., Deci & Ryan, 1991) holds that the self-regulatory styles of optimally functioning individuals consist primarily of identified and intrinsic regulation, rather than introjected and external regulation. Furthermore, Deci and Ryan (1995) suggest that contingent self-esteem is anchored in external and introjected self-regulatory processes, controlling forms of regulation that gain their power through the linking of behaviors and outcomes to self- and other-based (dis)approval. True self-esteem, as we described previously, is posited to emerge naturally out of more agentic processes associated with identified and intrinsic self-regulation.

To our knowledge, the relations of contingent and true self-esteem to self-regulatory styles have not been directly examined. However, it should be apparent from the current discussion that contingent and unstable self-esteem share a number of features, as do true and stable self-esteem (although they are not identical, an issue we take up in a later section). This overlap suggests that the more unstable individuals' self-esteem, the more they would engage in external and introjected self-regulation, and the less they would engage in identified and intrinsic self-regulation.

To test these hypotheses, Kernis et al. (2000) had participants complete measures of stability and level of self-esteem along with a measure of self-concept clarity (Campbell et al., 1996). In addition, participants generated a list of eight personal strivings, indicating the extent to which they engage in each striving because of reasons reflecting external, introjected, identified, and intrinsic self-regulatory processes. Approximately four weeks later, participants returned to the lab and indicated the intensity with which they experienced various emotions while engaged in each striving during the intervening time period. Although the use of retrospective accounts of emotion limit their definitiveness, we included them because of their potential to provide interesting information that can be pursued in future research.

The results offered strong support for our hypotheses. After controlling for the effects of self-esteem level, the more unstable people's self-esteem, the more external and the less identified and intrinsic were their self-regulatory styles. Interestingly, unstable self-esteem was not related to greater introjected self-regulation, which was measured by combining responses to two items. When each item was analyzed separately, unstable self-esteem was significantly related to one item ("I force myself to do it to avoid feeling guilty or anxious"), but was unrelated to the other ("I do it because I am supposed to do it"). It is unclear why the effect emerged for only one of the two items. Analyses of the retrospective accounts of emotion indicated that, compared to individuals with stable self-esteem, individuals with unstable self-esteem felt more tense when pursuing their strivings. Though subject to the limitation of retrospective accounts, this last finding provides additional support for our contention that unstable self-esteem individuals are chronically ego-involved as they go about their everyday activities.

As noted earlier, participants also completed the Self-Concept Clarity Scale (Campbell et al., 1996), which contains twelve items (e.g., My beliefs about myself often conflict with one another; In general, I have a clear sense of who I am and what I am). Kernis and Waschull (1995) suggested that having a poorly developed self-concept may contribute to unstable self-esteem by leading individuals to rely on, and be more affected by, specific evaluative information. In other words, the less confident and internally consistent one's self-knowledge, the less well-anchored one's feelings of self-worth are likely to be. Again the results offered strong support, as unstable self-esteem was associated with lower self-concept clarity (after controlling for self-esteem level).

In sum, past research has shown that compared to people with stable self-esteem, people with unstable self-esteem (a) experience greater increases in depressive symptoms when faced with daily hassles (Kernis et al., 1998), (b) have self-feelings that are more affected by everyday negative and positive events (Greenier et al.,1999), (c) take a more self-esteem protective (hence, less mastery oriented) stance toward learning (Waschull & Kernis, 1996), (d) focus relatively more on the self-esteem threatening aspects of aversive interpersonal events (Waschull & Kernis, 1996) and (e) have more impoverished self-concepts (Kernis et al., 2000). Importantly, each of these effects for self-esteem stability emerged after controlling for the role of self-esteem level. Taken as a whole, these findings point to the utility of using stability of self-esteem to distinguish between *fragile* and *secure* forms of high self-esteem. We turn now to this issue.

Self-esteem stability and fragile versus secure high self-esteem. Research has shown that people with unstable high self-esteem are more defensive and self-aggrandizing than are their stable high self-esteem counterparts, yet they are lower in psychological health and well-being. Defensiveness often manifests itself in frequent outbursts of anger and hostility, which often are aimed at restoring damaged self-feelings (Felson, 1984; Feshbach, 1970). As reported by Kernis, Grannemann, and Barclay (1989), unstable high self-esteem individuals scored the highest on several well-validated anger and hostility inventories (e.g., the Novaco Anger Inventory; Novaco, 1975), stable high self-esteem individuals scored the lowest, and low self-esteem individuals (whether stable or unstable) scored between these two extremes.[2] As evidence of self-aggrandizing tendencies, compared to stable high self-esteem individuals, persons with unstable high self-esteem said they would be more likely to boast about a success to their friends (Kernis et al., 1997), and after an actual success, they were also more likely to claim that they did so in spite of the operation of performance inhibiting factors (Kernis, Grannemann, & Barclay, 1992).

---

2. In the Paradise and Kernis (1999) study referred to earlier, the more unstable was women participants' self-esteem, the greater the intensity of the anger they reported in both the insult and control conditions, and these effects were not qualified by level of self-esteem. Additional main effects for self-esteem instability emerged on a number of the ARI subscales including anger intensity, malicious intent, constructive intent, and marginally for fractious intent. In the Kernis et al., (1989) study, self-esteem instability related to greater anger and hostility proneness only among high self-esteem individuals. This discrepancy may stem from differences in the measures used to assess anger and hostility proneness, differences in the sample (Paradise and Kernis included only women participants, whereas Kernis et al., 1989 included both men and women), or other unknown factors.

As would be expected if unstable high self-esteem represents a form of *fragile* high self-esteem, these enhanced tendencies toward self-glorification and self-defense for individuals with unstable high self-esteem do not promote greater psychological health and well-being. To examine this, Paradise and Kernis (1999) administered Ryff's (1989) measure of psychological well-being to a sample of college students who also completed measures of level and stability of self-esteem. Ryff's measure assesses six core components of psychological well-being: (1) *self-acceptance*, the extent to which one holds positive attitudes toward oneself ("I like most aspects of my personality"); (2) *positive relations with others*, the extent to which one has relations with others characterized by love, friendship, and identification ("I have not experienced many warm and trusting relationships with others"); (3) *autonomy*, the extent to which one is self-determining, independent, and self-regulating ("I judge myself by what I think is important, not by the values others think are important"); (4) *environmental mastery*, the extent to which one is able to deal successfully with environments and demands that constitute their everyday lives ("I am quite good at managing the many responsibilities of my daily life"); (5) *purpose in life*, the extent to which one has beliefs that reflect the feeling that there is purpose and meaning to life ("Some people wander aimlessly through life, but I am not one of them") ; and (6) *personal growth*, the extent to which one values and envisions continued development of one's potential ("I think it is important to have new experiences that challenge how you think about yourself and the world").

Note that Ryff's measure includes self-determination (autonomy), competence (environmental mastery, personal growth) and relatedness (positive relations with others), components of psychological functioning that SDT considers crucial. Therefore, it is of particular interest in the present context to note how unstable as compared to stable high self-esteem individuals fare on these indices. First we note that, consistent with previous findings (Ryff, 1989), high self-esteem individuals overall reported greater *autonomy, environmental mastery, purpose in life, self-acceptance, positive relations with others*, and *personal growth* than did low self-esteem individuals. Importantly, differences among high self-esteem individuals also emerged as a function of self-esteem stability. Specifically, relative to individuals with stable high self-esteem, individuals with unstable high self-esteem reported lower *autonomy, environmental mastery, purpose in life, self-acceptance*, and *positive relations with others*. Stated differently, whereas stable high self-esteem individuals reported that they functioned in a highly autonomous manner, possessed a clear sense of meaning in their lives, related effectively within both their physical and social environments, and were highly self-accepting, the same was less true of unstable high self-esteem individuals.

These findings suggest that possessing *stable* high self-esteem may provide the basis for functioning effectively in various realms, whereas *unstable* high self-esteem may undermine (or at least not promote) effective functioning. Given the correlational nature of the findings, an alternative explanation is that effective functioning in a variety of behavioral and psychological domains may foster well-anchored, positive self-feelings, whereas ineffective functioning may undermine the security and/or favorability of one's self-feelings. This latter explanation is consistent with the view of Deci and Ryan (1995) who assert that true high-esteem develops naturally out of the satisfaction of one's needs for self-determination, competence, and relatedness. A third explanation emphasizes the reciprocal influences that self-esteem and other aspects of psychological well-being may have upon each other. Each of these causal scenarios are likely to have their proponents and the data do not allow us to determine which is most viable. Nonetheless, it is important to note that all three explanations link self-esteem stability among high self-esteem individuals to factors that Deci and Ryan (1995) propose are important in distinguishing between contingent and true high self-esteem.

As we have noted on several occasions, our conceptualization of unstable self-esteem shares a number of features with Deci and Ryan's (1995) conceptualization of contingent self-esteem. First, both emphasize the link from specific outcomes to feelings of self-worth. Second, both describe enhanced tendencies to be caught up in the processes of defending, maintaining, and maximizing one's positive, though tenuous, feelings of self-worth. Likewise, stable and true high self-esteem both are taken to reflect secure, well-anchored feelings of self-worth that do *not* need continual validation. Pleasure following success and disappointment following failure are reactions thought to characterize people with either stable or true self-esteem, but these reactions are not tinged with the defensiveness or self-aggrandizement associated with unstable or contingent self-esteem (Deci & Ryan, 1995; Kernis et al., 1997).

Despite these multiple points of convergence, differences between the conceptualizations do exist. How important these differences will turn out to be remains to be seen, but we note them here so that they may be considered. One difference is that whereas we explicitly distinguish between typical and current feelings of self-worth, Deci and Ryan do not. We believe that it is important to maintain such a distinction, both conceptually and empirically. A number of contemporary "self" theorists (e.g., Markus & Kunda, 1986; Rosenberg, 1986; Swann & Hill, 1983) hold that transitory shifts in self-appraisals (self-evaluations, self-images, self-esteem) coexist along with self-appraisals that are more stable and resistant to change. Furthermore, stable and unstable self-appraisals are thought to relate in different ways to individuals' thoughts, feelings, and actions (Kernis & Johnson, 1990; Markus & Kunda, 1986). Kernis, Jadrich, Stoner, and Sun (1996) suggested "that the stable component is reflected in people's "typical self-appraisals" (How do you generally, or typically, feel about yourself?), whereas the unstable component is reflected in people's "current self-appraisals" (How do you feel about yourself right now?)" (p. 432). Importantly, the processses involved in the formation of current and typical appraisals differ. Typical appraisals reflect "evaluative judgments of personal qualities that are abstracted from numerous experiences whose self-relevant implications have been stored in memory" (Kernis & Johnson, 1990, p. 243). In contrast, current appraisals "reflect individuals' contextually based self-appraisals that are affected by a variety of factors, including self-evaluative thoughts, externally provided feedback, social comparisons, and task performance" (Kernis et al., 1996, p. 432). For further discussion and supportive evidence regarding the distinction between current and typical self-appraisals, see Kernis and Johnson (1990) and Kernis et al. (1996).

A second difference between our concepualization and that of Deci and Ryan is that, whereas by definition unstable self-esteem fluctuates, contingent self-esteem can be stable as long as standards or expectations are continually met. In Deci and Ryan's (1995) words: "A man who feels like a good and worthy person (i.e., has high self-esteem) only when he has just accomplished a profitable business transaction would have contingent self-esteem. If he were very successful, frequently negotiating such deals, he would have a continuing high level of self-esteem; yet that high level would be tenuous, always requiring that he continue to pass the tests of life, always requiring that he match some controlling standard (1995, p. 32)." Our view is that positive events (either internally generated or externally provided) will trigger short-term increases in unstable high self-esteem individuals' current feelings of self-worth. As discussed earlier, the self-feelings of unstable high self-esteem individuals are more affected by everyday positive events than are the self-feelings of stable high self-esteem individuals (Greenier et al., 1999).

A third difference is that whereas we focus on the association of impoverished self-concepts (i.e., low self-concept clarity) to unstable self-esteem, Deci and Ryan do not address the role of impoverished self-concepts in contingent self-esteem. A fourth difference is that whereas the assessment of contingent self-esteem seems to necessitate individuals' awareness that their self-esteem is dependent upon certain outcomes or self-evaluations (as measured by Crocker & Wolfe, 2001, and Paradise & Kernis, 1999), our research has demonstrated that people are not very good at knowing just how unstable their self-esteem is (Kernis et al., 1992). This discussion is not meant to take anything away from the important conceptualizations of contingent and true self-esteem, nor should it overshadow the significant implications that Deci and Ryan's framework has for our understanding of self-esteem stability. For the time being, though, it does support the usefulness of maintaining the distinction between unstable and contingent (and between stable and true) self-esteem. With the recent development of measures designed to assess contingent self-esteem, future research should include direct comparisons of the two sets of constructs.

Summary

In this chapter we have argued that self-esteem has multiple components and that, to fully understand its place in psychological functioning, we must go beyond whether it is high or low. Our major goal was to describe these components so as to demonstrate the value of distinguishing among various forms of high self-esteem, some of them *fragile*, and others *secure*. High self-esteem may be fragile or secure for a number of reasons. In one form of *fragile* high self-esteem (i.e., defensive high self-esteem), a person will deliberately misrepresent his or her self-feelings as positive, when in reality they are negative, because he or she is unwilling to admit to the negative self-feelings. The *secure* counterpart to this form (i.e., genuine high self-esteem) involves a person accurately depicting his or her feelings of worth as generally positive, while being willing to admit to the negative self-feelings that he or she has. A second form of *fragile* high self-esteem (high explicit/low implicit self-esteem) occurs when a person consciously holds positive feelings of self-worth but nonconsciously holds negative feelings of which he or she in *un*aware. The *secure* counterpart to this form (high explicit/high implicit) involves possessing positive conscious and nonconscious feelings of self-worth. Although research concerned with these forms is scarce, available findings do support our characterization of them.

A third form of *fragile* high self-esteem (contingent high self-esteem) occurs when a person bases his or her positive feelings of self-worth on specific attainments or evaluations. The *secure* counterpart to this form (true self-esteem) involves feelings of self-worth that do not require continual validation. SDT offers a rich theoretical analysis that has many empirical implications that are only beginning to be studied. The recent development of measurement scales to assess degree of contingent self-esteem is likely to produce a surge of research in the coming years. A fourth form of *fragile* high self-esteem (unstable high self-esteem) involves instances in which a person reports typically holding positive feelings of worth, yet his or her current, contextually-based feelings of self-worth exhibit considerable short-term fluctuations. The *secure* counterpart to this form (stable high self-esteem) involves contextually based feelings of self-worth that remain basically unchanged across time and contexts. SDT also offers many insights into the processes associated with unstable versus stable self-esteem, some of which have received empirical attention but many more of which remain to be examined.

Although there are differences among these various conceptualizations, they all share the conviction that there is more to self-esteem than whether it is high or low. For self-esteem research and theory to continue to progress it is critical that the various forms of self-esteem be taken into account. One question of interest is the extent to which these various forms of high self-esteem covary within individuals. Other important questions pertain to the extent to which they share similar etiologies and have similar consequences for psychological health and well-being. SDT holds a critical place in these endeavors, both as a rich source of hypotheses and as a broad theoretical framework within which seemingly diverse findings can be integrated.

References

Abend, T., Kernis, M. H., & Hampton, C. (2000). Discrepancies between explicit and implicit self-esteem and self-serving responses. Unpublished data, The University of Georgia.

Anderson, C. A., Anderson, J., & DeNeve, K. (1995). Competitive aggression without interaction: Effects of competitive versus cooperative instructions on aggressive behavior in video games. *Personality and Social Psychology Bulletin, 21*, 1020-1030.

Baumeister, R. F., Tice, D.M., & Hutton, D.G. (1989). Self-presentation motivations and personality differences in self-esteem. *Journal of Personality, 57*, 547-579.

Blascovich, J., & Tomaka, J. (1991). Measures of self-esteem. In J.P. Robinson, P. R. Shaver, & L. S. Wrightsman (Eds.), *Measures of personality and social psychological attitudes* (Vol. 1). New York: Academic Press.

Butler, A. C., Hokanson, J. E., & Flynn, H. A. (1994). A comparison of self-esteem ability and low self-esteem as vulnerability factors for depression. *Journal of Personality and Social Psychology, 66*, 166-177.

Campbell, J.D., Trapnell, P.D., Heine, S.J., Katz, I.M., Lavallee, L.F., & Lehman,D.R. (1996). Self-concept clarity: Measurement, personality correlates, and cultural boundaries. *Journal of Personality and Social Psychology, 70*, 141-156.

Carver, C. S., & Ganellen, R. J. (1983). Depression and components of self-punitiveness: High standards, self-criticism, and overgeneralization. *Journal of Abnormal Psychology, 92*, 330-337.

Crocker, J., & Wolfe, C. T. (2001). Contingencies of self-worth. *Psychological Review, 108*, 593-623.

Crocker, J., Thompson, L. L., McGraw, K. M., & Ingermane, C. (1987). Downward comparison, prejudice and evaluations of others: Effects of Self-Esteem and Threat. *Journal of Personality and Social Psychology, 52*, 907-916.

Crowne, D. P., & Marlowe, D. (1960). A new scale of social desirability independent of psychopathology. *Journal of Consulting Psychology, 24*, 349-354.

Deci, E. L., & Ryan, R. M. (1985). *Intrinsic motivation and self-determination in human behavior.* New York: Plenum.

Deci, E. L., & Ryan, R. M. (1987). The support of autonomy and the control of behavior. *Journal of Personality and Social Psychology, 53*, 1024-1037.

Deci, E. L., & Ryan, R. M. (1991). A motivational approach to self: Integration in personality. *Nebraska symposium on motivation: Vol. 38. Perspectives on motivation* (pp. 237-288). Lincoln: University of Nebraska Press.

Deci, E. L., & Ryan, R. M. (1995). Human agency: The basis for true self-esteem. In M. H. Kernis (Ed.), *Efficacy, agency, and self-esteem* (pp. 31-50). New York: Plenum.

Dunning, D., Leuenberger, A., & Sherman, D. A. (1995). A new look at motivated inference: Are self-serving theories of success a product of motivational forces? *Journal of Personality and Social Psychology*, *69*, 58-68.

Emmons, R. A. (1986). Personal strivings: An approach to personality and subjective well-being. *Journal of Personality and Social Psychology*, *51*, 1058-1068.

Epstein, S., & Morling, B. (1995). Is the self motivated to do more than enhance and/or verify itself? In M. H. Kernis (Ed.), *Efficacy, agency, and self-esteem* (pp. 9-30). New York: Plenum.

Farnham, , S. D., Greenwald, A. G., & Banaji, M. R. (1999).Implicit self-esteem. In D. Abrams, & M. A. Hogg (Eds.), *Social cognition and social identity*. London: Blackwell.

Felson, R. B. (1984). Patterns of aggressive social interaction. In A. Mummendey (Ed.). *Social psychology of aggression: From individual behavior to social interaction* (pp. 107-126). Berlin: Springer-Verlag.

Feshbach, S. (1970). Aggression. In P. H. Mussen (Ed.), Carmichael's manual of child psychology (Vol. 2, pp. 159-259). New York: John Wiley.

Fitch, G. (1970). Effects of self-esteem, perceived performance, and choice on causal attributions. *Journal of Personality and Social Psychology*, *16*, 311-315.

Greenier, K. D., Kernis, M. H., & Waschull, S. B. (1995). Not all high (or low) self-esteem people are the same: Theory and research on stability of self-esteem. In M. H. Kernis (Ed.), *Efficacy, agency, and self-esteem* (pp. 51-71). New York: Plenum.

Greenier, K. D., Kernis, M. H., Whisenhunt, C. R., Waschull, S. B., Berry, A. J., Herlocker, C. E., & Abend, T. (1999). Individual differences in reactivity to daily events: Examining the roles of stability and level of self-esteem. *Journal of Personality*, *67*, 185-208.

Harter. S. (1981). A scale of intrinsic versus extrinsic orientation in the classroom. Denver: University of Denver Press.

Horney, K. (1950). *Neurosis and human growth: The struggle toward self-realization*. New York: Norton

Kanner, A. D., Coyne, J. C., Schaefer, C., & Lazarus, R. S., (1981). Comparison of two modes of stress measurement: Daily hassles and uplifts versus major life events. *Journal of Behavioral Medicine*, *4*, 1-39.

Kernis, M. H. (1993). The roles of stability and level of self-esteem in psychological functioning. In R. F. Baumeister (Ed.), *Self-esteem: The puzzle of low self-regard* (pp. 167- 182). New York: Plenum.

Kernis, M. H., Cornell, D. P., Sun, C. R., Berry, A. J., & Harlow, T. (1993). There's more to self-esteem than whether it is high or low: The importance of stability of self-esteem. *Journal of Personality and Social Psychology*, *65*, 1190-1204.

Kernis, M. H., Grannemann, B. D., & Barclay, L. C. (1989). Stability and level of self-esteem as predictors of anger arousal and hostility. *Journal of Personality and Social Psychology*, *56*, 1013-1023.

Kernis, M. H., Grannemann, B. D., & Barclay, L. C. (1992). Stability of self-esteem: Assessment, correlates, and excuse making. *Journal of Personality*, *60*, 621-644.

Kernis, M. H., Greenier, K. D., Herlocker, C. E., Whisenhunt, C. R., & Abend, T. (1997). Self-perceptions of reactions to positive and negative outcomes; The roles of stability and level of self-esteem. *Personality and Individual Differences*, *22*, 846-854.

Kernis, M. H., Jadrich, J., Stoner, P., & Sun, C. R. (1996). Stable and unstable components of self-evaluations: Individual differences in self-appraisal responsiveness to feedback. *Journal of Social and Clinical Psychology*, *15*, 430-448.

Kernis, M. H., & Johnson, E. K. (1990). Current and typical self-appraisals: Differential responsiveness to evaluative feedback and implications for emotions. *Journal of Research in Personality, 24,* 241-257.

Kernis, M. H., Paradise, A.W., Whitaker, D., Wheatman, S., & Goldman, B. (2000). Master of one's psychological domain?: Not likely if one's self-esteem is unstable. *Personality and Social Psychology Bulletin, 26,* 1297-1305.

Kernis, M. H., & Waschull, S. B. (1995). The interactive roles of stability and level of self-esteem: Research and theory. In M. P. Zanna (Ed.), *Advances in experimental social psychology* (Vol. 27, pp. 93-141). San Diego, CA: Academic Press.

Kernis, M. H., Whisenhunt, C. R., Waschull, S. B., Greenier, K. D., Berry, A. J., Herlocker, C. E., & Anderson, C. A. (1998). Multiple facets of self-esteem and their relations to depressive symptoms. *Personality and Social Psychology Bulletin, 24,* 657-668.

Kuiper, N. A., & Olinger, L. J. (1986). Dsyfunctional attitudes and a self-worth contingency model of depression. In P.C. Kendall (Ed.), *Advances in cognitive-behavioral research and therapy,* (Vol. 5, pp. 115-142.)

Markus, H., & Kunda, Z. (1986). Stability and malleability of the self concept. *Journal of Personality and Social Psychology, 51,* 858-866.

Novaco, R. W. (1975). *Anger control: The development and evaluation of an experimental treatment.* Lexington, MA: D. C. Heath.

Paradise, A. W., & Kernis, M. H. (1999). Development of the Contingent Self-Esteem Scale. Unpublished data, University of Georgia.

Paradise, A. W., & Kernis, M. H. (in press). Self-esteem and psychological well-being: Implications of fragile self-esteem. *Journal of Social and Clinical Psychology.*

Paulhus, D. L. (1991). Measurement and control of response bias. In J. P. Robinson, P.R. Shaver, & L. S. Wrightsman (Eds.). *Measures of personality and social psychological attitudes* (pp. 17-60). San Diego: Academic Press.

Roberts, J. E., & Monroe, S. M. (1992). Vulnerable self-esteem and depressive symptoms: Prospective findings comparing three alternative conceptualizations. *Journal of Personality and Social Psychology, 62,* 804-812.

Rogers, C. R. (1951). *Client-centered therapy.* Boston: Houghton Mifflin.

Rogers, C. R. (1959). A theory of therapy, personality, and interpersonal relationships, as developed in the client-centered framework. In S. Koch (Ed.), *Psychology: A study of science* (Vol. 3, pp. 184-256). New York: McGraw-Hill.

Rosenberg, M. (1965). *Society and the adolescent self-image.* Princeton, NJ: Princeton University Press.

Rosenberg, M. (1986). Self-concept from middle childhood through adolescence. In J. Suls & A. G. Greenwald (Eds.), *Psychological perspectives on the self* (Vol. 2), Hillsdale, NJ: Erlbaum.

Ryan, R. M. (1982). Control and information in the interpersonal sphere: An extension of cognitive evaluation theory. *Journal of Personality and Social Psychology, 43,* 450-461.

Ryan, R. M. (1993). Agency and organization: Intrinsic motivation, autonomy, and the self in psychological development. In J. Jacobs (Ed.), *Nebraska symposium on motivation: Developmental perspectives on motivation* (Vol. 40, pp. 1-56). Lincoln, NE: University of Nebraska Press.

Ryan, R. M., & Connell, J. P. (1989). Perceived locus of causality and internalization: Examining reasons for acting in two domains. *Journal of Personality and Social Psychology, 57,* 749-761.

Ryan, R. M., Rigby, S., & King, K. (1993). Two types of religious internalization and their relations to religious orientations and mental health. *Journal of Personality and Social Psychology, 65,* 586-596.

Ryff, C. D. (1989). Happiness is everything, or is it? Explorations on the meaning of psychological well-being. *Journal of Personality and Social Psychology, 57,* 1069-1081.

Schneider, D. J., & Turkat, D. (1975). Self-presentation following success or failure: Defensive self-esteem models. *Journal of Personality, 43,* 127-135.

Swann, W. B., Jr., & Hill, C. A. (1983). The temporal stability of changes in self-ratings. Unpublished manuscript, University of Texas at Austin.

Tangney, J. P., Hill-Barlow, D., Wagner, P.E., Marshall, D. E., Borenstein, J. K., Sanftner, J., Mohr, T., & Gramzow, R. (1996). Assessing individual differences in constructive versus destructive responses to anger across the lifespan. *Journal of Personality and Social Psychology, 70,* 780-796

Tice, D. M. (1991). Esteem protection or enhancement? Self-handicapping motives and attributions differ by trait self-esteem. *Journal of Personality and Social Psychology, 60,* 711-725.

Waschull, S. B., & Kernis, M. H. (1996). Level and stability of self-esteem as predictors of children's intrinsic motivation and reasons for anger. *Personality and Social Psychology Bulletin, 22,* 4-13.

16: The Need for Competence

Andrew J. Elliot
Holly A. McGregor
Todd M. Thrash
University of Rochester

The competence construct has been integral to theories of personality and motivation since the advent of psychology as a scientific discipline (see James, 1890, pp. 309-311). Many theorists over the years have assumed that human beings strive to acquire competence and avoid incompetence, and researchers have conducted thousands of empirical studies designed to investigate the nature of competence-motivated behavior (Spangler, 1992). One contemporary theory that reserves a prominent place for the competence construct is Deci and Ryan's (1991) self-determination theory (SDT). SDT posits that all individuals possess an innate, appetitive form of competence motivation—a psychological need for competence. SDT's view of the need for competence is grounded in White's (1959) conceptualization of effectance motivation which posits that organisms are born with the urge to have an effect on and master their environment. In fact it seems, at times, that the two constructs, the need for competence and effectance motivation, may be viewed as essentially equivalent within SDT, as the terms "competence" and "effectance" are used interchangeably in explications of the need for competence construct (see Deci & Ryan, 1991; Ryan, 1995).

In this chapter we attempt to make the case for construing the need for competence in broader, more inclusive terms. Specifically, we propose that effectance motivation be construed as the initial manifestation of the need for competence, but that this inherent need becomes more elaborated and complex over the course of development. The chapter is organized as follows. First, we offer an

Thanks are extended to Anthony Capobianco, Richard Koestner, and Ken Sheldon for their helpful comments on earlier drafts of this chapter. Preparation of this chapter was supported in part by a grant from the Radcliffe Research Support Program of the Murray Center, and a Faculty Scholars grant from the W. T. Grant Foundation.

overview of White's effectence motivation concept in the context of his approach to personality and development. Second, we propose a broader conceptualization of the need for competence, and we overview developmental issues that suggest the viability of such a conceptualization. Third, we discuss this more inclusive view of the need for competence in terms of other forms of motivation that may be operative in competence-relevant settings. Finally, we close with a summary statement and consider the benefits of our proposed conceptualization.

White's Effectence Motivation

In 1959, Robert White published a now classic paper in which he introduced the concept of effectence motivation. In the paper, White detailed the shortcomings of the prevailing approaches to motivation based in drives and instincts, and marshalled evidence in support of an additional source of motivation—the desire for effective, competent interactions with the environment. This inherent motivational energy, labeled effectence motivation, represents an organismic urge or propensity that impels the individual to investigate, manipulate, and master the environment. The infant's natural tendency toward curiosity and exploratory play is considered the prototypic behavioral manifestation of effectence motivation. Effective engagement with the environment is said to produce an intrinsically pleasurable affective experience termed "a feeling of efficacy," an experience White (1965) later likened to "joy in being a cause" (p. 203).

Effectence motivation is viewed as a natural outgrowth of central nervous system functioning (rather than a response to tissue deficits), and is assumed to be in perpetual operation during waking hours, unless interrupted by homeostatic crisis. This source of motivation is posited to be universal among humans and higher mammals, and is thought to have the biological/evolutionary function of helping the organism adapt to his/her surroundings by fostering the development of skills and abilities. It is important to note that experientially, effectence motivated behavior is engaged in for the direct, immediate reward of having an effect on the environment, not for the sake of acquiring the resulting skills and abilities that maximize fitness and the probability of survival. White illustrated this point by drawing a parallel between sexual motivation and effectence motivation. The ultimate aim of sexually motivated behavior is survival and reproduction, but experientially, sex is engaged in for the immediate pleasure that accompanies the activity itself. Likewise the ultimate aim of effectence motivated behavior is the development of capabilities that afford survival, but experientially, such behavior is engaged in for the pleasure of the feelings of efficacy that accompany effective interaction with the environment.

White described effectence motivated behavior using both negative and positive criteria. He clearly stated that such behavior does *not* include reflexes and other automatic responses, action in the service of biologically-based drives, or random activity that may inadvertently have an impact on the environment. Behavior impelled by effectance motivation *is* characterized as persistent, focused effort intended to produce an effect, and is posited to be exhibited in the infant's earliest transactions with the environment (White, 1965). Early manifestations of effectance motivation simply entail the infant directing attention toward an object and attempting to effect a change of a *general* sort. White provided illustrative examples such as the infant's rudimentary attempts to fixate an object in vision, and the infant's poorly crdinated hand movements designed to knock into a suspended rattle. The changes in sensory input that follow from such efforts are experienced by the infant as feelings of efficacy (White, 1960). Effectance motivated behavior also includes actions intended to produce more *specific* types of change in the environment. In his 1963 monograph, White stated: "We are most familiar with the feeling of efficacy at a level of behavior where we act with intentions to produce particular effects. We feel efficacious when we throw the ball over the plate, swim to the raft, or mend the broken household appliance" (p. 35). Thus, whether the behavior entails ill-coordinated arm movements toward a rattle or highly controlled arm motions toward home plate, action impelled by effectance motivation involves at least some incipient form of intentionality (White, 1965), and is sustained by the pleasurable feelings of efficacy acquired directly and immediately from the activity itself (White, 1963).

In addition to the concepts of effectance motivation and feelings of efficacy, White introduced two other constructs: competence and sense of competence. He defined competence as the individual's actual skill and ability to interact effectively with the environment. Innate abilities were presumed to determine a person's competence to some extent, but it was thought to be primarily a product of learning via effectance and other means—"the cumulative result of the whole history of transactions with the environment" (White, 1963, p. 39). He defined sense of competence as the individual's subjective perception of his or her skill and ability to interact effectively with the environment that may or may not correspond to his or her actual competence. Sense of competence is viewed as a cognitive set or map representing one's confidence in one's skills and abilities, and like actual competence, it is thought to be a product of one's cumulative learning experiences (White, 1960; 1972). In contrasting effectance and feelings of efficacy with competence and sense of competence, White (1963) stated that the former are applicable to single episodes or experiences with the environment, whereas the latter represent structural elements of the self and personhood that cohere over many encounters with the environment.

White did not posit individual differences in effectance motivation (cf. Harter, 1978; Morgan, Harmon, & Maslin-Cole, 1990), opting instead to emphasize the inherent propensity in all human beings toward active exploration and mastery of their environment. White did, however, discuss various "constitutional" and environmental factors that facilitate or impede effective engagement with the environment. Constitutional factors include the individual's activity level, physique (discussed in terms of Sheldon's somatypes), and degree of manual dexterity, athletic talent, and intellectual ability; environmental factors include regular access to varied stimulation, parental responsiveness to the child's physical and emotional needs, and parental supportiveness of the child's initiatives and appreciation of his or her accomplishments (White, 1963; 1972; 1975). These factors are not construed as affecting effectance motivation per se, but by influencing effectance-relevant experiences, they are thought to have an important impact on interindividual variation in competence, sense of competence, self-esteem, and overall ego development.

Although White offered relatively clear definitions of effectance motivation, feelings of efficacy, competence, and sense of competence, the framework he constructed with these concepts to explain motivation and personality across the lifespan is imprecise and fragmentary, and lacks conceptual clarity (Harter, 1978; Maddi, 1996; Messer, 1993). One weakness of White's conceptualization is that it fails to clearly delineate how effectance motivation develops over the lifecourse. White stated that effectance motivation in infants and young children is undifferentiated, and argued that it gradually becomes differentiated into various motives such as "cognizance, construction, mastery, and achievement" (1959, p. 323). That is, each of these motives were said to have their root, at least in part, in effectance motivation and were thought to differentiate from it via life experiences focused on different aspects of effective functioning. Unfortunately, White did not elaborate on the relationship between effectance motivation and these other motives, and he was silent regarding how and why the motive differentiation process transpires.

A second weakness of White's conceptualization is that it does not clearly articulate the nature of the motivation underlying the competence and sense of competence constructs. White stated that competence and sense of competence result from learning via effectance motivation and other motivational sources; he also indicated that effectance motivation can fuse with other motives to produce behavior that results in competence and a sense of competence (White, 1960, 1963). In neither case did he suggest which other forms of motivation might be implicated, nor did he offer any details regarding these motivational processes. Most importantly, White did not speak to the issue of whether the desire for competence could represent a motivational source in and of itself. Although some who overview White's work state that he proposed a competence motivation construct parallel to the effectance motivation construct, this proposal is not to be found in White's writings. In fact, to the best of our knowledge, the term competence motivation is used only twice by White (both times in his seminal 1959 paper), and in both instances he simply used it to refer to effectance motivation in a non-technical, descriptive fashion.

A Broader Conceptualization of the Need for Competence

It is our contention that the need for competence construct is best conceptualized as an innate desire for competence broadly defined rather than an innate
desire for effectence per se. That is, we view the motivation that White referred
to as effectence motivation as a subset of a more general form of innate, appetitive competence motivation—a desire to be competent in one's actions, skills, and
abilities. This inherent urge has the experiential aim of being competent, and it
serves the biological/evolutionary function of adaptation to the environment.
From this standpoint, effectence motivation represents the first manifestation of
a broader motivational source; it is what the need for competence looks like initially, in infants and young children. It is posited that as the individual acquires
various representational capacities, is marked by experience, and encounters an
array of socialization experiences, his or her need for competence develops in
both a quantitative and qualitative fashion and becomes, over time, a multidimensional motivational disposition that includes, but is not limited to, effectence
motivation. In the following, we elaborate on this view of the need for competence, highlighting its link to White's conceptualization, the various developmental transitions and socialization factors that influence its growth and differentiation, its transformation into a motivational disposition, and the ways in which it
becomes an increasingly complex motivational construct as it operates in an
increasing complex and multiply motivated organism.

Differentiation of the Need for Competence

White described effectence motivated behavior as action engaged in "for its
own sake," a phrase he used to emphasize that effectence motivation was an
important source of energy in itself, independent of other drives and instincts.
Importantly, this phrase was not meant to connote that effectence motivated
behavior is engaged in simply for the pleasure of doing the activity per se (as
some have suggested); rather it is engaged in to experience the pleasure that
comes from doing the activity in an effective manner. If an infant seeks to fixate
an object in vision to produce a clearer image or swings his/her hand toward a
rattle to produce a noise, the mere act of fixating the object per se or swinging
his/her arm per se does not result in feelings of efficacy. If the child is able to
sharpen the image or cause the rattle to emit noise, he/she will then experience
feelings of efficacy; if the child is not able to sharpen the image or cause the rattle to emit noise he/she will not experience feelings of efficacy. Thus, behavior
motivated by effectence is outcome focused in that it represents striving to obtain
a desired result.

The result that effectence motivated behavior seeks to obtain is *task-referential* competence. That is, in effectence motivation, competence is defined in an absolute sense by the requirements of the task itself, and the individual's (experiential) aim is simply to accomplish what the task demands. Given that the standard for evaluating competence is inherent to the task, one may receive feedback regarding one's efficacy or competence directly and immediately during the course of task engagement. This direct and immediate receipt of feedback gives this form of competence motivation a very process-oriented, flow-like (Csikszentmihalyi, 1990) quality, enabling one to remain absorbed in the task even as one receives ongoing competence feedback. In sum, White's effectence motivation may be (re)construed as the initial manifestation of a more global need for competence, specifically, as a desire to attain task-referential competence.

In the neonate, the task and, therefore, competence are represented quite broadly and imprecisely as having some sort of general effect on the environment. Neonates are able to detect whether an environmental event is contingent upon their behavior (Watson, 1966; Papousek, 1967), and they display a positive orienting to and an anticipatory enjoyment of such behavior-event contingencies (DeCasper & Carstens, 1981). Within two to three months, infants clearly exhibit joyful pleasure in response to exerting an influence on the environment (Heckhausen, 1984). These rudimentary forms of task-referential competence motivation are obviously not guided by any consciously mediated desires or affective anticipations and may be construed as functioning in non conscious fashion, much like McClelland and colleagues' (McClelland, Koestner, & Weinberger, 1989) notion of implicit motivation.

By 18 months, children have developed the capacity to represent tasks cognitively with greater specificity and precision. Now, the child views task requirements and, therefore, competence in terms of fully completing or mastering activities, rather than simply exerting a general influence on the environment (Barrett & Morgan, 1995). This allows the child to evaluate his or her performance with more rigor and in a more deliberate fashion by explicitly comparing it to the task-referential standard of competence (Kagan, 1981). Thus, the need for competence at this age has begun to function in a more conscious, cognitively-elaborated fashion, akin, to some degree, to McClelland et al.'s (1989) notion of self-attributed motivation.

Prior to 18 months, the child's notion of self is limited to a sense of agency, commonly labeled the subjective self-concept or "I." By the age of 18 months to 2 years, children acquire an objective self-concept—a sense of self as a distinct entity that can become the object of one's knowledge (i.e., one can reflect on one's accomplishments; Harter, 1983). With the advent of this sense of "me," one's task-referential competence efforts can take on a new form of self-relevance, and, accordingly, task mastery can produce not only the pleasure of joy in accomplishment but also the pleasure of pride in accomplishment (Jennings,

1993; Mascalo & Fischer, 1995; Stipek, Recchia, & McClintic, 1992). In competence evaluation, joy and pride represent closely related emotional satisfactions; Heckhausen (1987) makes reference to "joyful pride" (p. 343), and Lewis (1993) describes the phenomenology of pride in terms of joy over an action well done. This affective experience corresponds directly to McClelland, Atkinson, and colleagues' (Atkinson, 1957; McClelland, Atkinson, Clark, & Lowell, 1953) conception of pride in success that served as the intrinsic satisfaction underlying their need for achievement construct. Importantly, although pride requires self-reflection and attribution to the self, the central focus is on the quality of the action that the self has produced, not on the self per se independent of the accomplishment (Lewis, 1997).

As the child's cognitive capacities continue to mature and develop, the child is able to represent tasks and cumulations of tasks in a more elaborate fashion and, eventually, can focus on the acquisition of skills and abilities as the desired accomplishment. For example, over time a child may move from seeking to play a single note on the piano, to seeking to play a chord, to seeking to play a song, to seeking to acquire piano skills more generally. In each case, if the satisfaction being sought is the joyful pride of accomplishing a challenge, the self-regulatory behaviors involved are a manifestation of the need for competence. Thus, the need for competence can be manifest in seeking to master a single act or set of actions, but it can also be manifest in seeking to master skills and abilities more broadly. These representational capacities are thought to emerge during the third year of life (Jennings, 1993; Kagan, 1981; van der Meulen, 1991).

Initially, children's conceptions of skills and abilities remain rather concrete and behaviorally focused. Over time, their conceptions can become more abstract and can take the form of underlying qualities such as ability (in contradistinction to abilities) and intelligence. Although there is currently much debate in the literature as to when this developmental transition occurs, researchers are beginning to think that children can conceive of underlying psychological abstractions as early as age 4 (Cain & Dweck, 1995; Heyman & Gelman, 1999). At this age, children construe ability and intelligence as malleable qualities that can be acquired through effort. Accordingly, this transition may not produce much of a change in the need for competence, as the need for competence is still manifest as a seeking to acquire competence, now simply construed in more abstract terms. It is interesting to note that children initially think of ability and intelligence in global terms across domains (e.g., academic and social) and gradually develop more specific representations of ability in distinct domains and distinct areas within domains (e.g., math ability and reading ability; Harter, 1983; Wigfield, Eccles, & Rodriguez, 1999).

A little researched issue concerns childrens' subtle shift from viewing competence in terms of task mastery to viewing it in terms of improvement and development. That is, once children have acquired the capacity to represent two outcomes simultaneously and to evaluate these outcomes with regard to temporal sequence, they can begin to define competence in terms of improvement—an increase in their present performance relative to their past performance. Most theorists have implicitly presumed that this *past-referential* form of competence motivation emerges rather early in development, around the time that children begin to focus on the acquisition of abilities and ability (Dweck & Elliott, 1983; Nicholls & Miller, 1984; Stipek & Mac Iver, 1989; Suls & Mullen, 1982). However, the minimal research that has been conducted on this issue has either failed to provide clear results or yielded evidence that temporal comparison is not utilized until a bit later (i.e., past the age of 5; Butler, 1998; Ruble, Eisenberg, & Higgins, 1994). At present, this issue remains unresolved. Past-referential competence motivation is a close derivative of task-referential competence motivation, and it seems likely that the two are often intertwined (Elliot, 1999; Elliot & McGregor, 2001), particularly during the time that children are just beginning to utilize temporal comparison. Like its predecessor, past-referential competence motivation affords a private, intrapersonal evaluative process that should help maintain task absorption. Nevertheless, past-referential competence motivation is not as likely as task-referential competence motivation to appear process-oriented or flow-like, given that the acquisition of competence feedback is more complex and relies on information beyond the immediate task performance.

Considerably more research has investigated a third component of the need for competence—*other-referential* competence motivation. The extant data suggest that children are able to define competence in terms of their performance relative to others as early as 3 years of age (Jennings, 1993). Specifically, children understand the concept of a simple competition to determine who can complete a task first, and they exhibit enhanced pleasure when they win a competition rather than simply master a task (Heckhausen, 1984; Stipek et al., 1992). Although children can comprehend the concept of other-referential competence at the age of 3, most researchers contend that children do not focus on acquiring this form of competence until 6 months to a year later (Butler, 1998; Jennings, 1993), and many believe that normative considerations do not become highly salient for children until the age of 6 or 7 (Jennings, 1993; Nicholls, 1989; Ruble & Frey, 1991; Stipek & Mac Iver, 1989; Veroff, 1969). Other-referential competence motivation may be contrasted with task-referential and past-referential competence motivation in that it necessitates an interpersonal evaluative process. In face-to-face competitions, competence information may be acquired rather directly during the process of task engagement, but in many instances, individuals do not have direct access to competence information and may not receive feedback until much later. Thus, although outperforming others may be as satisfying or even more satisfying than mastering a task or improving, other-referential competence motivation may not appear as process-oriented or flow-like as task-referential, or even past-referential, competence motivation.

Interindividual Variation in the Need for Competence

To this point, we have highlighted the role of cognitive maturation in the development of the need for competence in *all* individuals, but it is also important to note that there exists variation in this need *across* individuals. In fact, although the need for competence is innate and present in all individuals throughout the lifespan, we contend that there are biologically-based individual differences in this motivational source from birth onwards (see Elliot & Thrash, 2002). Interindividual variation in the need for competence is likely to be grounded, at least in part, in interindividual variation in neurophysiological activity such as behavioral activation system (BAS) sensitivity. The BAS represents an arousal system centered in the catecholaminergic pathways of the brain which is presumed responsible for activating approach-oriented responses to stimuli and for evoking positive anticipatory and reactive emotions (Gray, 1990; Sutton & Davidson, 1997). The need for competence is more specific than, and therefore clearly not isomorphic with, the BAS, but the BAS is likely to be one of a circuit of direct, biological contributors to the need for competence.

Early individual differences in the need for competence are likely to be manifest, in part, as variation in the infant's activity level. Activity level is a temperament variable representing the child's degree of motor activity, behavioral tempo, and physical energy level (Vondra, 1995). It has been shown to be heritable, and most developmentalists construe it as a foundational building block of adult personality (Buss & Plomin, 1984; Goldsmith et al., 1987). Although many factors clearly contribute to an infant's activity level, this temperament variable seems to reflect, in part, the child's inherent, biologically-based propensity to engage, interact with, and have an impact on the environment. As such, the infant's initial endowment of the need for competence is likely to be manifest (albeit in crude, imperfect form) in his or her degree of active, vigorous exploration of his/her environmental surrounds (see also Vondra, 1995).

A heritable, biologically-determined starting point for the need for competence does not mean that persons will possess the same amount of need for competence across the lifecourse. As with physiological needs, psychological needs change over time as a function of maturation and experience. Individuals begin life with a particular level of need for competence, and this level is posited to vary to some degree in either direction (i.e., become somewhat stronger or weaker) as a function of life experience (see Buss and Plomin, 1984, for a similar argument regarding temperament per se). In other words, experience impacts the strength of the individual's need for competence, but the degree to which experience can exert its influence is constrained by the individual's biological makeup. By experience we mean to connote cumulative experience. In any given situation, the degree to which a person's need for competence is satisfied is presumed to affect, in a cumulative fashion, his or her degree of well-being.

In addition to positing biologically-based individual differences in the need for competence from the womb, we believe that other aspects of the person's biological makeup impact the need for competence indirectly, by influencing the person's competence-relevant experiences. Infants born with greater sensorimotor intelligence or better symbolic representational skills or those with strong, muscular physiques are likely to have more success in interacting with their environment (McClelland, 1973; Vondra, 1995). Likewise, children blessed with abundant athletic skills or unusual musical or artistic talents are particularly likely to encounter feelings of efficacy and pride early and often. These success experiences and their accompanying affects are thought to maintain and facilitate the growth of the need for competence (Deci, 1980; Harter, 1981). Failure experiences can foster the need for competence to the extent that they provide information and are construed as a challenge to be overcome, but a disproportional number of successes to failures is certainly the ideal (Deci & Ryan, 1985; Harter, 1978)

The likelihood that a child will encounter mastery opportunities and experiences is further enhanced by the presence of a secure attachment with his or her caregiver(s). Securely attached children exhibit a greater desire to seek challenges in their environment and have been found to be more successful in conquering the challenges they undertake, even when variables such as IQ are held constant (Belsky, Garduque, & Hrncir, 1984; Maslin-Cole & Spieker, 1990; Pipp, Easterbrooks, & Harmon, 1992; van den Boom, 1989). Characteristics of the home environment can also have an important influence on the development of the need for competence. Parents who provide a stimulating and optimally challenging environment for their children create an ideal training ground for the need for competence. Parents themselves may provide direct stimulation for their children by engaging them in games that arouse curiosity and afford challenge (Yarrow et al., 1984). The provision of age-appropriate toys and ensuring access to a wide variety of stimulating activities and experiences throughout the home environment is another way that parents can facilitate mastery experiences and foster the need for competence in their children (Shaffer, 1999; Veroff, 1969). More generally stated, any home, school, or work environment that provides individuals with opportunities for optimal challenge should sustain and/or enhance the need for competence.

Socialization agents also impact the development of the need for competence. Socialization may be indirect or direct (Saarni, 1993). Parents and other caregivers may exert an indirect influence by exhibiting vigor, enthusiasm, and persistence in their own competence-relevant strivings (Katkovsky, Preston, & Crandall, 1964). Such modeling reinforces the importance and value of the child's own competence desires and provides him or her with concrete ideas as to how to go about channeling these urges into effective and structured pursuits (Harter, 1981). Caregivers may also exert a more direct influence by actively encouraging the child's competence-relevant actions and by responding to the child's successes and, importantly, efforts (independent of outcome) with approval and excitement (McClelland, 1973; Rosen & D'Andrade, 1959; Winterbottom, 1958). This positive reinforcement is presumed to sustain and facilitate the need for competence by enhancing or intensifying the affective experience of efficacy and pride, and by clearly communicating the importance and value of this internal motivational energy (Veroff, 1969). Space considerations prohibit the discussion of additional factors that contribute to the development of the need for competence, but the following may be acknowledged in passing: gender, socio-economic status, and family structure (see McClelland, 1973; Shaffer, 1999 for reviews). It is also likely that many of the factors discussed or listed above interact with each other in exerting their influence on the need for competence (see Vondra, 1995).

Thus far, we have highlighted the impact that various factors have on the quantitative nature (i.e., amount) of the need for competence, but it is important to note that many, if not most of the factors discussed or listed above may also influence the qualitative nature of the need for competence. Over time, an individual's need for competence may become weighted toward a desire for task-referential competence, past-referential competence, or other-referential competence. For example, a boy who daily strives to match the performance standards set by his near-age older brother may develop strong other-referential competence motivation (a process the senior author has observed in his own children); only children, in contrast, may be more likely to develop strong self-referential competence motivation given the absence of a live-in source of social comparison information. Likewise, parents who model competitiveness or directly encourage competitiveness in their children are more likely to raise children who have strong other-referential competence motivation. Indeed some have suggested that gender differences in competence-relevant motivation reflect the fact that males in our society are socialized to be more competitive than females (see Spence & Helmreich, 1983). Of course, the individual with the strongest overall need for competence would be the person who, over time, develops a high quantity of task-referential, past-referential, *and* other-referential competence motivation. Unfortunately, to date researchers have allocated little empirical attention to issues pertaining to the qualitative development of competence motivation.

A central feature of the conceptualization of the need for competence that we are espousing, and one that bears reiteration, is its innate nature. Although we acknowledge that experience plays an integral role in the shaping and molding of the need for competence over the lifecourse, we view this motivational source as inherent to the organism. Thus, in contrast to other conceptualizations of competence-relevant motivation that construe such energization as entirely a product of learning (e.g., McClelland, et al., 1953; although see McClelland's, 1985, later work on natural incentives), we believe that the motivational energy underlying competence strivings neither needs to be acquired via experience nor borrowed from some other source (see Hartman, 1958). The need for competence is present at birth, albeit in rudimentary form as a nonsconscious urge for effectence, and over the life course is filtered through cognitive structures of increasing complexity and channelled in various directions as a function of maturation, the individual's biological makeup, competence-relevant experiences, and socialization history. As the need for competence develops, it remains rooted in the effectence urge; new ways of defining or experiencing competence do not necessarily replace the old but differentiate from it and become integrated with it to form a multidimensional need for competence. Throughout the lifespan, all individuals possess the need for competence and require competence for optimal functioning and well-being. However, individual differences in the quantity and quality of the need for competence are clearly present such that some persons have a stronger desire for competence than others, and some persons have a desire for certain types of competence (i.e., task-referential, past-referential, or other-referential) relative to others. We believe that early life experiences have a disproportional impact on the strength and nature of the individual's competence (McClelland, 1951; Veroff, 1965), but we also contend that competence motivation remains somewhat malleable throughout childhood and even into the adult years (see McClelland & Winter, 1969).

Needs, Motives, and Goals

We would like to conclude this section on a general note, by briefly commenting on the distinction between the "need," "motive," and "goal" concepts in motivational theorizing. There is no consensual way to define the terms "need" and "motive;" some theorists over the years have considered them to be synonymous (Atkinson, 1964; McClelland, 1951), whereas others have offered various means of distinguishing between them (Liebert & Spielgler, 1994; Nuttin, 1984). Our view is that the need and motive concepts are similar to each other, but differ in one extremely important way. Needs and motives are similar to each other in that both represent affectively-based motivational dispositions that energize the individual and orient him or her toward valenced possibilities. Needs differ from motives in that they are part of the individual's inherent psychological makeup and, therefore, represent a psychological requirement, which means they must be attended to and satisfied for the individual to function in optimal fashion and experience well-being. In essence, a need may be seen as a motive that has innate roots.

Although this approach to distinguishing between the need and motive concepts is based on a single distinction, the ramifications of this distinction are far reaching, both conceptually (e.g., concerning the important issue of the number of motivational dispositions that should be considered needs in human personality) and functionally (e.g., concerning which motivational dispositions are likely to have the deepest and most pervasive impact on affect, cognition, and behavior).

The need for competence is conceptualized herein as an innate, multidimensional *need*, and is presumed to have a powerful and widespread influence on personality functioning and well-being. In accord with SDT (Deci & Ryan, 1991), we view many motivational dispositions that have been proffered in the literature (some of which carry the label "need") as *motives* rather than needs; examples include the need for closure, the need for dominance, the self-presentation motive, and the self-verification motive. Such motive dispositions clearly have an important influence on everyday functioning, but we suspect that their influence is qualitatively different from that of basic needs such as the need for competence (see Deci & Ryan, 2000).

As with the need and motive concepts, there is no consensual way to define the term "goal," nor is there a widely shared understanding of how goals differ conceptually from needs and motives (see, e.g., Austin & Vancouver, 1996; Locke & Latham, 1990; Pervin, 1982). Our view is that goals may be distinguished from needs and motives in that the latter are affectively-based dispositions that energize behavior and orient the individual in a general way, whereas the former are cognitive representations that serve a directional function for behavior by focusing the individual on more specific possibilities (Elliot, 1997; Thrash & Elliot, 2001). Goals are related to needs and motives in the self-regulatory process, in that individuals sometimes adopt goals that help serve their dispositional desires by channelling them in a more concrete direction. Needs or motives can and often do lead directly to behavior, but these general dispositional desires sometimes need to be strategically channelled in a specific direction to be satisfied in an effective and efficient manner. Thus, the need for competence can influence behavior in two ways: it can impel competence-based behavior directly, or it can lead to competence-based behavior indirectly by prompting the adoption of competence goals that proximally regulate behavior (Elliot & Thrash, 2001).

Like the need for competence, competence goals are differentiated in terms of the type of competence that the individual focuses on. Convention in the literature has been to collapse task-referential and past-referential competence together into a "mastery goal," and to distinguish this goal from a performance goal focused on other-referential competence (Ames & Archer, 1987; Dweck & Elliott, 1983; Maehr, 1983; Nicholls, 1984), but we have recently suggested the need to additionally consider bifurcating "mastery" goals according to the task-referential/past-referent distinction (Elliot, 1999; Elliot & McGregor, 2001). Interestingly, the relationship between the need for competence and competence goals may take on many different manifestations. For example other-referential competence motivation may straightforwardly prompt the adoption of an other-referential competence goal, but in many instances the desire for other-referential competence may actually be better served when it leads to a task-referential mastery goal that helps facilitate task absorption.

The Need for Competence and Competence Strivings in the Context of Other Sources of Motivation

Conceptually, the need for competence may be discussed in terms of a pure, isolated source of motivational energy, but in everyday life, the need for competence is often operative in conjunction with other forms of motivation. Furthermore, in some settings, competence strivings may be impelled by motivational sources in addition to, or even instead of the need for competence. In the following, we briefly discuss some (interrelated) ways in which the need for competence and competence strivings may become linked to other sources of motivation.

Links to Other Sources of Motivation

Self-enhancement motivation. With the advent of the objective self-concept, the child may not only evaluate the self's actions and accomplishments, but may evaluate the self in general. As such, competence strivings may emerge from a general desire for self-enhancement (Sedikides & Strube, 1997), and competence may become a means to the end of feeling good about the global self, rather than an end sought for its own sake. The emotional satisfaction accompanying competence may be seen as a marker of which form of self-relevant motivation is (or was) operative. In the need for competence, the emotional satisfaction is joyful pride in accomplishment, which represents a specific positive evaluation of the actions that the self has produced; in self-enhancement motivation, the emotional satisfaction is hubris, which represents a global positive evaluation of the entire self (see Lewis, 1997, for a discussion of the pride vs. hubris distinction). Accomplishments may be construed in terms of doing well on situation-specific tasks, developing skills or abilities, or even becoming the best person that one can become. This illustrates that it is not necessarily the globality/specificity dimension that distinguishes the need for competence from self-enhancement motivation, but whether the emotional satisfaction resides or does not reside in the accomplishment itself. However, it should be noted that the more general or abstract the focus of one's competence strivings, the more likely it is that the underlying motivation is separate from the accomplishment itself.

Instrumental competence motivation. Competence clearly has instrumental as well as inherent value. Early on, around the age of two, children become aware of the fact that their accomplishments can evoke smiles, hugs, and applause from others, in addition to feelings of joy and pride (Stipek et al., 1992; Thompson, 1998). Throughout the lifecourse competence is the gateway to multifarious benefits including money, material possessions, power, prestige, attention, fame, etc. These accompaniments represent concrete, symbolic indicators of competence and may be viewed simply as a source of competence information (Harackiewicz, 1989), but they may also supersede competence to become an end in themselves. As such, competence strivings may reflect an instrumental desire to acquire some external outcome that is completely independent of the accomplishment itself (see Harter's, 1981, conceptualization of extrinsic motivation), and this form of regulation has little to do with the need for competence per se.

Intrinsic motivation. Intrinsic motivation is commonly defined in terms of engaging in an activity for the enjoyment or interest of the activity itself (Deci & Ryan, 1985). When intrinsically motivated, the individual is not pursuing any separable outcome, but is simply seeking the pleasure that comes directly and immediately from the experience of the activity. Intrinsic motivation may be contrasted with competence motivation, in which the individual *is* pursuing a separable outcome, the pleasure of experiencing or attaining competence in the activity. Thus, conceptually, we view the need for competence and intrinsic motivation as distinct entities. Although conceptually distinct, the need for competence and intrinsic motivation are often closely related in any given experience of activity engagement. Intrinsic motivation is a descriptive term that refers to the pursuit of enjoyment and fun for its own sake, but an in-depth analysis of the construct requires a consideration of what it is that individuals experience as enjoyable or fun. Attaining competence at an activity is one important psychological determinant of enjoyment and fun, thus the pursuit of competence and seeking enjoyment/fun in the task can, in some instances, be inextricably intertwined. In addition, the relationship between competence and enjoyment is undoubtedly reciprocal (attaining competence is enjoyable and enjoyment yields greater competence), leading to a further entangling of the two constructs.

The intertwining of competence motivation and intrinsic motivation is most likely when the individual is seeking task-referential competence, as competence information in such instances is received directly and immediately from the task itself and allows the individual to remained fully absorbed in the enjoyment of task engagement. The pursuit of past-referential or other-referential competence can also be closely associated with intrinsic motivation, but only in situations in which competence information is readily available during or immediately after task engagement (e.g., a one-on-one competition such as a chess match or a racquetball game).

Self-worth motivation. The precise manner in which parents respond to their child's successful and unsuccessful competence pursuits has a deep and pervasive influence on the child's sense of self. To the extent that parents convey that their acceptance, approval, or love of the child is contingent upon his or her performance, competence will become linked to self-worth and security concerns, and the need for competence and competence strivings will suffer accordingly. Parents may establish competence-relevant contingencies in many ways, often unknowingly. For example, in response to a specific success, a parent may lavish person-focused praise on his or her child (e.g., "You're such a good boy/girl") or may comment on the child's broad-level attributes (e.g, "You're so smart"). Global feedback of this nature is likely to establish an association between the child's specific performances and his or her general value and worthiness (see Dweck, 1999, for related arguments). More invidiously, a parent may withdraw affection or love from his or her child upon failure, thereby sending an unequivocal message that the child's loveability and worth is contingent upon his or her performance in competence-relevant settings. In essence, these forms of socialization communicate to the child a lack of inherent self-worth and put the child in a position where he or she must earn approval, affection, and worth through his or her competence strivings (see Rogers', 1959, on conditions of worth). A child in this position is likely to develop a working model of the self as unworthy of love (Bowlby, 1973; Bretherton, 1990), and to manifest signs of ego-involvement in competence-relevant settings (Ryan, 1982). This view of the self is likely to be carried into adulthood, where it will be readily reinforced by a culture that implicitly presumes one must be competent to be a valuable member of society (Covington & Beery, 1976). The broad point to be made is that the need for competence is likely to be undermined to the extent that it becomes intermingled with self-worth and/or affiliation issues. Indeed, to the extent that competence becomes a means to the end of validating one's worth (Dykman, 1998) or gaining the approval of others (Smith, 1968), competence strivings are simply servants of other forms of motivation.

Self-presentation/self-assessment motivation. Implicit theories of intelligence (or ability) are likely to exert an important impact on the nature of competence strivings (Dweck, 1990). The tendency to view intelligence as a stable, fixed trait is thought to emerge sometime around the age of 7 (see Dweck & Elliott, 1983; Heyman & Dweck, 1998; Nicholls & Miller, 1984; Pomeranz & Ruble, 1997, Stipek & Mac Iver, 1989;). When intelligence is construed as stable, one's focus is no longer on being competent in a single act or set of actions, acquiring skill/abilities, or acquiring ability; rather, one's focus is on *determining* or *demonstrating* the degree to which one possesses immutable intelligence. Thus, when one holds an entity theory of intelligence, competence strivings are likely to be manifestations of self-assessment motivation (if one desires to *determine* one's intelligence) or self-presentation motivation (if one desires to *demonstrate* one's intelligence), rather than competence motivation per se (see Elliot, 1999). Given the consensual value of intelligence in our society, the competence strivings of entity theorists are also likely to be undergirded by (and laden with) self-worth and approval concerns.

A separate, learned competence motive? The need for competence is an innate form of appetitive competence motivation, and it is interesting to contemplate whether persons can develop an appetitive competence motive that is independent of the need for competence. McClelland et al. (1989) would likely answer in the affirmative, drawing on their distinction between implicit and self-attributed motives. McClelland and colleagues might argue that a person can learn, from one's parents or one's culture more broadly, that competence is something to value and, in response, may embrace this value to the point that it becomes, over time, a conscious, cognitively-elaborated, dispositional desire for competence (a self-attributed motive) separate from their non conscious, emotion-based, dispositional desire for competence (an implicit motive). Although we acknowledge this possibility, we would like to raise two points regarding the likelihood of a separate, entirely learned, appetitive competence motive. First, if one presumes, as we do, the existence of an innate desire for competence in all persons, it seems likely that information regarding the value of competence would simply bolster and reinforce the individual's inherent urges and tendencies (i.e., be incorporated into the existing motivational system), rather than establish an entirely separate motivational system. Second, to the extent that the conscious valuing of competence is based in a desire for social recognition or a desire to view or present oneself in a particular light (as McClelland and colleagues presume), we would question whether this motive disposition should be viewed in terms of competence per se. Indeed, Koestner and McClelland (1990) describe this self-attributed form of competence motivation as "extrinsic," a label that implies an interest in competence not as an end in itself, but as a means to some other end. At present, we remain open to the possibility of a separate, entirely learned, appetitive competence motive, but we prefer to emphasize the inherent nature of the desire for competence per se. We see the value of the implicit/self-attributed distinction but think it is best suited to address the fact that the need for competence may become cognitively-elaborated to varying degrees and that individuals may or may not be consciously aware of and, therefore, may or may not be able to accurately self-report their level of innate, appetitive competence motivation (see Thrash & Elliot, 2001 for a more detailed consideration of these issues).

Aversive competence motivation. To this point, we have discussed competence motivation exclusively in appetitive terms, but it is important to acknowledge that competence motivation also includes an aversive component—the desire to avoid incompetence. Aversive competence motivation clearly deserves a chapter in its own right; at present we will simply raise the question of whether such motivation should be conceptualized as an entirely learned motive that derives from the need for competence or as an innate source of energy independent of the need for competence (i.e., the need to avoid incompetence). On one hand, it seems reasonable to construe aversive competence motivation as derivative, essentially as the need for competence gone astray. Repeated failure experiences, insecure attachment, and socialization practices such as person-focused criticism or love withdrawal upon failure are all factors that can prompt the individual to reorient his or her desires toward avoiding incompetence rather than acquiring competence. On the other hand, aversive competence motivation may be construed as having an inherent basis to the extent that it is grounded in neuroanatomical structures such as the behavioral inhibition system (see Gray, 1990), and early individual differences in this motivational source might be manifest, in part, in the heritable, biologically-based infant temperament of fearfulness (see Rothbart & Ahadi, 1994) or behavioral inhibition (Kagen, Reznick, & Snidman, 1987). At present it is not clear which conceptualization is more accurate, although we suspect that the weight of the cumulative evidence will eventually support the latter. Regardless, it is important to note that aversive competence motivation is highly susceptible to becoming linked to other forms of motivation (i.e., self-worth concerns, affiliative concerns), and indeed much of what appears to be aversive competence motivation on the surface is probably not competence motivation at all, but is simply avoidance striving serving some other motivational aim (for further discussion of aversive competence motivation see Elliot & Church, 1997; Elliot & McGregor, 1999; Elliot & Sheldon, 1997).

The broader motivational context. Although the need for competence is clearly a positive and adaptive source of motivation, in the broad context of overall personality functioning there are instances in which the need for competence can interfere with optimal self-regulation. In addition to the need for competence, individuals possess a need for relatedness (Baumeister & Leary, 1995; Ryan, 1995), and to the extent that attending to the need for competence precludes sufficient attention to the need for relatedness, well-being will suffer. Specific manifestations of this would include the child who receives such strong gratification from developing Nintendo skills that interaction with peers is all but ignored, or the adult who becomes so absorbed in exciting accomplishments at the workplace that familial relations are neglected. Some aspects of the need for competence seem more likely to conflict with broader personality processes than others. A desire for other-referential competence, in particular, seems most likely to interfere with the need for relatedness, as in some situations, one's own competence may come at the direct expense of a relational other. The desire for other-referential competence can even interfere with other aspects of the need for competence itself, as when the individual ignores opportunities for challenge or skill development in the process of pursuing the thrill of competitive victory. It is even possible that the need for competence unrestrained by the occasional consideration of possible incompetence could be maladaptive, as individuals may find themselves so enthralled by the possibility of competence that potential pitfalls along the way are ignored or never even perceived (see Arnett, Smith, & Newman, 1997, for a conceptual parallel). Thus, satisfaction of the need for competence may lead to well-being in general, but balance within the need itself and within the broader context of personhood is important to ensure optimal functioning.

Closing Comments

In this chapter we have attempted to make the case for conceptualizing the need for competence in broad terms, as an innate, appetitive desire to be competent in one's actions, skills, and abilities. This broad conceptualization of the need for competence is grounded in White's notion of effectance motivation, but is not limited to it. Effectance motivation is clearly an important manifestation of the need for competence, and in many respects may be considered its prototypic form. The experiential aim of the need for competence is the pleasure of accomplishment *per se*, and the inherent urge to seek competence for its own sake is often witnessed most clearly and purely in the form of effectance pursuits. However, we believe equating the need for competence and effectance motivation unnecessarily restricts the scope of the need for competence construct. Accordingly, we posit that effectance motivation is best viewed as the initial manifestation of the need for competence and that this inherent desire for competence develops over time, both quantitatively and qualitatively, to the point that, in its "adult" form, it represents a multidimensional motivational disposition that includes a desire for past-referential and other-referential competence, in addition to a desire for task-referential competence (i.e., effectance).

Portraying the need for competence in broad, inclusive terms has many benefits. For example, extending the need for competence beyond effectance motivation enables SDT to account for more conceptual space in the competence domain. Furthermore, broadening the need for competence construct would seem to bring SDT's operationalization and conceptualization of the need for competence into concordance. In empirical research in the SDT tradition, competence is sometimes operationalized in terms of effectance, but other times it is operationalized in broader, more inclusive terms. For example, in recent research on need satisfaction, participants' state level of competence has been assessed by simply asking participants to report "how competent they felt" while doing selected daily activities during the previous 24 hours (Sheldon & Elliot, 1999, p. 488), and participants' trait level of competence has been assessed using the competence subscale of the Multidimensional Self-Esteem Inventory which is comprised of items such as "Most people who know me consider me to be a highly talented and competent person" and "How often do you approach new tasks with a lot of confidence in your ability?" (Reis, Sheldon, Gable, Roscoe, & Ryan, 2000; Sheldon, Ryan, & Reis, 1996). Thus, it seems that conceptually, SDT has often portrayed the need for competence as synonymous with effectance motivation, whereas operationally, it has allowed for a broader portrayal of the need for competence. Extending the need for competence construct to include task-referential, past-referential, and other-referential competence motivation would eliminate this problem.

In addition to benefitting SDT, we believe that the present portrait of competence motivation addresses an important shortcoming of White's theorizing. White's framework of motivation and personality has been critiqued for its lack of precision, specifically regarding the issues of how effectance motivation develops over the lifecourse and what type of motivation underlies the competence construct. We have directly discussed these issues in detail in the process of articulating the nature of the need for competence construct and, we believe, we have done so in a manner that is consistent with, and indeed maintains a prominent, foundational place for, White's classic conceptualization.

A further benefit of the proposed conceptualization of the need for competence is that it (implicitly) integrates two of the most influential analyses of competence-relevant motivation that have been offered to date—White's work on effectance motivation and the work of Murray (1938, 1948), McClelland (1951, 1985), and Atkinson (1957, 1964) on the need for achievement. Murray defined the need for achievement as the desire: "to accomplish something difficult. To master, manipulate, or organize physical objects, human beings, or ideas. To do this as rapidly, and as independently as possible. To overcome obstacles and attain a high standard. To excel one's self. To rival and surpass others. To increase self-regard by the successful exercise of talent." (1938, p. 164). The need for achievement was conceptualized as a motive disposition on which individuals vary considerably, and this disposition was presumed to be acquired via early learning experiences. McClelland and Atkinson embraced Murray's concept of the need for achievement but developed a more thorough analysis of the construct (including a clear explication of the nature of the satisfaction associated with the need—pride in accomplishment), and an objective scoring system to facilitate the assessment of individual differences.[1] Despite the clear overlap in

---

1. McClelland and Atkinson adopted an empirical rather than theoretical approach to operationally defining and devising a measure of dispositional need for achievement. Specifically, they used an experimental procedure whereby male university undergraduates (mostly ex-servicemen) encountered achievement-arousing cues or not prior to writing brief stories to TAT-like pictures. The achievement-arousing cues were characterized as "ego involving" and included instructions describing the story-writing task as a test of intelligence conducted by the Office of Naval Research designed to determine who was best suited to be a leader (interestingly, such cues had been shown to "frighten impressionable subjects into incoherence" in early pilot work; McClelland et al., 1953, p. 103). Any story content that differed between the achievement-arousing and neutral conditions was presumed to reflect need for achievement, and the need for achievement scoring system was derived on this basis. Consequently, the need for achievement was operationally defined as a desire for "success in competition with some standard of excellence" (McClelland et al., 1953, p. 110) and various types of achievement imagery were incorporated into the system including: competitive activity involving winning or doing better than others, self-imposed requirements for good performance such as doing a "thorough, workmanlike job" on a task, unique or extraordinary personal accomplishments, and striving to attain a long-term goal such as becoming a doctor or lawyer. An individual's need for achievement score is comprised of this achievement imagery category plus several subcategories representing processes (e.g., cognitive anticipation, affect) presumably associated with striving for the achievement standard. Many of these subcategories are positively valenced, but a number focus on failure-relevant processes such as anticipatory failure and negative affect upon failure. As such, although need for achievement was conceptualized by McClelland and Atkinson as a rather pure form of approach motivation (i.e., striving for achievement for its own sake), operationally it appears to be a somewhat heterogeneous compilation of motivational concerns (cf. Koestner and McClelland, 1990).

content domain, White made little mention of the work of Murray, McClelland, and Atkinson, and vice versa. White simply noted that effectence motivation differentiates over time into other motives including a motive for achievement; McClelland (alone) made passing reference to effectence motivation, but only in the context of discussing the rudiments of the power motive. Contemporary researchers working out of these two traditions have typically followed their pioneers by making little mention of the other tradition. The few who do discuss both usually contrast them and emphasize the ways in which they differ (Barrett, MacTurk, & Morgan, 1995; Harter & Connell, 1984; Heckhausen, 1987); for exceptions, see Dweck and Elliott (1983) and Nicholls (1989).

The need for competence, as conceptualized herein, incorporates aspects of both the effectence motivation and need for achievement traditions. Drawing on White, the need for competence is portrayed as an innate form of appetitive competence motivation, of which effectence motivation is an important component. Drawing on Murray, McClelland, and Atkinson, the need for competence is viewed as developing over time into a multidimensional disposition that includes the desire for task-referential, past-referential, and other-referential competence (each of which is represented in Murray's definition of the need for achievement) and varies across individuals. Although in the present chapter, we have focused primarily on the relationship between the need for competence and effectence motivation, our view of the need for competence is clearly grounded in the need for achievement tradition as well. We believe that further consideration of the links between these two highly influential and generative traditions promises to yield further insight into the nature of competence motivation.

References

Ames, C., & Archer, J. (1987). Mothers' beliefs about the role of ability and effort in school learning. *Journal of Educational Psychology, 79*, 409-446.

Arnett, P. A., Smith, S. S., & Newman, J. P. (1997). Approach and avoidance motivation in psychopathic criminal offenders during passive avoidance. *Journal of Personality and Social Psychology, 72*, 1413-1428.

Atkinson, J. W. (1957). Motivational determinants of risk taking behavior. *Psychological Review, 64*, 359-372.

Atkinson, J. W. (1964). *An introduction to motivation*. Princeton, NJ: Van Nostrand.

Austin, J., & Vancouver, J. (1996). Goal constructs in psychology: Structure, process, and content. *Psychological Bulletin, 120*, 338-375.

Barrett, K., MacTurk, R., & Morgan, G. (1995). Concluding comments: Origins, conceptualizations, and applications. In R. MacTurk & G. Morgan (Eds.), *Mastery motivation*. Norwood, NY: Ablex Publishing.

Barrett, K. C., & Morgan, G. (1995). Continuities and discontinuities in mastery motivation during infancy and toddlerhood: A conceptualization and review. In R. H.

MacTurk & G. A. Morgan (Eds.), *Advances in applied developmental psychology: Vol. 12. Mastery motivation: Origins, condeptualizations, and applications* (pp. 57-93). Norwood, NJ: Ablex Publishing.

Baumeister, R. F., & Leary, M. R. (1995). The need to belong: Desire for interpersonal attachments as a fundamental human motivation. *Psychological Bulletin, 117*, 497-529.

Belsky, J., Garduque, L., & Hrncir, E. (1984). Assessing performance, competence, and executive capacity in infant play: Relations to home environment and security of attachment. *Developmental Psychology, 20*, 406-417.

Bowlby, J. (1973). *Attachment and loss: Vol. 1. Attachment*. London: Hogarth Press.

Bretherton, I. (1990). Open communication and internal working models: Their role in the development of attachment relationships. In R. Thompson (Ed.), *Nebraska symposium on motivation* (Vol. 36, pp. 57-113). Lincoln, NE: University of Nebraska Press.

Buss, A. H., & Plomin, R. (1984). *Temperament: Early developing personality traits*. Hillsdale, NJ: Lawrence Erlbaum Associates

Butler, R. (1998). Age trends in the use of social and temporal comparison for self-evaluation: Examination of a novel developmental hypothesis. *Child Development, 69*, 1054-1073.

Cain, K. M., & Dweck, C. S. (1995). The development of children's achievement motivation patterns and conceptions of intelligence. *Merrill-Palmer Quarterly, 41*, 25-52

Covington, M., & Beery, R. (1976). *Self-worth and school learning*. New York: Holt, Rinehart, & Winston.

Csikszentmihalyi, M. (1990). *Flow: The psychology of optimal experience*. New York: Harper & Row.

DeCasper, A. J., & Carstens, A. A. (1981). Contingencies of stimulation: Effects on learning and emotion in neonates. *Infant Behavior and Development, 4*, 19-35.

Deci, E. L. (1980). *The psychology of self-determination*. Lexington, MA: D.C. Heath (Lexington books).

Deci, E. L., & Ryan, R. M. (1985). *Intrinsic motivation and self-determination in human behavior*. New York: Plenum Press.

Deci, E. L., & Ryan, R. M. (1991). A motivational approach to self: Integration in personality. In R. A. Dienstbier (Ed.), *Nebraska symposium on motivation* (Vol. 38, pp. 237-288). Lincoln, NE: University of Nebraska Press.

Deci, E. L., & Ryan, R. M. (2000). The "what" and "why" of goal pursuits: Human needs and the self-determination of behavior. *Psychological Inquiry, 11*, 319-338.

Dweck, C. (1991). Self theories and goals: Their role in motivation, personality, and development. In R. Dienstbier (Ed.), *Nebraska Symposium on Motivation* (vol. 38, pp. 199-235). Lincoln: University of Nebraska Press.

Dweck, C. S. (1999). *Self-theories: Their role in motivation, personality, and development*. Philadelphia: Psychology Press.

Dweck, C. S., & Elliott, E. S (1983). Achievement motivation. In P. H. Mussen (Series Ed.) & E. M. Hetherington (Vol. Ed.), *Handbook of child psychology: Vol. 4. Socialization, personality and social development* (4th ed., pp. 643-691). New York: Wiley.

Dykman, B. M. (1998). Integrating cognitive and motivational factors in depression: Initial tests of a goal-orientation approach. *Journal of Personality and Social Psychology, 74*, 139-158.

Elliot, A. J. (1997). Integrating the "classic" and "contemporary" approaches to achievement motivation: A hierarchical model of approach and avoidance achievement motivation. In M. Maehr & P. Pintrich (Eds.), *Advances in motivation and achievement* (Vol. 10, pp. 243-279). Greenwich, CT: JAI Press.

Elliot, A. J. (1999). Approach and avoidance motivation and achievement goals. *Educational Psychologist, 34,* 169-189.

Elliot, A. J., & Church, M. (1997). A hierarchical model of approach and avoidance achievement motivation. *Journal of Personality and Social Psychology, 72,* 218-232.

Elliot, A. J., & Harackiewicz, J. M. (1996). Approach and avoidance achievement goals and intrinsic motivation: A mediational analysis. *Journal of Personality and Social Psychology, 70,* 461-475.

Elliot, A. J., & McGregor, H. A. (1999). Test anxiety and the hierarchical model of approach and avoidance achievement motivation. *Journal of Personality and Social Psychology, 76,* 628-644.

Elliot, A. J., & McGregor, H. A. (2001). A 2 x 2 achievement goal framework. *Journal of Personality and Social Psychology, 80,* 501-519.

Elliot, A. J., & Sheldon, K. (1997). Avoidance achievement motivation: A personal goals analysis. *Journal of Personality and Social Psychology, 73,* 171-185.

Elliot, A. J. & Thrash, T. M. (2002). Approach-avoidance motivation in personality: Approach and avoidance temperaments and goals. *Journal of Personality and Social Psychology, 83.*

Goldsmith, H. H., Buss, A. H., Plomin, R., Rothbart, M. K., Thomas, A., Chess, S., Hinde, R. A., & McCall, R. B. (1987). Roundtable: What is temperament? Four approaches. *Child Development, 58,* 505-529.

Gray, J. (1990). Brain systems that mediate both emotion and cognition. In J. Gray (Ed.), *Psychobiological aspects of relationships between emotion and cognition* (pp. 239-288). Hillsdale, NJ: Lawrence Erlbaum Associates.

Harackiewicz, J. M. (1989). Performance evaluation and intrinsic motivation processes: The effects of achievement orientation and rewards. In D. Buss & N. Cantor (Eds.), *Personality psychology: Recent trends and emerging directions* (pp. 128-137). New York: Springer-Verlag.

Harter, S. (1978). Effectance motivation reconsidered: Toward a developmental model. *Human Development, 21,* 34-64.

Harter, S. (1981). A new self-report scale of intrinsic versus extrinsic orientation in the classroom: Motivational and informational components. *Developmental Psychology, 17,* 300-312.

Harter, S. (1983). Developmental perspectives on the self-system. In P. H. Mussen (Series Ed.) & E. M. Hetherington (Vol. Ed.), *Handbook of child psychology: Vol. 4. Socialization, personality and social development* (4th ed., pp. 275-385). New York: Wiley.

Harter, S., & Connell, J. (1984). A model of children's achievement and related self-perceptions of competence, control, and motivational orientation. In J. Nicholls (Ed.) *Advances in motivation and achievement* (Vol. 3, pp. 219-250). Greenwich, CT: JAI Press.

Hartman, H. (1958). *Ego psychology and the problem of adaptation.* New York: International Universities Press.

Heckhausen, H. (1982). The development of achievement motivation. In W. W. Hartup (Ed.), *Review of child development research* (Vol. 6, pp. 600-668). Chicago: University of Chicago Press.

Heckhausen, H. (1984). Emergent achievement behavior: Some early developments. In J. Nicholls (Ed.), *Advances in motivation and achievement* (Vol. 3, pp. 1-32). Greenwich, CT: JAI Press.

Heckhausen, H. (1987). Emotional components of action: Their ontogeny as reflected in achievement behavior. In D. Gorlitz & J. F. Wohlwill (Eds.), *Curiosity, imagination, and play: On the development of spontaneous motivational processes* (pp. 326-348). Hillsdale, NJ: Lawrence Erlbaum Associates.

Heyman, G. D. & Dweck, C. S. (1998). Children's thinking about traits: Implications for judgements of the self and others. *Child Development, 64,* 391-403.

Heyman, G. D. & Gelman, S. A. (1999). The use of trait labels in making psychological inferences. *Child Development, 70,* 504-619.

James, W. (1890). *The principles of psychology.* New York: H. Holt and Company.

Jennings, K. D. (1993). Mastery motivation and the formation of self-concept from infancy through early adulthood. In D. J. Messer (Ed.), *Mastery motivation in early childhood* (pp. 36-54). London: Routledge.

Kagan, J. (1981). *The second year: The emergence of self-awareness.* Cambridge, MA: Harvard University Press.

Kagan, J., Reznick, J. S., & Snidman, N. (1987). The physiology and psychology of behavioral inhibition in children. *Child Development, 58,* 1459-1473.

Katkovsky, W., Preston, A., & Crandall, V. J. (1964). Parents achievement attitudes and their behavior with their children in achievement situations. *The Journal of Genetic Psychology, 104,* 105-121.

Koestner, R., & McClelland, D. C. (1990). Perspectives on competence motivation. In L. A. Pervin (Ed.), *Handbook of personality: Theory and research* (pp. 527-548). New York: Guilford Press.

Lewis, M. (1993). The emergence of human emotions. In M. Lewis & J. Haviland (Eds.), *Handbook of emotions* (pp. 563-573). New York: Guilford Press.

Lewis, M. (1997). The self in self-conscious emotions. In J. G. Snodgrass, & R. L. Thompson (Eds.), *Annals of the New York Academy of Sciences: Vol 818. The self across psychology: Self-recognition, self-awareness, and the self concept.* (pp. 119-142). New York: New York Academy of Sciences.

Liebert, R., & Spielgler, M. (1994). *Personality: Strategies and issues.* Pacific Grove, CA: Brooks/Cole Publishing Company.

Locke, E., & Latham, G. (1990). *A theory of goal setting and task performance.* Englewood Cliffs, NJ: Prentice-Hall.

Maddi, S. R. (1996). *Personality theories: A comparative analysis* (6th edition). Pacific Grove, CA: Brooks/Cole Publishing.

Maehr, M. (1983). On doing well in science: Why Johnny no longer excels, why Sarah never did. In S. Paris, G. Olson, & H. Stevenson (Eds.), *Learning and motivation in the classroom* (pp. 179-210). Hillsdale, NJ: LEA.

Mascalo, M. F., & Fischer, K. W. (1995). Developmental transformations in appraisals for pride, shame, and guilt. In J. P. Tangney, & K. W. Fischer (Eds.), *Self-conscious emotions: The psychology of shame, guilt, embarrassment, and pride* (pp. 64-113). New York: Guilford Press.

Maslin-Cole, C., & Spieker, S. J. (1990). Attachment as a basis for independent motivation: A view from risk and nonrisk samples. In M. T. Greenberg & D. Cicchetti (Eds.), *Attachment in the preschool years: Theory, research, and intervention* (pp. 245-272). Chicago: University of Chicago Press.

McClelland, D. C. (1951). *Personality.* New York: Sloane.

McClelland, D. C. (1973). Sources of n achievement. In D. C. McClelland & R. Steele, *Human motivation: A book of readings* (pp. 319-375). Newark, NJ: General Learning Press.

McClelland, D. C. (1985). *Human motivation*. Cambridge, MA: Cambridge University Press.

McClelland, D.C., Atkinson, J. W., Clark, R. A., & Lowell, E. L. (1953). *The achievement motive*. New York: Appleton-Century-Crofts.

McClelland, D. C., Koestner, R., & Weinberger, J. (1989). How do self-attributed and implicit motives differ? *Psychological Review, 96*, 690-702.

McClelland, D. C., & Winter, D. (1969). *Motivating economic achievement*. New York: The Free Press.

Messer, D. (1993). Mastery motivation: An introduction to theories and issues. In D. Messer (Ed.), *Mastery motivation in early childhood*. London: Routledge.

Morgan, G., Harmon, R., & Maslin-Cole, C. (1990). Mastery motivation: Definitions and measurement. *Early Education and Development, 1*, 318-339.

Murray, H. A. (1938). *Explorations in personality*. New York: Oxford University Press.

Nicholls, J. (1984). Achievement motivation: Conceptions of ability, subjective experience, task choice, and performance. *Psychological Review, 91*, 328-346.

Nicholls, J. G. (1989). *The competitive ethos and democratic education*. Cambridge, MA: Harvard University Press.

Nicholls, J. G., & Miller, A. T. (1984). Development and its discontents: The differentiation of the concept of ability. In J. G. Nicholls (Ed.), *Advances in motivation and achievement* (Vol. 3, pp. 185-218). Greenwich, CT: JAI Press.

Nuttin, J. (1984). *Motivation, planning, and action: A relational theory of behavior dynamics* (R. P. Lorion & J. E. Dumas, Trans.). Hillsdale, NJ: Erlbaum. (Original work published 1980)

Papousek, H. (1967). Experimental studies of appetitivinal behavior in human newborns and infants. In H. Stevenson, E. Hess, & H. Rheingold (Eds.), *Early behavior: Comparative and developmental approaches*. New York: Wiley.

Pervin, L. A. (1982). The stasis and flow of behavior: Toward a theory of goals. In M. M. Page (Ed.), *Nebraska Symposium on Motivation* (vol. 30, pp. 1-53). Lincoln: University of Nebraska Press.

Pipp, S., Easterbrooks, M. A., & Harmon, R. J. (1992). The relation between attachment and knowledge of self and mother in one-year-old infants to three-year-old infants. *Child Development, 63*, 738-750.

Pomeranz, E. M., & Ruble, D. N. (1997). Distinguishing multiple dimensions of conceptions of ability: Implications for self-evaluation. *Child Development, 68*, 1165-1180.

Reis, H. T., Sheldon, K. M., Gable, S. L., Roscoe, J., & Ryan, R. M. (2000). Daily well-being: The role of autonomy, competence and relatedness. *Personality and Social Psychology Bulletin, 26*, 419-435.

Rogers, C. (1959). A theory of therapy, personality, and interpersonal relationships, as developed in the client-centered framework. In S. Koch (Ed.), *Psychology: A study of a science* (Vol. 3, pp. 184-256). New York: McGraw-Hill.

Rosen, B. C., & D'Andrade, R. (1959). The psychosocial origins of achievement motivation. *Sociometry, 22*, 185-218.

Rothbart, M. K., & Ahadi, S. A. (1994). Temperament and the development of personality. *Journal of Abnormal Psychology, 103*, 55-66.

Ruble, D. N., Eisenberg, R., & Higgins, E. T. (1994). Developmental changes in achievement evaluation: Motivational implications of self-other differences. *Child Development, 65*, 1095 – 1110.

Ruble, D. N., & Frey, K. S. (1991). Changing patterns of comparative behavior as skills are acquired: A functional model of self-evaluation. In J. Suls & T. A. Wills (Eds.),

Social comparison: Contemporary theory and research (pp. 79-113). Hillsdale, NJ: Lawrence Erlbaum Associates.

Ryan, R. (1982). Control and information in the interpersonal sphere: An extension of cognitive evaluation theory. *Journal of Personality and Social Psychology, 43,* 450-461.

Ryan, R. M. (1995). Psychological needs and the facilitation of integrative processes. *Journal of Personality, 63,* 397-427.

Saarni, C. (1993). Socialization of emotion. In M. Lewis & J. M. Haviland (Eds), *Handbook of emotions* (pp. 435-446). New York: Guilford Press.

Sedikides, C., & Strube, M. J. (1997). Self-evaluation: To thine own self be good, to thine own self be sure, to thine own self be true, and to thine own self be better. In someone and someone (Eds.), *Advances in Experimental Social Psychology* (Vol. 29, pp. 209-269). New York: Academic Press.

Shaffer, D. R. (1999). *Social and personality development* (4th ed.). Belmont, CA: Wadsworth.

Sheldon, K. M., & Elliot, A. J. (1999). Goal striving, need satisfaction, and longitudinal well-being: The self-concordance model. *Journal of Personality and Social Psychology, 76,* 482-497.

Sheldon, K. M., Ryan, R., & Reis, H. T. (1996). What makes for a good day? Competence and autonomy in the day and in the person. *Personality and Social Psychology Bulletin, 22,* 1270-1279.

Smith, M. B.(1968). Competence and socialization. In J. A. Clausen (Ed.), *Socialization and Society.* Boston: Little, Brown.

Spangler, W. D. (1992). Validity of questionnaire and TAT measures of need for achievement: Two meta-analyses. *Psychological Bulletin, 112,* 140-154.

Spence, J. T., & Helmreich, R. L. (1983). Achievement: Related motives and behaviors. In J. Spence (Ed.), *Achievement and achievement motives: Psychological and sociological approaches* (pp. 10-74). San Francisco: N. H. Freeman.

Stipek, D., & Mac Iver, D. (1989). Developmental change in children's assessment of intellectual competence. *Child Development, 60,* 521-538.

Stipek, D., Recchia, S., & McClintic, S. (1992). Self-evaluation in young children. *Monographs of the society for research in child development, 57* (1, Serial No. 226).

Suls, J., & Mullen, B. (1982). From the cradle to the grave: Comparison and self-evaluation across the lifespan. In J. Suls (Ed.), *Psychological perspectives on the self* (Vol. 1, pp. 97-125). Hillsdale, NJ: Lawrence Erlbaum Associates.

Sutton, S. K., & Davidson, R. J. (1997). Prefrontal brain asymmetry: A biological substrate of the behavioral approach and inhibition systems. *Psychological Science, 8,* 204-210.

Thompson, R. (1998). Early sociopersonality development. In W. Damon (Ed.), *Handbook of Child Psychology, Vol. 3* (5th ed., pp. 25-104). New York: Wiley.

Thrash, T., & Elliot, A. (2001). Delimiting and integrating the goal and motive constructs in achievement motivation. In A. Efklides, J. Kuhl, & R. Sorrentino (Eds.), *Trends and prospects in motivation research.* The Netherlands: Kluwer Academic Publishers.

van den Boom, D. C. (1989). Neonatal irritability and the development of attachment. In G. A. Kohnstamm & J. E. Bates (Eds.), *Temperament in childhood.* Chichester, England: John Wiley & Sons.

van der Meulen, M. (1991). "Toddlers" self-concept in the light of early action theory. In M. Bullock (Ed.), *The development of intentional action: Cognitive, motivational, and interactive processes.* Basel; New York: Karger.

Veroff, J. (1965). Theoretical background for studying the origins of human motivational dispositions. *Merrill-Palmer Quarterly*, *11*, 3-18.

Veroff, J. (1969). Social comparison and the development of achievement motivation. In C. P. Smith (Ed.), *Achievement-Related Motives in Children* (pp. 46-100). New York: Russell Sage Foundation.

Vondra, J. I. (1995).Contributions and confounds from biology and genetics. In R. H. MacTurk & G. A. Morgan (Eds.), *Mastery motivation* (pp. 165-199). Norwood: Ablex Publishing.

Watson, J. S. (1966). The development and generalization of "contingency awareness" in early infancy: Some hypotheses. *Merrill-Palmer Quarterly*, *12*, 123-135.

White, R. W. (1959). Motivation reconsidered: the concept of competence. *Psychological Review*, *66*, 297-333.

White, R. W. (1960). Competence and the psychosexual stages of development. *Nebraska Symposium on Motivation* (Vol. 8 pp. 97-141). Lincoln: University of Nebraska Press.

White, R. W. (1963). *Ego and reality in psychoanalytic theory* (Psychological Issues Series, Monograph No. 11). New York: International Universities Press.

White, R. W. (1965). The experience of efficacy in schizophrenia. *Psychiatry*, *28*, 199-211.

White, R. W. (1972). *The enterprise of Living*. New York: Holt, Rinehart & Winston. Inc.

White, R. W. (1975). *Lives in progress: A study of the natural growth of personality* (3rd ed.). New York: Holt, Rinehart and Winston.

Wigfield, A., Eccles, J. S., & Rodriguez, D. (1999). The development of children's motivation in school contexts. In P. D. Pearson & A. Iran-Nejad (Eds.), *Review of Research in Education* (Vol. 23, pp. 73-118). Washington DC: American Educational Research Association.

Winterbottom, M. R. (1958). The relation of need for achievement to learning experiences in independence and mastery. In J. W. Atkinson (Ed.), *Motives in fantasy, action, and society* (pp. 453-478). Princeton, NJ: Van Nostrand.

Yarrow, L. J., MacTurk, R. H., Vietze, P. M., McCarthy, M. E., Klein, R. P., & McQuiston, S. (1984). Developmental course of parental stimulation and its relationship to mastery motivation during infancy. *Developmental Psychology*, *20*, 492-503.

17: Three Views of the Agentic Self: A Developmental Synthesis

Todd D. Little
Patricia H. Hawley
Christopher C. Henrich
Katherine W. Marsland
Yale University

Although the concept of human agency has broad and deep philosophical roots (see Emirbayer & Mische, 1998), psychological inquiry into the nature of the agentic self has been rather fragmented. In this chapter, we examine the interrelationships among three psychological perspectives on human agency: self-determination theory (Deci & Ryan; 1985; Ryan & Deci, 2000), resource-control theory (Hawley, 1999a, 1999c), and action-control theory (e.g., Little, 1998; Skinner, Chapman, & Baltes, 1988). Our primary goal is to offer an elaborated conceptualization of the agentic self and, by so doing, to provide a broadened framework for understanding human behavior across the life span. First, we examine the common metatheoretical assumptions of these perspectives; namely, their organismic roots. Second, we define, in general terms, the concept of personal agency. Third, we discuss both basic and development features of the three views on human agency. Last, we integrate and clarify some of their commonalities in an effort to provide a broadened psychological view of the agentic self.

Common Metatheoretical Assumption

The three theoretical perspectives on human agency stem from a common organismic view of human behavior (for overviews see e.g., Miller, 1993;

We express our gratitude for the feedback and comments of our colleagues in the Agency in Development Lab of the Department of Psychology at Yale University. Partial support for this work was provided by a grant from Yale College, Yale University.

Overton, 1984; Reese, 1991). At its core, an organismic perspective views behavior as volitional, goal-directed action. Individuals are inherently active and self-regulating, and their actions are both purposive and self-initiated. Developmentally, an individual continually interacts with the environment while progressing along a predominantly self-guided path, giving form and meaning to his or her actions along the way. Moreover, an individual's actions result from selective choices that emanate primarily from the self.

An organismic approach to understanding the behavior of individuals also involves an explicit focus on the interface between the self and context (Little, in press; Ryan, Sheldon, Kasser, & Deci, 1996). Generally speaking, contexts reflect specific constellations of features at both the molar and micro levels that both constrain and afford behavior. At the same time, from an organismic perspective, the individual, when functioning optimally, is viewed as an integrated organism that both influences and is influenced by the contexts in which she or he acts and develops. In particular, this perspective presumes that individuals are active agents who plot and navigate a chosen course through the uncertainties and challenges of the social and ecological environments; however, like trade winds and currents, environments sometimes hinder, sometimes bolster, and other times change the course of a developmental route.

As part of their integrated functioning, individuals engage in a self-evaluative feedback process, continuously interpreting and evaluating actions and their consequences. As a result, across the episodes of activity in the varying constellations of context, the individual continually discovers and refines who she or he is and what she or he is capable of. Under optimal circumstances, this continually evolving and actively monitored self-system gives rise to a sense of personal agency.

A General Definition of the Agentic Self

On the basis of these organismic principles and assumptions, we define personal agency as the sense of personal empowerment, which involves both knowing and having what it takes to achieve one's goals. More broadly speaking, a well-adapted agentic individual is the origin of his or her actions, has high aspirations, perseveres in the face of obstacles, sees more and varied options for action, learns from failures, and, overall, has a greater sense of well-being. In contrast, a non-agentic individual can be a pawn to unknown extra-personal influences, has low aspirations, is hindered with problem-solving blinders, often feels helpless, and, overall, has a greater sense of ill-being (deCharms, 1968; Little, 1998; Ryan & Deci, 2000; Skinner, 1995; Weisz, 1990).

Individuals who have a sense of agency both try for ambitious goals and persist in their pursuits even in the face of obstacles. As a consequence, when individuals are high in agency, they can reach their goals more easily, and, in turn, their successes strengthen their feelings of personal agency and well-being. At the other extreme, when individuals have very little personal agency, they have low personal standards to which they aspire and often do not even try to initiate goal pursuit. Moreover, when goals are pursued, individuals low in agency find that goals are harder to reach and failures can further undermine trust in their own capabilities which, in severe cases, can lead to harmful consequences to the self and society such as alienation, amotivation, depression, helplessness, and antisocial behavior (Bandura, 1997; Ryan & Deci, 2000; Skinner, 1995).

Although these divergent profiles represent a wide continuum of variability in agentic functioning, various processes contribute to the quality and character of the agentic self, and numerous factors can influence the development of these processes. To address the nature of these influences, we endorse a stems approach to understanding human behavior; namely, an approach that underscores how the functioning of one system influences the functioning of another (e.g., Gottlieb, 1997; Lewis, 1997). From this view point, a thorough understanding of the behavior of individuals is best served by examining the various sub-systems together rather than in isolation (Magnusson & Cairns, 1996).

As mentioned, our primary goal in this chapter is to bring together the various subsystems that are the focus of the three theoretical views on personal agency and, thereby, to offer a broader perspective on motivation and self-regulation. In light of the fact that they share the fundamental assumptions of an organismic perspective, the three theoretical perspectives and their central concepts (e.g., motivated behavior, resource-directed activity, and self-regulated actions) complement one another in their characterization of individuals. Despite this complementarity, the processes that give rise to these concepts have generally been examined in isolation rather than in concert. Before examining the central points of overlap among the three theoretical perspectives, we turn to a brief overview of the specific features of each.

Specific Features of the Theoretical Perspectives on Agency

Self-Determination Theory

Basic Features. Self-determination theory posits three fundamental psychological needs for healthy functioning. The first, competence, is the basic need to successfully engage, manipulate, and negotiate the environment (see also White, 1959). The second need, relatedness, reflects the necessity for close emotional bonds and feelings of connectedness to others in the social world (see also Sroufe,

1990). The third need, autonomy, reflects the degree to which one's actions are precipitated by the self or, when non-autonomous, by causes external to the self (see also deCharms, 1968). According to self-determination theory, failure to meet any one of these needs leads to some form of psychological ill-being (for overviews see Deci & Ryan, 2000; Ryan & Deci, 2000).

The need for autonomy is perhaps the central need in self-determination theory. However, we suggest that autonomy seems to function more as an aspect of actions that support either the need for competence or the need for relatedness rather than as an independent need. In this sense, autonomy is a characteristic of one's actions, and satisfying one's need for autonomy is thereby mediated by actions that are directed toward competence or relatedness needs. For example, the act of learning basic algebra (i.e., competence) can be autonomous if the action is inherently satisfying and pursued because one experiences a genuine personal interest and sense of enjoyment from the act. On the other hand, learning basic algebra can be non-autonomous if the action is undertaken out of compliance, a desire for approval, or avoidance of a possible sanction. Likewise, having lunch with a friend (i.e., relatedness) can be autonomous if doing so is inherently satisfying and one experiences genuine personal fulfillment and enjoyment from the act; whereas it would be non-autonomous if it is done out of external obligation or social pressure.

Because controlled behavior involves action executed by the individual, it therefore involves personal agency in executing those actions. However, as we highlight in more detail below, for actions to be optimally agentic (i.e., to possess a full sense of personal empowerment), they must be autonomous. In this regard, autonomy is the quality of owning one's actions and making action choices that are integrated with the self and that serve the needs for competence, relatedness, or both. As Deci (1996) summarizes it, "without choice, there would be no agency, and no self-regulation" (p. 222).

Autonomy plays a central role in the distinction between intrinsic and extrinsic motivation as well as the variants of internalization along the self-determination continuum (e.g., integration, identification, introjection; Ryan & Deci, 2000). Intrinsic motivation describes behaviors and actions that are done of the self, by the self, and for the self. Such behaviors and actions are inherently satisfying and provide a deep sense of personal enjoyment. From the point of view of self-determination theory, intrinsically motivated behavior is fully autonomous. At the other end of the continuum, extrinsic motivation describes behaviors and actions that are done of others, by oneself, but for others (or rather, because of others). Such behaviors and actions are inherently unsatisfying, often engender a negative affective response, and rarely support one's need for autonomy (see Ryan & Deci, 2000).

Developmental features. The developmental features of self-determination theory have received only limited explication in the literature (see e.g., Ryan, Deci, & Grolnick, 1995; Grolnick, Deci, & Ryan, 1997), even though the basic features of the theory are also central aspects of core developmental theories, such as attachment theory. For example, self-determination theory posits that the needs for autonomy, competence, and relatedness are inextricably connected throughout development, and, particularly in infancy, parental support for autonomy is an important determinant of the quality of the caregiver-infant bond (Ryan et al., 1995). This view is quite consistent with attachment theory. Specifically, attachment theory, although it does not specify needs per se, nonetheless holds that beginning in infancy, competence, relatedness, and autonomy play integral roles in the development of the attachment system (Ainsworth, 1969; Ainsworth & Wittig, 1969; Bowlby, 1969; Sroufe, 1996). A secure attachment affords infants a "secure base" from which to explore the environment autonomously and develop an organized system of self as worthy, lovable, and capable. Conversely, insecurely attached infants lack the requisite affective tie with a caregiver which allows for sufficient autonomy support that, in turn, is needed for optimal self organization. In other words, attachment theory holds that a secure attachment affords a child the room to exercise autonomy and optimize both socio-emotional and cognitive competencies.

The balancing of the needs within the self is a primary self-regulatory task within self-determination theory. Consistent with this view, recent work on the longer-term implications of early infant-parent interactions conceptualizes attachment behavior as patterns of emotion or affect regulation during states of arousal or stress (e.g., Kogan & Carter, 1996). This perspective assumes that infants differ in both the degree to which they will become aroused in a frustrating or anxiety provoking situation (such as that used to measure attachment security), and the degree to which they can utilize various strategies to lower their arousal, or reorganize themselves. Moreover, recent studies on the emergence of children's motivational orientations suggests that this capacity to self-regulate and thereby pursue competence-directed and relatedness-directed goals autonomously is related to children's self-beliefs and implicit theories, even during early childhood (e.g., Smiley & Dweck, 1994).

Over the course of development, caregivers continue to influence adjustment in important ways. As posited by self-determination theory (Grolnick et al., 1997; Ryan & Deci, 2000), parenting styles that are autonomy supportive, such as authoritative parenting, are positively related to social adjustment and academic achievement (Fletcher, Darling, Steinberg, & Dornbusch, 1995; Grolnick & Slowiaczek, 1994). Thus, according to self-determination theory, caregivers promote intrinsic and internalized motivational orientations toward achievement in their children by supporting their inherent needs for autonomy, competence, and relatedness (Grolnick et al., 1997; Ryan & Deci, 2000). A primary influence on the development of competent and psychologically well individuals, then, is whether or not the early caregiver-child relationships foster an emotional bond and afford autonomous exploratory activity (see below).

Resource-Control Theory

The starting point of resource-control theory is the assumption that all organisms require resources for physical growth and development (Darwin, 1859; Ricklefs, 1979). From this decidedly evolutionary stance, an important aspect of meeting one's basic needs is to be a part of a social group where the presence of others facilitates acquisition of resources that are difficult or impossible to obtain individually. At the same time, the social group is a source of competition for the very resources it facilitates.

A history of wins and losses. Because there is within-group competition for resources, group members experience multiple wins and/or losses. That is, if resources are constrained—and many if not most are (e.g., food, social partners)—then some individuals are winning access to them while others are losing. Such within-group competition is the source of the dominance hierarchy which, from this point of view (cf. Bernstein, 1981; Strayer & Strayer, 1976), is an ordering of individuals according to their relative competitive abilities. Accordingly, socially dominant individuals by definition experience the lion's share of wins, while social subordinates experience a disproportionate quantity of losses.

These early (toddlerhood and before; Hawley & Little, 1999) and perhaps life long win-loss experiences set the stage for the development of personal agency. Indeed these early experiences may plant the seeds of agency. In any nursery group there must be winners and therefore also losers. Winners are learning that their goals can be met, they can control their environment, their efforts pay off, and future efforts are likely to pay off as well. Persistence may be a predictor of winningness (Hawley & Little, 1999), but so too may persistence be a consequence of it. Doubtless, persistence and agency are both cause and effect of present and future resource control attempts. Similarly, children who experience losses early on (in what are often viewed as trivial disputes over toys) may be in fact at risk for learning that they cannot achieve their goals and cannot control their environment in the presence of peers, that their efforts will not pay off, and that future efforts are futile. These profiles characterize the extremes of the dominance hierarchy.

Children of middle ranks experience both wins and losses depending on with whom they are interacting—those more dominant to themselves or less. Win experiences may foster a sense of personal agency in mid-ranking children that subordinates do not enjoy. It may be, however, that those occupying the highest ranks will be more likely to experience autonomy within the context of resource-directed behavior. Middle ranking children may resort to strategies such as cooperation, alliance formation, and ingratiation toward high-ranking others. They may know how and be able to achieve their goals, but they may nonetheless experience control of their behavior as external to themselves.

Balancing self and others' goals and the emergence of strategies. The necessity of meeting one's needs and simultaneously being a good group member underlies the evolution of much of human behavior and psychological organization: It implies that individuals must balance being egoistic and other-oriented (Alexander, 1977; Charlesworth, 1996; Humphrey, 1976; Trivers, 1971). Too much overt selfishness, for example, puts one at risk for alienating the very group members on which one relies. Importantly, resource-control theory explicitly recognizes that multiple strategies (e.g., prosocial, coercive) can be employed to control material resources (Hawley, 1999a, 1999c). One strategy (i.e., prosocial control), expertly capitalizes on the social group's mediation of material access by fostering cooperative relationships and treating others in ways that encourage good-will, reciprocity, and loyalty (e.g., helping, sharing, and appearing altruistic). Another strategy (coercive control) disregards positive bonds to gain direct access to resources by, for example, taking, monopolizing, and thwarting others. Both strategies underlie winningness and therefore lead to (and are the result of) personal agency. Yet, these divergent strategies may have distinct implications for the long-term psychological functioning of individuals employing them. Individuals employing prosocial strategies, for example, not only enjoy material resources, but also the regard of their peers. Coercive individuals may enjoy resource control but do not necessarily earn the regard of group members (e.g., Hopmeyer & Asher, 1997; Newcomb, Bukowski, & Pattee, 1993). Both prosocial and coercive strategies are superior to adopting no strategy: Subordinates neither orient toward resources in the environment nor capitalize on the mediating effect of others. Thus, these individuals would risk not meeting their material and social needs.

This evolutionary argument suggests that organismic adaptation requires basic motivation systems that move individuals to meet their material needs (i.e., competence needs) and to seek (resource-mediating) social relationships (i.e., relatedness needs). In other words, optimal adaptation implies drives that move the individual to seek both resources and social relationships simultaneously. This duality of motivation is especially true in infancy, where basic survival depends on both.

Developmental features. Resource-control theory has distinct developmental implications. The emergence of prosocial strategies, for example, necessitates recognizing that other group members may accept or reject you, that rejection has negative consequences, and that others have needs and desires that must also be considered. Although a certain amount of egocentricity appears to be adaptive during infancy and toddlerhood, by late preschool or kindergarten, children have refined their abilities to cooperate with peers (Cook & Stingle, 1974) and use cooperation to effectively access limited resources (LaFreniere & Charlesworth, 1987).

As a developmental theory, resource-control theory views the development of the strategies for resource control as a process of differentiation whereby development is directional and proceeds from the simple to the complex (Hawley, 1999a; Werner, 1957). The first behavioral manifestation of the motivation to acquire or control resources is primarily an undifferentiated coercive pattern.

During early development (around ages 3-5), more prosocial approaches to resource control and acquisition emerge and, after time (around ages 5-7), the two strategy types become distinct (Hawley, 1999a). Strategy employment, therefore, has differential implications depending on the age of the child.

Resource-control theory distinctly and uniquely views social dominance as relative success at controlling resources in the presence of others. That is, it is not a quality of individuals per se, but rather a characteristic of a relationship that is marked by inherent asymmetry resulting from relative ability and desire to compete. As such, social dominance is a consequence of a history of wins and losses between individuals (a matter of context). A history of winning resources at least partially underlies an individual's continued resource orientation and future attempts at resource control (i.e., agency). Similarly, a history of losses (in conjunction with personal factors) underlies a subordinate social role, and subsequently fewer resource control attempts are made in the presence of others.

Action-Control Theory

Basic features. Unlike the previous two theoretical perspectives, which focus on the motivational impetus of action, action-control theory focuses on the episodes of volitional activity — the act of goal pursuit. From this view point, the general agency system of individuals gives rise to a synergistic set of action-control beliefs and behaviors that provide the self-regulatory foundation that is called upon to negotiate the various tasks and challenges of the life course. More specifically, action-control theory focuses on the role of specific self-regulatory beliefs as mediators of motivated actions (i.e., they are the proximal links to behavior). Broadly speaking, action-control beliefs are self-perceptions about the means and competencies one has to reach one's goals (for an overview see Little, 1998). For example, action-control beliefs include (a) judgments about which specific means are most effective for reaching one's goals (means-ends beliefs), (b) beliefs about whether these means are personally available for use (agency beliefs) and (c), the general perception of the degree to which a person feels that he or she can attain a given goal (control-expectancy belief). As a general perception, control expectancy is not simply an aggregate of one's means-ends and agency beliefs (for details of these distinctions see Little, 1998; Skinner, 1995).

Under favorable conditions, such beliefs about one's own potential are a direct reflection of one's sense of agency. A highly agentic belief system would result in a specific profile of action-control beliefs that help individuals achieve successful outcomes and avoid potentially harmful influences. These beliefs are central to successful developmental outcomes because they are the proximal guides to one's actions and behaviors (Little, 1998).

Developmental features. Like children's resource control strategies, action-control beliefs differentiate over the elementary school years; they also become increasingly domain specific as well as means specific. The domain specificity of action-control beliefs results from the emerging understanding that different domains of functioning have different challenges and require different skills. That is, young children distinguish between physical, social, and academic domains of competence (Harter, 1998). By adolescence, however, these distinctions are made among both general and personal competencies in specific academic subjects, with even further distinctions made among different facets of physical, emotional, and social competence (Harter, 1998; Marsh & Yeung, 1998; Stipek & MacIver, 1989). Therefore, action-control theory posits unique profiles of self-regulation depending on the age of the individual, the domain of functioning, and, as we discuss in more detail below, the motivational orientation of the individual.

As mentioned, action-control theory also entails a means-specific view of self-regulation. The means-specificity also follows a pattern of developmental differentiation that emerges as children gradually come to distinguish among potential causes of competence. For example, young children fail to differentiate between causes such as luck, effort, ability, and powerful others. By about age 11, however, children clearly distinguish between effort and ability as causal factors (Little & Lopez, 1997; Skinner, 1990). At this time, children also begin to appreciate the inverse relation between effort and ability, inferring that greater effort implies lesser ability (Nicholls, 1978; Skinner, 1990).

Early in development, these beliefs emerge as a function of caregiver-child interaction insofar as they allow for the exercise of autonomy and competence within a given relatedness context. During early and later childhood, children bring these beliefs with them into their ever-expanding social context with caregivers, peers, and other important social figures. In turn, these social interactions also influence the further development of self-beliefs. Thus, the process is an iterative one that continues during adolescence and throughout adulthood. With age, both experience and increases in cognitive capacity influence the nature of one's action-control system.

Integrating the Three Views of Agentic Self

Self-determination theory posits central mechanisms of human agency that stem from the ontogenetic advantages of satisfying basic psychological needs for relatedness, competence, and autonomy. Resource-control theory posits central mechanisms of human agency that stem from an evolutionary perspective, emphasizing the advantages afforded individuals who are the beneficiaries of the finite resources of an environment (i.e., biologic needs). Action-control theory posits central mechanisms of human agency that stem from episodes of motivated activity. Together, these three perspectives on human agency provide an encompassing view of the agentic self.

Although there are numerous points of contact among these theoretical perspectives, we highlight three commonalties that we feel offer promising new directions for research and theorizing. In Figure 17-1, we provide an overview of these overlapping features. In the following section, we will first examine the interface between action-control regulation and the needs for autonomy, relatedness, and competence as well as the strategies of resource control. Second, we will examine the evolutionary underpinnings of the needs systems. Last, we will discuss the developmental implications of a synthesized view on the agentic self.

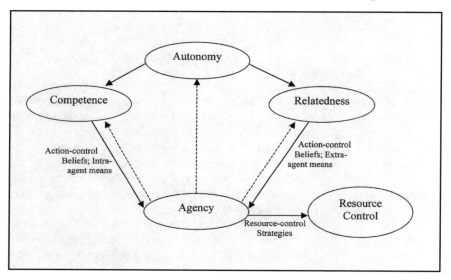

Figure 17.1. Conceptual Representation among the Key Constructs Represented in the Three Theoretical Perspectives on Human Agency.

Action-control regulation. Much of the work on action-control regulation has focused on the competence system, particularly as it occurs in the academic domain (see, e.g., Skinner, 1995). However, action-control regulation is a general process that applies to any domain of goal-directed activity, for example, social relationships (Little, 1998; Lopez & Little, 1996). Moreover, the profiles of action-control regulation that emerge across different domains of functioning provide a window that can inform how the basic needs systems operate within a given individual.

In our view, action-control theory provides a tool with which researchers can gain further insight into the interaction between the needs for competence, relatedness, and autonomy. For example, in action-control theory, causality beliefs (i.e., means-ends beliefs about the effectiveness of a given means) can include intra-agent means, such as effort or ability, and extra-agent means, such as luck and powerful others (e.g., parents, teachers, and peers). In order for children to develop an optimally agentic sense of self, they must understand that one can utilize not only intra-agentic resources, but also extra-agentic resources as means to meet their goals—a proposition held also by resource-control theory (Hawley, 1999a). However, for individuals to believe that they personally can utilize others prosocially as means to achieve their goals, they must feel connected to them. Furthermore, for individuals to be intrinsically motivated or integrated in their utilization of these means, they must feel that they are engaging in the process autonomously. In this way, the needs for relatedness and autonomy shape the motivations as well as the nature and quality of the agency beliefs guiding individuals' actions (e.g., beliefs in personal access to powerful others would be quite high in this case). These features of agency beliefs in turn influence the extent to which the need for competence is supported.

The causality beliefs, on the other hand, have distinct differential relations. By the early elementary years, most children readily learn that to perform at a certain level, more effort implies less ability and vice versa (Nicholls, 1978). Moreover, the relation between intra-agent and extra-agent means is generally independent (Little & Lopez, 1997). However, when examined as personal agency beliefs, effort, ability, and powerful others are all personal resources that one can call upon to surmount any obstacles. Thus, having (a) a sense that one possesses the ability to accomplish a goal, (b) a sense that one is capable of putting forth any needed expenditure of effort (should progress toward the goal become impeded), and (c) a sense that one can effectively utilize others in the process, reflect a powerful and adaptive profile for an individual.

Action-control theory posits that the set of control-related perceptions (i.e., action-control beliefs), because they are the proximal self-related resources that one calls upon during goal pursuit, would mediate motivational orientation (i.e., being intrinsically or extrinsically motivated). However, motivational orientation is, at the same time, a moderator of action-control perceptions. Here, for example, when intrinsically motivated, individuals should have greater beliefs in the intra-agentic means of effort and ability and these perceptions should mediate the well-documented effects of intrinsic motivation on performance and well-being (Ryan & Deci, 2000). On the other hand, externally regulated individuals should have lower intra-agentic beliefs and perhaps greater beliefs in the extra-agentic means of luck and powerful others. These self-regulatory beliefs and perceptions would function as the mediators of performance and well-being. In other words, the nature of a person's action-control beliefs will vary depending on the general motivational impetus for actions. Together, the motivational orientation and the action-control belief profiles reflect the overall quality of the agentic self.

Similarly, the action-control profile of individuals who employ different strategies of resource control would reflect the differential orientation of the strategies. For example, coercive strategies would be associated with a highly intra-agent profile and a strong belief that coercive means are effective for achieving one's goals. In contrast, prosocial strategies would be associated with a balanced profile of both intra- and extra-agent (prosocial) means viewed as most effective. In other words, the action-control belief system offers a window into the regulatory orientations that compel individuals in the service of their biological and psychological needs.

Evolutionary underpinnings. Although self-determination theory posits the three needs of competence, relatedness, and autonomy as fundamental and necessary for the individual to thrive psychologically, an evolutionary basis for these needs has only been suggested but not presented in great detail (Deci & Ryan, 2000; Ryan, Kuhl, & Deci, 1997). Clearly, the needs of competence and relatedness have direct evolutionary bases that support their inclusion as fundamental, biologically based, psychological needs. For example, fulfilling material needs (competence) is a must for all species, and members of social species can facilitate their resource control by being good group members (relatedness). Moreover, philosophical analysis of human behavior and research in psychology and sociology support the plausibility of the two-need view. Individuals, for example, are drawn to behave in self-serving ways in order to meet their needs and be effective in their environment (Bakan, 1966; Deci & Ryan, 1985; White, 1959) as well as in other-oriented ways in order to foster satisfying social relationships (Bakan, 1966; Ryan, 1995). Indeed, optimal social functioning is seen from many perspectives as a balancing of self and other priorities (Bakan, 1966; McDougall, 1933; Weinstein, 1969). An individual becomes socially dysfunctional when one goal is sought to the exclusion of the other (Ryan et al., 1995).

On the other hand, the need for autonomy may not have a direct evolutionary basis, but rather, an indirect relationship to human functioning that is likely a result of such adaptations as a highly developed cerebral cortex (i.e., an exaptation; Buss, Haselton, Shackelford, Bleske, &Wakefield, 1998; Gould & Vrba, 1982; cf. Deci & Ryan, 2000). Although we view the need for autonomy as a by-product of human intellectual capacity, its place as a fundamental psychological need is not undermined, nor is its role as a defining characteristic of optimal human agency undermine (see Figure 17-1).

Developmental implications. Throughout our discussion of the three views of the agentic self, we have highlighted specific developmental features of each. In our view, a more detailed developmental analysis is warranted. For example, successful resource control in young children, is associated with persistence, experience with peers, and social competence (Hawley, 1999b; Hawley & Little, 1999). In older children (around age 9), the group of children who are effective at resource control comprises both those who are drawn in positive ways to peers (e.g., agreeable and intrinsically motivated to pursue friendships) and those who are involved in less positive ways (e.g., hostile and extrinsically motivated to pursue friendships; Hawley, Pasupathi, & Little, 1999). This perspective thus focuses not only on how prosocially and coercively controlling individuals are different, but also on how they are the same (e.g., generally motivated to control). The long-term implications of these differences on development throughout adolescence and adulthood would likely yield new insights into the social behavior of individuals.

Although the developmental origins of the three needs appear to emanate from the attachment system, many processes of development during childhood, adolescence, and beyond do not appear to be explicitly integrated into self-determination theory. Clearly, identification via parental socialization is a key component (e.g., Grolnick et al., 1997); however, other central developmental issues, such as differentiation or de-differentiation of the needs, differential importance as a function of life phase, or the influence of other developmental acquisitions (e.g., perspective-taking), have not been explicated within the theory. In our view, further developmental analysis of self-determination would significantly bolster our understanding of human agency, particularly in light of the more explicit developmental focus of the other two views of the agentic self.

Summary Remarks

The three theoretical perspectives discussed offer different lenses through which the agentic self can be viewed. We believe, however, that rather than remain fragmented, the three perspectives can be brought together into a unified view of human agency. Moreover, a synthesis of these views opens up tremendously fertile grounds for future research. As we see it, a productive direction would be to focus on the synergism of the various processes that comprise the agentic self, the role of context (both broadly and narrowly defined) in shaping the synergism, and how these processes and their synergism change not only during childhood and adolescence but also into mid-life, old age, and beyond.

References

Ainsworth, M. D. S. (1969). Object relations, dependency, and attachment: A theoretical view of the infant-mother relationship. *Child Development, 40*, 969-1025.

Ainsworth, M. D. S., & Wittig, B. (1969). Attachment and exploratory behavior in one-year-olds in a strange situation. In B. Foss (Ed.), *Determinants of Infant Behavior (Vol. 4)*. London: Methuen.

Alexander, R. D. (1977). Natural selection and the analysis of human sociality. *The changing scenes in natural science, 12*, 283-337.

Bakan, D. (1966). *The duality of human existence*. Chicago: Rand McNally.

Bandura, A. (1997). *Self-efficacy: The exercise of control*. New York: Freeman.

Bernstein, I. S. (1981). Dominance: The baby and the bathwater. *Behavioral and Brain Sciences, 4*, 419-457.

Bowlby, J. (1969). *Attachment and loss. Vol. 1: Attachment.* London: Hogarth Press.

Buss, D. M, Haselton, M. G, Shackelford, T. K, Bleske, A. L., Wakefield, & J. C. (1998). Adaptations, exaptations, and spandrels. *American Psychologist, 53,* 533-548.

Charlesworth, W. R. (1996). Co-operation and competition: Contributions to an evolutionary and developmental model. *International Journal of Behavioral Development, 19,* 25-39.

Cook, H., & Stingle, S. (1974). Cooperative behavior in children. *Psychological Bulletin, 81,* 918-933.

Darwin, C. (1859). The origin of species. London: John Murray.

deCharms, R. (1968). *Personal causation: The internal affective determinants of human behavior.* New York: Academic Press.

Deci, E. L. (1996). Making room for self-regulation: Some thoughts on the link between emotion and behavior. *Psychological Inquiry, 7,* 220-223.

Deci, E. L., & Ryan, R. M. (1985). *Intrinsic motivation and self determination in human behavior.* New York: Plenum.

Deci, E. L., & Ryan, R. M. (2000). The "what" and "why" of goal pursuits: Human needs and the self-determination of behavior. *Psychological Inquiry, 11,* 227-268.

Emirbayer, M., & Mische, A. (1998). What is agency? *American Journal of Sociology, 103,* 962-1023.

Fletcher, A. C., Darling, N. E., Steinberg, L., & Dornbusch, S. (1995). The company they keep: Relation of adolescents' adjustment and behavior to their friends' perceptions of authoritative parenting in the social network. *Developmental Psychology, 31,* 300-310.

Gottlieb, G. (1997). Commentary: A systems view of psychobiological development. In D. Magnusson (Ed), *The lifespan development of individuals: Behavioral, neurobiological, and psychosocial perspectives: A synthesis* (pp. 76-103). New York: Cambridge University Press.

Gould, S. J., & Vrba, E. S. (1982). Exaptation: A missing term in the science of form. *Paleobiology, 8,* 4-15.

Grolnick, W. S., Deci, E. L., & Ryan, R. M. (1997). Internalization within the family: The self-determination theory perspective. In J.E. Grusec & L. Kuczynski (Eds.), *Parenting and children's internalization of values.* NY: John Wiley & Sons.

Grolnick, W. S., & Slowiaczek, M. L. (1994). Parents' involvement in children's schooling: A multidimensional conceptualization and motivational model. *Child Development, 65,* 237-252.

Harter, S. (1998). The development of self-representations. In W. Damon & N. Eisenberg (Eds.), *Handbook of child psychology: Social, emotional, and personality development* (5th Ed., Vol. 3, pp. 553-617). New York: Wiley.

Hawley, P. H. (1999a). The ontogenesis of social dominance: A strategy-based evolutionary perspective. *Developmental Review, 19,* 97-132.

Hawley, P. H. (1999b). *Social competence and prosocial and coercive strategies of resource control in preschoolers.* Manuscript submitted for publication.

Hawley, P. H. (1999c). Strategies of play and winning the game: A reply to Brian Vaughn. *Merrill-Palmer Quarterly, 45,* 363-369.

Hawley, P. H., & Little, T. D. (1999). On winning some and losing some: A social relations approach to social dominance in toddlers. *Merrill-Palmer Quarterly, 43,* 185-214.

Hawley, P. H., Pasupathi, M., & Little, T. D. (1999). *Winning friends and influencing peers: Strategies of control, social orientation, and well-being.* Manuscript submitted for publication.

Hopmeyer, A., & Asher, S. R. (1997). Children's responses to peer conflicts involving a rights infraction. *Merrill-Palmer Quarterly, 43,* 235-254.

Humphrey, N. (1976). The social function of intellect. In P. P. G. Bateson & R. A. Hinde (Eds.), *Growing points in ethology* (pp. 303-317). Cambridge: Cambridge University Press.

Kogan, N., & Carter, A. (1996). Attachment, coping and emotion regulation in 12-month-olds: Beyond the strange situation. *Infant Behavior and Development, 19*, 359-370.

LaFreniere, P. J., & Charlesworth, W. R. (1987). Effects of friendship and dominance status on preschooler's resource utilization in a cooperative/competitive paradigm. *International Journal of Behavioral Development, 10*, 345-358.

Lewis, M. D. (1997). Personality self-organization: Cascading constraints on cognition-emotion interaction. In A. Fogel, M. C. D. P. Lyra, & J. Valsiner (Eds.), *Dynamics and indeterminism in developmental and social processes* (pp. 193-216). Mahwah, NJ: Erlbaum.

Little, T. D. (1998). Sociocultural influences on the development of children's action-control beliefs. In J. Heckhausen & C. S. Dweck (Eds.), *Motivation and self-regulation across the life span* (pp. 281-315). New York: Cambridge University Press.

Little, T. D. (in press). Agency in development. In R. Silbereisen & W. H. Hartup (Eds.), *Expert views on human development*. East Sussex, England: Psychology Press.

Little, T. D., & Lopez, D. F. (1997). Regularities in the development of children's causality beliefs about school performance across six sociocultural contexts. *Developmental Psychology, 33*, 165-175.

Lopez, D. F., & Little, T. D. (1996). Children's action-control beliefs and emotional regulation in the social domain. *Developmental Psychology, 32*, 299-312.

Magnusson, D., & Cairns, R. B. (1996). Developmental science: Toward a unified framework. In R. B. Cairns & G. H. Elder (Eds.), *Developmental science: Cambridge studies in social and emotional development* (pp. 7-30). New York: Cambridge University Press.

Marsh, H. W., & Yeung, A.S. (1998). Top-down, bottom-up, and horizontal models: the direction of causality in multidimensional, hierarchical self-concept models. *Journal of Personality and Social Psychology, 75*, 509-527.

McDougall, W. (1933). *The energies of men*. New York: Charles Scribner's Sons.

Miller, P. H. (1993). *Theories of developmental psychology* (3rd ed.). New York: Freeman.

Newcomb, A. F., Bukowski, W. M., & Pattee, L. (1993). Children's peer relations: A meta-analytic review of popular, rejected, neglected, controversial and average sociometric status. *Psychological Bulletin, 113*, 99-128.

Nicholls, J. G. (1978). The development of the concepts of effort and ability, perception of academic attainment, and the understanding that difficult tasks require more ability. *Child Development, 49*, 800-814.

Overton, W. F. (1984). World views and their influence on psychological theory and research: Kuhn-Lakatos-Laudan. In H. W. Reese (Ed.), *Advances in child development and behavior* (Vol. 18). Orlando, FL: Academic.

Reese, H. W. (1991). Contextualism and developmental psychology. In H. W. Reese (Ed.), *Advances in child development and behavior* (Vol. 22). San Diego, CA: Academic.

Ricklefs, R. E. (1979). *Ecology*. Portland, OR: Chiron Press.

Ryan, R. M. (1995). Psychological needs and the facilitation of integrative processes. *Journal of Personality, 63*, 397-427.

Ryan, R.M. & Deci, E.L. (2000) Self-determination theory and the facilitation of intrinsic motivation, social development and well-being. *American Psychologist, 55*, 68-78.

Ryan, R. M., Deci, E. L., & Grolnick, W. S. (1995). Autonomy, relatedness, and the self: Their relation to development and psychopathology. In D. Cicchetti & D. J. Cohen (Eds.), *Developmental psychopathology, Vol. 1: Theory and methods* (pp. 618-655). New York: Wiley.

Ryan, R. M., Kuhl, J., & Deci, E. L. (1997). Nature and autonomy: An organizational view of social and neurobiological aspects of self-regulation in behavior and development. *Development and Psychopathology, 9,* 701-728.

Ryan, R. M., Sheldon, K. M., Kasser, T., & Deci, E. L. (1996). All goals are not created equal: An organismic perspective on the nature of goals and their regulation. In P. M. Gollwitzer & J. A. Bargh (Eds.), *The psychology of action: Linking cognition and motivation to behavior* (pp. 7-26). New York: Guilford.

Skinner, E. A. (1990). Age differences in the dimensions of perceived control during middle childhood: Implications for developmental conceptualizations and research. *Child Development, 61,* 1882-1890.

Skinner, E. A. (1995). *Perceived control, motivation, and coping.* Beverly Hills, CA: Sage.

Skinner, E. A., Chapman, M., & Baltes, P. B. (1988). Children's beliefs about control, means-ends, and agency: Developmental differences during middle childhood. *International Journal of Behavioral Development, 11,* 369-388.

Smiley, P. A., & Dweck, C. S. (1994). Individual differences in achievement goals among young children. *Child Development, 65,* 1723-1743.

Stipek, D., & MacIver, D. (1989). Developmental change in children's assessment of intellectual competence. *Child Development, 60,* 521-538.

Strayer, F. F., & Strayer, J. (1976). An ethological analysis of social agonism and dominance relations among preschool children. *Child Development, 47,* 980-989.

Sroufe, A. L. (1990). An organizational perspective on the self. In D. Cicchetti & M. Beeghly (Eds.) *The self in transition: Infancy to childhood* (pp. 281-307). Chicago, IL: University of Chicago Press.

Sroufe, A. L. (1996). *Emotional development: The organization of emotional life in the early years.* New York: Cambridge University Press.

Trivers, R. L. (1971). The evolution of reciprocal altruism. *Quarterly Review of Biology, 46,* 35-57.

Weinstein, E. A. (1969). The development of interpersonal competence. In D. Goslin (Ed.), *Handbook of socialization theory and research* (pp. 753-775). Chicago: Rand McNally.

Weisz, J. R. (1990). Development of control-related beliefs, goals, and styles in childhood and adolescence: A clinical perspective. In J. Rodin, C. Schooler, & W. Schaie (Eds.), *Self-directedness: Cause and effects throughout the life course* (pp. 19-49). Hillsdale, NJ: Erlbaum.

Werner, H. (1957). The concept of development from a comparative and organismic point of view. In D. B. Harris (Ed.), *The concept of development: An issue in the study of human behavior* (pp. 125-147). Minneapolis: University of Minnesota Press.

White, R. W. (1959). Motivation reconsidered: The concept of competence. *Psychological Review, 66,* 297-333.

18: An Educational-Psychological Theory of Interest and Its Relation to SDT

Andreas Krapp
Universität der Bundeswehr, München

In everyday thinking as well as in educational and psychological discussions of learning and development, the concept of interest plays an important role. One of the earliest theories of interest was developed by Herbart at the beginning of the nineteenth century (1806/1965), and by the beginning of the twentieth century, well-known authors were postulating that being interested was not only an important motivational condition for effective learning but was also central to people's personality and self-concept (Arnold, 1906; Berlyne, 1949; Claparède, 1905; Dewey, 1913; Thorndike, 1935). However, in the middle of this century, although the interest concept was still prominent in vocational training research, there was a noticeable decline in interest-related research in the field of learning and development.

Interest: A Rediscovered Motivational Concept in Educational Psychology

According to Krapp (1992) and Prenzel (1988) there are at least two reasons for the decline in the focus on interest: first, even in the same field of research, the concept of interest had several different meanings and there was no attempt to integrate these different concepts in an overarching theoretical framework; and second, the shift towards a focus on specialized research topics related to learning appeared to render the concept of interest superfluous. Specifically, instead of discussing the complex interrelations among different aspects of interest within a relatively broad approach to personality or human growth, research related to interest focused on phenomena such as attention (Deutsch & Deutsch, 1963), curiosity (Berlyne, 1960), emotion (Izard, 1977), flow (Csikszentmihalyi 1975), or intrinsic motivation (Hunt,1965; Deci, 1975). When used in discussions of these specific topics, the term "interest" tended to be given either a narrow and specialized meaning or a very general one that was not operationalized for purposes of research.

Over the past two decades, however, it has become clear that concepts and theories developed in these specialized fields of research do not adequately account for important phenomena that were addressed in earlier discussion on interest-based learning, especially those concerning important educational issues such as life-long learning and healthy development. As a result, researchers have shown a renewed interest in interest as a construct for describing and explaining processes and outcomes of learning in various educational settings (for a summary of recent research see Hoffmann, Krapp, Renninger, & Baumert, 1998; Krapp & Prenzel, 1992; Renninger, Hidi, & Krapp, 1992; U. Schiefele & Wild, 2000).

This rejuvenation of interest research has produced a variety of conceptualizations of interest and rather heterogeneous theoretical and operational definitions. Nevertheless, these concepts relate to one another, insofar as they address complementary aspects of the manifold phenomena. Krapp, Hidi, and Renninger (1992) have shown that theoretical and empirical research approaches in this new field can be reasonably integrated within the conceptual framework presented in Figure 18-1.

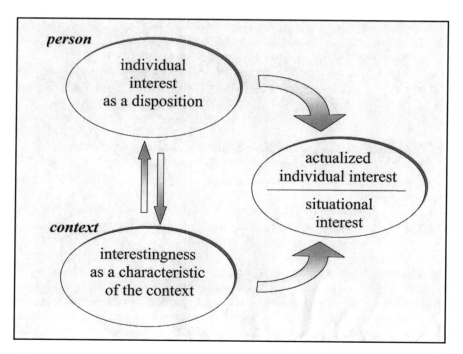

Figure 18.1. Conceptual Framework that Organizes Research on Interest

Most research on interest uses a concept of *individual interest* as a characteristic of the person. In other words, individuals are characterized by a more or less stable preference for a particular class of objects, topics, or learning tasks. Typically, individual interest is used as a predictor of academic achievement. However, there is also research about developmental changes in interest, such as gender-specific shifts in interest for various topics across years in school (Renninger, 1998) and about the effects of people's situation-specific states of interest. Such states are typically referred to as actualized individual interests. Finally, other interest research has focused on conditions in the context that affect interest and interest-based learning. From this perspective, interest is interpreted as the immediate outcome of a situation, characterized by a high level of . Such may be transitory or may provide the basis of an emergent individual interest (Hidi & Anderson, 1992; Hidi & Berndorff, 1998).

Research into interest has led to numerous results that are promising both theoretically and practically. However, there are still a number of shortcomings to this research field. A central problem is the lack of an overarching theoretical framework that could be used to summarize and systematically integrate results from different research programs (cf. Krapp, Renninger, & Hoffmann, 1998). I believe that the field of interest would benefit from a more general theory, much like the field of motivation has benefitted from general theories such as self-determination theory (SDT).

In Germany, the revival of interest as an educationally relevant motivational concept in its own right was initiated by Hans Schiefele in the late 1970s. Together with a small group of colleagues, he developed an educationally oriented theory of interest and stimulated research relevant to the theory (H. Siefele, Krapp, Prenzel, Heiland, & Kasten, 1983). He argued that the prevailing concepts of achievement motivation were insufficient from an educational standpoint for several reasons, the most important of which was its inability to address the content-specificity of a learner's motivation to learn. Therefore, a researchable concept of was needed that was motivational, could be used as the basis for an educational theory, and could be related to issues and concepts in existing motivational theories (e.g., SDT).

Looking back, it is surprising that, in 1983, H. Schiefele and his colleagues in Munich discussed the early work on intrinsic motivation by Deci (1975) and others but did not take notice of the empirical and theoretical work on SDT which had also begun by that time (Deci, 1980). Thus, their first theoretical conceptualizations of topic interest were developed without explicit reference to SDT. When we finally discovered the close compatibility of interest research and SDT, we began to explore the cross-relations and to specify some of our basic theoretical statements in accordance with SDT. In the remainder of this chapter, I present the *Person-Object Approach to Interest* (POI) (Krapp, 1993, 1999; Prenzel, Krapp & Schiefele, 1986; Prenzel, 1988, 1992), paying particular attention to its relation to SDT.

Person-Object Approach to Interest

POI is not a theory in the strict sense of the word, but rather a theoretical framework for structuring and elucidating interest-related concepts, hypotheses, and results. The POI approach includes metatheoretical principles of how to build and test a theory, a dynamic conception of personality, and specific models and investigation procedures for specialized questions (i.e. the development of interest). These will be discussed in terms of their relations to SDT.

Metatheoretical Premises

POI was developed by educational-psychological researchers who were committed to improving educational practice and for whom ,therefore, an essential feature of the theory was that it be applicable to practical research questions.

Another metatheoretical issue concerns the question of which "model of man" should be used as the starting point for building a theory. POI was from the start oriented toward a reflective-epistemological subject model (Groeben, 1986). This model, which was the basis for the German tradition of action theoretic models, assumes that people have reflective competencies for planning and realizing intentional actions—that is, that they have the ability to control rationally what they want to do. Although this has been useful as a metatheoretical starting point, additions and extensions were necessary. For example, it seems that analyzing issues about action goals or action control only at the level of conscious-rational processes, as is done in action-theoretic models, is not adequate for theoretically representing all of the influencing factors. As a consequence, POI began with a cognitive-rational action model but extended it to personality-theoretic framework to incorporate functional principles at different levels of action control.

The Underlying Conception of Personality and the Self

POI uses an approach to personality that reconstructs motivational aspects of the developing person not only with respect to individual differences, but even more importantly with respect to functional relations and general laws of human development. We agree with Deci and Ryan's position of thinking "of the person in terms of the concept of self " (Deci, 1998, p. 150; see also Ryan, 1993). Traditional approaches to differential psychology (Anastasi, 1958; Asendorpf, 1991) describe and explain psychological phenomena only from a limited perspective because they do not elaborate the dynamic and developing structure of the human being (Cronbach, 1957; Valsiner, 1986). A personality theory that considers these aspects of human development has to take into account that the person is aware of himself or herself, and that the "object" of this awareness is some sort of representation of the individual's personal "self."

According to Hausser (1983), an individual's self is manifest not only in the way the person perceives himself or herself (self-concept), but also in the way the person evaluates his or her capacities, goals, and attitudes (self-esteem), and in the way he or she assesses the potential for coping with actual and forthcoming life-tasks. In addition to cognitive representations, emotional and motivational aspects determine the structure of the self. The self can be seen as the central area of an individual's structure of personality. It represents a person's identity. Under normal circumstances, the different components of the self represent a unified structure: A mentally healthy person lives in relative harmony with his or her attitudes, goals, accumulated capacities, and knowledge structures.

Nevertheless, the self is subject to permanent change because the social and physical environments constantly require new adaptations and force the individual to set up new goals of action and development. However, only a limited selection of possible (and reasonable) goals correspond closely enough with the intentions of a person's self; other goals remain peripheral and do not particularly become significant to the person. Thus, we postulate that personality consists of a structure, which includes the self as well as other aspects that are more distant from this core.

The idea that personality is organized around an inner core not only corresponds with everyday experience but can also be found in numerous educational and psychological theories. According to Thomas (1989) all these concepts share a notion of *centrality*. Processes of high centrality are strongly self-referent, are characterized by a high degree of subjective significance, and have a pronounced readiness for (volitional) engagement and intensive emotional reactions under the conditions of success or failure.

With regard to the requirements and goals of education which involve optimizing individual development, the question arises as to how the cognitive and motivational structures represented in the self develop, that is, how the existing structure is elaborated and modified, how it changes over time, and which contextual conditions and psychological mechanisms are responsible for this development.

Development of the Self. Regarding development, POI has adopted several postulates and hypotheses of SDT. As in SDT, POI assumes "that the self is not simply a social construction or a reflection of social appraisals" (Deci, 1998, p. 151). Rather, we assume that individuals have a great influence on their own development, through an inborn tendency to interact with the social and physical environment in a constructive and self-determined way. Human beings are active by nature, and this "intrinsic proactivity" can be found from earliest childhood onwards. They are curious, explore their surroundings, manipulate things, try to affect the objects in their social and physical environment, and through these activities elaborate their own sense of self.

According to SDT, one can assume that, at the earliest stages of development, the aims and intentions that are visible in these activities belong to the child's actual state of self, although they would not exist as cognitive representations. As the child gets older the role of cognition becomes more important. During the course of life the self-system changes continually, such that already existing components become more differentiated and integrated. POI, as well as SDT and other theories, refer to these developmental changes using general concepts such as differentiation, integration, and "disintegration" (Fink, 1991).

Internalization and Integration. The ongoing developmental changes involve a continuous differentiation of the individual's structure of self, and it is only because there is an inborn propensity towards integration that this process of differentiation and reorganization does not lead to a compartmentalization of the self. The person tries to create and maintain a coherent image, a "good Gestalt" as his or her sense of self. As a consequence, the person cannot identify completely with all thoughts, actions, tasks, and strivings, even when they are experienced as important for his or her wishes and future goals at the moment. Simply stated, internalization signifies the process by which a goal that has been external to the person is taken into the self-related structure of one's personality. According to Deci (1998, p. 152), this is "the basis through which initially external regulation can become part of the self and extrinsic motivation can become autonomous."

General Characterization of the POI Approach

It is postulated that the individual, as a potential source of action, and an aspect of the environment, as the object of action, constitute a dynamic unit. Therefore, interest is conceptualized as a *relational concept*: An interest represents a specific relationship between a person and an object in his or her "life-space" (cf. Lewin, 1936). Toward some of these objects, a person will develop a close relationship that, under certain conditions, could become an individual interest.

An *object of interest* can refer to concrete things (Csikszentmihalyi & Rochberg-Halton, 1981), a topic (Schiefele, 1992; Schiefele & Krapp, 1996), a subject-matter, an abstract idea, or any other content of the cognitively represented life-space. The content of an interest object can be interpreted from two perspectives. On one hand, there is the person's knowledge about this object and his or her (emotional) assessments related to it. On the other hand, there is the object itself, apart from the person's subjective experience of it. Thus, an object of interest can be interpreted either as something that exists in an individual's mind, for example as a content-specific structure or "schema" in an individual's cognitive-emotional representation system, or as something that exists objectively in the real world, outside the individual's subjective representations.

The environment not only provides possibilities for experiencing new "objects" of interest but also represents a complex structure of conditions that influence developmental change. Here, the *social context* is of central importance.

The realization of an interest requires a situation-specific interaction between the person and the object. We use the term *object engagement* to indicate such an interaction at the most general level (cf. Prenzel, 1988). It refers to concrete, hands-on engagement with the object (e.g., a child playing with a truck), as well as to abstract cognitive working on a specific problem (e.g., the analysis of a scientific question) and to occupying oneself with certain ideas without conscious control (e.g., day-dreaming). An object engagement involves both a person and an environment and is often referred to as a *transaction* (Csikszentmihalyi & Rochberg-Halton, 1981; Fink, 1989). If the engagement occurs with purpose and intention, we refer to this as an *action of interest*. The action of interest is a special case of interest-oriented person-object-engagement insofar as the sequence of the event is subject to conscious and intentional control. This applies, for example, to all forms of intentional learning in formal schooling and training.

Under certain conditions, repeated engagements with specific aspects of the object stabilizes this relationship, creating a dispositional readiness or willingness to re-engage contents related to the domain of this object. The conditions and processes that are responsible for the emergence and development of interests are discussed later in this chapter.

This general characterization describes only the basic theoretical framework. A more detailed description requires further explication of both the object of interest and the defining characteristics of an interest-specific PO-relationship.

Objects of Interest

Although the object of an interest-related action is a fact that exists outside the person, the person's conception of the object is decisive for the action. This knowledge and evaluation of the object is represented in the person's memory system as a subjective construct, although this does not necessarily imply that the object of interest will be represented idiosyncratically. Perceptions of an object and object-related evaluations are influenced by the social context, that is, by socially shared thoughts and norms. Thus, object-related knowledge is to some extent shared and, thus, exhibits a certain degree of objectivity in the sense that an inter-subjective consensus can be found with regard to its meaning and can provide a basis for social communication about it (cf., Fink, 1989).

Because objects of interest are as a rule socially conveyed facts, each object of interest is part of societal reality (Valsiner, 1992). Moreover, individuals have contact with others who have similar or comparable interests, and they communicate about and evaluate these interests. Wherever the interests depend on direct cooperation with others (e.g., in sports or school subjects), the meanings of interest-objects are significantly defined by the social group as well as by tradition, standards, and habits.

The object of interest can be described on various levels of abstraction. The more general the characterization, that is, the more abstract the description of an object, the easier is an inter-subjective and in this sense "objective" communication about interests. However, in this way, the accuracy of the object's description is at the same time reduced. Individual interest in music, skiing, physics, or theater will surely differ from person to person with regard to the respective object conceptions when examining the micro-structure of the object conception, for example, whether one prefers the Berlin Philharmonic, the New York Philharmonic, or the Philadelphia Orchestra. However, at the intermediate level of abstraction one will find greater overlap among individuals' comparable objects of interest. You will find many music-lovers who agree that they are primarily interested in a particular form of music (e.g., classical music) and share preferred forms of engagement (e.g., going to classical concerts). Intersubjective agreement is achieved even more easily if one is satisfied with a very global characterization of preferred topics and engagements (e.g., if agreement requires only that one like music, whatever type it may be).

Regardless of the respective object domain and almost regardless of the respective level of abstraction of the object description, there are three general structural components that may be used for the descriptive analysis of almost any object of interest (cf., Fink, 1991; Krapp & Fink, 1992).

Real objects. This component refers to concrete objects toward which an interest may be directed or which are necessary for engaging in an interest. Examples would be records or instruments for the domain of music, or snowboard equipment for the domain of skiing. Objects of that kind often serve as clues for describing or empirically reconstructing an individual's interest. In qualitative analyses they have the function of reference objects (Fink, 1991; Prenzel, 1988, 1992).

Activities and types of engagement. An object of interest also includes activities and typical procedures to work on interest-related tasks. Listening to music, playing an instrument, talking about and discussing a topic, writing about a factual question, or painting a picture are examples for interest-related activities that are connected to specific areas of interest. Within the object domain of some interests, activities are of paramount importance because, so to speak, they represent the core of the interest (e.g., interest in fishing).

Topics. In almost all contexts of schooling, academic learning, professional training, or reading, the object of a learner's interest can best be described as a topic that represents a certain domain of knowledge. For example, Hidi and McLaren (1990) have defined a topic as a "coherent knowledge domain of subject matter" (p. 297). A topic can be used to describe the specific object of a situational interest (e.g., in the area of text-based learning) as well as the object of an individual interest.

Characteristics of the Interest Concept

When discussing the specific features of the interest concept, one has to bear in mind that it can be interpreted theoretically and investigated empirically either at the level of current engagements (e.g., an interest-triggered action) or at the level of dispositional structures (e.g., a student's stable subject matter interest). In any case, it differs from most other motivational concepts by its *content-specificity*. According to our determination to reconstruct interest on the basis of a PO-conception, the contents or the targets connected with an interest are important aspects for a theoretical and/or operational description. Interpreting interest as a content-specific concept fits well with modern theories on knowledge acquisition and instruction insofar as knowledge is always structured and acquired in particular domains.

In addition, four formal criteria have to be taken into consideration. They refer to cognitive aspects, emotional or feeling-related characteristics, the value component, and the intrinsic quality of interest-based activities.

Cognitive aspects. In the original conceptual framework (e.g., Prenzel, 1988; Schiefele et al., 1983) it was asserted that an action of interest is based on comparatively differentiated (complex) cognitive schemata concerning the object of interest and that it simultaneously increases cognitive complexity. This position was quite close to Renninger's (1990) characterization of an individual interest as a combination of high levels of stored knowledge and stored value for a class of objects, events, or ideas. There is indeed a lot of theoretical and empirical evidence for the assumption that an individual interest is cognitively characterized by a comparatively differentiated structure with regard to the domain of the interest object, and that each action of interest may lead to a further differentiation of this structure.

However, using a differentiated knowledge structure (i.e., high level of stored knowledge) as a criterion for defining and characterizing an interest raises serious theoretical and methodological problems because it creates a tautology. In other words, in studying the influence of interest on learning (i.e., knowledge acquisition), if one were to include stored knowledge in the definition of interest, one would, in essence, be examining whether stored knowledge predicted more stored knowledge. Thus, the postulated affect of interest would be part of the operational definition of interest. U. Schiefele (1991, 1996a) and Krapp (1992, 1999) have argued that this cognitive aspect might be appropriate for the identification of interest with small children whose knowledge acquisition is mainly interest determined but not for a definition of interests in general.

Nevertheless, cognitive aspects are still important for a comprehensive characterization of an interest. Two aspects seem to be especially important. First, an interest develops and the structural components change with respect to both cognitive and emotional representations. Thus, a developed interest differs from an interest at its earlier stages. This holds especially true for the amount of stored knowledge. As mentioned above, there is ample theoretical and empirical evidence for the assumption that a person's cognitive structure related to the knowledge domain of an established individual interest is highly differentiated and shows many connections to other cognitive domains.

Second, an interest has a tendency to grow. An interested person is not content with his or her current level of knowledge or abilities in the domain of an interest. Rather, there is a high readiness to test and to acquire new information, to learn and assume new knowledge, and to enlarge the competencies related to this domain. This means that the person needs metacognitive knowledge about things he or she does not know and is not yet able to perform. Prenzel (1988, p. 159ff.) refers to this as knowledge about "inherent object engagements" that goes beyond the domain of already executed interest-related actions. It is assumed that the knowledge structure concerning the object domain of an individual interest distinguishes itself by comparatively differentiated knowledge about opportunities for learning and development, which play an important role in the planning and execution of future interest-related actions. This trend to further develop and improve the pattern of interest related competencies is an essential indicator for the current dynamics and liveliness of a current interest. If this trend disappears completely, one would no longer speak of interest; rather it would be an indicator of the fact that the person has given up this interest.

Emotional characteristics. In the original conception of POI (e.g., H. Schiefele et al., 1983), the *emotional* characterization of an interest was limited to relatively global categories. However, Prenzel (1988, p. 156ff) expanded this by considering three components: (1) tension, in the sense of an optimal level of arousal (Berlyne, 1960); (2) empathic content-specific emotional experiences; and (3) feelings of competence. He, along with U. Schiefele (1992) and U. Schiefele & Krapp (1996), suggested that feelings of enjoyment, involvement, and stimulation are the most typical emotional aspects of an interest-based activity, and I argued that it would be theoretically fruitful to consider the concept of basic needs, which means that the emotional characteristics of an interest-based action would be experienced positively because the action satisfies basic needs such as those proposed by SDT.

From these discussions about the emotional qualities of an interest action, we conclude the following: (1) an optimum level of activation and arousal is experienced as a pleasant tension; (2) feelings of competence result from an optimal fit between a person's perceived level of competence and the requirements of the object-specific task, an aspect that is closely related to self-efficacy (Bandura, 1977; Schunk, 1991); (3) feelings of autonomy or self-determination result from the individual's experiencing freedom from external and internal pressures and being able to do what he or she wants; and (4) interest-oriented actions involving social interactions will result in positive socially-oriented emotions if the intentions of the action are compatible with the conceptions and expectations of relevant significant others.

On the whole, many aspects of an interest-triggered action are connected with positive emotional experiences. Under extremely congenial conditions, flow, or optimal experience, may be experienced (Csikszentmihalyi, 1990; Csikszentmihalyi & Csikszentmihalyi, 1988). In a person's cognitive-emotional representation system these states and experiences that precede, accompany, or follow activity involving the object of interest are stored as positive *feeling-related valences* (U. Schiefele, 1992, 1996a).

Value-related characteristics. A third aspect of interest is the component referred to as its *value* to a person. There is, however,. the question of how "high value" should be theoretically portrayed. Seen from a cognitive point of view, one could say that the individual assigns positive *value-related valences* (U. Schiefele, 1992, 1999) to the goals, contents, and actions related to the domain of interest. It would be asserted that if something is an interest it would have a prominent position within the individual's hierarchy of values. Such a description is, however, appropriate for only a small range of an individual's total pattern of interests. That portrayal would exclude all PO-relationships that are in an early or transitional stage of development. Furthermore, the assumption that a person's values are clearly and hierarchically structured is an idealistic one that does not fit real life. Thus, the value of an interest requires a different theoretical explication.

In early phenomenological analyses (cf., Allport, 1961; Dewey, 1913), and in more recent theories (e.g., Hannover, 1998; Todt, 1978; Renninger, 2000), including SDT, it is frequently asserted that a person's valuing of an activity or content is closely related to his or her self-system, and this idea can be readily applied to the value component of the interest concept. From such a theoretical perspective, the fact of positive evaluation of an interest object results either from a person's experiencing the object as intrinsically interesting or identifying with its relevance and importance for him or her. The person feels subjectively affected because it has a more or less stable relevance to his or her sense of self. Therefore, in POI the value component of an interest is referred to with the concept of *self-intentionality* in order to make clear that the goals and intentions related to the object area of an individual interest are compatible with the attitudes, expectations, and values of the person's self-system.

Intrinsic quality. The theoretical idea that an interest is characterized by a combination of emotional and value oriented components is closely related to the concept referred to as undivided interest or serious play by Rathunde (1993, 1998) and used by Rathunde and Csikszentmihalyi (1993) to describe an optimal mode of task engagement. Dewey (1913) had already characterized an interest as an undivided activity in which no contradiction is experienced between the assessment of personal importance of an action and positive emotional evaluations of the activity itself. From the POI perspective, this is the main reason why an interest based action (including knowledge acquisition in an area of interest) has the quality of intrinsic motivation: There is no gap between what a person has to do in a specific situation and what the person likes to do.

Not only in POI, but in many other conceptions of interest, the intrinsic quality of the activity is considered its most obvious feature of an interest. Here, the definition of intrinsic is based on an action-theoretical model. In his extended model of learning motivation, Rheinberg (1989, 1998) considered two different kinds of incentives: *consequence-related incentives,* which refer to future events with respect to an action-episode, and *activity-specific incentives,* which refer primarily to positive emotional experiences while performing an activity regardless of future results and consequences (e.g., enjoyable states in sports activities). The latter concept is the most closely aligned with intrinsic motivation but it still cannot cover all forms of intrinsic motivation, especially with respect to teaching and learning. Most important is the fact that this view does not take into account the content or the object of the learning activity. "From the standpoint of interest theory, a learner is intrinsically motivated when his or her main incentive for learning is related to qualities of the respective knowledge domain" (U. Schiefele, 1998, p. 93). Insofar as a person's relationship toward this knowledge domain fits the above mentioned criteria of an interest, the individual will experience a related learning task or learning episode (Boekaerts, 1996) as intrinsically motivated.

Development of Interest

With respect to the aims of the educational endeavor, the question of how interests develop and which conditions in family, school, and/or society have influenced the emergence and changes of interest is of central importance (Krapp, 1998, 2000).

Description and Explanation of General Developmental Trends

A great deal of research on the development of interest has been descriptive. Findings from studies in kindergarten and preschool (Krapp & Fink, 1992; Renninger, 1989, 1990; Renninger & Leckrone, 1991) indicate that even at this young age relatively stable interests can be identified, although the object-specific structure becomes progressively more differentiated over time. Empirical studies using cross-sectional as well as longitudinal methods have revealed negative trends across the years in students' interest for school. Indicators of such a general decline of subject interests have been found as early as the first year of elementary school (Helmke, 1993), but they have been particularly evident in secondary school. The decline has been most evident in the fields of physics, chemistry, and mathematics, and it seems to be more prominent for girls than for boys in these subjects (Gardner, 1985; Hoffmann et al., 1998).

There is now a growing body of research exploring *conditions* of interest development at different ages and in different areas of the educational system. Recent research, for example in the field of preschool and elementary education (cf., Renninger, 1998), science education (Gardner, 1998; Lehrke, Hoffmann, & Gardner, 1985), especially physics (Häussler & Hoffmann, 1998), and vocational education and training (Krapp & Lewalter, 2001; Nenniger, 1998; Prenzel, Kramer, & Drechsel, 1998; Wild et al. 1998), has examined specific conditions of interest development. At a relatively general level, the results have shown that in comparison to family and/or peers, the influence of school seems to be relatively small (Todt & Schreiber, 1998). However, a variety of different developmental trends can be found if the data are analyzed for subgroups and specific content areas. Häussler et al. (1998), for example, have reanalyzed the results of a nationwide study about the development of interest in the specific content areas of physics, using a mixed Rasch model. This methodological approach made it possible to take into consideration *qualitative* differences among students with regard to the interest structure and *quantitative* differences in the degree of interest. Students could be empirically allocated to different types of interest groups (e.g., interest in physics as formalized science vs. interest in applications and matters of societal relevance of physics). The researchers found that developmental changes in secondary school (between the sixth to tenth grade) refer primarily to differences in the distribution of types and not so much to the intensity of physics-related interest.

One problem with descriptive survey studies of interest development is that they have not specified how restructuring the conditions of learning and development could effect interest. In contrast to the results from the survey studies mentioned above, qualitative approaches (such as longitudinal case studies using retrospective interviews (Gisbert, 2001; Lewalter et al., 1998) have provided evidence that parents and teachers can have a crucial influence on the course of a student's interest development. This result is supported by intervention studies that have tried to improve the curriculum and the quality of instruction on the basis of theoretical considerations and empirical results in the field of interest research. Hoffmann & Häussler (1998) carried out a large scale intervention project to support students' development of interest in introductory physics (grade 7) – giving particular consideration to girls' negative attitudes towards natural sciences. In addition to other reform measures, new teaching materials were developed which embedded the contents of physics into contexts that girls generally find more interesting. The intervention had favorable effects on the girls' interest in physics, as well as their physics-related self-concept and achievement at the end of the school year– without any negative side effects for the boys. Referring directly to POI, Prenzel, Eitel, Holzbach, Schoenheinz, and Schweiberer (1993) found similar positive effects for a curricular revision in the interest development of medical students in the area of surgery training.

An Explanation at the Level of Psychological Processes: The Role of Basic Needs

The results from intervention studies demonstrate that the formation and change of interests can be influenced to a considerable extent by the curriculum and the quality of instruction concerning the topic. However, there remains the question of what are the psychological processes underlying the change in interests. Further, correlational studies, which are very prominent in this field, path coefficients and estimates of the percentage of variance explained by the curriculum and instruction variables fail to elucidate the general psychological processes and mechanisms that are operative for all individuals in those settings (Valsiner, 1986).

In a recent attempt to specify a functional model of interest development (Krapp, 1998, 2000), I suggested that both the explanation of maintaining a situational interest that has been newly stimulated by interestingness factors and the explanation of developmental changes in people's existing structure of individual interests depend on two components of action control, which follow different psychological principles. The *first* component is based on cognitive-rational processes and refers primarily to the problem of intention formation or the deliberate selection of learning goals. This aspect has been the focus of attention in the more cognitively oriented motivation research and has been studied thoroughly in traditional research approaches based on expectancy-value-models (cf. Heckhausen, 1991; Pintrich & Schunk, 1996). The *second* component refers to the quality of subjective experiences and the immediate emotional feedback during action. Whereas the first component of action control typically takes place at the level of conscious-reflective information processing, the second component very often functions at a non conscious level of information processing. The psychological phenomena related to this emotional component have received comparatively little attention in recent research – at least in the field of educational psychology. In accordance with SDT and other process-oriented concepts of action control (e.g. Boekaerts, 1996; Epstein, 1990) POI assumes that these factors play a crucial role in interest development.

It is postulated that a person will engage continuously in a certain topic area only if he or she assesses it, on the basis of rational considerations, as sufficiently valuable and if he or she experiences the course of interactions on the whole as positive and emotionally satisfactory (Krapp, 1999, see also Deci, 1992, 1998). In recent research within the POI framework, we have tried to specify those emotional experiences that play a functional role in development on the basis of the concept of basic psychological needs. In line with SDT (e.g., Ryan, 1995) and Nuttin's (1984) Relational Theory of Behavioral Dynamics, we assume that emotional feedback concerning the degree to which the three basic psychological needs for competence, autonomy, and social relatedness have been satisfied is especially important among the wealth of possible emotional aspects that might have a positive or negative influence on the quality of experience during motivated learning.

In fact, several studies have revealed significant relationships between empirical indicators of need-satisfying experiences and different criteria of interest development. The majority of these studies were carried out with students and young adults in vocational settings (Prenzel, Kramer & Drechsel, 1998). We are currently studying the conditions and processes of interest genesis in the context of vocational education on the basis of a longitudinal study. Here, especially the mechanisms of need-related qualities of experience are being studied with both quantitative and qualitative methods (Lewalter, Krapp, Schreyer, & Wild, 1998; Wild & Krapp, 1996; Wild, Krapp, Schreyer, & Lewalter, 1998). The quantitative analyses are based on data from questionnaires and ESM studies and observational techniques. The qualitative analyses are based on retrospective interviews with a smaller number of randomly chosen participants from the main study. Although the results from different aspects of the research differ in several important respects, they seem to support the overall hypothesis that need-related experiences with respect to an interest object will lead to the emergence and stabilization of longer-lasting interests (Krapp & Lewalter, in press; Lewalter et al., 1998).

Interest, Learning and Academic Achievement

When conditions and processes of development are under consideration, interest is interpreted as a dependent variable, and the work focuses on the questions of how and why interests change over time. Another research perspective refers to the question of how and to what degree interests influence learning and academic achievement. Most empirical research in educational psychology has been devoted to this second question. Findings prior to 1990 have been presented and summarized in Renninger, Hidi, and Krapp (1992). Many researchers now have adopted the distinction between situational and individual (or personal) interest (see Figure 18-1). According to Hidi and Berndorff (1998) and Mitchell (1993), the personal interest approach tends to focus on individual differences, whereas the situational interest approach centers on creating appropriate environmental settings to create interest and motivate learning.

Results from both approaches have demonstrated positive effects of interest-based learning on educationally relevant outcome criteria. In reviewing past research on the relation between individual interest and academic achievement, Schiefele, Krapp, and Winteler (1992) and Schiefele, Krapp and Schreyer (1993) have conducted meta-analyses with respect to global indicators (grades, achievement tests) and specific indicators of learning (e.g., recall of a specific text). On average, across different subject areas, types of schools, and age groups, the level of interest has accounted for about 10% of the observed variance in achievement. Gender turned out to be a strong moderator variable: female students' academic performance tends to be less associated with their interests than male students' performance. In principle, research on situational interest has also shown that an interest-triggered learning activity leads to better learning results, especially with respect to qualitative criteria such as a higher degree of conceptual or deep-level learning (see Hidi & Anderson, 1992; Hidi & Berndorff, 1998; U. Schiefele, 1996a).

In recent years, research on interest and learning has become more differentiated. New research questions have been raised, for example the role of interest in text learning (U. Schiefele, 1992, 1996a, 1999), the interrelation between interest personal goals and self concept (Hidi & Harackiewcz, 2001; Hannover, 1998), or the effects of interest based learning at different developmental stages and in different educational surroundings, including preschool and elementary school (Prenzel, Lankes, & Minsel, 2000; Renninger, 1998), secondary school (Baumert & Köller, 1998), colleges and universities (Krapp, 1997), and vocational education and training (Prenzel et al., 1998; Krapp & Wild, 1998). Another important line of research is concerned with the search for mediating variables that can explain the (positive) effects of interest-based learning at the level of functional processes (Schiefele, 1998; Schiefele & Rheinberg, 1997). Among the few variables that have been analyzed in detail are attention (for a summary see Hidi, 1995), learning strategies (Wild, 2000), emotional experiences (Krapp & Lewalter, 2001; Lewalter et al., 1998; U. Schiefele, 1996b; U. Schiefele & Csikszentmihalyi, 1994).

Conclusions

The Person-Object Conception of Interest (POI) has been developed in the field of educational psychology. It is based on metatheoretical premises and central ideas about the structure and dynamics of human personality which are closely related to SDT.

According to POI, interest is a relational construct. It refers to a "person-object-relation," which is characterized by several specific features including both, feeling- and value-related aspects. An interest-based PO-relationship can be investigated and theoretically substantiated at two levels of analysis: at the level of current events, states, or processes when an individual is realizing an interest (*action of interest*) and at the level of (motivational) disposition, indicating a relatively stable tendency to become occupied with an object of interest (*personal* or *individual interest*). With respect to educational practice, the question of how educationally relevant interests develop is of special importance. A good deal of empirical research has been devoted to analyzing general trends of interest development with regard to different educational settings, student populations, and object areas. Other approaches have tried to explore institutional, curricular, or individual conditions of interest development.

POI has proposed that the wide variety of developmental trends and effects can be explained not only with respect to the emergence of interindividual differences but also with respect to general principles of human growth and development. The functional model of interest genesis postulates that the control of single interest actions and, on a long-term basis, the facilitation of interest development takes place on two different levels of information processing: in the conscious-reflective level concerning decisions about future learning goals and the emotional level which provides continuous and often non conscious feedback about the quality and/or efficacy of the ongoing action. Here, experiences referring to the fulfillment of the three basic needs discussed in SDT play a crucial role. Results from several longitudinal studies in the area of vocational education using quantitative as well as qualitative data provide empirical evidence that supports the basic theoretical ideas represented in this model.

Besides interest development, the effects of interest on learning and development make up another important field of interest research. Results from many different approaches confirm the hypothesis that interest-based learning tends to have many advantages with respect to educationally desirable outcomes. What will have to be explored in more detail in the future is the question of how these positive effects can be explained at the level of psychological principles which ultimately can be used to optimize the educational endeavor.

References

Allport, G. W. (1961). *Pattern and growth in personality.* New York: Holt.

Anastasi, A. (1958). *Differential psychology (3rd ed.).* New York: Macmillan.

Arnold, F. (1906). The psychology of interest. I/II. *Psychological Review, 13,* 221-238/291-315.

Asendorpf, J. (1991). *Die differentielle Sichtweise in der Psychologie.* Göttingen, Germany: Hogrefe.

Bandura, A. (1977). Self-efficacy: Toward a unifying theory of behavioral change. *Psychological Review, 84,* 191-215.

Baumert, J., & Köller, O. (1998). Interest research concerning secondary level I: An overview. In L. Hoffmann, A. Krapp, K. A. Renninger, & J. Baumert (Eds.), *Interest and learning. Proceedings of the Seeon-Conference on interest and gender* (pp. 241-256). Kiel, Germany: Institut für die Pädagogik der Naturwissenschaften.

Berlyne, D. E. (1949). Interest as a psychological concept. *The British Journal of Psychology, 39,* 184-195.

Berlyne, D. E. (1960). *Conflict, arousal and curiosity.* New York: Grove Press.

Boekaerts, M. (1996). Personality and the psychology of learning. *European Journal of Personality, 10,* 377-404.

Claparède E. (1905). *Psychologie de l'enfant et pedagogie expérimentale.* Genève, Switzerland: Kundig.

Cronbach, L. J. (1957). The two disciplines of scientific psychology. *American Psychologist, 12,* 671-684.

Csikszentmihalyi, M. (1975). *Beyond boredom and anxiety. The experience of play in work and games.* San Francisco: Jossey-Bass.

Csikszentmihalyi, M. (1990). *Flow.* New York: Harper & Row.

Csikszentmihalyi, M., & Csikszentmihalyi, I. S. (1988). *Optimal experience.* New York: Cambridge University Press.

Csikszentmihalyi, M., & Rochberg-Halton, E. (1981). *The meaning of things.* New York: Cambridge University Press.

Deci, E. L. (1975). *Intrinsic motivation.* New York: Plenum Press.

Deci, E. L. (1980). *The psychology of self-determination.* Lexington, MA: D. C. Heath.

Deci, E. L. (1992). The relation of interest to the motivation of behavior: A self-determination theory perspective. In K. A. Renninger, S. Hidi, & A. Krapp (Eds.), *The role of interest in learning and development* (pp. 43-47). Hillsdale, NJ.: Erlbaum.

Deci, E. L. (1998). The relation of interest to motivation and human needs: The self-determination theory viewpoint. In L. Hoffmann, A. Krapp, K. A. Renninger, & J. Baumert (Eds.), *Interest and learning. Proceedings of the Seeon-Conference on interest and gender* (pp. 146-162). Kiel, Germany: Institut für die Pädagogik der Naturwissenschaften.

Deutsch, J. A., & Deutsch, D. (1963). Attention: some theoretical considerations. *Psychological Review, 70,* 80-90.

Dewey, J. (1913). *Interest and effort in education.* Boston: Riverside Press.

Epstein, S. (1990). Cognitive-experiential self theory: Implications for developmental psychology. In M. Gunnar & L. A. Sroufe (Eds.), *Minnesota symposia on child psychology: Self processes and development* (Vol. 23, pp. 79-123). Hilsdale, NJ: Erlbaum.

Fink, B. (1989). *Das konkrete Ding als Interessengegenstand.* Frankfurt, Germany: Lang.

Fink, B. (1991). Interest development as structural change in person-object relationships. In L. Oppenheimer & J. Valsiner (Eds.), *The origins of action: Interdisciplinary and international perspectives* (pp. 175-204). New York: Springer.

Gardner, P. L. (1985). Students` interest in science and technology: an international overview. In M. Lehrke, L. Hoffmann, & P. L. Gardner (Eds.), *Interests in science and technology education* (pp. 15-34). Kiel, Germany: Institut für die Pädagogik der Naturwissenschaften.

Gardner, P. L. (1998). The development of males´ and females´ interest in science and technology. In L. Hoffmann, A. Krapp, K. A. Renninger, & J. Baumert (Eds.), *Interest and learning. Proceedings of the Seeon-Conference on interest and gender* (pp. 41-57). Kiel, Germany: Institut für die Pädagogik der Naturwissenschaften.

Gisbert, K. (2001). *Geschlecht und Studienwahl.* Münster, Germany: Waxmann.

Groeben, N. (1986). *Handeln, Tun, Verhalten als Einheiten einer verstehend-erklärenden Psychologie.* Tübingen: Francke Verlag.

Hannover, B. (1998). The development of self-concept and interests. In L. Hoffmann, A. Krapp, K. A. Renninger, & J. Baumert (Eds.), *Interest and learning. Proceedings of the Seeon-Conference on interest and gender* (pp. 105-125). Kiel, Germany: Institut für die

Pädagogik der Naturwissenschaften.

Hausser, K. (1983). *Identitätsentwicklung.* New York: Harper & Row.

Häussler, P., & Hoffmann, L. (1998). Qualitative differences in student's interest in physics and the dependence on gender and age. In L. Hoffmann, A. Krapp, K. A. Renninger, & J. Baumert (Eds.), *Interest and learning. Proceedings of the Seeon-Conference on interest and gender* (pp. 280-289). Kiel, Germany: Institut für die Pädagogik der Naturwissenschaften.

Häussler, P., Hoffmann, L., Langeheine, R., Rost, J., & Sievers, K. (1998). A typology of students' interest in physics and the distribution of gender and age within each type. *International Journal of Science Education, 20,* 223-238.

Heckhausen, H. (1991). *Motivation and action (German Original 1989: Motivation und Handeln).* Berlin: Springer-Verlag.

Helmke, A. (1993). Die Entwicklung der Lernfreude vom Kindergarten bis zur 5. Klassenstufe. *Zeitschrift für Pädagogische Psychologie, 7,* 77-86.

Herbart, J. F. (1965/1806). Allgemeine Pädagogik, aus dem Zweck der Erziehung abgeleitet. In J. F. Herbart (Hg.), *Pädagogische Schriften* (Vol.2, p. 9-155). Desseldorf, Germany: Kepper.

Hidi, S. (1995). A reexamination of the role of attention in learning from text. *Educational Psychological Review, 7,* 323-350.

Hidi, S., & Anderson, V. (1992). Situational interest and its impact on reading and expository writing. In K. A. Renninger, S. Hidi, & A. Krapp (Eds.), *The role of interest in learning and development* (pp. 215-238). Hillsdale, NJ.: Erlbaum.

Hidi, S., & Berndorff, D. (1998). Situational interest and learning. In L. Hoffmann, A. Krapp, K. A. Renninger, & J. Baumert (Eds.), *Interest and learning. Proceedings of the Seeon-Conference on interest and gender* (pp. 74-90). Kiel, Germany: Institut für die Pädagogik der Naturwissenschaften.

Hidi, S., & Harackiewicz, J. M. (2001). Motivating the academically unmotivated: A critical issue for the 21st century. *Review of Educational Research, 70,* 151-179.

Hidi, S., & McLaren J. (1990). The effect of topic and theme interestingness on the production of school expositions. In H. Mandl, E. De Corte, N. Bennett, & H. F. Friedrich (Eds.), *Learning and instruction* (pp. 295-308). Oxford: Pergamon Press.

Hoffmann, L., & Häussler, P. (1998). An intervention project promoting girls´ and boys´ interest in physics. In L. Hoffmann, A. Krapp, K. A. Renninger, & J. Baumert (Eds.), *Interest and learning. Proceedings of the Seeon-Conference on interest and gender* (pp. 301-316). Kiel, Germany: Institut für die Pädagogik der Naturwissenschaften.

Hoffmann, L., Krapp, A., Renninger, K. A., & Baumert, J. (Eds.) (1998). *Interest and learning. Proceedings of the Seeon-conference on interest and gender.* Kiel, Germany: Institut für die Pädagogik der Naturwissenschaften.

Hunt, J. McV. (1965). Intrinsic motivation and its role in psychological development. In D. Levine (Ed.), *Nebraska symposium on motivation* (pp. 189-282). Lincoln: University of Nebraska Press.

Izard, C. E. (1977). *Human emotions.* New York: Plenum.

Krapp, A. (1992). Interesse, lernen und leistung. *Zeitschrift für Pädagogik, 38,* 747-770.

Krapp, A. (1993). *The construct of interest: Characteristics of individual interests and interest-related actions from the perspective of a person-object-theory.* (Studies in Educational Psychology). Munich: Institut für Empirische Pädagogik und Pädagogische Psychologie der Universität der Bundeswehr.

Krapp, A. (1997). Interesse und Studium. In H. Gruber & A. Renkl (Eds.), *Wege zum*

Können. Determinanten des Kompetenzerwerbs (pp. 45-58). Bern, Switzerland: Huber.

Krapp, A. (1998). Entwicklung und Förderung von Interessen im Unterricht. *Psychologie in Erziehung und Unterricht, 45,* 186-203.

Krapp, A. (1999). Interest, motivation and learning: An educational-psycholgical perspective. *European Journal of Psychology in Education, 14,* 23-40.

Krapp, A. (2000). Interest and human development during adolescence: An educational-psychological approach. In J. Heckhausen (Ed.), *Motivational psychology of human development* (pp. 109-128). London: Elsevier.

Krapp, A., & Fink, B. (1992). The development and function of interests during the critical transition from home to preschool. In K. A. Renninger, S. Hidi, & A. Krapp (Eds.), *The role of interest in learning and development* (pp. 397-429). Hillsdale, NJ: Erlbaum.

Krapp, A., Hidi, S., & Renninger, K. A. (1992). Interest, learning and development. In K. A. Renninger, S. Hidi, & A. Krapp (Eds.), *The role of interest in learning and development* (pp. 3-25). Hillsdale, NJ: Erlbaum.

Krapp, A., & Lewalter, D. (2001). Development of interests and interest-based motivational orientations: A longitudinal study in school and work settings. In S. Volet & S. Järvelä (Eds.), *Motivation in learning contexts: Theoretical and methodological implications,* (pp. 201-232). London: Elsevier.

Krapp, A., & Prenzel, M. (Eds.) (1992). *Interesse, Lernen, Leistung.* Münster, Germany: Aschendorff.

Krapp, A., Renninger, A., & Hoffmann, L. (1998). Some thoughts about the development of a unifying framework for the study of individual interest. In L. Hoffmann, A. Krapp, K. A. Renninger, & J. Baumert (Eds.), *Interest and learning Proceedings of the Seeon-Conference on interest and gender* (pp. 455-468). Kiel, Germany: Institut für die Pädagogik der Naturwissenschaften.

Krapp, A., & Wild, K. P. (1998, August). *The development of interest in school and work settings: A longitudinal study based on experience-sampling data.* Paper presented at the 24the International Congress of Applied Psychology, San Francisco.

Lehrke, M., Hoffmann, L., & Gardner, P. L. (Eds.) (1985). *Interests in science and technology education.* Kiel, Germany: Institut für die Pädagogik der Naturwissenschaften.

Lewalter, D., Krapp, A., Schreyer, I., & Wild, K. P. (1998). Die Bedeutsamkeit des Erlebens von Kompetenz, Autonomie und sozialer Eingebundenheit für die Entwicklung berufsspezifischer Interessen. In K. Beck, & R. Dubs (Eds.), *Kompetenzentwicklung in der Berufserziehung - Kognitive, motivationale und moralische Dimensionen kaufmännischer Qualifizierungsprozesse. Zeitschrift für Berufs- und Wirtschaftspädagogik* (Vol. Beiheft Nr. 14, pp. 143-168.). Stuttgart, Germany: Steiner.

Lewin, K. (1936). *Principles of topological psychology.* New York: McGraw-Hill.

Mitchell, M. (1993). Situational interest: Its multifaceted structure in the secondary school mathematics classroom. *Journal of Educational Psychology, 85,3,* 424-436.

Nenniger, P. (1998). Changes of interests in academic and vocational learning. In L. Hoffmann, A. Krapp, K. A. Renninger, & J. Baumert (Eds.), *Interest and learning Proceedings of the Seeon-Conference on interest and gender* (pp. 420-429). Kiel, Germany: Institut für die Pädagogik der Naturwissenschaften.

Nuttin, J. (1984). *Motivation, planning, and action.* Hillsdale, NJ: Erlbaum.

Pintrich, P. R., & Schunk, D. H. (1996). *Motivation in education. Theory, research and applications.* Eglewood Cliffs: Prentice-Hall.

Prenzel, M. (1988). *Die Wirkungsweise von Interesse. Ein Erklärungsversuch aus pädagogisch-*

er Sicht. Opladen, Germany: Westdeutscher Verlag.

Prenzel. M. (1992). Selective persistence of interest. In K. A. Renninger, S. Hidi, & A. Krapp (Eds.), *The role of interest in learning and development* (pp. 71-98). Hillsdale, NJ.: Erlbaum.

Prenzel, M., Eitel, F., Holzbach, R., Schoenheinz, R. J., & Schweiberer, L. (1993). Lernmotivation im studentischen Unterricht in der Chirurgie. *Zeitschrift für Pädagogische Psychologie, 7*, 125-137.

Prenzel, M., Kramer, K., & Drechsel, B. (1998). Changes in learning motivation and interest in vocational education: Halfway through the study. In L. Hoffmann, A. Krapp, K. A. Renninger, & J. Baumert (Eds.), *Interest and learning. Proceedings of the Seeon-Conference on interest and gender* (pp. 430-440). Kiel, Germany: Institut für die Pädagogik der Naturwissenschaften.

Prenzel, M., Krapp, A., & Schiefele, H. (1986). Grundzüge einer pädagogischen Interessentheorie. *Zeitschrift für Pädagogik, 32*, 163-173.

Prenzel, M., Lankes, E. M., & Minsel, B. (2000). Interessenentwicklung in kindergarten und grundschule. In U. Schiefele & K. P. Wild (Eds.), *Interesse und lernmotivation* (pp. 11-30). Münster, Germany: Waxmann.

Rathunde, K. (1993). The experience of interest: A theoretical and empirical look at its role in adolescent talent development. In M. Maehr, & P. R. Pintrich (Ed.), *Advances in motivation and achievement* (Vol. 8, pp. 59-98). London: Jai Press Inc..

Rathunde, K. (1998). Undivided and abiding interest: comparisons across studies of talented adolescents and creative adults. In L. Hoffmann, A. Krapp, K. A. Renninger, & J. Baumert (Eds.), *Interest and learning. Proceedings of the Seeon-Conference on interest and gender* (pp. 367-376). Kiel, Germany: Institut für die Pädagogik der Naturwissenschaften.

Rathunde, K., & Csikszentmihalyi, M. (1993). Undivided interest and the growth of talent: A longitudinal study of adolescents. *Journal of Youth and Adolescence, Vol. 22, No. 4*, 1-21.

Renninger, K. A. (1989). Individual patterns in children's play interests. In L. T. Winegar (Ed.), *Social interaction and the development of children's understanding* (pp. 147-172). Norwood, NJ: Ablex.

Renninger, K. A. (1990). Children's play interests, representation, and activity. In R. Fivush & J. Hudson (Eds.), *Knowing and remembering in young children (Bd. III. Emory Cognition Series* (pp. 127-147). Cambridge, MA: Cambridge University Press.

Renninger, K. A. (1992). Individual interest and development: Implications for theory and practice. In K. A. Renninger, S. Hidi, & A. Krapp (Eds.), *The role of interest in learning and development* (pp. 361-395). Hillsdale, NJ.: Erlbaum.

Renninger, K. A. (1998). The role of individual interest(s) and gender in learning: An overview of research on preschool and elementary school-aged children/students. In L. Hoffmann, A. Krapp, K. A. Renninger, & J. Baumert (Eds.), *Interest and learning. Proceedings of the Seeon-Conference on interest and gender* (pp. 165-174). Kiel, Germany: Institut für die Pädagogik der Naturwissenschaften.

Renninger, K. A. (2000). Individual interest and development: Implications for theory and practice. In C. Sansone & J. M. Harackiewicz (Eds.), *Intrinsic and extrinsic motivation. The search for optimal motivation and performance* (pp. 375-404). New York: Academic Press.

Renninger, K. A., Hidi, S., & Krapp, A., (Eds.) (1992). *The role of interest in learning and development.* Hillsdale, NJ: Erlbaum.

Renninger, K. A., & Leckrone, T. G. (1991). Temperament and task engagement: Individual patterns in children's play. In L. Oppenheimer, & J. Valsiner (Eds.), *The origins of action: Interdisciplinary and international perspectives* (pp. 205-238). New York: Springer.

Rheinberg, F. (1989). *Zweck und Tätigkeit.* Göttingen, Germany: Hogrefe.

Rheinberg, F. (1998). Theory of interest and research on motivation to learn. In L. Hoffmann, A. Krapp, K. A. Renninger, & J. Baumert (Eds.), *Interest and learning. Proceedings of the Seeon-Conference on interest and gender* (pp. 126-145). Kiel, Germany: Institut für die Pädagogik der Naturwissenschaften.

Ryan, R. M. (1993). Agency and organization: Intrinsic motivation, autonomy and the self in psychological development. In J. Jacobs (Ed.), *Nebraska symposium on motivation: Development perspectives on motivation*

Ryan, R. M. (1995). Psychological needs and the facilitation of integrative process. *Journal of Personality, 63 (3)*, 397-427.

Schiefele, H., Krapp, A., Prenzel, M., Heiland, A., & Kasten, H. (1983). *Principles of an educational theory of interest.* (Paper presented at the 7th Meeting of the International Society for the Study of Behavioral Development in Munich).

Schiefele, U. (1991). Interest, learning and motivation. *Educational Psychologist, 26 (2 & 3)* 299-323.

Schiefele, U. (1992). Topic interest and levels of text comprehension. In K. A. Renninger, S. Hidi, & A. Krapp (Eds.), *The role of interest in learning and development* (pp. 151-182). Hillsdale, NJ: Erlbaum.

Schiefele, U. (1996a). *Motivation und Lernen mit Texten.* Göttingen, Germany: Hogrefe.

Schiefele, U. (1996b). Topic interest, text representation, and quality of experience. *Contemporary Educational Psychology, 21,* 3-18.

Schiefele, U. (1998). Individual interest and learning - what we know and what we don´t know. In L. Hoffmann, A. Krapp, K. A. Renninger, & J. Baumert (Eds.), *Interest and learning. Proceedings of the Seeon-Conference on interest and gender* (pp. 91-104). Kiel, Germany: Institut für die Pädagogik der Naturwissenschaften.

Schiefele, U. (1999). Interest and learning from text. *Scientific Studies of Reading, 3,* 257-279.

Schiefele, U., & Csikszentmihalyi, M. (1994). Interest and the quality of experience in classrooms. *European Journal of Psychology of Education, IX (3),* 251-270.

Schiefele, U., & Krapp, A. (1996). Topic interest and free recall of expository text. *Learning and Individual Differences, 8,* 141-160.

Schiefele, U., Krapp, A., & Schreyer, I. (1993). Metaanalyse des Zusammenhangs von Interesse und schulischer Leistung. *Zeitschrift für Entwicklungspsychologie und Pädagogische Psychologie, 25,* 120-148.

Schiefele, U., Krapp, A., & Winteler, A. (1992). Interest as a predictor of academic achievement: A meta-analysis of research. In K. A. Renninger, S. Hidi, & A. Krapp (Eds.), *The role of interest in learning and development* (pp. 183-212). Hillsdale, NJ: Erlbaum.

Schiefele, U., & Rheinberg, F. (1997). Motivation an knowledge acquisition: searching for mediating processes. In M. L. Maehr, & P. Pintrich (Eds.), *Advances in motivation and achievement, Vol 10.* (pp. 251-301). London: Jai Press

Schiefele, U., & Wild, K. P. (Eds.), (2000). *Interesse und lernmotivation.* Münster, Germany: Waxmann.

Schunk, D. H. (1991). Self-efficacy and academic motivation. *Educational Psychologist, 26,* 207-231.

Thomas, M. (1989). *Zentralität und Selbstkonzept.* Bern, Switzerland: Huber.

Thorndike, E. L. (1935). *Adult interests.* New York: Macmillan.

Todt, E. (1978). *Das Interesse.* Bern, Switzerland: Huber.

Todt, E., & Schreiber, S. (1998). Development of interests. In L. Hoffmann, A. Krapp, K. A. Renninger, & J. Baumert (Eds.), *Interest and learning. Proceedings of the Seeon-Conference on interest and gender* (pp. 25-40). Kiel, Germany: Institut für die Pädagogik der Naturwissenschaften.

Valsiner, J. (1986). Between groups and individuals. Psychologists' and laypersons' interpretations of correlational findings. In J. Valsiner (Ed.), *The individual subject and scientific psychology* (pp. 113-151). New York: Plenum Press.

Valsiner, J. (1992). Interest: A Meta-Theoretical Perspective. In K. A. Renninger, S. Hidi, & A. Krapp (Eds.), *The role of interest in learning and development* (pp. 27-41). Hillsdale, NJ.: Erlbaum.

Wild, K. P. (2000). Lernstrategien im studium. Münster/New York: Waxmann.

Wild, K. P., & Krapp. A. (1996). Die Qualität subjektiven Erlebens in schulischen und betrieblichen Lernumwelten. Untersuchungen mit der Erlebens Stichproben Methode. *Unterrichtswissenschaft, 24,* 195-216.

Wild, K. P., Krapp, A., Schreyer, I., & Lewalter, D. (1998). The development of interest and motivational orientations: gender differences in vocational education. In L. Hoffmann, A. Krapp, K. A. Renninger, & J. Baumert (Eds.), *Interest and learning. Proceedings of the Seeon-Conference on interest and gender* (pp. 441-454). Kiel, Germany: Institut für die Pädagogik der Naturwissenschaften.

PART V

❖ ❖ ❖

CONCLUDING COMMENTS

19: Self-Determination Research: Reflections and Future Directions

Edward L. Deci
Richard M. Ryan
University of Rochester

Three decades have passed since publication of the first experiments on intrinsic motivation in humans (Deci, 1971, 1972a, 1972b; Kruglanski, Friedman, & Zeevi, 1971; Lepper, Greene, & Nisbett, 1973). These studies, which found that extrinsic rewards can undermine intrinsic motivation, were anomalous with respect to existing paradigms in psychology, and they suggested many fascinating questions that have occupied researchers ever since. For example, a recent meta-analysis (Deci, Koestner, & Ryan, 1999) revealed more than 125 articles reporting laboratory experiments that examined the effects of extrinsic rewards on intrinsic motivation. Additional studies have examined the effects of rewards on such outcomes as creativity, problem solving, learning, and well-being, to which intrinsic motivation is hypothesized to be related. And still other studies have moved beyond rewards to examine the effects of such factors as threats, deadlines, imposed goals, competition, and interpersonal climates on intrinsic motivation and related outcomes. These various studies have been conducted in field settings as well as in the laboratory, and some of them have examined the mediating processes through which the effects are produced.

Subsequently, when studies began to focus on the differentiation of extrinsic motivation using the concept of internalization (e.g., Ryan, Connell, & Deci, 1985), the field of self-determination truly mushroomed. Laboratory experiments as well as field studies using interview, questionnaire, and observational methods have examined the conditions that promote more versus less self-determined forms of extrinsic motivation, both developmentally and in particular situations, and these studies have also related the different forms of extrinsic motivation to such important outcomes as persistence, learning, prosocial activity, healthy behaving, and psychological well-being. This work all added to the development of self-determination theory (SDT), and increasing numbers of researchers have been using SDT to organize or inform their motivational research.

The Diversity of Self-Determination Research

In this volume, more than 30 researchers report on their programs of SDT-related research. Reading through the chapters, one is struck by both the breadth and the depth of the issues covered. The chapters present sophisticated theoretical discussions integrating the results of investigations concerned with topics as varied as levels of analysis, the nature of self, the motivational basis of effective coping, differentiated styles of autonomous regulation, the motivational potential of values, the processes of achievement, types of self-esteem, the complexity of perceiving motivation in others, and interest as a motivational force. As such, they test, extend, and refine the tenets of SDT and point the way to important issues that await further attention.

These chapters also demonstrate how readily the concepts of SDT can be applied to life domains as diverse as medicine, parenting, education, work, cultural values, sports, environmentalism, and institutional reform. In these chapters concerning the ongoing activities of life, one sees that differentiation of the concept of motivation according to the degree of autonomy experienced has been useful for predicting behavioral, affective, and mental health outcomes. Furthermore, characterization of social environments in terms of the extent to which they allow satisfaction of basic psychological needs for competence, relatedness, and autonomy has served well for explaining variance not only in the degree of self-determination but also in the various behavioral and well-being outcomes.

The concepts that underlie SDT have shown themselves to be enduring, yet they have ongoingly been refined and applied. The concepts include, of course, the classic distinction between intrinsic and extrinsic motivation (Ryan & Deci, 2000b) and the relation of these types of motivation to amotivation. As well, there are the central concepts of the basic needs for autonomy, competence, and relatedness, and of autonomy support, competence support, and relational support. And there are additional constructs such as causality orientations, ego-involvement versus task-involvement, psychological vitality, the specific forms of internalization (e.g., introjected, identified, and integrated regulation), and the distinctions among needs, motives, and goals (Deci & Ryan, 2000). These various constructs have been operationalized in multiple ways by researchers, they have been used to integrate research findings from a multitude of studies, and they have proven useful for devising prescriptions and proscriptions in many applied domains. Still, all of these concepts gain their true meaning from the metatheory out of which they evolved, so the organismic-dialectical metatheory is an integral, defining aspect of SDT.

The SDT Metatheory

Self-determination theory was built on the assumption, based in the organizational principle of the life sciences, that humans are active, growth-oriented organisms, with an inherent tendency toward integrating experiences into a unified regulatory process. This integrative tendency is understood to be dependent upon specific nutriments from the social environment to operate effectively. It is the organismic-dialectical metatheory, as detailed in the introductory chapter and elsewhere (e.g., Ryan & Deci, 2000c), which captures the interplay of these discrepant human tendencies and is therefore significantly different from the metatheories guiding other current motivational theories, particularly those with behavioral or social-cognitive orientations. The metatheory has also led self-determination theorists to make predictions and interpretations that frequently differ in profound and interesting ws from those of other theories. One finds these predictions and interpretations scattered throughout the chapters of this book.

The very concept of autonomy, of being self-determined, of acting from an integrated sense of self, necessitates starting with the assumption of an active, growth-oriented organism. However, the ubiquitous evidence that human beings are often quite passive, unintegrated, and reactive requires both a metatheory that can accurately encompass the interplay of proactivity and vulnerability in human nature and a theory that differentiates the varied types of regulation which result from that interplay. Most mainstream theories of human motivation in contemporary psychology continue to use a relatively mechanistic metatheory and to view motivation as a unitary phenomenon—something that varies in amount but not kind. Thus, most motivational researchers, other than those focused on SDT, have been unable to capture the multiple forms of regulation that reflect differing degrees of activity and passivity. These different qualities and types of self-regulation are routinely observed in clinical and applied settings and are well recognized by dynamic and phenomenologically based perspectives, but the empirically based theories that fail to recognize these different types of motivation are unable to address some of the most critical aspects of human behavioral regulation.

Fortunately, the growing interest in SDT and the elaboration of the SDT framework by researchers such as those represented in this volume have led to the explication of processes and conditions that promote effective functioning and psychological health, and in so doing have shed further light on the psychological nature of human freedom and connectedness.

In spite of the progress that has been made and is well presented in the chapters of this book, there is much work remaining to be done. Several major theoretical problems remain to be solved, new areas of application await careful consideration, and countless refinements would help to make the theory more exhaustive and precise. We mention just a few of the obvious areas where important additional work is needed.

Future Directions

One of the unique aspects of SDT is its postulate of the universal psychological needs for competence, relatedness, and autonomy (Deci & Ryan, 2000). SDT has been very clear (1) in its definition of needs as essential nutriments for growth, integrity, and well-being, and (2) in its assertion that the concept of basic needs is necessary for integrating diverse empirical phenomena.

The concept of basic psychological needs serves three important functions. First, it provides a theoretical basis for predicting which environmental factors are likely to facilitate versus undermine natural processes such as intrinsic motivation and internalization of ambient social values. Specifically, those factors in the social context that would be logically expected to facilitate need satisfaction are predicted to promote intrinsic motivation and the integration of values and regulations. Second, the concept of needs provides a basis for relating motivation and behavior not only to performance but also to psychological development and health. Because the needs specify necessary nutriments, behaviors that are expected to yield such nutriments are predicted to promote healthy development and well being, as well as constructive and creative outputs. Third, the concept of innate needs provides a basis for the design of social systems such as schools, health clubs, work places, and, yes, even cultures. By understanding people's basic psychological needs, psychologists can play a role in establishing policies and procedures and in designing activities and interactions that will allow or facilitate individuals' need satisfaction so that the social systems will function more effectively and the systems' members will display greater vitality, productivity, and satisfaction.

The Universality of Needs

The concept of innate or basic needs is quite controversial in modern motivational psychology, and it stands in sharp contrast to the cultural relativism and postmodernism that is so prevalent in the social sciences today. Specifically, most current theories of motivation still fail to acknowledge any human nature or deep design to the human psyche other than plasticity and docility—a viewpoint that Tooby and Cosmides (1992) referred to as the "standard social science model." From this perspective, people's goals and motives are shaped largely by cultural and social forces, and well-being and other positive outcomes are expected to accrue when the people are efficacious at achieving their goals, whatever the goals might be (see, e.g., Bandura, 1989; Oishi, Diener, Lucas, & Suh, 1999). All goals "are created equal," so to speak.

Advocates of this viewpoint suggest that competence, autonomy, and relatedness are important motivators only to the extent that individuals have adopted them as goals through some type of social learning process, so these motivators will be differentially important in different groups or cultures that value them to differing degrees. For example, theorists such as Heine, Lehman, Markus, and Kitayama (1999) have maintained that whereas a focus on autonomy character-izes western societies, eastern societies place greater emphasis on relatedness, and in so doing these researchers have aligned autonomy with the western value of individualism and have aligned relatedness with the eastern value of collectivism. Other commentators such as Jordan, Kaplan, Miller, Stiver, and Surrey (1991) have similarly argued that autonomy is more central for males and relatedness is more central for female.

SDT asserts, in contrast, that all humans, regardless of culture or gender, need to feel both related and autonomous in order to be healthy, even though these needs may be expressed and satisfied in different ways within different cul-tural contexts or by people at different ages or of different genders. Thus, SDT suggests that there is not a clear alignment of cultural orientations or genders with the different human needs. Individualism does not ensure satisfaction of the need for autonomy, and collectivism does not ensure satisfaction of the need for relatedness. Rather, the psychological effects of both individualism and collec-tivism depend, to a large extent, on how those values are transmitted and to what extent they have been meaningfully integrated by the individuals exposed to them. People can be autonomous in their enactment of collectivist values just as they can in their enactment of individualistic values, and they can find satisfac-tion of their relatedness need while holding either value. Similarly, being male does not differentially facilitate satisfaction of the need for autonomy nor does being female facilitate satisfaction of the need for relatedness, unless of course political or religious values and practices interfere with satisfaction of one or the other needs by one or the other genders. For example, it seems perfectly clear that, like men, women suffer psychologically when they are deprived of autono-my, as they are in many cultural, societal, and interpersonal contexts.

We maintain that, in spite of being a unique and controversial aspect of SDT, the idea of universal needs that are differentially expressed and satisfied as a function of differing social contexts is consistent with recent work in evolution-ary psychology and genetics. One of the most significant conclusions from mod-ern genetic research is that, to an extent not anticipated three decades ago, humans across the globe share a basic genetic makeup. Indeed, we are one species, with a common nature. Exploration of the invariant aspects of that nature and how it is expressed under varied developmental and cultural condi-tions is thematic in recent SDT work.

Accordingly, a major current and future direction of SDT work is the con-tinued examination of cross-cultural variation in the relation of motives and needs to mental health. Recent studies (e.g., Chirkov & Ryan, 2001; Deci, Ryan, Gagné, Leone, Usunov, & Kornazheva, 2001; Ryan, Chirkov, Little, Sheldon, Timoshina, & Deci, 1999; Yamauchi & Tanaka, 1998) have provided evidence in support of the universal importance of SDT's proposed basic needs, but much work remains to be done and represents an important direction for future research.

Similarly, more work to ground the basic human needs in evolutionary psychology is warranted. This will, however, involve some controversy. The current tendency in that field is to search for narrow, "lock-and-key" mechanisms that solved very particular adaptive problems during the era of evolutionary adaptation, and important things are being learned using that approach. However, some evolutionary thinkers who have taken that approach have also disparaged the examination of any multipurpose, broad-band, or organizational features in the deep design of the human psyche, and that is a position with which we take strong exception. The position holds in essence that the design of organisms is accretive in nature, and that view is conceptually parallel to the accretive, associationist view adopted by behaviorists early in the twentieth century. Elsewhere (Deci & Ryan, 2000), we referred to this as the "heap of stones" model of organismic design, pointing out that the view lacks a conception of an organization within living entities which plays a role in what features could emerge or be added and in what functions and features of organisms are subserved by adaption and could in turn either directly or indirectly influence selective processes. Accordingly, an important future direction for SDT is to interface constructively with evolutionary psychological theories and, in so doing, to help emphasize the deep design features of the human psyche which concern the needs to be related to others, to experience competence, and to be an origin and organizer of one's behavior. This agenda, while still relatively nascent has nonetheless received increasing attention (e.g., Deci & Ryan, 2000; Ryan, Kuhl, & Deci, 1997).

The Relation of Integration to Autonomy

One of SDT's central features is the relative autonomy continuum—that is, the theoretical characterization of motivational or regulatory types in terms of the degree to which they represent autonomous or self-determined functioning. Further, the developmental component of SDT emphasizes that people become more autonomous with respect to behaviors or domains as the organismic integration process leads the behaviors to become more integrated within one's unified sense of self. This feature of the theory, like the feature of universal needs, is both unique and controversial. Still, abundant research has shown that identified and integrated forms of extrinsic motivation are associated with the experience of greater autonomy than are introjected or externally-based regulations, and that regulations accompanied by greater autonomy are also associated with more effective performance and greater well-being.

Nonetheless, there is an interesting and related phenomenon that has yet to be fully explicated within SDT. Specifically, there are regulations and values which individuals hold and with which they identify that are not coherent with respect to their integrated selves. That is, people may identify with certain values that are quite inconsistent with other aspects of their sense of self, leading them to compartmentalize these identifications so they will not experience the discomfort resulting from a conflict between these values and other aspects of their psychological makeup.

An interesting case in point concerns Nazi values that were apparently endorsed by many Germans during the 1930s and early 1940s. The espoused value of annihilating an ethnic minority within their culture was certainly inconsistent with values contained within the integrated selves of many of the individuals—values of kindness and promoting humanity, for example. Yet, a recent argument by Goldhagen (1996) suggested that, [in the language of SDT] although some individuals may have enacted Nazi atrocities out of external or introjected forms of regulation, a large number of people appear to have identified strongly with these values. In other words, they seem to have identified with a set of politico-cultural values that could not have been easily integrated with their true sense of self. In previous writings, we have referred to the concept of compartmentalized identifications, and it is that concept to which we here refer. One of the extremely important empirical agendas facing SDT is to clarify the workings of these unintegrated identifications.

Within-person Variations in Motivation and Well-being

Along with the rest of the field of personality and social psychology, SDT is being reshaped by the advent of methodological tools that allow the exploration of within-person variations in functioning. In particular, the relation of need satisfaction to well-being has typically been studied at only the between-person level, which has shown that individuals whose needs are generally supported have more positive well-being outcomes. Multilevel modeling allows a deeper examination of the functioning of needs. To show that each individual is more fully functioning and has more optimal experience at the times or in the contexts where needs are satisfied relative to times or contexts where they are frustrated is an even more powerful result concerning the postulate of universal needs. Already, several studies have shown within-person covariation between basic needs and well-being across time and contexts (e.g., Reis, Sheldon, Gable, Roscoe, & Ryan, 2000; Sheldon, Ryan, & Reis, 1996). Moreover, a recent study highlighted an association between the formation and maintenance of attachments to specific others and the satisfaction of basic needs at the within-person level (La Guardia, Ryan, Couchman, & Deci, 2000), pointing toward a need-based theory of interpersonal connectedness. As SDT applies multilevel modeling to variation in need satisfaction, psychological vitality, and performance, the dynamics of motivation and its functional underpinnings will become increasingly well specified.

Emotional Integration

It has long been a tenet of SDT that emotions as well as psychological needs are energizers of action. However, most of our attention has focused on the dynamics of psychological needs, and relatively little consideration has been given to emotions other than the emotion of *interest*, which is a key element in intrinsic motivation and integrative processes. Particularly little empirical attention within the SDT framework has been given to the so-called negative emotions such as anger and contempt and to the associated expressions of aggression toward others or toward oneself. These issues are indeed central ones in life, and from the SDT perspective the darker sides of human existence are unarguably associated with lack of basic need satisfaction and with ineffective regulation of the corresponding negative emotions (Ryan & Deci, 2000a). Still, much work remains to be done in order to present a consistent and comprehensive analysis of emotional regulation.

Certainly this analysis will recognize that emotions are innate to the human organism, yet effective regulation of emotions requires that they become managed by the self. SDT, of course, has a unique handle on the issue of self-management. Specifically, people can be either self-controlling or self-regulating in managing their emotions, and the consequences of these two different forms of regulation, which reflect differing degrees of relative autonomy, will be quite different. In the former case, emotions are ignored, suppressed, or denied, whereas in the latter case they are attended to, "owned," and used as sources of information. Healthy emotional regulation requires internalization of the regulatory processes in a way that will permit awareness of the feelings and satisfaction of basic needs that is associated with effective regulation. Investigation of the phenomenology and dynamics of regulatory processes with respect to emotions is thus a key issue for SDT research. More generally, in fact, the nature of awareness and mindfulness in self-determination is an area in need of greater specificity and research-based examination.

Additional Applied Considerations

Within each of the domains to which SDT has been applied there are numerous unanswered questions that will occupy the attention of interested researchers for years to come. However, perhaps the one applied area that has received the least attention but is ripe for exploration is that of psychotherapy.

The concept of autonomy has been addressed extensively by theories formulated within the psychoanalytic and humanistic traditions where the ideas of holistic functioning and volitional self-regulation are considered important. Angyal (1965), for example, proposed that the two fundamental life trajectories are toward greater autonomy and greater homonomy. In other words, the direction and meaning of development involve simultaneously achieving greater personal integrity and volition (autonomy) and more meaningful relationships with others (homonomy). Miller (1981), in discussing the meaning of true self, which closely resembles our concept of integrated self, suggested that children require an atmosphere of respect and tolerance to develop their autonomy and identity. These and other such theories (see, e.g., Ryan, Deci, & Grolnick, 1995) are fully consistent with the SDT postulate of basic psychological needs for autonomy, competence, and relatedness and with the ideas that satisfaction of these needs is essential for healthy development and for psychotherapeutic change. Further, many of the therapeutic approaches that have been developed within these traditions are relatively congruent with the tenets of SDT. Still, we have yet to provide a clear and comprehensive analysis of the processes of psychotherapeutic change, and that is another important agenda for the future.

Conclusions

The chapters of this volume make clear that SDT provides a coherent and comprehensive basis for understanding human motivation and personality development, that a remarkable body of research supporting SDT has accumulated over the past three decades, and that the theory has been useful for guiding applications and interventions in a variety of domains. Based on an organismic-dialectical metatheory, the empirical programs summarized herein have added substantial breadth and depth to the theory and have helped to point the way toward further important problems that remain to be tackled. Our hope is that this volume will serve to stimulate greater interest in the SDT approach and that those who are curious about the dynamics of motivation and the essential features of human nature will engage these questions that bear on the optimal functioning of human beings and on the communities that nurture them.

References

Angyal, A. (1965). *Neurosis and treatment: A holistic theory.* New York: Wiley.

Bandura, A. (1989). Human agency in social cognitive theory. *American Psychologist, 44,* 1175-1184.

Chirkov, V. I., & Ryan, R.M. (2001). Parent and teacher autonomy support in Russian and U.S. adolescents. *Journal of Cross-Cultural Psychology, 32,* 618-635.

Deci, E. L. (1971). Effects of externally mediated rewards on intrinsic motivation. *Journal of Personality and Social Psychology, 18,* 105- 115.

Deci, E. L. (1972a). Effects of contingent and non-contingent rewards and controls on intrinsic motivation. *Organizational Behavior and Human Performance, 8*, 217-229.

Deci, E. L. (1972b). Intrinsic motivation, extrinsic reinforcement, and inequity. *Journal of Personality and Social Psychology, 22*, 113- 120.

Deci, E. L., Koestner, R., & Ryan, R. M. (1999). A meta-analytic review of experiments examining the effects of extrinsic rewards on intrinsic motivation. *Psychological Bulletin, 125*, 627-668.

Deci, E. L., & Ryan, R. M. (2000). The "what" and "why" of goal pursuits: Human needs and the self-determination of behavior. *Psychological Inquiry, 11*, 227-268.

Deci, E. L., Ryan, R. M., Gagné, M., Leone, D. R., Usunov, J., & Kornazheva, B. P. (2001). Need satisfaction, motivation, and well-being in the work organizations of a former Eastern Bloc country. *Personality and Social Psychology Bulletin, 27*, 930-942.

Goldhagen, D. J. (1996). *Hitler's willing executioners*. London: Little, Brown.

Heine, S. J., Lehman, D. R., Markus, H. R., & Kitayama, S. (1999). Is there a universal need for positive self-regard? *Psychological Review, 106*, 766-794.

Jordan, J. V., Kaplan, A. G., Miller, J. B., Stiver, I. P. & Surrey, J. L. (1991). *Women's growth in connection: Writings from The Stone Center*. New York: Guilford.

Kruglanski, A. W., Friedman, I., & Zeevi, G. (1971). The effects of extrinsic incentive on some qualitative aspects of task performance. *Journal of Personality, 39*, 606-617.

La Guardia, J., Ryan, R.M., Couchman, C., & Deci, E.L. (2000). Within-person variation in security of attachment: A self-determination theory perspective on attachment, need fulfillment, and well-being. *Journal of Personality and Social Psychology, 79*, 367-384.

Lepper, M. R., Greene, D., & Nisbett, R. E. (1973). Undermining children's intrinsic interest with extrinsic rewards: A test of the "overjustification" hypothesis. *Journal of Personality and Social Psychology, 28*, 129-137.

Miller, A. (1981). *The drama of the gifted child: The search for the true self* (R. Ward, Trans.). New York: Basic Books.

Oishi, S., Diener, E., Lucas, R. E., & Suh E. (1999). Cross-cultural variations in predictors of life satisfaction: Perspectives from needs and values. *Personality and Social Psychology Bulletin, 25*, 980-990.

Reis, H. T., Sheldon, K. M., Gable, S. L., Roscoe, J., & Ryan, R. M. (2000). Daily well-being: The role of autonomy, competence, and relatedness. *Personality and Social Psychology Bulletin, 26*, 419-435.

Ryan, R. M., Chirkov, V. I., Little, T. D., Sheldon, K. M., Timoshina, E., & Deci, E. L. (1999). The American dream in Russia: Extrinsic aspirations and well-being in two cultures. *Personality and Social Psychology Bulletin, 25*, 1509-1524.

Ryan, R. M., Connell, J. P., & Deci, E. L. (1985). A motivational analysis of self-determination and self-regulation in education. In C. Ames & R. E. Ames (Eds.), *Research on motivation in education: The classroom milieu* (pp. 13-51). New York: Academic Press.

Ryan, R. M., & Deci, E. L. (2000a). The darker and brighter sides of human existence: Basic psychological needs as a unifying concept. *Psychological Inquiry, 11*, 319-338.

Ryan, R. M., & Deci, E. L. (2000b). Intrinsic and extrinsic motivations: Classic definitions and new directions. *Contemporary Educational Psychology, 25*, 54-67.

Ryan, R. M., & Deci, E. L. (2000c). Self-determination theory and the facilitation of intrinsic motivation, social development, and well-being. *American Psychologist, 55*, 68-78.

Ryan, R. M., Deci, E. L., & Grolnick, W. S. (1995). Autonomy, relatedness, and the self: Their relation to development and psychopathology. In D. Cicchetti & D. J. Cohen (Eds.), *Developmental psychopathology Vol. 1.* (pp. 618-655). New York: Wiley.

Ryan, R. M., Kuhl, J., & Deci, E. L. (1997). Nature and autonomy: Organizational view of social and neurobiological aspects of self-regulation in behavior and development. *Development and Psychopathology, 9*, 701-728.

Sheldon, K. M., Ryan, R. M., & Reis, H. T. (1996). What makes for a good day? Competence and autonomy in the day and in the person. *Personality and Social Psychology Bulletin, 22*, 1270-1279.

Tooby, J., & Cosmides, L. (1992). The psychological foundations of culture. In J. H. Barkow, L. Cosmides, & J. Tooby (Eds.), *The adapted mind: Evolutionary psychology and the generation of culture* (pp. 19-136). New York: Oxford University Press.

Yamauchi, H., & Tanaka, K. (1998). Relations of autonomy, self-referenced beliefs and self-regulated learning among Japanese children. *Psychological Reports, 82*, 803-816.

CONTRIBUTORS

Nicholas H. Apostoleris
Department of Family Medicine and Community Health
UMASS Medical School
55 Lake Avenue North
Worcester, MA 01655
e-mail: Nicholas.Apostoleris@umassmed.edu

Paul P. Baard
Departments of Communications and Management
Graduate School of Business Administration
Fordham University
113 West 60th Street
New York, NY 10023
e-mail: baard@fordham.edu

Edward L. Deci
Department of Clinical and Social Sciences in Psychology
University of Rochester
Rochester, NY 14627
e-mail: deci@psych.rochester.edu

Kathleen Edge
Psychology Department
Portland State University
P.O. Box 751
Portland, OR 97207-0751

Andrew J. Elliot
Department of Clinical and Social Sciences in Psychology
University of Rochester
Rochester, NY 14627
e-mail: andye@psych.rochester.edu

Michael E. Enzle
Department of Psychology
P-220 Biological Sciences Bldg.
University of Alberta
Edmonton, Alberta, CANADA T6G 2E9
e-mail: mike.enzle@ualberta.ca

Christina M. Frederick-Recascino
Human Factors Department
Embry-Riddle Aeronautical University
600 Clyde Morris Blvd.
Daytona Beach, FL 32114-3900
email: frederic@cts.db.erau.edu

Wendy S. Grolnick
Frances L. Hiatt School of Psychology
Clark University
950 Main Street
Worcester, MA 01610
e-mail: wgrolnick@clarku.edu

Patricia H. Hawley
Department of Psychology
Southern Connecticut State University
501 Crescent Street
New Haven, CT 06515
e-mail: Hawley@scsu.ctstateu.edu

Christopher C. Henrich
Department of Psychology
Georgia State University
University Plaza
Atlanta, GA 30303
e-mail: psycch@langate.gsu.edu

Holley S. Hodgins
Department of Psychology
Skidmore College
Saratoga Springs, NY 12866
e-mail: hhodgins@skidmore.edu

Tim Kasser
Department of Psychology
Knox College
Galesburg, IL 61401
e-mail: tkasser@knox.edu

Michael H. Kernis
Department of Psychology
University of Georgia
Athens, GA 30602
e-mail: mkernis@arches.uga.edu

C. Raymond Knee
Department of Psychology
University of Houston
Houston, TX 77204-5022
e-mail: knee@uh.edu

Richard Koestner
Department of Psychology
McGill University
1205 Dr. Penfield Avenue
Montreal, Quebec, CANADA H3A 1B1
e-mail: koestner@hebb.psych.mcgill.ca

Andreas Krapp
Faculty of Social Sciences
University of the Bundeswehr, Munich
85577 Neubiberg, GERMANY
e-mail: andreas.krapp@unibw-muenchen.de

Todd D. Little
Department of Psychology
Yale University
P.O. Box 208205
New Haven, CT 06520-8205
e-mail: Todd.Little@Yale.edu

Gaëtan F. Losier
École de Psychologie
Université de Moncton
Moncton, NB, CANADA E1A 3E9
e-mail: losierga@umoncton.ca

Katherine W. Marsland
Department of Psychology
Yale University
P.O. Box 208205
New Haven, CT 06520-8205
e-mail: Katherine.Marsland@Yale.edu

Holly A. McGregor
Department of Clinical and Social Sciences in Psychology
University of Rochester
Rochester, NY 14627
e-mail: mcgregor@psych.rochester.edu

Andrew W. Paradise
Department of Psychology
University of Georgia
Athens, GA 30602

Luc G. Pelletier
Research Laboratory on Human Motivation
School of Psychology
University of Ottawa
P.O. Box 450, Stn. A
Ottawa, Ontario, CANADA K1N 6N5
e-mail: social@uottawa.ca

Catherine F. Ratelle
Laboratoire de recherche sur le comportement social
Départment de Psychologie
Université du Québec à Montréal
Box 8888, Succursale Centre-Ville
Montréal (Québec) CANADA H3C 3P8

Johnmarshall Reeve
Division of Psychological and Quantitative Foundations
361 Lindquist Center
University of Iowa
Iowa City, IA 52242
e-mail: johnmarshall-reeve@uiowa.edu

Richard M. Ryan
Department of Clinical and Social Sciences in Psychology
University of Rochester
Rochester, NY 14627
e-mail: ryan@psych.rochester.edu

Kennon M. Sheldon
Department of Psychology
112 McAlester Hall
University of Missouri, Columbia
Columbia, MO 65211
e-mail: sheldonk@missouri.edu

Ellen Skinner
Psychology Department
Portland State University
P.O. Box 751
Portland, OR 97207-0751
e-mail: Skinnere@pdx.edu

Todd M. Thrash
Department of Clinical and Social Sciences in Psychology
University of Rochester
Rochester, NY 14627
e-mail: thrash@psych.rochester.edu

Robert J. Vallerand
Laboratoire de recherche sur le comportement social
Départment de Psychologie
Université du Québec à Montréal
Box 8888, Succursale Centre-Ville
Montréal (Québec) CANADA H3C 3P8
e-mail: vallerand.robert_j@uqam.ca

T. Cameron Wild
Addiction and Mental Health Laboratory
Centre for Health Promotion Studies, and
Department of Public Health Sciences
University of Alberta
13-133 Clinical Sciences Bldg.
Edmonton, Alberta, CANADA T6G 2G3
e-mail: cam.wild@ualberta.ca

Geoffrey C. Williams
Departments of Medicine and of
Clinical and Social Sciences in Psychology
University of Rochester
Box 270266
Rochester, NY 14627
e-mail: Geoffrey_Williams@URMC.rochester.edu

Index of Names

Csikszentmihalyi, I. S., 415, 422
Csikszentmihalyi, M., 115, 117, 119,
    121, 279, 286, 291, 366, 382, 405,
    410-1, 415, 420, 422, 425-6
Cunningham, J., 150, 157
Curry, S. J., 52-53, 60, 247, 251

D

d'Ailly, H., 196, 200
d'Andrade, R., 371, 385
Darley, J., 152, 156
Darling, N. E., 393, 402
Darwin, C., 394, 402
Davey, J., 259, 274
Davidson, R. J., 369, 386
Dawson, S., 130, 139
Debeis, P., 109, 121
DeCasper, A. J., 366, 382
deCharms, R., 8, 10-11, 15, 17, 29,
    48, 60, 104, 119, 142, 155, 193,
    197, 200, 259, 273, 301-4, 312,
    332, 390, 392, 402
Deci, E. L., 5, 7-15, 17-18, 20-23, 25-
    29, 32-33, 37, 42-44, 46, 48-50, 53,
    56, 60-63, 66-68, 72, 75-76, 82-83,
    85-87, 91, 93, 98, 100-102, 104,
    106, 114-5, 118-9, 121, 127, 129,
    131-3, 136-142, 145-9, 151, 154-7,
    161, 168, 177, 179, 181, 184, 187,
    189, 192, 195-7, 199-200, 202-3,
    206, 211-2, 214, 224-5, 229, 235,
    237-9, 242-5, 248, 250-1, 253-4,
    256-262, 264, 273-5, 279-280, 283,
    286-7, 291-3, 298-9, 301-5, 309,
    313-5, 317, 329, 332, 339, 344-5,
    348-351, 354-5, 357, 361, 370, 373,
    375, 382, 389-393, 399-405, 407-
    410, 418, 422, 431-441
DeCourcey, W., 170, 180
DeJong, W., 12, 28, 141, 155, 197,
    199
DeNeve, K., 346, 357
Denton, F., 133, 139
Deutsch, D., 405, 422
Deutsch, J. A., 405, 422
Dewey, J., 141, 155, 405, 415, 422
DeYoung, R., 210-1, 214, 229

DiDio, L., 118, 120
Diener, C. I., 170, 179
Diener, E., 22, 30, 75, 83, 434, 440
Dobreva-Martinova, T., 282, 290
Dodge, K. A., 163, 179, 317, 332
Dolmat-Connell, J., 255, 274
Dornbusch, S., 393, 402
Doty, R. M., 176, 179
Dowd, D. A., 285, 292
Drechsel, B., 417, 419-420, 425
Druckman, D., 206, 232
Duda, J. L., 277-8, 283, 291, 293-4
Duff, K. J., 90, 99
Duncan, N., 96, 99, 106, 120, 141, 156
Dunning, D., 344, 358
Dutton, K. A., 50, 59
Dweck, C. S., 170, 179, 192, 201,
    278, 291, 298, 302-4, 309-310, 313,
    332-4, 367-8, 373, 376, 381-2, 384,
    393, 404
Dwyer, W. O., 209, 229, 234, 251
Dykman, B. M., 376, 382

E

Easterbrooks, M. A., 301, 334, 370, 385
Eccles, J. S., 183, 201, 367, 387
Edge, K., 305, 307, 314, 320, 336
Edwards, T. C., 209, 230
Eghari, H., 20, 29, 46, 60, 115, 119,
    189, 196, 200, 224, 229, 239, 251,
    304, 332
Eisenberg, N., 321, 333
Eisenberg, R., 368, 385
Eisenberger, R., 11, 29, 142, 155
Eitel, F., 417, 425
Elder, G. H., 163, 179
Elliot, A. J., 13, 32, 65-66, 68, 72-75,
    85, 91, 100, 115-6, 119-121, 141,
    143, 155-6, 213, 229, 231, 368-9,
    373, 376-9, 382, 386
Elliott, E. S., 170, 179, 368, 373, 376,
    381-2
Emel, J., 218, 230
Emery, J., 184, 202
Emirbayer, M., 389, 402
Emmons, R. A., 44, 60, 65, 67-68, 70,
    83, 123, 135, 138, 350, 358

Subject Index

A

action-control theory, 396-399
action tendencies, 307-8, 323
adherence
    to exercise, 286-8
    to medications, 243-4
adult development, 98
agency
    see human agency
agentic self
    see self, agentic
alcohol treatment, 242, 247
amotivation, 15-17, 40-43
    in organizations, 258
    measurement of, 45-47
aspirations, 24-26, 123-138
    and autonomous regulation, 90
    and basic needs, 24-26
    and well-being, 134-7
    intrinsic and extrinsic, 128-132
authenticity, 89-91
    see also self
autonomous motivation, 235-6
    and values, 128
    in educational settings, 183
autonomous orientation, 21, 94
    and responsibility, 97
autonomous regulation, 89
    and defensiveness, 89-90, 95
autonomy, 5
    see also need for autonomy
    and coping, 298-9, 309-327
    and integration, 436-7
    is not independence, 236
    and openness, 96
    and relationships, 326-7
    and religious behavior, 269-270
    and work behaviors, 262-264
autonomy support
    among the elderly, 247-8
    and pro-environmental behavior, 220-7
    and regulatory styles, 196
    and self-system processes, 303-4
    and structure, 114-5, 193-4
    in coping, 319, 324-6
    in educational settings, 183
    in health care, 238-240
    in managers, 260
    in parenting, 161-5
    is not permissiveness, 304
autonomy supportive teaching, 185-190
    effects on students, 186-8
    learning how, 188-190
    taking the students' perspective, 189-190
    what undermines it, 190-3
active organism, 3-4

B

basic needs theory, 22-27
    and well-being, 22-23
basic psychological needs, 6-8, 87,
    235, 300-302
    and agency, 391-2, 397-8
    and aspirations, 24-26
    and ego-involvement, 93
    and environmental behaviors, 224
    and interest, 418-9
    and organizational behavior, 259
    and sports, 279
    and values, 126-7, 132-4
    satisfaction of, 26-27
    universality of, 434-6
    when thwarted, 132-4
behavioral confirmation, 152

C

causality orientations theory, 20-22
coercion
    see also stress, coercion as
    versus loss of control, 312-3